More Praise for Nancy Dunnan and *Dun & Bradstreet Guide to $Your Investments$®*:

"An invaluable reference tool loaded with useful information and advice. I turn to it regularly in researching issues important to my clients."
>—Edward J. Sullivan, Senior Vice President, Fleet Investment Services/Fleet Bank

"In this high-tech, ever-changing financial world, it takes a true artist to absorb, understand and translate the material for us average guys. Nancy Dunnan is our financial Picasso."
>—Bob Harris, KFGO Radio, Fargo, ND

"This book is bursting with useful information on personal finance. An excellent source for consumers and a handy reference for professionals. Clear, concise, complete. Nancy Dunnan knows her stuff."
>—Mark Mills, WCVB-TV, Boston

"*The Dun & Bradstreet Guide to $Your Investments$®* is a clear, comprehensive and accurate guide through the money jungle. Nancy Dunnan knows her stuff."
>—Julie Tripp, *The Oregonian*

"Nancy Dunnan's insight is useful and pertinent. She has the ability to handle many things at one time, and she's equally at ease offering advice to people who want to invest $50 or $5,000."
>—Kenn Peters, Syracuse (NY) *Herald-Journal*

"Nancy Dunnan is one of those rare but increasingly important figures in the financial world. She is a highly astute combination of writer, analyst, advisor, speaker and book author. She has a remarkable talent for covering the vast spectrum of money-related issues in a perceptive yet delightful, easy-to-understand way."
>—Michael C. Hodes, Moderator, "Financial Focus" Legends Broadcasting Network

"I've known Nancy Dunnan and her work for many years. I'm constantly amazed at how she can turn out such high quality material year after year. To my further amazement, Ms. Dunnan covers a very wide range of subjects—everything from stocks and bonds and taxes to commodities, options, precious metals and collectibles."
>—Richard Russell, Publisher, *Dow Theory Letters*

DUN & BRADSTREET

Guide to
$YOUR INVESTMENTS$®
1997

ALSO BY NANCY DUNNAN

Never Call Your Broker on Monday

How to Invest $50-$5,000

Your First Financial Steps

DUN & BRADSTREET

Guide to
$YOUR INVESTMENTS$®
1997

NANCY DUNNAN

HarperPerennial
A Division of HarperCollinsPublishers

GRATEFUL ACKNOWLEDGMENT IS MADE FOR PERMISSION TO REPRINT:

"How to Calculate the Effect of Inflation" table reprinted with permission from *Encyclopedia of Banking and Financial Tables,* copyright © 1980, 1986, Warren, Gorham & Lamont, Inc., Boston, Mass. All rights reserved.

"The Power of Compound Interest" table reprinted with permission from *Encyclopedia of Banking and Financial Tables,* copyright © 1980, 1986, Warren, Gorham & Lamont, Inc., Boston, Mass. All rights reserved.

"Calculating Growth Rates" table from *Security Analysis,* Fourth Edition, by Benjamin Graham et al. Copyright © 1962 by McGraw-Hill, Inc. Reprinted by permission of McGraw-Hill, Inc.

"Dun & Bradstreet" is a registered trademark of The Dun & Bradstreet Corporation and is used under license. The title *$Your Investments$*® is a registered trademark of HarperCollins Publishers, Inc.

HarperCollins books may be purchased for educational, business, or sales promotional use. For information, please write to: Special Markets Department, HarperCollins Publishers Inc., 10 East 53rd Street, New York, New York 10022.
Designed by Gayle Jaeger

ISSN 73–18050
ISBN 0–06–273289–7 (pbk.)

97 98 99 00 ❖/RRD 10 9 8 7 6 5 4 3

*With profound thanks to
these New York University doctors who helped
make my life happier, healthier, and longer:
Matthew N. Harris, M.D.; David T. Liu, M.D.;
Tibor Moskovits, M.D.; and Govin Gopinathan, M.D.*

CONTENTS

PART THREE
When the Bulls Are Running

PART FOUR
High Risk for High Returns

PART FIVE
You and Your Account

PART SIX
Financing Your Lifestyle

PART SEVEN
Taxes and Your Investments

PART EIGHT
Your Customized Portfolio

APPENDIXES
Investment Analysis and Information Sources

Acknowledgments

I wish to thank the following people for their expertise and willingness to provide valuable, accurate information:

American Stock Exchange	New York, NY	Kristin Winter
Bureau of Public Debt	Washington, DC	Dale Vanderhagen
Burnham Securities, Inc.	New York, NY	Jay J. Pack
Certified Financial Planner Board of Standards	Denver, CO	Noel May
Credit Union National	Madison, WI	Jerry Karbon
Dow Theory Forecasts	Hammond, IN	Charles B. Carlson
Dow Theory Letters	La Jolla, CA	Richard Russell
F.D.I.C.	Chicago, IL	John S. Stevens
Federal Reserve Bank	New York, NY	Bart R. Sotnick
Health Care Financing Administration	Washington, DC	Ann Verano
Internal Revenue Service	Washington, DC	Don Roberts
International Strategy & Investment Group	New York, NY	Joel Fein
NASDAQ Stock Market, Inc.	Washington, DC	Richard B. Myers
National Association of Investment Clubs	Madison Hts, MI	Kenneth S. Janke, Barry Murphy
New York Stock Exchange	New York, NY	James Buck, Margaret Draper, Brad Mills
100 Highest Yields	North Palm Beach, FL	Robert Heady
Securities Investor Protection Corp.	Washington, DC	Michael Don
Social Security Administration	Washington, DC	Carolyn Cheezum
Standard & Poor's Corp.	New York, NY	Arnold Kaufman, Jon Diat
T. Rowe Price Associates	Baltimore, MD	Steven E. Norwitz
Thomas Heller Tax Services	New York, NY	Thomas Heller
Wertheim Schroder & Co.	New York, NY	Thomas Byrne, John Murray, Andrew Wooten

And, with special thanks to:
Robert Wilson, HarperCollins
Joseph Spieler
Marcy Ross

DUN & BRADSTREET
Guide to
$YOUR INVESTMENTS$®
1997

This book is intended and written to provide the author's opinions in regard to the subject matter covered. This book is prepared solely by Nancy Dunnan and not by The Dun & Bradstreet Corporation and its subsidiaries; The Dun & Bradstreet Corporation does not give out investment advice. The author, the publisher, and The Dun & Bradstreet Corporation are not engaged in rendering legal, accounting, or other professional advice, and the reader should seek the services of a qualified professional for such advice.

The author, the publisher, and The Dun & Bradstreet Corporation cannot be held responsible for any loss incurred as a result of the application of any of the information in this publication.

Every attempt has been made to assure the accuracy of the statistics that appear throughout *$Your Investments$* ®. In some cases, data may vary from your reports because of interpretations or accounting changes made after the original publication. In others, there may be errors—for which we apologize. Please remember that *$Your Investments$*® is a *guide,* not a definitive source of financial information. When you have a question, check with your broker's research department.

Getting Started on Your Investment Portfolio

INTRODUCTION

Sophie Tucker put it well when she said, "I've been rich and I've been poor, and believe me, rich is better." You too can start on the road to riches or increase the riches you already have during 1997 by heeding the suggestions and advice in this year's edition of *Dun & Bradstreet Guide to $Your Investments$® 1997*. It doesn't matter whether you have $5,000, $50,000, or $550,000. At all three levels and those in between there are many investment choices; so many, in fact, you may have difficulty deciding where to put your money.

That is what this section, Part One, will help you sort out. It will simplify what can otherwise be a tough decision-making process. Gathering and understanding the information needed to make those decisions is your first step in building up your riches and becoming at ease in the world of finances.

BEGINNING INVESTORS

Please start by reading all of Part One, "Getting Started on Your Investment Portfolio." Here you will find information on basic, time-tested choices, as well as on:

- How to pick a money market fund

- How to get the best deal at your bank

- The advantages of a credit union

- When to move into mutual funds, and which ones to choose

- How to protect and insure your money

SEASONED INVESTORS

You should begin by reading Chapter 1, which contains new and timely advice on special investments for 1997. Then move on to the "Investors Almanac" where we discuss "hot" collectibles, and Part Two to size up the risks and rewards of more sophisticated investments.

WHAT YOU CAN DO TO IMPROVE YOUR FINANCIAL LIFE

1. *Be aware.* Take time to learn how to handle your money. You know perfectly well that the stock market dips, and that inflation, changing interest rates, unemployment, and generally hard times are, now and then, unfortunately part of our lives. So don't passively put your financial matters in the hands of your spouse or your parents, a stockbroker or financial planner, or even the corporation you work for. To do so, I feel, is childlike and courting disaster.

   Although many regulatory agencies, as well as the Securities and Exchange Commission, the stock exchanges, and the Federal Reserve Board, make every effort to maintain orderly markets and a stable economy, you too should take steps to protect yourself in this fully globalized investing world.

   To choose to remain uninvolved or ignorant about the stock market, the direction of the economy, and the workings of the financial world will eventually cost you money.

2. *Be informed.* The two best defenses you have against trouble are relatively simple: The first is *information,* and the second is *diversification.* After taking time to learn how the economy, individual companies, the banks, interest rates, the dollar, and inflation affect your investments, you may still lose money some of the time, but you will win far more often—if you are both diversified and informed.

   Begin by reading at least one intelligent financial publication each week. Select one that matches your level of sophistication. Carry it with you (see the box below). Watch the market news on CNN, CNN-FN, CNBC, or PBS television or listen to broadcasts on public radio. Know what's happening, in this country and abroad.

Your Financial Library

Read one of these 16 publications each week or month. I've arranged them by approximate level of sophistication, beginning with the most elementary. Subscriptions are available for each and many are available over the newsstand.

1. *USA Today*	8. *Smart Money*
2. Your local newspaper	9. *Money*
3. *Bottom Line Personal*	10. *The New York Times*
4. *U.S. News & World Report*	11. Standard & Poor's *The Outlook*
5. *Better Investing* (National Assn of Investment Clubs)	12. *BusinessWeek*
	13. *Barron's*
6. *Consumer Reports*	14. *Value Line Investment Survey*
7. *Your Money*	15. *Investor's Business Daily*

---

3. Then, *diversify*—among types of investments and risk levels. Check your holdings against the investment pyramid on page 14. Make certain you have dollars invested in several levels.

HOW TO PICK WINNERS

There was a time when all an investor had to do was pick attractive stocks or bonds. Now, however, you're faced with a bewildering variety of choices, often involving hefty commissions. It's important to determine whether they are speculations or investments. To boost your success ratio:

- **Don't become involved with special "opportunities"** until you've developed a balanced portfolio. Stay away from futures, commodities, most new issues, and other complicated investments. These are dominated by the professionals, who have more skill, knowledge, and money than most individuals—and even they get hurt.

- **Don't follow the crowd.** The majority opinion is often wrong. Every significant market advance has begun when pessimism was loudest and prices lowest.

- **Don't dash in and out of the market.** You'll find your profits eaten up by commissions.

- **Don't be in a hurry to invest your money.** If you miss one opportunity, there will be another just as good and possibly better along soon.

- **Don't fall in love with your investments.** There is always a time to be in a stock, a bond, a money market account, and a CD and a time to be out. Remember, with few exceptions most investments eventually become overpriced, and no tree ever grows to the sky.

How to Calculate the Effect of Inflation

YEARS FROM NOW	4%	5%	6%	7%	8%
5	1.22	1.28	1.34	1.40	1.47
10	1.48	1.63	1.79	1.97	2.16
15	1.80	2.08	2.40	2.76	3.17
20	2.19	2.65	3.21	3.87	4.66
25	2.67	3.39	4.29	5.43	6.85
30	3.24	4.32	5.74	7.61	10.06

SOURCE: Reprinted with permission from *Encyclopedia of Banking and Financial Tables,* copyright © 1980, 1986, Warren, Gorham & Lamont, Inc., Boston, Mass. All rights reserved.

THE MAGIC OF COMPOUNDING

No matter what the market or the economy does, there's one given, one technique that works continually and that's the positive impact of compounding, or earning interest on interest, by prompt reinvestment of all interest, dividends, and capital gains. As shown in the tables in this chapter, with compounding your savings will grow at an astonishing rate over the years.

☑ *HINT: The Rule of 72: For a quick calculation on how long it takes to double your money, use the rule of 72: divide 72 by the yield. Thus, at 9%, it will take 8 years; at 10% about 7 years; and at 12%, 6 years to double your money.*

The Power of Compound Interest

A REGULAR INVESTMENT OF $100 PER YEAR, INVESTED AT:	WILL, COMPOUNDED ANNUALLY AT THE END OF EACH YEAR, GROW TO THIS SUM AFTER THIS NUMBER OF YEARS:							
	5	10	15	20	25	30	35	40
6%	$564	$1,318	$2,328	$3,679	$5,486	$7,906	$11,143	$15,476
8	587	1,449	2,715	4,576	7,311	11,328	17,232	25,906
10	611	1,594	3,177	5,727	9,835	16,449	27,102	44,259
12	635	1,755	3,728	7,205	13,333	24,133	43,166	76,709
14	661	1,934	4,384	9,102	18,187	35,679	69,357	134,202
16	688	2,132	5,166	11,538	24,921	53,031	112,071	236,076

To get the corresponding total for any other annually invested amount (A), multiply the dollar total given above for the yield and the number of years by A/100. Example: You plan to invest $75 per month, $900 a year. What capital sum will that provide after 35 years, at 12% compounded annually? Check where the lines cross for 12% and 35 years: $43,166 ¥ 900/100 = $388,494. *Note:* The totals will be greater if: (1) the deposits are made at the beginning of the year; (2) compounding is more frequent.

LISTENING TO THE PROS

John Kenneth Galbraith, in his book *The Great Crash,* reminds us that John D. Rockefeller told the press after the crash of October 29, 1929, "Believing that fundamental conditions of the country are sound, my son and I have for some days been purchasing sound common stocks." To this Eddie Cantor replied, "Sure, who else had any money left?"

After reading the *Dun & Bradstreet Guide to $Your Investments$*® and becoming an informed investor, you too will be able to decide if you wish to follow Rockefeller's notion or side with Mark Twain, who said, "October. This is one of the peculiarly dangerous months to speculate in stocks. The others are July, January, September, April, November, May, March, June, December, August, and February."

If you follow Rockefeller's path, I urge you to keep in mind that it's terribly important to cut your losses—when and if you have any. As Warren Buffett, the chairman of Berkshire Hathaway, Inc., said in one of his annual reports, "Should you find yourself in a chronically leaking boat, energy devoted to changing vessels is likely to be more productive than energy devoted to patching leaks."

Personally, I like Mae West's attitude best: "Too much of a good thing can be wonderful." May 1997 be a wonderful year for you and your investments.

Financial Resolutions for 1997

I resolve to:

- *Pay* myself every month—to make savings the first check/deposit I make after my mortgage or rent
- *Set* up a realistic, automatic savings plan
- *Live* within my income
- *Organize* my financial papers
- *Review or write* my will and health care proxy
- *Subscribe* to a financial publication...and then actually read it
- *Aim to be* an informed investor, not a timid one or a speculator
- *Spend* half an hour each day listening to or reading about financial matters
- *Invest* only in things I understand and learn about those I don't
- *Keep* a financial notebook handy in which to write down ideas, questions

And finally,

- *Read* most of this book and deduct the cost from my taxes.

1

Special Advice for 1997

"The safest way to double your money is to fold it over once and put it in your pocket."

There's some debate about which great wit first offered this advice. Most say it was Frank McKinney Hubbard, who worked on the *Indianapolis News* in the 1930s, where, under the name Kim Hubbard, he wrote and illustrated amusing stories about the rustic philosopher Abe Martin.

However, there's absolutely no debate over the fact that it's never easy to double your money, whether it was in 1930 or in 1997. Yet there are a number of steps you can take to increase your personal wealth during 1997, in addition to folding over any spare bills you might have on hand.

AN INVESTOR'S ROAD MAP FOR 1997

Although it's impossible to predict precisely what will happen in the financial world during 1997, there are eight possibilities you should seriously consider.

1. The U.S. stock market will continue to rise, interrupted by occasional corrections.

2. Interest rates will probably move up slightly to counteract any rise in inflation.

3. Terrorism will continue to be a factor in our lives.

4. We will do more trading of securities by computer and gain more of our information about stocks, bonds, mutual funds, and personal finance from the Internet.

5. More and more of us will work at home or find work through placement companies.

6. It will become easier and easier to invest in foreign securities.

7. Due to competition, more companies will offer stocks directly to investors, bypassing the need to use a stockbroker.

   And ...

8. We will all grow one year older.

These observations lend themselves to unique investing opportunities for you during 1997, and with some old-fashioned research and thought, you just may be able to make money on them. Add your own special spin to the following 13 ACTION STEPS.

YOU AND THE STOCK MARKET IN 1997

The market had several severe corrections last year, due largely to the fact that investors and institutions thought the technology stocks were wildly overpriced. You can expect several corrections during 1997 as well. Use these price dips to buy shares of stocks you like, particularly blue chip stocks, which tend to recover quickly.

Action Step #1

Buy blue chips on dips.
Six suggestions:

- Abbott Laboratories
- Bristol-Myers Squibb
- Coca-Cola
- Johnson & Johnson
- Procter & Gamble
- Schering-Plough

Action Step #2

Add high yielding stocks to your portfolio.
They will provide some downside protection if the market drops.

$TIP: Investors generally hesitate to sell their income stocks because they enjoy the income, therefore their prices do not decline as much as other stocks when the market takes a dive.

Six suggestions:

- Alliance Capital Management
- BCE Inc.
- Central & Southwest
- Health & Retirement Properties
- 1838 Bond Debenture Fund
- Weingarten Realty

Action Step #3

Invest in companies that are involved in the world of computers, the Internet, and the year 2000.

- Cheyenne Software
- Computer Associates*
- Computer Sciences Corp.*
- Data Systems & Software
- Electronic Data Systems*
- Microsoft
- Sterling Software

Those with an * are equipped to deal with the problem known as The Year 2000, when software must be updated. These three companies have developed tools to use in this specialized transformation. In fact, the U.S. Department of Commerce estimates that some $200 billion will have to be spent between 1997 and 2000 to meet this task.

Action Step #4

Invest in stocks involved in home office equipment and services and placement agencies for those seeking work.

- IBM
- Kelley Services
- Manpower
- Olsten Corp.
- Robert Half Int'l
- Staples, Inc.
- Viking Office Products

Action Step #5

New business starts are on the rise. Look for publicly traded companies whose products and services you like, keeping in mind that this is a speculative arena.
Add several smaller cap and/or lesser known stocks to your portfolio.

- Boston Chicken
- Correction Corp. of America
- DeVry Inc.
- Pep Boys
- Verifone
- Youth Services Int'l
- Steinway Musical Instruments

Action Step #6

Consider stocks in the bomb detector business.
The downing of TWA Flight 800, the bombing at the Summer Olympics in Atlanta, and other acts

of terrorism have led to a demand for tighter security systems at airports and other public places. Consider these stocks, knowing that they are a speculative play on the current national concern:

- American Science & Engineering
- Barringer Technologies
- InVision Technologies
- Thermedics

YOU AND INTEREST RATES IN 1997

As we go to press, it appears as though interest rates might rise during 1997 in order to keep the lid on inflation. Watch rates carefully, and in the meantime:

Action Step #7

Move money out of your bank savings account.

If you still have money earning the typically low bank rate, move it immediately to a money market fund.

Example: The Strong Money Market Fund, one of the ones with a consistently high yield, as of September 1996 was yielding 5.96%. Call 800–368–1030 for details. (And remember, you get free checking provided you write checks in amounts of $500 or more.)

Action Step #8

Buy Treasuries.

Not only is this consistently a safe place to put money, but the interest you earn is exempt from state and local taxes. Read Chapter 9 for details on how to buy Treasuries without using a broker. As we go to press, the rate on T-bills was 4.97% and on a three year T-note, 5.30%. *NOTE:* the longer the maturity the higher the rate.

Action Step #9

Put money in a tax-advantaged fund.

If you are in the 28% bracket or higher, find a money market fund on which you won't have to pay federal, state, or local taxes on the income earned.

Example: The United Services Government Securities Saving Fund (800–873–8637) invests only in U.S. government or government-backed obligations. The three states where investors don't get this tax break are Maine, New Hampshire, and Pennsylvania.

Action Step #10

Add high-yield corporate bonds to your portfolio.

However, select only those rated B or above by Standard & Poor's. For example:

Issuer	Current Yield	Maturity
■ SPX Corp.	10.6%	2002
■ Storer Communications	9.9%	2003
■ AK Steel Corp.	9.8%	2004
■ Eckerd	9.6%	2004
■ Beverly Enterprises	9.4%	2006
■ Genesis Health Ventures	9.5%	2005

YOU AND THE INTERNATIONAL SCENE IN 1997

In Chapter 19 you'll find lots of pointers on investing in foreign securities. However, I want to highlight here a new technique for purchasing foreign stocks without using a broker.

Action Step #11

Buy foreign stocks directly.

A new program, launched in the summer of 1996 by Morgan Stanley, lets you make your initial purchase directly from over 15 foreign companies. The minimum initial investment for each is $250. There's an annual $15 administration fee and a transaction fee of $5 plus brokerage commissions of about 12 cents per share. For details, 800–711–6475.

Among the companies available:

Banco de Santander	Spain
British Airways	UK
British Telecom	UK

Fiat	Italy
National Westminster	UK
Nippon Telegraph & Telephone	Japan
NorskHydro	Norway
Novo-Nordisk	Denmark
Pacific Dunlop	Australia
Reuters Holdings	UK
Sony	Japan
Telefonos de Mexico	Mexico

Action Step #12

Buy U.S. stocks directly.

Continue to explore the growing number of stocks that are sold directly to the individual investors, making it unnecessary to use a stockbroker. A handful are listed below. For more information, see Chapter 13.

Atlantic Energy	609–645–4506
Barnett Banks	904–791–7720
Bob Evans Farms	614–492–4952
Dial Corp.	800–453–2235
Exxon Corp.	800–252–1800
Johnson Controls	414–228–2363
Kellwood Co.	314–576–3100
Kerr-McGee Corp.	405–270–1313
Morton Int'l	201–324–0498
Procter & Gamble	800–742–6253
Tenneco, Inc.	800–446–2617
Texaco, Inc.	800–283–9785

U.S. West	800–537–0022
Wisconsin Energy	800–558–9663

YOU AND THE LONG LIFE

I'm sure you're aware of the fact that Americans are living longer and longer. Babies born in 1997 can expect to live well into their mid- and late eighties. And as we become a nation of older citizens, we are generating a huge, ongoing need for new types of places in which to live, new types of medical care and coverage, new drugs, medicines, medical equipment, even new vitamins.

Action Step #13

Add health care and/or drug stocks to your portfolio.

Some suggestions; keep in mind that these stocks are not risk-free.

- Columbia Healthcare
- Community Psychiatric
- General Nutrition
- Healthsource
- Manor Care
- Medpartners/Millikin
- Merck & Co.
- Oxford Health Plans
- Physician Corp. of America
- Scheing Plough
- U.S. Healthcare

2

Building Your Own Investment Pyramid

One of the questions I am asked most frequently is, "How do I get started investing? I just don't know where to begin." It's a very valid question and one you should not be embarrassed to ask.

There are hundreds of choices out there and many more people willing to sell them to you. How do you decide between stocks and bonds, mutual funds and bank CDs, Spiders and LEAPS, zeros and derivatives, options and commodities, foreign stocks or foreign currencies? Real estate or gold? One way to develop a winning porfolio is to envision it, literally as an INVESTMENT PYRA-MID—it works whether you are a new investor or a sophisticated money manager who has weathered numerous bull and bear cycles.

It's a visual way in which to see how much risk accompanies each type of investment...and exactly when it's appropriate to add each on to your own portfolio.

YOUR HOMEWORK ASSIGNMENTS

Random purchases of stocks, bonds, and mutual funds may work out for you initially, but they are unlikely to fulfill your long-range goals. To make the most money, you need to be prepared, like the Boy and Girl Scouts—and to do your homework. Here are your four assignments.

Lesson #1: Know Thy Worth

Before making any type of investment expenditure, whether it's buying a stock, a bond, or a house, you need to know your approximate net worth—not down to the last penny, but within several thousand dollars or so. This is one of the first questions stockbrokers, money managers, and bank mortgage officers ask potential clients. If, like most people, you're not sure, don't panic. Figuring it out is easy—all you need is a free evening, a calculator, your checkbook, bills, and a record of your income. Then follow these two easy steps:

1. Add up the value of everything you own (your assets).
2. Subtract the total of all you owe (your liabilities).

The amount left over is your net worth. You can use the worksheet on the following page as a guide for arriving at the correct amount. When figuring your assets, list the amount they will bring in today's market, which could be more or less than you paid for them originally. Assets include cash on hand, your checking and savings account balances, the cash value of any insurance policies, personal property (car, boat, jewelry, real estate, investments), and any vested interest in a pension or retirement plan. Your liabilities include money you owe, charge account debts, mortgages,

Finding Your Net Worth

ASSETS as of _____ (date)		LIABILITIES as of _____ (date)	
Cash on hand	$_____	Unpaid bills	
Cash in checking accounts	_____	Charge accounts	$_____
Savings accounts	_____	Taxes, property taxes, and	
Money market fund	_____	quarterly income taxes	_____
Life insurance, cash value	_____	Insurance premiums	_____
Annuities	_____	Rent or monthly mortgage payment	_____
Retirement funds		Utilities	_____
IRA or Keogh	_____	Balance due on:	
401(k) plan	_____	Mortgage	_____
Vested interest in pension		Automobile loans	_____
or profit-sharing plan	_____	Personal loans	_____
U.S. savings bonds, current value	_____	Installment loans	_____
Investments		**Total liabilities**	$_____
Market value of stocks, bonds,			
mutual fund shares, etc.			
Real estate, market value of real			
property minus mortgage	_____	Assets	$_____
Property		Minus liabilities	–_____
Automobile	_____	**Your net worth**	$_____
Furniture	_____		
Jewelry, furs	_____		
Sports and hobby equipment	_____		
Equity interest in your business	_____		
Total assets	$_____		

auto payments, education or other loans, and any taxes due.

Lesson #2: Know Where Thy Worth Is Going: aka: Budgeting

You may not be thrilled with the idea of doing a budget, but if you're serious about taking good care of your net worth, then a little budgeting is part of the deal. In fact, it's really the only accurate way to know how much you're spending and on what, and it's also a way to set aside money for investing, the reason you probably bought this book in the first place.

If you need help in establishing a budget for saving and investing, use the fill-in worksheet on page 13. Try to set aside a certain dollar amount on a regular basis, even if it's not an impressively large number. Mark it immediately for "savings/investing." Ideally you should try to save 5% to 10% of your annual income; if you make more than $70,000 a year, aim for 15%.

☑ *HINT: Here's my favorite gimmick for those of you who need one to get you going: Begin by saving 1% of your take-home pay this month and increase it by 1% each month for a year so that at the end of 12 months you'll be saving 12%.*

What Happens to a $1,000 Investment at 5¼% Compounding

FREQUENCY OF COMPOUNDING	1 YEAR	5 YEARS	10 YEARS	20 YEARS
Continuous	$1,054.67	$1,304.93	$1,702.83	$2,899.63
Daily	1,054.67	1,304.90	1,702.76	2,899.41
Quarterly	1,053.54	1,297.96	1,684.70	2,838.20
Semiannually	1,053.19	1,295.78	1,679.05	2,819.21
Annually	1,052.50	1,291.55	1,668.10	2,782.54

In the meantime, take a look at the table below which shows what happens to $1,000 over 20 years when you put it in an investment yielding 5¼% and the income earned is reinvested or compounded.

Lesson #3: Know Thy Goals and Priorities

After you've accumulated money to invest, your next homework assignment is to decide what you want to accomplish by investing. If you were to take a trip to Europe or travel by car across the country, you would bring along a good road map. So, too, it is with saving and investing. However, the road map consists of financial, not geographic, destinations. When you travel through Italy, you decide what towns, cathedrals, or monuments you want most to visit; how long it will take you to get from one to the next; and approximately what it will cost. Just do the same as you plot out your financial journey through life.

Your highlights or destination points may include some of these:

- Building a nest egg for emergencies
- Establishing an investment portfolio
- Reducing taxes
- Preparing for retirement
- Paying for a college education
- Buying a house, car, or boat
- Traveling or taking a cruise
- Investing in art or antiques
- Adding on a room or installing a swimming pool
- Setting up your own business

Goal setting, you will discover, enables you to take firm control of your financial life, especially if you actually write down your goals. The process of listing goals on paper, perhaps awkward at first, forces you to focus on how you handle money and how you feel about risk versus safety. I think it's best to divide your goals into two sections: immediate goals (those that can be accomplished in a year or less) and long-range goals.

If you're single, your immediate goals could be:

- Obtain a graduate degree
- Join a health club
- Save for summer vacation
- Start to pay off college loans

Longer-term goals:

- Buy a car
- Set up a brokerage account or buy shares in a mutual fund
- Purchase a co-op or condo with a friend

If you're married and raising a family, the goals might shift to include:

- Buying a house
- Setting up educational funds for children
- Building a growth portfolio
- Travel with the family

Singles and marrieds closer to retirement tend to seek other goals:

- Shift bulk of portfolio to safe, income-producing vehicles
- Increase contribution to retirement plan

Your Cash Flow

Where It Comes From	Annual Amount	Where It Goes	Annual Amount
Take-home pay	$_____	Income taxes	$_____
Bonus and commissions	_____	Mortgage or rent	_____
Freelance consulting	_____	Property taxes	_____
Interest	_____	Utilities	_____
Dividends	_____	Automobile	
Rent	_____	maintenance	_____
Pensions	_____	insurance	_____
Social Security	_____	Commuting or other transportation	_____
Annuities	_____	Insurance	
Tax refunds	_____	Homeowner's or renter's	_____
Alimony	_____	Life	_____
Other	_____	Health	_____
Total	$_____	Disability	_____
		Child care	_____
		Education	_____
		Food	_____
		Medical Expenses	_____
		Clothing	_____
		Household	
		miscellaneous	_____
		Home improvements	_____
		Entertainment	_____
		Vacations, travel	_____
		Books, magazines, club dues	_____
		Contributions to charities or	
		organizations	_____
		Total	$_____
		Surplus or deficit	_____

- Find appropriate short-term tax shelters
- Set up a consulting business; incorporate
- Pay off mortgage
- Be debt-free

Regardless of your age or income, individual goals make it easier and more meaningful to stick to a budget and to save for investing. Putting aside that 5% to 15% every month for an investment program suddenly has a very tangible purpose—one that you personally decided on.

Lesson #4: Building Your Investment Pyramid

Once you know why you want to invest, you are ready to think about your investments as part of a pyramid in which each level builds on the earlier ones. This approach to investing offers a carefully designed, diversified system that provides for financial growth and protection regardless of your age, marital status, income, or level of financial sophistication. As you can see by looking at the illustration, you begin your financial program

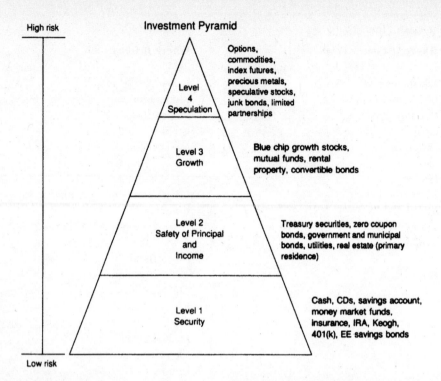

Investment Pyramid

High risk

Low risk

Level 4 Speculation — Options, commodities, index futures, precious metals, speculative stocks, junk bonds, limited partnerships

Level 3 Growth — Blue chip growth stocks, mutual funds, rental property, convertible bonds

Level 2 Safety of Principal and Income — Treasury securities, zero coupon bonds, government and municipal bonds, utilities, real estate (primary residence)

Level 1 Security — Cash, CDs, savings account, money market funds, insurance, IRA, Keogh, 401(k), EE savings bonds

on the pyramid at *Level 1*. It is the lowest in terms of risk and the highest in safety. As your net worth grows, you automatically move up to the next level, increasing both the amount of risk involved and the potential for financial gain.

Level 1 covers life's basic financial requirements and includes:

- An emergency nest egg consisting of cash or cash equivalents, such as savings account, CDs, money market funds
- Health, life, and disability insurance
- A solid retirement plan, including an IRA, Keogh, or 401(k)

Before leaving this level, you will have saved enough cash or cash equivalents to cover a minimum of 6 to 9 months' worth of living expenses. This minimum is your emergency reserve, and when you've achieved this goal, you're financially solid enough to advance to Level 2.

Level 2 is devoted entirely to safe income-producing investments, such as corporate or municipal bonds; Treasury securities; longer-term CDs; zero coupon bonds; and real estate (your primary residence)—all of which are described in this book.

Although safety is key at this step, the liquidity factor emphasized in Level 1 is now traded off for a higher return or yield. And because some of these items, notably zero coupon bonds and CDs, are timed to mature at a definite date, they provide ideal means to meet staggering college tuition bills and retirement costs.

Money to buy real estate is also included, not only because it gives you a place to live, but also because historically real estate has appreciated significantly in value. At the same time, it offers tax benefits in the form of deductions for mortgage and home equity interest payments and for real-estate taxes.

Level 3 involves investing for growth. At this point you can afford to be more adventuresome, more risk-oriented, and less conservative; and this book shows you how to turn away from liquidity and assured income and toward growth and blue-chip stocks, conservative mutual funds, convertible bonds, and rentable property. If you find you're interested in the stock market, this is the ideal time to join an investment club and learn by doing so.

Level 4, the pinnacle of the pyramid, is given over to the riskiest investments, which may or may not yield spectacular returns. These include speculative stocks, stocks in new companies, takeover candidates, options, commodities, index futures, gold and precious metals, junk bonds, and limited partnerships, all vehicles discussed in detail in the following chapters.

FOUR DUMB INVESTMENT MISTAKES YOU CAN AVOID

You may think that only novices make investment mistakes—not true. Here are four traps into which the pros as well as new investors often fall, along with practical solutions for each. Chapter references are to further material on the topic within this book.

1. *Merely chasing yields.* When CD and money market funds pay attractive yields, it's easy to park our money in CDs and money market funds. This is appropriate with some of your money, but it's no way to keep up with inflation let alone beat inflation.
   Solutions: (1) Stagger bond and CD maturities so you continually have money coming in for reinvestment should rates go up. (2) Put only one-quarter of your income portfolio in risky, high-yield bonds or bond mutual funds. (See Chapter 6.)
2. *Failing to diversify.* It's easy to keep doing what works and overlook the importance of dividing your portfolio into different investments—

ones that work in different ways so you are protected when interest rates move up or down or when the market is bullish or bearish.
   Solutions: Divide your money among these categories: (a) money funds, CDs, and Treasury bills; (b) domestic stocks; (c) foreign stocks; (d) domestic bonds; (e) international bonds; and (f) real estate. Then, within each category, you can diversify even further. With stocks, divide your money among blue chips, small-caps, utilities, growth stocks, and some new issues, for example.

   Within the bond category, you can further divide your investments into different maturities (ranging from short- to long-term); into tax-free municipals; and into different risk levels: government bonds, AAA-rated corporate bonds, and higher-risk junk bonds. (See Chapters 9 and 12.)
3. *Not taking advantage of dollar cost averaging.* Most investors either put too much or too little into stocks or mutual funds at one time.
   Solution: Instead, invest a set amount on a regular basis, say once a month, to smooth out market fluctuations. You'll generally wind up making purchases at a lower cost per share than if you bought all at once (see page 256).

☑ **HINT: Need a little arm-twisting to get going on a regular savings plan? Set aside a certain amount weekly or monthly and look at what can happen. The accumulation of interest and/or dividends is impressive. Here's what happens when you invest $100, $300, and $500 every month, assuming a fixed rate of 5¼%:**

What Happens When You Save at 5¼%

MONTHLY AMOUNT	NUMBER OF YEARS				
	5	10	15	20	25
$100	$7,348	$18,295	$34,604	$58,902	$85,103
$300	22,043	54,884	103,811	176,706	285,308
$500	36,738	91,473	173,019	294,510	475,513

4. Hanging onto a losing investment. Too often we are taken with a stock or other investment, so that it's hard to admit we made a mistake.

Solution: Set a percentage loss figure and stick to it. Write it down in your investment book or on your computer disk. When you sell, note why the investment turned out to be a loser so you can avoid repeating your error.

WHAT TO DO WHEN: A MONEY STRATEGY CHECKLIST

In Your 20s and 30s

- *Write* your will
- *Set up* a savings plan
- *Buy* a house
- *Invest* for growth
- *Get* insurance coverage
- *Begin* contributing to a retirement plan
- *Start* your IRA

In Your 40s and 50s

- *Do* all of the above if you haven't already
- *Invest* for income as well as growth
- *Look* into tax-exempt investments
- *Fund* your retirement plan to the max
- *Draw up* a durable power of attorney or living trust, and a living will
- *Consult* an attorney if your estate is over $600,000
- *Pay* off your mortgage before you retire

In Your 60s or at Retirement

- *Invest* more for income but keep some growth stocks
- *Aim* to reinvest income and gains to beat inflation
- *Review* your will and estate plan
- *Investigate* retirement housing
- *Talk* to your family about your estate plans and funeral wishes
- *Revise* your will if it's out of date

Hints for the Beginning Investor

1. *Don't think you'll get rich overnight.* Few people do.
2. *Don't rush into stocks or bonds* until you've saved the equivalent of 6 to 9 months of living expenses in a money market fund, CDs, or treasuries.
3. *Know whether you're investing for income or growth.* Many people never bother to figure this out and are disappointed with their returns.
4. *Pick stocks and bonds of leading companies* at the beginning. They have proven track records, a lot of research is available for them, and there will always be a buyer should you wish to sell.
5. *Buy a stock* only if you can state at least two reasons why it will appreciate in price or continue to pay high dividends.
6. *Resist churning your own account* so that commissions won't eat up your profits.
7. *Spread out your risks.* Every company and mutual fund has the potential to be a loser some of the time. Therefore, never put all your eggs in one basket.
8. *Decide on the maximum amount* that you're willing to lose and stick to it.
9. *When you lose money,* if you do, try to determine why your choice was a poor one.
10. *Study investing* and investments on a regular basis.

3

Finding Safe Places for Your Money: Banks, Money Market Funds, CDs, and Credit Unions

Throughout your investment life there will be many times when varying portions of your assets should be kept liquid—liquid meaning readily available. Far too many people interpret this to mean keeping it in their bank savings account. NO! Don' be foolish — the interest rate is always way, way too low.

Fortunately, you have six other options:

1. Interest-bearing checking accounts (sometimes called NOW accounts)
2. Bank money market deposit accounts
3. Bank certificates of deposits (CDs)
4. Money market mutual funds
5. U.S. savings bonds
6. U.S. Treasuries (the latter two are discussed in Chapters 9 and 10)

All of these are safe and readily available and will preserve your capital, as illustrated on Level 1 of *"Your Investment Pyramid"* (page 14).

Use the table on page 18 to compare the current yields for each one (as we went to press), as well as their average minimum dollar requirements and the amount of time you can have your money invested in each one. I don't by any means suggest you put all your money in these safe havens—even their yields are too low—but you should certainly earmark about one-quarter of your assets for this Level 1 category. Investors—amateurs and pros—have come to realize that the stock market is unpredictable, and diversification is not just mumbo jumbo from the mouths of conservative financial advisers and writers such as myself: It is the basis of protecting one's investments in economic climates of all kinds.

☑ *HINT: Be sure you know the difference between interest rate and yield. Interest rate is the annual return without compounding. The effective yield reflects compounding—daily, monthly, quarterly, annually. If you have a CD, compare yields if you plan to leave your earned interest the bank. Compare interest rates if you are taking out your earned interest.*

AT YOUR BANK

In late 1992, the Federal Insurance Deposit Corporation (FDIC) limited the interest rates that our weaker banks can give customers, while at the same time permitting well-capitalized banks to determine their own interest rates. So, undercapitalized banks and savings and loans can no longer pay extremely high rates; however, it pays to shop around, because rates, fees, products, and services continue to vary from bank to bank. Although it's time-consuming to get on the phone, do. It could mean you're landing as much as 1½% more.

☑ *HINT: All things being equal, however, there's something to be said for having all or most of your banking at one institution. Called "relationship banking," it may mean you can get higher interest on your savings, lower fees on your checking, and better terms on your loans. That's because when all your banking is lumped together, you become a more important customer. But find out.*

⊘ CAUTION: *Unless you have a very small amount to save or are opening an account for a child, avoid savings accounts; better interest rates are available through the accounts described in the rest of this chapter.*

To get the most out of your bank:

1. Ask for overdraft checking privileges—that is, a permanent line of credit that prevents you from bouncing a check. The bank will automatically cover your check even if you don't have enough money in the account, for up to a predetermined dollar amount. You will have to pay back the loan plus interest.

2. Once you have more than $2,500 in your NOW account (or whatever the minimum balance required is), move the excess into a money market deposit account at the bank or to a money market mutual fund—whichever has better rates.

3. Don't buy bank-printed checks. You can save money by ordering checks from Checks in the Mail (800–733–4443) or Current, Inc. (800–426–0822).

Bank Money Market Deposit Accounts

The counterpart of a money market mutual fund at a bank is a money market deposit account. They pay relatively competitive interest rates, offer liquidity, and—like all bank accounts including savings and NOWs—are insured up to $100,000 by the FDIC, or, at a savings and loan, by the FSLIC. They tend to pay slightly lower yields than money market mutual funds and Treasury bills and their rates change periodically with fluctuations in overall short-term rates, which is also true of money market mutual funds. The minimum to open ranges from $100 to $10,000.

These accounts also offer convenience—most

Safe Havens

INVESTMENT	YIELD (OCTOBER 1996)	AVERAGE MINIMUM INVESTMENT
■ **1 to 3 Months**		
Money market mutual funds	4.81%	$1,000
Bank money market accounts	2.64	1,000
NOW bank accounts	2.50	2,500
Short-term CDs	4.79	500
3-month Treasury bills	5.01	10,000 initial; 1,000 thereafter
Passbook savings account	2.50	50
Credit union savings	3.65	50
■ **3 Months or Longer**		
12-month CD	5.14	500
1-year Treasury bills	5.64	10,000 initial; 1,000 thereafter
7-year Treasury notes	6.42	5,000 (1- to 4-year maturities)
		1,000 (4- to 10-year maturities)
10-year Treasury bonds	6.66	1,000
EE savings bonds	4.06	25

banks let you write checks on them for any dollar amount, although they limit the number of checks you can write to third parties (anyone but your-self)—typically to three checks per month to a third party and three pre-authorized transactions (as might occur when you arrange in advance to pay a specific bill, such as a mortgage payment). Generally, you may withdraw cash in person as often as you like. On the other hand, money market mutual funds let you write as many checks as you like, but you must write them for a minimum amount—usually $250 or $500.

Yields and penalties for falling below the required minimum vary from bank to bank. So find out if your bank avoids paying interest on a money market deposit account if the balance drops below a certain minimum.

Certificates of Deposit (CDs)

CDs, also known as time certificates of deposit, are safe, reliable savings instruments available at most every local bank. The certificate indicates that you have deposited a sum of money for a specified period of time (6 months, 1 year, etc.), at a specified rate of interest. The fact that they're insured up to $100,000 has made them popular with savers seeking a high level of safety.

Banks are free to set their own minimum amounts, but they tend to range from $500 to $5,000 and more. Those that are $100,000 or over are called "jumbo CDs" and pay a slightly higher yield.

Although CD rates, terms, and dollar amounts vary from bank to bank, the following are generally available:

Determining how long to tie up your money is not always easy. If you've invested in a 3-year CD and interest rates rise, you'll be stuck with the old lower rate. On the other hand, if rates fall, you'll be glad to have locked in the high yield. In general, if rates are falling, buy longer-term CDs, and if they are rising, keep the maturities short.

You should also ask the bank how you will find out when your CD is due. The bank should either send you a reminder or call you a few weeks beforehand so you can decide whether to withdraw your certificate or roll it over into a new CD.

☑ HINT: *To maximize your return, buy a CD in which the interest is not actually paid out until maturity. This gives you the benefit of compounded interest.*

Remember, too, that if you take out your CD before it matures, you will be penalized; however, early withdrawal penalties are usually waived in three instances:

- If the owner dies or is found to be mentally incompetent
- If the CD is in a Keogh or IRA retirement plan and the depositor is over 59½ years old
- If the bank offers penalty-free early withdrawals

How Compounding Boosts Returns on a $1,000 CD over a 1-Year Period

RATE	DAILY	MONTHLY	QUARTERLY	ANNUALLY
5%	$1,051.27	$1,051.16	$1,050.95	$1,050.00
6	1,061.83	1,061.69	1,061.37	1,060.00
7	1,072.50	1,072.28	1,071.86	1,070.00
8	1,083.28	1,083.00	1,082.44	1,080.00

SOURCE: Carteret Savings Bank, Morristown, New Jersey.

CDs with a Twist

To remain competitive with money market mutual funds and other banks, some institutions market CDs with added incentives. For example, there are adjustable-rate CDs, in which the interest rate fluctuates weekly along with the average T-bill rate or some other stated rate. Other banks have "designer CDs," in which you set your own maturity date so you can time it to come due when your child goes off to college, when you retire, or when you will need a lump sum of money. There are also CDs with yields tied to the Standard & Poor 500 Stock Index, to the price of gold, even to the cost of college tuition.

CAUTION: Before rushing out to buy one of the atypical CDs, find out precisely how the yield is caculated, whether it is tiered (the larger your deposit, the greater the interest rate), if it is automatically renewed upon maturity, and if so, whether at the same rate or a new one.

☑ *HINT: If you have $50,000 to $100,000 to invest in a CD, negotiate your rate. Banks may pay between ¼% and 1% more on large CDs.*

Zero CDs

Some brokerage firms offer zero coupon CDs in a variety of maturities. This type of CD does not pay interest on a regular basis. Instead, it is sold at a discount from face value. The interest accrues annually until the CD matures. You must report the income for tax purposes each year as it accrues.

Retirement CDs

This new product, available from a relatively small number of banks, is aimed at those who want safety rather than growth. Also known as an annuity CD, it combines a bank deposit with an annuity. As with the standard CD, your principal and interest are insured by the FDIC, up to $100,000. And, as with an annuity, all earnings are tax-deferred until you withdraw them. At that time you receive a monthly income for life.

CAUTION: The FDIC does NOT insure your lifetime payments; if the bank fails and is liquidated, you would get back your principal and interest, minus whatever payouts you'd already received.

In general, however, it's a safer investment than the straight insurance company annuity because when insurance companies go belly-up, part of your money can be lost. The tradeoff—retirement CDs have a lower yield.

Among the banks with sound financial reputations (according to Veribanc rating service) that offer these CDs are:

- Blackfeet National Bank, Browning, Mont.
- First National Bank, Santa Fe, N. Mex.
- Deposit Bank, Du Bois, Pa.
- CenWest National Bank, Johnstown, Pa.

What Is the True Rate?

Bank CD ads are often very confusing, with two rates given: fixed rate and yield. The yield figure is always higher, but to earn it, you must have your

CDs with a Twist

BANK		SPECIAL FEATURE
Hudson City Savings, Hudson, NY	(518–828–4600)	Interest rate rises over 2 years
College Savings Bank, Princeton, NJ	(800–888–2723)	Rises with college tuition
Eagle Federal, Hartford, CT	(203–947–7790)	9 month liquid CD
Wells Fargo Bank, San Francisco, CA	(415–781–2235)	Continual deposits; expandable CDs

CD at the bank for 1 full year at the same annual rate. For example, if your bank advertises a fixed rate of 6.5% and a yield of 6.75%, and you buy a 6-month CD and take it out at maturity, you will earn only the 6.5% fixed rate.

☑ *HINT: Roll over your 6-month CD so that it is on deposit the full year in order to earn the effective annual yield. In most institutions, the original yield is applicable even if the yield falls.*

CDs from a Stockbroker

Buying a CD through your stockbroker is often a better deal than buying it through a bank because yields tend to be higher. That's because brokers have access to CDs from banks across the nation and are not limited to just one institution. Merrill Lynch, for example, can tap about 160 banks, which gives investors more choices in terms of maturity, yield, and risk factor. And because brokered CDs are still bank CDs, they are insured up to $100,000.

Stockbrokers usually do not charge fees for CDs because they receive their commission from the issuing bank. Brokered CDs are also more liquid than those available at banks because they can be sold by your broker in a "secondary market." And there's no penalty for selling prior to maturity as there is when you cash in a bank CD.

However, the value of CDs, just like bonds, rises and falls in direct relationship to interest rates: If interest rates rise, the price of your CD will fall and you'll receive less than face value if you sell. If interest rates fall, you may be able to sell your brokered CD at a premium because it's worth more, because its rate is higher than that being paid on newly issued certificates.

💣 *CAUTION: CDs purchased from a broker seldom pay compounded interest. The broker typically puts each interest payment into a money market fund that is part of your account at the firm. The interest is often lower than that being paid on your CD. Check with the broker first, so you understand exactly how your interest will be handled.*

Out-of-State CDs

If you're seduced by ads for higher yields at out-of-state banks, remember that the grass isn't always greener. Proceed with caution and steer clear of troubled banks and S&Ls. Even though your money is insured up to $100,000, if the institution is closed, there may be a delay in getting your money out, and there have even been cases where high yields have been reduced.

☑ *HINT: Robert Heady, publisher of 100 Highest Yields, a newsletter ranking federally insured*

Brokered CDs

FIRM	TELEPHONE	MINIMUM
A.G. Edwards	800–999–4448	$1,000
Fidelity	800–544–8888	5,000
Edward D. Jones	314–851–2000	5,000
Merrill Lynch*	local office	1,000
Piper Jaffray & Hopwood	612–342–6000	1,000
Prudential-Bache	local office	1,000
Charles Schwab	800–435–4000	5,000
Smith Barney	local office	1,000

*Merrill Lynch's CDs are rated by Standard & Poor's.
(Data current as of October 1996.)

banking institutions, suggests purchasing CDs only from banks whose net worth exceeds 5% of assets and have recorded a profit for the previous two quarters.

To find the nation's best CDs, check:

- Heady's newsletter, *100 Highest Yields*, P.O. Box 088888, North Palm Beach, FL 33408; 800–327–7717; 8 issues, $48; 52 issues, $124.
- The Wednesday issues of the *Wall Street Journal*, which lists the top-yielding CDs for 1-, 2-, 3-, and 6-month, and 1-, 2-, and 5-year maturities.
- Personal finance magazines, such as *Money* and *Your Money*, which run lists of high-

yielding CDs and bank money market deposit accounts.

MONEY MARKET MUTUAL FUNDS

These funds are pooled investments sold by mutual funds, insurance companies, and brokerage firms. They take your cash and invest in something called the money market—a term that describes the way in which the government, banks, corporations, and securities dealers borrow and lend money for short time periods. Money market mutual funds invest in such short-term financial instruments as Treasury bills and notes (government IOUs), CDs (bank IOUs), and com-

Four Ways to Make More Money at Your Bank

1. *Stagger your CD maturities* by purchasing a variety of maturity dates, say, for 6 months, 12 months, and 15 months. If interest rates rise, you can reinvest CDs that mature at the new rate. If rates fall, your longer-term CDs will be earning the old, higher rate.
2. *Invest your CD interest.* Ask your bank to invest your CD interest automatically in a money market deposit account. You'll earn interest on your interest yet have access to the money without incurring a withdrawal penalty.
3. *Snowball* your CD. If your bank offers higher rates on larger CDs, it may pay to roll over several small CDs into one big one. Select a target date, say 1 month after your longest-term CD matures. When you renew your smaller CDs, have them mature on that date. Then all your CDs will mature on the same day and you can reinvest in one large CD with a high rate.
4. *Establish* your own interest-bearing checking account. Instead of depositing your paycheck into your checking account, put it in your money market deposit account. Several times during the month, transfer money to cover your checks. You will earn money market rates and be less tempted to spend without thinking about it first.

Money Market Funds with Competitive Yields

Alger Fund	800–992–3863
Dreyfus Liquid Assets	800–645–6561
Dreyfus Worldwide Dollar Fund	800–645–6561
Evergreen Fund	800–235–0064
Fidelity Spartan*	800–544–8888
Strong Money Market Fund	800–368–1030
Vanguard Prime Portfolio	800–662–7447

*Fidelity Spartan charges $2 per check if there's less than $50,000 in the account.

mercial paper (corporate IOUs). Many also invest in repurchase agreements, bankers' acceptances, federal agency securities, Eurodollar CDs, and Yankeedollar CDs.

Money market funds are an excellent parking place for your money while trying to decide where to invest. They are not a true investment except when rates are high. Their rates are almost always slightly higher than the bank equivalent, a money market deposit account.

To buy shares in a money market fund, you simply call the fund directly or your stockbroker. You can get your money out at any time, either by writing a check (the fund provides the checks) or by wire.

You can find a list of money market funds in the financial pages of most newspapers, and several financial magazines list those with the highest yields. Or see the box on page 22 for suggestions.

The Money Market: What It Is

Contrary to popular belief, the money market does not exist in the heart of Wall Street, or in London, Brussels, or even Washington, DC. Nor is it housed in an impressive Greek Revival building. The money market runs throughout the country and is made up of large corporations, banks, the federal government, and even local governments.

When any of these institutions need cash for a short period of time, they borrow it from this seemingly elusive money market by issuing money market instruments. For example, the U.S. government borrows through Treasury bills, large corporations through commercial paper, and banks via jumbo CDs.

These instruments are purchased by other large corporations, banks, and extremely wealthy investors. The instruments pay high interest rates

---

The Advantages of Money Market Funds

1. *Daily income.* Dividends are credited to your account each day, which means that your money is always working for you.
2. *Liquidity.* There is no minimum investment period, and there are no early withdrawal penalties. Money can be withdrawn quickly by telephone, mail, wire, or check.
3. *Stability of principal.* Most money market funds have a constant share price of $1. This makes it easy to determine the value of your investment at any time. Earnings are also paid in shares, so the value of a share never increases above $1. For example, if your interest in a money market mutual fund averaged 5% and you invested $1,000, at the end of 1 year you would have 1,050 shares worth $1,050.
4. *No fees or commissions.* When you buy shares, all your money goes to work immediately.
5. *Small minimum investment.* Some funds require as little as $500 initial investment; most minimums are between $1,000 and $2,000. In general, funds do not require shareholders to maintain a minimum investment.
6. *Safety.* Your money is used to buy prime debt of well-rated corporations or the U.S. government and its agencies. If you choose a fund that invests only in U.S. government securities, your yield will be ½% or so lower, but you can count on Uncle Sam's guarantee. Money market funds bought through your stockbroker are protected by the SIPC. (See pages 35–37 for details on SIPC.)
7. *Check-writing.* Most funds offer this service free, although some require that checks written be for at least $250 or $500.
8. *Continual high yields.* If rates drop, you will receive the higher interest rate for about a month afterward until the high-yielding securities are redeemed. With a bank, the yield changes more frequently, usually on a weekly basis.

Major Uses of Money Market Funds

- As a nest egg
- As a place to accumulate cash for a large expenditure, such as a house, a car, taxes, or a vacation
- As a temporary place to deposit large amounts of cash received from the sale of a stock or a property, an inheritance, an IRA rollover, etc.
- As a parking place until you find a desirable stock, bond, or other investment
- As a resting place for funds when switching from one mutual fund to another within a family of funds

---

because the dollar amounts involved are so large, the maturity lengths are so short (1 year or less), and the borrowers are well known and considered excellent risks. These money market instruments, not stocks and bonds, constitute a money market mutual fund's portfolio.

Selecting the Right Money Market Fund

Although there are several hundred money market mutual funds, they fall into four basic categories. Knowing which one is best for meeting your investment goals will help narrow the search.

- *General funds.* Available from your stockbroker or directly from the fund itself (by calling its toll-free number), general funds invest in nongovernment money market securities.
- *Government-only funds.* Also available directly from the fund or from a broker, government-only funds limit their investments to U.S. government or federal agency securities. Because their portfolios are backed by the "full faith and credit" of the U.S. government, they are regarded as less risky; consequently, they have lower yields than general funds.
- *Federal tax-free funds.* Available directly from the fund or from a broker, tax-free funds restrict their portfolios to short-term tax-exempt municipal bonds. Their income is free from federal tax but not necessarily from state and local taxes. These are generally advisable

---

What the Money Market Mutual Funds Buy

- *Bankers acceptances:* drafts issued and sold by banks with a promise to pay upon maturity, generally within no more than 180 days
- *Certificates of deposit:* large-denomination CDs sold by banks for money deposited for a minimum time period (14 days, 91 days, etc.)
- *Commercial paper:* unsecured IOUs issued by large institutions and corporations to the public to finance day-to-day operations, usually in amounts of $100,000 for up to 91 days
- *Eurodollar CDs:* dollar-denominated certificates of deposit sold by foreign branches of U.S. banks or by foreign banks; payable outside the United States, the minimum is generally $1 million, with maturities of 14 days or more
- *Government-agency obligations:* short-term securities issued by U.S. government agencies
- *Repurchase agreements ("repos"):* short-term buy/sell deals involving any money market instrument in which there is an agreement that the security will be resold to the seller on an agreed-upon date, often the next day. The money market fund holds the security as collateral and charges interest for the loan. Repos are usually issued as a means for commercial banks and U.S. government securities dealers to raise temporary funds.
- *U.S. Treasury bills and notes*

only for investors in the 28% tax bracket or higher. Their yields are, of course, much lower, sometimes about half those of a regular money market fund.

Even though their yields are lower, tax-free money market funds are more appealing, now that other ways of sheltering income are limited by the 1986 Tax Reform Act.

■ *Double or triple tax-exempt money funds.* Designed for residents of high income-tax states, such as New York, California, Massachusetts, and Connecticut, these invest in short-term tax-exempt municipals and are free from federal, state, and often local taxes for residents of the states and localities that issue them.

By shopping around you will find that some funds have higher yields than others (see the lists in this chapter). At various times the yield discrepancy has been as much as 3% to 3½% on taxable funds, but the current yield is not the only factor to consider; look also at the 12-month yield and the character of the fund's holdings.

☑ *HINT: To determine how you would fare in a taxable versus a tax-exempt fund:*
1. *Subtract your tax bracket from 1*
2. *Divide that number into the tax exempt yield times 100*

The Risk Factor

The risk factor—even though it's quite minimal with money market funds—rises with the portfolio's maturity. By law, any money market fund that says it keeps its net asset value at $1 per share is required to limit its average portfolio maturity to 90 days. If you're a conservative investor, select a fund with maturities of 90 days or less. If you're willing to assume more risk, you may get a slightly higher yield.

Lower-quality portfolios lead to higher yields but also higher risk.

Ultrasafe Money Market Funds

MUTUAL FUNDS SPECIALIZING IN U.S. TREASURY SECURITIES		YIELD
Capital Preservation Fund	800–321–8321	4.77%
Fidelity Government Reserves	800–544–8888	4.81
Fidelity U.S. Treasury Money Market	800–544–8888	4.83
Vanguard U.S. Treasury Money Market	800–662–7447	4.96
TAX-FREE MONEY MARKET FUNDS		
Calvert Tax-free Reserves	800–368–2748	3.28
Dreyfus Tax-exempt Money Market	800–645–6561	2.94
Franklin Tax-exempt Money Fund	800–342–5236	2.92
Lexington Tax-free Money Market	800–526–0056	3.00
USAA Tax-exempt Money Market	800–531–8181	3.28
HIGH-INCOME STATES: TRIPLE TAX-EXEMPT		
Fidelity Mass Tax-free MM Portfolio*	800–544–8888	3.02
Vanguard Tax-free Calif Money Market	800–662–7447	3.34

*Double-exempt.
(Yields as of November 1996)

Expenses

Money market funds take an annual management charge, called the *expense ratio*, from the investor's assets. These fees range from about 0.48% to 0.80%.

☑ HINT: *The average money fund's expense ratio as a percentage of assets is about 0.58%. Therefore, a fund earning 10% gives a yield to investors of 9.42%.*

WHEN INTEREST RATES CHANGE

Now that you've been introduced to three of the key "safe havens" for your money—bank money market deposit accounts, money market mutual funds, and CDs—it's time to understand what to do when interest rates change and how to track such changes. The best indicator of trends in CD and money market account rates is something called the federal funds rate—the rate banks charge each other for overnight loans. If a bank must pay more itself to borrow money, it will try to raise more money to pay for this increased cost by offering higher yields to potential depositors. The federal fund rate is listed in the financial pages of major newspapers.

CREDIT UNIONS

A credit union is a cooperative, not-for-profit financial institution organized to provide checking, savings, loans, and other financial services for members. Membership is limited to those having a common bond—occupation, association, etc.—and to groups within a community or neighborhood. Many credit unions allow members to remain members even if they move away or change jobs.

Credit unions are member owned and controlled, with each member having an equal vote and the opportunity to serve on the board of directors. The board, elected by the membership, sets dividend and interest rates. Board members are volunteers, except for the treasurer, and they may not receive payment for their services.

Credit unions are either state or federally chartered. State-chartered unions are supervised by a state regulatory agency. Federally chartered ones are supervised by the National Credit Union Administration, an independent agency in the executive branch of the federal government. Member share accounts are insured up to $100,000 per account by the National Credit Union Share Insurance Fund.

There are approximately 12,175 credit unions representing more than $330 billion in assets and nearly 70.5 million individual member--owners.

Credit union CDs, sharedraft accounts (interest-bearing checking accounts), and money market deposit accounts pay extremely competitive rates, often ½% higher than banks. Loans may be ½% to 1% lower. Credit unions can afford to undercut their competitors because they are non-

---

How to Take Advantage of Interest Rate Changes

1. *When rates are low:* Buy short-term CDs.
2. *When rates begin to rise:* Put more money into your money market account so you can ride up with the rates.
3. *When rates are high:* Lock in yields with long-term CDs. Move money out of money market accounts into higher-yielding CDs.
4. *When rates are falling:* Immediately lock in with a CD before they fall further.
5. *When rates are low:* Invest over the short term and add to your money market account so that your cash will be available for reinvesting when rates begin to rise.

profit corporations, don't pay federal taxes, and are essentially volunteer directed. Credit unions are also available for students.

FOR FURTHER INFORMATION

Material on Credit Union Loans, Savings, Services

Credit Union National Association
P.O. Box 431
Madison, WI 53701

Material on Banking

Money in the Bank: How To Get the Most For Your Dollar by Consumer Federation of America and the AARP (New York: Perigee Books, 1995).

Your Bank: How To Get Better Service by Jeff Davidson (Yonkers, New York: Consumer Reports Books; 1995).

Is Your Money Safe? by Warren G. Heller (New York: Berkley Books, 1995).

4

Protecting Your Investments and Cash

*T*umultuous markets, changing interest rates, bank failures, mergers of financial institutions, and the occasional dishonest broker cause even the most trusting investors and savers to question how safe their securities and cash are in the nation's banks, mutual funds, brokerage firms, and insurance companies—and rightly so.

Here's what you need to know.

AT YOUR BANK

Over the past decade, more banks and savings and loan associations have been liquidated or merged than at any time since the Great Depression. However, the pace has slowed down recently and in fact the number of commercial and savings banks on the FDIC's trouble list now numbers only 193, down from 318 a year ago. These troubled banks hold about $31 million, only a fraction of the banking industry's total assets. Hopefully, you are not one of their customers.

The Facts

Most of the country's commercial banks are insured by the Federal Deposit Insurance Corporation (FDIC), an independent government agency. To be eligible for membership in the FDIC, a bank must meet certain standards and be regularly examined by both federal and state agencies. Member banks pay insurance fees, which are in turn invested in federal government securities. These securities constitute the FDIC's Bank Insurance Fund. In addition, the FDIC may borrow several billion dollars from the U.S. Treasury if it needs to.

Most savings and loan associations (also known as thrifts), which prior to August 9, 1989, were insured by the Federal Savings & Loan Insurance Corporation (FSLIC), are now insured by the FDIC through the Savings Association Insurance Fund (SAIF). Some savings and loan associations are insured by state insurance, a very few are privately insured, and a handful have absolutely no insurance at all.

CAUTION: Make certain you are with an insured S&L.

Most credit unions (97%) are insured by the National Credit Union Administration (NCUA); others, by state agencies.

The FDIC and NCUA are backed by the federal government, and money insured by them is considered safe since the government would presumably come to their rescue. Banks that are insured by a state or privately, however, do *not* have the backing of the federal government.

WHAT YOU CAN DO

The solution is not to tuck your money under the mattress, but to bank only at federally insured

Government Protection

Federal Deposit Insurance Corporation Bank Insurance Fund

- Insures depositors for up to $100,000
- Consumer hotline: 800–934–3342
- Address for more information on deposit insurance: 550 17th Street NW, Washington, DC 20429

Savings Association Insurance Fund
- Insures depositors for up to $100,000
- Consumer affairs: 800–934–3342
- Address for more information on evaluating SAIF: 550 17th Street NW, Washington, DC 20429

National Credit Union Share Insurance Fund
- Insures depositors for up to $100,000
- Telephone: 703–518–6300
- Address for more information on your credit union: 1775 Duke Street, Alexandria, VA 22314

institutions and know the facts about insurance coverage; here they are:

Rules for Existing Accounts

- Contrary to popular opinion, or wishful thinking, the government does not insure $100,000 per account. Instead, it insures $100,000 per person at any one bank or savings and loan in any "one right and capacity." If you have several savings accounts, even at different branches of the same institution, and they are all in the same name, they are lumped together for insurance coverage. In other words, if you have four accounts in the same name in one institution, you are insured only for a total of $100,000, not $400,000.
- The $100,000 figure applies to both principal and interest. So, if you have $98,000 in an account and you then earn $5,000 in interest, your account will be insured for $100,000, leaving $3,000 uninsured.
- If you have money in a checking account, a savings account, and a CD at one bank, in your name, you do not get $100,000 of insurance for each account—you only get a total

coverage of $100,000. And, changing your name on different accounts, by using a middle initial, for example, will not boost your coverage.
- If you are married, you can get coverage for more than one account: You and your spouse can each have an individual savings account. You may also have one joint account. In addition, you can set up two trust accounts, known as revocable testamentary accounts, one in trust for your spouse, the other being your spouse's, in trust for you. This type of account pays the balance to the beneficiary upon the death of the grantor of the trust. And you could each have an IRA account. That's a total of seven accounts. With $100,000 in each, all $700,000 would be insured even though it's all in the same bank.

CAUTION: If you left that $700,000 in one single account, $600,000 of it would not be insured.

- Some other types of testamentary accounts are insured separately if the beneficiary or beneficiaries are qualified as kinship—a child, stepchild, grandchild, step-grandchild, or spouse. An account in trust for a parent, niece, or friend is treated as another account in your name and does not get separate coverage. Note that these types of accounts are insured to $100,000 per qualifying beneficiary. Thus, an account in trust for your three children is insured to $300,000.

- Joint accounts are insured separately from individual accounts, but with certain limitations—you are insured for up to $100,000 on the money you have in all joint accounts at any one bank. If, for instance, you have $100,000 in three joint accounts at the same bank—one with your wife and one with each of your two daughters—your share of each would be $50,000, or half, for a total of $150,000. Of that only $100,000 will be insured.

- The FDIC treats all joint accounts owned by the same combination of people at the same bank as being one account. So, if you and your spouse have a joint checking and a joint savings account, the two together are insured for up to $100,000. And don't try reversing the order of your names or using your Social Security number on one and your spouse's on another—it doesn't work.

☑ *HINT: If you have a loan or home equity line of credit at your bank, check its financial condition (see ways to obtain reports below). If your bank should fail, you could lose access to your credit line—a real problem if you need the money.*

Remember, too, that changes in your life can affect your FDIC coverage. For example, death could convert your joint account to an individual account and thus put you over the $100,000 limit. Or, your interest accrual or a large cash payment, say from the sale of a home, insurance proceeds, inheritance, or a lump sum pension distribution, could likewise toss your balance above the insurance limit.

Choose Only Insured Bank Products

Banks offer both insured and uninsured products. If you are uncertain about a particular product, ask the bank to give you written assurance regarding its coverage. Products that are typically insured include: checking accounts, savings accounts, NOW accounts, Christmas club accounts, certificates of deposit, money market deposit accounts, and trust fund accounts.

Banking products that are not typically insured include: annuities, mutual funds, life insurance, stocks, bonds, government securities (Treasury bills, bonds, notes), repurchase agreements, and commercial paper, which includes shares of the bank's stock.

HOW TO CHECK UP ON YOUR BANK

You can protect your money by getting an overview of the financial health of your bank, savings and loan, or credit union through reports offered by these two private rating companies:

Veribanc, Inc.
P.O. Box 461
Wakefield, MA 01880
617–245–8370; 800–442–2657

Bauer Financial Reports
Box 145510
Coral Gables, FL 33114–5510
800–388–6686

And also, request and read the Report of Condition on your bank (not available for branches, only main banks). It will tell you how much the bank is making, what its loan portfolio is made up of, and what percentage of loans is nonperforming. The FDIC will bill you $6. Do not send cash. Order from:

FDIC
Disclosure Group, Room F–518
550 17th Street NW
Washington, DC 20429
800–945–2186

Help from Regulators

If you're having a problem with your bank, call one of the regulatory authorities listed below. They are surprisingly accessible, often more so than your local bank official. If you need to file a written complaint, include a brief statement describing the problem and a list of the steps you've taken to try to resolve it. Include your bank account number and copies of all documents. Keep a copy for your files.

Ask the customer service department which regulator oversees your bank—they are legally obligated to tell you.

FDIC
Office of Consumer Affairs
550 17th Street NW
Washington, DC 20429
800–934–3342

Office of Thrift Supervision
Consumer Affairs Division
1700 G Street NW
Washington, DC 20552
202–906–6237 or
800–842–6929

Federal Reserve Board
Consumer Affairs
Mail Stop 800
20th and C Streets NW
Washington, DC 20551
202–452–3946

U.S. Comptroller of the Currency
Compliance Management
Mail Stop 7-5
250 E Street SW
Washington, DC 20219
202–874–4710

If Your Bank or Savings and Loan Fails

Should the unthinkable happen and a federally insured bank or savings and loan fail, the FDIC or the Savings Association Insurance Fund (SAIF) will either liquidate the institution's assets to pay off depositors or transfer assets to a healthy institution. You may have to wait, but you will receive your principal and interest, up to $100,000.

In most cases, in fact, a solvent institution takes over the failed institution's assets and liabilities. For example, the April 1990 collapse of Seamen's Bank for Savings in New York, the largest bank failure of the year, was estimated to cost the FDIC $2.8 billion. Seamen's 13 branches, valued at $2.1 billion, were sold to Chase Manhattan Bank for $5 million.

CAUTION: When accounts of a failed institution are transferred, the new management can lower the interest rate being paid on CDs or increase the rate you pay on a home-equity loan or other credit line. However, you must be given prior notice and time to make penalty-free switches to another institution that has more favorable rates. If bank officials won't let you know whether they are honoring your existing terms, take it as a warning and begin looking for a new bank or savings and loan.

If you have a loan, the loan cannot be called in by the new bank under any conditions not spelled out by the original loan agreement. Check your agreement for loopholes. If you don't understand it, ask your lawyer.

CAUTION: If a federally insured institution fails, regulators will liquidate the assets, and insured depositors will be paid usually within 5 business days. If you have money in excess of the $100,000 insured limit, however, you will have a pro rata stake for that portion in excess of $100,000, along with other creditors, and you may or may not get that portion of your money back.

How Safe Is Your Safe Deposit Box?

If your bank fails, the acquiring institution will take over the safe deposit boxes and you will be notified. If there is no acquirer, you will receive written instructions about coming in and removing the contents.

Even under normal circumstances your safe deposit box may not be so safe. The contents are not insured by FDIC or by the bank that rents you the box. Take time to read the rental contract to see if there's any insurance coverage.

I suggest that you purchase fire or theft insurance if you do not have safe deposit box coverage as part of your homeowner's or tenant's insurance policy; check with your agent.

Stolen funds may be covered at the bank by a blanket bond which is a multi-purpose insurance policy banks buy to protect the institution from fire, flood, earthquake, embezzlement, and just plain old-fashioned robberies and stickups. If a bank employee messes around with a customer's account, the blanket bond insurance will probably cover your loss. On the other hand, if a third party gains access to your account and transacts business using your checks or ATM number, you must notify both the bank and the police.

IN A MUTUAL FUND

The mutual fund industry is governed by the Investment Company Act of 1940—but that does not guarantee total protection. Here are the facts:

- BANKRUPTCY. The assets of a mutual fund belong to the shareholders, and all securities are held in trust by a third party. A fund's directors can theoretically ask shareholders to allow the fund to close down its assets have dwindled away and it's no longer profitable to operate, for example. To date, this has never happened.

    It's far more likely that a troubled fund will merge into a larger, healthier one; this often happens when a bank, S&L, or broker-

age firm goes bankrupt. However, a very small fund that is poorly managed might be unable to attract a merger candidate.

If a fund were to liquidate, the shareholders fortunes would depend on market conditions and the quality of the fund's holdings. The SEC would oversee the sale and subsequent distribution of assets. A small fund with large holdings of thinly traded securities or little cash on hand could be in for losses if the market were down.

- SUSPENSION OF TRADING. Trading can be suspended only in the case of a national emergency—if the New York Stock Exchange closes, there's a presidential assassination, war, etc. Yet, even in these situations, you can place a redemption order and it will lock in the fund price at the close of the trading day.

- IMPORTANCE OF CASH RESERVES. The fund managers almost always hold cash and Treasury securities in their reserves, plus proceeds from security sales. Funds also have bank credit available to them: They can borrow $1 for every $3 of assets. Yet, a heavily invested fund, when faced with a barrage of redemption requests, might have to sell stocks even when it would prefer not to.

☑ *HINT: Invest only in a fund that has at least 10% or more in cash reserves.*

- PROTECTING YOURSELF. I urge you to find out if your mutual fund has a local office; if so, keep some of your money there so you can have access to it in person. Secondly, prepare the fund's official redemption form or letter and be prepared to send it by Express Mail should the telephone redemption lines become overloaded and you can't get through. Third, get your fund's redemption fax number if it has one.

☑ *HINT: It doesn't matter what time of day you put in your mutual fund buy or sell order; as long as it's in before 4 P.M., Eastern time; you're guaranteed the closing share price that day. Phones are busiest in the morning.*

IN A MONEY MARKET FUND

Everyone wants to know how safe their money market fund or account is. It's very safe. But every investment has some degree of risk. Money market funds have an excellent safety record, primarily because they invest in short-term securities of the government, large institutions, and corporations.

The basic principle to keep in mind is: The shorter the maturity of an investment, the lower the risk. Why?

Short portfolio maturities keep a fund's risk level to a minimum, because a bank or corporation whose securities are sold in the money markets is not very likely to default in such a short time. In addition, securities that mature so quickly seldom fluctuate in value. A money market mutual fund's securities must mature in 1 year or less, and no one individual security may make up more than 5% of a fund's assets.

HINT: *The average maturity is about 40 days. You can check maturities in the financial section of your newspaper.*

For the ultimate in safety, select a fund that invests only in Treasury issues (see list on page 25). These are backed by the full faith and credit of the U.S. government. They are called government or Treasury-only funds. The yields are about 1% lower than nongovernment money market funds.

Money market funds must have:

■ Ninety-five percent of their assets in short-term debt, such as the highest-grade commercial paper. The other 5% can be held in second-tier paper, such as A–2 or P–2, but no more than 1% of this can come from the same issuer.

■ No more than 5% of a fund's total assets can be invested in the securities of a single issuer, except for those of the U.S. government.

■ The average maturity of a fund's portfolio can be no more than 90 days.

CAUTION: *If your account is with a bank that has FDIC or a savings and loan that has FSLIC, it is insured up to $100,000 per account name. Money market mutual funds with your stockbroker are protected by the SIPC. Money market mutual funds purchased directly from the fund are not insured unless the fund itself indicates that they are. Be sure to ask.*

HINT: *Invest in a large money market fund, one with at least $1 billion in assets. it's more likely to protect shareholders than a small fund.*

FROM DERIVATIVES

Since 1994, the "D" word has been making financial headlines—at that time some leading corporations such as Procter & Gamble and Gibson Greeting suffered losses on investments and Orange County, California, one of the richest in the country, filed for bankruptcy because of investments in derivatives.

Most mutual fund have derivatives and for that reason, Morningstar Mutual Funds, the Chicago research and rating service, has information on how funds use derivatives. For each fund it lists the four basic categories of derivatives:

■ Options and futures
■ Illiquid securities
■ Exotic mortgages
■ Structured notes

It then gives the percentage of assets the fund invests in each type.

Just What Are Derivatives?

A derivative is a financial instrument whose price is derived from other prices—prices typically of an underlying security, asset, or index.

The most familiar and oldest of derivatives are found in the commodities markets where farmers and those who purchase farm products used *options* and *futures contracts* to protect themselves in the price they either pay or receive for wheat, cattle, corn, coffee, etc.

They are also used to control the risk of volatile interest rates and exchange rates as well as for purely speculative purposes. Some of them have fairly complex features that make them particularly sensitive to any changes in the underlying security's price.

In addition to basic options, forwards, and futures, there's a more complicated type known as a synthetic security. These include indexed securities whose values are tied to the movement of what is known on Wall Street as an unmanaged market index, such as the Standard & Poor's 500 floating rate notes (which reset their interest rates periodically to reflect changes in other rates), and mortgage-backed securities in which the interest and principal payments from the underlying mortgages are sold as separate securities.

Pools of home mortgages cut up and packaged as collateralized mortgage obligations, or CMOs, are technically derivatives.

All types of derivatives come with risks. Market risk is a key one—the risk of loss due to changes in the prices of securities underlying the derivatives. There's also income risk—risk that the stream of income will change. This is particularly applicable to derivatives based on a security or index. Another risk is called valuation risk—that the instrument has not been priced accurately. Two other risks: liquidity risk—that the security cannot be sold at a good price; and finally, counter-party risk—the risk that one party to an agreement cannot meet its obligation.

The Advantages of Derivatives

If your mutual fund owns index futures or options (two of the more common types of derivatives),

don't panic. In fact, if they are used intelligently and carefully they may even reduce your risks.

Many sound portfolio managers use derivatives to counterbalance the movements of stocks, bonds, commodities, and currencies, by creating separate but related deals to the actual markets for these investments. Strategies involving derivatives to offset market activity are known as hedges.

Managers of international stock and bond portfolios very often use currency forwards and options to keep the portfolio stable because the value of the portfolio's international investments fluctuate with changes in the value of currencies.

In another situation, a portfolio manager might buy a futures contract on the S&P 500 index in order to put new cash to work while seeking more suitable stocks.

How Derivatives Work

Let's look at options, a common type of derivative. Its value depends on the movements in a stock's price. It has a specific shelf life—often 3 months. There are two types of options: calls and puts. Call options let the holder buy shares at a specified price (known as the strike price) whereas put options let the holder sell shares at a specified price. The value of a call increases when the stock goes up; the value of a put increases when the stock price falls.

You might want to write a call on your stock as a way to make money. If your stock is trading at $50, you write an option and sell it to another investor to purchase shares at $60 for $2 a share. If the stock doesn't reach $60 before the option expires, you gain $2 per share in income and also collect any dividends the stock pays out.

Options are explained in detail in Chapter 16.

The Disadvantages

The trouble, however arises when the portfolio manager uses borrowed money or invests only a fraction of the cost of the securities underlying the derivatives. Known as leveraged investing, it back-fires completely if the manager guesses wrong.

What Derivatives Mean to You

Although some derivatives are relatively safe and liquid, others have been deemed inappropriate, especially for money market mutual funds. To make this point clear, the SEC has stated that these derivatives are unsuitable for money funds:

- Inverse floaters
- Leveraged floaters
- CMT floaters
- Capped floaters
- Dual-index floaters
- COFI floaters

☑ *HINT: You should feel free to call your mutual fund and ask its policy on derivatives. To avoid derivatives altogether, stick with funds that are 100% invested in U.S. Treasuries.*

And, if you'd like a slightly higher yield (accompanied by a bit more risk), look into money funds that invest in Treasuries and repurchase agreements, aka repos. A standard repro agreement works like this: The fund manager buys a position in government agency securities from a bond dealer, agreeing to sell them back the next day at the same price plus a little interest. Although the fund has taken on a degree of risk, it also has the securities as collateral in the event that the bond dealer can't make good on the repurchase agreement.

AT A BROKERAGE FIRM

Your money, or at least much of it, is protected at your broker's firm by the Securities Investor Protection Corp. SIPC, as it's called, consists of a $1½ billion fund supported by some 7,600 member brokerage firms. It also has a $1 billion credit line with the government that can be activated only by the SEC, as well as a $1 billion credit line with banks.

SIPC is neither a government agency nor a regulatory agency. Rather, it is funded through assessment of dealer members. All brokers and dealers registered with the SEC and national stock exchanges must contribute, except those dealing exclusively with mutual funds.

If There's a Failure

If a member brokerage firm fails, the SIPC applies to a court, which appoints a trustee to liquidate the firm and perhaps transfer customer accounts to another broker. (If the firm is small, the SIPC may decide to cover losses from its funds directly.)

If it has the securities on hand, the liquidating firm will send the securities registered in customers names directly to them. If it does not have enough securities to meet all customer claims, they would be secured on the open market. Any remaining claims will be settled in cash. However, this ties up your money for several months.

If the brokerage house in liquidation does not have enough securities or funds to settle all claims, the rest will be met by the SIPC—up to $500,000 per customer, including $100,000 for any cash held in the brokerage account.

Your Account

If you have investments in a brokerage account, SIPC will cover the market value of your stocks, bonds, CDs, mutual funds, notes, and warrants on securities. Commodities and commodity options, gold, and silver are *not* covered. Coverage is up to $500,000 in securities and $100,000 in cash.

☑ *HINT: Extend your coverage by opening a second account as a joint account with your spouse, as a trustee for a child, or as a business account. Each account receives full protection—$500,000.*

Keep in mind that the SIPC covers losses due to the failure of the firm, not losses because investments turned out to be of poor quality or because securities fell in price. And many brokerage firms carry additional insurance, about which you can ask your broker. In the past 24 years, SIPC has liquidated about 250 firms. In 1995, only four were liquidated.

Burned by the poor performance of the stock market in 1987 and American investors' subsequent flight to safety, brokerage firms and sponsors of various investment products have added a new enticing feature to their advertisements, touting them as guaranteed or insured. The idea, of course, is to make high-risk investments appear safe. Many of these guarantees have questionable value—don't be taken in by such comforting terms.

Ask your broker or financial planner these questions when you're faced with what appears to be a come-on:

■   How much of my money is being invested in the primary product? Where will the rest be invested?
■   How long is the guarantee or insurance good for?
■   Am I protected against market loss?
■   If the project or investment fails, who is responsible for covering the losses?
■   Who backs the insurance or guarantee?

IN A PENSION PLAN

Think of pension plans like any other investment—one that requires safeguarding.

■   Defined benefit plans promise a set amount upon retirement, usually based on factors such as age, earnings, and years of service. Most are insured by the Pension Benefit Guaranty Corporation, an FDIC-like agency that will pay each employee up to about $30,000 a year if the company fails.
■   A company can terminate a fully funded pension plan at any time and pay benefits in a lump sum or buy annuities from insurance companies to take over monthly benefit pay-

ments. When that happens, you have lost your protection.
■   Defined contribution plans, which include 401(k)s, profit-sharing plans, and employee stock option plans, include more than 80% of all private pensions. The amount contributed to the plan by you and by your employer is typically a percentage of your pay or the company's profits.
■   You are not guaranteed a specific amount upon retirement. You get the contributions made plus any earnings. And, this type of plan is *not insured* by the Pension Benefit Guaranty Corporation.
■   About one-third of the money in defined contribution plans is invested in a Guaranteed Investment Contract (GIC), which, like bank CDs, pay a guaranteed interest rate for a set time. GICs are sold by insurance companies; if you do not live in one of the states that insures these plans, your money is backed by the insurer only. If the insurance company is in bad shape, then so is the GIC it sells.
■   Ask your company's plan administrator for a copy of Form 5500, the financial report the plan is required to file with the Labor Department.
■   If your pension money is invested with an insurance company, read the section that follows for safety tips.

AT AN INSURANCE COMPANY

In recent years several life insurance giants became insolvent. And, consumers have less protection when life insurers fail than they do when banks tumble. Insurance companies are regulated by state commissioners, not by federal authorities, and there is no national fund to cover losses.

Each state has a life and health insurance guarantee association insurance fund. These nonprofit organizations were created by state law to provide money to policyholders. Typically they cover individual policies up to $100,000 of cash value or $300,000 of life insurance and death benefits.

Each insurance company is assessed 2% of premiums received in the state for policies and contracts covered by the guarantee association. This money is turned in effect into an insurance pool. Depending upon how well funded the insurance pool is and how large the losses, you might have to wait for your money.

If a major insurer runs into trouble, a state regulator could intervene. This was the case when the failed Executive Life Insurance lost some $900 million in the 1990 market. Its assets, valued at $13 billion, plunged; then policyholders, hearing about the problem, began to cash out and Executive Life had to pay about $4 billion in policy redemptions.

Policyholders were protected, but even now they are earning the policy's guaranteed minimum rate, about 5% on their cash values, considerably less than the 11% before the company went under.

Until policies can be transferred to another company or some other arrangements are made, insurers typically lose access to the cash value of their contracts, sometimes for periods of a year or more. It is possible that, in the final analysis, they may get less than the contract's full value.

☑ *HINT: Call your state insurance commission to make certain you would be covered under the state guaranty system if your insurer became insolvent. Some state plans cover contract holders of companies headquartered in that state regardless of where they live; others guarantee only their own residents and only if they are insured by companies licensed in that state.*

The best way to avoid problems is to do business with financially sound life insurance companies—those that have A+ or A++ ratings by A.M. Best or AA or AAA by Standard & Poor's and Moody's. Firms rated B+ or better by

Weiss Research are regarded as solid. All are independent services that rate the financial conditions of companies, including insurance companies.

Standard & Poor's
212–208–1527
free

Moody's
212–553–0377
free

Duff & Phelps
312–368–3157
free

Weiss Research
800–289–9222
$15/verbal report
$25/written report

A.M. Best
800–424–BEST
$2.50/minute

WITH THE GOVERNMENT

You often hear the phrase, protected by the full faith and credit obligation of the U.S. Government. It applies to investments in EE Savings Bonds, Treasury bills, notes and bonds, and Ginnie Maes (Government National Mortgage Association bonds.) It means you don't have to worry about default of principal and interest when you invest with our government.

However, it does not protect you if the price of your Treasury or Ginnie Mae fluctuates due to changes in interest rates.

Government agencies that issue bonds carry what is known as a moral obligation against default and timely payment of principal and interest by the U.S. government. That means you're protected if you invest in bonds issued by the Small Business Administration, Federal National Mortgage Association, and other agency bonds.

WITH GICS

Guaranteed Investment Contracts, or GICs, are fixed rate investments issued by insurance companies that are part of 401(k) retirement plans and other tax-deferred investments.

They tend to pay high fixed rates of interest, but they are only as good as the insurance company. Deal only with insurance companies that are rated at least A+ by A.M. Best and carry at least AA claims-paying ratings by Standard & Poor's and Moody's.

☑ *HINT: Ask your employer to provide you with information about the insurance company before you invest in a GIC.*

WITH MUNICIPAL BONDS

Many municipal bonds carry insurance against default. These bond issuers have to be financially sound to get the coverage in the first place. Insured bonds yield about one-quarter of one percent less than uninsured bonds.

Most are insured by either the American Municipal Bond Assurance Corp. (AMBAC) and by the Municipal Bond Insurance Association (MBIA). Both are well capitalized for covering defaults. In addition, at least one-third of bonds covered by insurers are also backed by tax revenue.

PROTECTING YOURSELF AGAINST SCAMS

A surprising number of intelligent people are taken in by scam artists, who seem to know just how to swindle money out of investors and savers alike. The best of the scam artists tie their pitch to current events, thereby improving their credibility and creating a sense of urgency. They do best among the elderly, who tend to be more passive (or kindly) when it comes to dealing with strangers.

As the American public becomes increasingly tired of telephone solicitations, scam artists are switching to other means, primarily church groups, professional societies, and group help organizations. Some have even managed to infiltrate organizations that help families of AIDS victims. Once the swindler has made (or says he has) a substantial amount of money for one member, he then tries, often with success, to work the whole group.

According to Barry Guthary, president of the North American Securities Administrators Association (NASAA), cold callers are enticing investors to replace CDs with higher-yielding investments at much greater risk, even when there are penalties for early withdrawal of the certificates. The majority of the victims are people on fixed incomes. An Investor Alert, published by NASAA and the Council of Better Business Bureaus, warns that banks, in an effort to keep depositor's money, are offering investments, mutual funds, and annuities that may not be covered by federal deposit insurance.

☑ *HINT: To protect yourself, never give a cold caller your credit card number, your bank account number, your Social Security number, or write him a check.*

IF YOU ARE ELDERLY OR HAVE ELDERLY FRIENDS, YOU SHOULD KNOW THAT:

- Con artists study obituaries, notices of probate proceedings, and real-estate transactions to find elderly victims.
- Con artists know that the elderly often have substantial savings or proceeds from pension and insurance policies.
- Widowed men and women often lack experience in managing finances if their spouse took care of such matters.
- The elderly are often home alone with no one to ask them to think twice about an impulsive investment.

- Elderly people tend to be less suspicious of strangers and more willing to talk to them, even to invite them into their homes.
- Today's elderly grew up thinking a handshake was the right way to make a business deal.

FOR FURTHER INFORMATION

For Information About the SIPC and What It Covers

SIPC
805 15th Street NW, Suite 800
Washington, DC 20005
202–371–8300

If you have a complaint or a question about your bank, write to the Consumer Services Division of your State Banking Commission or Department in your state capital.

If you live in New York, write to:
Consumer Services Division
New York State Banking Department
2 Rector Street
New York, NY 10006
212–618–6445

For Information About a Brokerage Firm and Its Insurance

Office of Consumer Affairs
Securities & Exchange Commission
Mail Stop 11–2
450 Fifth Street NW
Washington, DC 20549
202–942–7040

For the booklet *How to Get Safety Information from Your Financial Institution*, send $2 to:
Weiss Research
4176 Burns Road
Palm Beach Gardens, FL 33410
800–289–9222

It includes postcard questionnaires you can send to your bank, savings and loan, insurance company, or stock broker, along with simple instructions on how to interpret the answers.

For Information on Scams

The Consumer's Resource Handbook is free from: U.S. Office of Consumer Affairs, 800–664–4435.

Tells you what steps to follow if you've been taken; includes sample complaint letters, addresses, telephone hot lines, government agencies, etc.

The National Financial Fraud Exchange
800–822–0416

Collects public information about financial and real estate frauds from some 100 government and private watchdog groups.

You can run a name through the system for $29; if the person you're checking up on has had a complaint filed and is in the system, you'll be told on the telephone; a written or faxed report is an additional $5.

An individual is in the system if he or she has SEC violations or infractions, fines, sanctions or other official complaints.

5

Moving from Saver to Investor

Now that you have set aside money in several safe places where it is earning well above the savings account rate, you are ready to stretch your wings and move into the arena of the true investor. Incidentally, before you leap from saver to investor, you should have a minimum of 6 months worth of living expenses in one of the safe havens discussed in the previous chapters. That means if you need $4,000 per month to operate comfortably, set aside $24,000 in a combination of CDs, Treasuries, and money funds. Then if you are hit with a financial emergency, such as losing your job or becoming ill, you will have immediate liquid resources to draw upon.

☑ HINT: *If you feel your job may be in jeopardy, set aside at least 9 months of expenses—it often takes that long to find a new position.*

Moving from saver to investor is a step many people, especially those with a conservative bent, find difficult to take. Some, in fact, never manage to make the move at all. Although there's nothing inherently wrong with leaving your money in a safe haven, during inflationary periods you may actually lose money, and during a bull market, even a mini one, you'll be on the sidelines. And, if you're facing high taxes, these safe investments are not truly safe at all, for instead of reducing your federal income tax bite, they add to it.

Of course, no investment is for all seasons. Review the boxes on pages 47–48 to help you determine which vehicles are best during various economic periods. Keep in mind that the greater the risk you take, the greater the potential return.

MUTUAL FUNDS VS. INDIVIDUAL SECURITIES

One of the first key decisions you will have to make as you move from saver to investor is whether to select your own stocks and bonds or to buy shares in a mutual fund. Mutual funds, in which professional portfolio managers make all the buy and sell decisions, are described fully in Chapter 6.

There's no reason, however, to shy away from picking individual stocks, especially if you're willing to spend some time researching them.

Where to Begin

Why not start in your own backyard? Investigate your local utility company or a corporation headquartered nearby.

For additional research information:

1) Call for the annual report and ask a local broker.

2) Another easy way to dip into the market is by purchasing shares in the company you work for or one whose products or services you use and like. If you are wedded to your Nikes or if you love

40

Moving from Saver to Investor

INVESTMENT	WHERE TO FIND	FACTS TO KNOW
Savings account	Bank, credit union	What is the interest rate? How often is it compounded? Is it federally insured?
Money market deposit account	Bank, credit union	What is the interest rate? How often does it change? Are there withdrawal penalties/limitations?
Certificate of deposit (CD)	Bank, credit union	How much money will I have at maturity? Can I roll it over at the same or a higher rate? Are there withdrawal penalties?
Brokered CD	Stockbroker	Will my interest compound? If I sell my CD back to you before maturity, will I lose money? Is the originating bank sound?
Money market mutual fund	Brokerage firm, mutual fund	What is the yield? What is the portfolio's average maturity?
EE Savings Bonds	Bank, Federal Reserve, Bureau of Public Debt	What is the current rate? When do the bonds mature?
Treasury issues	Federal Reserve, Bureau of Public Debt, stockbroker	What is the current rate? Is there a purchase/sales fee? When do they mature?
Stocks	Brokerage firm, investment club dividend reinvestment plan	What is the commission? What is the *Value Line* rating? Is there a dividend?
Bonds	Brokerage firm	What is the commission? Can the bond be called? What is the yield? What is the rating?
Mutual funds	Mutual fund, brokerage firm	What is the total return for 6 months, 1 and 5 years? Are there fees?

Kellogg cereals, you might like to start down the investor's path by purchasing stocks in those familiar companies.

Seven Ways Beginners Can Win in the Stock Market

If you are averse to risk or want to reduce your risk quotient, here are seven easy techniques that will enable you to maintain a healthy portfolio and weather declines in the market.

- *Diversify.* To some extent you can protect yourself from market swings by owning a mixture of stocks, bonds, precious metals, real estate, and other investments because rarely does everything decline at the same time.

- *Buy for the long haul.* If you plan in general to hold your stocks 1 to 3 years, day-to-day and month-to-month fluctuations can largely be ignored.
- *Select investments on the basis of quality.* Take advantage of low-priced, high-quality stocks. Ignore rumors and study the fundamentals.
- *Include high-yield investments.* Common stocks with high dividends, preferred stock, good quality high-yielding bonds, and closed-end bond funds all help cushion dips in the market.
- *Investigate convertibles.* Their yields are higher than the underlying stock of the same company, and should the stock fall in price, the convertible (CV) will fall less. (See Chapter 10)
- *Use dollar cost averaging.* With both mutual funds and stocks, this approach enables you to buy more shares at lower prices and fewer shares at higher prices, as well as to ignore short-term market gyrations. (See page 255 for more on dollar cost averaging.)
- *Don't buy on margin.* You will be able to hold your stock through all kinds of weather if you buy for cash. With a margin account, you are subject to margin calls from your broker. (See Chapter 25)

The Perils of Being Too Cautious

Even though it's important to sleep at night, you should also avoid taking the path of least resistance—that of being an ultraconservative investor who stashes large amounts of money in savings accounts or money market funds or, even worse, buys stocks and hold them until forced to sell because of the need for cash or money to live on.

The conservative approach provides peace of mind, but it's very poor protection against inflation and low interest rates. If, for instance, the cost of living rises 4% a year, and your conservative investments don't keep pace, you will actually lose. With a 4% rise, the real purchasing power of every $1,000 is cut to $822 in 5 years and to $703 in 10 years.

Conservative investments should, of course, constitute a portion of everyone's portfolio, but they are most appropriate for people who are retired, or soon to be, are fixed incomes, or earn low to modest salaries.

☑ *HINT: For additional suggestions on equating your appetite for risk with your investment choices, see the INVESTMENT PYRAMID on page 14.*

FINDING MONEY TO INVEST

Obviously, you need money to invest, to achieve your financial goals and to lead a stress-free life. You won't accomplish any of these if you set aside money sporadically — you need to save on a regular basis.

Painless sources of money to invest:

- Dividend checks
- Gifts
- Bonuses
- A raise
- Tips
- Automatic payroll deduction plan
- Inheritance
- Freelance and consulting activities
- Company savings plans
- Tax refunds
- The lottery

☑ *HINT: Another "automatic" technique for saving money to invest: Once you've paid off your mortgage, college loan, car loan, etc., save that amount. You have been living without the cash all these years; now stash it in your money market fund until you're ready to invest it in stocks, bonds or mutual funds.*

SPOTTING ECONOMIC TRENDS

To build and maintain a profitable portfolio, you must develop a sense of the country's economic strength or weakness. By following these key short-term market indicators, all of which are reported in the media, you can take the pulse of the nation.

- *Capacity utilization.* Measures the activity of U.S. manufacturers and the percentage rate at which factories are operating. A healthy rate is about 85%. When it drops, unemployment is high.
- *Consumer price index.* Also known as the cost-of-living index (COLA), it measures price changes for goods and services. Its components include housing, food, transportation, clothing, medical care, and electricity.
- *Gross domestic product.* The GDP measures the total value of all goods and services produced and sold in the United States over a particular time period. It tells whether the U.S. economy is expanding or contracting. Less than 2% is regarded as slow growth; over 5% is a boom. When the GDP declines two quarters in a row, it indicates that a recession has begun.
- *Index of leading economic indicators.* This index represents 11 components of economic growth, ranging from stock prices to housing permits. If it falls for 3 or 4 consecutive months, an economic downturn is likely.
- *New car sales.* Consumer buying trends are reflected in this purchase pattern, reported every 10 days. Keep track over a minimum of 2 months.
- *Retail sales.* Compares monthly sales with those of the previous month, 6 months, and 1 year.
- *Department store sales.* These reflect both regional and seasonal trends but can be an accurate indicator if they confirm other trends.
- *Housing starts.* Any improvement indicates optimistic consumer attitudes and, quite often, lower interest rates.
- *Unemployment.* This statistic reflects the over-all status of the country's economy. Watch it regularly.
- *Federal funds rate.* This figure, which fluctuates daily, tracks the interest rate banks charge each other overnight.
- *Prime rate.* Interest rate banks charge their most creditworthy customers. Follow at least 3 months.
- *Broker loan rate.* Interest rate for brokers borrowing money from banks.

☑ HINT: *For more information on how to use economic trends, read:* Market Movers, *by Nancy Dunnan and Jay J. Pack (New York: Time-Warner Books, 1993).*

TAKING ADVANTAGE OF CHANGES IN INTEREST RATES

Interest rates continually move up and down, and as they do, they impact directly on the appeal of many investment choices that are popular with those of you who are conservative investors, such as Treasury bills and notes, money market funds, and CDs. And so . . .

1. When rates peak and start to head down, high yields suddenly become history. When that happens, you want to be locked in with high-yielding CDs and Treasuries, not only to profit from high rates but also to benefit from rising bond prices that always accompany falling rates.
2. On the other hand, when rates are low, you want to be in short maturities so you can reinvest as rates rise. Use the box on page 47 as a guideline for timing your investments with changing rates.

To help you decide when to purchase long-term bonds, CDs, and Treasuries, use these three basic indicators:

- *Money market maturities.* The average maturity of money market fund portfolios indicates what direction the professional fund managers think interest rates will take. This maturity statistic, available by calling a fund, gives the average maturity of Treasury bills, CDs, and other short-term securities in the fund's portfolio. A fund with short maturities indicates that the manager thinks rates will climb even higher. Rates tend to turn downward when maturities reach 39 or 40 days.

■ *Prime rate.* A drop in prime usually occurs after other short-term rates have fallen, indicating that banks anticipate the downward interest rate spiral to continue. When prime drops, investors should lock in the highest yields available.

■ *Yield curve.* This illustrates the relationship between short- and long-term interest rates. Usually long-term rates are higher than short-term rates to reward investors for tying up their money for many years. When short-term rates are higher, the yield curve is inverted. An inverted yield curve generally indicates that interest rates have not yet peaked.

15 DO'S FOR SUCCESSFUL INVESTING

1. *Do investigate* BEFORE *you invest.* Do not buy on impulse, hunch, or rumors heard on the golf course. Make all investments according to your goals for income and/or growth. Take nothing for granted. Get the facts lest the lack of facts gets you.

2. *Do limit your purchases until your forecast is confirmed.* When you feel you have latched onto a winner, buy half the amount of shares you have money for. You may lose a few points profit by waiting, but you will also minimize your losses. Watch the action in the marketplace, and when your judgment appears accurate, buy the other half of your position.

3. *Do focus on the downside risk.* An important consideration in buying stocks is not how much you can make, but how much you can lose. If a stock's dividend, asset value, or price history clearly indicates a limited downside risk, it's probably a good investment.

4. *Do buy only stocks quoted regularly* in the *Wall Street Journal, The New York Times,* or *Barron's.* You want a ready (or secondary) market that will attract other investors when you sell.

5. *Do research* AFTER *you invest.* There is no such thing as a permanent winner. (Even IBM has bounced up and down over the years.) This caveat applies especially to small companies that show great promise at the outset but all too soon fall by the wayside.

6. *Do watch trends:* of the economy, the stock market, industry groups, and the stocks in which you are interested. Stock market leaders change almost monthly, so what was favorable in January may be sliding in June.

7. *Do set target prices when you make your original purchase.* Roughly, these should be 35% to 50% higher than your cost, and the time frame should be 24 to 36 months. Once in a while, a stock will zoom up fast, but investments usually move up slowly and steadily, with interim dips, to new highs.

8. *Do diversify, but carefully.* As a rule of thumb, a $100,000 portfolio should have no more than 10 securities, with no more than 20% in any one company or industry. However, you can put as little as 5% of your assets in special high-risk investments. Above $100,000, add one new security for each additional $10,000.

9. *Do stay flexible.* This will let you make the most profitable use of your money during any specific period. When yields on bonds, CDs, money market funds, and Treasuries are 6% or more, move part of your savings into these areas. When the yield drops, take your profits and invest the proceeds in quality common stocks where the chances of appreciation are greater.

10. *Do keep a list of 10 future investments.* Review them periodically to determine whether any offer greater prospects for faster rewards than the holdings you now have. This list should include stocks, REITs, convertibles, bonds, and Treasuries. Don't switch as long as your original investments are profitable and appear to have reasonable prospects of reaching your goals.

11. *Do watch the market, but never be in a hurry to spend your money.* If you miss one opportunity, there will be another soon.

12. *Do be patient.* Never flit from one stock to another. This will make your broker rich, but it will cut your potential profits and, unless you are very wise and very lucky, will not increase your capital. Four trades a year, at an average cost of 1% of stock value, equals 4% of income.

13. *Do upgrade your portfolio periodically.* Review all holdings quarterly and plan to sell at least one security every 6 months. Replace the weakest securities with those on your futures list. Be slow to sell winners, because this will leave you with less profitable holdings. On the average, a successful portfolio will be turned over every 5 years, about 20% annually.

14. *Do average up when you choose well.* Buy more shares as the price of the stock rises.

15. *Do set selling prices,* preferably stop-loss orders at 15% to 20% below your cost or the recent high. This is discussed in greater detail in Chapter 25, but it is a key factor in successful investing. It is just as important to keep losses low as to keep profits high. If the company runs into temporary difficulties, don't panic, but if research concludes that profits will be below projections, it's usually smart to sell now. You can always buy back later.

. . . AND 10 DO NOT'S FOR SUCCESSFUL INVESTING

1. *Don't invest in a vacuum.* You must have a systematic, sensible, long-range plan for your personal, business, and retirement monies.

2. *Don't be overly conservative.* This means limiting the portion of your savings allocated to fixed asset or income investments, such as money market accounts, CDs, preferred stocks, and treasuries. These are safe, but they rarely grow in value. Most of these holdings should be viewed as temporary parking places while you wait for more rewarding opportunities, or as a segment of our total portfolio.

3. *Don't be overly optimistic or pessimistic* about the market or the securities that you own. Even the best corporations falter now and then: their growth slows or their markets change. Smart professionals recognize when this occurs and also when the stock price soars to an unrealistic level. When any stock becomes clearly overvalued by your standards, sell or set stop-loss orders.

4. *Don't be lured by the greater fool theory:* that the price will keep rising because someone else will be foolish enough to pay far more than the stock is worth. When you have a pleasant profit, cash in.

5. *Don't rush to buy bargains,* regardless of the pressure from your adviser or broker. When a stock is at a low price, there is usually a reason. It may not appear to be logical, but major investors are either skeptical or uncomfortable. Once you spot a bargain, wait until the price and volume start to rise, and then proceed cautiously, buying in small lots.

6. *Don't average down.* A stock that appears to be a good buy at 20 is seldom more attractive at 15. When there's a serious decline in your current favorite, either your research is inaccurate or your access to the latest information is inadequate. Ask your broker to check with his/her research department. If you are wrong and keep buying as the price declines, you'll only compound your mistake.

7. *Don't assume that a quality rating will continue.* With cost squeezes, foreign competi-

tion, governmental regulations and edicts, and fast-changing financial and market conditions, even stable corporations can become less attractive in a few months.

8. *Don't heed rumors.* Wall Street is a center of gossip, hopes, and fears, but a rumor is never a sound reason for investment decisions. By the time you hear or read it, the professionals have made their move.

9. *Don't forget that a stock does not care who owns it.* The price per volume of the trading of its shares is the result of forces far stronger and wealthier than you are or probably ever will be.

10. *Don't look back.* There's no way that you can reverse your decision. If your judgment was wrong, try to learn from it.

REDUCE SALES FEES AND COMMISSIONS: A PAINLESS WAY TO BOOST YOUR RETURNS

There are three basic types of investing costs: (1) sales commissions, which you pay when you buy stocks, bonds, and load mutual funds; (2) mutual fund expenses; and (3) the spread: the difference between the ask price at which dealers sell a security to the public and the bid price at which they buy it back. Spreads are particularly heavy in purchasing zero coupon bonds, municipals, and over-the-counter stocks.

Here's how to cut costs when investing in:

U.S. Treasuries

Banks and brokerage firms charge sales commissions for buying and selling Treasury securities, which range from $25 to $75+ for up to $10,000 worth of securities. The discount broker Charles Schwab (800–442–5111) charges a flat fee of $49 whether you purchase one bond or many of them. Check out fees at several brokers before making a Treasury purchase.

☑ *HINT: Avoid commissions entirely by purchasing directly from the Treasury through its Treasury Direct system. For a free brochure, call your Federal Reserve Bank. (See pages 102–103 for the telephone number and address of the one in your area.)*

Review Your Portfolio When. . .

- There's a significant move up or down in the stock market
- Prime and other bank interest rates change
- A new tax law is passed
- The dollar becomes substantially stronger or weaker in the international market
- There's been a major scientific breakthrough
- Regulatory agencies adopt a new policy
- The inflation rate changes
- There's a change in political leadership
- Foreign-trade restrictions are put into effect
- A new international trade agreement is reached
- New rules are passed on margin accounts
- War begins or ends
- The economy changes from boom times to recessionary times, or vice versa
- Bond interest rates change
- There's a shortage in a key commodity or energy source

. . . And Then Take These Steps:

- Buy more stock of a proven company when the market falls and prune out losers when it rises.
- As rates move up, lock in higher yields in CDs and longer-term bonds; as rates fall, invest short term—under 2 years—and look to stocks.
- Determine your new tax bracket and talk to your accountant about ways to cut taxes.
- When the dollar is stronger, go to Europe on vacation; when it weakens, buy foreign currencies.
- Select one or two stocks within the industry to buy.
- Look for investments that will benefit from new attitudes and legislation, such as environmental mutual funds, waste and hazardous waste removal stocks, engineering companies, and water purification stocks.
- If inflation increases, interest rates will rise, so turn to money market funds and high-yielding CDs. If inflation decreases, stocks will do well.
- Read the newspaper to determine the current administration's priorities—military buildup or reduction; concern about education, the environment, or health care; protection of the rich—and position on taxes. Invest in areas where there's likely to be increased spending.
- Reduce holdings in companies or mutual funds heavily dependent on foreign sales.
- Look for corporations already operating or prepared to operate in that country.
- Call your broker to discuss implications for your account.
- If war starts, buy military stocks or investigate which commodities may be in short supply, depending on location of the conflict—copper, gold, wheat, oil.
- If war ends, decrease military holdings.
- If the economy is booming, take profits. If a recession starts, build up cash reserves and buy stocks at their lows.
- If rates go up, buy longer-term bonds. If rates decline, keep shorter-term bonds.

Money Market Funds

These mutual funds are sold without any sales charge or commission; however, their management expenses can take a bite out of your yield.

☑ *HINT: Call several funds or read their prospectuses to find a fund with an expense ratio below 0.6%. But remember, an extremely low expense ratio often means that management is absorbing some of the costs to push up the fund's yield and attract customers. This is often the case with new funds. Once the fund has new investors, it may raise expense charges.*

Stock and Bond Mutual Funds

Funds sold by brokers, called load funds, charge front-end loads or fees of as much as 8.5%. Many funds have back-end loads of up to 1.5%, which go into effect when you sell your shares. Still others have 12b–1 fees—an annual fee of up to 1% to cover marketing costs to bring in new shareholders. These 12b–1 fees are on top of annual management fees, which range from 0.3% to 1.5%. (Management fees are highest for international stock funds, which must be actively managed.)

The SEC passed a ruling in the spring of 1988 that all sales charges and fees must be listed in the fund's prospectus, accompanied by a table showing their precise effect on a $1,000 investment after 1, 3, 5, and 10 years.

☑ *HINT: Buy no-load funds directly from the mutual fund company and you'll have no sales fees, unless it's a low-load fund. Most of the funds recommended in this book are no-loads.*

Individual Stocks

The smaller the number of stocks you buy and sell, the wider the spread. With actively traded stocks, which includes most blue chips, the spread is typically narrow—say 12¢ per share. Yet a thinly traded stock that sells over the counter (OTC) could have an ask price of $5 and a bid price of just $4.50. Another point to keep in mind with OTC stocks: If you buy from the market maker (a broker/dealer firm that keeps the stock in its inventory), then you pay only the spread. On the other hand, if you buy through a broker who must in turn get the shares from a market maker, you wind up paying the spread plus the broker's commission.

CAUTION: *If you buy fewer than 100 shares of any stock (100 shares being a round lot), you wind up paying the same commission as though you'd purchased 100 shares. So, buy in round lots; buy OTC stocks from the market maker, listed in the pink sheets directory available from most brokers. (See chapter 14 for more on pink sheet listings.)*

Discount Brokers

You can cut sales commissions significantly by purchasing stocks through discount brokerage firms, although you have to give up the research and personal feeding and care you get from a full-service firm. However, you'll save as much as 50% to 80%. (See Chapter 24 for more on discount firms.)

Discounters also relieve you of another fairly new expense: annual fees for customers who do not actively trade their accounts. The leader of this charge, Merrill Lynch, charges $40 a year if you do not trade but simply store securities with the firm. Other firms have similar charges.

BUY STOCKS DIRECTLY

A handful of companies let investors buy their shares directly, thus bypassing a stockbroker. To find out, call the company's Investor Relations division. Among those that do are Central Vermont Public Service, Citizens First Bancorp, Exxon, Procter & Gamble, and Texaco.

You can also purchase stock directly from a number of public utility companies if you live in an area serviced by them. These include Carolina Power & Light, Cleveland Electric Illuminating Co., Duke Power, Hawaiian Electric Industries, Minnesota Power & Light, Philadelphia Suburban, San Diego Gas & Electric, and Wisconsin Energy.

Yet another way to reduce your cost of buying stocks is to have your dividends automatically reinvested in additional shares. (See page 255 for full details.)

When Investments Perform Best

INVESTMENT	ADD TO YOUR PORTFOLIO	RISK LEVEL
Growth stocks	When economy is growing at above average rate When interest rates are stable	Medium to high
Blue-chip stocks	During slow to moderate growth periods When interest rates are falling	Medium
Utility stocks	When interest rates are falling When energy costs are falling	Low to medium
Long-term bonds	When interest rates are falling	Low to medium
Short-term notes and bills	When interest rates are stable or falling	Low
Money market funds and CDs	When interest rates are rising	Low

Municipal Bonds

Spreads, which are built into the bond's price, are higher for odd-lot purchases. With munis, an odd lot is less than $25,000. If you buy a municipal bond in the secondary or aftermarket from a broker who does not have it in inventory, your yield is further reduced by about an eighth of a percentage point to cover the broker's costs in getting the bonds from another dealer.

☑ HINT: *Buy actively traded bonds, and new issues in particular. Spreads are typically 0.75%, compared to as much as 4% to 5% for odd lots. Try to pick bonds from your broker's inventory.*

Zero Coupon Bonds

The pricing of zeros tends to be confusing, and hefty spreads are not uncommon. Some brokers have been known to charge as much as 5%.

☑ HINT: *Shop among several brokers, asking how much you must invest per $1,000 face value for the particular zero you want. Then ask what the effective yield to maturity is. Buy from the broker with the lowest price and the highest yield.*

INVESTMENT CLUBS

If you're skittish about picking your own stocks or nervous about working with a stockbroker, you can circumvent these problems by purchasing stocks through an investment club, a team approach that is used by thousands of Americans.

An investment club is a group of individuals, often neighbors, coworkers, or friends, who meet once a month, contribute a set dollar amount, and invest the common pool in stocks. Every member is responsible for doing research on individual stocks on a rotating basis. They then report their findings to the club, and members debate the risks and rewards of each stock and finally take a vote on which ones to buy.

☑ HINT: *Much of the guidance for clubs comes from the National Association of Investors Corporation (NAIC), a nonprofit organization operated by and for the benefit of member clubs. This association, which has been the force behind the investment club movement in the United States since the 1950s, has about 23,000 clubs with 360,000 members. Membership is $35 for clubs plus $14 for each club member and $39 for individuals who are not members of a club.*

Join an Investment Club

If you'd like to start building a portfolio of stocks, but feel uncertain about making your own selections, join an investment club in your area. By pooling your money with that of 15 to 20 other people and sharing research, you can comfortably begin to develop investment savvy.

Kenneth S. Janke, president of the National Association of Investors Corporation, says the following three guiding principles followed by clubs enable them to frequently outperform the S&P 500:

1. Invest a fixed amount regularly to eliminate the guesswork of trying to time the market.
2. Reinvest earnings to take advantage of the magic of compounding.
3. Invest in stocks growing faster than the economy.

For details on joining a club, contact:

National Association of Investors Corp.
711 West 13 Mile Rd.
Madison Hts., MI 48071
810–583–6242

The association offers detailed information on how to start a club, how to analyze stocks, and how to keep records.

Another great plus: Clubs and individual members of NAIC can also dispense with brokerage commissions by participating in NAIC's Low-Cost Investment Plan. Under this program, clubs can buy as little as one share directly from about 150 major participating companies, such as Kellogg, PepsiCo, Mobil, Quaker Oats, and Whirlpool, for a one-time charge of $7 per firm. Most of these corporations do not charge a commission, although some have a nominal fee ($1 to $3) for each transaction to cover their expenses. All of these companies also have dividend reinvestment programs, so instead of taking dividends in cash, the club or individual members automatically reinvest the dividends in additional shares of the company's stocks.

☑ **HINT:** *According to a recent NAIC survey, clubs bettered the Standard & Poor's 500 for 26 out of the last 38 years.*

The most famous of the clubs, the Beardstown Ladies Club, made up of 16 Illinois women (average age: 63½) has walloped the stock market since 1983, averaging a 23% annual return. One of their big winners: Rubbermaid, which captured their attention because it had a double-digit growth record and made products that we know and use.

KEEPING GOOD RECORDS: IT PAYS TO BE A PACKRAT

You don't need to turn into the Collier brothers, but tossing out papers you need can lead to lots of trouble and hours trying to recreate lost records.

Here's a look at the documents you need to keep:

Tax Records

The IRS has three basic rules you must keep in mind:

1. It has three years from your filing date to audit your return if it suspects "good faith" errors. The three year deadline also applies if YOU discover a mistake in your return and decide to file an amended return to claim a refund.
2. It has six years to challenge your return—but only if it thinks you underreported your gross income by 25% or more.
3. It can come after you forever if you failed to file your return or filed a fraudulent return . . . Keep tax-related cancelled checks and receipts for six years; including your W–2 forms and 1099s as well as cancelled checks or receipts for:
   ■ Alimony
   ■ Charitable contributions
   ■ Child care
   ■ Medical expenses
   ■ Mortgage interest
   ■ Professional dues
   ■ Retirement plan contributions
4. If you made a nondeductible contribution to an IRA (for which you must use IRS Form #8606), keep the records forever. When it comes time for you to start withdrawing, you will be able to prove that you've already paid taxes on this money.

NOTE: If your IRA contributions are all deductible, you don't need to file Form #8606.

Brokerage Statements

■ *Stocks.* Keep the purchase/sales slips from your brokerage or mutual fund until you sell these securities; you need them to prove whether you have a capital gain or loss when you file your taxes. (*NOTE:* Some brokerage firms give you all the needed documentation on the monthly statement, but some show only the settlement date and total dollar amount of the transaction. Check to see how specific your monthly statements are before tossing any sales slips.

■ *Bonds.* The same record-keeping rules that apply to stocks also apply to bonds. In other words, keep the confirmation slips if you are buying a bond for which you have to pay some accrued interest to the seller at the time of purchase. For example, if the last interest payment was 2 months ago and the next one is 4 months in the future, you must pay the seller the 2 months' interest due him or her, because you will be receiving the full payment. This amount returned to the seller can be subtracted from your taxable income. This amount should be noted on your confirmation slip.

■ *Dividend Notices.* Save these until you receive your annual 1099-DIV form from each issuer. Save dividend reinvestment slips until the end of the year when you receive a summary of all purchases and reinvesments.

■ *Stock & Bond Certificates.* Save until you sell them.

☑ **HINT: *Photocopy your certificates and store in a separate location from the originals. If your safe-deposit box is broken into, the copies will help you prove ownership.***

Mutual Funds

With mutual funds, as with stocks and bonds, you must pay taxes on any price appreciation when you sell your shares. Therefore, when you buy shares in a mutual fund, save the confirmation slip indicating the number of shares you bought and what you paid for them.

Certain funds pay interest or dividends. In addition, you may get distributions of capital gains from the sale of investments held in the fund's portfolio. Taxes are due on these payouts in the year in which you receive them. Should you reinvest this money in more fund shares, save the statements recording this reinvestment transaction. Otherwise you may forget to include these distributions as part of your cost basis when you

sell. Some firms send out cumulative statements, in which case you need to save only the December one, which lists all transactions for the year.

If you decide to sell only some of your shares, your records will help you decide which ones to unload. The IRS assumes that you are selling the first shares you purchased unless you specify to the contrary. This is called first in, first out (FIFO), and can be unnecessarily costly if you have regularly purchased shares in a fund that has continually increased in value.

There are two other options besides FIFO: the identifiable-cost and average-cost approaches. With the identifiable-cost approach, you specify to the fund that you are selling a certain number of shares purchased on a particular date or dates. With a rising fund, this approach enables you to sell the most costly shares—those purchased most recently—and postpone taxes on the cheaper shares purchased earlier. If you sell by phone, send the mutual fund a letter confirming this fact. Keep a copy of your letter plus the transaction statements for 6 years.

With the average-cost method, you find the total cost of all shares ever purchased, including reinvestments, and divide by the number of shares you own to arrive at the cost per share. Then, multiply this by the number of shares you plan to sell to find your total tax cost. This method must be entered on tax Schedule D when you report the sale, and you must use the same method for future sales.

Banking Records

Go through your checks each year, keeping those relating to your taxes, business expenses, housing and mortgage payments. You can toss out those that have no long-term importance, such as those written for minor purchases and cash.

Housing Records

If you own a house, co-op, or condominium, keep all records documenting the purchase price and the cost of all permanent improvements—remodeling, additions, installations. Also keep records of expenses incurred in selling and buying the property (real estate agent's commission, legal fees, etc.) Even though it's a pain, keep all of these papers for as long as you own your house plus another six years after you sell it.

☑ HINT: *Co-op owners often get an annual tax information letter from the building's accountant indicating additions to your cost basis from amortization payments on the building's mortgage—keep these as well.*

And, keep IRS Form #2119 ("Sale of Your Home") on which you report the sale or exchange of your house and purchase of a new one.

Paycheck Stubs

Keep these until you receive your annual W–2 form from your employer. Make certain the informaton matches; if it does, toss the stubs. If it doesn't, get in touch with your employer's accounting department and ask for a corrected form, known as a W–2c. You should also save your final paycheck stub for the year because it records deductions for pension contributions and possibly for dedutible medical insurance premiums, charitable contributions and union dues.

Bills

Once a year, when you go through your checks, also sort out your bills. Basically, once you've paid a bill and the cancelled check has been returned, you can throw out the bill. However, bills for big ticket items—jewelry, rugs, appliances, antiques, cars, collectibles, computers, furniture, etc., should be kept to use as proof of their value in event of loss or damage.

Ways to Earn Interest

PART OF YOUR MONEY SHOULD BE PUT TO WORK EARNING MORE MONEY. HERE ARE WAYS TO DO JUST THAT. (DATA AS OF OCTOBER 1996)

Investment	Risk Level	Yield
Bank money market account	Low	2.64%
Money market mutual fund	Low	4.81
Certificate of deposit (6 month)	Low	4.79
Certificate of deposit (1 year)	Low	5.14
Certificate of deposit (5 year)	Low	5.73
Treasury bill (3 months)	Low	5.01
Treasury bill (1 year)	Low	5.64
Savings bonds	Low	4.06
Treasury note (5 years)	Low	6.42
Treasury bond (10 year)	Low	6.66
Ginnie Mae certificate	Low to medium	8.19
Utility stocks	Medium	6.87
Utility bonds (A-rated)	Medium	7.15
Corporate bonds (A-rated)	Medium	8.62
Utility bonds (BBB-rated)	Medium	8.65
Preferred stocks (Utility)	Medium	8.70
Preferred stocks	High	8.73

Credit Card Receipts and Statements

Keep your original receipts until you get your monthly statement; if there are no errors, discard the receipts. Keep the actual monthly statements for six years if tax-related expenses, charitable contributions and other documentations are involved. *NOTE:* If your credit card gives you buyer protection or has an extended warranty plan, keep related receipts until these perks expire.

Expired CDs and Bankbooks

Save these until January of the following year after they've expired—that's when you will get Form #1099 from the bank showing the amount of interest you earned. Compare this figure with the amount of interested entered in your bankbook or on your CD form. If everything matches, toss the expired certificates and bankbooks.

Retirement/Saving Plan Statements

Keep your quarterly statements from your 401(k) or other plan until the end of the year when you receive the annual summary; if everything matches, toss the quarterlies but keep the annual summaries until you either retire or close your account.

FOR FURTHER INFORMATION

Books

The Beardstown Ladies' Common-Sense Investment Guide (New York: Hyperion, 1995), $19.95.

The Hometown Investor: How to Find Investment Treasures in Your Own Backyard by Richard J. Maturi (New York: McGraw-Hill, 1995), $22.95.

Newsletters

Call or write for sample issues if you are interested in receiving continual data on the funds.

Income & Fund Outlook
Institute for Econometric Research
2200 SW Tenth Street
Deerfield Beach, FL 33442
800–327–6720; 954–421–1000
Monthly; $49 per year.
Covers money market funds, Ginnie Maes, and tax-free bonds.

100 Highest Yields
P.O. Box 088888
North Palm Beach, FL 33408
800–327–7717; 407–627–7330
Monthly; 8 issues for $48; 52 issues for $124.

Pamphlets

Money Market Mutual Funds
Publications Division
Investment Company Institute
1401 H Street
Washington, DC 20005
202–326–5800
$0.25; explains how money market funds are regulated.

Why You Should Belong to a Credit Union
Credit Union National Association, Inc.
P.O. Box 431
Madison, WI 53701
608–231–4000
Free

New York Stock Exchange Investors Information Kit.
Contains:

- *Capital Market Book*
- *Understanding Stocks and Bonds*
- *Understanding Financial Statements*
- *Getting Help When You Invest*
- *Glossary*
- *Margin Trading Guide*

$12; prepay by check or money order. Send to:
New York Stock Exchange
P.O. Box 5020
Farmingdale, NY 11736
516–454–1800

Record-Keeping

The Standard Homefile
$19.95 + $3.50 shipping from:

Financial Advantage
2606 Turf Valley Road
Ellicott City, MD 21042
800–695–3453
Includes plastic-coated file dividers and a helpful 48-page handbook.

Recordkeeping for Individuals; IRS Publication #552
Free; 800–829–3676

6

Investing with Mutual Funds

Although there's no one ideal investment for everyone, mutual funds come closest for many of us.

A mutual fund is an investment company in which an investor's dollars are pooled with those of thousands of others; the combined total is invested by a professional manager in various securities—primarily in stocks, bonds, government securities, foreign currencies, and options—or in different combinations of these vehicles.

Because you can buy shares in a fund for minimums ranging from several hundred to several thousand dollars, funds give all investors, even those without deep pockets, access to the entire market. And once you buy shares you can add to your account with as little as $100 or $500.

Funds also offer a wide range of investment objectives and philosophies—from conservative to middle-of-the-road to extremely aggressive, so there is a fund to match every conceivable investment goal.

12 ADVANTAGES OF MUTUAL FUNDS

Funds have a number of key advantages over owning individual stocks or bonds, especially for those with less than $30,000.

1. *Diversification.* Unless you have at least $30,000, it is almost impossible to have a properly diversified portfolio. Mutual funds, on the other hand, with 30, 40, even 100 securities in their portfolios, provide excellent diversification.

2. *Professional management.* Mutual fund managers are professionals with experience and a wealth of research to assist them in managing their portfolios. If their fund's performance falters in comparison with those of its peers, the fund manager may be replaced.

3. *Switching privileges.* When a management company, such as T. Rowe Price, Fidelity, or Vanguard, sponsors more than one type of fund (and most do), you may switch from one fund to another within this so-called family, as the market changes or as your goals change. Most funds offer free switching, although some impose nominal fees.

☑ *HINT: Select a fund that permits the portfolio manager to shift out of stocks and into U.S. Treasury bills, jumbo CDs, and other higher-yielding cash instruments if it looks like the stock market may decline. This gives you added protection when the market or interest rates change direction.*

4. *Paperwork.* Mutual funds handle the details of all transactions efficiently, mail dividend checks promptly, provide accurate year-end summaries for income tax purposes, and are always ready to answer questions on their toll-free phone lines.

5. *Savings and checking.* Many funds will set up an automatic monthly savings plan, wiring money from your bank into the fund. If your employer has a direct deposit payroll program, you can have part or all of your payroll check automatically invested in certain funds. U.S. government checks, federal salary, and veterans benefits can also be automatically invested. More and more funds are offering to sweep dividends and capital gains earned in one fund into another fund within the same family. Money market funds and some bond funds have check-writing privileges. However, unlike bank checking accounts, there's usually a $250 or $500 per check minimum, and you may be allowed only to write a limited number of checks per month, but the checks are free.

6. *Dollar cost averaging.* This involves regularly investing a set dollar amount in a fund—say, $150 to $500 per month. Many funds will automatically transfer money from your bank account into the fund every month. For example, you put $100 into a mutual fund every month: The shares fluctuate in price between $5 and $10. The first month you buy 10 shares at $10 each for a total of $100. The second month, because the market dropped, the shares are selling at $5 each, so you buy 20 shares at $5 and so on. At the end of 4 months you have acquired 60 shares for your $400 at an average cost of $6.67 per share (400 ÷ 60). *NOTE:* During this same period, the average price per share was $7.50.

☑ HINT: *For a free brochure on Dollar Cost Averaging, contact: T. Rowe Price, 100 East Pratt Street, Baltimore, MD 21202; 800–638–5660.*

7. *IRAs.* Most funds permit investors to open IRAs with considerably smaller dollar amounts than they require for their regular funds. This is a smart way to invest in a fund whose minimum otherwise is too high.

8. *Telephone trading.* Most funds sold directly to the public allow you to buy, sell, or switch fund shares over the telephone.

9. *Distribution or reinvestment of income.* You earn money from a fund in one of two ways, other than selling your shares at a profit: dividend income and capital gains distributions. Income dividends represent the interest and/or dividends earned by the fund's portfolio holdings, minus the fund's expenses. Capital gains distributions represent a fund's net realized capital gains—when there are profits in excess or losses on the sale of any of the portfolio securities. Both income dividends and capital gains distributions can usually be reinvested in the fund automatically, usually at no cost.

   A summary of the distributions made to each shareholder annually, called a Form 1099, is sent to the shareholder and to the IRS.

⊘ CAUTION: *Automatic reinvestment may not always be in your best interest. Mutual funds pay their largest distributions when the stock market is relatively high. Instead of reinvesting at the high level, you may do better to take the cash and wait for the market to decline. Then your cash will buy more shares.*

10. *Beneficiary designation.* You can name your beneficiary by means of a trust agreement so that your investment goes directly to your designated heir when you die, with none of the delays and expenses of probate. Consult your lawyer, because some states prohibit this transfer.

11. *Regular income checks.* You can set up monthly or quarterly income in several ways: (a) by buying shares in several funds, each with different dividend payout months; (b) by arranging for regular quarterly dividends to be paid out; or (c) by arranging to redeem automatically the dollar value of the number of shares

you specify. There's usually a $50 or $100 minimum per month. The fund will mail a check to you monthly, quarterly, or annually.

12. *Information and service.* Almost all investment companies provide toll-free numbers. Call to learn about prices, minimum investments, charges, and types of other funds available for switching. You can also ask for forms for setting up automatic withdrawals and for switching into other funds.

Systematic Withdrawal Plans

SWPs, long a favorite with retired people, are also ideal for making mortgage payments, paying insurance premiums, or other regular commitments. SWPs are an alternative to traditional written or telephone requests for withdrawal of your money from a mutual fund. Under an SWP, the fund periodically redeems the dollar value or percentage you request. Payment is made by check to you, to a third party, or to your bank account.

The amount required to maintain an SWP varies with each fund, but typical SWPs require a $5,000 or $10,000 minimum opening balance and a minimum $50 per month withdrawal. You can withdraw money monthly, bimonthly, or quarterly. Some funds permit you to withdraw only on the same day each month; others are more flexible.

SWPs offer several advantages:

- Steady stream of controlled income prevents overspending.
- Paperwork is reduced.
- Plan eliminates telephoned withdrawal requests.

And two definite disadvantages:

- You may draw out more money than you need or than you earn on the principal.
- May lead to apathetic attitude about saving.

Funds offer one or more of four types of withdrawals: (1) straight dollar amounts, (2) a fixed number of shares, (3) a fixed percentage, and (4) a declining balance based on your life expectancy.

☑ HINT: *If you don't wish to tap your principal, remove your money at a lower rate than the fund's increase in net asset value.*

Keep in mind that withdrawing a regular dollar amount is in effect reverse dollar cost averaging. In dollar cost averaging (see page 257) you invest an equal dollar amount every month and in this way buy more fund shares for the same amount when the market is down and fewer shares when it's up. In a fixed-amount withdrawal plan, you are forced to redeem more shares when the market is down to meet the set dollar amount and to sell fewer shares when the market is up.

💣 CAUTION: *Withdrawals are reportable as sales for tax purposes, whether the result is a gain, loss,*

Uses for Systematic Withdrawal Plans
- To pay your mortgage
- As a monthly living allowance for college students
- As income while on maternity leave
- For retirement
- To provide care for someone in a nursing home
- To meet insurance premiums
- As income while on sabbatical
- For alimony or child support payments

or breakeven. Keep records of your withdrawals to simplify year-end tax calculations.

HOW FUNDS WORK

All mutual funds operate along the same lines: They sell shares to the public at net asset value (NAV) price. (NAV per share equals the total assets of the fund divided by the outstanding shares minus liabilities.) The money received is then pooled and used to buy various types of securities. So when you buy into a fund, you are really buying shares in an investment company, but the assets of this company consist not of a plant or equipment, but of stocks, bonds, and cash instruments. The price of your shares rises and falls every day with the total value of the securities in the fund's portfolio.

As the owner of mutual fund shares, you receive periodic payments, provided your fund does well. Of course, if the fund has a poor year, you stand to lose money; that is, your NAV will fall. Most funds pay dividends every quarter and capital gains distributions annually. Capital gains distributions result when a fund sells some of its securities at a profit. You may elect to have your earnings reinvested automatically in additional fund shares, usually at no cost.

Open vs. Closed

Funds are either open- or closed-ended. In an open-end fund, shares are continually available to the public at NAV. The fund's shares are always increasing or decreasing in number, depending on sales to the public.

A closed-end fund has fixed capitalization and makes one initial issue of shares. After that it trades as a stock on the major stock exchanges or over-the-counter. In other words, it closes its doors to new investors, and shares can be purchased only by buying the stock. Prices are determined by supply and demand: When buyers are plentiful, the price of the stock rises, and vice versa. Depending

on market conditions, the price will be above or below NAV. When a closed-end fund is selling at a discount from NAV, the investor has an opportunity to see profits from price appreciation. (See Chapter 7 for more on closed-end funds.)

HOW TO SELECT MUTUAL FUNDS

There are thousands of mutual funds available, so how do you go about finding those that are right for you?

Know Why You're Investing and Pick a Fund to Meet That Purpose

Your basis choices are: income, growth, and/or a tax-free return.

Has the Fund Made Money?

There are three ways to judge this:

■ Follow other price of its shares, officially known as its Net Asset Value, or NAV.
■ Track its yield—the amount of income it's paying out to shareholders.
■ Look at its total return.

The total return figure takes into consideration changes in the price of shares and then adds in the results of reinvesting income or dividends, plus any capital gains or losses after expenses. (Capital gains and losses result from the sale of securities by the fund's portfolio manager.)

Although all three figures are important, the third—the total return figure—is the only overall indicator of how well a fund is doing, because it shows the total profit generated by the fund. (*NOTE:* A capital gains payment serves to reduce the fund's NAV because the fund pays out money that prior to payout counted toward the value of the entire portfolio.) The total return figure is also the best one to use when comparing one fund with another, or one type of fund with another type of fund.

The total return figure over 1, 3, and 5 years, as well as from the beginning of the year to date, is given in financial publications and from the funds directly.

☑ **HINT: Keep in mind that in a growth fund, the yield figure is not terribly important because the stocks in the fund were selected for their potential price appreciation, not for their dividends income. In fact, the stocks may not even pay dividends. What is important in a growth fund is whether the share price has been rising steadily for several years. On the other hand, in an income or bond fund, the yield is important because you selected the fund for income.**

Study the total return figures for several years, in both up and down markets. Many fine funds have never been first in any one year, but have done better than the market in good periods and have lost less in bear markets. One of the best guides is the annual *Forbes Magazine* report in late August. This issue rates funds on the basis of per-formance in both rising and falling markets. To get a high score, the fund must perform consistently in relation to other funds, in both up and down periods. Adjustments are made to prevent exceptional performance (good or bad) in any one period from having undue influence on the fund's average performance.

Other popular periodicals such as *Money, Your Money,* and *Kiplinger's Personal Finance* track fund performance in every issue. Morningstar, a weekly reference service, updates mutual funds and their performance; it is the most thorough in coverage. (See For Further Information at the end of this chapter for details.)

Take a Look at the Fund's Fees

The more of your money that goes into fees, the less you have actually invested.

For example, if you put $1,000 into a fund with an 8.5% commission or sales load, you will be purchasing only $915 worth of shares.

Yield vs. Total Return

It is important to know the difference between yield and total return when evaluating a fund.

- *Yield.* Measures the income (dividends or interest) per share paid out to shareholders by a bond or money market fund for a specified time. It is expressed as a percentage of the current offering price per share.

To calculate yield:

$$\frac{\text{distribution per share} \quad \$00.47}{\text{price per share} \quad \$10.00} = \text{Yield (\%)} = 4.7\%$$

- *Total return.* This measures the per-share change in the total value of a fund, from the beginning of the year to any given date. Total return is derived from dividend and interest income, capital gains distributions, any unrealized capital gains or losses, plus the effect of any re-invested dividends and capital gains.

To calculate total return:

current value	$22,000
−cost of initial investment	$20,000
difference	$ 2,000

$$\frac{\text{difference} \quad \$ 2,000}{\text{cost of initial investment} \quad \$20,000} = \text{Total Return (\%)} = 10\%$$

The law requires all funds to list their fees at the beginning of the prospectus, and it must give an easy-to-understand illustration in actual dollars of how much the fees are.

- *No-load funds.* These funds do not charge a sales fee, known as a load (or burden). Most are sold directly by the fund through advertising. Money market mutual funds, even those sold by stockbrokers and banks, are virtually all no-load.
- *Low-load funds.* There are some funds that have loads of 2% to 3%.
- *Load funds.* These are sold by stockbrokers, financial planners, or brokerage divisions of banks, who charge a commission every time you buy new shares. The legal limit is 8.5% of the amount invested. This amount is deducted from the amount of your initial investment. Thus, on a $10,000 purchase, the dollars that go to work for you are reduced by the 8.5% load to $9,150 ($10,000 − $850).

    There is no evidence that load funds perform better than no-loads, so if you don't need help in selecting a fund, go with a no-load and save the fee. And, if you plan to invest for 1 year or less, always select a no-load. One year is seldom long enough to make up an 8.5% sales fee.
- *Back-end loads* (also called redemption fees). Some funds charge this fee when you sell your shares, thus reducing your profit or making your loss even greater. They are levied against the net asset value.
- *Deferred loads* (also called contingent deferred sales fees). These are deducted from your original investment if you sell shares before a specified time passes after buying them. They may be based on a sliding scale, often 6% the first year, moving down to 0% in year six.
- *12b–1 fees.* These are named after the SEC regulation that authorized them in 1980. It allows the fund to deduct the costs of advertising and marketing directly from the fund's assets. They typically range from .25% to .30%, but can be as high as 1.25%.
- *Reinvestment loads.* These take a small amount out of the interest, dividends, and capital gains that are reinvested in your account. The maximum is 7.25% of the total investment. For example, if you receive a capital gains distribution of $100 and you automatically reinvest these gains, the fund can retain $7.25 as a selling fee and reinvest only $92.75 in new fund shares.
- *Management fee.* Every fund, load and no-load, charges a management fee to pay the adviser who manages the portfolio. The typical management fee is ½% to 1% of the fund's assets. It may be a flat rate or a sliding scale that gets smaller as the fund's portfolio gets larger.

☑ *HINT: Avoid funds with an expense ratio above 1.25%. The highest fees tend to be tied to funds with the highest risks—those with options, futures, short-selling, etc.*

Find Out the Turnover Rate

This shows the dollar amount of stocks or other holdings sold in relation to total assets. Thus, if a fund had assets of $100 million and sold $75 million in stocks in one year, the turnover would be 75%. This is considered high for a blue-chip stock fund and may indicate the manager is either speculating for short-term profits or not making successful choices.

    A high turnover rate also means the fund will be paying high commission costs and that you'll have higher capital gains distributions, which are taxed in the year distributed. For example, T. Rowe Price Growth fund, which contains primarily high quality stocks, has had a turnover rate that fluctuated from 30% to 51% over the last 5 years, while its Intermediate U.S. Treasury fund, which

---

The Five Best-Performing Equity Mutual Funds

According to *Forbes Magazine* these five funds did well over the past years, in both up and down markets.

- First Eagle Fund of America
- Legg Mason Value Trust-A
- Nicholas Limited Edition
- Clipper Fund
- Fidelity Growth & Income

---

holds Treasuries of 3- to 7-year maturities, had a turnover ranging from 175% to 195%.

☑ *HINT: Two excellent sources for studying turnover rates are Morningstar and The Individual Investor's Guide to No-Load Mutual Funds. (See For Further Information at the end of this chapter.)*

Size Is Also Important

The larger the assets of a mutual fund, the smaller the amount each investor pays for administration. However, stay away from funds whose assets have been under $50 million for over 5 years. If a fund hasn't grown, its performance must have been so poor that new shares could not be widely sold.

Study Volatility

This is measured by a component called "beta." You can use this figure to compare the fund's volatility with that of the stock market as a whole. (the market's beta is always 1.0 and a money market fund's beta is always 0.) If your mutual fund has a beta of 1.0, it will move with the market. In other words, if the market is up 5%, the fund will be up on average 5%. A mutual fund with a beta of 1.5 is 50% more volatile than the market, so if the market is up 10%, the fund will be up on average 50% more, or 15%.

The beta essentially compares the risk of the fund with the risk of the overall market. It is helpful in selecting a stock fund; less so for a bond fund. Bond funds respond to changes in interest rates, not the market. If you are selecting a bond

fund, you should check the ratings given the bonds by Standard & Poor's and Moody's as well as the maturity of the portfolio, rather than its beta.

Look for Adequate Diversification

Although the 5 percent rule, which limits investments in any one issue to 5% of a fund's assets, provides some protection, bear in mind that the rule applies to just 75% of a fund's assets. That means it could have 25% of its assets into one security and still be within the law. Check the fund's prospectus carefully.

HOW TO BUY FUND SHARES

You can buy shares in no-load funds directly from the funds themselves. You'll find toll-free numbers for many, as well as performance figures, listed in several financial magazines, including *Money, Your Money,* and *Kiplinger's Personal Finance Magazine.* Simply call the number and request the prospectus of the fund in which you're interested. Many no-load mutual fund companies have offices in cities throughout the country where you may stop in and pick up prospectuses and general literature.

☑ *HINT: Whenever you see a mutual fund with a telephone number listed in this book, it is a no-load (or low-load) fund and can be purchased by calling the fund.*

To buy shares in a load fund, you must contact a stockbroker or other commissioned sales person. Banks and some discount brokerage firms also sell load funds.

Load and no-load funds and their net asset values are also listed in the financial pages of major newspapers. *Barron's* has one of the most complete listings.

Closed-end funds, which trade as stocks and have a limited number of shares available, are sold by stockbrokers. The next chapter is devoted exclusively to closed-end funds.

HAND-HOLDING

If you want someone else to monitor your portfolio of funds, there are financial planning firms that will do just that—for a yearly fee. The fee includes asset allocation, fund selection, performance reports, and year-end tax summaries.

☑ *HINT: In addition to the ones listed below, you can get the names of fee-only planners in your area from the National Association of Personal Financial Advisors, 800–366–2732.*

BUYING MUTUAL FUNDS THROUGH A DISCOUNT BROKER

One rather easy way to buy a wide variety of funds is by opening a mutual fund account with a discount stockbroker. You can invest in some 300+ funds from more than 25 fund families with absolutely no transaction fees. Or, you can pick from several hundred other funds that have transactions fees based upon the amount you invest.

For example:

- *Charles Schwab Onesource* (800–526–8600). Offers more than 900 funds, 300 of which have no transaction fees. If you want to purchase funds outside these, you can do so if you pay a transaction fee. With an investment of $15,000 or less, the commission is 0.7% of the principal. The minimum transaction fee is $39.

- *Fidelity Fundswork* (800–544–9697). Has some 350 funds selected from about 10 fund families with no transaction fees. For funds with transaction fees, Fidelity charges are based upon the dollar amount of the investment, with a $28 minimum for a $1,000 investment.

- *Jack White & Co.* (800–323–3263). Has 500 no-transaction fee funds within 52 fund families plus another 400 funds for which there is a transaction fee. The minimum fee is $27 and the maximum, $50.

The Prospectus

You must read the prospectus before investing in a fund. Although it may appear formidable at first glance, a half-hour with this step-by-step guide will crystallize the entire process and enlighten you about the fund. Here's what to look for:

- What the fund's investment objectives are. These will be spelled out at the beginning.
- A risk factor statement
- What strategies will be used to meet the fund's stated goals
- The degree of diversification. How many issues does it hold?
- What is the portfolio turnover? A low rate, below 75%, reflects a long-term holding philosophy, whereas a high rate indicates an aggressive strategy.
- Fees and expenses. Check in particular the cost of redeeming shares, which should not exceed 1% per year.
- Rules for switching within a family of funds and fees, if any
- Restrictions. Will the fund sell securities short, act as an underwriter, engage in selling commodities or real estate? What percentage of total assets is invested in any one security? Be wary of a fund that is not adequately diversified. Does it use derivatives?
- How much the fund has gained or lost over 1, 5, and 10 years

☑ *HINT: Pick a fund that has an experienced man-*
ager. According to a recent Morningstar study,
stock funds with managers who've been with the
fund a number of years have higher returns.
Why? Poor fund managers lose their jobs.

SHOULD YOU BUY MUTUAL FUNDS FROM YOUR BANK?

More than 3,500 banks now sell mutual funds, and some of them market their funds very aggressively. Some sell funds from an independent mutual fund company, such as Fidelity, Franklin, or others, while about 125 banks sell their own line of funds.

According to a study done by *Consumer Reports,* the investment advice about mutual funds given by bank personnel to an investigative reporter was often inappropriate, sometimes wildly so. Only 16 of the 40 bank salespeople asked the potential investor the necessary questions about income, risk level, what other investments he owned. The magazine's conclusion: The odds of getting good advice at a bank that sells mutual funds are worse than 1 in 6.

After you've read this chapter you should be able to judge a bank's funds on your own, but keep these points in mind:

■ The phrase "a government-guaranteed fund" doesn't mean your money is 100% safe—the fund's shares could drop in value.

■ SIPC insurance does not insure the performance of your investment in a bank's mutual fund. SIPC insures bank brokerage accounts for up to $500,000 each, but pays off only if the brokerage firm goes bankrupt.

■ FDIC insurance does not cover annuities, mutual funds, insurance policies, stocks, bonds, or money market funds purchased from a bank.

■ Banks charge commissions on their funds.

■ Before heading to your bank for funds, take time to read the report in the March 1994 issue of *Consumer Reports,* available at your library.

HOW TO READ FUND QUOTES

You will find a listing of mutual funds in the financial pages of the newspaper (see the following table). Funds are listed under the sponsor's name, such as Vanguard or Fidelity. The first column is the name of the fund, then the NAV, or Bid as it may be called. (The NAV is the price at which fund shareholders sold their shares the previous day.) The next column, Offer Price, is the price paid by new investors the previous day.

When the offer price is higher than the NAV, there is a load: The difference between the NAV and the offer price is the sales commission. Funds with NL in the offer column are no-loads. A small r next to a fund's name indicates that a redemption charge may apply. Funds do not always have an r when they should, according to a study done

How Mutual Fund Shares Are Quoted

	NAV	OFFER PRICE	NAV CHANGE
Dreyfus Funds			
Cap V p	12.35	12.93	+.12
Index	17.21	NL	−.14
Interm	13.93	NL	−.02
Levge	17.63	18.46	−.14

p—distribution costs apply

NAV—net asset value

NL—no-load

recently by the American Association of Individual Investors. (Redemption fees are also called back-end loads.) The p denotes that a fund charges a fee from assets for marketing and distribution costs, also known as a 12b–1 plan.

☑ *HINT: When a distribution is made to shareholders, the NAV is reduced by the amount of the distribution per share. So, buy shares just after a distribution to save paying tax on the distributed amount. Call the fund to get exact dates.*

Don't panic if a fund's quoted price doesn't change much over the year. You may buy shares at $10 per share and find them the same a year later. That's because 90% of income and capital gains have been distributed to shareholders. Instead, judge the fund's total performance (capital appreciation plus dividend income) as a percentage gain or loss. The figure is available by calling the fund.

TYPES OF FUNDS

Mutual funds come in all sizes, shapes, and combinations. It is extremely important that you match your personal investment objectives with those of the fund. The accompanying list summarizes the broad objectives and should be read carefully in order to familiarize yourself with the various terms or bits of jargon the funds use to describe what they do with your money.

Keep in mind that there are scores of other mutual funds, many of which are described in chapters relating to specific types of securities. Before you commit any money to a fund, do your homework and make certain you understand exactly what you are investing in.

HOW MANY FUNDS SHOULD YOU OWN?

With about 4,000 funds out there, it's not easy to decide which ones to own or how many. Although there's no magical "right" number, common sense suggests somewhere between 3 and 10, not including a money market fund—10 being the maximum most people can track on a regular basis. Of course, it also depends upon how much money you have to invest. If you have $5,000 saved in addition to your emergency nest egg, then one or two is appropriate. In the long run, your goal is to cover different aspects of the market and thus protect your investments from wide economic and industry swings. Aim to pick funds that will do well at different points in the economic cycle.

☑ *HINT: Begin by picking a fund that is already diversified, such as Vanguard Star or T. Rowe Price Spectrum Growth. Both hold a mix of other funds within their own mutual fund family.*

SECTOR FUNDS

If you're confident about what industry or industries will do well during 1997 and 1998, consider a sector fund, one that invests in a single industry. Keep in mind, however, that although such funds offer greater profit potential than broader-based funds, they're also far riskier. This risk factor is reflected in their great price volatility.

💣 *CAUTION: Stocks in a given group tend to fall in unison. Most sector funds stay fully invested or nearly so even when their industry has a slide. They are less likely to switch portfolios into Treasuries or cash equivalents. Select a fund that's part of a family of funds so you can switch out when your industry turns sour.*

It's difficult to use past performance to predict future performance in this group.

Read one or two of the newsletters listed at the end of this chapter, plus *Value Line Investment Survey* and Standard & Poor's *Outlook* to keep up-to-date on industry developments.

☑ *HINT: Limit your investment in sector funds to 10%. Because they focus on one economic area, you'll reduce your chances for loss if that particular sector experiences a downturn.*

Types of Mutual Funds

FUND	OBJECTIVE
Aggressive growth funds	Seek maximum capital gains, not current income. May invest in new companies, troubled firms. Use techniques such as option writing to boost returns. Highly risky.
Balanced funds	Aim to conserve principal, generate current income, and provide long-term growth. Have portfolio mix of bonds, preferred stocks, and common stocks.
Corporate bond funds	Seek high level of income. Buy corporate bonds, some U.S. Treasury bonds or bonds issued by federal agencies.
Flexible portfolio funds	May be 100% in stocks or bonds or money market instruments. Have the greatest portfolio flexibility of all funds.
Ginnie Mae funds (GNMAs)	Invest in mortgage-backed securities. Must keep majority of portfolio in these securities.
Global bond funds	Invest in debt of companies and countries throughout the world, including the United States.
Global equity funds	Invest in securities traded worldwide, including the United States.
Growth funds	Invest in common stock of well-established companies. Capital gains, not income, is primary objective.
Growth and income funds	Invest in common stock of dividend-paying companies. Combine long-term capital gains and steady stream of income.
High-yield bond funds	Keep two-thirds of portfolio in lower-rated corporate bonds (junk bonds) to achieve high income.
Income bond funds	Invest at all times in corporate and government bonds for income.
Income equity funds	Invest in companies with good dividend-paying records.
Income mixed funds	Seek high current income by investing in equities and debt instruments.
Index funds	Buy stocks to match an index such as the S&P 500.
International funds	Invest in equity securities of companies located outside the United States.
Long-term municipal bond funds	Invest in bonds issued by states and municipalities. In most cases, income earned is not taxed by the federal government.
Money market mutual funds	Invest in short-term securities sold in the money market. Safe, relatively high yields.
Option/income funds	Seek high current return by investing in dividend-paying stocks on which call options are traded.
Precious metals/gold funds	Keep two-thirds of portfolio in securities associated with gold, silver, platinum, and other precious metals.
Sector funds	Concentrate holdings in a single industry or country.
Short-term municipal bonds	Invest in municipals with short maturities—2- to 5-year maturities.
Single-state municipal bond funds	Portfolios contain issues of only one state so that income is free of both federal and state taxes.
Socially conscious funds	Avoid investments in corporations known to pollute, have poor records in hiring minorities, and are involved in the military, tobacco, and liquor industries.
U.S. government income funds	Invest in a variety of government securities, including U.S. Treasury bonds, mortgage-backed securities, and government notes.

Buying on Margin

If you're an aggressive trader, you can buy mutual funds on margin. You must pay 50% of the total cost of your transaction up front. The rest you borrow from your broker. Before doing so, see pages 259–262 on how a margin account works, and beware of the pitfalls.

Among the brokerage firms offering mutual fund shares on margin are:

- Charles Schwab & Co. (800–435–4000)
- Jack White & Co. (800–233–3411)
- Quick & Reilly (800–672–7220)

Building a Basic Mutual Fund Portfolio

DOLLARS TO INVEST	NUMBER OF FUNDS	TYPE
$4,000 or less	1	A money market fund
$4,000 to $5,000	2	and a government income fund
$5,000 to $10,000	3	and a balanced fund
$10,000 to $20,000	4	and a growth and income fund
$20,000 to $30,000	5	and a high quality corporate bond fund
$30,000 to $40,000	6	and a tax-exempt municipal bond fund
$40,000 to $50,000	7	and an aggressive growth fund
$50,000 to $60,000	8	and an index fund
$60,000 to $70,000	9	and a small cap stock fund
$70,000 to $80,000	10	and a sector fund
$80,000 to $100,000	11	and an international stock or bond fund

INVESTING IN GOOD CAUSES

Earth Day, held in April, heightens the country's awareness of the urgent need to save our environment, specifically the importance of developing better methods of energy conservation, waste management, and pollution control. Wall Street offers ways to invest in the emerging business of environmental housecleaning.

Socially Responsible Mutual Funds

According to the Social Investment Forum, a trade group, about 670 money managers invest $162 billion in socially screened investment portfolios. These funds share fairly similar goals ranging from avoiding firms that deal in liquor, tobacco, or military weapons, to championing the environment. Others look for companies that are involved in community development and low-income housing projects.

1) The granddaddy of socially responsible investing, *The Pax World Fund* of Portsmouth, New Hampshire, is a balanced stock and bond fund that was started in 1971. The fund, which has $495 million in assets, will not buy companies in the liquor, tobacco, or gambling industries, and it emphasizes health care and education stocks.

2) *The Dreyfus Third Century,* started a year later in 1972, is a large fund with $480 million in assets. It invests in companies that protect or improve the environment, that make careful use of our natural resources, and that are involved in occupational health and safety and consumer protection. All companies must be equal opportunity employers. Dreyfus will, however, invest in firms with military sales. For the 10-year period through

Types of Sector Funds

Agriculture	Health care
Biotech	International
Chemicals	Leisure
Computers	Precious metals/gold
Defense/aerospace	Real Estate
Energy	Socially responsible
Environment	Technology
Financial services	Transportation
Foreign countries	Utilities

May 31, the fund chalked up an annual return rate of 11.56%.

3) *The Parnassus Fund* in San Francisco was named for a sacred Greek mountain overlooking the oracle at Delphi. It follows a contrarian philosophy, investing only in stocks that are out of favor with the investment community. Among the factors used in building its portfolio: Companies must produce a product or service of high quality,

be sensitive to the communities where it operates, and treat its employees fairly and well.

4) *The Calvert Social Investment Fund* invests in companies that make quality products and environmentally responsible goods. They must be equal opportunity employers, promote women and minorities, and provide safe workplaces. The fund will not buy companies primarily engaged in the production of nuclear energy or weapons systems.

Socially Responsible Equity Funds

FUND	TELEPHONE	TOTAL RETURN/ JAN–JULY 1996
Calvert Social Investment	800–368–2748	12.1%
Dreyfus Third Century	800–645–6561	18.0
Parnassus Fund	800–999–3505	15.2
Pax World Fund	800–767–1729	11.9
Pioneer Fund (stocks)		15.7
Pioneer II (stocks)		18.1
Pioneer III (stocks)	800–225–6292	15.4
Pioneer Bond Fund		7.1
Pioneer American Income		7.0

Socially Responsible Money Market Funds

FUND	TELEPHONE	YIELD AS OF OCTOBER 1996
Calvert Money Market Fund	800–368–2748	5.10%
Pioneer Cash Reserves		5.00
Pioneer U.S. Government	800–225–6292	4.91
Pioneer Tax-Free Money Fund		4.62
Working Assets Money Fund	800–533–3863	4.04

5) The 25 funds operated by *The Pioneer Group* rule out investments in liquor, tobacco, gambling, or firearms.

Socially Responsible Money Market Funds

In addition to these stock funds, there are several socially responsible money market funds for those who want a parking place for their cash. The largest, working assets money fund, was started in 1983 with $100,000 by a group of eight bay area people interested in educating the public on social issues. It invests in money market instruments that help finance housing, small businesses, family farms, higher education, and certain types of energy.

INDEX FUNDS

These funds actually buck the odds and often win. According to Investability, a Louisville, Kentucky, firm that tracks funds, of the 462 regular, non-index stock funds with 10-year records, fewer than one out of four beat the S&P 500 over the past decade (adjusted for up-front charges).

With an index fund you are the index.

These funds buy the same securities that make up an index and therefore their performance mirrors that of the index, such as the S&P 500, the Small Cap Index, or the S&P 100. They offer an easy way for you to participate in the long-term growth of the overall stock market, at a relatively low cost. (Index funds are pretty inexpensive because they don't need a hot-shot portfolio manager to buy and sell stocks.)

There are more than 70 index-linked funds. Because they are designed to closely match the performance of major market yardsticks, they have several unique advantages:

1. During bull markets they provide full market participation.
2. They're relatively cheap. Because their portfolio turnover is low and they don't require large research staffs, most have low operating costs, thereby boosting your returns. (These funds sell shares only when a stock is deleted from an index or when net redemptions force stock sales.) The average equity fund has an expense ratio of about 1.4% versus a little under 1% for index funds. The Vanguard 500 Index, which tracks the S&P 500, has an annual expense of only 0.19%.
3. Taxes are not a big factor. These funds rarely sell stock, so their capital gains distributions are far less than for actively managed funds. Therefore, taxes on such gains are deferred for the most part until you sell your shares.
4. These funds provide excellent diversification, and you know exactly what stocks you're invested in at all times.

Index Funds

FUND	INDEX TRACKED	TELEPHONE
Dean Witter Value-Added Equity	S&P 500	800–869–3863
Fidelity Market Index	S&P 500	800–544–8888
Peoples Index (Dreyfus)	S&P 500	800–645–6561
Peoples MidCap Index	S&P MidCap	800–645–6561
Schwab-1000*	Schwab-1000	800–435–4000
Vanguard Index Trust 500	S&P 500	800–662–7447
Vanguard Index Trust Extended Mkt	Wilshire 4500	800–662–7447

*Index of 1,000 largest publicly traded U.S. companies.

FUNDS-OF-FUNDS

If you don't have the time, energy, or expertise to put together your own portfolio of funds, you can get into what's known as a funds-of-funds. As the name implies, these are funds that invest in other funds.

There are about two dozen of these hybrids, the largest being Vanguard Start Portfolio and the two T. Rowe Price Spectrum funds. One point to take into consideration is that the funds-of-funds pay expenses on each investment in the portfolio. The fund then adds on its own costs, creating a hefty layer of expenses. Both T. Rowe Price and Vanguard cut the expenses by investing within their own family of funds, but then that also cuts diversification.

Bottom line: Use it if you know you can't make the decision yourself regarding which funds to own, and you're willing to get instant diversification but also pay for it.

TAXES AND MUTUAL FUNDS

Each time you touch your mutual fund shares there are tax implications that must be reported to the IRS, including these:

- When you switch from one fund to another within a family, the IRS considers this a sale in one fund and a purchase in another. You must report your profit or loss.
- When your fund earns dividends and taxable interest and passes them on to you, you must pay taxes on this distribution.

- When your dividends are automatically reinvested in more shares, you must report this as dividend income.
- When there are capital gains distributions, these must also be reported.
- For further information, read IRS booklet No. 564, *Mutual Fund Distributions*, and contact T. Rowe Price for a free copy of *Tax Considerations for Investors*, 100 East Pratt Street, Baltimore, MD 21202; 800–638–5660.

☑ HINT: *If you buy shares in a fund just prior to its annual earnings distribution, you will be taxed on this distribution even though the value of your new shares drops to reflect this distribution. Buy just after distribution.*

TAX-FREE FUNDS

Should you be in a tax-free mutual fund? To compute how much you need to earn on a taxable investment to equal a tax-free one, use the following formula:

$$\frac{\text{tax-exempt yield}}{1 \text{ minus your tax bracket}} = \text{equivalent of a taxable investment}$$

For example, if you're in the 28% tax bracket and a tax-exempt bond is yielding 10%, you would have to receive a yield of 13.88% on a taxable investment to be equivalent:

$$\frac{.10}{1-.28} = .1388 = 13.88\%$$

Funds-of-Funds

Here are the best performers; call for 1- and 5-year total returns:

API Growth	800–544–6060
FundTrust	800–344–9033
New Century	800–244–7055
T. Rowe Price	800–638–5660
Vanguard	800–662–7447

In the 31% bracket, a tax-exempt bond yielding 7% is the equivalent of a 10.14% yield on a taxable investment:

$$\frac{.07}{1-.31} \quad = \quad .1014 = 10.14\%$$

☑ *HINT: In all states, dividends from U.S. Treasury money funds or bond funds are also tax-free, even though you have to pay federal tax on them. And you may be eligible for a foreign tax credit if you own a mutual fund that invests in stocks or securities of foreign corporations. Watch for an indication on your 1099-DIV form of foreign tax paid on your behalf.*

SMART WAYS TO BULLET-PROOF YOUR FUNDS

The key to making money in mutual funds is knowing what type of funds to buy and when. Two such times are when the market is having a sharp correction and when interest rates move up or down substantially. Here's how to reallocate your funds under those situations.

When the market drops:

■ *Buy a bear fund,* one that is specifically managed to perform well when stock prices are declining by selling short some of its holdings. Selling short means betting that stock prices will decline. *Suggestion:* Robertson Stephens Contrarian Fund, 800–766–3863.
■ *Buy a low-volatility stock fund* that invests in a mixture of dividend-paying companies, bonds, and out-of-favor stocks. *Suggestions:* Fidelity Puritan Fund, 800–544–8888, and Mutual Beacon Fund, 800–553–3014.

   When interest rates rise:

■ *Buy short-term bond funds.* Rising rates depress bond fund shares, especially funds with long-term holdings. *Suggestion:* Vanguard Short-Term Corporate Portfolio, 800–662–7447.

■ *Buy high-yield junk bond funds,* which are less sensitive to changing rates. *Suggestion:* Fidelity Capital & Income Fund, 800–544–8888.

   At any time:

■ *Buy foreign stock funds.* Other economies do not have economic cycles parallel to ours, so a foreign fund may be a hedge against a declining U.S. market.

WHEN TO SELL YOUR MUTUAL FUND SHARES

A fund is not forever. Just as you revise your stock portfolio, you should do the same with mutual funds. They should be evaluated periodically and weeded out, for no fund is perfect for your needs forever. Unquestionably the toughest decision you will face is knowing when to sell. Here are some objective signals for selling and/or switching funds:

■ If the portfolio manager quits
■ If the fund's performance ranks in the bottom third of funds of its type for over a year
■ If the fund lags the market averages, such as the S&P 500
■ If the stock market shifts dramatically. Equity funds generally suffer during bear markets. Switch from stock to money market funds at the beginning of a bear market. As a bull market begins, move into conservative blue-chip funds. As the bull begins to roar, put more dollars into aggressive growth funds.
■ If interest rates rise. Bond funds tend to be hurt when interest rates move up. Sell bond fund shares when rates start to decline, but buy bond funds with longer maturities when rates seem to be at or near their peak in order to lock in the new higher yields.

WHEN A MUTUAL FUND MANAGER LEAVES

Just when you've found a fund that's making money, the portfolio manager suddenly leaves to run another fund. Do you stay or follow him to his new home? Generally you're all right to stay put, at least for 6 months, during which time you can see how the new manager is performing. This is particularly true if switching means paying high redemption fees. If it's a money market fund or an index fund, the manager has relatively little to do with performance, so there's no need to change. However, consider following the manager to his or her new fund after 6 to 12 months if:

1. Its investment goals match yours.
2. Your current fund, under the new manager, is underperforming in its category 6 to 12 months after the changeover.
3. The new manager revises the fund's strategies so it no longer fits your needs—it becomes too conservative or too aggressive, for example.

FOR FURTHER INFORMATION

General Directories

Individual Investor's Guide to Low-Load Mutual Funds
American Association of Individual Investors
625 North Michigan Avenue
Chicago, IL 60611
312–280–0170

An annual guide evaluating 800+ no-load and low-load funds; $24.95.

Mutual Fund Almanac
Agora Financial Publishers
1217 St. Paul Street
Baltimore, MD 21202
800–433–1528
An annual with data on more than 4,000 funds; $34.95

The Handbook for No-Load Fund Investors
P.O. Box 318
Irvington, NY 10533
800–252–2042
An annual directory with useful ideas on how to pick a no-load fund; performance data on 1,700 funds; $45.

The Investor's Guide to Low-Cost Mutual Funds
Mutual Fund Education Alliance
1900 Erie Street
Kansas City, MO 64116
816–471–1454
Performance figures, assets, turnover rates on 900 funds; updated twice a year; a bargain at $9.

Comparing Your Fund with Others

In your fund's annual report you will find the index that the fund manager uses as a benchmark for measuring the fund's performance. You can use that figure or you can compare your fund with other similar funds. Stick to a single time period for both your fund and the benchmark.

Your Fund Average Annual Total Return	Index's Annual Total Return	Other Fund Average Annual Total Return

Year
19__ _____
19__ _____
19__ _____
19__ _____

Mutual Fund Fact Book
Publications Division
Investment Company Institute
1401 H Street NW
Washington, DC 20005
202–326–5800
$25

Books

Warren Boroson, *Keys to Investing in Mutual Funds* (Hauppauge, NY: Barron's Educational Publishing, Inc., 1992), $4.95.

Greg Dougherty, *Consumer Reports Guide to Mutual Funds* (Yonkers, NY: Consumer Reports Inc., 1995), $22.95.

Carole Gould, *New York Times Guide to Mutual Funds* (New York: Random House, 1994), $14.00.

Sheldon Jacobs, *How to Pick the Best No-Load Mutual Funds for Solid Growth and Safety* (Homewood, IL: Business One Irwin, 1992), $15.

Pamphlets

Publications Division
Investment Company Institute
1401 H Street NW
Washington, DC 20005
202–326–5800
A *Close Look at Closed-End Funds*, $0.25.
What Is a Mutual Fund? $0.25.
Discipline: Dollar Cost Averaging, $0.20.

Newsletters

Morningstar Mutual Funds
Morningstar Inc.
225 West Wacker Drive
Chicago, IL 60606
800–876–5005

Like *Value Line;* covers 1,500 funds in detail; updated every other week; $425 /year; 3-month trial, $55.

The No-Load Fund Investor
P.O. Box 318
Irvington, NY 10533
800–252–2042
A monthly analysis of the no-load funds; $129.

No-Load Fund X
DAL Investment Co.
235 Montgomery Street, Suite 662
San Francisco, CA 94104
415–986–7979; 800–323–1510
Monthly; lists top performers by investment goals; $75.

Mutual Fund Forecaster
2200 SW Tenth Street
Deerfield Beach, FL 33442
954–421–1000
Monthly; ranks funds by risk and profit potential; $100.

Sector Funds Newsletter
P.O. Box 270048
San Diego, CA 92198
619–748–0805
Monthly; tracks the sector funds; $117: 3-month trial, $27.

In order to sample a variety of newsletters, contact:
Select Information Exchange
244 West 54th Street
New York, NY 10019
212–247–7123
SIE is a financial publications subscription agency providing a group of trial subscriptions to various investment newsletters. One trial group comprises 20 different mutual fund services for $19.96.

The Clean Yield Newsletter
P. O. Box 117
Greensboro, VT 05841
802–533–7178
Bimonthly; $80/year.
Written for socially concerned individual investors and financial professionals, this stock market newsletter profiles 2 stocks per issue and updates 8 others. It screens companies for their environmental practices and weapons production.

The Social Investment Forum
1612 K Street NW
Suite #600
Washington, DC 20006
202–872–5340
National trade association for socially responsible professionals in the financial field; has quarterly publication on socially responsible investments with periodic updates; $20

7

Using Closed-End Funds

Many investors shy away from closed-end funds because they simply don't understand how they work. Yet overlooking these hybrid creatures—part mutual fund, part stock—can mean missing a good investment opportunity. Many offer investors the opportunity to buy their portfolio assets at a discount.

WHAT THEY ARE

Closed-end funds, also called *Publicly Traded Investment Companies,* are similar in some ways to open-end mutual funds, described in the previous chapter. Both are investment companies that take money from thousands of investors and assemble portfolios of stocks, bonds, convertibles, and other securities to meet the fund's stated investment goal, and then issue shares to the public. Both use professionals to manage their portfolios.

However, the similarities end there. There are key differences: *Open-end* mutual funds continually issue new shares as people invest their money and they buy back their shares when investors sell. Not so with a *closed-end* fund—these funds raise their initial capital by issuing a fixed number of shares in a process similar to selling a new stock issue. After this initial offering the fund is closed, hence its name. It does not issue new shares (unless it has a secondary offering later), nor does it redeem shares.

From this point on, the fund's shares trade in the secondary market on one of the stock exchanges or over-the-counter as regular stocks. That is why they are sometimes called publicly traded funds. Shares cannot be purchased directly from the fund itself. Instead, you must buy and sell them through a stockbroker, and you pay a commission, just as you do when trading common and preferred stocks.

UNDERSTANDING DISCOUNTS AND PREMIUMS

The relationship between a closed-end fund's market value and its net asset value (NAV) is quite different from that of an open-end mutual fund.

Each closed-end fund has a NAV and, like a mutual fund, it changes daily depending on the market value of the stocks and bonds in its portfolio. When you sell shares in an open-end mutual fund, you receive the net asset value per share, minus any redemption fees. But the NAV is not used to determine the market price of the fund's shares; i.e., its price on an exchange or over-the-counter.

Because they are traded on the exchanges, their shares fluctuate in price based upon demand, just as with any stock. And this price moves independently of the portfolio value. When buyers of the fund outnumber sellers, the price rises, and when sellers outnumber buyers, the price declines. The result: The price of a closed-end fund's shares may sell at a premium to (above) or at a discount (below) from its NAV, depending upon investor interest in the fund. (The NAV is the market value of the fund's portfolio divided by the total number of shares outstanding, minus any liabilities.)

For example, if a fund has a NAV per share of $15, based on the current market value of its portfolio, but is priced at $12, it is selling at a 20% discount. Or to look at it another way, when a share of a closed-end fund is selling at a 20% discount, every $12 invested in a share puts $15 in assets to work for you.

The NAV for each closed-end fund and its stock price plus whether it is selling at a premium or a discount from NAV (expressed as a percentage) are listed in the financial press (see box on page 77).

You'll find that most newly issued closed-end funds trade at a premium to NAV, reflecting the start-up costs of the fund. That's because a portion of your investment, often 7% to 8%, goes toward paying underwriting expenses and commissions to brokers who sold the fund at the initial offering. For example, if you pay $10 per share to buy at the initial offering, approximately $9.30 would go toward actual investments.

☑ **HINT: Generally avoid buying shares at the initial offering. Wait until the share price drops below NAV in the secondary market.**

TYPES OF CLOSED-END FUNDS

There are several types of closed-end funds:

- *Closed-end stock funds.* These invest in common and preferred stocks. Some specialize in a given sector, such as health care or energy. (*Examples:* Gabelli Equity, Blue Chip Value, Cypress.)

- *Closed-end bond funds.* These invest in a range of bonds, including high-quality corporates, low-rated, or junk bonds. Some invest only in U.S. government bonds, municipal bonds, or bonds of foreign governments. As with any fixed-income investment, the price of closed-end bond funds moves in the opposite direction from interest rates. (*Examples:* 1838 Bond-Debenture, ACM Government Opportunity, Nuveen NY Muni, First Australian Prime Income.)

- *Closed-end convertible bond funds.* These have portfolios consisting of bonds that can be converted into common stock. Convertibles offer relatively high yields in comparison to some other investments, and they also have a potential for capital gains. (See Chapter 10 for more on convertibles. *Example:* Lincoln National Convertible.)

- *Closed-end single country funds.* These specialize in stocks of a given country or geographical area. (*Examples:* The New Germany Fund, the Asia Pacific Fund, or the Irish Investment Fund.)

- *Closed-end dual purpose funds.* These funds have two classes of shares. The income shares are entitled to all of the dividends paid out or interest earned. The capital shares receive all the capital gains. Dual-purpose funds usually end 10 to 15 years after being launched. When they are terminated, income shares are redeemed at a specific price. Owners of capital shares divide up the fund's remaining assets, either by liquidating the fund or by converting it to an open-end status and permitting investors to sell their shares at NAV. The closer the ending date, the more likely the fund's discount will disappear. If you are a long-term investor and buy at a discount and hold your shares until the termination date, you will make a nice profit. (*Examples:* Quest for Value Capital Shares, Quest for Value Income Shares, Hampton Utilities Capital Shares.)

BUYING A CLOSED-END FUND

You should go about selecting a closed-end fund just as you would any other investment: Determine your investment goal and the amount of risk you wish to take, and then find a fund that meets your requirements.

Unlike open-end mutual funds, most closed-end funds issue a prospectus only when they are launched, or on the rare occasion when they issue new shares. You can learn about a closed-end fund's investment objectives, services, extent of portfolio turnover, the proportion of a fund's shares owned by officers and directors, and other facts from the fund's reports to shareholders. Funds will supply copies upon request. As a shareholder, you will receive an annual report.

Be certain to study the fund's performance record and its expense ratio. The average expense ratio for open-end stock funds is 1.3%, so avoid funds with ratios much higher than this, with the exception of single country funds, whose expenses run higher than average.

Closed-end bonds funds can use their capital to maintain their dividends (and investor interest), even when it's not earning enough to cover the payouts. The dividend will probably be cut, eventually.

 CAUTION: When buying a fund you should also be aware of the discounts and premiums to NAV. The rule of thumb is, all other things being equal, avoid selling at a premium to NAV and aim to buy when the fund's price is at a discount to NAV. Funds tend to trade at a premium when the portfolio contains issues of foreign companies located in countries that have a promising outlook for growth. (See Chapter 19 for more on single-country closed-end funds.)

It's important to keep in mind that the discount or premium is primarily a function of investor sentiment, rather than changes in the fund's underlying portfolio value.

HOW TO MAKE MONEY IN CLOSED-END FUNDS

There are three basic kinds of return for investors in closed-end funds:

- *Dividend income.* Funds receive interest and dividend income from the securities in their portfolios. This income, minus fund operating costs, is distributed to shareholders as dividends.
- *Capital gains distributions.* Most funds buy and sell portfolio securities throughout the year. If a net gain is realized from these sales, most funds pay all or most of this money to shareholders as a capital gains distribution.

Government Closed-End Bond Funds

- ACM Government Income Fund   NYSE:ACG   Price: $10   Yield: 9%
  Portfolio consists primarily of U.S. government and agency debt and some foreign government debt. Managed by Alliance Capital of New York.
- Putnam Intermediate Government Income Trust   NYSE:PGT   Price: $7   Yield: 8%
  Has most assets in U.S. government securities, cash, and some foreign government debt.

(Prices as of October 1996)

■ *Capital gains.* If you sell shares in the fund for more than you paid for them, you then make your own capital gain through the sale.

SHAREHOLDER SERVICES

Services vary from fund to fund. Some of them offer:

■ Automatic reinvestment of dividends and/or capital gains distribution. By reinvesting, you automatically buy more shares, which adds to your original investment and allows even larger holdings to earn still more.
■ Cash investment plans let you invest a specified dollar amount in the fund at various intervals.
■ Cash withdrawal plans let you receive a specific amount from the fund at certain intervals. Payments come from selling shares only if dividend income and capital gains distributions become insufficient.

FOLLOWING CLOSED-END FUND PRICES

By checking the daily prices of closed-end funds in the stock listings of most daily newspapers, you can get still more information, including the fund's high and low prices for the past 52 weeks; dividend payments made in the past year; the volume of sales for the previous day; and the change that price represents from one day earlier. (*Note:* Even publicly traded funds that invest in bonds are included in some stock tables.) Barron's lists net asset values, discounts, and premiums in each weekly issue.

Value Line Investment Survey reports on about 40 closed-end funds among the many companies it follows. For extra protection, you may wish to confine your purchases to those given high rankings for safety and timeliness by its analysts. *Value Line* is available at most libraries and brokerage firms.

WHEN TO SELL YOUR SHARES

As with all your investments, you should determine a selling point when you make your initial purchase. But before you achieve that profit, two conditions may appear, indicating that you should sell your shares:

■ If the market is at a high. Traditionally, closed-end fund premiums and discounts reach their best levels when the market tops, not when it bottoms.

Checking Closed-End Fund Prices

Each week the financial newspapers list closed-end fund prices and net asset values per share. The listings vary depending upon the paper but are typically divided into various categories, such as:

■ General Equity Funds
■ World Equity Funds
■ U.S. Government Bond Funds
■ National Muni Bond Funds
■ Single State Muni Bond Funds

For each you will find: the fund name; the symbol for the exchange on which it trades, such as NYSE; the NAV or net asset value (given in dollars and cents); the stock price and the percentage difference; a plus or minus figure that indicates how much above or below the fund's net asset value per share the shares are trading.

For example:

Kemper High Income	NYSE	$9.06	$8 ¾	−3.42%

■ If new, similar funds are brought to market. For example, in November 1989, the Berlin Wall fell and the existing Germany Fund, which had been around a long time, catapulted to an 80% premium in two months. Then, during the first quarter of 1990, three new Germany funds were launched and by the end of April, all four funds were selling at discounts and their underlying NAVs had also declined.

FOR FURTHER INFORMATION

Investor's Guide to Closed-End Funds
Thomas J. Herzfeld Advisors

Box 161465
Miami, FL 33116
305–271–1900
Monthly; $365/year or $75 for two-month trial.

Wiesenberger's Investment Companies Yearbook
CDA/Wiesenberger
1355 Piccard Drive
Rockville, MD 20850
800–232–2285
An annual directory of open-end and closed-end funds, and variable annuities; $295 + $19.95 shipping.

The Investor's Almanac for 1997

*L*ove to rummage through flea markets and antique shops? Or take your chance at an auction? Perhaps you're looking for exciting, less traditional ways to spend your bonus, inheritance, or windfall.

There are endless numbers of offbeat investment choices if you're willing to be experimental. In this special section we highlight three of the most timely of such choices. These do not come with a guarantee that you'll make a huge killing, but they do come with a guarantee that you'll have fun learning about a new field.

Before you invest in any one of the three Investor's Almanac picks, do a little background research. A reading list is provided for each choice. And, if you know experts in the area, call and ask for advice.

When considering a collectible:

- Buy only what you like. If later on the value should fall or if you should decide to sell only part of your collection and keep the rest, you will still be left with something you cherish.
- Focus on something. Random collecting tends to be considerably less valuable over the years. Decide on an art form or category and then specialize in an artist, period, craftsman, or country. Unrelated individual pieces have less marketability than a cohesive collection.
- Set aside a limited dollar amount. You can revise this amount annually. Don't take all the money in your CDs or Microsoft stock and move it into exotic investments. If you should suddenly need cash and everything's tied up in prints by old masters or baseball cards, you'll be forced to sell, perhaps at a low price.
- Buy in your price range. Begin small if the amount of extra money you have is limited. As circumstances and your financial situation improve, you can always go after more elaborate and expensive items. So don't take out a second mortgage to get started in the world of collectibles.

HOW TO PROTECT YOURSELF AT AN AUCTION

Many collectibles, including the three described on the following pages, are found in antique shops and galleries and through dealers, as well as at shows and flea markets. When you buy from these sources, you have enough time to study each object. But when making a bid at an auction, the gavel swings fast and decisions must be made almost instantly. In this pressurized atmosphere, keep these points in mind to protect yourself from "auction fever" and buy the right piece at the right price.

■ DO YOUR HOMEWORK. Study up on the item. Know the price range.

■ READ THE CATALOG. Purchase the catalog well in advance of the auction. It will give dollar estimates as well as a description of the items for sale. During the auction, write down what each item sold for and use these figures as price guidelines in the future.

■ ATTEND THE PREVIEW. Study the lots on display and make notes in the catalog regarding their size, age, condition, etc. Take a pen, notebook, small flashlight, magnifying glass,

Leading U.S. Auction Houses

Christie's
  502 Park Avenue
  New York, NY 10022
  212–546–1000
Sotheby's
  1334 York Avenue
  New York, NY 10021
  212–606–7000
Phillips
  406 East 79th Street
  New York, NY 10021
  212–570–4830

C.G. Sloan & Co.
  4920 Wyaconda
  North Bethesda, MD 20852
  301–468–4911
Skinner, Inc.
  63 Park Plaza
  Boston, MA 02116
  617–350–5400
DuMouchelle's
  409 Jefferson Avenue
  Detroit, MI 48226
  313–963–6255

and a tape measure with you. At the preview, open drawers, look for cracks, plug in lamps, search for identifying marks, signatures, initials; and turn everything over and/or upside down.

■ MAKE A LIST OF THE ITEMS YOU REALLY WANT. This will help you avoid auction fever and going home with a trunkload of stuff you didn't want.

Then, at the auction:

- After registering, you will be given a number and something to bid with, most likely a paddle.
- Next, find out what the incremental dollar amounts are. Some auctioneers move up by $10, others by $100. Ask or check in the catalog.
- If you don't want your bidding noticed, sit either near the front, a little to the side so you can see the others bidding, or in the back rows.
- Listen to the bidding terminology. "Silver looking" is not the same as "sterling silver."
- Wait to place a bid until after you've become at ease with the auctioneer's patter. Know if you are bidding by the piece or by the lot.
- Get a feel for the timing of the auction. The most important items are generally brought out toward the middle of the sale, when the crowd has been "warmed up." After the major items are sold, the audience may thin out, leaving less competition for the remaining items. This is an excellent time to bid if you're interested in the remaining items.
- Never be the first to bid on an item you want. Auctioneers often set an arbitrary opening price, which may turn out to be artificially high. If so, it will drop if there are no bidders. Watch who else is bidding. You certainly want to avoid bidding against yourself. Bid as you sense the prices rising, or when they are near the top.

Deciphering Auction Catalogs

Auction catalogs are excellent resources and should be read carefully. Often they are available well in advance, giving you time to comparison shop and study various subject areas. Catalogs spell out:

1. *Terms of the sale,* including deposit requirements, methods of payment, how to place absentee bids, buyer's fees or premiums, and when and how purchased items should be picked up and paid for.

2. *Policy on reserves.* Although all items are sold to the highest bidder, in practice it may be somewhat different. Certain lots have a "reserve" or minimum price. If a lot does not actually bring this price, it can be withdrawn. Some auction houses use an "R" to designate that a lot has a reserve price.

3. *Descriptive statements.* These are usually given to help the bidder if the piece is by a well-known artist, craftsman, or designer. Beware of such phrases as "attributed to" and "in the school of," which indicate that the experts are not 100% sure that the work is indeed by a certain person.

4. *Descriptive information.* Catalogs often tell the style, patterns, colors, ounces, measurements. The term "style" may signal a reproduction. For example, a Queen Anne table means the table is from the chronological period of Queen Anne; on the other hand, a Queen Anne–style chair means it is a reproduction of that style and may have been made yesterday.

5. *Guarantees or warrantees.* Catalogs are not perfect. Neither are the experts and appraisers. If you buy an item described as silver and it turns out to be silver plate, or mahogany that is really walnut, you may have a claim against the auction house.

6. *Presale estimates.* Estimates represent the auctioneer's opinion based on the current market. If an item seems way above your price limit, don't despair. The estimate may be too high, or interested people may not show up at the auction—any number of circumstances can reduce the sale price.

Getting an Appraisal

To get an official evaluation or appraisal of your collectible or artwork, you need to hire an appraiser. An appraisal, which is a statement of an accurate and realistic value of a possession made by a knowledgeable person, can be used for establishing an item's worth, either for insurance coverage or to arrive at a price when selling. Appraisals are also required by the IRS when something of value is donated to a charity and you wish to declare a tax deduction.

An official appraisal must be written, dated and signed. It should also indicate whether the appraisal is the fair market value (used for selling the item, dividing an estate, or donating it to charity), or replacement value (for insurance reimbursement). The object appraised should be described in as much detail as possible and the number of pieces being appraised should be made very clear. For example, if the value given is for a pair of vases, a set of 12 water goblets, etc., these numbers should be given.

Before hiring an appraiser, ask what he or she charges and for an estimate regarding how long it will take. Some appraisers charge a flat fee, others an hourly rate.

☑ **HINT: *Never hire an appraiser who asks to be paid a percentage of the dollar value of the items appraised.***

FOR FURTHER INFORMATION

Although there are no federal licensing or educational requirements for becoming an appraiser, you can find a reliable one through these sources:

The American Society of Appraisers
Box 17265
Washington, DC 20041
703–478–2228
Ask about their free/inexpensive brochures on a number of topics.

The Appraisers Association of America
386 Park Avenue South
New York, NY 10016
212–889–5404
Publishes "Elements of a Correctly Prepared Appraisal."

Jewelers of America
1185 Avenue of the America (30th floor)
New York, NY 10036
212–768–8777

GLOBES AND MAPS

Maps and globes of all types and sizes have been popular with collectors for centuries. They range widely in price, depending upon their age, rarity, and condition—and whether or not they are signed. It won't be difficult to find either a map or a globe (or both) within your price range with which to begin a collection.

About Globes

Interestingly, the very first globes were used not to map the earth but rather to record what man could see in the sky—the stars and planets. These early globes were largely based on the calculations made some 2,000 years ago by the Greek astronomer Claudius Ptolemaeus, whom we know today as Ptolemy.

Then in the late-fourteenth and early-fifteenth centuries, Europeans began making hand-painted, instructional yet decorative globes. The German mathematician Schoner is generally thought to be the first official globemaker because he actually had a shop on a main street in Nuremberg around 1515–1520. He printed segments or parts of maps first and then glued them onto a sphere. At the time, Schoner thought our Earth was the exact center of the universe.

One of the earliest printed celestial or star maps was made by the German artist Albrecht Dürer in about 1515. Most of these star maps were made from woodcuts or even copperplate engravings. They were then printed in black and white, and hand-colored later on, often by someone else. Some were bound into atlases, which in later years were taken apart and the maps sold individually.

Another major globemaker was Delamarche, a Frenchman of the eighteenth century. He created what are known as armillary spheres out of wood. Today these spheres range in price from $4,000 to nearly $8,000.

One of the most famous examples of the armillary sphere style globe can be seen at Rockefeller Center in New York City. It's carried on the back of the huge statue of Atlas.

A good place to begin is with American-made globes. The George F. Cram Co. of Indianapolis, for example, made some 2,500 seven-inch globes each year from 1934 to 1965. Back in the 1930s they cost around $4 each; today they are worth several hundred dollars, provided they're in good condition.

About Maps

Wall maps, as we know them today, date back about 500 years. The Germans were among the leading early makers, using large wood block prints, joined together to cover a geographical area. Many were highly decorated in order to capture the public's attention.

Antique maps, easily recognized by their elaborate ornamentation and detailed design, were largely the result of the age of exploration and patronage of mapmakers by the nobility. Among the first known printed maps were those showing the streets of London in 1559–60. All ancient maps are extremely expensive.

However, far more within the average collector's budget are maps produced since the middle of the nineteenth century, in great demand largely because of the settlement of new territories.

Then, with the discovery of the New World, mapmakers had plenty of new material with which to work. In fact, among Americans, Benjamin Franklin was one of the first map enthusiasts—he had Henry Popple's "Map of the British Empire In America's" hung in Independence Hall. (You can see it there today.) Franklin loved this one in particular because it was the first English map to include and name the thirteen original colonies.

Another mapmaker of the New World was John Mitchell, whose maps often covered much of the territory that today we call the Midwest. One of his most famous maps, actually used to carve out state/territorial boundaries, also acknowledged the thirteen colonies. It is estimated today to be worth over $50,000.

Military maps, even dating as far back as the American Revolution, are not uncommon. Look, too, for maps of subsequent wars, including the Civil War and World Wars I and II. Battle maps were often reproduced in newspapers and magazines.

As the country was settled, the need for maps grew. And both community pride and increased prosperity in the later 1800s led to three distinctly different types of maps.

First, was the so-called "bird's eye" view of a town—one that shows the houses, stores, pathways, school, churches, all as if you were drawing it from the top of a hill or steeple. Indeed, historians speculate that some mapmakers may have done this from balloons. Second, there were more ordinary or traditional town maps, and third, county atlases that documented ownership of land and territorial boundaries.

At that time, each town was "sold" maps in advance of publication, with private mapmaking companies charging anywhere from $1 to $10 for a map. For a bit more, a businessman, landowner, or farmer could have the mapmaker add illustrations of his land or buildings to the map's border. As a result, these maps often have drawings of "mansions," farmhouses, prize pigs, etc.

The advent of the automobile lead to the first road maps, dating back to around 1901. These were first issued by automobile companies as a means of free advertising. Then oil firms started giving them away in their filling stations—free until the late 1970s when they began to charge for them. Those most likely to be worth collecting have interesting cover designs or a special historical interest or viewpoint.

NAMES TO LOOK FOR

Among the early names to look for when collecting:

Globes	Maps
Johann Schoner	Martin Waldseemuller
Willem Blaeu	Henry Popple
Vincenzo Coronelli	John Mitchell
Charles Delamarche	Jay Gould
Malby & Co.	Willem Blaue
Delamarche	Nicolas Sanson
George Mercator	John Speed

PRICES

Prices range from several hundreds of dollars for nineteenth- and twentieth-century globes to several thousands of dollars. The highest price in recent times was almost $1.8 million dollars for a pair of Gerard Mercator globes that were made for the Sultan Murad II, who was so taken with astronomy that he built an observatory in Istanbul in the late-sixteenth century.

However, there are plenty of globes in good condition in the $2,000 to $5,000 range, especially at special auctions and shows. Recently, a Rand McNally World Globe on a walnut stand, measuring about 39" by 22", made in 1925, brought $600.

On the other hand, map prices are considerably less. You can buy local ones for less than $100, but don't expect them to escalate quickly in price. More rare types can be $10,000, with truly superb examples in the $50,000 neighborhood. A folded map of Yellowstone National Park, entitled "The Wonders of Yellowstone," in color and dated 1874, went for under $75. A Standard Oil map of the state of Wisconsin in 1936 is worth about $20 today.

FOR FURTHER INFORMATION

The Hispanic Society of America
New York City
212–926–2234

The New York Public Library
Fifth Ave at 42nd Street
New York, NY 10018

National Maritime Museum
Greenwich, England
011–44–181–858–4422

American Geographical Society Collection
University of Wisconsin
Milwaukee, WI 53201

The Hermon Dunlap Smith Center for
the History of Cartography
The Newberry Library
Chicago, IL 60610

Library of Congress
Geography & Map Division
Alexandria, VA 22304

Collectors Organizations
California Map Society
c/o Bancroft Library
University of California
Berkeley, CA 94720

The Chicago Map Society
60 West Walton Street
Chicago, IL 60610

Dealers
Richard B. Arkway
New York City
212–751–8135

W. Graham Arader
Philadelphia, PA
215–735–8811

High Ridge Books
Rye, NY
914–967–3332

George Glazerr
212–535–5706

WHAT TO BUY IN 1997 AT FLEA MARKETS, GARAGE SALES, AND SWAPS

The key to success in these arenas is to focus on a particular type of collectible, learn all about it and purchase as many examples as you can find, in good condition and at the right price. To determine what may go up in price in the future, fast-forward your mind—think about what's fairly common, but interesting, unique, and/or attractive in today's world that might be rare 25 or 50 years from now.

Here are some suggestions; add your own to the list.

- Stadium seats from major parks that have gone or are going out of business or that are remodeling.
- Memorabilia from the Gulf War: posters, uniforms, flags, stamps, newspaper coverage banners, etc.
- Olympics stuff: the Atlanta Summer Olympics and others. T-shirts and caps in mint condition, buttons, banners, programs and anything autographed by a winner.
- Political items from the forthcoming presidential election: Focus on anything that's autographed or unique. One of the thousands of buttons being given out is unlikely to bring much a decade from now, but a unique button, banner, or cap of which only a handful were manufactured are good bets.
- Lucille Ball items: as well as those of other popular figures whose movies or TV shows are continual reruns. Recently, a 1952 "I Love Lucy" baby doll, in its original box, went for just over $800.
- Original artwork for MAD magazine, which was published between 1966 and 1992.
- Golf cards: According to "Kovel's Sports Collectibles," 50 of the oldest golf cigarette cards were sold at auction for over $5,000, while a collection of 80 modern cards (including a Tom Morris and a Bobby Jones series from the 1990s), went for almost $140.

- Hawaiian Shirts. We've known about these since Hawaii became the fiftieth state in the 1920s. Now they're becoming collectors' items, especially those from what's called the "golden era" between 1935 and 1950. Look for shirts with a historical tie (king or queen), a military division, etc.

  For info: "The Hawaiian Shirt," Abbeville Press, 800–278–2665.
- Anniversary items: plates, spoons, and other items manufactured to celebrate the anniversary of a country, city, county, state.
- Teenage Mutant Ninja Turtles
- Hello Kitty stuff
- Dungeons and Dragons video
- Pac Man and other video games
- Decorative glass jars since everything's going to plastic
- Caps, jackets with logos, and other unworn items from Warner Bros., Disney, Hard Rock Cafe, Planet Hollywood, and from hit plays, such as *Angels in America*, *Rent*, *Chorus Line*, *Les Miserables*, *Phantom of the Opera*.
- Always worth considering at the right price: Star Trek, the Beatles, Elvis, Barbie, Mickey, Minnie, Superman, Power Rangers, and, of course, Batman and Robin.

FOR MORE INFORMATION

Kovel's Antiques & Collectibles Price List; New York: Crown Publishers; an annual.

Hake's Americana & Collectibles. Numerous catalogs, price lists, and books available.
Post Office Box 1444
York, PA 17405
717–843–1333

IRISH ART

People tend to think of Ireland as the land of great novelists, playwrights, and poets, and so it is. But it has also produced a number of wonderful painters. These painters have gone largely unnoticed until just recently, perhaps because, as one expert noted, Irish art has been regarded as a subdivision of English art, not as a school of art on its own.

But a handful of the best Irish artists are beginning to gain recognition. The best of the older ones, including William Butler Yeats' overlooked brother, Jack Butler Yeats, sell for over $500,000 a canvas. Don't be discouraged. There are a number of less well-known painters and a good many prints well within the means of the average art lover.

You'll find that many painters focus on farms, families, wooded landscapes, gardens, portraits, and, of course, horses.

Leading Painters

George Nairn	1799–1850
Jack Butler Yeats	1871–1957
Walker Osborne	1859–1903
William Opren	1878–1931
John Lavery	1856–1941
Roderic O'Conor	1860–1940
Frank O'Meara	1853–88
Paul Henry	1876–1958
William Leech	1881–1968
Gerard Dillon	1916–71

FOR MORE INFORMATION

Museums

National Gallery of Ireland
Dublin, Ireland

Hugh Lane Municipal Gallery of Modern Art
Dublin, Ireland

Yale Center for British Art
New Haven, CT

Hirshhorn Museum
Washington, DC

Walters Art Gallery
Baltimore, MD

And read:
Irish Painting by Brian P. Kennedy, Town House, 1993; 800–352–1985; $39.95.
Irish Arts, a quarterly.

Auction Houses

In London: both Christie's and Sotheby's auction Irish paintings in the spring.
In Dublin: the leading auction houses are James Adam & Sons, and de Veres Art Auctions.

When the Bears Are Out of the Cave

Most people initially feel more at ease with bonds than stocks, perhaps because they know bonds provide fixed income, during any kind of market, any kind of economy.

Yet bond prices can be almost as volatile as stocks. So even if you have always looked upon bonds as your safe investment, take time to read Part Two and update your position. You'll learn about the safest bonds (those issued by the government) as well as the riskiest (junk or high-yield bonds).

In between there is information on how to evaluate bonds, use the rating services, read the quotes in the newspaper, and get call protection.

Part Two covers these broad categories:

- Corporate bonds
- Bond mutual funds
- U.S. Treasury issues
- Savings bonds
- Convertibles
- Municipal bonds
- Junk bonds
- Ginnie Maes and Ginnie Mae funds
- Zero coupon bonds
- CMOs

8

Bond Basics: How to Make Money with Corporate Bonds

*I*f you want to protect your principal and also set up a steady stream of income, bonds, rather than stocks, are the answer. Most investors buy bonds for their income because they generally generate greater returns than CDs, money market funds, and stock dividends. They have another key advantage: As long as you hold your bonds until maturity, you know exactly how much money you will get back typically $1,000 per bond and precisely when you will get it.

Bonds also offer greater security than most common stocks since the issuer must pay interest on its bonds before it pays dividends on its common or preferred stock. On the other hand, a corporation can and often does cut back or eliminate the dividend on its common stock.

Bonds are issued by corporations, by the U.S. government and its agencies, and by states, municipalities, and their agencies. The latter group, also called "munis," are discussed in Chapter 11; high-yield or junk bonds appear in Chapter 12; and Treasuries, or government issues, in Chapter 9. This chapter is devoted to corporate bonds and corporate bond funds.

HOW BONDS WORK

Bonds, unlike stocks, are debt. They can best be described as IOUs, or as contracts to pay back money. In other words, when you buy a bond, you become a lender, loaning money to the issuer. In return the issuer owes you the dollar amount shown on the face of the bond plus interest. (You may actually get a bond certificate to put in your safe deposit box, although increasingly bond ownership is recorded in the form of book entry. This means the issuer maintains a record of bond buyers' names but does not send them certificates.)

The interest rate, officially called the *coupon rate,* is fixed—that means the issuer pays no more and no less for the entire life of the bond. Bondholders receive their interest payments on a regular schedule, generally every 6 months. The amount you get back when the bond matures is called the *face value or par*—typically $1,000, although sometimes $5,000.

Bonds mature anywhere up to 40 years, although those that mature in 1 to 10 years are known as *notes*. Those that mature in 5 to 10 years are called intermediate-term bonds; those issued for over 10 years are called long-term bonds.

Many investors mistakenly think of bonds as being stable in price, almost stodgy. This is simply not true. When bonds are first issued by a corporation or the government, they are sold at face value or par, but immediately afterward they move up and down in price, trading in what is called the secondary market. If they are selling at above par—above $1,000—they are said to be at a *premium;* if they are trading below par, at a *discount.*

The reason they move in price is in response to changes in interest rates, as explained in greater detail below. The formula is easy to remember:

- When interest rates move down, bond prices move up.
- When interest rates move up, bond prices move down.
- The further away the bond's maturity date, the more volatile its price.

This price fluctuation actually offers you another way to make money with bonds in addition to earning a fixed rate of interest, and that is by selling your bonds at a higher price than you paid.

NOTE: You'll find that in the financial pages of newspapers, the prices for bonds are quoted on the basis of $100, so always add a zero to the price—a bond quoted at $108 is really selling at $1,080.

FIVE REASONS WHY YOU SHOULD OWN BONDS

- DIVERSIFICATION. When stock prices are depressed, bond prices tend to be high and therefore are a viable alternative to stocks.
- CURRENT INCOME. Annual interest payments must be made to bondholders at the stated rate unless the company files for bankruptcy or undergoes a restructuring of its debt. Therefore your steady stream of income is guaranteed in all but the worst situations. And, if the company restructures its debt, it will issue new securities in exchange for existing bonds.
- CAPITAL GAINS. If you buy a bond at a discount (below $1,000 or par) and sell it for more than you paid, you'll have a profit.
- SENIORITY. Interest on corporate bonds must be paid before dividends on common and preferred stocks of the same company, again protecting your income.

- SAFETY RATINGS. These are available on corporate bonds that help determine how safe they are as an investment. Both Moody's and Standard & Poor's, independent rating services, rate the financial solidness of corporation's and their bonds on a continuing basis.

UNDERSTANDING BOND YIELDS

In order to be successful with bonds, it's necessary to understand how bond yields and price fluctuations work. Like stocks, bonds move up and down in price, their market value changing any number of times a day in reaction to interest rate movements. This is because bonds have a fixed rate of interest, and the only way the market can accommodate the changes in overall interest rates is by changing the price of bonds.

For example: If you buy a bond at par ($1,000) and it has a coupon rate (the annual rate paid to bondholders) of 10%, you will receive $100 each year in interest payments. Now let's say that interest rates move up and the corporation that issued your bond needs to raise more money. The new bonds it issues must pay a higher interest rate in order to attract investors, otherwise no one will buy them. The new rate may be 10.5%. Now, the corporation's older bonds—the ones you own —will fall in price, perhaps to $960, in order to compensate for the fact that their yield of 10% is less appealing than the new 10.5% rate. The older bonds are now selling at a discount.

What if interest rates fall?

Exactly the opposite occurs: the corporation will be able to issue new bonds paying a lower rate of interest and the older bonds, the ones you own, will rise in price, immediately becoming more desirable, due to their higher coupon rate. They now will sell at a premium.

Here's an example of how bond prices move with interest rate changes, supplied by the Vanguard Group. If you own a 30-year bond that yields 8%:

If the yield…	The price will…
rises to 9%	fall 10%
rises to 10%	fall 19%
falls to 7%	rise 12%
falls to 6%	rise 28%

When dealing with bonds, you'll come upon five different types of yields:

■ COUPON YIELD. This is the interest rate stated on the face of the bond: 6.75%, 7%, etc. It is determined by the issuing corporation and it depends on the prevailing cost of money at the time the bond is issued.

■ CURRENT YIELD ON THE PURCHASE PRICE. This is the annual interest payment based on the bond's current market price. It is higher than the coupon yield if you buy the bond below par and lower if you buy the bond above par. For example, an 8% coupon bond selling below par at $900 has a current yield of 8.9%. (Take the annual interest payment, which is $80, divide it by the current bond price [$900] and multiply by 100.)

■ YIELD TO MATURITY. This is the current yield and the gain or loss you will get if you hold the bond to maturity.

Because maturities vary and the current yield measures only today's return, the bond market relies on the yield to maturity (YTM). This is the total return, comprising both interest and gain in price. Put another way, it is the rate of return on a bond when held to maturity. It includes the appreciation to par from the current market price when bought at a discount or depreciation when bought at a premium.

To approximate the YTM for a discount bond:

1. Subtract the current bond price from its face value.

2. Divide the resulting figure by the number of years to maturity.

3. Add the total annual interest payments.

4. Add the current price to the face amount and divide by 2.

5. Divide the result of step 3 by the result of step 4.

   Example: A $1,000 7% coupon bond due in 10 years is selling at 72 ($720). The current yield is 9.7% ($70 ÷ $720). The YTM is about 11.4%.

$$1,000 - 720 = 280$$
$$280 ÷ 10 = 28$$
$$28 + 70 = 98$$
$$720 + 1,000 = 1,720 ÷ 2 = 860$$
$$98 ÷ 860 = 11.4\%$$

The YTM is the yardstick used by professionals, because it sets the market value of the debt security. But to amateurs, the spread—between the current and redemption prices—is what counts, because this appreciation will be added to your income. You get a competitive return while you wait—usually over 8 years, because with shorter lives, the current yield is modest. *For example,* AT&T 5⅛, 2001 at 8.8. That's a current yield of 5.8%, but each year there will be an additional $20 price appreciation per $1,000 bond if the bond is held to maturity in 2001.

■ DISCOUNT YIELD. This is the percentage from par or face value, adjusted to an annual basis, at which a discount bond sells. It is used for short-term obligations maturing in less than 1 year, primarily Treasury bills.

   It is roughly the opposite of YTM. If a 1-year T-bill sells at a 6% yield, its cost is 94 ($940). The discount yield is 6 divided by 94, or 6.38%.

■ YIELD TO CALL. This is the same as yield to maturity, except it is based on the assumption that the bond will be redeemed by the issuer at the call date.

☑ *HINT: Yield to maturity and yield to call are not listed in the newspaper. Your broker can give it to you or you can find it in Standard & Poor's Bond Guide, available at many libraries.*

THE BOND PROSPECTUS

In addition to using the S&P and Moody ratings and your stockbroker's research, you can evaluate bonds on your own by looking at the bond's prospectus. This document details the issue's financial features, the means of payment, what the money raised will be used for, and what analysts think about the issuer's creditworthiness.

The two key points to look for are:

■ *The amount of debt the company has already issued.* Heavy debt means that much of the money raised by this issue could go toward interest payments on the company's debt.

■ *The bondholder's claim on the company's cash flow.* Is it a first claim or subordinated? You want one with first claim. Often the employee pension plan has a higher claim on earnings than bondholders, should there be a default. Note, too, whether the pension plan is funded or unfunded; if a large part is unfunded, discuss the appropriateness of the investment with your broker.

YOUR BOND-BUYING CHECKLIST

There are a number of factors to keep in mind when selecting corporate bonds for your portfolio. A bond's value depends first and foremost on the credit quality of the issuing corporation. Bonds of a solid successful corporation are certainly a better investment than bonds of a weaker firm. Use this checklist to select the right bonds for your portfolio:

■ *The bond's quality rating.* Bond issuers are rated by independent research services, such as Moody's and Standard & Poor's. They analyze the financial strength of the corporation, project future prospects, and determine how well the corporation is prepared to cover both interest and principal payments. These two top services tend to reach the same conclusions about each bond.

Watch, too, for changes in bond ratings. When a bond is upgraded, its market price will probably rise and the yield dip a bit. Downgrading of a bond signals possible trouble and so the value of the bond may decline.

How Bonds Are Rated: 1997

GENERAL DESCRIPTION	MOODY'S	STANDARD & POOR'S
Best quality	Aaa	AAA
High quality	Aa	AA
Upper medium	A	A
Medium	Baa	BBB
Speculative	Ba	BB
Low grade	B	B
Poor to default	Caa	CCC
Highly speculative	Ca	CC
Lowest grade	C	C
In default	–	D

Ratings may also have a + or – sign to show relative standings in class. Bonds at BBB level and above are considered investment grade.

(Downgraded bonds are called fallen angels on Wall Street.) However, if the rating is not too low, and you are not adverse to risk, you can sometimes make money purchasing a fallen angel you believe will be eventually upgraded, either as the economy improves or as the corporation makes changes that puts it on a more solid financial footing. *NOTE:* Slight rating shifts are not terribly important as long as the rating is A or better.

And remember, the lower the rating, the higher the yield a bond must pay in order to attract investors. That's why very high-yielding bonds are called junk bonds.

■ *The interest rate, or coupon rate.* This is the fixed dollar amount you will be receiving. You obviously want a competitive rate.

■ *The maturity date.* This is the date when you will be paid the face value of the bond. Pick maturity dates that meet your needs, say to pay college tuition or fund your retirement. Remember that by staggering your maturity dates, you will have a stream of income coming due that can be reinvested if interest rates go up. On the other hand, if rates fall, you will have locked in the higher yields.

■ *The current yield.* This is the coupon rate divided by the current market price of the bond.

■ *The yield to maturity.* This combines the current yield with the price you paid for the bond if that price was more or less than the face value.

■ *The yield to call.* This gives you the yield, assuming the bond will be called in or redeemed before maturity date. (Calls are explained on page 96.)

■ *The bond's backing or collateral.* Bonds are categorized as either secured bonds or debentures. *Secured bonds* are backed by the corporation's plant, equipment, or other assets. If the collateral is real estate, the bonds are called mort-

gage bonds; if the collateral is equipment, they are called equipment certificates. If the corporation defaults on its bond payments, these assets can be sold to pay off the bondholders.

Debenture bonds are riskier in that they are unsecured, backed only by the overall ability of the corporation to meet its bills and other obligations. If the company declares bankruptcy, debentures cannot be paid off until secured bondholders are paid.

■ *Poison put provisions.* These guarantee that bondholders in a company that is taken over can redeem their bonds at par. Poison puts accomplish two things: They protect investors and discourage unwanted takeovers. (This was more important during the 1980s when there were a rash of corporate takeovers.)

■ *Special terms.* Most bonds issued by the federal government and corporations carry a fixed coupon as well as a fixed date of maturity. But there are occasionally serial bonds in which a portion of the issue will be paid off periodically. Usually, the earlier the redemption date, the lower the interest rate, by $\frac{1}{4}$% to $\frac{1}{2}$% or so. These bonds are excellent if you have a specific date by which you need money.

Picking the Right Bond or Note

If you want to invest $10,000 in bonds for 10 years, you have these choices:

■ A 6-month T-bill that will be rolled over at each maturity.

■ A 2- to 3-year Treasury note that at maturity will be turned into a 7- to 8-year note at a somewhat more rewarding yield if interest rates go up.

■ A 10-year bond to be held to redemption. This would be best if you expect interest rates to decline or stay about the same.

■ A 15- to 20-year bond to be sold at the end of 10 years, best if you expect rates to fall, but the longer the maturity, the greater the risk if rates climb.

SHORT-TERM VS. LONG-TERM BONDS

When deciding what maturity of bond to buy, keep in mind that:

- The shorter the maturity rate, generally the lower the yield, but:
- The shorter the maturity, the less the bond is affected by interest rate changes and inflation.
- The longer the maturity, the higher the yield.
- The longer the maturity, the more likely the bond will be redeemed or called early; then you will be paid off, but will be forced to reinvest this money at lower rates.
- To get the highest yields, invest for the shortest time possible while rates are rising. When rates have peaked, sell and buy longer-term bonds to lock in those high yields.
- You can protect yourself against price declines to some extent by purchasing high-grade bonds at a discount—that is, below face value. This is especially true if their maturity is not far away.
- Rather than having all your bonds come due at the same time, own a spread of bonds to come due every year or so. That way you'll periodically receive cash, which you can reinvest to keep the cycle going. Spreading out maturities also tends to average out the effects of price changes.
- If you have less than $50,000 to invest, diversify through a bond mutual fund or unit investment trust, which will also help reduce your risk.

Changes in Bond Ratings

UP:	Borden
	BBB- to BB+
DOWN:	Air Products
	A+ to A

SOURCE: Standard & Poor's, June 1996.

THE NEWSPAPER LISTINGS

When reading a bond listing in the newspaper, keep in mind that:

- Bonds are issued at par ($1,000), but in the financial pages they're quoted on the basis of $100, so always add a zero to the price; for example, a bond quoted at $108 is really selling at $1,080.
- Current yield is the annual yield you will receive if you buy the bond at that day's price. If it's selling at a discount from par (the issue price), the price given in the "Last" column will be under 100. If the bond is selling at a premium or above par, the price will be above 100.
- Sales stands for the number of $1,000 bonds traded that day. (Bonds are usually priced at issue time at $1,000 each.)
- The small "s" that sometimes follows the interest rate means "space" and is used to separate the interest rate from the next group of numbers—the year in which the bond matures.
- The letters "cv" indicate that the issue is a convertible bond and can be exchanged for a fixed number of shares of common stock of the issuer.
- The letters "zr" before the maturity date indicate that the issue is a zero coupon bond.

Debt for Equity

A variation on the sinking fund is *defeasance*, which is used by corporations to discharge debts without actually paying them off prior to maturity. The company arranges for a broker to buy a portion of the outstanding bond issues for a fee. The broker then (1) exchanges the bonds for a new issue of corporate stock with a market value equal to that of the bonds and (2) sells the shares at a profit. The corporate balance sheet is improved without harming operations or prospects.

How to Read Corporate Bond Listings

The table below shows a listing in *Barron's* for an A-rated NY Telephone bond with a coupon of 7⅞% and a 2017 maturity date. The high price was 100, and the low 98⅛, with the last sale at 99½, up 1⅞ from the last sale of the previous week. Altogether 93 $1,000 bonds changed hands.

STANDARD & POOR'S STANDARD RATING*	ISSUE	CURRENT YIELD	SALES	HIGH	LOW	CLOSE	CHANGE**
A	NYT 7⅞, 2017	7.9%	93	100	98⅞	99½	+1⅞

Each bond pays $78.75 in annual interest, so the current yield is 7.9%. In the year 2017 each bond will be redeemed at 100 ($1,000) for a gain of ½ a point, or $5 per bond.

*The rating is not shown in the press.
**From previous week.

HOW TO GET CALL PROTECTION

To attract investors for long-term commitments, corporations usually include call protection when they issue new bonds.

When a bond is called, the issuer exercises a right (which will appear in the prospectus) to retire the bond, or call it in, before the date of maturity. This right to call gives the issuing corporation the ability to respond to changing interest rates. If, for example, a corporation issued bonds with an 11½% rate when rates were high and then rates dropped to 7%, it would be to the issuer's advantage to call in the old bonds and issue new ones at the lower prevailing rate. In fact, it is often so advantageous that a corporation is willing to pay a premium over par to call its bonds.

There are three types of call provisions you should know about:

- *Freely callable:* Issuer can retire the bond at any time, therefore it has no call protection.
- *Noncallable:* Bond cannot be called until date of maturity.
- *Deferred call:* Bond cannot be called until after a stated number of years, usually 5 to 10.

The *call price* is the price the issuer must pay to retire the bond. It's based on the par value plus a premium, which in theory often works out to be equal to 1 year's interest at the earliest call date. *For example*, an 8% bond would theoretically have an initial call of $1,080—the $80 being the premium. However, there are many variations. For example, the call price can be specified, or it can be based on a declining scale, with greater premiums given for calling in during the earlier years.

 CAUTION: *A call on a bond is nearly always bad news for the investor. That's because issuers seldom call a bond when interest rates are rising and when getting your money out would enable you to reinvest at the higher rates. On the contrary, bonds are generally called when rates are declining and you would prefer to lock in your higher yield by keeping the bond. So try to purchase bonds with call protection. Check the prospectus or ask your broker.*

Example: Safeway Stores, 10% debentures, due 2001, are noncallable to maturity. This means that an investor who buys these bonds in 1997 can look forward to almost 5 years of receiving a 10% coupon.

SINKING FUND PROVISIONS

Often a corporation borrows millions of dollars in any one bond issue, so quite obviously that amount of money must be available when the bond matures and the bondholders are paid back the full face value.

In order to retire a portion of that enormous debt, some issuers buy back part of it early — before the maturity date, leaving less to be paid off (to the bondholders) at one time in a lump sum. In this process, the issuer shrinks the corporation's debt. The money used to do this repurchasing is called a *sinking fund*.

When a corporation sets up a sinking fund, it must make periodic predetermined cash payments to a special custodial account set up for this purpose.

Advantages

■ By setting up this process and establishing a sinking fund, the corporation winds up paying less total interest. *For example*, with a 25-year issue set up to buy back 3.75% of the debt annually, 75% of the bonds will be retired before maturity. This means that the average life of the bonds will be about 17 years, not the 25 years anticipated by the investor.

■ A sinking fund also adds a margin of safety for investors: The periodic purchases provide price support and enhance the probability of repayment when the bond matures.

Disadvantages

■ It actually narrows the time span or length of the bond, so that there will be less total income for the long-term investor. The bottom line: Sinking funds benefit the corporation more than the bondholder.

BOND MUTUAL FUNDS

If you have a small amount to invest or simply don't wish to select your own bonds, you can buy bonds through a mutual fund or closed-end fund. (see Chapter 6 on mutual funds.)

Although funds are extremely popular with investors, it's important that you understand that your return in a fund is not as assured as with an individual bond—in other words, with a bond you know what your annual income will be and how much you will get back when your bond matures.

On the other hand, with a bond mutual fund, your return fluctuates, depending upon the holdings in the portfolio and, when you go to sell your shares, it is possible that your shares will be worth less than what you paid for them—on the other hand, they could be worth more. Make certain before you purchase shares in a bond mutual fund that you understand this concept—that a bond mutual fund's return is in continual flux.

Then,

- CHECK THE PERFORMANCE. Follow performance over at least 5 years, long enough to include both bad and good years for debt securities.
- LOOK FOR FREQUENT DISTRIBUTIONS. A mutual fund that pays monthly ensures a steady cash flow. If this is reinvested, compounding will be at a more rewarding rate.
- CONSIDER CLOSED-END BOND FUNDS. They do not issue new shares or units after their initial offering. Instead, they trade on one of the exchanges or over-the-counter. The capitalization of this type of fund is fixed at the outset, and investors must buy shares either at the initial offering or later in the secondary market or aftermarket. This means that the price of a closed-end fund is determined by two variables: (1) the public's demand for its shares and (2) the value of its portfolio. Therefore such funds sell either at a premium or at a discount from the portfolio's

Closed-End Bond Funds

FUND	YIELD	PRICE	SYMBOL
CNA Income Shares	9.6%	$10	CNN
Transam Income	8.1	23	TAI
American Gov't Income	12.7	5	AGF
John Hancock Inc. Sec.	8.0	15	JHS
Duff & Phelps Util. & Corp	9.2	13	DUC
New America High Yield	9.8	5	HYB

SOURCE: Barron's, Fall 1996.

net asset value. Like their open-end cousins, closed-end funds are professionally managed, contain a wide variety of bonds, and make monthly distributions. (See Chapter 7 for more on closed-end bond funds.)

FOR FURTHER INFORMATION

Books and Pamphlets

Marcia Stigum and Frank J. Fabozzi, *The Dow Jones-Irwin Guide to Bond and Money Market Investments* (Homewood, IL: Dow Jones-Irwin, 1994).

Newsletters and Newspapers

The Bond Buyer
One State Street Plaza
New York, NY 10004
212–803–8200
Published daily; $1,897/year; $15 per copy; 3-week trial, free.

Investor's Guide to Closed End Funds
Thomas J. Herzfeld Advisors
P.O. Box 161465
Miami, FL 33116
305–271–1900
Monthly; $75 for 2-month trial; $365/year.

Closed-End Bond Funds

PROS
↑ Closed-end funds do not have to sell off their portfolios when the market declines as open-end funds must do in order to meet redemption demand by investors.
↑ The managers tend to have greater flexibility in portfolio composition. A fund selling at a deep discount is sometimes a takeover candidate.

CONS
↓ Funds react very quickly to interest rate changes: When rates rise, bond prices fall and vice versa.
↓ Many funds buy lower-quality bonds to boost yields and to compete with older funds that sell at a discount.

9

U.S. Treasuries: Bills, Notes, Bonds and EE Savings Bonds

You've heard it over and over—there are no safer securities than U.S. Treasury obligations, which are backed by the full faith and credit of the U.S. government. And it's basically true—if you're looking for a risk-free investment, invest in the federal government. Uncle Sam is continually borrowing money, and thus far has an excellent reputation for paying back his debts.

ADVANTAGES

In addition to safety and affordability, Treasuries provide interest that is exempt from state and local income taxes—a plus for anyone, but especially those who live in high-tax states. And if interest rates fall, you can sell your Treasury for more than you paid.

Treasuries are also easy to unload because of the enormous size of the government bond market. In fact, the Treasury market is the world's largest securities field, with average trading volume in excess of $100 billion annually.

DISADVANTAGES

So, are there any disadvantages? Yes. If interest rates rise after your purchase, the value of that Treasury will fall because new issues will pay a higher annual interest; to make up for that, buyers will pay only a discounted price for the older issues. Of course, if you hold your Treasuries until maturity, this won't affect you as you're guaranteed to get the full face value.

U.S. Treasury bonds and notes are noncallable unless they have an alternate earlier maturity date. These dates are given in their newspaper lists, for example: 2000–2005. Or, ask your broker if specific Treasuries are callable.

Another disadvantage: the rates are lower than on corporate bonds with comparable maturities—but then, corporates are also a riskier investment.

BUYING NEW TREASURIES

Buying Treasuries is not difficult. You can, of course, buy them from a broker, but you'll pay a minimum commission ranging from $25 to $100, which lowers your yield. Because fees vary, call several full-service and discount brokers.

☑ *HINT: Even though you pay a fee or commission, if convenience is important to you, use a broker; and certainly do if you plan to sell Treasuries before maturity; the paperwork is much easier than if you buy from the Federal Reserve, as explained right below.*

You can sidestep the commission by buying them yourself at one of the 36 Federal Reserve Banks or branches, or by mail.

Just follow these 8 steps:

■ **Step 1.** Contact your Federal Reserve Bank for a tender form and information on how to purchase Treasury securities through the Treasury Direct System. You'll find the telephone number for the one in your area on pages 102–103. You can also pick up the tender forms in person or by writing to: U.S. Treasury, Division of Consumer Services, Washington, DC 20239–0001.

■ **Step 2.** Fill out the form for opening a Treasury Direct account and for entering a noncompetitive bid. Note that you must fill in your bank's routing number if you wish to have payments made directly to your bank account. This number is printed on your checks.

Although the Treasury prefers that you submit the official tender form, you may actually submit a tender by letter. If you do, be sure to type or print the following information and then sign the letter in dark ink: (a) the face amount of the securities you wish to purchase; (b) the maturity; (c) whether you are submitting a noncompetitive or competitive bid (specify yield when making a competitive bid); (d) your name and mailing address; (e) your Social Security number (if the securities are being purchased in two names, you must supply the Social Security number of the first-named purchaser); (f) your telephone number during business hours; (g) your Treasury Direct Account number, if you have one.

If you do not yet have a Treasury Direct Account, then include: (h) your Direct Deposit information—the name of the financial institution and its routing number, your account name, number, and type (checking or savings account). You will also need to include a W–9 certificate or a signed statement by the first-named owner certifying, under penalty of perjury, that you are not subjected to backup withholding tax. (Call 800–TAX–FORM to order the W–9, or pick up one at your bank.)

■ **Step 3.** Mail the tender and payment to your Federal Reserve Bank or its branch. Print or type in large letters on the front of the envelope: TENDER FOR TREASURY SECURITIES.

■ **Step 4.** If you bid in person, your noncompetitive tender must be in by noon the day of the auction. If you're bidding by mail, your tender must be postmarked by midnight the day before the auction and received by the Federal Reserve Bank or branch by the issue date to be accepted for that auction. A cashier's check is necessary for T-bills, but a personal check is acceptable for notes and bonds. Checks are made payable to the Federal Reserve Bank of *(city)*. All checks must have the name and Social Security number of the purchaser on the face of the check. Endorsed checks are not accepted. If you're paying in person you can use cash. You may also use Treasury securities maturing on or before the issue date of the new T-bills.

■ **Step 5.** Auction results are announced by the Treasury in the afternoon of the auction day. Many Federal Reserve Banks have 24-hour recorded messages giving the results as well.

■ **Step 6.** The government will set up a Treasury Direct Account, called a Master Record, when you submit your first tender form. You may review your account at any Federal Reserve Bank or branch, or request that a Statement of Account be mailed to you. It consists of your name, address, phone number, Treasury Direct Account number, tax information, and payment instructions. It also provides detailed information on all your Treasury securities maintained in the account. Whenever a change is made to the account information, such as when you receive interest payments or when money is received upon maturity of a security, you will receive a copy of the updated record. (T-notes and bonds pay interest twice a year. T-bill interest, which is slightly more complicated, is described below.)

- **Step 7.** Through the direct deposit payment method, interest, discount, and principal payments are electronically deposited into your account at the bank you designated on the tender form.
- **Step 8.** You can also specify that interest and principal payments be automatically deposited into your bank account, and that the Treasury roll proceeds over into future auctions. However, unlike a mutual fund investment, in which all interest, dividends, and capital gains can be reinvested in more fund shares, the Treasury rollover involves only your original investment.

☑ *HINT: Buying Treasuries directly at auction works best for those who plan to keep them until they mature. You can sell Treasuries on the secondary market, but only through a broker or bank, which again entails paying a commission.*

A Potpourri of Rates for Savers

INVESTMENT	YIELD/RATE
Bank money market account	2.64%
6-month CD	4.79
1-year CD	5.14
5-year CD	5.73
Taxable money market fund	4.81
Tax-free money market fund	3.04
3-month Treasury bill	5.01
6-month Treasury bill	5.25
1-year Treasury bill	5.64
2-year Treasury note	6.05
5-year Treasury note	6.42
10-year U.S. government note	6.66
30-year U.S. government bond	6.93

(As of October 1996)

NOTE: If you are already holding Treasuries in your bank or brokerage account and wish to transfer them to the Treasury Direct system, submit New Account Request Form PD 5182, available from a Federal Reserve Bank.

THE FEDERAL RESERVE BANKS AND BRANCHES

- ATLANTA. Securities Service Division, 104 Marietta St., NW, Atlanta, GA 30303; 404–521–8653
- BALTIMORE. Box 1378, 502 South Sharp St., Baltimore, MD 21203; 410–576–3300
- BIRMINGHAM. Box 830447, 1801 Fifth Ave. North, Birmingham, AL 35283; 205–731–8708
- BOSTON. Box 2076, 600 Atlantic Ave., Boston, MA 02106; 617–973–3800
- BUFFALO. Box 961, 160 Delaware Ave., Buffalo, NY 14240; 716–849–5000
- CHARLOTTE. Box 30248, 530 East Trade St., Charlotte, NC 28230; 704–358–2100
- CHICAGO. Box 834, 230 South LaSalle St., Chicago, IL 60690; 312–322–5369
- CINCINNATI. Box 999, 150 East Fourth St., Cincinnati, OH 45201; 513–721–4787
- CLEVELAND. Box 6387, 1455 East Sixth St., Cleveland, OH 44101; 216–579–2490
- DALLAS. Securities Dept., Box 655906, 2200 North Pearl St., Dallas, TX 75265; 214–922–6770
- DENVER. Box 5228, 1020 16th St., Denver, OCO 80217; 303–572–2473
- DETROIT. Box 1059, 160 West Fort St., Detroit, MI 48231; 313–964–6157
- EL PASO. Box 100, 301 East Main St., El Paso, TX 79901; 915–544–4730
- HOUSTON. Box 2578, 1701 San Jacinto St., Houston, TX 77252; 713–659–4433
- JACKSONVILLE. Box 2499, 800 West Water St., Jacksonville, FL 32231; 904–632–1190
- KANSAS CITY. 925 Grand Blvd., Kansas City, MO 64198; 816–881–2409

■ LITTLE ROCK. Box 1261, 325 West Capital Ave., Little Rock, AK 72203; 501–324–8272

■ LOS ANGELES. Box 2077, Terminal Annex, 950 South Grand Ave., Los Angeles, CA 90051; 213–624–7398

■ LOUISVILLE. Box 32710, 410 South Fifth St., Louisville, KY 40232; 502–568–9236

■ MEMPHIS. Box 407, 200 North Main, Memphis, TN 38101; 901–523–7171

■ MIAMI. Box 520847, 9100 N.W. 36th St., Miami, FL 33152; 305–471–6497

■ MINNEAPOLIS. Box 291, 250 Marquette Ave., Minneapolis, MN 55480; 612–340–2075

■ NASHVILLE. 301 Eighth Ave. North, Nashville, TN 37203; 615–251–7100

■ NEW ORLEANS. Box 61630, 525 St. Charles Ave., New Orleans, LA 70161; 504–593–3200

■ NEW YORK. Federal Reserve P.O. Station, 33 Liberty St., New York, NY 10045; 212-720–6619

■ OKLAHOMA CITY. Box 25129, 226 Dean A. McGee Ave., Oklahoma City, OK 73125; 405–270–8652

■ OMAHA. Box 3958, 2201 Farnam St., Omaha, NE 68103; 402–221–5636

■ PHILADELPHIA. Box 90, 100 North Sixth St., Philadelphia, PA 19105; 215–574–6680

■ PITTSBURGH. Box 867, 717 Grant St., Pittsburgh, PA 15230; 412–261–7802

■ PORTLAND. Box 3436, 915 S.W. Stark St., Portland, OR 97208; 503–221–5932

■ RICHMOND. Box 27622, 701 East Byrd St., Richmond, VA 23261; 804–697–8000

■ SALT LAKE CITY. Box 30780, 120 South State St., Salt Lake City, UT 84111; 801–322–7900

■ SAN ANTONIO. Box 1471, 126 East Nueva St., San Antonio, TX 78295; 210–978–1303

■ SAN FRANCISCO. Box 7702, 101 Market St., San Francisco, CA 94120; 415–974–2330

■ SEATTLE. Securities Services Dept. Box 3567, 1015 Second Ave., Seattle, WA 98124; 206–343–3605

■ ST. LOUIS. Box 14915, 411 Locust St., St. Louis, MO 63166; 314–444–8703

TREASURY BILLS

Treasury bills mature in 3 months, 6 months, or 1 year. T-bills, as they are often called, are issued in minimum denominations of $10,000, with $1,000 increments. New issues are sold at a discount from face value and are redeemed at full face value upon maturity. If, for example, you buy a T-bill through the Treasury Direct System, you write a check for $10,000. Shortly after the auction you are refunded by mail or electronic deposit into your account—the discount that is equal to the interest rate determined at the auction.

Let's say the discount or interest rate is 4%: You'll get a check for $400. When the T-bill matures, the Treasury will pay you $10,000, the full face value. Because they are guaranteed by the full faith and credit of the U.S. government, investors have no risk of default. In fact, if the federal government goes into bankruptcy, it won't matter what types of investments you have!

T-bills constitute the largest part of the government's financing. They are sold by the Treasury at regular auctions where competitive bidding by major institutions and bond dealers takes place. Auctions are held weekly for 3- and 6-month maturities, monthly for 1-year bills. (Occasionally the government issues a 9-month T-bill.) The yields at these auctions are watched very carefully as indications of interest rate trends. Floating-rate loans, mortgages, and numerous other investments tie their rates to T-bills.

■ FIGURING YIELDS. Because T-bills are sold at auction at a discount from face value, there is no stated interest rate. You can determine their yield by using the formula in the box on page 104.

■ TO DEFER INCOME WITH T-BILLS. Because Treasury bills are sold at a discount price—that is, at less than face value—and are redeemed at maturity at full face value, they do not pay an annual interest. Therefore, in the following example, you would not have to pay taxes until your T-bill matured in 1997. This is to your advantage if you expect your income to be lower in 1997.

Example: You buy a $10,000 1-year bill in February 1996, for $9,380. Your real yield is 6.6% ($10,000 − $9,380 ÷ $9,380). When you cash in the bill in February 1997, you will receive $620 on a cash investment of only $9,380.

☑ *HINT: Use T-bills as a short-term parking place for money received in a lump sum, say from the sale of a house or yacht, as a bonus, or from a royalty check. Think of them as interest-bearing cash.*

Determining the Yield on a 1-Year T-Bill

$$\frac{\text{Face value} - \text{price}}{\text{price}} = \text{"annual interest rate"}$$

$$\frac{10,000 - 9,100}{9,100} = \frac{900}{9,100} = 9.9\%$$

Thus a 1-year 9.9% bill will be purchased for $9,100 and redeemed 12 months later at full face value, or $10,000. This gain of $900 is interest and subject to federal income tax, but is exempt from state and local taxes.

TREASURY NOTES

These intermediate-term securities mature in 2 to 10 years. They are issued in $1,000 and $5,000 denominations. The $1,000 minimum is usually available only on notes of 4 to 10 years. Notes maturing in 2 to 3 years are issued in $5,000 denominations. The interest rate is fixed and determined by the coupon rate as specified on the note. It is calculated on the basis of a 365-day year. Interest earned is paid semiannually and is exempt from state and local taxes. Two-year notes are issued monthly; 3-year notes, quarterly; and 4- to 10-year notes, also quarterly.

T-notes are growing in popularity with investors, primarily because they are more affordable than T-bills (which have hefty $10,000 minimums), but also because their longer maturities usually give investors a higher yield. Another plus is the fact that they are not callable, so you are guaranteed a steady stream of income until maturity.

TREASURY BONDS

These long-term debt obligations are also issued in $1,000 minimums, with $5,000, $10,000, $50,000, $100,000, and $1 million denominations also available. They range in maturity from 10 to 30 years.

NOTE: As we go to press, only 30 year bonds are being sold.

A fixed rate of interest is paid semiannually. The interest earned is exempt from state and local taxes. Unlike T-notes, these bonds are sometimes subject to a special type of call. If a specific bond is callable, its maturity date and call date are both listed in hyphenated form in the newspaper. In the example described on page 105, the 12% bond due to mature in 2013 could be called in at any time starting in 2008.

☑ *HINT: Because government bonds come in so many maturities, stagger your portfolio to meet future needs and to take advantage of any rise in interest rates.*

BUYING ON THE SECONDARY OR AFTER MARKET

After a Treasury issue is first sold, it then trades in the secondary or aftermarket—not on the major exchanges, but over-the-counter. This type of trading is subject to the same market forces that affect corporate bonds (see Chapter 8) and stocks (see Chapter 13). And you will need a broker to handle your trades—all previously issued Treasuries must be purchased through securities dealers, commercial banks, or a stockbroker, not from the Federal Reserve Banks. Very often you will wind up buying directly from the broker's own portfolio of Treasuries, and you may not have to pay a direct commission or transaction fee. Instead, the extra cost of the securities covers the broker's costs and gives him a profit.

You may wish to buy in the secondary market if you want to have money come due on a certain date. In this case, check the Treasury listings in the newspaper to find a maturity date that meets your goals. You'll note that there's a bid and an asked figure. The bid price is what you're offered if you sell, while the asked is what it will cost you to buy. The figures in the paper, however, are for trades of $1 million. Since you'll most likely be buying less than a million, you'll wind up paying slightly more than the price listed in the newspaper and your yield will be slightly less. (See box.)

☑ HINT: *Be certain you check with several brokers, including a discount broker. Charles Schwab, for example, charges $39 per transaction up to $150,000. Fidelity does not charge those who are already Fidelity customers with active accounts.*

HOW TO READ THE QUOTES

All Treasury issues are quoted daily in dollars plus units of ½ of a dollar (0.03125), with the bid, asked change in price, and yield given in the newspaper. The quotations for each note or bond are per $1,000 face value.

The first line in the table at right shows notes due in 1998 with a coupon of 7⅛%, a bid price of 102–12 ($1,023.75), and an asked price of 102–18 ($1,025.63) with a yield of 6.48%. An investor who holds these notes for 4 years until maturity will get $71.25 per year less the premium of $25.63, for a yield to maturity of 6.48% when redeemed in October of 1998.

The 12% bond due to mature in 2008–2013 has what is known as a double maturity, sometimes referred to as a call date. Its yield is calcu-

How Government Notes and Bonds Are Quoted

ISSUE	BID	ASKED	CHANGE	YIELD
Oct. 98, 7⅛	102–12	102–18	–6	6.48%
Aug. 08–13, 12	141	141–04	–24	7.30
May 16, 7¼	97–27	97–29	–22	7.44
May 18, 9⅛	118–09	118–11	–30	7.47

SOURCE: Barron's, September 1996.

lated on the earlier maturity, 2008; however, at the Treasury's choice, the maturity may be extended to 2013. Notification appears in the newspaper, and in some cases by letter. All Treasury issues with this modified call feature can be identified in the paper by the hyphenated listing. A small n indicates that the issue is a note rather than a bond.

SELLING YOUR TREASURIES

If you hold Treasury issues in a Treasury Direct Account, you will have to transfer them out and into an account at a brokerage firm or bank. They then will sell the securities for a fee.

To transfer securities, fill out Form PD 5179, Security Transfer Request, available from your Federal Reserve Bank or branch. You will need to include the routing number of the financial institution you will be using.

USING THE YIELD CURVE

A yield curve is a diagram that illustrates the relation between bond yields and maturities on a particular day. Use it to decide which type of bond to buy at a certain period. It is published daily in the *Wall Street Journal*.

To draw a yield curve, professionals set out the maturities of like bonds—all Treasuries or all AA-rated corporates—on graph paper on a horizontal line, from left to right, starting with the shortest maturities (30 days) and continuing over days or years to the longest (30 years). Then they plot the yields on the vertical axis and connect the dots with a line that becomes the yield curve.

☑ *HINT: When short-term rates are more than a percentage point above long-term rates, the yield curve is inverted. A recession typically follows, usually within 6 months.*

NOTE: The curve is used to tell whether short-term rates are higher or lower than long-term rates. When short-term rates are lower, it is called a positive yield curve. When short-term rates are higher, it's a negative or inverted yield curve. If there is only a modest difference between the two, it's known as a flat yield curve.

Generally, when the yield curve is positive, investors who are willing to tie up their money long term are rewarded for their risk by getting a higher yield.

Although any fixed-income securities can be plotted on a yield curve, the most common one illustrates Treasuries, from a 3-month T-bill to a 30-year bond.

SAVINGS BONDS

Savings bonds are an ultra-safe and extremely easy way to put aside money. They are not just for timid investors or grandparents who are at a loss over what to give their grandchildren. Today these bonds offer several special tax breaks that make them a good deal for families within certain income brackets who will be facing college tuition.

And they're inexpensive to purchase—the minimum is only $25.

From 1941 until 1979 the government issued Series E bonds. Starting in 1980, Series EE and Series HH bonds were issued.

Their True Advantages

- *Easy to buy.* You can buy EE savings bonds at your bank, through the Bureau of Public Debt, or through automatic payroll deduction plans—certainly a painless way to save. And, there are no fees or commissions involved, so all your money immediately goes to work for you.

- *Low minimums.* EE bonds have denominations ranging from $50 to $10,000, but you pay only half the face value. In other words, a bond with a $50 face value costs only $25; a $10,000 bond, $5,000. The maximum annual investment in EE bonds is $30,000 face value per calendar year per person—that's $15,000 in cash.

- *Safety.* Savings bonds are backed by the full faith and credit of the U.S. government and are redeemed at full face value upon maturity. Even if you lose your bond, all is not really lost. You may get it replaced by writing to: Bureau of Public Debt, 200 Third St., Parkersburg, WV 26106–1328. Give as much information as you have: serial number; issuance date; name, address, and Social Security number of the original owner. You'll be asked to fill out Form PD-F1048.

- *Floating interest rates.* Starting May 1, 1995, bonds held less than 5 years earn 85% of the average earned on 6-month Treasuries. Those bonds held 5 to 17 years will earn 85% of the 5-year Treasury. Different rates apply to bonds purchased before May 1, 1995.

☑ *HINT: To get the current rates, call 800–US–BONDS.*

- *Easy to redeem.* EE Bonds may be redeemed at any time after 6 months from issue date at most banks or other financial institutions. HH Bonds are redeemable at any Federal Reserve Bank or branch, or at the Bureau of the Public Debt in Parkersburg, West Virginia, any time after 6 months from issue.

- *No probate.* If, upon the death of an owner, there is a surviving co-owner or beneficiary named on the bonds, the bonds do not form a part of a decedent's estate for probate purposes. Subject to applicable estate or inheritance taxes, if any, they become the sole property of the survivor.

■ *Special tax break with savings bonds.* The interest you earn on savings bonds is exempt from state and local taxes, and you have a choice when it comes to paying federal taxes. You can either pay the federal tax each year as the interest accrues, or wait and pay the tax when you cash in the bonds, give them to someone else, or when the bonds mature.

☑ *HINT: If you defer paying federal tax, that money, which would otherwise be going to the IRS, can be invested elsewhere.*

■ *More tax breaks.* There's yet another tax-related choice: You can exchange or roll over your EE bonds for HH bonds and continue delaying taxes on the amount you roll over until you cash in the HH bonds or they (the HH bonds) mature. However, the interest on HH bonds is paid out in semiannual installments and taxed in the year received. That rate since March 1, 1993, has been 4%.

HH bonds cannot be purchased. They are available only by exchanging at least $500 in Series E or EE bonds. Series HH bonds are issued in denominations from $500 to $10,000. Unlike EEs, they pay interest semiannually and are sold at full face value. You get your interest twice a year by Treasury check, and at redemption receive only your original purchase price.

■ *As a tax shelter.* When you swap Es for EEs or HHs, the interest—unlike that from savings accounts, money market funds, and other bonds—does not have to be reported to the IRS annually until you cash them in. By swapping, you can postpone the tax on the accumulated interest for a number of years. When cashed in, the amount of the accrued income is stamped on the face of the HH

bonds, and from then on, you must pay taxes on the semiannual payments. To make the transfer, fill out form PD 3523.

How Interest Is Calculated

EE bonds do not pay out current interest to bondholders. Instead, they sell for one-half their face value and are redeemed at full face value upon maturity. In other words, they are accrual-type bonds, which means that the interest is paid when the bond is cashed in—on or before maturity date, and not regularly over the life of the bond, as is the case with corporate bonds, Treasury notes, and bonds.

Rulings for Bonds Issued after May 1, 1995

There's good and bad news surrounding the new EE bond rulings. The good news is that interest is more competitive, based at 85% of 6-month Treasuries for bonds held 5 years or less, and at 85% of the return on 5-year Treasuries for savings bonds held longer than 5 years.

The really bad news is that the new rulings eliminate one of the most appealing features of EEs, a guaranteed minimum rate. Until now, bonds were guaranteed to pay at least 4%. As we go to press the rate is 5.25%, but if interest rates drop, so too will the rates on newly issued EEs.

Series HH bonds, which pay interest semiannually, still pay 4% if issued after March 1, 1993. HH bonds issued from November 1986 until March 1992 earn a flat 6%. Older HH bonds continue to receive their previous guaranteed rates, either 8.5% or 7.5%, to the end of the maturity period.

☑ *HINT: If you have old EE bonds or if you converted EE bonds to HH bonds before the rate declines, KEEP THEM. The EE bonds you hold for 5 years or more will continue to earn their original minimum until their original maturity of 12 years from when you purchased them. And if you have old HH bonds paying 6%, they will continue to pay 6% for 10 years from when you purchased them. After that, these bonds will earn the current rate until final maturity.*

Using EE Bonds to Pay for College: Tax Benefits

For generations Americans have used savings bonds as a way to pay for their children's college degrees, putting them in their child's name. Before doing so, you should be aware of the tax rulings:

1. The first $650 of investment income (also called unearned income) a child receives is tax-free. This dollar amount is adjusted to reflect inflation, so check for annual changes.

2. If the child is under age 14, the next $650 of unearned income is taxed at the child's rate, which is probably 15%. Investment or unearned income over $1,300 is taxed at the parent's rate, which is usually higher than the child's rate—most likely 28%, 31%, or 36%.

3. Once your child is 14, all his income—earned and unearned—is taxed at his rate, again usually 15%.

4. Because tax is deferred on EE bonds until they are redeemed, you can purchase them in a child's name and, assuming they are not cashed in before the child is 14, the interest will be taxed at the child's rate, which is presumably lower than the parent's.

5. If a parent is a co-owner of the bonds with the child, the parent is required to pay any tax due.

6. However, under certain circumstances it may make sense to report the interest income each year as it is earned; for instance, if the child has little or no other income, then, depending upon how many bonds the child owns and the amount of interest earned, there might be very little or no tax due at all.

7. Fairly complicated rules apply when it comes to using EE bonds to pay for college. True,

interest earned on EE bonds can be totally tax-free, that is, free from state, local, and federal income tax if the bonds are used to pay a child's college tuition. In order to qualify for this tax break, the bonds must be purchased in the parent's name, not the child's, and the parent must be at least 24 years old when the bonds are purchased. Bonds purchased before 1990 do not qualify.

CAUTION: There are also income requirements: Single parents who make less than $43,500 and married couples earning less than $65,250 can completely avoid federal taxes on the interest EE bonds earn if they sell the bonds to pay tuition. NOTE: The income requirements are not set in stone and change with inflation; you cannot predict what the figures will be in advance.

HINT: What if you've purchased EE bonds in your child's name? There's an out, but not a well-publicized one. If you purchased the bonds after 1990 and mistakenly put them in your child's name, you can file a reissue form PD F 4000 with the Bureau of Public Debt, Parkersburg, WV 36106–1328, and try to get them changed.

EE Bonds and Qualifying For Financial Aid

But remember, the interest earned will be tax-free only if it's used to pay for qualifying educational expenses, which means tuition and fees (not room and board) at a college, university, technical institute, or vocational school.

For example, if parents redeem bonds worth $20,000 and pay $20,000 in tuition and fees, then all interest earned will be tax-free; if only $10,000 is paid in education expenses, then just 50% of the interest will be tax-exempt.

CAUTION: Keep college savings bonds separated from others you may own. Record the serial numbers, face amounts, and issue and redemption dates. When you redeem them, record the total dol-

lar amount received (interest plus principal) and the name of the school to which you paid tuition.

☑ **HINT:** *Although grandparents cannot buy the bonds and meet the requirements for this tax break, they can, of course, give the money to the child's parents and let them buy the bonds.*

EE Savings Bonds

PROS

↑ Safe; principal and interest guaranteed

↑ No fees or commissions

↑ If lost, replaced free of charge

↑ Get a floating rate of interest tied to Treasury yields

↑ Federal taxes can be deferred

↑ No state or local taxes

↑ Market value does not drop when interest rates rise as with other bonds

CONS

↓ Cannot be used as collateral

↓ Limited purchase: $30,000 face value in 1 year per person

↓ Other vehicles often pay higher rates

↓ Cannot redeem during the first 6 months

↓ Bonds issued after May 1, 1995, do not have a guaranteed minimum rate

---

FOR FURTHER INFORMATION

Pamphlets

U.S. Savings Bonds Buyer's Guide
free from:
Department of the Treasury
U.S. Savings Bond Marketing Office
Washington, DC 20226
202–377–7715

Basic information on Treasury bills is free from your nearest Federal Reserve Bank or:
Federal Reserve Bank of New York
Issues Division, 1st floor
33 Liberty Street
New York, NY 10045
212–720–5000
For material on the Treasury Direct program, call or write your area Federal Reserve Bank or write:
Bureau of Public Debt
Division of Consumer Services
Washington, DC 20239–0001
202–874–4000 (recorded message)

Buying Treasury Securities is available for $4.50 from:
Federal Reserve Bank of Richmond
Public Affairs Department
P.O. Box 27622
Richmond, VA 23261
804–697–8000
For information and reports on the value of your savings bonds, contact:
Dan Pederson, President
Savings Bond Informer
800–927–1901
This is a national fee-based service located in Detroit.
Cost is $12 for one to 12 bonds

10

Convertibles: Income Plus Appreciation

*I*f you're interested in a stock but its price is too high, check to see if there's a convertible available. Convertibles, which are usually bonds but occasionally are stocks, can be exchanged for a set number of common shares, and their prices tend to track the stock on its way up.

WHAT ARE CONVERTIBLES?

A convertible is a bond that pays a fixed rate of interest with a unique feature—it can be exchanged for a specified number of the issuing company's common shares, if those shares move up to a certain price. In other words, you can have your cake and eat it too: You collect the high interest rate from the bond and, if the common shares rise sufficiently in price, make a profit by converting into the shares of the company's common. But if the common does not rise in price, you can simply keep collecting your bond's interest payments. (Unlike common stock dividends, which can be cut, postponed, or eliminated, a convertible's interest income is secure.)

NOTE: There are also some convertible preferred stocks, but they are not nearly as common as convertible bonds.

HOW MUCH DOES IT COST TO CONVERT?

This conversion feature does not come cheap. Conversion prices are set at 15% to 20% above the price of the common stock when the convertible is issued, and some premium continues to exist. In fact, convertibles tend to trade at prices that are 5% to 20% above that of the common stock into which they can be converted. The reason behind this premium over the conversion price is that convertibles tend to yield 3% to 5% more than common stock dividends, but less than what you would collect on the same company's straight bonds or preferred stock.

Before considering convertibles, you must know that:

1. If the issuing company's common stock rises above the conversion price, you can exchange your convertibles for the common shares and make a profit.
2. If the issuing company's common stock goes down in price, your convertible will usually hold its value better than the common stock, and you will still be collecting your regular income.

So, this hybrid investment combines the security and fixed income of bonds with the potential price appreciation of common stock. Convertibles pay higher income than common stocks and have greater price appreciation than regular bonds. Their convertibility factor links their price movement with that of the underlying stock, so even though a convertible bond has the low-risk char-

Tips for Investing in CVs

- Buy a CV only if you like the common stock.
- Avoid CVs of potential takeover companies; you may be forced to convert early.
- Buy only high-rated issues—BB or above as rated by Standard & Poor's or Ba by Moody's.
- Know the call provisions; if a CV is called too early, you may not recover your premium.
- Select a CV whose common stock is expected to rise considerably in price.

acteristics associated with straight bonds (safety of principal and regular interest payments), they usually fluctuate in price more than straight bonds.

The bottom line: You give up some safety in exchange for potential capital gains.

Sometimes the issuing company calls the convertible bonds, forcing a conversion—but never below their conversion value. Bonds are sometimes called when the corporation can replace the convertible debt with new common stock.

If the CV is called when the market value of the stock is greater than the conversion price of the bond, you should opt to convert.

HOW CONVERTIBLES WORK

Company ABC needs to raise capital for expansion but does not want to dilute the value of its common stock by issuing new shares at this time. It also rejects selling a straight bond because it would be forced to pay the going interest rate, which for this example is 12%. Instead, management offers a bond that can be converted into its own common stock.

Because of this desirable conversion feature, investors are willing to buy the CV bond at a lower rate of only 10%. Bonds are quoted as a percentage of par, or face value, which is $1,000, so this bond is listed as 100. This is the market price,

the price at which the CV can be bought and sold to investors.

When Company ABC issues the CV bonds, its common stock is selling at $32 per share. Management decides its offering will be attractive to the public if each $1,000 bond can be converted into 25 shares of common. This is the conversion ratio—the number of shares of common stock you receive by converting one bond. The conversion price of the ABC bond is $40 (divide 25 into $1,000). The current value of the total shares of ABC Corp. to which a bond can be converted is the conversion value. With ABC stock trading at $32 and a CV ratio of 25, the conversion value is $800.

On the day of issue, the difference between $40 (the conversion price) and $32 (the current market price) is $8. To determine the conversion premium, $8 is divided by $32 to yield 0.25, or a 25% CV premium. Another way to figure the conversion premium is to take the price of the bond ($1,000), subtract the CV value ($800), and divide the remainder ($200) by the CV value.

The investment value of ABC's CV is an estimated price, usually set by an investment advisory service, at which the bond would be selling if there were no conversion feature. For ABC it is 75.

The premium-over-investment value is the percentage difference between the estimated investment value and the market price of the bond. Here the investment value is 75 and the market price is 100, so the difference is 25, or 33% of 75. The premium-over-investment value is therefore 33.

HOW YOU CAN MAKE A PROFIT WITH CONVERTIBLES

If the Stock Goes Up . . .

In general, a CV's price will accompany the rise in price of the company's common stock, although it never rises as much. For example, let's say the underlying stock rises by 50%, from $32 to $48. To find the value of the CV bond, multiply the higher price by the conversion ratio: $48 × 25 = $1,200 (or 120, as bond prices are expressed). During the time in which this rise has taken place, the investor has received 10% interest on the bond and has participated in the appreciation of the common stock by seeing the value of the CV bond appreciate by 20%, from $100 to $120.

If the Stock Goes Down . . .

If the underlying stock falls in price, the CV may also fall in price, but less so. Let us assume that the price of ABC, instead of appreciating by 50% to $48, drops by 50% to $16 per share. Its conversion value is now only $400 ($16 5 the CV ratio of 25). What happens to the price of the CV? The senior position of the bond as well as the 10% interest rate payable to bondholders serve as a brake on its decline in price. Somewhere between $100 and $40 the safety features inherent in a CV bond become operative, usually at the investment value, which in this case is 75. At 75 the bond's yield will rise to 13.33%.

☑ *HINT: When you want to make an investment but you fear that the company's common stock is too volatile and therefore risky, check to see if there are any convertible bonds or preferreds outstanding.*

To Convert or Not to Convert

By and large, holders of CVs should stay with the security of the CV and not convert. Stock markets are uncertain, and prices of individual stocks have been known to fall 50% or even more. Therefore the holder of a CV, which is senior to the common stock, should surrender or convert only under certain circumstances such as these:

■ The company, in a restructuring, makes a tender offer for a large percentage of its outstanding common stock at a price well above the market price. The CV bondholder must convert to common stock in order to participate in this tender offer.

■ In another type of restructuring, the company pays stockholders a special dividend equal to most of the price of the common stock. Here again, the CV bondholder must convert in order to receive this special dividend. For example, in July 1988, USG Corp. paid for each common share outstanding $37 in cash, plus other securities, in a corporate restructuring.

■ Corporations in cyclical businesses pay oversized year-end dividends. General Motors, for instance, did this for many years. To receive a special dividend, CV bondholders must convert prior to the ex-dividend date.

Convertible Bonds to Consider

COMPANY/BOND	CV PRICE OF BOND	PRICE OF COMMON	PRICE OF BOND	S&P RATING
AES Corp. 6½, 2002	$26.20	$18	$92	B+
Beverly Ent 7⅞, 2003	$20.47	12	94	B
EMC Corp. 4¼, 2001	$19.84	22	112	B+
Gen Instru 5, 2000	$23.75	31	139	BBB–

SOURCE: Standard & Poor's *Bond Guide,* August 1996.

HEDGING WITH CVS

For experienced investors, CVs offer excellent vehicles for hedging—buying one security and simultaneously selling short its related security. The hedge is set up so that if the market goes up, one can make more money on the purchase than one can lose on the sale, or vice versa if the market goes down. Such trading is best in volatile markets (of which there have been plenty in recent years).

Here's an example cited by expert John Calamos, president of Calamos Asset Management in Naperville, Illinois:

The CV debenture carries a 10% coupon and is convertible into 40 shares of common stock. The CV trades at 90; the common at 20. Buy 10 CVs at 90 at a cost of $9,000; sell short 150 common at 20—$3,000. Since the short sale requires no investment, the cost is $9,000 (not counting commissions).

- If the price of the stock falls to 10, the CV's estimated price will be 72, so there will be a loss of $1,800 ($9,000 – $7,200). But 150 shares of stock can be acquired for $1,500, for a profit of $1,500. Add $500 interest (10% for 6 months), and the net profit is $200.
- If the price of the stock dips to 15, the CV will sell at 80 for a $1,000 loss, but this will be off-set by the $750 profit on the stock plus $500 interest, for a return of $250.
- If the price of the stock holds at 20, the CV will stay at 90. There will be no profit on either, but the $500 interest will represent an annualized rate of return of 11%.
- If the stock rises to 25, the CV will be worth 104, for a $1,400 profit, but there will be a $750 loss on the shorted stock. With the $500 interest, there'll still be a $1,150 profit.
- And if the stock soars to 40, the CV will trade at 160, for a whopping $7,000 gain, which will be offset by a $3,000 loss on the stock but enhanced by the $500 income, for a total of $4,500 on that $9,000 investment—all in 6 months!

Says Calamos: Selling short stock against undervalued CVs can eliminate risk while offering unlimited gains if the stock advances.

Best bet with hedges of CVs: Try out the if projections on paper until you are sure that you

Convertibles

PROS
- ↑ When the stock market falls, CVs do not fall as much as the underlying stock.
- ↑ You can keep collecting regular income no matter what happens to the stock.
- ↑ When a takeover bid is made, the common stock usually soars in price.

CONS
- ↓ You do not receive the full price gain when the stock goes up in price.
- ↓ You do not earn as much interest as you would had you bought a bond that is not convertible.
- ↓ CVs are often issued by companies with poor credit ratings.

CV Mutual Funds

If you have limited capital or prefer to let someone else make the selections, there are mutual funds that use a substantial portion of their assets to buy CVs and, in some cases, to write options.

When considering CV mutual funds, keep these tips in mind:
- Usual minimum investment is $1,000.
- Shares can be purchased directly from the fund or from a stockbroker.
- Read the fund's prospectus before investing.
- Check the quality of the fund's underlying stocks.
- Convertibles offer a hedge against volatile changes in the stock market.
- Automatic reinvestment of distribution into additional fund shares is available.
- If you invest in a family of funds and your yield declines, you can switch to higher-yielding funds within the family.

understand what can happen. By and large, the actual transactions will follow these patterns. At worst, the losses will be small; at best, the profits will be welcome.

WRITING CALLS WITH CVs

Writing calls is a conservative way to boost income and, when properly executed, involves minimal risks and fair-to-good gains. Because the CVs represent a call on the stock, they provide a viable base. Let's say that a $1,000 par value CV debenture can be swapped for 40 shares of common; the CV is at 90, the stock at 20; the calls, exercisable at 20, are due in 6 months and carry a premium of 2 ($200) each.

Buy 10 CVs for $9,000 and sell 3 calls. (Because the CVs represent 400 shares of stock, this is no problem.) The $600 premium will reduce the net investment to $8,400. If the stock jumps to 40, the CV will sell at 160, for a $7,000 gain. Add $500 interest to get $7,500 income. But there will be a $5,400 loss because the calls will have to be repurchased with a (tax-advantageous) deficit of $1,800 each. The net profit will thus be $2,100.

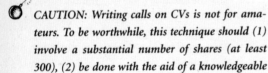 *CAUTION: Writing calls on CVs is not for amateurs. To be worthwhile, this technique should (1) involve a substantial number of shares (at least 300), (2) be done with the aid of a knowledgeable broker who watches for sudden aberrations in price spreads, (3) be initiated with adequate cash or margin reserves that may be needed to buy back*

Leading Convertible Bond Mutual Funds

FUND	TOTAL RETURN, JANUARY 1 TO JUNE 30, 1996
American Capital Harbor Fund (800–421–5666)	9.62%
Putman Convertible Income Growth (800–354–4000)	11.59
Calamos Convertible Income Fund (800–323–9943)	14.67
Value Line Convertible Fund (800–223–0818)	9.10
Phoenix Convertible Fund (800–243–1574)	11.13

calls early, and (4) be undertaken only by individuals in a high enough tax bracket to benefit from the short-term losses.

FOR FURTHER INFORMATION

Books

Thomas C. Noddings, *Superhedging* (Chicago: Probus Publishing Co., 1995).

Newsletters

Value Line Convertible Strategist
220 East 42 Street
New York, NY 10017
800–833–0046
48 times per year; $625.

11

Municipal Bonds: Last of the Tax Shelters

Municipals are tax-exempt debt obligations or IOUs issued by states, counties, cities, and other public agencies, such as school districts, sewer and water districts, airport, bridge and tunnel authorities, and highway authorities.

ADVANTAGES OF MUNIS

Their great advantage is that what the interest investors collect is exempt from federal income tax and, if the bonds are issued in the investor's state of residence, they are also exempt from state and local income taxes. For example, if you live in Minnesota, interest on munis (as they are called) issued by the state of Minnesota is exempt from federal and state income taxes. They are known as double tax-free bonds. (exceptions: Illinois, Iowa, Oklahoma, and Wisconsin impose some limitations on tax exemptions.)

☑ *HINT: Munis issued by U.S. Territories—Puerto Rico, Guam, and the Virgin Islands—are tax-exempt in all states.*

DISADVANTAGES

Because of their tax-exempt status, munis pay a lower interest rate than taxable corporate bonds. They are issued in units of $5,000 or, occasionally, $10,000. Most stockbrokers are reluctant to sell just one bond and many have $20,000 minimums. Some discount brokers will accept small-sized orders. But to have an adequately diversified portfolio, you probably need $40,000 to $60,000. Certainly if you have only $20,000 you may want to invest through a mutual fund or unit investment trust, described at the end of this chapter.

SHOULD YOU BUY MUNIS?

You don't have to be a millionaire to benefit from tax-exempt investments. On the other hand, municipal bonds make sense only if the interest earned is more than the after-tax yield of a taxable investment. For most people, that means being in the 28% tax bracket or higher. Tax brackets are adjusted for inflation each year, but generally if your taxable income is about $25,000 for a single return or $40,000 for a joint return, you will be in the 28% bracket.

To really determine whether to buy a municipal or not, use this formula:

1. Subtract your tax bracket from the number 100. For example:

    1 − .28 (tax bracket) = .72

2. Then divide the tax-free yield the fund is paying by .72 to find the taxable equivalent:

    6% ÷ .72 = 8.33%

3. The result—in this case, 8.33%—is the yield you need on a taxable investment to match the tax-free yield of 6%.

The bottom line: As you can see, even though a taxable corporate bond might pay 7% or even

7.5%, a muni paying only 6% is actually a better investment in this case. If you live in a high-tax state, such as New York, California or Minnesota, a municipal bond issued by your state would have even greater benefit.

Let's look at another example: If you're in the 31% tax bracket, a muni yielding 5.5% is the equivalent to a taxable bond yielding about 8%.

$$1 - .31 = .69$$
$$5.5\% \div .69 = 7.97\%$$

Again, you would need a taxable bond yielding at least 8% to equal your tax-free muni with only a 5.5% yield.

 CAUTION: There's no point, of course, in putting a tax-free municipal in an IRA or other tax-advantaged account.

Use the table above for additional comparisons.

TYPES OF MUNICIPAL BONDS

If you decide to buy individual bonds, you'll find a number of choices:

General Obligation Bonds (GOs)

Also known as public purpose bonds, these are sold to finance roads, schools, and government buildings. They are the most conservative of the municipals and are backed by the full taxing power of the state or local government that issues them. The interest and principal are repaid to bondholders out of a government's general revenue, primarily its taxes. Therefore, they generally have the highest safety ratings. Most are voter approved.

Revenue Bonds

These are issued to finance public works projects; their interest and principal are repaid only from the revenues generated by the project that bonds were issued to build—an airport, highway, tunnel, toll bridge, or a sewage treatment plant, for example. Because of this limited source of income, they are generally regarded as less safe than gos.

Taxable Municipals

For many years, all munis were tax-free, but that's no longer the case. Bonds issued to finance private business activities and ventures, such as shopping malls, sports stadiums, convention and trade shows, industrial parks, and parking facilities, are exempt often from state and local taxes where issued, but subject to federal income taxes. Yet income from certain kinds of private activity bonds, such as those to build a hospital, is still fully exempt. These taxable municipals, or private activity bonds as they're also called, generally yield 2 to 3 percentage points more than fully tax-exempt municipals.

Your Tax Bracket	28%	31%	36%	39.6%
TAX-EXEMPT YIELD	TAXABLE EQUIVALENT YIELDS			
3%	4.17%	4.35%	4.69%	4.97%
4	5.56	5.80	6.25	6.62
5	6.94	7.25	7.81	8.28
6	8.33	8.70	9.38	9.93
7	9.72	10.14	10.94	11.59
8	11.11	11.59	12.50	13.25

SOURCE: Federated Mutual Funds, Pittsburgh.

CAUTION: for investors in high tax brackets who have a sizable amount of tax-sheltered income, interest from such bonds issued after August 7, 1986, may be subject to the alternative minimum tax (AMT). The AMT taxes so-called preference income above a certain level at a flat rate.

Zero Coupon Munis

These bonds provide no interest income to the owner until they mature. Instead they are sold at a discount (below par) and you receive the full face value at maturity. Because they are sold far below face value, zero coupon munis are an inexpensive way for small investors to participate in the municipal bond market. Stripped munis, as they are called, literally have their semiannual interest rate coupons stripped off. Both parts then are sold separately—the principal and the series of coupon interest payments. By dividing the bond into two pieces, maturities are created that otherwise would not exist. Prior to the existence of stripped munis, bondholders had to wait 20 to 40 years for a municipal bond to mature; zeros, on the other hand, mature in less than half that time. So when you buy a stripped muni, you are in essence buying a couponless bond with zero interest, hence the name zero coupon.

These bonds have true tax advantages: If, for example, you buy a zero at $800, when it matures you'll receive the face value of $1,000, but there will be no federal income tax due on the $200 profit made during the holding period. Another advantage: Bonds used for stripping are non-callable, so you know they can be held to maturity. (The call feature of bonds is explained beginning on page 96.) Strips are sold by bond dealers.

 HINT: Zero coupon bonds are an excellent way to pay for college or set money aside for retirement or other distant goals. Whoever owns the bonds does not have to pay federal income tax on them.

Stripped Munis

PROS

↑ Can time your balloon payment
↑ No problem of where to reinvest income
↑ Noncallable
↑ Know exactly how much you will receive
↑ Shorter maturity dates than regular munis

CONS

↓ Interest is locked in; yields could rise
↓ Should be held to maturity
↓ Slim secondary market

Zero Coupon Convertible Munis

Like other zeros, these sell at a deep discount to face value. They have a unique feature, however, and that is that at a certain time they convert into regular interest bonds.

For example, a 25-year zero coupon convertible muni bond pays no interest during its first 10 years. Then in the tenth year, it converts into a regular municipal bond. At that point the investor starts to receive the stated interest rate in cash and continues to receive it for the remaining 15 years. At maturity, the bond returns its full face value of $1,000 to the investor. Both appreciation and interest income are free of federal income taxes.

 CAUTION: Some zero coupon convertible munis can be called early.

Prerefunded or Escrowed-to-Maturity Bonds

Sometimes a municipality floats a new bond issue when interest rates have dropped, in order to pay off the first bond. The proceeds from the sale of the second bond are invested in U.S. Treasury securities that are held in escrow until the old bonds can be redeemed—at their next call date in the case of prerefunded bonds, or at their maturity date in the case of escrowed-to-maturity bonds.

Because the money to repay the bonds is set aside and safely invested in Treasuries, these bonds are considered very safe.

Example: New York State Urban Development 8⅞s, yield 7.3%, due to be called in 1997.

Variable-Rate Option Munis

These are long-term municipals whose interest rates are adjusted, up or down, each year based on current market rates. You can usually cash in a variable-rate option muni on a daily, weekly, monthly, or yearly basis and get back what you paid for it. They are best if you know you might need your money within a year, or at least before the bond matures.

Single-State Bonds

If you live in a high-tax state, look for munis issued by your own state and, if possible, local governments. By avoiding state and local taxes you can improve your after-tax return, often adding as much as 1½ percentage points to your yield. Among the highest-taxed states are California, Massachusetts, Minnesota, and New York.

Funds that specialize in single-state bonds are forced to purchase bonds from a smaller pool than regular bond funds, and consequently have less choice when it comes to bond grade, type, and maturity. This adds a small element of risk to these funds. Single-state municipal bond funds are listed in the table on page 119.

Serial Maturities

Unlike most corporate bonds, which usually have the same redeption date, municipals often mature serially: a portion of the debt comes due each year until the final redemption. Select maturities to fit future needs: college tuition, retirement, house, etc.

PICKING A MUNI BOND

These are the key points to keep in mind when building a portfolio of individual municipal bonds:

- *Safety.* Like corporate bonds, municipals are also rated for safety—or how likely they are to default—by Standard & Poor's and Moody's. The safest are rated AAA or Aaa. And, of course, the higher the rating the less interest the bond issuer needs to pay to attract investors. The opposite is also true: The highest interest rates are paid on the riskiest bonds. (see page 94 for rating information.)

  Before purchasing municipals, ask your stockbroker for a research report and bond ratings. Muni prices are rarely listed in the newspaper, so you must use an experienced, reliable broker. Stick with those rated AD or above.

- *Maturity date.* For bonds with the same rating, the shorter the maturity, the lower the yield and the greater the price stability. Unless you plan to buy municipals regularly, it is usually prudent to stick to those with maturities of less than 10 years. In many cases, these will be older bonds selling at a discount. Select maturities to match your financial goals.

- *Type of bond.* Start with general obligation bonds, which typically yield less than other municipals, or an insured bond. Then consider revenue bonds backed by high, steady streams of income, such as utility bills. Suggested water revenue bonds and electric revenue bonds are given in Chapter 15.

☑ *HINT: Keep in mind bonds of the commonwealth of Puerto Rico. Their income is free from state, local, and federal taxes no matter where you live in the United States. To date, Puerto Rico has never defaulted on a bond issue.*

- *Unrated bonds.* You may run across bonds that are not rated. An unrated bond is not necessarily high in risk. It is often unrated because the municipality is so small or has such modest debt that its bonds have never been rated. If you personally know the community and if it is run well, you can add them to your portfolio. But plan to hold them to maturity as there probably is very little secondary market.

- *Marketability.* If you have to sell bonds before maturity, you want there to be an active secondary market. The most saleable municipals are general obligation bonds of state governments and revenue bonds of large, well-known authorities. Smaller issues can be tough to sell.
- *Call provision.* Larger issues usually permit the bonds to be called, that is, redeemed before maturity. In fact, many municipals are issued with a 10-year noncallable provision. If your bond is called, you will have to reinvest that money, probably at lower rates. Try to buy bonds that cannot be called or have call protection. (see pages 96–98.)
- *Insured bonds.* It's very rare for a municipal bond issuer to default. A recent study shows that between 1980 and 1991, only 1.9% of the $155 billion of nonrated bonds sold during that period defaulted. Of the $1.24 trillion of rated bonds sold, only 0.27% defaulted.

Nevertheless, you can boost your safety level by purchasing insured bonds. With these bonds, the insurance company agrees to pay the principal and interest to bondholders if the issuer defaults. The insurance policy lasts for the life of the bond.

NOTE: Once a bond is insured, it is given an AAA rating by Standard & Poor's even if the bond originally had a BBB rating. So remember that if you are purchasing an AAA insured bond, it may really be a BBB bond with insurance.

Insured municipal bonds pay lower yields, usually 1 to 1½ percentage points less than comparable uninsured bonds.

HINT: Insurance does not protect you against market risks: if interest rates go up, the value of bonds still goes down.

To insure its bonds, the issuer pays an insurance premium ranging between 0.1% and 2% of total principal and interest. In return, the insurance company will pay the principal and interest to the bondholders should the issuer default. Policies for new issues cannot be canceled, and the insurance remains active over the lifetime of the bond. With a bond fund or unit trust, the insurance is generally purchased for the entire portfolio. The oldest insurers are the American Municipal Bond Assurance Corp. (AMBAC) and the Municipal Bond Insurance Association (MBIA). Both are rated AAA by Moody's and AAA by Atandard & Poor's.

UNDERSTANDING THE RISKS INVOLVED

There are two primary risks: interest rate risk and default.

Electric Revenue Bonds

ISSUER	S&P RATING	APPROXIMATE YIELDS
South Carolina Public Service Authority	AA–	5.50%
Intermountain Power Agency (UT)	AA–	5.20
New York State Power Authority	AA–	5.00
Orlando Utilities Commission (FL)	AA	4.80
Muscatine Electric Revenue (IA)	AAA	4.80

(As of October 1996)

Puerto Rico Municipal Bonds

ISSUER	S&P RATING	APPROXIMATE YIELDS
Puerto Rico Electric Power	A–	5.50%
Puerto Rico Muni Finance	A–	5.50
Puerto Rico Telephone Authority	A+	5.30
Commonwealth of Puerto Rico	A	5.90
Puerto Rico Public Building Authority	A	5.80

(As of October 1996)

1) As with any bond, the interest rate it pays is fixed. If interest rates rise, the value of a municipal bond will fall. This presents a problem if you sell before the bond's maturity. It's not a problem, of course, if you hold until maturity because you will receive the bond's full face value.

In fact, interest rate risk is a greater problem than defaults for municipal bonds.

2) The second risk is that of default—if the issuer cannot make the interest and principal payments. To protect against default, purchase insured bonds.

CAUTION: Munis rated below A are regarded by many bond experts as risky. (The ratings are behind the true credit risk—they're a lagging indicator.) But because there is a shortage of municipals, many fund managers and others buy them anyway. Certain housing and health care bonds fall into this risk category. When buying a muni fund, trust, or individual bond, check the exact ratings.

Four Water Revenue Bonds

ISSUER	S&P RANKING	COUPON
Dallas Water & Sewer	AA	6.00%
Los Angeles Dept. Water/Power	AA	6.35
Phoenix Water System	AA	5.00
NY City Municipal Water	A–	6.30
MA Water Resources	AAA	4.50

(As of October 1996)

MUNICIPAL BOND MUTUAL FUNDS

For small investors, one of the best ways to buy municipals is through a mutual fund. Mutual funds provide diversification (by type, grade, coupon, and maturity), continuous professional management, the opportunity to add to your portfolio with relatively small dollar amounts, the ability to switch to other funds under the same sponsorship, and, most important, prompt reinvestment of interest to buy new shares and benefit from compounding.

A fund contains bonds with varying maturities. The manager continually buys and sells bonds in order to improve returns, switching from short to long-term maturities when yields are high and doing the opposite when yields decline. When interest rates shift quickly, some funds do extremely well; some do not. Keep in mind that your income from the fund will fluctuate, unlike that from an individual bond or a unit trust, where the yield is locked in.

TYPES OF MUNICIPAL BOND MUTUAL FUNDS

There are five types of mutual funds to consider:

- *Nationally diversified tax-exempt funds.* These hold bonds issued by states and municipalities throughout the country. Income is usually free from federal income tax.
- *Single-state funds.* These invest in bonds of a single state so investors who are residents of

10 Tax-Exempt Bond Funds

FUND	YIELD (OCTOBER 1996)
Calvert Tax-free Long Term (800–368–2748)	5.59%
Dreyfus Intermediate Tax-exempt (800–645–6561)	5.10
Fidelity Municipal Bond (800–544–8888)	4.98
New York Muni Fund (800–225–6864)	4.01
T. Rowe Price Tax-free Intermediate (800–638–5660)	5.64
Scudder Managed Municipal (800–225–2470)	5.06
SteinRoe Intermediate Municipal (800–338–2550)	4.45
Vanguard Long-Term Municipal (800–662–7447)	5.52

that state can have income that is free from federal and state income tax.

■ *Triple-exempt funds.* These invest in municipal bonds of a given municipality, and income earned is free from federal, state, and local income tax.

■ *Tax-free money market funds.* These were discussed in Chapter 3. Income is free of federal taxes and, if it's a single-state tax-free money market fund, from federal and state income tax as well.

■ *High-yield bond funds.* These invest in lower-rated tax-exempt bonds. Although they are higher in risk than top higher-quality bonds, they also have higher yields. They are suitable only for investors who knowingly wish to assume a high risk for a high return.

☑ *HINT: Before investing in your state's bonds or bond fund, check on the financial health of your particular state's economy. If you have any reservations, limit your holdings, perhaps to a 50–50 division between single-state and multi-state funds.*

MUNICIPAL BOND UNIT TRUSTS

These trusts have fixed portfolios of municipal bonds that remain in the trust until maturity, unless they are called. The trust aims to lock in the highest yield possible with good-quality issues at the time of the initial offering. Each trust has a limited number of shares for sale, but new trusts are continually being brought to the market. Sponsors also buy back existing units from investors who want to sell before the trust matures—so you could also buy one in the secondary market.

Trusts are mostly sold through brokers and carry up-front sales charges of 3.5% to 4.9%. A typical national trust issued by Nuveen or Van Kampen Merritt will have about 20 bonds, held typically until maturity unless one is called.

If you purchase a uit (unit investment trust) it will be registered in your name and monthly, quarterly, or semiannual checks will be mailed to you, although some unit investment trusts have reinvestment privileges.

☑ *HINT: The monthly payouts from a uit are more stable than those of a long-term bond fund, giving you a more predictable stream of income. Most are long term, with average maturities of 25 to 30 years, but trusts running 10 to 15 years are not uncommon.*

The New Laddered Trust

The newest type of trust is laddered with various maturities. It returns 20% of your principal each year for 5 years.

In either the old-fashioned or the newer laddered trusts, when the bonds mature, are sold

Leading Single-State Municipal Bond Funds

STATE	MUTUAL FUND	YIELD (OCTOBER 1996)
Minnesota	Franklin Minnesota Insured (800–632–2180)	5.30%
New York	Putnam New York (800–225–1581)	5.36
West Virginia	MFS Managed West Virginia (800–225–2606)	5.01
California	MFS Managed California (800–225–2606)	5.28
Oregon	Oregon Municipal Bond Fund (800–541–9732)	4.90

Insured Municipal Bond Mutual Funds

FUND	YIELD (OCTOBER 1990)
Vanguard Muni Bond Insured Long Term (800–662–7447)	5.31%
Merrill Lynch Muni Insured Portfolio (609–282–2800)	5.67
American Capital Tax-exempt Insured (800–421–5666)	4.01
Dreyfus Insured Tax-exempt Bond Fund (800–645–6561)	5.00
Fidelity Insured Tax-free (800–544–8888)	5.01

(rarely), or are called, the principal is returned to the investor as a return of capital. If the sponsor feels a bond is endangering the trust's interest, it can be sold and proceeds paid out.

If you need to sell your trust before maturity date, you can do so in the secondary market, but doing so entails a commission. If interest rates have fallen, you could make a profit, but if they've gone up, you may not get back your original investment. Unit trust prices are based on the price of the securities in the portfolio and are determined either by the sponsor or by an independent evaluator. Nuveen, for instance, which has a number of trusts, sets the price on a daily basis. Although unit prices are not given in the newspaper, you can call the sponsor for up-to-date quotes.

General and State Trusts

General trusts include bonds from various states and territories, while state trusts have bonds only from a single state, hence the name single-state unit trusts. Income is generally free from state and local taxes in the issuing state, as well as from federal taxes.

Unit trusts are usually sold in $1,000 units, but with a $5,000 minimum. The sales charge plus the annual fee or trust expenses, which both run about 0.2%, are factored into the yield. Mutual funds, by contrast, may be subject to a sales charge (load) or not (no load).

Mutual Fund vs. Unit Trust

- A managed mutual fund is generally a better investment for people who expect to sell in less than 10 years. Check the 1-, 5-, and 10-year performance records of several before investing.
- Unit trusts are best for long-term holdings, especially when the initial yield is high enough that you want to lock it in.

YOUR TAXES AND MUNICIPALS

Believe it or not, unfortunately interest on some municipal bonds is now subject to taxation. You'll want to be aware of this before investing in a muni. Here are the facts:

Private activity bonds. Interest on these bonds, issued after August 7, 1986, to finance private business activities, such as shopping malls, is generally taxable at the federal level for individuals subject to the alternative minimum tax (AMT). The AMT affects investors in high tax brackets who also have a sizable amount of tax-sheltered income. Interest on these private activity bonds may be subject to the AMT. The AMT taxes so-called preference income above a certain level at a rate of 26% or 28%. Check with your accountant before investing in private activity bonds.

☑ *HINT: Because of their tax disadvantage, private activity bonds usually have higher yields than public purpose munis. That makes them appealing to those who remain below the AMT threshold.*

An exception: bonds issued by private, nonprofit hospitals and universities, called 501(c) bonds, are not subject to taxation.

> ### A Freebie for Readers
> The Franklin fund family has a free slide rule that lets you figure out your combined state and federal marginal income tax rate. The data are available for every state and for the 28%, 31%, 36%, and 39.6% tax brackets. Call 800–342–5236.

Social Security and Munis—Tax Consequences. Municipal bond income is added to other income to determine whether a retiree must pay taxes on his/her social security benefits. Up to 85% of a retiree's social security benefits can be taxed if municipal bond interest income plus adjusted gross income plus half of social security payments is more than $32,000 for couples or $25,000 for singles. Again, check with your accountant, as these dollar amounts are subject to change.

FOR FUTHER INFORMATION

David L. Scott, *Municipal Bonds: The Basics and Beyond* (Chicago: Probus Publishing Co., 1995).

12

Nontraditional Bonds: Maes, Junk, Zeros, and the Mae Family

*H*igh yields, safety, and convenience—that's what the various mortgage-backed securities in the Mae family offer. These securities, which are shares in pools of secured mortgages, are often called pass-throughs because the sponsor who packages the mortgages passes through the income (minus a modest fee) directly to you, the investor.

You'll receive payments on a monthly basis and you can expect the yields to be 1.5+ points higher than those on comparable treasury bonds. This higher yield is due in part to the fact that Maes are slightly more risky than treasuries and also because your monthly payments include principal as well as interest.

CAUTION: This is an important concept that many investors don't fully understand. To state it another way: Mortgage-backed securities do not behave like regular bonds, which provide a return of principal upon maturity. Instead, with members of the Mae family, your monthly check includes both interest and principal. It is important to understand this distinction. Many investors mistakenly believe that these monthly checks are interest only. They are both interest and part payment of principal.

The pass-through technique allows individual investors to share the income derived from monthly mortgage payments and prepayments.

They are similar to mutual funds in that investors do not own one particular mortgage but pieces of many mortgages.

HINT: Ginnie Maes are the only securities, other than U.S. Treasury issues, that carry the direct full faith and credit guarantee of the U.S. Government. Others in the Mae group, described below, carry an indirect guarantee.

GINNIE MAES

Ginnie Mae stands for the government national mortgage association (GNMA), a wholly owned corporation of the U.S. Government that functions as part of the department of housing and urban development.

The objective of Ginnie Mae is to stimulate housing by attracting capital and guaranteeing mortgages. A GNMA certificate represents a portion of a pool of 30-year FHA- or VA-insured mortgages. It provides payment of interest and principal on a monthly basis.

How They Work

When a home-buyer takes out a mortgage, the house is pledged as collateral. The bank or savings and loan pools this loan with others of similar terms and rates, thus creating a package of mortgages worth $1 million or more. Ginnie Mae reviews the mortgages to make certain they meet certain standards and then assigns a pool number. Stockbrokers and others sell pieces of this pool, called certificates, to the public.

Home-buyers then make their payments (interest and principal) to the bank, which deducts a handling fee as well as a Ginnie Mae insurance fee. The rest of the money is passed on to the investors from the mortgage bankers.

Because GNMA certificates carry the guarantee of the U.S. Government, they have made mortgage investments especially safe. And because certificates can be traded in the secondary market, they also offer liquidity.

Where and How to Buy Ginnie Maes

You have two choices: to buy a Ginnie Mae Certificate or shares in a Ginnie Mae Mutual Fund.

1. The minimum investment for a GNMA certificate is $25,000, with $5,000 increments thereafter. Monthly interest in considered ordinary income and is taxed, whereas monthly principal payments are considered a return of capital and are exempt from taxes. Monthly payments are not uniform—they are based on the remaining principal in the pool. As homeowners make their mortgage payments, the mortgage pool gets paid down, and although you receive the stated coupon interest, it is on a declining amount of debt. In other words, each month the proportion of interest received is slightly less and the proportion of principal slightly more. Over the long term, GNMAs are therefore self-liquidating. When the pool of mortgages is paid in full by homeowners, that's it. You don't receive a lump payment or a return of face value as you do with a zero or straight bond.

CAUTION: When interest rates fall, homeowners pay off their mortgages and refinance at lower rates. This means your Ginnie Mae is paid off quickly.

2. You can purchase Ginnie Maes for less than $25,000 through mutual funds (discussion follows), or you can buy older Ginnie Mae in the secondary market. Older Ginnie Maes have been partially paid down and are usually bid down in value to compensate for the declining stream of income.

CAUTION: Ads for Ginnie Maes and their mutual funds often claim they are totally safe and 100% government guaranteed. This is not true. Ginnie Maes are not completely risk-free:

- The government does not guarantee the yield.
- The government does not protect investors against declines in either the value of the fund's shares or the yield.
- The government, however, does indeed protect investors against late mortgage payments as well as foreclosures. If homeowners default, you will still receive payments on time.

HINT: If you're considering Ginnie Maes, bear in mind that the average 30-year Ginnie Mae is repaid in about 12 years.

GINNIE MAE MUTUAL FUNDS

If you don't want to invest $25,000, Ginnie Maes are available through unit investment trusts and mutual funds for as little as $1,000. In a unit trust, once the trust's portfolio is assembled, it's set. The

---

Hidden Risks in Ginnie Maes for Retirees

- If you spend each monthly check, you are using up both interest and principal.
- You may want to reinvest your monthly payments. Finding a better rate with equal safety is often difficult.
- Monthly checks are not all the same, which is worrisome if you need a set dollar amount to live on.

portfolio manager cannot make adjustments, so if interest rates drop, you face exactly the same dilemma you do in owning a GNMA certificate. Unit investment trusts are explained in greater detail on page 121.

Here are the points you need to understand about these funds:

1. A Ginnie Mae mutual fund is not a pass-through security like the certificates. The fund itself receives interest and principal payments from the certificates in its portfolio. You then own shares in the fund, which in turn pays you dividends. The market value of your shares fluctuates daily, and the interest rate does, too.

   CAUTION: *The fund's yield is not fixed, nor is it guaranteed. If interest rates fall, as mortgages are paid off, principal payments are received by the mutual fund. The manager then must reinvest this money, usually in lower-yielding certificates. So if interest rates are declining, your fund yield will fall also.*

   HINT: *Because of this volatility, Morningstar Mutual Funds says investors should hold fund shares at least 3 to 5 years.*

2. An advantage of a fund over a unit trust is that portfolio managers can shift the maturities of the certificates in the fund to reflect changing economic conditions. For example, if it appears that inflation is returning, they will move to shorter maturities to protect the return. And in certain types of funds, part of the portfolio can be shifted into other types of investments. The Kemper U.S. Government securities fund, for instance, also invests in intermediate treasury bonds.

3. An advantage the funds have over straight Ginnie Mae certificates is that they will reinvest the principal payments received from home-owners in more fund shares if you so request.

4. Funds are best for investors who want high current income rather than capital appreciation. Plan on a long-term play, because these funds are volatile and subject to market risks.

5. In seeking high yields, many GNMA funds use almost speculative strategies, investing in put and call options, interest rate futures contracts, etc. Others invest in mortgage-related securities that do not carry the full government guarantee. Check the prospectus, and remember that a fund's shares may go down in value as well as its yield.

6. For every 1% change in interest rates, the value of the average Ginnie Mae fund will move in the opposite direction almost 6%. Therefore Ginnie Maes are well suited to tax-deferred portfolios, where regular contributions over a period of time cushion any negative effects of price swings.

FREDDIE MACS

The Federal Home Loan Morgage, Corp., known as Freddie Mac, issues its own mortgage-backed securities, which are called participation certificates, or PCs. Freddie deals primarily in conventional single-family mortgages, which are backed by the veterans administration, but it also resells nongovernment-backed mortgages.

If homeowners do not make their mortgage payments on time, you will receive your monthly payment on time, but you may have to wait several months to a year to receive your share of the principal.

NOTE: A key difference between Freddie and Ginnie is that Ginnie Maes are backed by the U.S. Government; Freddies are guaranteed by private mortgage insurance. Even though they're not quite as secure as GNMAs, they are considered very safe. Because of the discrepancy in safety, Freddie often pays slightly higher yields.

Freddie Macs are sold for $25,000. Because the market is dominated by institutional investors,

GNMA Issues

RATE	ASK	CHG.	YIELD
6.00	86:02	86:10	8.07
6.50	89:18	89:26	8:07
7.00	93:00	93:08	8:12
7.50	96:05	96:13	8:18
8:00	99:01	99:09	8:24
8.50	101:16	101:24	8:33
9.00	103:27	104:03	8:34
9:50	106:00	106:08	8:28
10.00	107:20	107:28	8:30
10.50	109:12	109:20	8:31
11.00	111:08	111:16	8:38
11.50	112:24	113:00	8:46
12.00	113:24	114:00	8.26

SOURCE: Barron's, October 1996.

there are fewer mutual funds: Vanguard and Federated investors are two. The U.S. AA income fund divides its assets between Ginnie and Freddie.

FANNIE MAES

The Federal National Mortgage Aassociation (FNMA, or Fannie Mae) is a private shareholder-owned corporation that buys conventional mortgages, pools them in $1 million lots, and sells them in $25,000 units. Although not backed by the full faith and credit of the U.S. Government, Fannies are AAA-rated by both Standard & Poor's and Moody's. Fannie Mae shares also trade on the NYSE.

Both Freddie Mac and Fannie Mae are corporations chartered by Congress and are not officially part of the federal government. Therefore they do not carry the unconditional guarantee of Ginnie Mae. One advantage of this discrepancy in safety is a slightly higher yield. Another is that the mortgage pools are larger than the Ginnie Mae pools. The more mortgages, the more accurately you can predict how fast the principal will be returned.

After their initial offering, both Freddie and Fannie PCs trade in the secondary market.

CMOs

Collateralized mortgage obligations (CMOs) were introduced in 1983 by the Federal Home Loan Mortgage Corp. Their advantage is a more predictable payout of interest and principal than with Ginnie Maes. Instead of buying mortgage securities directly, you buy an AAA-rated bond. These bonds are sold against mortgage collateral comprised of GNMA-or FNMA-guaranteed mortgages.

Each bond is divided into four classes, or tranches, having different dates of maturity ranging from 3 to 20 years. Each CMO has a fixed coupon and pays interest like a traditional bond—monthly or quarterly—but, and here's the difference, principal payments are initially passed through only to investors in the shortest maturity class, class A. Once that group has been paid in full, principal payments go to the next class. In the fourth and final class, investors get all interest and all principal in one lump sum.

These certificates generally have slightly lower yields than the regular pass-throughs, because the size and length of payments can be more accurately determined and you have some protection against prepayments. CMOs are available from larger brokerage firms in $5,000 units.

CAUTION: Although CMOs improve on traditional mortgage securities by smoothing the rate of early principal payments, they are less liquid, more expensive to trade, and harder to track. They also entail record-keeping and reinvestment problems that most individuals want to avoid.

SALLIE MAES

Created in congress in 1972 to provide a nationwide secondary market for government guaranteed student loans, Sallie Mae (the Student Loan Marketing Association) is to students what Ginnie

Mae is to homeowners. It issues bonds, rather than certificates, based on a pool of loans.

Each bond is backed by Sallie Mae, and because its assets are made up of loans that have a government guarantee, these bonds are regarded as almost as safe as Treasuries. However, and this is key, this federal backing is only implied, not explicit. They yield about 3½% more than equivalent Treasury bonds.

Student Loan Marketing is a publicly owned company chartered by the government. Its stock trades on the New York Stock Exchange. Originally issued at $20 per share, it split a 2.5 for 1 in 1988; as of September 1996, it was selling at $73/share. It also issues floating-rate notes and convertible bonds. The need for student loans is expected to continue through the 1990s.

GOVERNMENT AGENCY BONDS

These bonds, although they have slightly lower interest rates than those of the Mae family, are almost as safe as U.S. Treasuries. They are either affiliated with or owned by the government and so are mostly insured against default by some type of federal guarantee. No agency has defaulted on its debt. The distinguishing feature of Government Agency Bonds is whether they are guaranteed by the government.

Here's a guide to who's who in agency bonds:

- FULLY GUARANTEED AGENCIES. These bonds are guaranteed against deffault by the U.S. government and include:
  1. Federal housing administration (FHA). Insures mortgages made by private lending firms to individual home-buyers, thus lowering the costs.
  2. Government National Mortgage Association (GNMA). Ginnie Mae improves liquidity of the mortgage trading market by guaranteeing securities backed by pools of federally insured mortgages, for example, by the FHA.

  3. Tennessee Valley Authority (TVA). U.S. Government-owned utility providing electricity to the Tennessee River Valley and area. Created in 1933 to promote regional growth.
- UNGUARANTEED AGENCIES. These do not carry an unconditional guarantee. They are stockholder-owned:
  1. Federal Home Loan Mortgage Corporation (or Freddie Mac). Increases liquidity of mortgage market by buying mortgages from lending institutions and selling them to individual investors.
  2. Federal National Mortgage Association (Fannie Mae). Performs same function as Freddie Mac.
  3. Student Loan Marketing Association (Sallie Mae). Improves liquidity of student loan market by providing financing to state student loan agencies and buying loans made by private sources.
- PARTIALLY GUARANTEED AGENCIES. The United States and most other industrialized nations are obligated to contribute funds to these agencies:
  1. Asian development bank. Makes loans to developing countries in Asia.
  2. Inter-American development bank. Makes loans to developing nations in Latin America.
  3. World bank. Makes loans to developing countries throughout the world.

JUNK BONDS

If you're looking for very high yields, a solution is the so-called high-yield or junk bond, which yields substantially more than higher-quality, safer bonds.

Junk bonds are those rated BB or lower by Standard & Poor's and BA or lower by Moody's. Some have no ratings at all. The world of junk bonds comprises new or old companies with uncertain earnings coverage of their fixed obligations (bond interest payments), along with blue-chip companies that have been forced into heavy debt in order to fend off a takeover or to finance an acquisition or a buyback of their own stock. For example, Kroger Co., In an effort to avoid a takeover attempt, paid its shareholders a special distribution of $40 per share and financed it by raising its debt level to $4.6 billion.

When these situations occur in a blue-chip company, a new set of circumstances comes into being:

- Low-earning or unprofitable assets are sold off.
- Costs are cut, reflecting corporate efforts to become lean and mean.

The credit rating gradually improves as these changes are implemented. Thus a good junk bond is always one in which the coverage of fixed charges increases with time.

However, default is not out of the question, which is why, unless you have sufficient money with which to speculate, you should invest in junk bonds only through a mutual fund, where the element of risk is diversified.

JUNK BOND MUTUAL FUNDS

High-yield junk bond mutual funds offer professional management plus portfolio supervision. As with other mutual funds, track records vary, so care must be exercised. The publicity attached to the Drexel Burnham/Ivan Boesky insider trading scandals sent shock waves through the junk bond markets, but junk bonds have fared well despite the adverse publicity provoked by these and other notorious cases.

 CAUTION: Like any fixed-income security, junk bond funds are vulnerable to broad changes in interest rates, and as those rates rise, the value of the fund falls.

Junk Bonds to Consider in 1997

COMPANY	S&P RATING	PRICE
HealthSouth 9½, 2001	B+	$103
Genesis Health, 2005	B 9¾	102
Kroger 9s, 1999	B−	101
Webb (Del) 9¾, 2003	B−	98

(As of June 1996)

Junk Bonds: A Two-Tier System

During 1997, expect high-yield junk bonds to vary widely in quality, ranging from speculative (risky) to those with improving credit-worthiness and therefore less speculative. In fact, some junk bonds will continue to rise from junk to investment grade—BBB. Here are four to watch in both categories:

HIGH RISK

Genesco	10⅜%
Service Merchandise	9
Stone Container	10¾
Trump Casino	11¾

LOWER RISK

Health South*	9½%
Jack Eckerd	9¼
Safeway Stores	10
Viacom Int'l.	10¼

*Guaranteed by Promus Corp.
(As of June 1996)

High-Yielding Junk Bond Mutual Funds

FUND	YIELD (OCTOBER 1996)
Oppenheimer High Yield (800–525–7048)	9.53%
T. Rowe Price High Yield (800–638–5660)	8.47
American Capital High Yield (800–421–5666)	9.00
Prudential-Securities High Yield Corp. Fund (800–648–7637)	9.72
Fidelity Spartan High Income (800–544–8888)	8.12

Some of the top-yielding junk bond funds are listed in the table below. If one bond in a fund defaults, it means a decrease in the overall fund yield, certainly less of an impact than if you owned the bond directly. However, if several bonds default, the fund share price will suffer.

JUNK BOND UNIT INVESTMENT TRUSTS

Unit investment trusts have fixed portfolios. Their yields are more predictable than those of a mutual fund. However, they have far less flexibility in terms of adjusting the portfolio and getting rid of poor bonds. Because they are not actively managed, *investors may suffer losses should there be a default*. The unit investment trust is fine for quality bonds but should be avoided for junk issues.

ADVICE FOR 1997

Junk bonds can be a mine field for the unsophisticated investor. Yet it's hard to say no to an 8%-to-11% yield. Here are nine ways to protect yourself if you decide to take the risk.

1. Put no more than 10% of your portfolio in junk bonds.
2. If you want to buy individual bonds, use a broker who knows the area well.
3. Watch the market closely and be prepared to sell quickly and swallow losses.

4. If you buy individual bonds, diversify among types: fallen angels (companies facing difficulties), emerging growth (companies that have yet to achieve quality ratings), and bonds of companies emerging from a leveraged buyout or takeover.
5. Buy only publicly listed bonds—they are quoted daily and are much easier to buy and sell.
6. Avoid bond issues under $75 million; they tend to be illiquid.
7. Watch the price of the common stock that underlies your bonds. If it suddenly drops in price, it often forecasts trouble for the company's bond.
8. Use a mutual fund for diversification unless you can afford to buy 10 to 15 bonds.
9. If you buy a mutual fund, select it based upon total return, not just yield. A solid fund should generate capital gains along with income. Also, pick a well-diversified fund with no more than 2% to 3% of its assets in any one company's bonds. This broad base helps the fund to weather any adverse economic conditions.

ZERO COUPON BONDS

Zero coupon bonds (zeros) are an excellent choice if you know you will be needing a lump sum of money at a certain date in the future. These bonds, offered by corporations, municipalities, and the U.S. Government, are sold at a deep discount from face value ($1,000), and pay no interest. Worthwhile? Yes, as long as you understand the facts.

These bonds are stripped of their interest coupons and, instead of being paid out to you, you get this interest in a balloon payment when the zeros mature. In this respect they are much like EE savings bonds. In other words, they are fully redeemed at par or face value. The difference between the fractional price paid initially and the

High-Yielding Municipal Bond Funds

FUND	YIELD (OCTOBER 1996)
Franklin High Yield Tax-free Income (800–342–5236)	6.19%
Fidelity Aggressive Tax-free Portfolio (800–544–8888)	5.78
SteinRoe High Yield Muni (800–338–2550)	5.24
T. Rowe Price Tax-free High Yield (800–638–5660)	5.99

value at maturity is the return on your investment, that is, the yield to maturity. *For example,* a zero coupon the Treasury is selling for $485 will be worth $1,000 at maturity in 2006. That is a yield to maturity of 7.05%.

Taxation

The annual appreciation (or undistributed interest) is subject to tax. You must pay taxes annually all along the way, just as if you had actually received the interest payments. Zeros tend to be volatile in price because of this compounding effect; in fact, because there are no interest payments to cushion market swings, zeros can fall dramatically in price when interest rates rise. Therefore, if you buy zeros, plan to hold them to maturity.

Ways to Use Zeros

Zeros are tailor-made for retirement accounts, such as IRAs and Keoghs, so you can avoid paying taxes every year on interest you don't actually receive. For example, an Allied Corp. zero due 2007 sold at 45 ($450 per bond) with a yield of 7.5%. In December 2007, bondholders will receive $1,000 per bond.

☑ *HINT: Zeros are also ideal for saving for a specific goal, such as college tuition payments or a vacation home. If you use zeros to finance a child's college education, have your broker select ones that come due in the years your child will be in school. Better yet, put them in your child's name; when they mature, they'll be taxed at the child's lower rate after age 14.*

How to Avoid the Drawbacks

Locking in your yield can turn out to be a disadvantage if interest rates rise over the life of your zero so that other investments are offering higher yields. To tackle the dual problem of rising interest rates and increasing inflation:

- Select zeros with medium-term maturities— 3 to 7 years, possibly 10—and avoid being committed to an interest rate over the long term.
- Purchase zeros continually—say every year— as part of your IRA, to take advantage of changing rates.
- Purchase zeros with varying maturities to cover yourself in case interest rates rise.

☑ *HINT: Zero coupon Treasuries are backed by the full faith and credit of the U.S. Government and are one of the safest and simplest ways to invest for your retirement. You lock in a fixed rate of return, thus eliminating uncertainty.*

The Power of Compounding

How Much $1,000 in Zeros Will Grow, before Taxes, at Various Compounding Rates

| MATURITY | SEMI-ANNUAL COMPOUNDING RATE | | | | |
	6%	7%	8%	9%	10%
5 Years	$1,343	$1,410	$1,480	$1,553	$1,629
10 Years	1,806	1,990	2,191	2,412	2,653
15 Years	2,427	2,807	3,243	3,745	4,322
20 Years	3,262	3,959	4,801	5,816	7,040
30 Years	5,892	7,878	10,520	14,027	18,679

SOURCE: Merrill Lynch.

Types of Zeros

- GOVERNMENT ZEROS. In 1982 Merrill Lynch devised the idea of Treasury zeros by purchasing long-term government bonds, placing them in an irrevocable trust, and issuing receipts against the coupon payments. This created a series of zero coupon treasuries, one for every coupon date. In other words, Merrill stripped the interest coupons from the principal of the treasury bond and sold each portion separately. Merrill called these TIGRs (Treasury Investment Growth Receipts). Then along came Salomon Brothers with their version—CATs (Certificates of Accrual on Treasury Securities). All are certificates held in irrevocable trust in a custodial bank.

- TREASURY STRIPS. In 1985 the government entered the act, introducing its own coupon-stripping program called strips (separate trading of registered interest and principal securities). Because they are issued directly by the Treasury, they are safer than all other types of zeros. Yields are slightly less than those of TIGRS, LYONs, and CATs, because of the greater degree of safety. Treasury strips must be purchased from a stockbroker.

  Example: A 20-year bond with a face value of $20,000 and a 10% interest rate could be stripped into 41 zero coupon instruments: the 40 semiannual interest coupons plus the principal. The body upon maturity is worth the $20,000 face value. The other coupon zeros would be worth $1,000 each, or half the annual interest of $2,000 (10% of $20,000) on the payment date.

- MUNICIPAL ZEROS. Issued by state and local governments, these are exempt from federal taxes and also from state taxes in the state where issued. They are suggested for investors in high-tax brackets. An A-rated muni zero issued by New York City Water

Authority, due 2011, with a yield of 5.6%, recently sold for $433. That means that in the year 2011 you would receive $1,000 for each $433 invested.

CAUTION: *Zeros issued with call features should be shunned.*

- MORTGAGE-BACKED ZEROS. These are backed by securities issued by Ginnie Mae, Fannie Mae, and Freddie Mac. The securities are secured by AAA-rated mortgages. You'll see some of them referred to as ABCs (agency-backed compounders).

- ZERO COUPON CONVERTIBLES. This hybrid vehicle allows you to convert the bond into stock of the issuing company. Merrill Lynch, the leading marketer of zero CVs, calls them LYONs (Liquid Yield Option Notes). Conversion premiums on LYONs are generally lower than on traditional coupon issues; therefore, they offer potential appreciation if the underlying stock moves up in price. LYONs are sold at a substantial discount from par. They give the holder the right, after a certain date, to sell the issue back to the issuer at the original issue price plus accrued interest. This so-called put feature can reduce some of the market risk that accompanies convertibles. (see Chapter 10 on convertibles.)

  For example, a Rite Aid zero due in 2006 sold recently for $525 for a yield of 6.9%. It converts into 15.933 shares.

- COLLEGE ZEROS. A number of states issue tax-exempt zero coupon bonds as a way to help parents pay for their children's college education. They often have good yields and their interest is exempt from state taxes for the state's residents. The first state to sell these bonds was Illinois—it sold a zero coupon general obligation bond. Some states sell these bonds on an annual or semiannual basis. Check with your stockbroker or state department of education.

The bonds vary in maturities and interest rates, but are united by the fact that they are low in risk. Most are general obligation bonds, which are high in safety because they are backed by the taxing power of the state itself. Most are also noncallable, so if interest rates fall the state cannot call in your bond.

Although you can use the money you earn with these bonds for any purpose, the states often give added incentives if you use the proceeds to pay for college expenses at one of the state's own schools. Illinois, for example, pays an added yield if you use the money to pay for an education in Illinois. Others do not count the income in their formulas for determining if you or your child is eligible for state financial aid.

These special education bonds, like other municipals, are sold through brokers, not by the states directly. Many states advertise their bonds when they are about to be issued. Some, such as Iowa, give announcements to public school students to take home to their parents. You must move quickly, however. These bonds tend to sell out quickly—often within a week or so.

Zero Coupon Bond Mutual Funds

Zeros, like straight bonds, rise in price when interest rates fall and fall when rates rise. And since they are even more sensitive to interest rates, they should be held until maturity. If this is not your plan, use a mutual fund. You'll avoid both being forced to sell early and paying a broker's commission.

■ Benham Target Maturities Trust (800–4 SAFETY)

■ Scudder U.S. Government Zero Coupon Target Portfolio (800–225–2470)

☑ *HINT: These bonds are sometimes available in the secondary market. Tell your broker if you're interested; it may take him some time to locate the maturity you want.*

ZERO COUPON FICO STRIPS

These zero coupon obligations derived from bonds issued by the federally sponsored agency FICO, the financing corp., first appeared on the scene in May 1988. They were the first zeros created from the bonds of a federally sponsored agency.

FICO was created by Congress to raise money for the ailing Federal Savings & Loan Insurance Corp. (FSLIC.)

The principal of these bonds is secured by U.S. Treasury securities that match the maturities on FICO bonds. Interest on the bonds is paid from assessments made on the savings and loan industry.

Zero Coupon Treasury Bonds

PROS

↑ Lock in fixed yield

↑ Maturity dates can be tailored to meet future needs

↑ Call protection available

↑ Predictable cash payment

↑ Guaranteed by U.S. government

↑ Tax-deferred in retirement accounts

↑ No reinvestment decisions

↑ Less expensive than most bonds

CONS

↓ If interest rates rise, you're locked in at a lower yield

↓ Inflation erodes purchasing power of the bond's face value

↓ Commissions and/or sales markups not always made clear

↓ Many zeros have call provisions permitting issuer to redeem them prior to maturity

FICO zeros have higher yields than Treasury bonds. The longest-maturing FICOs pay the highest returns.

Although Standard & Poor does not assign credit ratings to FICOs, it has stated that it believes these bonds are very high quality, the equivalent of AAA issues, based on a commitment of Congress to both FICO.

FICO strips trade over-the-counter and can be purchased through a stockbroker. Like other bonds, when interest rates rise, their value drops, and vice versa. The minimum face value of a FICO coupon strip is $1,000; of a principal strip, $20,000.

A WORD OF CAUTION

A recent survey revealed the fact that brokers' fees for trading Ginnie Maes and zeros can vary by as much as 7%. Sometimes discount brokers are more expensive than full-service brokers, particularly for over-the-counter bonds, and less so for corporate and U.S. Treasury issues. (The vast majority of zero coupons trade over-the-counter.) Most brokers charge a commission ranging from $5 to $10 per bond. Stick to this range, which is fair, considering that even at $10 per bond the commission is only 1% of the bond's price.

FOR FURTHER INFORMATION
Freddie Mac

Shareholder Relations Department
Federal Home Loan Mortgage Corp.
Mail Stop #485
8200 Jones Branch Drive
Mclean, VA 22102
800–424–5401

Sallie Mae

Investor Relations
Student Loan Marketing Association
1050 Thomas Jefferson Street, NW
Washington, DC 20007
202–333–8000

CMOs

Pension Investment Memorandum: CMOs
Research Division
Gabriele, Hueglin & Cashman
World Financial Center
200 Liberty Sreet
New York, NY 10281
212–607–4100; 800–422–7435
Free

When the Bulls Are Running

At the heart of every portfolio are, of course, stocks. Whether you have only dreamed about owning a stock or whether you and your broker are trading hundreds of shares every morning and afternoon, we suggest you read this entire section. The basic information is essential to the beginner and the lists of suggested stocks and the tips on trading options, getting in on new issues, and making money with rights and warrants, can help even the most wizened investor.

In Part Three you will learn about:

- Common and preferred stocks
- How to pick stocks that go up in price
- When to buy and when to sell
- Over-the-counter stocks
- Electric utilities and water company stocks
- High-dividend stocks
- Low-debt companies
- Options
- Stock rights and warrants
- New issues

13

Stocks: Common and Preferred

WHY OWN STOCKS?

The two basic tools of investing are stocks and bonds, or equity and debt, to use a little Wall Streetese. We discussed the various types of bonds and their pros and cons in Part Two. Now, we're going to discuss common and preferred stocks—the backbone of any portfolio.

The ongoing bull market is certainly the most compelling reason for investing in stocks. Yet even in a less impressive market, there are two other equally impressive reasons to be in the market:

Those two facts are:

1. *Over the long run, stocks outperform bonds—*although sometimes it may indeed be a very long run. Both trade in the marketplace, which historically rewards risk rather than caution. There are, of course, periods when you're better off in T-bills or corporate bonds, but the fact that stocks are better profit-makers remains a truism of investing.

2. *Stocks tend to keep pace with inflation.* With stocks, at least you have a fighting chance of staying even. Not so with bonds: Once you buy a bond, the interest rate is locked in. If, for example, oil prices go up, it doesn't matter—your bond will pay exactly the same whether crude is at $18 or $35 a barrel. (Bonds do compensate for this factor by moving up or down in price, however.) If you own shares in Exxon or Occidental Petroleum, however, you'll participate in the increase in oil prices through higher dividends *and* a rising price for your shares. Stocks, in fact, respond directly to inflation: If the buying power of your dollar is reduced to 50¢ by rampant inflation, you and everyone else buying Exxon will have to pay more for the company's shares. At the same time, inflation will eat away at interest earned on fixed-income securities.

THE TWO TYPES OF STOCKS

Despite the pull of the bull market, it's important to remember that there's no such thing as a stock that's always an excellent holding. It's a mistake, in fact, to expect all things from any one stock. A great number of investors are unaware of the fact that stocks are *not* all designed to do the same thing. In fact there are two distinct types of stocks: those that generate income and those that appreciate in price.

Success with Stocks

Over the past 20 years, stocks, as measured by the S&P 500 Stock Index, provided an annualized return of 11.9% compared to 9% on 10-year Treasury bonds and 7.7% for 90-day Treasury bills. Inflation averaged 6.3% during this period.

- Income stocks, such as utility stocks, real estate investment trusts (REITs), and closed-end funds that trade on the exchanges, should be held primarily for income; you definitely should not also expect them to appreciate much in price.
- Stocks selected for appreciation are an entirely different matter. Within this growth category you must narrow your selection even further, to low-risk growth stocks or speculative stocks. Throughout this book you will find various lists of stocks suggested for growth, income, or total return.

Selected Low-Risk Stocks

These stocks were ranked #1 (highest) for safety by *Value Line* in late 1996. Utility stocks, which also have high yields, are not included in this list.

ACM Gov't. Income Fund	Lilly (Eli)
Abbott Labs	Long's Drug Stores
Amer. Home Products	McDonald's Corp.
AT&T	McGraw-Hill
Anheuser-Busch	Merck & Co.
Boeing	Mobil Corp.
Bristol-Myers Squibb	New Plan Realty Trust
British Telecom	Procter & Gamble
Campbell Soup	Raytheon Co.
Chevron Corp.	Reader's Digest
Clorox Co.	Royal Dutch Petroleum
Coca-Cola	Schering-Plough
Deluxe Corp.	Shell Canada
1838 Bond Debenture	Texaco, Inc.
Emerson Electric	Toyota Motor (ADR)
Gannett Co.	Unilever
General Electric	Union Pacific
General Mills	Vulcan Materials
Hanson plc	Walgreen Co.
Heinz (H.J.)	Washington Post
Hershey Foods	Washington REIT
Imperial Oil	Weis Markets
Johnson & Johnson	Winn-Dixie Stores
	Wrigley (Wm.) Jr.

KNOWING THE LINGO

To help sort out the who, what, where, when, and how of making money in stocks, you'll need to be familiar with the following terms, used not only by financial wizards and pundits, but also by your broker, the business news person, and other media.

- *Blue-chip stocks* represent ownership in a major company that has a history of profitability and continual or increasing dividends with sufficient financial strength to withstand economic or industrial downturns.

  Examples: General Electric, Exxon, Du Pont, Procter & Gamble.
- *Growth stocks* represent ownership in a company that has had relatively rapid growth in the past (when compared with the economy as a whole) and is expected to continue in this vein. These companies tend to reinvest a large part of their earnings in order to finance their expansion and growth. Consequently, dividends are small in comparison with earnings.

  Examples: Cascade Corp., Tonka Corp., Brown & Co., Reader's Digest, and UST, Inc.
- *Cyclical stocks* are common stocks of companies whose earnings move with the economy or business cycles. They frequently have lower earnings when the country is in a slump and higher earnings when the economy is in a recovery phase.

  Examples of cyclical industries: aluminum, steel, automobiles, machinery, housing, paper, airlines, and travel and leisure.
- *Income stocks* have continually stable earnings and high dividend yields in comparison with other stocks. Income stocks generally retain only a small portion of earnings for expansion and growth, which they are able to do because there is a relatively stable market for their products.

Examples: public utility companies, international oil companies, closed-end bond funds, and REITs.

Now you're ready to start selecting stocks for your own personal portfolio, keeping the following key consideration in mind: *Every investment involves some degree of risk.* Stocks vary in their degree of risk, depending on the stability of their earnings or dividends and the way they are perceived in the marketplace.

☑ HINT: *The general rule is that return is correlated to risk: The greater the risk, the greater the expected return.*

HOW STOCKS WORK

When you buy shares in a company, you become part owner of that company, and you can make money in one of two ways: through dividends or through price appreciation when you sell your shares at a profit.

Dividends, a distribution of earnings, are generally declared when the company is comfortably profitable. The dollar amount is decided by the board of directors and is traditionally paid to shareholders quarterly.

A stock may *appreciate in price* for a variety of reasons, not all of which are completely rational:

■ The company is profitable.
■ It has an exciting new product.
■ It is part of an industry that is performing well.
■ It is the subject of takeover rumors or actual attempts.
■ Wall Street likes it.

If a corporation earns 15% on stockholders' equity (the money invested by shareholders), it ends the year with 15¢ per dollar more. After payment of a 5¢-per-share dividend, 10¢ is reinvested for future growth: research and development, new plants and equipment, new products and markets, etc. Thus the underlying value of the corporation doubles in about 7½ years. Eventually, these gains will be reflected in the price of the common stock. That's why the best investments are shares in companies that continue to make the most money!

As you might expect, it can fall in price for similar reasons and others: a poor earnings report, ineffective management, negative publicity, or even a mass dumping that feeds on itself, perhaps unrelated to the performance of the company.

It's All in the Timing

No where is this more true than with stocks. In general there are times when you should move out of the market and times when you should be in high-yielding fixed-income securities. Just think about the world around you: Industries change with the times, and so do common stocks. Utilities face regulatory problems; the electronics and computer field is full of new competition; the Koreans make cheaper steel; the Japanese and Germans give us a run for our money when it comes to cars. Woe to the investor who psychologically locks into a stock as though it were a CD. To make a profit, always be prepared to sell your stock when the time is right.

The single most common mistake of investors is *inertia*. The market constantly changes, and no one stock (or any other investment) is right for all seasons. Do not buy a stock, even a solid blue chip, and then never look at it again. While your back is turned the company could be taken over, enter bankruptcy, or just have a bad year. In each case, you should be ready to take some form of action—buy more shares, sell all your shares, or sell some of your shares.

One of the most difficult aspects of investing is timing—should you put money into stocks or mutual funds this week, next week, or months from now? There's a simple formula you can use to get around this age-old dilemma—dollar cost averaging. It involves investing the same amount of money in a stock or mutual fund at fixed inter-vals, monthly or quarterly, for instance. It may seem dull, but it requires some personal discipline in down markets when the temptation is not to invest.

COMMON STOCKS VS. BONDS

Stocks are *live* investments. The market value of a common stock grows as the corporation pros-pers, whereas the face value of bonds remains the same, so that over the years, their real value, in terms of purchasing power, decreases.

The prices of bonds are almost completely controlled by interest rates and change almost immediately when rates do. When the cost of money rises, bond values drop to maintain com-petitive returns; when interest rates decline, bond prices rise. Bonds, therefore, are traded by yields; stocks, by what investors believe to be future cor-porate prospects.

Stocks also offer the potential of increased dividends; a bond, however, has a set interest rate—your payout will remain the same as long as you own the bond.

☑ *HINT: The S&P 500, which tracks the stock price changes of 500 leading U.S. companies, rose 385% in the 15 years that ended December 31, 1993. With dividends reinvested, that increase actually more than doubled, to 795%.*

SEVEN STOCKS WITH YIELDS ABOVE 6%

STOCK	SYMBOL	YIELD
Alliance Cap Mgmt	AC	7.6%
Central & South West	CSR	6.4
Florida Progress	FPC	6.2
Health & Retirement	HRP	8.2
Kansas City P & L	KLT	6.5
Meditrust SBI	MT	8.0
Weingarten Realty	WRI	6.5

(As of Summer 1996)

Dividends Every Month in 1997

You can receive a dividend check every month of the year by purchasing a group of stocks with dif-ferent dividend-payment dates. The following is a list of issues broken down by payout dates. By pur-chasing stocks from each of the groups, you will have a portfolio of stocks producing dividend checks every month of the year.

JANUARY, APRIL, JULY, OCTOBER

Burlington Northern	Kimberly-Clark
CIGNA	McKesson
Dexter	Morgan (J.P.) & Co.
Dow Chemical	Northern States Power
Eastman Kodak	Ogden
General Electric	Philip Morris
Genuine Parts	Companies
Hanson plc	SCEcorp
Heinz (H.J.)	Thomas & Betts

FEBRUARY, MAY, AUGUST, NOVEMBER

American Tel. & Tel.	Lincoln National
BellSouth	Orange & Rockland
Betz Laboratories	Utilities
Bristol-Myers Squibb	Penney (J.C.) Co.
Brooklyn Union Gas	Procter & Gamble
Clorox	Rochester Telephone
Colgate-Palmolive	Southwestern Bell
Consolidated Natural	TECO Energy
Gas	WPL Holdings

MARCH, JUNE, SEPTEMBER, DECEMBER

American Brands	Kmart
American Home	Minnesota Mining &
Products	Mfg.
Amoco	Norfolk Southern
Atlantic Richfield	Potomac Electric Power
Chevron	South Jersey Industries
Du Pont (E.I.)	Southern Indiana Gas &
Dun & Bradstreet	Electric
Exxon	Tambrands
Indiana Energy	Times Mirror

SOURCE: Dow Theory Forecasts, 7412 Calumet Avenue, Hammond, IN 46324; 219–931–6480.

Four Stocks with Longest Record of Dividends	
Bank of Boston	1784
Fleet/Norstar Financial	1791
Midlantic	1805
First Maryland Bancorp	1806

SOURCE: Standard & Poor's Corp.

RISKS OF OWNING COMMON STOCK

There are, of course, risks associated with owner-ship of common stocks. The risks are far less with quality corporations and, to a large degree, can be controlled by setting strict rules for selling and by using common sense. As long as the company continues to make more money, its stock price is likely to rise, but this may take time, often longer than you are prepared to accept financially or mentally.

To reduce your risk with common stocks, fol-low these four guidelines:

1. Buy stocks with low betas: (see page 143 for a full explanation of how beta works)
2. Diversify by type of stock and industry
3. Spread out your risk over a number of stocks and industry groups
4. Be defensive by moving in and out of the market when appropriate.

You Should Also Understand Interest Rate Risk

Certain stocks are interest-sensitive, which means they are directly affected by changes in interest rates. These stocks include utilities, banks, finan-cial and brokerage companies, housing and con-struction, REITs, and closed-end bond funds. You can cut your risk in these stocks by moving to other investments when interest rates are high or on the way up.

The reason why these industries suffer during high-interest-rate seasons is because:

Companies with Sixteen Straight Quarters of Increased Profits	
Stock	**S&P Ranking**
Abbott Labs	A+
Automatic Data Proc	A+
Avery Dennison	B+
Bank of New York	B+
Coca-Cola	A+
Cracker Barrel	A
Green Tree Fin'l	A-
Int'l Dairy Queen	B+
Johnson & Johnson	A+
Meditrust	nr
Norwest Corp.	A
Oxford Health Plans	B-
Sealed Air	A-
SunAmerica Inc.	A-
Sysco Corp.	A+
Textron Inc.	A

1. Utility companies have to pay more on monies borrowed for expansion or upgrading of facilities.
2. Banks and finance companies are forced to pay more on money deposited in their insti-tutions as well as for money they borrow.
3. Building falls off because of higher interest rates.

EIGHT WAYS ANYONE CAN ANALYZE STOCKS LIKE THE PROS

Use these Wall Street analytic tools — they are the most reliable and proven ways to judge a stock:

■ EARNINGS PER SHARE. For the average investor, this figure distills the company's finan-cial picture into one simple number. Earnings per share is the company's net income (after taxes and preferred stock dividends) divided by the number of common shares outstanding. When a company is described as growing at a certain rate, the growth is then usually stated in terms of earnings per share.

9 Stocks for Long-Term Appreciation

COMPANY	S&P RATING	PRICE FALL 1996	P/E RATIO
Abbott Laboratories	A+	$46	19.3
CocaCola	A+	39	12.7
ConAgra	A+	43	16.2
Du Pont	B+	71	11.0
Emerson Electric	A+	85	18.8
Federal Home Loan	nr	90	13.3
Merck & Co.	A+	69	22.2
Microsoft	B+	125	30.5
Procter & Gamble	A	89	18.2

(As of October 1996)

Look for a company whose earnings per share have increased over the past 5 years; 1 down year is acceptable if the other 4 have been up. You will find earnings per share in Moody's, Value Line, Standard & Poor's, or the company's annual report.

Calculating Growth Rates

ANNUAL RATE OF EARNINGS INCREASE PER SHARE	JUSTIFIED P/E RATIOS			
	5 YEARS	7 YEARS	10 YEARS	15 YEARS
2%	15	15	13	12
4	17	17	16	16
5	18	18	18	18
6	19	19	20	21
8	21	22	24	28
10	23	25	28	35
12	25	28	33	48

Note that there should be only a small premium when a low growth rate remains static over the years. A 5% annual gain in EPS justifies the same P/E no matter how many years it has been attained. But when a company can maintain a high rate of earnings growth, 10% or more, the value of the stock is enhanced substantially.

SOURCE: Graham and Dodd, *Security Analysis,* 4th ed. (New York: McGraw-Hill, 1962).

■ PRICE-EARNINGS RATIO (P/E). This is one of the most common analytic tools of the trade and reflects investor enthusiasm about a stock in comparison with the market as a whole. Divide the current price of a stock by its earnings per share for the last 12 months: That's the P/E ratio, also sometimes called the multiple.

You will also find the P/E listed in the daily stock quotations of the newspaper. A P/E of 12, for example, means that the buying public is willing to pay 12 times earnings for the stock, whereas there is much less interest and confidence in a stock with a P/E of 4 or 5. A company's P/E is of course constantly changing and must be compared with its own previous P/Es and with the P/Es of others in its industry or category.

It is important to realize that the P/E listed in the paper is based on the last 12 months' earnings; however, Wall Street professionals refer to the earnings of the current year. So when considering a stock to buy or sell, remember to focus on its future, not its past.

Although brokers and analysts hold varying views on what constitutes the ideal P/E, a P/E under 10 is regarded as conservative. As

15 Stocks For $15

Analysts expect these stocks, selling for $15 per share or less as of fall 1996, to increase their earnings by at least 10%. None has a P/E ratio higher than 15.

 CAUTION: These stocks are more volatile than the market as a whole.

STOCK	SYMBOL
Advocat Inc.	AVC
Armco Inc.	AS
Buffets Inc.	BOCB
Cornerstone Imaging	CRNR
Electroglas Inc.	EGLS
Kellwood Co.	KWD
Mariner Health	MRNR
Mentor Graphics	MENT
Monro Muffler Brake	MNRO
NetManage Inc.	NETM
Property Capital	PCT
RehabCare Group	RHBC
Ryan's Family Steak Houses	RYAN
Sceptre Resources	SRL
Thera Tx Inc.	THTX

the P/E moves above 10, you start to pay a premium. If the P/E moves below 5 or 6, it tends to signal uncertainty about the company's prospects and balance sheet.

- BOOK VALUE. This figure, also known as stockholders' equity, is the difference between a company's assets and its liabilities, in other words, what the stockholders own after all debts are paid. That number is then divided by the number of shares outstanding to arrive at book value per share. The book value becomes especially important in takeover situations. If book value is understated—that is, if the assets of the company are worth substantially more than the financial statements say they are—you may have found a real bargain that the marketplace has not yet recognized. (This is often true with in-the-ground assets such as oil, minerals, gas, and timber.)

- RETURN ON EQUITY (ROE). This number measures how much the company earns on the stockholders' equity. It is a company's total net income expressed as a percentage of total book value and is especially useful when comparing several companies within one industry or when studying a given company's profitability trends. To calculate a simple ROE, divide earnings per share by book value. A return under 10% is usually considered poor.

- DIVIDEND. Check the current and projected dividend of a stock, especially if you are building an income portfolio. Study the payouts over the past 5 years as well as the current dividend. There are times when a corporation reinvests most of its earnings to ensure its future growth, in which case the dividend will be small. Typically, the greater the current yield, the less likelihood there is of stock price appreciation. However, it's best if a company earns $5 for every $4 it pays out.

- VOLATILITY. Some stocks go up and down in price like a yo-yo; others trade within a relatively narrow range. Those that dance about obviously carry a greater degree of risk than their more pedestrian cousins.

The measurement tool for price volatility, called *beta*, tells how much a stock tends to move in relation to changes in the Standard & Poor's 500 Stock Index. The index is fixed at 1.00, so a stock with a beta of 1.5 moves up and down 1½ times as much as the Standard & Poor's index, whereas a stock with a beta of 0.5 is less volatile than the index. To put it another way, a stock with a 1.5 beta is expected to rise in price by 15% if the Standard & Poor's index rises 10%, or fall by 15% if the index falls by 10%. You will find the beta for stocks given by the investment services as well as by good stockbrokers.

■ TOTAL RETURN. Most investors in stocks tend to think about their gains and losses in terms of price changes, not dividends, whereas those who own bonds pay attention to interest yields and seldom focus on price changes. *Both approaches are mistakes.* Although dividend yields are obviously more important if you are seeking income, and changes in price play a greater role in growth stocks, the total return on a stock is extremely important. It makes it possible for you to compare your investment in stocks with a similar investment in corporate bonds, municipals, Treasuries, mutual funds, and unit investment trusts.

☑ *HINT: To calculate the total return, add (or subtract) the stock's price change and dividends for 12 months and then divide by the price at the beginning of the 12-month period. For example, suppose you buy a stock at $42 a share and receive $2.50 in dividends for the next 12-month period. At the end of the period, you sell the stock at $45.00. The total return is 13%.*

Dividend	*$2.50*
Price appreciation	*+ 3.00*
	$5.50 ÷ $42 = 13%

■ NUMBER OF SHARES OUTSTANDING. If you are a beginning investor or working with a small portfolio, look for companies with at least 5 million shares outstanding. You will then be ensured of both marketability and liquidity, because the major mutual funds, institutions, and the public will be trading in these stocks. You are unlikely to have trouble buying or selling when you want to. In a smaller company, your exposure to sharp price fluctuations is greater.

PROVEN WAYS TO FIND WINNERS

In addition to the eight analytical tools just described, you can boost your ability to build a winning portfolio by using these guidelines:

■ CONTINUITY. For investors who place safety first, the best common stocks are those of companies that have paid dividends for 20 years or more. Many have familiar names: Abbott Labs, Bristol-Myers, H.J. Heinz, Olin Corp., Wells Fargo, and Woolworth.

Always check a company's annual report to see if (1) the dividends have increased fairly consistently as the result of higher earnings and (2) the company has been profitable in recent years and appears likely to remain so in the near future. It's great to do business with an old store, but only if the merchandise is up-to-date and priced fairly.

■ INSTITUTIONAL OWNERSHIP. Pick stocks chosen by the experts—managers of mutual funds, pension plans, insurance portfolios, endowments, etc. With few exceptions, these are shares of major corporations listed on the New York Stock Exchange.

Institutional ownership is no guarantee of quality, but it does indicate that some professionals have reviewed the financial prospects and for some reason (not always clear) have recommended purchase or retention. Without such interest, stocks are slow to move up in price.

In most cases, these companies must meet strict standards of financial strength, investment acceptance, profitability, growth, and, to some extent, income. But institutions still buy name and fame and either move in after the rush has started or hold on after the selling has started.

Institutions are not always smart money managers, but since they account for nearly three-fourths of all NYSE transactions (and a high percentage of those on the AMEX and OTC), it's wise to check their portfolios when you consider a new commitment.

☑ *HINT: Every investment portfolio should contain at least three stocks whose shares are owned by at least 250 institutions.*

- MOST PROFITABLE COMPANIES. You obviously want to own shares in a profitable company. Profitability can be determined by calculating the rate of return on shareholders' equity, a minimum annual average of 11%. By sticking to these real winners, you will always make a lot of money—in time.

  A list of companies that are expected to achieve high total returns because of higher profits and current undervaluation appears on page 143.

- INDUSTRY LEADERS. Companies that capture the business within their industry are creative and well managed.

- STOCK SPLITS. With many stocks at or near new highs, stock splits are on the rise. (The record was 225 in 1983.) In a purely technical way, a stock split provides no advantage to shareholders, but the history of the market shows that more often than not a stock will rise in price at about the time the directors vote a split. And, often an increase in the cash dividend accompanies a split. A stock split calls the public's attention to the company, to its earnings progress, and this often results in increased buying and eventually a higher price for the company's shares. And, with the new reduced price per share, small investors are attracted to the stock.

Stocks with P/Es Below Five-Year Earnings Growth Rates

COMPANY	P/E RATIO
Aaron Rents (Cl B)	13.9
Chaparral Steel	11.5
Crestar Financial	10.2
Helix Technology	11.0
Lam Research	8.3
Nouvellus Systems	9.2
Texas Industries	9.3

SOURCE: Standard & Poor's *The Outlook,* Spring 1996.

To find stock split candidates, look for a sharply higher market price, a history of stock splits, or large stock dividends.

☑ HINT: Standard & Poor's **The Outlook** *generally publishes a list of stock-split candidates once or twice a year.*

Guidelines for Selecting Growth Stocks

- *Read the annual report backward.* Look at the footnotes to discover whether there are significant problems, unfavorable long-term commitments, lawsuits, etc.
- *Analyze the management's record* in terms of growth of revenue and earnings and, especially, return on stockholders' equity.
- *Find a current ratio of assets to liabilities of 2:1 or higher.* This indicates that the company can withstand difficulties and will probably be able to obtain money to expand.
- *Look for a low debt ratio with long-term debt no more than 35% of total capital.* This means that the company has staying power and the ability to resist cyclical downturns.
- *Compare a stock's price-earnings ratio* to those of other companies in the same industry. If their ratios are higher, this may be a sleeper. If the P/E multiple is above 20, be wary. Such stocks tend to be volatile.
- *Look for stocks with strong management,* little debt, and a return on investment high enough to generate internal growth.
- *Concentrate on companies whose earnings growth rate has been at least 15%* annually for the past 5 years and can be projected to be not much less for the next 2 years.

Keep in mind that (1) you are buying the future of the company, (2) increasing revenues are not enough (the real test is increasing profits), and (3) the stock market is built on hype, and that's easy with new companies that do not have a long, successful record.

Established Companies

The corporation does not have to be young to have growth potential. There are opportunities with old companies where there's new management, a turnaround situation, or R&D-based developments. These developments are indicators of growth:

- *Strong position in an evolutionary market.* Find an industry or market that is bound to move ahead and check the top half-dozen corporations. The leaders are probably the best bets, but do not overlook the secondary companies. They may provide a greater percentage gain on your investment.

- *Ability to set prices at profitable levels.* This is important in service industries where greater volume can bring proportionately higher profits as overhead remains relatively stable. The same approach applies to companies making or distributing branded merchandise.
- *Adequate funds for R&D.* With few exceptions, future growth of any corporation is dependent on finding new and better products, more efficient methods of doing business, etc. Look for a company that is building for that sort of future.
- *Control of a market.* For example, General Electric is in a dominant position, not because of price but because of its ability to engineer new computers and office equipment and to provide good, continuing service at reasonable cost to the customer.
- *Strong technology base.* This is a valuable, but not essential, asset. Growth companies usually start with expertise in specific areas and then move out into other products and markets.
- *Growing customer demand.* This means a total market that is growing faster than the GNP. In the early years of new items, almost any company can prosper, because the demand is greater than the supply. Later, when production has caught up, the strong, better-managed firms will survive and expand their positions.
- *Safety is always important,* but with common stocks, the foremost consideration should be profitable growth: in assets, revenues, and earnings.
- *Improving profit margins.* This is an excellent test, because wider PMs almost always indicate increased earnings per share within a short period of time.

The gross profit margin (sometimes called the operating profit margin) shows a company's operating income, before taxes, as a percentage of revenues. It is listed in many annual reports and most statistical analyses. It can be calculated by dividing the operating income (total revenues less operating expenses) by the net sales. Generally, a gross PM of 12% indicates a company that deserves further study. Anything below that, especially when it is lower than the previous year, is a danger signal.

The gross profit margin is useful in comparing companies within a given industry. However, because it varies widely among industries, avoid interindustry comparisons. For example, supermarket stores have lower gross PMs than many others.

- *Plowed-back earnings.* The fastest-growing companies will almost always be the stingiest dividend payers. By reinvesting a substantial portion of its profits, preferably 70% or more, a company can speed expansion and improve productive efficiency. Any corporation that plows back 12% of its invested capital each year will double its real worth in 6 years.

- *Strong research and development.* The aim of research is knowledge; the aim of development is new or improved products and processes. A company that uses reinvested earnings largely for new plants and equipment will improve its efficiency and the quality of its products, but it may not grow as fast in the long run as a company that spends wisely to develop new and better products.

A prime test for aggressive growth management is whether the company is spending a higher than average percentage of its revenues for research and new process and product development. With good management, dollars spent for R&D constitute the most creative, dynamic force for growth available for any corporation. It is not unusual for the thousands of dollars used for research to make possible millions of dollars in additional sales and profits.

What Stocks to Avoid

To spot the nonachievers among companies in a growth industry, look for these two danger signals:

- *Substantial stock dilution.* This means that a company repeatedly and exclusively raises funds through the sale of additional common stock, either directly or through convertibles. There's no harm in small dilution, especially when there are prospects that the growth of earnings will continue. But beware of any company with heavy future obligations. Too much dilution merely enlarges the size of the company for the benefit of management and leaves stockholders with diluted earnings.

- *Vast overvaluation as shown by price-earnings ratios of 30 or higher.* This is a steep price to pay for potential growth. Take your profits, or at least set stop-loss prices. When any stock sells at a multiple that is double that of the overall market (usually around 14.56), be cautious.

Finding Bargains

Benjamin Graham, the grandfather of security analysis in his book by the same title, looks for bargains in stocks, which he defines as the time when they trade at:

- A multiple of no more than twice that of the prevailing interest rate: that is, a P/E ratio of 16 versus an interest rate of 8%
- A discount of 20% or more from book value
- A point where current assets exceed current liabilities and long-term debt combined
- A P/E ratio of 40% less than that of the S&P index P/E. For some examples of stocks with low P/Es as of Spring 1996, see box on page 145.

How to Determine a High Compound Growth Rate

Despite some temporary setbacks, American business continues to make more money and to pay out higher dividends.

In selecting stocks, check the growth of earnings and dividends. Select companies that have posted rising earnings and dividends, not for just a year or two, but fairly consistently over a 5-year period.

Look for a high compound growth rate: at least 15% to 20% annually. Compounding means that every year earnings are 20% higher than in the prior year. The table below shows a theoretical example of earnings growth of 20% compounded annually.

Example: To find earnings growth for any one year, subtract the earnings per share of the prior year from the earnings per share of the year in question. Then divide the difference by the base year (i.e., the prior year) earnings.

For example, a company earned $1.20 per share this year and, in the prior year, it earned $1.00 per share.

$1.20
−1.00
0.20 ÷ $1.00 = 20% growth rate

In the next year, in order to maintain a 20% growth rate, it would have to report an increase of 20% of $1.20, or $1.20 × 0.20% = 24¢. Therefore, earnings expectations are $1.44 per share in the third year ($1.20 + 24¢ = $1.44).

HOW TO DETERMINE A COMPANY'S EARNED GROWTH RATE

A fundamental measure of corporate growth and profitability is the *earned growth rate* (EGR). It measures the ability of management to make the money entrusted to them by stockholders grow over the years. You can use the same technique.

Earnings Growth Rate

Year 1	$1.00 × 20% = 0.20 = $1.20
Year 2	$1.20 × 20% = 0.24 = $1.44
Year 3	$1.44 × 20% = 0.29 = $1.73
Year 4	$1.73 × 20% = 0.35 = $2.08

What Are Earnings Worth?

ANNUAL GROWTH RATE	WHAT $1.00 EARNINGS WILL BECOME IN 3 YEARS AT GIVEN GROWTH RATE	THE P/E RATIO YOU CAN PAY TODAY TO MAKE 10% ANNUAL CAPITAL GAIN AND EXPECT P/E RATIO IN IN 3 YEARS TO BE	
		15x	30x
4%	$1.12	12.6	25.3
5	1.16	13.1	26.2
6	1.19	13.4	26.8
7	1.23	13.9	27.7
8	1.26	14.2	28.4
9	1.30	14.7	29.3
10	1.33	15.0	30.0
12	1.40	15.8	31.6
15	1.52	17.1	34.3
20	1.73	19.5	39.0
25	1.95	22.0	44.0

SOURCE: Knowlton and Furth, *Shaking the Money Tree* (New York: Harper & Row, 1979).

EARNED GROWTH RATE. The EGR is the annual rate at which the company's equity capital per common share is increased by net earnings after payment of the dividend—if any. *It is a reliable measure of investment growth because it shows the growth of the capital invested in the business.*

EGR = $E – DE$ = earnings
BVD = dividend
BV = book value

The book value is the net value of total corporate assets, that is, what is left over when all liabilities, including bonds and preferred stock, are subtracted from the total assets (plant, equipment, cash, inventories, accounts receivable, etc.). It is sometimes called stockholders' equity and can be found in every annual report. Many corporations show the book value over a period of years in their summary tables. A good growth company will increase its equity capital at a rate of at least 6% per year.

A Dozen Stocks with Consistent Earnings

Abbott Laboratories	International Dairy
Bristol-Meyers	Queen
Cisco Systems	Johnson & Johnson
DuPont	Microsoft Corp.
Exxon Corp.	Mobile Corp.
General Motors	Schering-Plough
	Squibb

(As of October 1996)

To determine the EGR for a company, take the per-share earnings, say $5.73, and subtract the $3.34 dividend to get $2.39. Then divide this by the book value at the *beginning of the year*. Let's say it was $17.42. Thus, the EGR for that year was 13.7%:

$$EGR = \frac{5.73 - 3.34}{17.42} = \frac{2.39}{17.42} = 13.7\%$$

GUIDELINES FOR SELECTING THE BEST INCOME STOCKS

Dividend-paying stocks are not just for retirees and ultraconservative investors. They are important to everyone because they both boost the value of a stock and generally indicate that the company is a mature one, no longer in the throes of expensive expansion. A company that can afford to pay high dividends is no longer reinvesting all its profits in the company.

Another reason why high-dividend stocks are looked upon with such favor is that the dividend is likely to increase if the company's earnings grow—unlike a bond, whose coupon rate remains the same throughout its life.

✓ *HINT: Dividend-paying stocks fall less in price when the market falls. A study by Avner Arbel, professor of finance at Cornell University, shows that high-dividend stocks fell only 21% in the 1987 crash while nondividend payers dropped 32%.*

10 Stocks with High Dividends

Stocks with comparatively high dividends give income plus some protection against a falling stock market. But remember, the higher the yield, the higher the risk. This list does not include utility stocks, which traditionally have high yields.

COMPANY	PRICE	OCTOBER 1996 YIELD
Alliance Capital Management	$26	7.7
ACM Government Income Fund	10	9.8
Pennsylvania REIT	24	8.1
BRE Properties	33	8.0
Bankers Trust NY	83	4.0
Weingarten Realty	38	6.5
New Plan Realty	22	6.5
Meditrust	35	7.9
Royce	12	10.3

(As of October 1996)

To determine if a company is likely to continue making dividend payouts:

■ Check the dividend-payout history for the past 10 years in *Standard & Poor's Stock Guide* or *Value Line Investment Survey.* Those with uninterrupted payouts are your best bet.
■ Check the company's payout ratio: total dividends paid divided by net operating income. If the payout ratio is less than 50%, the company will probably continue to pay dividends.
■ Check the company's cash flow per share. If cash flow is three times the dividend payout, dividends will probably continue to be paid.
■ Avoid or invest very carefully in stocks that have extraordinarily high yields for the industry group. Extremely high yields can signal trouble.
■ Don't buy a high-yield stock near the ex-dividend date. That is the beginning of the time period during which purchasers of the stock cannot receive the next quarterly dividend, generally paid 3 to 4 weeks later. Usually stock

prices are inflated just before the ex-dividend date, and on that date they tend to fall. If you buy the stock at an inflated price in order to receive the dividend, you may not break even because you'll be paying tax on the dividend income.

✓ *HINT: Sign up for a company's dividend reinvestment plan so your dividends will automatically be reinvested in additional shares of stock. Most companies do not charge a brokerage fee for these purchases, and some companies offer a 5% discount off market price for shares purchased through dividend reinvestment. Approximately 1,000 companies have dividend reinvestment plans.*

✓ *HINT: Call the investor relations division of any company you own shares in to see if it has a dividend reinvestment plan, or obtain the book: Directory of Dividend Reinvestment Plans ($39.95) from:*
Standard & Poor's Corp.
Direct Marketing
25 Broadway
New York, NY 10004
800–221–5277
This annually updated guide lists 700+ companies that offer such programs, telephone numbers, S&P rankings, and other details.

CYCLICAL STOCKS

The performance of cyclical stocks, as their name implies, is closely tied to the economic and consumer cycles. As economic activity picks up, these stocks should have earnings gains. Many have cleaned up their balance sheets, reduced serious debt, and increased marketing efforts. Nevertheless, pick cyclicals carefully—they usually make large price moves within relatively short time periods. In fact, there is no guarantee that the cyclicals will perform as well as Wall Street analysts say they will. Before investing in any cyclical stock, check

Six Top Cyclical Stocks for 1997

Catepillar
Deere & Co.
Dover
Ford Motor Co.
Genuine Parts
Sherwin-Williams Co.
Home Depot
May Department Stores
Whirlpool
Sigma-Aldrich Chemicals

to see that: (1) the nation's GNP is increasing, (2) unemployment has eased, and (3) auto and retail sales are starting to rise.

The key cyclical industry groups are: aluminum, autos, building and home-building materials, chemicals, diversified machinery, household furnishings and appliances, machine tools, steel, airlines, newspapers, restaurants, oil, and railroads.

Cyclical stocks that could conceivably perform well in 1997–1998:

- Southwest Airlines
- Citicorp
- Squibb
- Phelps Dodge
- Chevron
- Exxon
- Burlington Northern
- Norfolk Southern
- SBC Communications
- Penney

TWO WINNING TECHNIQUES FOR SMALL INVESTORS

Dollar Cost Averaging

One of the most difficult aspects of investing is timing—should you put money into stocks or mutual funds, this week, next week, or months from now? There's a simple formula to get around this age-old dilemma—dollar cost averaging.

It involves investing the same amount of money in a stock or mutual fund at fixed intervals, monthly or quarterly, for instance. It may seem dull, but it actually requires personal discipline in down markets when the overwhelming temptation is NOT to invest.

Basically, what it does is force you to buy more of a stock or fund when its price is low and less when it is high. Over the long haul, your average cost will be lower than the average price of the security.

CAUTION: Although this is a fine technique, it will not turn a poor investment choice into a winner. If a stock keeps falling in price forever, you wind up buying more losses. To avoid this, select stocks and funds that have a record of long-term upward trends.

Most mutual funds require an initial investment of $1,000 or more, but subsequent investments may be as little as $100. You may be able to dollar cost average with a fund that automatically transfers a preset amount from your bank checking account into the fund's portfolio.

Dividend Reinvestment

You can also dollar cost average with individual stocks. And if the shares are in your name (rather than held by your broker in street name), you may be able to participate in a dividend reinvestment plan. Over 750 companies have such plans in which your dividends are automatically reinvested in additional shares of stock rather than paying you the cash. Many of these companies also allow shareholders to make additional cash investments. This means you can dollar cost average without using a broker.

WHEN TO SELL A STOCK

Financial whiz kids and Wall Street gurus are always weaving complex theories about when to

Stocks with Dividend Reinvestment Plans that Permit Cash Investments

STOCK	MINIMUM/MAXIMUM CASH PURCHASE
AT&T	$100/$50,000 annually
American Brands	$100/$10,000 quarterly
Block (H&R)	$25/$2,000 monthly
Bristol-Myers Squibb	$105/$10,025 monthly
Browning-Ferris	$25/$60,000 annually
Exxon	$50/$100,000 annually
First Alabama Bancshares	$20/$10,000 monthly
Houston Industries	$50/$120,000 annually
PepsiCo	$10/$60,000 annually
Walgreen	$10/$5,000 quarterly

buy a stock. That's the easy part. They shy away from explaining when to sell, which is a much trickier business.

Although there's no foolproof system for making certain you always buy low and sell high, you can make an educated decision.

The first basic rule to follow in mastering the art of selling is to know precisely whether you bought the stock for growth or income.

1. *Growth.* If you purchased the stock for growth and price appreciation, hold it as long as the company's earnings keep rising at a steady pace. If profits slow down, find out why. Sell unless you discover a truly viable reason why profits will increase within the year.

2. *Income.* Keep the stock as long as the company is financially solid and its earnings per share exceed the dividend by at least 10% and they (i.e., earnings) are rising more than 5% a year. If earnings stagnate for several quarters, or if an independent rating agency (Standard & Poor's or Moody's) downgrades the firm's creditworthiness, seriously consider selling.

Other guidelines that work:

- You should consider selling when you think the market is headed for a serious setback. But, of course, not all stocks react to a declining market to the same degree. So, to judge how much an individual stock fluctuates against broad market drops, check its beta in *Value Line Investment Survey*. The higher the beta, the more it moves and the faster you should sell (*see following list*).
- You should also consider selling if you think the company is in serious trouble and its earnings prospects are poor and not likely to recover quickly.
- If your stock suddenly drops in price by 20% or more within a short period—a month or less—you need to find out why and then consider selling.
- If your stock has become overvalued—you can tell if its P/E suddenly moves up and is way above the average P/E of the S&P 500. Find out if it's soared because of good news,

---

Consider Increasing or Decreasing Your Position in an Individual Stock When. . .

- The price changes substantially.
- New management takes over.
- Earnings increases or decreases are announced.
- A new product comes on line.
- A merger or acquisition takes place.
- The company is listed on or unlisted from one of the exchanges.
- Substantial legal action is brought against the company.
- Dividends are increased, cut, or canceled.
- The P/E multiple changes dramatically.
- The stock is purchased or sold by the institutions.
- The company spins off unprofitable divisions or subsidiaries.

---

in which case hold, or because it's out of line, in which case sell and take your profit.

Four Indicators That It's Time to Sell

These four indicators, all reported in the *Wall Street Journal* as well as most major newspapers, should be your signposts for selling.

1. *Stock prices are inflated.* This is indicated by a high P/E ratio for the S&P 500. In August 1987, just before the crash, it hit 23. Check the ratio regularly. In August 1996, it was around 14.
2. *There's a rise in interest rates.* Escalating interest rates hurt stocks as money moves to CDs and bonds. Watch the 3-month T-bill rate and the Federal Reserve discount rate. The market tends to fall when the Fed has raised the discount rate three or four consecutive times. It also falls if the T-bill rate is double the S&P 500 dividend yield. In October 1996, the 6 month T-bill rate was 5.13% and the dividend yield on the S&P 500 was 2.10%.
3. *A recession is in the wings.* The market tends to decline 6 to 9 months before an economic slump. Watch the Department of Commerce's leading economic indicators, which are reported monthly. If they are down for 3 consecutive months, the market may soon follow.
4. *The market breadth is narrowing.* Often a group of stocks pushes the Dow Jones Industrial Average (or some other indicator) higher even though most other stocks are declining. This is called a narrowing of the market's breadth. You can spot this trend by following the advance/decline line that is reported in *Barron's*. It reflects the difference between the number of stocks that gain and lose each day. In August 1987 the market was moving up but the advance/decline line was moving down. In fact, the Dow reached a high of 2722 during that period.

FOUR SMART WAYS TO KEEP YOUR PROFITS

Of course the most obvious way to keep your gains is simply to sell your investment when you've made a profit. This approach has several drawbacks—you have to pay taxes on the gain, and if the market goes up you won't benefit. Here are four ways to protect your position on the downside and profit on the upswings.

■ *Enter stop orders.* Have your broker sell your stock if it drops to a particular price. This protects you against major declines.

■ *Sell into strength.* Each time the market makes a major move on the up side, sell a portion of your holdings. For example, if you own 500 shares of Xerox and you have big gains, sell 100 shares each time it appreciates 10%. You reduce your risk, and at the same time you're selling your stock at higher prices.

■ *Buy put options.* This gives you the right to sell 100 shares of a stock at a particular price within a certain time period, up to 9 months. These options set a selling floor. For example, if you own a $50 stock, you buy a put allowing you to sell 100 shares for $45 at any time within the next 6 months. The put costs about 75¢ per share and it limits your loss to $5 per share.

■ *Switch to convertibles.* Move out of common stock into convertibles to lower your risk and still profit from a rise in the market. Buy stocks for the long term.

PREFERRED STOCK

Individual investors usually gravitate toward preferred stocks because of their high, secure dividends. Many are issued by utilities.

As their name implies, preferred stocks enjoy preferred status over common stocks. Preferred shareholders receive their dividend payments after all bondholders are paid and before dividends are paid on common shares. Like bonds, preferreds have a fixed annual payment, but it's called a dividend. It is set at a fixed dollar amount and is secure for the life of the stock. If a payment is skipped because of corporate losses, it will be paid later when earnings recover. That's why preferreds are sometimes called *cumulative*, because the dividends accumulate and must be paid out before common. Most preferreds are cumulative and are indicated by the initials cm in the stock guides.

There are also *noncumulative preferreds:* If a dividend is skipped, it is not recovered. It's best to avoid this type of preferred.

■ PROS. Although there have been a few incidents of corporations skipping preferred divi-

Selected Preferred Stocks

COMPANY	DIVIDEND	PRICE	YIELD
Alabama Power "A"	$1.90	$25	7.6%
Bank of Boston	2.15	26	8.3
Du Pont (E.I.) "B"	4.50	63	7.2
Georgia Power "P"	1.90	25	7.7
Niagara Mohawk Power "K"	2.04	25	8.2
Pennsylvania Power "A"	4.40	56	7.9
So. Calif Edison "P"	1.84	23	7.9

SOURCE: Quotron as of Fall 1996.

dends, on the whole these securities have an excellent safety record. And if the yield is high, it remains permanently high.

■ CONS. Inflation and high interest rates can have a large negative impact on preferreds. That's because the dividend is fixed, and when rates rise, holders are locked in at the old lower rate. Not only are they shut out of rising interest rates, but the opportunity for substantial price appreciation of their shares is limited.

Although preferreds trade like bonds on the basis of their yields, unlike bonds they have no maturity date. With a bond you know that at a specified time you will get back your initial investment, the face value. There is no such assurance with a preferred. Market conditions are the sole determinant of the price you will receive when you sell.

Selecting Preferreds

The basic criteria for selecting preferreds are *quality* of the issuing corporation, as shown by financial strength and profitability; *value*, as indicated

---

> ### Preferred Stock
>
> **PROS**
> ↑ Generally pays higher dividends than common
> ↑ Receive your dividend before common stockholders
> ↑ Dividends generally cumulative; if dividend skipped, made up in future
> ↑ Know what your dividend income is
> ↑ Possibility of capital gain in price of stock
>
> **CONS**
> ↓ If company's earnings rise, you don't share in increases unless it is a participating preferred
> ↓ Dividend fixed, with few exceptions
> ↓ Call provisions allow company to redeem your stock at stated price
> ↓ No protection against inflation

---

by the yield; and *timing*, taking into account the probable trend of interest rates. Then:

■ *Deal with a brokerage firm that has a research department that follows this group of securities.* Not every broker is familiar with preferreds, and many will not be able to provide enough pertinent information.

■ *Recognize the inherent volatility because of limited marketability.* Preferreds listed on a major stock exchange may drop (when you want to sell) or rise (when you plan to buy) 2 or 3 points the day after the last quoted sale. If you have to sell in a hurry, this can be expensive. Preferreds sold over-the-counter (OTC) may fluctuate even more because of their thin markets. As a rule, place your orders at a set price or within narrow limits.

☑ HINT: *Ask your broker about* **adjustable-rate preferreds.** *The quarterly dividend fluctuates with interest rates and is tied to a formula based on Treasury bills or other money market rates.*

☑ HINT: **Participating preferreds** *entitle shareholders to a portion of the company's profits. In* **nonparticipating preferreds,** *shareholders are limited to the stipulated dividend.*

Quality

Choose preferred stocks rated BBB or higher by Standard & Poor's or Baa or higher by Moody's if you are conservative. But if you are willing to take greater risks, you can boost your income by buying BB-rated preferreds, such as Philadelphia Electric 7.80% cm pfd selling at $89 with a yield of 9.2%.

Usually, but not always, the higher rating will be given to companies with modest debt. Since bond interest must be paid before dividends, the lower the debt ratio, the safer the preferred stock. For example, look for utilities with balanced debt and then check the preferred stocks. Buy several different preferreds so you can benefit from diversification.

Call Provision

This provision allows the company to redeem or call in the shares of a preferred, usually at a few points above par (face value). When the original issue carries a high yield, say over 10%, the company may find it worthwhile to retire some shares (1) when it can float new debt or issue preferred stock at a lower rate, say, 8% or (2) when corporate surplus becomes substantial. In both cases, such a prospect may boost the price of the preferred by a point or two.

CAUTION: Preferred stock, especially of small, struggling corporations, often has special call or conversion provisions. And utilities sometimes take advantage of obscure provisions in their charters to use other assets to call in their preferreds. You may end up with a modest profit, but if the redemption price is less than that at which the stock was selling earlier, you will lose money. Always check a preferred's call features.

Sinking Fund

Corporations use sinking funds to accumulate money on a regular basis in order to redeem the corporation's bonds or preferred stocks from time to time so that the entire issue is retired before the stated maturity date. For example, starting 5 years after the original sale, a company might buy back 5% of the stock annually for 20 years. The yields of such preferreds will usually be slightly less than those for which there is no such provision.

IF YOU DARE: Look for a company that has omitted dividend payouts for several years. It will probably be selling at a discount. Should earnings recover, it will pay off all accumulated dividends, and the price of the stock is likely to rise.

HINT: Buy participating preferreds to ensure receiving a percentage of any exceptional profit gain, as for example, if the corporation sells a subsidiary and has excess profits for the year.

Continual Dividends

Sharp investors may get as many as 12 dividends a year by rolling over preferred stocks. By buying shares just before the dividend date, they get the full payout. They sell the next day and buy another preferred with an upcoming dividend payment date. Because of the commission costs and need for constant checking, this technique is difficult for amateurs. Yet it can work well when it involves 500 shares or more and you work with a discount broker.

Timing is the key. After the payout date, the price of the preferred may drop almost as much as the value of the dividend. A 12% preferred thus might trade at $100 before the dividend date and drop back to just over $97 the next day. If you sell, you take a small loss. If you wait a week or so and are lucky in a strong market, you may be able to sell at 100. If you have the time, money, and a feel for this type of trading, you could make substantial profits.

HINT: You can also purchase preferreds through the Lindner Dividend Fund (314–727–5305), which is about 50% invested in preferreds. Its largest holdings are in utilities. This no-load fund has a 5-year annualized return of about 15%.

Getting Current Info on Stocks

Call Standard & Poor's Research Reports ($9.95; 800–642–2858) or Schwab's Investment Reports Service (800–752–9295) to get five or more pages on each of about 4,000 publicly traded companies. Reports tell you how many analysts like the company and how many don't, plus earnings estimates, news about the company, future outlook for the industry, along with Standard & Poor's grade, ranging from one star (sell) to five stars (strong buy).

FOR FURTHER INFORMATION

General Guides

Louis Engel and Brendon Boyd, *How to Buy Stocks* (Boston: Little, Brown & Co., 1982).

Lawrence J. Gitman and Michael D. Joehnk, *Fundamentals of Investing* (New York: HarperCollins, 1990).

Benjamin Graham and David L. Dodd, *Security Analysis*, 5th ed. (New York: McGraw-Hill, 1988)(updated by S. Cotile).

Thomas O'Hara, *Taking Control of Your Financial Future: Making Smart Investment Decisions with Stocks and Bonds* (Homewood, IL: Dow Jones–Irwin, 1995).

Richard J. Teweles and Edward S. Bradley, *The Stock Market* (New York: John Wiley & Sons, 1992).

Andrew Tobias, *The Only Investment Guide You'll Ever Need* (New York: Bantam, 1995).

Philip B. Capelle, *Investing in Growth* (Chicago: Probus Publishing Co., 1992).

Michael B. Lehman, *The Dow Jones–Irwin Guide to Using the Wall Street Journal* (Homewood, IL: Dow Jones–Irwin, 1990).

Dividend Reinvestment Guides

Directory of Companies Offering Dividend Reinvestment Plans (Laurel, MD: Evergreen Enterprises, Box 763, Laurel, MD 20725; $32.45; 301–549–3939).

Charles Carlson, editor, *The Drip Investor* (newsletter)
Monthly; $79/year
NorthStar Financial, Inc.
7412 Calumet Avenue
Hammond, IN 46324
212–931–6480

14

Nasdaq and Over-the-Counter Stocks

A good investment is not always an obvious one, dancing in the limelight of the New York or American stock exchanges. Even the venerable Benjamin Graham, father of security analysis, subscribed to this belief. He advised investors to consider making one out of three securities in their portfolios a stock trading elsewhere—in the Nasdaq market, over-the-counter, or on regional exchanges. And he was right. Nasdaq, which stands for National Association of Securities Dealers Automated Quotations, is the fastest-growing stock market in the United States. Stocks that trade on Nasdaq are listed separately in the financial pages under the heading Nasdaq National Market Issues.

THE NASDAQ STOCK MARKET

Nasdaq is operated by the Nasdaq Stock Market, Inc., a wholly owned subsidiary of the National Association of Securities Dealers, Inc. This non-profit association, known as NASD, was created in 1939 by amendments to the Securities Exchange Act of 1934. This market is distinctly separate from the over-the-counter (OTC) market, described below, although both are regulated by the NASD.

Uunlike the New York and American stock exchanges, Nasdaq does not have a centralized trading floor. Instead it is an electronic market, and in fact was the world's first electronic stock market when it was created in 1971. Today, with

millions of investors around the world, Nasdaq has more companies listed than any other market—some 4,500. Of these, many are leaders in the fields of computers, data processing, biotechnology, and financial services.

Interestingly, many of the large companies that trade on Nasdaq (see box on page 158) meet the more stringent financial requirements for listing on the New York State Exchange. Yet they have chosen Nasdaq, largely because of its competitive market-maker system—a system of multiple trading by many dealers rather than the centralized approach of the New York Stock Exchange, where all trading in a stock must go through the exchange specialist in that stock.

Another important role Nasdaq plays is that of listing many new public companies. Consistently, many of the fastest growing companies in the United States are listed on Nasdaq.

Nasdaq lists more:

- Companies than any other U.S. stock market
- Foreign-based issues than the New York and American stock exchanges combined
- Initial public offerings (IPOs) than any other U.S. stock market

How Nasdaq Differs

There are two ways in which Nasdaq differs from the traditional stock exchanges: (1) its use of competing market makers; and (2) its advanced technology.

Each company that lists its shares on Nasdaq has several competing securities firms that make the market in its stock. In fact, a minimum of two market makers is required for a company to be listed on Nasdaq. There are some 490 of these multiple dealers, including such firms as Merrill Lynch, Morgan Stanley, Goldman Sachs, PaineWebber, etc., all aggressively competing with one another for investor orders by buying and selling for their own accounts. The typical Nasdaq stock has 11 market makers, although some of the most popular stocks have 40 or more.

These market makers are required to quote a firm bid and ask price. (The bid is the price at which a market maker is willing to buy; the ask is the price at which he/she is willing to sell.)

These trades take place over Nasdaq's electronic network of terminals or screen-based workstations. If, for example, you place an order with your broker to buy 100 shares of Biogen, your broker will route that order to the firm's trading room. If your brokerage firm makes a market in Biogen, it will execute the order internally at a price equal to or better than the best price being quoted in Nasdaq by all of the competing market makers.

If your firm is not a maker in Biogen, it will buy shares from a market maker at another firm. (A market maker is to Nasdaq what a specialist is on the exchanges; a specialist is a member of a stock exchange who maintains a fair and orderly market in one or more securities.)

Your trade and all other Nasdaq trades can be viewed by brokers and investors around the world—there are some 250,000 terminals receiving Nasdaq trading information in 55 countries.

QUALIFYING FOR A NASDAQ LISTING

Every company listing its shares on a U.S. stock market must register them with the SEC and then

---

Actively Traded Nasdaq Stocks for 1997

■ **UNITED STATES**
Amgen
Apple Computer
Intel
MCI Communications
McCormick
Microsoft
Nordstrom
Novell
Oracle
Seagate Technologies
Sun Microsystems
Tele-Communications

■ **FOREIGN**
Akzo (Netherlands)
Cadbury Schweppes (UK)
L.M. Ericsson (Sweden)
Fuji (Japan)
Newbridge Networks (Canada)
Pacific Dunlop (Australia)
Reuters (UK)
Scitex (Israel)
Teva Pharmaceutical (Israel)
Toyota (Japan)
Waterford Wedgewood (Ireland)

---

must provide the SEC with periodic reports on its financial condition. U.S. companies file these reports quarterly while foreign companies file twice a year. These reports are available to the public.

To list on the Nasdaq, a company must meet Nasdaq qualifications, either for the Nasdaq National Market, which has some 3,200 companies, or the Nasdaq Small Cap Market, which has about 1,300 companies. Nasdaq's requirements are less difficult to meet than those of the NYSE and AMEX, and therefore it encourages smaller companies to go public. For instance, to be listed on the NYSE, a company must have pretax income for the most recent year of $2.5 million; on the

American Stock Exchange, $750,000. Nasdaq's requirement is just $400,000 in the latest fiscal year or in two of the last three fiscal years. There are other, more complicated requirements for listing that include size, trading activity, etc.

THE NASDAQ–100 INDEX

This Index, which is market-value weighted, measures the price performance of Nasdaq stocks. In January 1993, the Nasdaq–100 Index was halved, the result of the soaring growth of the Nasdaq Stock Market. Launched in 1985 with a value set at 250, in mid-September 1996, it stood at 707. The index is a widely watched barometer of large capitalization growth stocks trading on Nasdaq. The composition of the index was not affected by the split.

THE OTC MARKET

The term over-the-counter stems from the days when securities were sold over the counter in banks and stores, right along with money orders and dry goods. Today it refers to a security not listed and traded on an organized exchange. Over-the-counter companies tend to be smaller, newer, and less well known than those trading on Nasdaq or on the New York and American exchanges.

Over-the-counter (OTC) stocks are listed in a publication known as the Pink Sheets (named for its color) and on the OTC Bulletin Board, an electronic version of the Pink Sheets. The Pink Sheets, which is published daily by the National Quotation Bureau, gives the bid and asked prices for 13,000 OTC stocks as well as listing who makes a market in the stock. (The National Quotation Bureau is a subsidiary of the Commerce Clearing House, a financial publishing company.) For the most part, these stocks are thinly traded and not carried in the newspaper's daily OTC listing. Corporate bonds are listed separately on the Yellow Sheets.

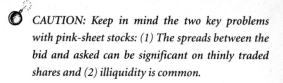 CAUTION: *Keep in mind the two key problems with pink-sheet stocks: (1) The spreads between the bid and asked can be significant on thinly traded shares and (2) illiquidity is common.*

SIX GUIDELINES FOR SELECTING WINNING OTC STOCKS

- Start in your own backyard. Do research on companies in your region. Check with a local stockbroker for ideas. Read annual reports and visit the company personally.
- Buy only companies with established earnings growth and, if possible, low debt. Ideally the assets-to-current liabilities ratio should be 2:1.
- Study wide economic and industrial trends and select companies that have a timely product or service.
- Find companies that have a market niche.
- Allow 2 to 10 months for price and/or earnings movement.
- Avoid penny stocks (stocks that sell for less than 50¢); the bid/asked price spread is often over 25%.

Eight Nasdaq Stocks for 1997

Biosys (BIOS)	Nontoxic pesticides
Ha Lo Indus (HALO)	Specialty advertising
Logic Works (LGWX)	Database design
Logan's Roadhouse (RDHS)	Restaurants
Mariner Healthcare (MRNR)	Low-cost provider
Movie Gallery (MOVI)	Video rental
Netmanage (NETM)	Applications for Windows
PMT Services (PMTS)	Credit card authorization
Remedy (RMDY)	Software that tracks data
Rock Bottom (BREW)	Microbrewed beer

USING THE KEY INDICATORS TO PICK THE BEST STOCKS

If and when you believe the big stocks are overpriced, it's time to move some of your portfolio into smaller issues. To help you time your move, watch these key indicators:

- NASDAQ COMPOSITE INDEX. Listed in the major newspapers, its direction and progress can be compared with those of other major indexes. If its trend is up, the environment is favorable.
- OTC VOLUME VOLUME. Tends to verify the direction, up or down, of a market or individual issue. If the market rises on low volume, for example, generally the rise will be short.
- NEW HIGHS AND LOWS. A number of new highs over new lows is a positive buy sign.
- BLOCK TRADING. When trades of 10,000 shares or more take place, it probably signals institutional participation and future interest in the stock.
- S&P OTC 250 INDEX. Like the Nasdaq index, Standard & Poor's indicates the overall direction of secondary issues. It is especially valuable to compare it to the S&P 500. Since the beginning of 1988, many OTC stocks have recovered from their lows of October–November 1987.
- SHADOW STOCK INDEX. In January 1986 the American Association of Individual Investors, a nonprofit educational organization, introduced this index, which covers less well-known stocks. The market value of a company's outstanding stock must fall between $20 million and $100 million to qualify for inclusion. This means that all companies in the shadow stock index have some sort of track record. Most trade OTC.

SMALL-CAP STOCKS

Another area that is often overlooked by investors is small cap stocks, those with a limited

---

Over-the-Counter Stocks

PROS
↑ In an OTC mutual fund, professional management, diversification, liquidity, possibility of switching into other funds within the same family
↑ Prices often low
↑ Potential capital appreciation

CONS
↓ May be thinly traded
↓ Can be difficult to sell when negative news appears
↓ Research difficult to find, sometimes nonexistent
↓ Losses can be large
↓ Value of fund shares can decline

---

number of shares outstanding and small capitalization. (Capitalization is determined by multiplying the number of shares by the current market value of one share.) These are discussed in Chapter 23.

USING MUTUAL FUNDS

If you want a professional to make the buying and selling decisions in the OTC market, you can invest in stocks of small companies. But remember, higher interest rates and inflation will hurt stocks.

Tips for selecting a fund:

- *Invest only* in a fund that has $100 million or less in assets. A larger fund may have to buy stocks of larger companies, or its portfolio may become too unwieldy to manage effectively.
- *Portfolio turnover* should be 30% per year or less.
- *Check the prospectus and quarterly reports* to make certain the fund is indeed investing in small companies with capitalization below $100 million.

OTC Mutual Funds

FUND	TOTAL RETURN JAN 30 TO SUMMER 1996
Fidelity OTC Portfolio (800–544–8888)	+37.2%
T. Rowe Price OTC (800–638–5660)	+24.7%
American Capital Emerging Growth (800–421–5666)	+31.9%

SPECIAL NASDAQ TERMS

The National Association of Securities Dealers and Nasdaq use several unique terms in daily trading. Here are some you should know if you trade Nasdaq-listed securities.

- *Affirmative obligations.* Requirements imposed on Nasdaq market makers by the NASD, including quoting firm prices and making two-sided markets on a continuous basis.
- *Aftermarket.* Trading activity in a security immediately following its initial offering to the public.
- *Best-execution requirement.* An NASD rule requiring member firms to execute customer orders at the best prices available.
- *Broker/dealer.* A firm that buys and sells securities as an agent for public customers (broker) and as a principal for its own account and risk.
- *Capital commitment.* The monies invested by market makers in carrying inventories of the stocks in which they make markets. More than 470 Nasdaq market makers carry inventories valued at some $1 billion.
- *Central computer complex.* The facility in Trumbull, Connecticut, where the Nasdaq Stock Market's mainframe computers are located. It is connected to more than 3,400 Nasdaq terminals in securities firms and financial institutions.

- *Firm quotation.* The NASD requirement that a market maker receiving an order from another broker/dealer execute it at its displayed Nasdaq price.
- *Last-sale reporting.* Notification by a market maker to the Nasdaq Stock Market of the price and number of shares involved in a transaction in a Nasdaq security. The notification must be made within 90 seconds of the execution of an order.
- *Market makers.* Dealers that buy and sell securities at publicly quoted prices for their own account and risk. Market makers are subject to NASD and SEC rules.
- *Nasdaq Composite Index.* The market-value, weighted measure of the price performance of Nasdaq National Market securities, except warrants, and all Nasdaq Small-Cap Market domestic common stock. The Index is one of the broadest-based and among the most widely followed major market indexes.
- *Nasdaq Small-Cap Market securities.* The smaller capitalization tier of the Nasdaq Stock Market. Requirements for listing in this market are significantly lower than those for Nasdaq National Market companies.
- *NASD.* The National Association of Securities Dealers, Inc., is the largest self-regulatory organization for the securities industry in the United States. It is responsible for the operation and regulation of Nasdaq and the over-the-counter securities markets. It operates under the 1938 Maloney Act Amendment to the Securities and Exchange Act of 1934.
- *OTC Bulletin Board.* An electronic, screen-based market for small, developing companies that are not eligible for listing on Nasdaq. Operated and regulated by the NASD, this market also includes the ADRs of foreign companies, some of which are of considerable size.
- *Over-the-counter securities.* OTC securities are those not listed on Nasdaq or any of the other

exchanges, including the New York, American, and regional exchanges.

- *Self-regulatory organization.* An entity, such as the NASD, responsible for regulating its members through enforcement of rules and relations governing its members.
- *Small-order execution system.* The SOES is an automatic trade/execution system for customer agency orders of up to 1,000 shares. It guarantees the best bid or asked price available in Nasdaq at the time the order is entered. SOES participation is mandatory for market makers in Nasdaq National Market securities.
- *Third market.* The buying and selling of exchange-listed securities in a dealer market. The Nasdaq system facilities are used by third-market firms to quote and execute trades in this market.
- *Two-sided market.* The obligation imposed by NASD regulations that Nasdaq market makers quote both a bid and ask price for each security in which they make a market and to execute orders at those prices.

FOR FURTHER INFORMATION
Books

The 1996 Nasdaq Company Directory and Fact Book
NASD
Media Source
Box 9403
Gaithersburg, MD 20898
202–728–8000
$20.
Lists all Nasdaq stocks with their symbols, addresses, and telephone numbers.

Magazines

Equities
160 Madison Avenue
New York, NY 10016
212–213–1300
Monthly; $36 per year.
Contains studies of individual stocks.

Newsletters

Growth Stock Outlook
4405 East-West Highway
Bethesda, MD 20814
301–654–5205
Twice monthly; $195 per year.
Published by Charles Allmon; covers stocks with potential appreciation.

The OTC Profiles
Standard & Poor's
25 Broadway
New York, NY 10004
800–221–5277
$85 per year.
Published three times/year; lists historical data and prices for the larger OTC companies. Check your library.

Value Line OTC Special Situations
220 East 42 Street
New York, NY 10017
800–833–0046
Bimonthly; $428 per year; trial: $39 (6 issues). Reliable coverage of OTC and small-cap stocks.

15

Utilities

*I*nvestors have always been attracted to utility stocks for their traditionally high yields. And with good reason—you can get an idea of just how high the yields are by checking the boxes on the following pages. Yet high yields come with a down side: Utility stocks are extremely sensitive to interest rates and behave like bonds. When interest rates rise, share prices head down.

One of the most dramatic examples of just how sensitive utility stocks are took place in the spring of 1994 when the Fed started boosting interest rates—utilities immediately began falling in price—the total plunge for that year was in the neighborhood of 19%.

THE NEW ERA OF DEREGULATION

The National Energy Policy Act passed in October 1992 is bringing about a new world for utilties. This law requires power companies to give independent power producers access to their transmissions lines. This means that industrial customers can shop around for the best price on power, and then have the local utility company deliver it to their factories and office buildings.

The Act has also given large industrial customers the right to bypass their local utility company and purchase power directly from remote, lower-cost utilities. Within the industry, this is known as "retail wheeling."

A number of states have announced their goal of putting full competition into operation around the year 2000. Some have already begun—for example, customers selected at random in New Hampshire can now choose their electricity supplier. And, starting in 1998, the largest customers in California will be able to pick a supplier other than their local utility.

Competition and deregulation, in the long run, will have a positive impact on the financially solid utility companies. Many had grown rather fat and now they are starting to cut costs and trim their work forces, just as other industries have been forced to do. And, utilities are no longer building huge, expensive plants. Some are responding to growing competition by merging with each other. These mergers are likely to lead to a wider variety of available fuels, a broader customer base, and greater overall financial strength.

DIVERSIFICATION

Another way many utilities are reacting to the end of their monopolistic way of life is diversification—into cogeneration projects, in this country as well as into utility operations in foreign countries. Moves have already been made into the UK, Latin America, Asia, and the Pacific Rim.

As foreign countries gain economic strength, especially the third world economies, demand for power will increase at a rapid rate. U.S. utility companies with an overseas presence will certainly stand to benefit. *NOTE:* Utility earnings derived from foreign countries are not subject to a regulatory cap.

INVESTING TIPS

Before automatically buying a utility stock, here's what you need to know:

- The utility business is facing increased competition.
- Only companies that cut costs and seek means of diversification will be successful.
- Companies that invest in rapidly growing foreign economies should be among the most profitable.
- Utility stocks can no longer be held forever; the scene is continually changing and utilities, like any other stock, must be watched on a regular basis.

GUIDELINES FOR SELECTING UTILITY STOCKS

In the past, utility stocks moved pretty much as a group, but today the difference between the best and the poorest has widened and skepticism should be your guiding principle. When making a utility selection you should ask:

Nine Utilities with Secure Dividends

COMPANY	SYMBOL	YIELD
Allegheny Power	AYP	6.7%
Brooklyn Union Gas	BU	5.4
Connecticut Natural Gas	CNG	6.1
Delmarva Power	DEW	7.8
FPL Group	FPL	4.4
Kansas City P&L	KLT	6.2
Orange & Rockland	ORU	7.3
Public Service Enterprises	PEG	7.0
Union Electric	UEP	6.5

SOURCE: Quotron, Fall 1996.

Utilities for Long-Term Holding

STOCK	SYMBOL	YIELD
Eastern Utilities	EAU	6.5%
Florida Progress	FPC	6.0
FPL Group	FPL	4.2
Montana Power	MTP	6.4
NIPSCO Industries	NI	4.9
PacifiCorp	PPW	5.3
Pinnacle West Capital	PNW	4.1
SCANA Corp.	SCG	6.0

(As of Fall 1996)

- How good is management?
- Is the dividend well covered by earnings?
- Is management addressing deregulation? How?
- Is the company planning to make a move overseas?
- What is the reserve margin? (Reserve margin is power capacity above peak-load usage; if it is especially high, the company may have unused plants and high costs. The industry-wide average is around 25%.)

Moreover:

- Don't select a utility stock solely on the basis of its yield. (A high return often reflects Wall Street uncertainty about the safety of the dividend.)
- Do select stocks that have expectations for higher earnings and growth rates. (Check write-ups in *Value Line Investment Survey* for up-to-date analysis of this.)
- If all other things are equal, select a utility that has a dividend reinvestment plan. You will save on commissions.
- Diversify. Buy utilities from several states, to avoid any one state's unfavorable regulatory policies.

You should also study:

- *Bond rating*, as determined by Standard & Poor's or Moody's. A company's bond rating is a realistic measure of the company's financial strength.
- *Regulatory climate.* The attitude of state authorities toward permitting the utility to earn an adequate rate of return is an important factor.
- *Return on equity.* This is that basic standard of quality—the ability of management to make money with your money. It is often a reflection of the state authorities, who may or may not permit an adequate rate of return.
- *Main fuel.* This is a key criterion for many analysts. Utilities that use water (hydroelectric plants) have no cost worries.
- *Consider high quality* preferred utility stocks (Preferred stocks are discussed in Chapter 13).

But bear in mind that preferred have no possibility of increased dividends although they do offer high yields, although generally less high than public utility bonds. Preferreds are a no-brainer

Four High-Quality Preferred Utility Stocks

Consolidated Edison	7.5%
Duke Power	6.6
Florida Power & Light	7.5
Northern States Power	6.0

The Bell Companies

SYMBOL	COMPANY	PRICE	RATIO	YIELD
T	ATT Corp	$39	15	3.3%
AIT	Ameritech	56	16	3.7
BEL	Bell Atlantic	60	13	4.8
BLS	Bell South	38	12	3.7
NYN	NYNEX	43	17	3.0
PAC	Pacific Telesis	35	14	3.6
SBC	SBC Communications	49	15	3.5
USW	U.S. West	30	12	7.0

(As of August 1996)

way to lock in a high yield and you prefer not to add bonds to your portfolio.

☑ *HINT: Look for utilities with strong internal cash flow that have completed construction programs, have cut costs, and are addressing the issues surrounding deregulation of the industry.*

UTILITY MUTUAL FUNDS

If you prefer not to select individual utilities, there are mutual funds that invest in these stocks. The funds, however, are not all alike. It is imperative that you read each prospectus before investing. Some have a portion of their assets in utility bonds while others own natural gas and telephone stocks whose growth potential is greater than that of electric utilities. Some funds invest in foreign utilities and high-yielding equities. Some prefer electric utilities in a certain area.

☑ *HINT: The more diversified the fund's portfolio, the lower its interest rate sensitivity.*

For example, the Pittsburgh-based Federated's Utility Fund (created by a merger of two of the company's funds in 1996), owns these utility sectors, as of summer 1996:

33.33%	Electrics
22.08%	Telecommunications
8.96	Natural gas
22.70	Non-utility
9.48	International utilities
2.36	Cash

Federated has taken the precaution of holding non-utility convertibles that have high yields as a means of cushioning the fund against changing interest rates.

NOTE: You should also be aware of the fact that some mutual funds have two types of shares: Class A and Class B. Class A has a front-end load, while Class B usually has a 1% per annum 12b–1 fee to defray marketing expenses and levy a

Six Utility Mutual Funds

FUND	YIELD OCTOBER 1996	TELEPHONE
Colonial Utilities: A	4.70%	800–345–6611
Fidelity Utilities Income	3.62	800–544–8888
Franklin Utilities	5.21	800–342–5236
IDS Utilities Income	6.00	800–328–8300
Stratton Monthly Dividend	5.01	800–634–5726
Vanguard Utilities Income	5.91	800–662–7447

(As of October 1996)

deferred sales charge if you redeem your shares within a certain number of years, often 5 or 6. If you know you're going to hold your shares 5 or 6 years, you're better off with the Class A shares so you can avoid the ongoing 12b–1 charges.

☑ *HINT: If you are retired, you may want a fund that pays out dividends on a monthly basis, or set up your own automatic payout with individual utility stocks. For example, according to the Dow Theory Forecasts, these six, high-quality utility stocks pay out dividends as follows:*
Jan, April, July, Oct:

Ipalco Enterprises
Northern States Power

Feb, May, Aug, Nov:

Teco Energy
WPL Holdings

March, June, Sept, Dec:

SIGCPORP
Southern Co.

BUYING UTILITY STOCKS DIRECTLY

A number of utility companies allow customers to buy stock directly in the company, without a broker.
Among those that do are:

- Centerior Energy
- Central Maine Power
- Dominion Resources
- Idaho Power

- Nevada Power
- San Diego Gas & Electric
- Central Hudson Gas & Electric
- Central Vermont Public Service
- Hawaiian Electric Industries
- Minnesota Power
- Philadelphia Electric
- Union Electric

NOTE: Call the investor relations department of your local utility company to see if you can purchase shares directly.

WATER COMPANIES

Telephone and electric companies have always been in the spotlight, hogging center stage in the utilities industry. Yet stocks of public water companies are a good way to tap into the group. These stocks have low institutional ownership and are still reasonably priced.

Consider water companies because they:

- Provide a commodity everyone needs
- Have no competition; there is no alternative to water
- Have no nuclear exposure

Although there are approximately 59,000 water companies in the United States serving 248 million people, most are municipally owned and regulated by city governments. However, 24,000 systems are investor-owned and of these 18 are publicly traded. American Water Works is the largest. It serves 1.5 million customers in 21 states; its largest customer is Monsanto. It has one of the best dividend records in the industry, having increased its dividend over 10% compounded annually over the past 11 years.

If you decide to invest in a water company, keep in mind that rate increases are determined by area regulatory bodies and that various local situations, including the weather and the economy, have a major effect on earnings. Residential customers dominate the industry, and companies therefore tend to benefit from hot weather spells when Americans use more water. Companies must continually meet the water standards set by the Environmental Protection Agency.

The larger better-known water firms are listed in the table below. You may also want to investigate your local water company—find out if it is publicly traded—but read the last two annual reports and the current quarterlies before purchasing shares.

UTILITY BONDS

Utility bonds are no longer the well protected investment they were just a few years ago. Mergers and takeovers have come to the utility industry and only those bonds with AA ratings should be considered during the next couple of years — or at least until the industry settles down and adjusts to deregulation. Check the list below and/or ask your broker for a list of high rated issues. As we go to press, yields on new bond issues ranged from 6½% to 7½%.

Four High-Quality Utility Bonds

- Dayton Power & Light   Aa3
- Duke Power   Aa2
- Florida Power Corp.   Aa3
- Southern Indiana G & E   Aa2

☑ *HINT: Buy only bonds rated A or above and check the call feature. Most utilities have only 5-year call protection, whereas Treasuries are essentially noncallable. Avoid bonds of companies with nuclear or regulatory problems, or that have not cut costs as a way of addressing deregulation.*

💣 *CAUTION: Many high-yielding utility bonds have special, early redemption clauses built into their issues. These call provisions permit a utility to buy back its bonds at face value or even a bit higher, but more often than not at prices below the current market. Utility companies are allowed to use these special calls to cut expenses by retiring high-yield or high-coupon bonds.*

Leading Water Companies

COMPANY	EXCHANGE: SYMBOL	PRICE	YIELD
American Water Works	NYSE:AWK	$37	4.1%
Citizens Utilities	NYSE:CZN.A	12	none
Connecticut Water	OTC:CTWS	28	6.7
Consumers Water	OTC: CONW	19	7.2
E'Town Corp.	NYSE:ETW	29	7.1
Middlesex Water Co.	OTC: MSEX	16	6.5
Philadelphia Suburban	NYSE:PSC	21	6.0
Southern Calif. Water	NYSE:SCW	23	6.4
United Water Resources	NYSE:UWR	19	6.3

(As of Fall 1996)

16

Options

You know that over the long term, stocks are one of the best ways to achieve long-term total returns. Options can be equally effective, provided you understand how to use them. In fact, when used correctly, they can actually increase the profit on stocks you already own and/or reduce the potential for losses in a declining market. They also enable you to take advantage of the concept of leverage, for, with a small amount of money, you can control a large investment. However, you must be disciplined and adept to make options work.

You should also realize that options are derivatives, which means they derive their value from an underlying asset. Those assets can be common stocks or indexes of common stocks.

If the idea of trading in derivatives is nerve-wracking, think of it this way: A novelist sells an option on his book to a Hollywood movie producer. The option gives the producer the right to buy the story for a movie within a specified time, but it does not actually force or oblige the producer to do so.

In exchange for giving Hollywood a crack at his novel, or an option on it, the novelist receives a payment. If the producer likes the story and decides to make a movie before the option expires, the novelist then must sell the screen rights to the producer, at the agreed-upon price. If the producer decides not to go ahead with the project, the novelist keeps the option payment and

his novel and the producer's rights end or expire when the option's time is up.

So, too, it is with Wall Street options. They are very much the same.

☑ *HINT: Before actually allocating money to trading options, test several hypothetical examples on paper—follow them in the newspaper to see how options really work. Once you have done this learning exercise, you are ready to take the plunge and spend real money.*

Then, talk to your broker. Depending upon the brokerage firm, you may be asked for your net worth statement, or perhaps to open a margin account (see Chapter 25). And remember, to be successful with options you must be prepared to devote time watching the calendar.

WHAT ARE OPTIONS?

Options are the contractual right, but not the obligation, to buy or to sell something. A put is the right to sell, whereas a call is the right to buy. In a way, options are a cross between trading in stocks and trading in commodities. They enable you to control a relatively large amount of stock with a relatively small amount of capital for a fixed period of time. To be more specific: An option represents the right, but not the obligation, to buy or sell a specific stock at a specific price, called the strike price for a specified time. You do not need to own the stock to buy an option on it.

If, for example, you believe a stock will go up in price in the future, you can buy a call on it. This enables you to purchase 100 shares near its current price. On the other hand, if you have reason to believe the stock will fall in price, you can buy a put on that stock, which gives you the right to sell 100 shares near its current price. (You may also sell puts and calls.)

How long a time do options run? Most options are available for 3-, 6-, or 9-month periods, or remaining fractions thereof. (As their expiration date approaches, they may have as little as 1 or 2 weeks or days.)

However, in a small number of stocks there are options that last a year or two years. These long-term options are known as LEAPS, which stands for Long-Term Equity Appreciation Security. All the same rules apply to LEAPS as to regular options, but the premiums you must pay for such extended times are higher. LEAPS are quoted in a separate section of the Wall Street Journal and financial press.

Now let's look at a very simple example of how options work. You bought a 3-month call on IBM at $100 when the stock was selling at $90. The option's selling price or premium was $300 (or $3 per share). One month later, IBM's shares move up to $110. You now have two choices (or options, hence the name of this vehicle): (1) you can exercise your option and buy the IBM shares at $100/share; or (2) you can sell your call, which is now worth approximately $1,000, based on the price of IBM plus whatever the option is now worth—probably around $1,000. (When a stock rises in price, as in this example, the premium [$3] tends to diminish.)

You may wonder, Why not buy the 100 shares of IBM to begin with? It would have moved from $90 to $110 and you would have had a nice profit. First of all, you would have had to invest much more money—$9,000 rather than just $300. Had the stock dropped in price, you would have lost much more than you would with the option.

Options trade on the Chicago Board of Options Exchange, the American Stock Exchange, the Philadelphia Stock Exchange, the Pacific Stock Exchange, and the New York Stock Exchange. You may also buy and sell puts and calls on the major stock market indexes and on foreign currencies.

COMMISSIONS

Commissions vary with the number of contracts traded: For a single call, the maximum is often $25; for 10 calls, about $4 each. As a guideline, make your calculations, in multiple units, at $14 per contract, less if you use a discount broker. Ask your broker his rates prior to trading.

You may be able to save on commissions when you write calls for a premium of less than 1 ($100). A call traded at $15/16$ ($93.75) will cost $8.39, compared with $25 for one priced at 1 or higher.

LEAPS

This is a leap you may or may not want to take. Long-Term Equity Anticipation Securities (LEAPS) are put and call options that expire in 2 or 3 years instead of the conventional 8 months for equity options. They are offered on about 100 large-cap stocks, on the S&P 500 and the S&P 100 indexes. About half of them trade on the CBOE, the rest on the AMEX and Pacific stock exchanges.

Since they were introduced in October 1990 by the Chicago Board Options Exchange, they've been gaining in popularity. Why? Because regular options expire or disappear so fast, yet leaps are longer running, with some that expire up to 2 to 3 years away. Their long life is an advantage for most traders.

Each LEAPS has puts and calls on the underlying stock with at least three strike prices: in-the-money, at-the-money, and out-of-the money. At their start, the out-of-the-money strikes are approximately 20% to 25% away from the stock's market value. Initial prices tend to be under $10.

Let's look at how they work. This example is supplied by Standard & Poor's: You have a gain in Microsoft, selling at $84. You write a LEAPS call expiring in January with a strike price of $95. That means the option is 11 points out of the money or selling above the current market price. The call represents 100 shares, so you wind up with $1,300 for each. The buyer now can buy Microsoft shares from you at $95/share by January.

Writing this call merely provides a cushion; it does not guarantee a profit. If the stock rises above $95 by the expiration date, the buyer will exercise the option and take your stock. At any price between $95 and $71, you will have a paper gain because of the $1,300 received for the call. If the stock falls, it can reach $71 before you have a paper loss.

Or you can buy a LEAPS put. Let's say you bought AT&T stock at 38\frac{3}{4}$. It's now March and the stock is at 58\frac{3}{4}$. You could buy a January put with a price strike of 60 for 5. Owning the put gives you the right to sell the stock at 60, which guarantees you an out price of at least $55. If AT&T goes to $61, the put goes to zero, but you can then sell your shares for a put price of $56. In any case, you will always get at least $55, which in this example would lock in 16$\frac{1}{4}$ points or 81% of your $20 paper profit.

See "For Further Information" at the end of this chapter for useful sources of material on LEAPS.

HOW PREMIUMS WORK

The cost of the option is quoted in multiples of $\frac{1}{16}$ for options priced below $3, $\frac{1}{8}$ for those priced higher. To determine the percentage of premium, divide the current value of the stock into the quoted price of the option. When there's a difference between the exercise price of the option and the quoted price of the stock, add or subtract the spread.

Here's how options were quoted in the financial pages when EFG stock was at 32$\frac{3}{8}$ (see the table below):

The April 30 call prices ranged from a high of 4$\frac{3}{4}$ ($475) to a low of 2$\frac{3}{4}$ ($275), and a closing price of 3$\frac{1}{8}$ ($312.50) for a net change from the previous week of $\frac{1}{8}$ ($12.50). There were 1,317 sales of contracts for 100 shares each.

The second line lists the action with April 30 puts: a high of $\frac{9}{16}$ ($56.25), a low of $\frac{1}{4}$ ($25), and a closing price of $\frac{3}{8}$ ($37.50). For the week, the net change was $\frac{1}{16}$ ($6.25). There were 996 contracts traded.

Traders looking for quick profits were pessimistic, as shown by the heavy volume in puts: 1,422 contracts for the April 35s and 2,219 for the April 40s. But there were fairly sharp differences of opinion, as the April 35 puts were up $\frac{5}{16}$ and the April 40s up $\frac{3}{8}$.

Investors were more optimistic and appeared to believe that EFG stock was ready for an upswing: April 40 calls, due in a few weeks, were quoted at $\frac{1}{8}$, whereas the farther-out October 40s were quoted at 1$\frac{5}{8}$. Much of the spread, of course, was due to the time factor.

Relative Premiums

As a Percent of Price of Underlying Common Stock When Common Is at Exercise Price

MONTHS TO EXPIRATION	LOW	AVERAGE	HIGH
1	1.8\-2.6	3.5\-4.4	5.2\-6.1
2	2.6\-3.9	5.2\-6.6	7.8\-9.2
3	3.3\-5.0	6.7\-8.3	10.0\-11.7
4	3.9\-5.9	7.9\-9.8	11.8\-13.8
5	4.5\-6.8	9.0\-11.2	13.5\-15.8
6	5.0\-7.5	10.0\-12.5	15.0\-17.5
7	5.5\-8.2	10.9\-13.7	16.4\-19.2
8	5.9\-8.9	11.8\-14.8	17.7\-20.6
9	6.4\-9.5	12.7\-15.9	19.0\-22.2

Terms Used in Option Trading

Before moving on to some more sophisticated examples and techniques, let's review the terms involved.

- At-the-money: when a strike price is exactly the same as the price of the underlying stock
- Call: the right, but not the obligation, to buy a stock at a specified price
- Closing transaction: buying or selling an option to close a previously held position
- Covered option: an option written against shares of a stock you already own. This is the most popular and a fairly conservative option strategy, letting you get a little more value out of your stock. It involves selling a call option on a stock that is already in your portfolio. The investor who buys the call then has the right to buy your shares (called the "underlying stock") at a predetermined strike price. In other words, the investor can "call" the stock away from you at a certain price. However, the investor will not exercise the call (that is, take possession of the shares) unless the stock rises above the option strike price.

    When you sell a covered call option, you collect some income—the premium. If the price of the stock rises a lot, the investor will exercise the option and you then lose your stock and the ability to benefit from any further appreciation above the strike price.

 CAUTION: This strategy works well if the stock price remains unchanged or stays under the strike price, because then the option expires worthless and you've collected the premium plus any dividends.

- Diagonal spread: buying and selling options at the same time on the same stock, but with different expiration dates and different strike prices
- Dividends and rights: as long as you own the stock, you continue to receive the dividends. That's why calls for stocks with high yields sell at lower premiums than those for companies with small payouts.

    A stock dividend or stock split automatically increases the number of shares covered by the option in an exact proportion. If a right is involved (see Chapter 17), its value will be set by the first sale of rights on the day the stock sells ex-rights.
- Expiration date: options last 3, 6, or 9 months, then they expire. The expiration date is the third Friday of the month in which it can be exercised.
- Horizontal spread: buying and selling options at the same time on a stock with the same strike price, but with differing expiration dates
- In-the-money: an option that will make a profit if exercised
- Married put: a put on shares that you already own
- Naked option: opposite of a covered option; an option written (sold) against shares you do not already own
- Out-of-the-money option: an option that will not be profitable to exercise
- Premium: an option's selling price. Premiums vary with the price of the underlying stock and its volatility.
- Put: the right to sell a stock at a specified price for a specified time
- Restricted option: This may occur when the previous day's price closed at less than 50¢ per option and the underlying stock price closed at more than 5 points below its strike price for calls, or more than 5 points above its strike price for puts. Opening transactions (buying or writing calls) are prohibited unless they are covered. Closing transactions (liquidations) are permitted. There are various exceptions, so check with your broker.
- Spread: buying and selling options on a stock at the same time in order to lock in a closing transaction and limit the risk involved
- Strike price: the price a stock must reach in order for the owner of the option to exercise the option
- Vertical spread: buying and selling options on the same security with the same expiration dates, but different strike prices

The prices of the options reflect temporary hopes and fears, but over a month or two they will tend to move with the underlying stock. But do not rely solely on this type of projection: Near the expiration date, the prices of options move sharply.

One key factor to keep in mind is that the premium at the outset reflects the time factor. This will fall rapidly as the expiration date nears. In the last 3 months of a call, the premium can be cut in half because of the dwindling time.

WRITING CALLS

When you write or sell calls, you start off with an immediate, sure, limited profit rather than an uncertain, potentially greater gain, which is the case for puts. The most you can make is the premium you receive, even if the price of the stock soars. If you write calls on stock you own, any loss of the value of the stock will be reduced by the amount of the premium. Writing covered calls (on stock you own) is a conservative use of options. You have these choices:

On-the-Money Calls

These are written at an exercise price that is at or close to the current price of the stock.

Example: In December, Investor One buys 100 shares of Company A at 40 and sells a July call, at the strike price of 40, for 3 ($300). He realizes that A's stock may move above 43 in the next 7 months, but is willing to accept the $3 per share income.

Investor Two is the purchaser of the call. He acquires the right to buy the stock at 40 at any time before the expiration date at the end of July. He anticipates that A's stock will move up well above 43.

Investor One will not sustain a dollar loss until the price of A goes below 37. He will probably keep the stock until its price goes above 43. At this price, the profit meter starts ticking for

How Options Are Quoted

NAME, EXPIRATION DATE, AND PRICE	SALES	HIGH	WEEK'S LOW	LAST	NET CHG.
EFG Apr30	1,317	$4\frac{3}{4}$	$2\frac{3}{4}$	$3\frac{1}{8}$	−1/8
EFG Apr30 p	996	$\frac{9}{16}$	$\frac{1}{4}$	$\frac{3}{8}$	−1/16
EFG Apr35	3,872	$1\frac{1}{4}$	$\frac{3}{8}$	$\frac{1}{2}$	−3/16
EFG Apr35 p	1,422	$3\frac{1}{8}$	$1\frac{5}{8}$	$2\frac{15}{16}$	+5/16
EFG Apr40	1,526	$\frac{3}{16}$	$\frac{1}{16}$	$\frac{1}{8}$	−1/16
EFG Apr40 p	2,219	$7\frac{7}{8}$	$5\frac{7}{8}$	$7\frac{7}{8}$	+3/8
EFG Jul30	426	6	$4\frac{1}{2}$	$4\frac{1}{2}$	−1/2
EFG Jul30 p	805	$1\frac{3}{8}$	$\frac{7}{8}$	$1\frac{3}{8}$	+1/8
EFG Jul35	1,084	3	2	$3\frac{1}{16}$	−3/16
EFG Jul35 p	870	$3\frac{7}{8}$	$2\frac{3}{4}$	$3\frac{7}{8}$	+1/4
EFG Jul40	1,145	$1\frac{1}{8}$	$\frac{3}{4}$	$\frac{3}{4}$	−1/8
EFG Jul40 p	523	$7\frac{3}{4}$	$6\frac{1}{8}$	$7\frac{3}{4}$	+3/8
EFG Oct35	346	$4\frac{3}{8}$	$3\frac{1}{8}$	$3\frac{1}{4}$	−1/4
EFG Oct35 p	261	$4\frac{3}{8}$	$3\frac{1}{2}$	$4\frac{3}{8}$	+3/8
EFG Oct40	137	$2\frac{1}{4}$	$1\frac{5}{8}$	$1\frac{5}{8}$	−1/4
EFG Oct40 p	326	$7\frac{7}{8}$	$6\frac{1}{2}$	$7\frac{3}{4}$	+1/4

Stock price: $32\frac{3}{8}$. Table does not show open interest because of space limitations.

Investor Two, so let's see what happens if company A's stock jumps to 50. At any time before late July, Investor Two can exercise his option and pay $4,000 for stock now worth $5,000. After deducting about $400 (the $300 premium plus commissions), he will have a net profit of about $600, thus doubling his risk capital.

Investor Two will sell the call at $2 and lose $1 per call. Investor One will end up with about $375: the $300 premium plus two dividends of $50 each minus the $25 commission for the sale of the call.

In-the-Money Calls

In-the-money calls are those where the exercise price is below the price of the underlying stock. This is a more aggressive technique that requires close attention but can result in excellent profits.

Example: In January, Karen buys 300 shares of Glamor Electronics Co. (GEC) at 105 ($31,500) and sells three June 100 calls at 8 each ($2,400). If GEC stock drops below 100, she keeps the premiums and the stock. If it goes to 110, she can buy back the calls at, say, 11, $1,100 ($3,300 total), to set up a loss of $900.

Deep-in-the-Money Calls

These are calls that are sold at strike prices far below the current quotation of the stock—8 to 20 points below. Writing them is best when the investor is dealing in large blocks of stock because of the almost certain commissions that have to be paid when the underlying stock is called. With this approach, the best selection is a stable, high-dividend stock. Your returns may be limited, but they are likely to be sure.

The technique used by professionals is called using leverage: When the exercise price of the call is below that of the current value of the stock, both securities tend to move in unison. Because the options involve a smaller investment, there's a higher percentage of return and, in a down market, more protection against loss.

Example: Pistol Whip, Inc. (PWI), is selling at 97⅝. The call price at 70 two months hence is 28, so the equivalent price is 98. If PWI goes to 105, the call will keep pace and be worth 35.

If you bought 100 shares of the stock, the total cost would be about $9,800. Your ultimate profit would be about $700, close to a 7.1% return. If you bought one option, your cost would be $2,800 and you would have the same $700 profit. Your return would be about 25%.

NOTE: All too often, this is more theory than practice. When an option is popular, it may trade on its own and not move up or down with the price of the stock. This separate value will shift only when the expiration date is near.

When one volatile stock was at 41 in March, the November 45 call was trading at 2⅟₁₆. Three weeks later, when the stock fell to 35½ (−16%), the call edged down to 2: a 3% decline. The professionals had moved in and set their own terms.

But remember that at times the price of the call may drop further percentage-wise than that of the stock.

A variation of this use of deep-in-the-money calls is to create cost by basing the return on the total income received from premiums plus dividends.

Example: In January, one professional money manager seeking extra income for his fund bought 1,000 shares of Wellknown Chemical at 39½. He then sold April 35 options for 6⅞ each, thereby reducing the price per share to 32⅝. He could count on a 45¢-per-share dividend before the exercise date.

When the call is exercised at $35 per share, the profit on the $32.625 investment will be $2.375 plus the 45¢ dividend, or $2.825 for a return of 8.66% in a 4-month period.

Out-Of-The-Money Calls

This is when the strike price is above the market price of the underlying stock for a call or the

> ### Rules for Writing Options
>
> - Define your goal.
> - Work on a programmed basis.
> - Concentrate on stocks that you would like to own.
> - Set a target rate of return.
> - Buy the stock first.
> - Write long-term calls.
> - Calculate your net return.
> - Keep your capital fully employed.
> - Be persistent.
> - Watch the timing.
> - Protect your capital.
> - Use margin to boost profits.
> - Watch the record date of high-dividend stocks.
> - Keep a separate bookkeeping system.

strike price is below the market price of the underlying stock of a put.

WRITING NAKED CALLS

Some calls are sold by speculators or investors who do not own the underlying stock. This is referred to as writing a naked call. The writer is betting that the stock will either remain at its current price or decline. He receives a premium, which he pockets if the stock does not rise above the call price. But if it does, he then must buy back his call at a loss.

☑ *HINT: Don't get involved unless you maintain a substantial margin account, have considerable experience, and feel confident that the price of a stock will stay flat or decline. It's risky, because if the stock hits the strike price before or at the exercise date, you are obligated to deliver the shares you do not own.*

You can, of course, cover your position by buying calls, but if the stock price soars, the loss can be substantial. At best, your premium income will be reduced.

One technique that works well is to write two out-of-the-money calls for every 100 shares you own. This gives you double premiums. Do not go too far out, because a lot can happen in a few months.

Example: You own 300 shares of Company XYZ at 32. The 35 call, due in 4 months, is 3, but you are not convinced that the market, or the stock, will rise soon. You sell six calls, pocket $1,800 (less commissions), and hope that the stock stays under 35. If it moves to 36, you can buy back three calls for, say, 1½ ($450) and let the stock go. But if the stock jumps to 40, you're in deep trouble.

BUYING CALLS

Investors buy calls in anticipation of an increase in the price of the underlying stock. If that happens, the call may also rise in price and you can sell at a profit. Buying calls means you can invest a fraction of the cost of the stock and obtain greater leverage. You also limit your risk because the most you can lose is the cost of the option.

The basic problem with buying options is that calls are wasting assets. At expiration date, their values can decline to zero if the stock price moves opposite to your expectations or stays fairly stable.

Example: On February 15, ABC's common is selling at $40 per share. An October 40 call can be purchased for $500 (100 shares at $5 per share). On April 15, ABC is selling at $46 per share and the October 40 call is trading at a value of $750. The investor, anticipating an increase in the value of ABC, had purchased the call for $500 and sold it for $750, realizing a $250 profit.

Here are the ways leverage works in this situation:

In this example, the call buyer can lose no more than the $500 he paid for the October 40 call, regardless of any decline in the stock, but he can lose the entire $500 if he is wrong. However,

	STOCK	CALL
Bought—February 15	$4,000	$500
Sold—April 15	4,600	750
Profit	600	250
Return on investment	15%	50%

he may be able to resell his option in time to recover some of his cost. Keep in mind that if he had purchased the stock itself for $4,000 and it had gone down in price, he would have lost more than $500 if he had sold. If he decided to hold the stock and it appreciated, he would have another opportunity to make a profit.

A put buyer does not have to resell a profitable call, but can instead exercise it and take delivery of the underlying stock. He can then sell the stock for a gain or hold it for long-term appreciation.

☑ *IF YOU DARE: In an up market, buy calls on up stocks on either of these terms:*

Long-term, out-of-the-money options at a low premium, typically 1 or less. By diversifying with four or five promising situations, you may be lucky enough to hit it big with one and make enough to offset the small losses on the others.

Short- or intermediate-term in-the-money or close-to-the-money options of volatile stocks: 2 months to expiration date, a stock within 5% of the strike price, and a low time premium. If the price of the premium doubles, sell half your holdings. Advice from one expert: Never pay a premium of more than 3 for a call on a stock selling under 50, or more than 5 for one trading over 60. Both prices should include commissions.

☑ *HINT: The strike price of the option and the market price of the stock should change by about half as many points as the change in the stock price: For example, if a 30 option is worth 5 when the stock is at 30, it should be worth 2½ when the stock falls to 25 and worth 8 when the stock moves up to 36.*

PUTS FOR PROFIT AND PROTECTION

In a broad sense, a put is the opposite of a call: It is an option to sell a specified number of shares (usually 100) of a specified stock at a specified price before a specified date. Puts have the same expiration months and price intervals as listed calls. The put buyer profits when the price of the underlying stock declines significantly. Then he sells the put at a profit, with the holder buying the stock at the lower current market price and selling it at the higher exercise or striking price.

The value of a put moves counter to that of the related stock: up when the price of the stock falls, down when it rises. You buy a put when you are bearish and anticipate that the market or stock will decline. Vice versa with selling puts. As with all options, a put is a wasting asset, and its value will diminish with the approach of the expiration date.

Here again, the attraction of puts is leverage. A few hundred dollars can acquire temporary control of thousands of dollars' worth of stock. The premiums are generally smaller than those of calls on the same stock because of lower demand, reflecting the small number of people who are pessimistic. Sharp traders take advantage of this situation, because they realize that most people tend to be optimistic about the stock market.

Selling (Writing) Puts

This provides instant income but involves your responsibility to buy the stock if it sells, before the expiration date, at or below the exercise price.

Example: Ed owns Xanadu stock, now selling at 53, well above the purchase price. He's hopeful that the market will keep rising, but decides to write a put at 50 for 2 ($200).

As long as the stock stays above 50, the put will not be exercised and Ed keeps the $200 per contract. But once the stock falls below 50, Ed must buy the shares or buy back the put, thus cutting or eliminating the opening profit.

Buying Puts

These can be used to protect positions and, of course, to score a quick gain. The profits come when the price of the stock falls.

Example: In March, Ann becomes skittish about the stock now trading at 47. She buys a July put at the strike price of 50 for 4 ($400). This put has an intrinsic cash value of 3, because the stock is selling 3 points below the exercise price. In effect, she is paying 1 ($100) to protect her position against a sharp market or stock decline.

If Ann's prediction is right and the price of the stock drops, the value of the put will rise to over 7 when the stock falls to 43.

In late July, the stock price is 45, so Ann sells the put for 5 for a $100 gross profit. If the price of the stock goes below 43, her profit will be greater.

As with calls, the important factor in profitable puts is the related stock. The best candidates for both writing and buying puts are stocks that:

- *Pay small or no dividends.* You are hoping that the value of the stock will decline. Dividends tend to set a floor because of their yields.
- *Sell at high price-earnings ratios.* These are more susceptible to sharp downswings than stocks with lower multiples. A stock with a P/E of 25 runs a greater risk of a quick decline than one with a P/E of 10.
- *Are historically volatile*—with patterns of sharp, wide swings in price. Stable stocks move slowly even in an active market.
- *Are unpopular with institutions.* At the outset, when selling starts, the price drops can be welcome. Later, however, when panic selling is over, there's likely to be minimal action, because there will be few buyers.

TECHNIQUES FOR HIGH ROLLERS

Spreads

A spread is the dollar difference between the buy and sell premiums. Spreads involve buying one option and selling another short, both on the same stock. If the cost of the option is greater than the proceeds of the option sold, it is a debit. If the reverse is true, it's called a credit. If the costs and proceeds are the same, the spread is even money. Your goal: to capture at least the difference in premiums—at least ½ point between the cost of options exercisable at different dates and/or at different prices. Make your calculations on paper first, and make no commitments until you are sure you understand the possibilities or probabilities.

Example: Here's an example involving POP stock priced at 50 in April. The premiums for 50 calls are 3½ for July, 4 for October.

If POP is below 50 in July, you keep $350 and still own an option worth $250 to $300.

Sell July 50 for 3½	+$ 350
Buy October 50 for 4	− 400
Cash outlay	− 50
Commission	− 25
Total cost	− $75

If POP goes up by October, the option will be worth $500 or more, so you have a profit of $850.

If POP is at 60 at the end of July, that month's option will be worth 10, so you have to buy it back at a loss of about $650 plus in-and-out costs. But the October call might be at 14, so you could sell that for a gross profit of $1,000 to offset the July loss.

If the stock falls below 46½, you will lose money unless there's a recovery by October. But with such a stable stock in a rising market, this is not likely. The key factor is the small spread, which keeps the maximum loss low.

Perpendicular Spread

Also called a price or vertical spread, it is based on buying and selling options with the same exercise date but different strike prices.

Example: Easy Rider (ER) is at 101¾ . The market is moving up and you are bullish. Sell 10 ER October 100s at 12¼ and buy October 90s at 16⅞. This requires an outlay of $4,625. Your maximum loss will occur if ER plunges below 90.

If it goes to 95, you will still make $375. At 100 or higher, your profit will be a welcome $5,375, a 120% return on your investment.

If the market is declining, set up a bearish spread. Psychologically, the risk is greater, so it is best to deal with lower-priced stocks, selling at, say, 24⅝.

Buy 10 October 25s at 2⅛ and sell 10 October 20s at 5⅜. This brings in $3,250 cash. Because the October 20 calls are naked, you'll need $5,000 margin (but the premiums cut this to $1,750) to control nearly $50,000 worth of stock.

If the stock goes to 22, you will make $1,250. At 20 or below, your profit is $3,250 for a 180% return. With perpendicular spreads, you know results at any one time. With horizontal spreads, there's the added risk of time.

Straddle

A straddle is a double option, combining a call and a pu0t on the same stock, both at the same price and for the same length of time. Either or both sides of a straddle may be exercised at any time during the life of the option—for a high premium. Straddles are profitable when you are convinced that a stock will make a dramatic move but are uncertain whether the trend will be up or down.

Traditionally, most speculators use straddles in a bull market against a long position. If the stock moves up, the call side will be exercised and the put will expire unexercised. This is more profitable than writing calls, because the straddle premiums are substantially higher than those of straight calls.

But this can be costly in a down market. If the underlying stock goes down, there's a double loss:

in the call and in the put. Therefore, when a straddle is sold against a long position, the straddle premium received must, in effect, protect 200 shares.

In a bear market, it is often wise to sell straddles against a short position. The odds are better.

Here's how one self-styled trader did it:

Example: In January, QRS stock was at 100. This was close to the last year's high, and because the stock had bounced as low as 65, I felt the best straddle was short term, so I picked a February expiration date. Simultaneously, I bought a call and a put, both at 100: 5 ($500) for the call and 4 ($400) for the put. With commissions (for buying and selling) of about $100, my exposure was $1,000.

To make money, QRS had to rise above 110 or fall below 90. I guessed right. The stock's uptrend continued to 112. I sold the call for $1,300 and was lucky to get rid of the put at $50: profit—$350 in one month!

I would do OK if the stock fell to 88. Then the call would be worth ½ but the put would bring at least $1,200, so I end up with about $250.

The risk was that the stock's price would hold around 100. This would mean an almost total loss. But from experience I know that I'll lose on about 25% of my straddles, so I have to shoot for a high return on the other deals.

Strip

A strip is a triple option: two puts and one call on the same stock with a single option period and striking price. A strip writer expects the stock to fall in the short term and rise over the long term. He offers to sell 100 shares that he owns above the market price or take 200 shares below the market. The premium is higher than for a straddle.

Strap

This is also a triple option: two calls and one put on the same stock. The writer gets top premium—

bullish over the long term but more negative than the strip seller on short-term prospects.

Insurance

To protect a profit, buy a put on stock you own. *Example:* Your stock has soared from 30 to 60, so you expect a setback. You buy a short-term put, at 60, for $400. If the stock dips to 50, the put will be worth 10 ($1,000), so you sell for a profit of $600 and still own the stock. If the stock keeps moving up to 70, the put expires worthless. You lose $400, but you have a paper profit of $1,000 on the stock, so you are $600 ahead.

Lock in Capital Gains

The same technique can be used to lock in a capital gain. By buying the put at 60 for $400, you reduce the stock value to 56. If it falls to 50, you sell the stock at the exercise price of 60 for $6,000. Deduct the $400 premium from the $3,000 profit (from cost of 30) and you still have $2,600. That's $600 more than if you had held the stock until its price fell to 50.

MAKING MONEY WITH OPTIONS ON INDEXES

When the market is at an all-time high, as it was when we went to press, it's a good time to consider using options. This way you can hold onto your profits without selling your stocks.

Index options settle in cash—most of them for $100 × the index value. One exception: LEAPS (discussed above) which settle at $100 × 10% of the index value.

When protecting your stock portfolio with index options, bear in mind that the price-weighted indexes, such as the Major Market Index, are most influenced by the movements of the highest-priced stocks within their index, while capitalization-weighted indexes are most influ-

---

Making Your Own Put

Options are flexible and can be combined so that the stock purchases, sales, or short sales protect positions and make profits. Here's an example, by Max Ansbacher, of how to create your own put. Assume that in late summer, your stock is at 69⅞ and the January 65 call is 9¼. You sell short 100 shares of the stock and buy the call. Here are the possibilities:

- If the stock falls to 55 by the end of January, the call will be worthless, so you lose $925. But your profit from the short sale is $1,487.50 ($6,987.50 sale; $5,500 buyback cost) for a net profit of $562.50 (not counting commissions and fees).
- The option limits your risk of loss on the short sale even if the stock price should rise. Thus if the stock jumps to 100, an unprotected short sale would mean a loss of $3,012.50 ($10,000 purchase price minus $6,987.50 received from the short sale).
- But with a short sale of the stock and a purchase of a call, the loss will be only $437: the purchase price of 9¼ ($925) minus $488 (the spread between the stock price of 69⅞ and the exercise price of 65)—again not counting costs.

---

enced by movements in price of their largest stocks.

FOR FURTHER INFORMATION
Books

Kenneth H. Shaleen, *Technical Analysis and Options Strategies* (Chicago: Probus Publishing Co., 1992).

Pamphlets

Characteristics and Risks of Standardized Options
You are required to obtain a copy of this brochure if you want to trade options. Copies are available from the options exchanges and from brokerage offices.

Options Clearing Corporation
440 South LaSalle Street
Chicago, IL 60605
800–537–4258 or 800-OPTIONS
Has a number of inexpensive brochures for the public.

American Stock Exchange
Derivative Securities Dept
86 Trinity Place
New York, NY 10006
212–306–1000

Has general information brochures and strategy sheets describing in fairly easy, but detailed terms, how to make money with options.

LEAPS Investing Kit
The Options Exchange
400 South La Salle
Chicago, IL 60605
312–786–5600

17

Stock Rights and Warrants

STOCK RIGHTS

Stock rights are a special type of option that permits current shareholders in a corporation to buy more of that corporation's securities, usually common stock, ahead of the public, without commissions or fees, and typically at a discount of 5% to 10%. All of these factors can make certain rights a very good deal.

In most rights offerings, stockholders are allowed to purchase only a fractional share of the new common stock, based on the number of shares of common they already own. That means two or more rights are often required to buy one new share. The price, given in the rights offering or prospectus, is called the exercise or subscription price, and as already stated, it is below the current market price of the stock.

Rights offerings have a short market life, frequently running only for several weeks. If they are not used by their expiration date, they expire and lose all their value.

Why Do Rights Exist?

Rights are a convenient way for corporations to raise additional capital at a modest cost. They are often used by utilities eager to issue more common stock to balance their heavy debt obligations. The fact that they are offered at a discount from the regular market price of the stock makes it possible for investors (who obviously have confidence in the company) to acquire additional shares at a bargain price or to pick up a few extra dollars by selling the rights in the open market. In this sense, they are a type of reward to existing shareholders.

CAUTION: Keep in mind that rights are worthwhile only when the additional money raised by the company is expected to generate more corporate profits, eventually leading to increased dividends on the additional shares. This is an important aspect of judging rights, because essentially they represent a dilution of your ownership in the company.

How to Find Stock Rights

First, you must already own the common stock as of a stated date. If you do you will be notified in writing of the offering. Because most offerings must be exercised within a short time, usually less than 30 days, read your mail. Or, if your common shares are held in street name by your broker, ask him or her to keep you informed. You will then exercise your rights through your broker, or in some cases through the company itself. Failure to take advantage of a rights offering could turn out to be a financial mistake.

How Rights Work

The obvious advantages of a stock right is that it allows the holder to purchase stock at a reduced price and to do so without paying a broker's commission.

In addition, however, rights may have a speculative value because of the high leverage they offer: A 10% rise in the price of the stock can mean as much as a 30% jump in the value of the right, or vice versa on the loss side.

Let's assume that the stock is trading at $28 per share, that shareholders get one right for every 5 shares, and that each right entitles the holder to buy 1 new share at $25 each.

$$VR = \frac{MP - EP}{NR + 1}$$

Where: VR = value of right

MP = stock's market price

EP = exercise price

NR = number of rights needed to buy one share

To calculate the value of one right *before* the ex-date, add 1 to the number of rights:

$$VR = \frac{28 - 25}{5 + 1} = \frac{3}{6} = 0.50$$

Thus each right is worth 50¢, and the stock at this time is worth that much more to investors who exercise their rights.

After the stock has gone ex-right, there'll be no built-in bonus for the stock, and the right will sell at its own value, or possibly higher, if the price of the stock advances, lower if it declines.

The Advantages of Rights to Shareholders

■   *Maintenance of ownership position.* If you like a company well enough to continue as a share-holder, pick up the rights. Historically, 80% of stocks bought with rights have outperformed the market in the year following the issue. That's logical; management was optimistic.

■   *Bargain price.* For example, when Southwestern Public Service issued 29.2 million rights, the offer permitted shareholders to buy one additional common share at $10.95 for each 10 shares already held. At the time, the stock was trading at $11.50, so the new shares were available at a 4.8% discount. If you owned 1,000 shares, you could save about $55 on the deal, because there were no transaction costs.

■   *Profits from rights themselves.* If you do not want to acquire more stock, you can sell the rights in the open market, through your broker or through a bank designated by the company. With Southwestern, each right was worth 4⅝¢ ($4.625 for each 100 rights).

■   *Trading rights.* You can buy rights either to exercise them or as a speculation. Trading in rights starts as soon as the offer is announced. For a while, the prices of both the basic stock and the rights are quoted—the latter on a when issued (wi) basis, as shown with XYZ Corp. in the table above. As a rule, it's best to buy rights soon after they are listed in the financial press; it's best to sell a day or two before the lapse date.

Special Benefits

There are several other investment advantages to rights:

How Rights Are Quoted

52 WEEKS					WEEK'S	
HIGH	LOW	STOCK	SALES 100S	YIELD	HIGH	LOW
68	42	XYZ Corp.	132	3.7	64	62¼
1	⅜	XYZ Corp. rts.	27		⅞	½

1. *You can purchase the shares* offered with a very low margin requirement in a special subscription account (SSA). An SSA is a margin account set up for this purpose. Your broker will explain what is required to open this type of account.

   The key advantage is that the margin requirement for rights is only 25%, compared with 50% for regular stocks. You also have a year to pay, provided you come up with 25% of the balance due each quarter.

   Example: You have rights to buy ABC common, selling at 63, for 56 on the basis of 1 new share for 10 old shares. You acquire 100 rights, so you need $5,600 to complete the purchase. You can borrow up to 75% ($4,200), so you can make the deal with only $1,400 in cash or collateral. Every 3 months you must reduce the outstanding balance by 25%.

   CAUTION: The SSA has two critical disadvantages, however: (1) the price of the stock may decline and you will have to come up with more margin, and (2) you cannot draw cash dividends or use the securities for collateral as long as they are in this special account.

2. *Another advantage:* Neither the receipt nor the exercise of the right results in taxable income to the stockholder, but you will have to pay taxes on ultimate profits when the stock is sold.

3. *Oversubscription privileges.* Some shareholders will not exercise their rights, so after the expiration date, you can buy these rights, usually on the basis of your original allotment. You must indicate your wish to participate in the oversubscription early, preferably when you send in your check for the new shares.

WARRANTS

Warrants, unlike options, are issued by the corporation typically with new issues, bonds, or preferred stock. They are traded on the exchanges.

A warrant is an option to buy a stated number of shares of a related security (usually common stock) at a stipulated price during a specified period (5, 10, 20 years, or, occasionally, perpetually). The price at which the warrant can be exercised is fixed above the current market price of the stock at the time the warrant is issued. Thus when the common stock is at 10, the warrant might entitle the holder to buy 1 share at 15. (This differs from a right, where the subscription price is usually lower than the current market value of the stock and the time period is typically several weeks.)

Because the two securities tend to move somewhat in parallel, an advance in the price creates a higher percentage gain for the warrant than for the stock.

Example: Let's say that the warrant to buy 1 share at 15 sells at 1 when the stock is at 10. If the stock soars to 20 (100% gain), the price of the warrant will go up to at least 5 (400% gain).

But the downside risk of the warrant can be greater than that of the stock. If the stock drops to 5, that's a 50% loss. The warrant, depending on its life span, might fall to ⅛, an 88% decline.

A warrant is basically a call on a stock. It has no voting rights, pays no dividends, and has no claim on the assets of the corporation. Warrants trade on the exchanges and are usually registered in the owner's name. Some warrants are issued in certificate form, although most are not. On expiration date, a warrant loses all its trading value.

The value of a warrant reflects hope that the price of the stock will rise above the exercise price. When the stock trades below that call price, the warrant has only speculative value: With the stock at 19 and the exercise price at 20, the warrant is theoretically worthless. But it will actually trade at a price that reflects the prospectus of the company and the life of the warrant. When the price of the stock rises above the specified exercise price, the warrant acquires a tangible value, which is usually inflated by speculation plus a premium, because it is a lower-priced way of playing the common stock. However, the closer a warrant gets to its expiration date, the smaller the premium it commands. Conversely, the longer the life of the warrant, the higher the premium if there is real hope that the price of the stock will rise. After expiration, the warrant is worthless.

☑ *HINT: The main advantage warrants have over options is that they run for much longer. The longest an option lasts is 9 months. Warrants, however, run for years and some in perpetuity, which gives the investor a chance to speculate on a company over the long term at a relatively low cost. This time frame makes warrants less risky than options.*

Calculating the Value of a Warrant

The speculative value of a warrant is greatest when the warrant price is below the exercise price. If the stock moves up, the price of the warrant can jump fast. The table at right shows guidelines set by warrant expert S.L. Pendergast for the maximum premium to pay. For example, when the stock price is at the exercise price (100%), pay at most 41% of the exercise price. Thus with a stock at the exercise price of 30, the maximum price to pay for a warrant (on a one-for-one basis) would be about 12. In most cases, better profits will come when the warrant is bought at a lower price.

An actual example is Atlas Corp. warrants that are perpetual; that is, they do not expire. They trade on the ASE at $3, with an exercise price of $15.625. The market price of the stock, as of July 1995, was $1¾.

$3 \div 15.625 = 19\%$

These percentages fall outside the acceptable buying range using the table at right.

How to Select Profitable Warrants

Warrants are generally best in bull markets, especially during periods of great enthusiasm. Their

Maximum Premium to Pay

STOCK PRICE AS PERCENT OF EXERCISE PRICE	WARRANT PRICE AS PERCENT OF EXERCISE PRICE
80	28
90	34
100	41
110	46

low prices attract speculators who trade for quick gains. At all times, however, use these checkpoints:

■ BUY ONLY WARRANTS OF A COMMON STOCK THAT YOU WOULD BUY ANYWAY. If the common stock does not go up, there's little chance that the warrant's price will advance.

The best profits come from warrants associated with companies that have potential for strong upward swings due to sharp earnings improvement, a prospective takeover, news-making products or services, etc. It also helps if they are temporarily popular.

In most cases the warrants for fast-rising stocks, even at a high premium, will outperform seemingly cheap warrants for issues that are falling.

At the outset, stick with warrants of fair-to-good corporations whose stocks are listed on major exchanges. They have broad markets.

When you feel more confident, seek out special situations, especially warrants of small, growing firms. Many of these new companies rely on warrants in their financing. Their actual or anticipated growth can boost the price of their warrants rapidly.

💣 *CAUTION: But be wary of warrants where the related stock is limited or closely controlled. If someone decides to dump a block of stock, the values can fall fast.*

- BUY WARRANTS WHEN THEY ARE SELL-ING AT LOW PRICES. The percentages are with you when there's an upward move, and with minimal costs the downside risks are small. But watch out for super-bargains, because commissions will eat up most of the gains.

    Also watch their values and be cautious when their prices move to more than 20% of their exercise figure.

- WATCH THE EXPIRATION OR CHANGE DATE. After expiration, the warrant has no value. If you're conservative, stay away from warrants with a life span of less than 4 years. When you know what you are doing, short-life warrants can bring quick profits if you are smart and lucky. But be careful. You could end up with worthless paper.

- SPREAD YOUR RISKS. If you have sufficient capital, buy warrants in five different companies. The odds are that you may hit big on one, break even on two, and lose on the others. Your total gains may be less than if you had gambled on one warrant that proved a winner, but your losses will probably be less if you're wrong.

- LOOK FOR SPECIAL OPPORTUNITIES SUCH AS USABLE BONDS WITH WAR-RANTS ATTACHED. Some bonds are sold along with detachable warrants. In many cases the bonds can be used at par ($1,000) in paying the exercise price. In other words, they can be used in lieu of cash to pay for the stock at the specified warrant price.

    Should the bond trade at 90, a discount to par, the discounted price of the bond also discounts the exercise price of the warrant.

    Except in unusual situations, all warrants should be bought to trade or sell and not to exercise. With no income, usually a long wait for appreciation, and rapid price changes, warrants almost always yield quick gains to speculators who have adequate capital and time to watch the market.

10 Points for Evaluating Warrants

1. *Underlying stock price.* The higher the stock price, all other things being equal, the higher the value of the warrant.
2. *Stock volatility.* The higher the volatility of the underlying stock, the higher the value of the warrant. Volatile stocks are more likely to appreciate or depreciate substantially. A warrant, too, will benefit from appreciation.
3. *Dividend.* The higher the dividend on the underlying stock, the lower the value of the warrant. Warrant holders are not entitled to receive dividends paid to stockholders.
4. *Strike price.* The lower the exercise price, all other things being equal, the higher the value of the warrant.
5. *Time to expiration.* The longer the warrant's life, the higher the value of the warrant.

Some Popular Warrants

COMPANY	EXERCISE PRICE	PRICE OF COMMON	PRICE OF WARRANT
Kroger Equity	$8.00	$27	$1.75
Lone Star Industries	18.75	14¾	7.75
Manville Corp.	9.40	12	2.75
Saga Communications "A"	15.00	23	2.75

SOURCE: Standard & Poor's *Stock Guide,* Fall 1996.

6. *Interest rates.* Higher rates tend to increase the value of warrants.
7. *Call features.* Call features shorten the life of the warrant and detract from its value.
8. *Usable bonds.* A usable bond can be used at par to pay the exercise price of a warrant. This gives a warrant added value.
9. *Ability to borrow the underlying stock.* This tends to depress the warrant's value.
10. *Takeovers.* If the company is taken over at a high price, warrants will appreciate.

Selling Warrants Short

Selling short means selling a security you do not own, borrowing it from your broker to make delivery. This is done in anticipation of a decline in price. Later you expect to buy it at a lower price and make the profit between that lower price and your original short sale.

But short selling is always tricky, and with warrants there can be other problems: (1) limited markets because of lack of speculator interest; (2) exchange regulations—e.g., the American Stock Exchange prohibits short selling of its listed warrants several months before expiration date; (3) the possibility of a short squeeze—the inability to buy warrants to cover your short sales as the expiration date approaches; (4) the possibility that the life of the warrants may be extended beyond the stated expiration date, advancing the date when the warrants become worthless, so a short seller may not be able to cover a position at as low a price as was anticipated.

Where to Find Warrants

Warrants Are Issued:

■ with bonds as a sweetener to buy them
■ as part of initial public offering packages consisting of shares of common as warrants
■ in conjunction with mergers and acquisitions

Where to Find Warrants:

■ Brokerage firm research lists
■ Newspaper securities listings, where they are identified by the letters "wt"

18

New Issues

New issues are one of the liveliest and most appealing areas of investment—perhaps because they represent part of the American dream, that start-up companies can succeed in this country. If you're one of those who find the idea of investing in start-ups tempting, it's essential that you follow the guidelines for selecting such companies and make your decision based on the facts, not your emotions.

It is indeed possible to make money in IPOs, but it requires far more research than most investments, as well as an understanding of the market. Norman G. Fosback, editor of *New Issues*, favors companies that have reported profits for at least 5 years and whose earnings are trending upwards.

If you don't buy an IPO when it's first issued, you can buy shares in the aftermarket when they trade OTC. If it's a weak market, chances are you won't pay much more, if anything; but in a hot market, expect a 20% to 25% increase in the aftermarket. If you are enamored of the issue but cannot buy at a reasonable price, follow the stock's progress carefully. Wait for the first blush to fade, and move in when it takes a tumble. Often a new company will lose its initial luster or report lower earnings, thus pushing the price down temporarily.

☑ *HINT: Learning about new issues is less difficult than you might think. A number of the larger brokerage firms publish a list of them on a regular*

basis, but unless you're a major client, you won't hear about them. Your broker or library may subscribe to the bible in the field, Investment Dealer's Digest, *which lists all IPOs as they are registered with the SEC.*

THE UNDERWRITER

Your chances for success will be increased if you select IPOs from reputable investment bankers. First-class underwriters will not allow themselves to manage new issues that are of poor quality or highly speculative. Moreover, if a fledgling company runs into a need for additional financing, a first-rate banker will be ready to raise more capital. Thus the prime consideration is the reputation of the underwriters. However, this guideline is not written in stone.

THE PROSPECTUS

Once you learn about a new issue, your first investigative step is to read a copy of the prospectus, generally available when an offering is registered with the SEC. (It's also called a red herring because of the red-inked warning that the contents of the report are not final.) Despite its many caveats, the prospectus will help you form a rough opinion about the company and what it may be worth. Look for:

Details about Management

The success of a company is often determined by the quality of the management team. The officers and directors should have successful experience in the company and/or similar organizations; they should be fully involved in the firm and should not treat it as a part-time activity.

Type of Business

New ventures have the best chance of success in growth areas, such as electronics, specialty retailing, and biotechnology. Software companies, environmental cleanup, waste disposal stocks, and health care are expected to do well. The risks are greatest with companies in exciting but partially proven fields such as biotechnology, genetic engineering, and AIDS research. These companies are tempting but pay off only after heavy capital investments and successful R&D. Try to invest in an area you know something about or a business located near you. A good prospectus will also list some of the company's customers.

Financial Strength and Profitability

Apply the following criteria to the current balance sheet. Glance at the previous year's report to catch any major changes.

- Modest short-term debt and long-term obligations of less than 40% of total capital. With $40 million in assets, the debt should not be more than $16 million.
- Current ratio (of assets to liabilities) a minimum of 2:1 except under unusual, temporary conditions.
- Sales of at least $30 million to be sure that there's a market for products or services. Double-check if revenues exceed $50 million. That's the threshold for the big leagues, where competition is sure to heighten.

- High profitability: a return on equity of 20% annually for the past 3 years—with modest modifications if recent gains have been strong. This will assure similar progress in the future.

Earnings

The company should be able to service its debt. Look for the most recent P/E and compare it with P/Es of competitors, listed in the newspaper. If a P/E is significantly higher than the industry average of a similar-sized company, shares are overpriced.

☑ *HINT: Because a young company has not had sufficient time to build up profits and earnings, you should also study the ratio of total offering price to annual sales. On the whole, this market-capitalization-to-sales ratio should not be greater than 2:7.*

Use of Proceeds

Check out what the company plans to do with the newly raised capital. It should not be devoted to repaying the debt or bailing out the founders, management, or promoters. Most of it should be used to expand the business. If 25% or more is going toward nonproductive purposes, move on. Avoid firms whose management or a founding shareholder is selling a large percentage of the shares (30% or more).

☑ *HINT: Whenever the public is chasing after new issues, beware of telephone solicitations from high-pressure salesmen who guarantee that you'll double your money once the company goes public. Careful: You're skating on very thin ice.*

FINDING OUT ABOUT IPOS

Many brokers will let their clients know about new issues that their firm either knows about or is

Six Mutual Funds that Invest in Small, Emerging Companies

FUND	TELEPHONE
Govett Smaller Companies	800–634–6838
PBHG Growth	800–809–8008
Goldman Sachs Small Cap	800–526–7384
Seligman Frontier A	800–221–2783
Putnam OTC Emerging Growth	800–225–1581
Franklin Small Cap Growth	800–324–5236

(As of October 1996)

underwriting. Make certain your broker knows of your interest. In addition, check the publications listed below. Several, such as *Barron's* and *Investment Dealer's Digest*, cover IPOs along with all types of financial news. They will give you the following information:

- Name of stock and symbol
- Expected date
- Use of proceeds
- Name of underwriter
- Financial data and balance sheet
- Write-up of what the company has done and plans to do, plus an evaluation of the IPO as an investment

FOR FURTHER INFORMATION

To help you spot the winners and avoid the losers when firms go public, you may want to read one of the following advisory newsletters for background data:

Newsletters

Emerging and Special Situations
Standard & Poor's Corp.
25 Broadway
New York, NY 10004
800–221–5277; 212–208–8000
Monthly; $259 per year; 3-month trial: $65.

New Issues
Institute for Econometric Research
2200 SW Tenth Street
Deerfield Beach, FL 33442
800–327–6720; 954–421–1000
Monthly; $95 per year.

Barron's
200 Burnett Road
Chicopee, MA 01020
800–568–7625
Weekly; $140 per year.

New Issues Outlook
50 Main Street
White Plains, NY 10606
800–477–3331; 914–421–1500
Every 10 days; $335 per year; 6-week trial: $39.
Full-page, advance reports on all IPOs, plus follow-up material in the aftermarket for nine months.

Magazines

Investment Dealers Digest/IDD Magazine
2 World Trade Center (18th floor)
New York, NY 10048
212–227–1200
Weekly; $625 per year. Full-page, advance reports on all IPOs, plus follow-up in the aftermarket for 9 months.

PART FOUR

High Risk for High Returns

At a certain point in your investment life, a portion of your portfolio should be earmarked for more speculative plays. You know, of course, that you could lose money, so limit your commitment to no more than 15% of your funds. If you are smart—and lucky—enough to make a killing, immediately put half of your winnings into a money market fund, certificate of deposit, or Treasuries in order to earn interest and wait for the next investment opportunity.

Speculations are not entirely investments. This statement sounds simple-minded, but most people fail to make the distinction. Investments are designed to preserve capital and to provide income. The decisions are made on the basis of fundamentals: the quality and the value of the investment.

Speculations involve risks and are profitable primarily because of market fluctuations. They should not be part of your retirement portfolio. They should be entered into only when you understand what you are doing and with money that you can afford to lose. To be on the safe side, keep in mind that with any speculative choice:

- There is usually a sound reason why a security is selling at a low price or paying a very low yield. Find out just exactly why.
- In making projections, cut in half the anticipated upward move and double the potential downswing.
- Speculate only in a rising market unless you are selling short. Worthwhile gains will come when more people buy more shares—not likely in a down market.
- Be willing to take quick, small losses, and never hold on in blind hope of a recovery.
- When you pick a winner, sell half your shares (or set a protective stop-loss order) when you have doubled your money.

On the next few pages you will read about:

- Foreign stocks, bonds, currencies, and CDs
- Commodities
- Precious metals
- Financial futures and market indexes
- Splits, spin-offs, small-caps, Spiders, and stock buybacks

19

Foreign Stocks, Bonds, CDs, and Currencies

Americans have always been enchanted by products from abroad—French champagne, Swiss chocolate, Japanese cars, German beer, and more recently Australian wine and South African diamonds. During the last few years we've also become aware of the importance and at the same time, riskiness of investing abroad.

The electronic age has made the flow of money and information almost instantaneous, so whatever happens on the Hong Kong stock exchange or to the price of gold in London has a direct impact on investors in Des Moines, Duluth, and Davenport. As we draw closer and closer to one global market, it is essential to widen your investment horizons.

If you're not convinced, consider this awesome statistic: Two-thirds of the total value of the world's stock markets is outside the U.S.

THE RIPPLE EFFECT

A key positive for going global is the so-called international ripple effect: At various times and in certain economic cycles, you can make money, because each country's economic cycle is a separate one. When one nation is in the midst of a recession, others are inevitably thriving. However, timing overseas investments is tricky.

PRECAUTIONARY TIPS FOR BEGINNERS

- International investing is far more complicated than investing in the United States. Stock markets in other countries have different listing requirements for issues, often requesting fewer financial disclosures and having much looser accounting standards.
- When you invest in a foreign stock, you invest also in foreign currency. Changes in the value of the dollar can reduce your profits or reduce your losses.

For example, if you buy a French stock for 42 French francs and the dollar is worth 4 francs, your cost is $10.50/share. If a year later the stock has risen to 50 francs, you may want to sell and take your profit. In the meantime, however, the dollar has also gotten stronger and is now worth 5 francs. If you sell you will actually get only $10/share and you will have a loss of 50¢. The rule of thumb is:

Foreign stocks tend to do well if the dollar drops against that foreign currency. Even if the stock doesn't actually rise in price but the dollar declines against the currency of that country, you will make a profit when you sell. Why? Because the foreign currency you receive from the stock sale, when converted into dollars, converts into more dollars than it cost you to buy the stock. If the stock should also independently rise in price, you will achieve even more profits.

On the other hand, a decline in the foreign currency will eat into potential profits.

In other words, an investment in a foreign stock offers at least two ways to make a profit or loss:

- The price of the stock can go up (or down) in its local currency.
- The value of the foreign country's currency can rise (or drop) relative to the U.S. dollar, thereby increasing or decreasing the value of your stock.

The best situation obviously exists when the price of the stock rises and the value of the country's currency likewise rises against the dollar.

However, it's not easy for anyone, even the professional managers of mutual funds that invest abroad, to call the shots right all of the time, And, despite the compelling reasons for international investing, many otherwise clever investors still remain unschooled in the mechanics involved. The necessary guidelines, given here, can be mastered by anyone with the time and inclination to do so.

We'll discuss the major ways to invest in foreign countries, with the exception of real estate; they are, in order of coverage within this chapter:

- U.S. multinational companies
- American Depository Receipts (ADRs)
- Mutual funds
- Closed-end foreign country funds
- Foreign CDs
- Currencies and futures

U.S. MULTINATIONAL COMPANIES

American multinationals—companies with at least 25% to 30% of earnings and profits derived from foreign business—make it possible to invest globally while sitting at home. Among the large number of U.S. blue-chip corporations that fall into this multinational category are:

- Abbott Labs
- Avery Dennison
- Avon Products
- Coca-Cola
- Colgate-Palmolive
- Compaq
- CPC International
- General Electric
- Gillette
- Exxon
- Hewlett-Packard
- IBM
- McDonald's
- Microsoft
- Mobil Oil
- Motorola
- PepsiCo
- Procter & Gamble
- Westinghouse
- Wrigley

You'll find it's simple to find solid research on any of these companies, get copies of their annual and quarterly reports, and know what products and services they offer and how good they are.

Among those with less well-known names are:

- AMP Inc.
- Arwin Ind.
- Donaldson Co.
- Dresser Ind.
- Kennametal
- Mallinckrodt
- Medtronic
- Nucor
- Perkin-Elmer
- Praxair Inc.
- Premark Int'l
- Witco Corp.

Foreign Investment

PROS

↑ Provides diversification

↑ Provides additional investment opportunities not available in U.S. markets

↑ Provides hedge against U.S. monetary or economic troubles such as inflation, dollar depreciation, slump in stock market

↑ As vitality shifts from one country to another, foreign firms may represent attractive alternatives

CONS

↓ Currency fluctuations

↓ Local political situations

↓ Less information available on foreign companies than on U.S. firms

↓ Foreign firms not required to provide the same detailed type of information as U.S. firms

↓ Different accounting procedures, which can make accurate evaluation complex

↓ Foreign brokers and foreign exchanges seldom bound by regulations as strict as those imposed by the SEC (every country has its own set of regulations)

↓ Quotes sometimes difficult to obtain

Special Advice For 1997

With new markets rapidly opening up due to the European Community as well as in the Pacific Rim, Eastern Europe, and South and Central America, many of the multinationals with strong balance sheets are well positioned to take advantage of the surging demand for their goods and services. In fact, the multinationals are often the first to establish trade agreements in the emerging markets.

Look in particular to multinationals in these industries: chemicals, drugs, household products, American-style food and restaurants, appliances, telephones, and computers.

Think Argentina

This country's economy, in the summer of 1996, began to come back from the negative fallout from the collapse of the Mexican peso. Argentinian banks lost about 20% of their deposits within just five months in 1995; now their vaults are overflowing. Experts are predicting 3% to 5% growth in the GDP for 1997. Among industries that could prosper: autos, chemicals, communications, and banks. If you're interested in a potentially high growth (but risky) overseas investment, these five companies have millions of dollars committed to Argentina:

- Ford Motor Co.
- Fiat
- Dow Chemical
- Banamex
- Telefonica

INVESTING GUIDELINES

When selecting a multinational stock, keep in mind that:

- When foreign currencies rise relative to the dollar, earnings from an American company's foreign operations are instantly worth more.
- A strong dollar tends to hurt these stocks; it makes U.S. products expensive for foreign buyers and foreign products cheaper for American consumers.
- A strong dollar also creates an exchange loss—that is, if the money an American earns abroad loses value against the dollar, the earnings for the company and its stockholders are reduced.
- The more a U.S. multinational depends on exports for sales, the more it will benefit from a weaker dollar. That means multinationals are a good hedge against a declining dollar.

Select a multinational that:

1. Has a sound, sophisticated management team
2. Is not burdened by too much debt
3. Has products and/or services that are unique or better than their foreign counterparts
4. Has sizable U.S.-generated earnings as a cushion against a decline in foreign revenues
5. Has rising earnings
6. Is ranked #1 or #2 in timeliness and in safety in *Value Line Investment Survey*

TWO MULTINATIONAL STOCKS TO CONSIDER IN 1997

These stocks are well positioned to take advantage of a European, Far Eastern, and Latin American recovery.

- *BellSouth.* Through subsidiaries, this regional Bell has cellular interest in a number of countries, including Argentina, Australia, Chile, Denmark, Germany, India, Israel, Venezuela; it has received a 20-year license to build and run Panama's first cellular telephone network. It also owns almost one-fourth of Optus, a company licensed by the government of Australia to build and operate that country's second telecom network.
- *Deere & Co.* Strong demand for this manufacturer of farm equipment exists in many overseas countries, especially in Asia and the former Soviet Union. Export sales are up.

USING BASKETS AND WEBS

Two new financial projects launched in March of 1996, CountryBaskets and WEBS (World Equity Benchmark Shares) are designed to make overseas investing simpler. Both offer stocks that represent holdings in individual countries—the Country-Baskets has nine and there are 17 in WEBS.

CountryBaskets is managed by Deutsche Morgan Grenfell/C.J. Lawrence, a U.S. arm of Germany's Deutsche Bank, and WEBS is managed by BZW Barclays Global Fund Advisors, a British outfit.

Prices for these new investments will change continually (with mutual funds, the prices for purchases and redemptions are determined only at the end of the trading day and investors don't know what price they'll pay when they place their order. With these new stocks you'll trade shares just as with any other stock, knowing the price at trading time.

Both CountryBaskets and WEBS are built around a single-country index fund that mirrors the fluctuations of the nation's market:

- COUNTRYBASKETS, on the NYSE, has stocks of Australia, France, Germany, Hong Kong, Italy, Japan, South Africa, United Kingdom, and the United States.
- WEBS, on the AMEX, has stocks of Australia, Austria, Belgium, Canada, France, Germany, Hong Kong, Italy, Japan, Malaysia, Mexico, the Netherlands, Singapore, Spain, Sweden, Switzerland, and the United Kingdom.

A MULTINATIONAL DIRECTORY

These corporations derive at least 30% of sales from international operations. Read their current write-ups in Value Line or get your broker's research.

Auto Industry

Cummins Engine
Echlin Inc.
Goodyear Tire & Rubber
TRW Inc.

Chemicals

Dow Chemical
Lubrizol Corp.
Monsanto Co.
PPG Industries

Computer/Software

Apple Computer
Hewlett-Packard
Microsoft Corp.
Sun Microsystems

Food and Beverages

Coca-Cola
Heinz (H.J.)
McDonald's Corp.
Ralston Purina
Sara Lee

Drugs

Abbott Labs
American Home Products
Bausch & Lomb
Bristol-Myers Squibb

Household Products

Avon
Black & Decker
Procter & Gamble

Other

Eastman Kodak
Emerson Electric
Millipore Corp.
Minnesota Mining & Mfg.
Polaroid Corp.
United Technologies
Xerox Corp.

AMERICAN DEPOSITORY RECEIPTS (ADRs)

ADRs are negotiable receipts representing owner-ship of shares of a foreign corporation that is traded in an American securities market. They are issued by an American bank, but the actual shares are held by the American bank's foreign deposi-tory bank or agent. This custodian bank is usually, but not always, an office of the American bank (if there is one in the country involved). If not, the bank selected to be custodian is generally a foreign bank with a close relationship to the foreign com-pany for which the ADRs are being issued.

ADRs allow you to buy, sell, or hold the for-eign stocks without actually taking physical pos-session of them. They are registered by the SEC and are sold by stockbrokers. Each ADR is a con-tract between the holder and the bank, certifying that a stated number of shares of the overseas-based company have been deposited with the American bank's foreign office or custodian and will be kept there as long as the ADR remains out-standing. The U.S. purchaser pays for the stock in dollars and receives dividends in dollars.

When the foreign corporation has a large capitalization so that its shares sell for the equiva-lent of a few dollars, each ADR may represent more than 1 share: 10, 50, or even 100 shares in the case of some Japanese companies, where there are millions of shares of common stock.

ADRs are generally initiated when an American bank learns that there is a great deal of interest in the shares of a foreign firm, or when a foreign corporation wants to enter the American market. In either case, the bank then purchases a large block of shares and issues the ADRs, leaving the stock certificates overseas in its custodian bank.

If you decide to buy ADRs, select those actively traded in the United States—i.e., listed on one of the exchanges. (Those that are not listed trade over-the-counter. Their prices are not given in the newspaper, but available from brokers.)

IMPORTANCE OF DIVERSIFICATION

As with any investment, diversification greatly reduces the level of risk involved. With foreign ADRs, stocks, or funds it is especially important to avoid reliance on the performance of any one

ADR or stock, any one industry, or even one country. Risk reduction is best achieved by spreading your investment dollars in at least one of the following ways:

■ *By country.* When some foreign stock markets fall, it is inevitable that others will rise. Diversification by country offers a hedge against a poor economic climate in any one area. Keep in mind that the U.S. market tends to be an anticipatory one, reflecting what the American investor thinks will happen in the forthcoming months.

■ *By type of industry.* Buying shares in more than one industry—high-tech, computers, oil, automobiles, etc.—likewise provides protection.

■ *By company within the industry.* For example, an energy portfolio could include stocks from a number of companies located in the North

Sea area, Southeast Asia, Canada, and the United States.

■ *By region.* Diversify among the regions of the world. Never become too dependent on any one area.

MUTUAL FUNDS

Another way to go global with relative ease and little paperwork, especially if you do not have the time or inclination to do your own research, is to purchase shares in one of the funds specializing in foreign investments. In this way, you can participate in a diversified portfolio and, as with domestic funds, reap the advantages of professional management—in this case, with foreign expertise. Although most of these funds are American owned and operated, they have foreign consultants (and offices) providing up-to-the-minute

ADRs to Consider in 1997–1998

ADR	SYMBOL	BUSINESS
Amway Japan	AJL	Distributor
Barclays plc	BCS	British bank
British Airways	BAB	Airline
British Gas	BRG	Gas
British Petroleum	BP	Oil
British Telecom	BTY	Telephone
Cable & Wireless	CWP	UK phone co
Elf Aquitaine	ELF	French oil co
Glaxco Holding plc	GLX	Pharmaceuticals
Honda Motor	HMC	Japanese cars
Hong Kong Telecom	HKT	Telephone
Imperial Chemical	ICI	Chemicals
Korea Electric Power	KEP	Utility
National Westminster	NW	British bank
News Corp., Ltd.	NWS	Publishing
Shell Transport	SC	Refining
SmithKline Beecham plc	SBH	Drug/Tagament
Stet	STEI	Italian telecom
Tele Danmark	TLD	Danish telecom
Unilever	UN	Consumer goods
Vodafone	VOD	UK cellular phone

research on specific stocks as well as on the country's political situation and outlook.

There are two basic types of foreign funds: international funds, which invest exclusively abroad, and global funds, which mix U.S. and foreign equities. Among those whose prospectuses you should read are:

- *For global funds*: Fidelity Worldwide, Scudder Global Small Company, and Lexington Global Fund
- *For international funds:* T. Rowe Price International Stock Fund, Scudder International Fund, Oakmark International, Warburg, Pincus International Equity Fund, and Twentieth Century International Equity
- *For emerging markets:* Fidelity Emerging Markets and Montgomery Emerging Markets
- *For Europe:* Invesco European Fund, Financial Strategic European Portfolio, and T. Rowe Price European
- *For Latin America:* Scudder Latin American Fund
- *For Asia*: T. Rowe Price New Asia and Fidelity Pacific Basin

FOREIGN BOND FUNDS

Most of these funds are global and include some U.S. bonds in their portfolios. The individual funds have different requirements that determine what they can invest in. Some, such as the

Mutual Funds that Invest in Foreign Bonds

FUND	YIELD	TELEPHONE
Fidelity Global Bond	4.21%	800–544–8888
GT Global Government Income	6.51	800–824–1580
PaineWebber Global	5.32	800–457–0849
Scudder International Bond	4.96	800–225–2470
T. Rowe Price International Bond	5.53	800–638–5660
Templeton Global	5.71	800–237–0738

(As of November 1996)

Five Short-Term Global Income Funds

FUND	YIELD	TELEPHONE
Alliance	8.10%	800–221–5672
Blanchard	5.59	800–922–7771
Eaton Vance	8.21	800–225–6265
Fidelity	5.21	800–544–8888
Scudder	4.94	800–225–2470

(As of November 1996)

T. Rowe Price Global Government Bond Fund, invest primarily in high-quality U.S. and foreign government bonds. A more aggressive philosophy allows the GT Global High Income to buy debt of emerging countries, such as Mexico and Argentina.

SHORT-TERM GLOBAL INCOME FUNDS

High yields in short-term global funds are enticing, but take care. This type of fund has risk and volatility. These funds invest primarily in high-grade foreign debt with maturities of 3 years or less, and usually have some portion of their assets in dollar-denominated securities.

For example, Fidelity's Short-Term World Fund, yielding nearly 5.21% in late 1996, is primarily invested in the United States, Canada, Sweden, France, Mexico, and Italy. Its aim is to purchase A-rated securities, yet up to 35% of its assets may be in BBB- or BB-rated securities, and within that 35%, 10% in BB debt.

The oldest of the short-term global funds, the Alliance Short-Term Multi-Market Trust, has had remarkably stable share prices—$7.51 when first sold in 1989 and, as of September 1996, $7.67.

CAUTION: Although these funds are often marketed as relatively low-risk alternatives to money market funds or CDs, don't be misled. They are not a substitute for either. Their share price, unlike that of a money market fund, fluctuates with interest and currency swings, making them considerably higher in risk.

CLOSED-END COUNTRY FUNDS

These funds are an excellent way for investors to participate in foreign bull markets without having to select individual stocks. However, they are not risk-free and should not be confused with international mutual funds.

They are still less popular than their close cousin, open-end mutual funds, and there are fewer to select from: 135 closed-end foreign country sector funds versus over 2,000 open-end mutual funds.

Unlike open-end funds, which continually issue new shares to the public, closed-end funds sell their shares just once, when they begin operating. After that, shares can be bought or sold only on stock exchanges or over-the-counter through a broker. Their prices then move up and down with investor demand just like any stock. Consequently, their price is often above or below net asset value (NAV), the value of the holdings in the portfolio divided by the number of shares. When the price of a fund is above NAV, it is being sold at a premium; when it falls below NAV, it's at a discount (see box on page 199). Before purchasing shares, read Chapter 7.

☑ *HINT: Buy at a discount. Closed-end funds provide investors with the possibility of buying a dollar's worth of common stock for less than $1. This occurs if you buy shares at a discount and thereafter the shares move up to or above NAV.*

This can work negatively in reverse: If you're forced to sell your shares at the same or a larger discount, you'll lose money.

Most closed-end shares trade at a premium to NAV for a spell just after their initial public offering. Then, if they continue to sell at premium, it's often because they've cornered the market. Generally, however, closed-end funds trade at a discount to NAV, partly because there are no salespeople keeping them in the public eye.

☑ *IF YOU DARE: Purchase closed-end shares at a discount and hold until they are selling at or above NAV. When funds reach NAV, they may become takeover targets or be converted into a regular mutual fund, at which point they are automatically repriced at 100¢ on the dollar.*

FOREIGN CDs

Yet another path to foreign investing is through foreign-currency CDs. They're available at large U.S. branches of overseas banks, through some currency traders, and at the three U.S. banks listed below.

These foreign CDs can be a good investment if the dollar is weak and/or the foreign interest rate is higher than you can get at home. If the dollar rises, however, you could wind up with a huge loss.

Citibank, for example, has accounts available in a number of different currencies. The minimum deposit requirement is the equivalent of $25,000.

Seven Foreign Stocks and ADRs for 1997

COMPANY	COUNTRY	BUSINESS	PRICE/SPRING 1996
Banco Santander	Spain	Banking	$45
Cable & Wireless	UK	Telecom	20
Ericcson	Sweden	Telecom	21
Fletcher Challenge	New Zealand	Paper	18
Norsk Hydro	Norway	Energy	44
Philips Electronics	Netherlands	Electronics	35
Singer	Hong Kong	Sewing machines	25

Closed-End Country Funds for 1997

NAME	SYMBOL
Asia Pacific	APB
Austria	OST
Chile	CH
First Australia	IAF
First Iberian	IBF
First Philippine	FPF
India Growth	IGF
Italy	ITA
Korea	KF
Malaysia	MF
Mexico	MXF
New Germany	GF
ROC Taiwan	ROC
Scudder New Asia	SAF
Singapore Fund	SGF
Spain	SNF
Swiss Helvetia	SWZ
Taiwan	TWN
Templeton Emerging Markets	EMF
Thai	TTF
Turkish Inv. Fund	TFK
United Kingdom	UKM

Foreign Country Sector Funds

PROS

↑ Professionally managed
↑ Offer diversifications within a country, which reduces risk
↑ Provide a hedge against U.S. market
↑ Way to maintain position in overseas markets
↑ High liquidity
↑ May be able to buy shares at a discount

CONS

↓ If foreign currency declines, value of your investment drops
↓ Value of stocks in fund can fall
↓ May be special taxes for Americans
↓ Political uncertainty
↓ Price of funds subject to fluctuations, like any stock
↓ Foreign markets less well regulated than U.S. market

At the Mark Twain bank it's $20,000. Although these accounts are protected by FDIC insurance up to $100,000, they are not protected from losses due to currency swings. And, at the First Union Bank the minimum is a hefty $100,000.

For specific details on buying foreign Cds, these three banks will help you out:

- Citibank, Tarrytown, New York, 800–755–5654
- First Union National Bank, Charlotte, North Carolina, 800–736–5636
- Mark Twain Bank, St. Louis, Missouri, 800–926–4922

TRAVELER'S CHECKS

A low-cost way to play the game is to purchase traveler's checks in the currency you feel will rise against the dollar. Cash them in when that currency rises to pocket your gains.

The key disadvantage with traveler's checks is that you do not earn interest on your money.

FOREIGN CURRENCY TRADING

Currency Options

Before investing in currency options, take time to read Chapter 16 on options. Then, if you think a given currency will rise against the U.S. dollar, you can buy a call. If you think it will fall, then purchase a put.

Let's say, for example, you believe that the dollar will fall against the Japanese yen. By purchasing

Four Ways to Make a Profit Overseas

- When the price of a stock rises
- When a foreign currency rises against the U.S. dollar
- When you buy shares in a closed-end investment company at a discount to NAV, and the discount narrows because of increased demand
- When both the stock and the foreign currency advance, creating a compounding effect

In the Know: 10 Terms to Impress Your Broker

- *ADR* American Depository Receipt; document indicating you own shares in a foreign stock held by a U.S. bank. ADRs trade on the exchanges or over-the-counter.
- *Big Bang* October 27, 1986, when the London Stock Exchange ended fixed brokerage commissions
- *Bourse* French word for stock exchange (from purse). Also used by exchanges in Switzerland and Belgium.
- *Denationalization* When a corporation is turned over to private ownership
- *ECU* European currency unit; developed by nations of the European Common Market
- *Eurobond* Bond issued in one European country's currency but sold outside that country
- *Gilts* Government bonds and money market securities in Britain
- *Out-sourcing* Shopping the world for the least-expensive suppliers of parts or products and services
- *SDRs* Special drawing rights; credits issued by the International Monetary Fund to its member countries; can be traded on the open market to stabilize the value of a currency in the foreign exchange market
- *Supranationals* Agencies formed by groups of countries to help their economies; International Monetary Fund, World Bank

a call option on the yen, you gain the right to purchase a stated number of yen at a predetermined strike price in dollars. You have that right until the expiration date—usually at 3-month intervals.

CAUTION: If the option exercise date comes up and the yen is below your strike price, your entire investment is lost.

Options of seven countries are traded on the Philadelphia Exchange. They are for the deutsche mark (DM), pound sterling, Canadian dollar, Japanese yen, Australian dollar, French franc, and Swiss franc. The premiums run from $25 for a short-life out-of-the-money option to $2,000 for a long-term deep-in-the-money call or put.

These options expire at 3-month intervals.

The quotations are in U.S. cents per unit of the underlying currency (with the exception of the yen, where it's $\frac{1}{100}$¢): Thus, the quote 1.00 DM means 1¢ per mark, and because the contract covers 62,500 DM, the total premium would be $625.

Futures Contracts

Futures contracts on various foreign currencies are traded on the International Monetary Market Division (IMM) of the Chicago Mercantile Exchange.

For the most part, positions are taken by importers and exporters who want to protect their profits from sudden swings in the relation between the dollar and a specific foreign currency. A profit on the futures contract will be offset by a loss in the cash market, or vice versa. Either way, the businessperson or banker guarantees a set cost.

The speculation performs an essential function by taking opposite sides of contracts, but unlike other types of commodities trading, currency futures reflect reactions to what has already happened more than anticipation of what's ahead.

For small margins of 1.5% to 4.2%, roughly $1,500 to $2,500, you can control large sums of money: 100,000 Canadian dollars, 125,000 German marks, 12.5 million Japanese yen, etc.

The attraction is leverage. You can speculate that, at a fixed date in the future, the value of your contract will be greater (if you buy long) or less (if you sell short).

The daily fluctuations of each currency futures contract are limited by IMM rules. A rise of $750 per day provides a 37.5% profit on a $2,000 investment. That's a net gain of $705 ($750 less $45 in commissions). If the value declines, you are faced with a wipeout or, if you set a stop order, the loss of part of your security deposit, and vice versa when you sell short.

One of the favorite deals is playing crosses, taking advantage of the spread between different currencies: buying francs and selling liras short, etc. For example, when the German mark was falling faster than the Swiss franc relative to the U.S. dollar, an investor set up this spread:

April 15: He buys a June contract for 125,000 francs and sells short a June contract for 125,000 marks. The franc is valued at .6664¢, the mark at .5536¢. Cost, not including commissions, is the margin: $2,000.

May 27: The franc has fallen to .6461, the mark to .5120. He reverses his trades, selling the June contract for francs and buying the mark contract to cover his short position.

Result: The speculator loses 2.03¢ per franc, or $2,537.50, but he makes 4.16¢ per mark, or

$5,200,00. The overall gain, before commissions, is $2,662.50, a return of 133% on the $2,000 investment—in about 6 weeks.

CAUTION: *Trading in foreign currencies can be exciting and profitable. It can also be hazardous to your financial health. Small margins tempt novices overlooking the fact that they are financially liable for the full extent of any losses. So:*

- *Don't* trade currencies or futures on currencies unless you know the full extent of your potential loss. Write it down.
- *Don't* get involved at all unless you have a reliable and trustworthy stockbroker or adviser.

FOR FURTHER INFORMATION
Books

You can add to your list of multinationals by studying one of the standard reference books such as Moody's *Handbook* and Standard & Poor's *Stock Market Guide* or *Value Line*. All three give the percentage of a company's earnings and sales derived from foreign operations. You should also read various company annual reports to learn what areas their sales come from. Earnings from Western Europe and Japan are currently more stable than those from Latin America.

Moody's International Manual and News Reports
Moody's Investors Service
99 Church Street
New York, NY 10007
800–342–5647; 212–553–0546
3-volume annual; $3,175.
Contains financial information on 9,000 stocks and institutions in 100 countries.

Nancy Dunnan and Douglas Schaf, *How to Make Money Investing Abroad* (New York: HarperCollins, 1995) covers the topics discussed in this chapter in greater detail.

Why Exchange Rates Fluctuate

Exchange rates among currencies fluctuate for a number of reasons. Here are the key factors to watch.

- Inflation. Rates move to reflect changes in the currencies' purchasing power.
- Trade deficits. Countries with large trade deficits usually have a depreciating currency. Inflation is often a cause of this deficit, making country's goods more expensive and less competitive, which in turn reduces demand for its currency abroad.
- Productivity. If a country produces superior products, foreigners will pay more for them. Those products and the country's currency will tend to rise in value.
- Interest rates. High rates usually boost currency values in the short term by making these currencies appealing to investors. If high rates are the result of high inflation, in the long run the currency will fall in value.
- Political instability. Upheaval makes a country a hazardous place in which to invest.

Periodicals

The following periodicals cover foreign markets as well as individual stocks:

Wall Street Journal, 800–568–7625
Financial Times (London), 800–628–8088
Asian Wall Street Journal, 800–568–7625
The Economist, 800–456–6086
International Herald-Tribune, 800–882–2884

Newsletters

These newsletters regularly cover foreign stocks:

Capital International Perspective
Morgan Stanley
1585 Broadway
New York, NY 10036
212–703–2965
Monthly; $3,000 per year.

Dessauer's Journal
P.O. Box 1718
Orleans, MA 02653
508–255–1651
Monthly; $99 per year.

Frank Cappiello's Closed-End Fund Digest
1224 Coast Village Circle
Santa Barbara, CA 93108
805–565–5651
Monthly; $199 per year; $65 for three month trial.

International Economic Trends
Federal Reserve Bank of St. Louis
P.O. Box 442
St. Louis, MO 63166
314–444–8809
Quarterly; free.

International Living
105 West Monument Street
Baltimore, MD 21201
410–223–2605

20

Commodities

The concept of buying and selling agricultural goods at a price agreed upon today, but with actual delivery of the goods sometime in the future, is a time-honored practice dating back to the early 19th century. But don't allow the long history of commodities trading lull you into thinking it's an easy way to make money.

Trading commodities is one of the riskiest games on Wall Street—some studies indicate that well over half the people who invest in commodities lose their money. In fact, commodities futures are almost always 100% speculation because you must try to guess, months in advance, what will happen to the prices of food products, natural resources, metals, and foreign currencies.

The greatest appeal of trading commodities lies in the impressive amount of leverage they provide. Your broker will require you to meet certain net worth requirements and make a margin deposit. Nevertheless, there are low cash requirements: 5% to 10% of a contract's actual value, depending on the commodity and the broker's standards. That means $2,000 could actually buy, say, $29,000 worth of soybeans. So if you're good at it, you can make sizable profits with very little money.

CAUTION: Don't get involved unless you have some money you can afford to lose, an ability to follow trends, and a lot of emotional stability and calmness. If prices move against you, your broker

will require more money, and unless you have the cash readily available, he will sell out your position and you could suffer huge losses.

HINT: To help reduce the risks involved, you can give your broker a stop-order loss on each futures contract, thus establishing a price at which you will automatically sell your position rather than suffer greater losses. (See Chapter 25 for details on stop-order sales.)

WHICH COMODITIES ARE TRADED WHERE

- *Chicago Board of Trade* (CBOT)
  Corn, Ginnie Mae mortgages, gold, oats, paper, plywood, silver, soybeans, soybean meal, soybean oil, Treasury bonds, wheat
- *Chicago Mercantile Exchange* (CME)
  Broiler chickens, cattle, certificates of deposit, currencies, eggs, Eurodollars, gold, hogs, lumber, pork bellies, potatoes, silver coins, S&P 500 Index futures, Treasury bills
- *Coffee, Sugar & Cocoa Exchange* (New York City)
  Aluminum, copper, gold, silver
- *Kansas City Board of Trade*
  Wheat, Value Line Stock Index futures
- *Mid America Commodity Exchange* (Chicago)
  Corn, gold, oats, soybeans, wheat
- *Minneapolis Grain Exchange*
  Sunflower seeds, wheat

- *New York Cotton Exchange*
  Cotton, orange juice, propane gas
- *New York Futures Exchange* (part of the NYSE)
  New York Stock Exchange Composite Index, options on futures
- *New York Mercantile Exchange*
  Beef (imported), gasoline, gold, heating oil, palladium, platinum, potatoes, silver coins

WHAT ARE COMMODITIES FUTURES?

A futures contract is an agreement to buy or sell a certain amount of a commodity at a particular price within a given period of time. The price of the contract is established on the floor of a commodities exchange.

Futures are traded in many areas: grain, meat, poultry, lumber, meats, gold, foreign currencies, petroleum, Treasury bonds and notes, and even stock indexes.

You can make money in one of two ways: by going long, which means buying a contract to take ownership of a product to be delivered on a certain date at a predetermined price; or by going short, which means agreeing to hand over a product on a certain date at a predetermined price. To take your profits or to cut your losses, you cancel your contract by offsetting it with a contract for the opposite trade. In other words, a futures contract obligates the buyer to buy and the seller to sell unless the contract is closed out by an offsetting sale or purchase to another investor before the so-called settlement date.

For example, if you had purchased a May 1996 wheat contract and you wanted to get out of the market, you would sell a May 1996 contract, thus closing out the position. The two positions cancel each other out. If you don't offset, you are obliged to take physical delivery. It would be cumbersome and costly to have wheat unloaded into your living room.

The theory or rationale behind futures trading is twofold: (1) futures are supposed to transfer risk from one party to another; and (2) they are designed to even out price fluctuations. Although this theory tends to be true in agricultural markets, the proliferation of financial and stock index futures has led to increased volatility and speculation.

Farmers use futures as a hedge against changes in prices for agricultural prices; manufacturers use them to lock in the price of raw materials they need, such as orange juice, oil, rubber, corn, wheat, and sugar. International traders lock in values for currencies. Others, especially institutional investors, use futures to protect against stock market drops, using futures on indexes, such as S&P's 500 Stock Index.

HOW THE MARKET OPERATES

Commodity trading is different from investing in stocks. When you buy a common stock, you own a part of the corporation and share in its profits, if any. If you pick a profitable company, the price of your stock will eventually rise.

With commodities, there is no equity. You basically buy hope. Once the futures contract has expired, there's no tomorrow. If your trade turned out badly, you must take the full loss. And it's a zero sum game: For every $1 won, $1 is lost by someone else.

Agricultural Commodities Contracts

COMMODITY	SYMBOL	ONE CONTRACT EQUALS
Soybeans	S	5,000 bushels
Soybean oil	BO	60,000 pounds
Soybean meal	SM	100 tons
Oats	O	5,000 bushels
Wheat	W	5,000 bushels
Corn	C	5,000 bushels
Silver	AG	1,000 troy ounces
Gold	K	1 kilogram

SOURCE: Chicago Board of Trade.

Hedging

Let's say a hog farmer has animals that will be ready for market in 6 months. He wants to assure himself of today's market price for these hogs. He does this by selling a contract of today's market price for these hogs, which he does by selling a contract for future delivery. When the hogs are ready for market, if the price has dropped, he will be forced to take a lower price on the actual hogs, but he will have an offsetting gain, because the contract he sold 6 months ago was at a higher price. In other words, he closes that contract with a profit.

- *The advantage to the sellers*: They have themselves locked in a price, thereby protecting themselves from any future fall in the price of hogs. In effect, they have transferred this price risk to the buyers.
- *The advantage to the buyers*: They also have locked in a price, thereby protecting themselves from any future rise in the price of hogs. The buyer in this hypothetical case might be a speculator, a meat packer, or a meat processor.

Margin

Because payment is not received until the delivery date, a type of binder or good faith deposit is required. It is called margin. The margin in the world of commodities is only a small percentage of the total amount due, but it serves as a guarantee for both buyer and seller. Unlike margin for stocks, which is an interest-bearing cost, margin for commodities is a security balance. You are not charged interest, but if the price of your futures drops by a certain percentage, more money must be deposited in the margin account or your position will be closed out by your broker.

In reality, most futures trading is not this simple. More often than not, the opposite side of each transaction is picked up by speculators who believe they can make money through favorable price changes during the months prior to delivery.

Trading Limitations

The commodity exchanges set day limits, based on the previous day's closing prices, specifying how widely a contract's trading price can move. The purpose of these limits is to prevent excessive short-term volatility and therefore also to keep margin requirements low. But trading limits can also lock traders into positions they cannot trade out of because the contract held is either up or down to the daily limit.

For example, an investor buys one gold contract (100 ounces) at $500 per ounce on June 30. On July 1 gold falls to $470 an ounce. The trading limit on gold is $20 per day, which means that on that day gold can be traded anywhere from $480 to $520 per ounce. Because the price has dropped below $480, trading is halted and the investor is locked into his position, unable to sell on that day. On the next day, July 2, the trading limits change to $460 to $500.

Price Quotations

Commodity prices are printed in the papers in various ways. In general you'll find the "high" (highest price of the day), the "low", and the "close". "Net change" refers to the change from the prior day's settlement price. The final column gives the high-low range for the year. Grain prices are given in cents per bushel; for example, wheat for December may be listed at a closing price of 3.71 per bushel.

Important Protective Steps to Take

Choose an Experienced Broker
Deal only with a reputable firm that (1) has extensive commodities trading services and (2) includes a broker who knows speculations and can guide you. Never buy or sell as the result of a phone recommendation until it has been confirmed in written or printed form.

Special Terms in Commodities Trading

- *Arbitrage.* Simultaneous purchase and sale of the same or an equivalent security in order to make a profit from the price discrepancy
- *Basis.* The difference between the cash price of a hedged money market instrument and a futures contract
- *Contract month.* Month in which a futures contract may be fulfilled by making or taking delivery
- *Cross hedge.* Hedging a cash market risk in one financial instrument by taking a position in a futures contract for a different but similar instrument
- *Forward contract.* An agreement to buy or sell goods at a set price and date, when those involved plan to take delivery of the instrument
- *Hedge.* Strategy used to offset an investment risk that involves buying and selling simultaneously in the futures market
- *Index.* Statistical composite that measures the ups and downs of stocks, bonds, and commodities; reflects market prices and the number of shares outstanding for the companies in the index
- *Long position.* Futures contract purchased to protect the investor against a rise in cost of a future commitment or against a drop in interest rates
- *Mark to the market.* Debits and credits in each account at the close of the trading day
- *Open interest.* Contracts that have not been offset by opposite transactions or by delivery
- *Physical.* The underlying physical commodity
- *Selling short.* A popular hedging technique involving sale of a futures contract that the seller does not own. A commodity sold short equals a promise to deliver at a future date.
- *Spot market.* Also known as the actual or physical market, in which commodities are sold for immediate delivery
- *Spread.* Holding opposite positions in two futures contracts with the intent of profit through changes in prices

Zero in on a Few Commodities

Preferably those in the news. For instance, during the drought in the Midwest in the spring of 1988, soybeans and grains experienced wild price gyrations. Watch for such movements and remember that in commodities the trend is your friend.

Commodities

PROS
↑ Large potential capital gains
↑ High amount of leverage available
↑ Small initial investment
↑ High liquidity

CONS
↓ Extremely risky
↓ Requires expertise
↓ Highly volatile
↓ Must continually monitor position
↓ Could lose total investment

Avoid Thin Markets

You can score when such a commodity takes off, but the swings can be too fast and may send prices soaring or plummeting, and the amateur can get caught with no chance of closing a position.

Look for a Ratio of Net Profit to Net Loss of 2:1

Because the percentage of losses will always be greater than that of profits, choose commodities where the potential gains (based on confirmed trends) can be more than double the possible losses.

Prepare an Operational Plan

Before you risk any money, test your hypothesis on paper until you feel confident that you understand what can happen. Do this for several weeks to get the feel of different types of contracts in different types of markets.

With an active commodity, buy contracts at several delivery dates and calculate the potential profits if the price rises moderately.

Never Meet a Margin Call
When your original margin is impaired, your broker will call for more money. Except in most unusual circumstances, do not put in more money. Liquidate your position and accept your loss. This is a form of stop-loss safeguard. When a declining trend has been established, further losses can be expected.

Be Alert to Special Situations
Information is the key to profitable speculation. As you become more knowledgeable, you will pick up many points, such as these:

- If there's heavy spring and summer rain in Maine, buy long on potatoes. They need ideal weather.
- If there's a bad tornado over large portions of the Great Plains, buy wheat contracts. Chances are the wheat crop will be damaged, thus changing the supply and demand.

Trade with the Major Trend, Against the Minor Trend
With copper, for example, if you project a worldwide shortage of the metal and the market is in an uptrend, buy futures when the market suffers temporary weak spells. As long as prices keep moving up, you want to accumulate a meaningful position.

The corollary to this is never to average down. Adding to your loss position increases the number of contracts that are returning a loss. By buying more, you put yourself in a stance where you can lose on more contracts if the price continues to drop.

Generally, if the trend is down, either sell short or stay out of the market.

Watch the Spreads Between Different Delivery Dates
In the strong summer market, the premium for January soybeans is 8¢ per bushel above the November contract. Buy November and sell January.

If the bull market persists, the premium should disappear and you will have a pleasant limited profit. Carrying charges on soybeans run about 6½¢ per month, so it is not likely that the spread will widen to more than 13¢ per bushel. Thus with that 8¢ spread, the real risk is not more than 5¢ per bushel.

Never Spread a Loss
Turning a long or short position into a spread by buying or selling another contract month will seldom help you and in most cases will guarantee a locked-in loss. When you make a mistake, get out.

Watch the Price Peaks and Lows
Never sell at a price that is near the natural or government-imposed floor, and never buy at a price that is near its high.

Similarly, do not buy after the price of any commodity has passed its seasonal high or sell after it has dropped under its seasonal low.

Risk No More than 10% of Your Trading Capital in Any One Position
And risk no more than 30% of all capital in all positions at any one time—except when you have caught a strong upswing and can move with the trend. These limits will ease the effect of a bad decision. Few professionals count on being right more than half the time.

COMMODITY ADVISERS

One avenue for help is the trading adviser. These professionals must be registered with the Commodity Futures Trading Commission. They charge in one of two ways: a percentage, usually 6%, of the funds turned over to them, or an incentive fee, typically 15% of any profits generated by the adviser.

Commodity Futures Options

COMMODITY	SYMBOLS	ONE CONTRACT EQUALS
Options on T-bond futures	CG, PG	One T-bond futures contract
Options on soybean futures	CZ, PZ	One soybean futures contract
Options on corn futures	CY, PY	One corn futures contract
Options on silver futures	AC, AP	One 1,000-ounce silver futures contract
Options on 10-year Treasury futures	TC, TP	One 10-year Treasury futures contract

SOURCE: Chicago Board of Trade.

☑ *HINT: Select an adviser who has an annual rate of return of at least 25% for a minimum of 3 years.*

Burlington Hall Asset Management, in Hackettstown, New Jersey, offers a software program, called La Porte Asset Allocation System, which evaluates trading advisers. For details, call 908–852–1694.

Performance records of major advisers are also tracked by several of the publications listed below.

FOR FURTHER INFORMATION

Periodicals

Commodity Traders Consumer Report
141 West 28 Street
New York, NY 10001
800–832–6065
Monthly; $225 per year; one trial issue: $20

Tracks commodities advisers and provides useful information on how to trade.

Managed Account Reports
220 Fifth Avenue
New York, NY 10001
212–213–6202
Monthly; $299 per year; one free sample copy.

Tracks commodity funds and futures funds.

Books

Dwight A. Jackson, *The Individual Investor's Guide to Commodities* (Chicago: Probus, 1991).

21

Precious Metals

Some say it's a hedge against inflation; doom-sayers swear it's our only protection against the inevitable downfall of our entire economic system. And in between are those who believe in diversification. Precious metals have a place, albeit a small place, in every portfolio as long as one realizes they are volatile—you have to know when to sell or else be willing to hold long term.

If you decide to invest, here are your choices:

- *Bullion.* You can buy actual bars of the metal itself, called ingots, through larger banks, brokerage firms, and major dealers. It must be assayed (certified for weight and purity) before reselling. Bullion requires storage and does not pay dividends or benefit from compounding.
- *Bullion certificates.* Unless you want to fill up your living room with bars or coins, buy certificates. The minimum is typically $1,000, and they are sold at roughly 3% over the price of the metal.
- *Bullion coins.* Not to be confused with rare coins, these have very little or no value as a collectible. Bullion coins, issued by the United States and a handful of other countries (see box below), also must be stored. Their price is based on their gold content, whereas rare coins purchased at auctions or from dealers

have a numismatic value, which is based upon their age, rarity, and popularity.
- *Mining stocks.* Another route is to purchase the individual stocks of mining companies. Stocks offer potential price appreciation and dividend income, yet leave you subject to political upheavals, mining strikes, and the overall trend of the stock market. Mining stocks tend to rise faster in price than the gold itself when the market is up, and they usually drop faster than the metal when its price drops.
- *Mutual funds.* Funds specializing in precious metals are one of the easier ways to invest. However, this is not a pure play because you are buying partial shares of stocks of companies that mine metals. Your profit will depend on how well the fund is managed.
- *Options.* Options on metals and mining stocks are listed in the newspaper. (See Chapter 16 for more on options.)
- *Futures contracts.* These are available on precious and industrial metals and are the riskiest choice because they involve betting on the future direction of prices. With a gold, silver, or platinum futures contract, you agree to buy or sell a certain quantity at a specified price. You are required to put up 5% to 10% of the value of the contract as margin.

Although you control a large amount of metal for a relatively small amount of money, you can lose your entire investment if your bet is wrong. (See Chapter 22 for more on futures.)

A PURIST'S VIEW

The true gold buffs shun mutual funds, stocks, and certificates, maintaining that if the world caves in, only the real tangible metals will be valuable. If you're less of a purist, then you may be content with a certificate or shares of a stock or a fund. After all, gold, silver, and platinum do not pay dividends and can never benefit from compounding.

 CAUTION: Put no more than 5% to 8% of your portfolio in precious metals.

Before Buying a Precious Metal

Follow these guidelines and heed these warnings:

- Paper trade for at least 1 month. Make decisions, calculate margins, set stop-loss prices, and monitor how well you are doing in theory.
- Never commit more than 5% of your risk capital to metals. If you are trading contracts, keep the balance in a money market account to meet any margin calls.
- Read the commodity columns in the Wall Street Journal and Barron's. Ask several dealers to send you their research reports.
- Track the direction of interest rates, inflation, and the spot prices of the metals. (Spot price is the cash price for metals that are delivered at once.)
- Never give discretionary powers to anyone in the business.
- Never place an order over the phone with someone who has called you cold.

GUIDELINES FOR BUYING PRECIOUS METALS

Here are the key facts to keep in mind:

Gold

To enhance your potential profits in gold, watch for changes in these leading indicators:

- Political situation in South Africa
- The trend of inflation and the Consumer Price Index
- Movement of interest rates
- Direction of the dollar
- Third-world debt and related banking problems
- Changes in gold production

Remember, gold vies with the dollar as the world's safest currency. When the dollar is strong, gold tends to be low in price and vice versa.

In 1960, gold was $35 per ounce; in 1970, also $35 per ounce; in 1980, $612 per ounce; in 1990, $383 per ounce; and as we go to press, $384 per ounce.

Silver

Silver is primarily an industrial metal; its price is directly related to supply and demand and less (as is the case with gold) to inflation, interest rates, and politics. Silver is used in coins, jewelry, and silverware, but its greatest demand is in the photo-

---

Leading Gold Coins

- American Gold Eagle
- Austrian 100 Corona
- Canadian Maple Leaf
- Australian Nugget
- Mexican 50 Peso
- Hungarian Corona
- Mexican Onza
- Chinese Panda

graphic, electronic, dental, and medical fields. Its industrial uses are so great, in fact, that the world consumes as much silver as is mined.

In 1980 the Hunt brothers tried to corner the market in silver, and at that time the price soared to $48 an ounce, only to fall rapidly. As we go to press it's $4.95 an ounce. The American silver bullion coin is called the Silver Eagle.

Platinum

Although platinum has generally been considered more valuable than gold or silver because of its limited availability, it has never been as popular with investors. Its primary uses are in the electronics, chemical, and automobile industries. It is an essential ingredient in the production of catalytic converters for pollution control in cars.

Its use as an antipollutant is expected to create more demand as emission control regulations become increasingly strict in both the United States and Europe. Platinum coins include the Noble, Canadian Maple Leaf, and Australian Koala.

As we go to press, it is selling at $390 per ounce.

BUYING METALS BY PHONE

Although you should never succumb to a high-pressure salesman, you can buy bullion bars and coins by phone from reliable dealers; however, check and compares the prices and fees of those listed below before purchasing.

- *Wilmington Trust Refined Investments* allows clients to use their Visa or MasterCard to buy precious metals, provided you store the metals with them. Call: 800–223–1080. (Their 24-hour Quoteline gives the latest spot prices: 302–427–4700.)

No-Load Gold Funds

FUND	TELEPHONE
Bull & Bear Gold Investors	800–847–4200
U.S. World Gold	800–873–8637
Lexington Gold Fund	800–526–0056
Vanguard Spec Portfolio-Gold	800–662–7447

- *Merrill Lynch's Blueprint* program has a minimum purchase of only $100, with $50 thereafter. Call: 800–637–3766.
- *Benham Certified Metals* has a discount brokerage division. The minimum for silver is $1,000 and $2,000 for gold and platinum. Call: 800–447–4653.
- *Rhode Island Hospital Trust National Bank of Providence* sells certificates. Call: 800–343–8419.

FOR FURTHER INFORMATION
Newsletters

Dow Theory Letters
P.O. Box 1759
La Jolla, CA 92038
619–454–0481
$250 per year.

Pamphlets

Your Introduction to Investing in Gold and *Your Introduction to Investing in Silver* from:

The Gold and Silver Institute
1112 16th Street NW
Washington, DC 20036
202–835–0185
$5 each.

22

Financial Futures and Market Indexes

FINANCIAL FUTURES

If trading corn and pork bellies is too tame for you, you can move along to another type of commodity: interest-bearing securities, such as Treasury bonds and notes, CDs, and Ginnie Maes. For amateurs, financial futures and stock indexes are just about the riskiest areas of Wall Street. Yet professional money managers use them as investment tools, as a way to hedge their portfolios. Just as agribusinesses rely on commodities futures, so money managers and others use financial futures to protect their profits.

Financial futures trading requires an ability to predict correctly the short-term or intermediate movements of interest rates, because futures involve debt issues whose values move with the cost of money; that is, with interest rates. With tiny margins (as small as $800 to control $1 million), a shift of ½% in the interest rate can double your money—or lose most of your capital.

☑ **HINT: If you are a modest investor, skip this chapter. If you have over $100,000 in a portfolio, read it rapidly. If you are a speculator who can afford to lose half your stake, study the explanations and then deal with an experienced broker.**

HOW FINANCIAL FUTURES WORK

Basically, these are contracts that involve money. They are used by major investors, such as banks, insurance companies, and pension fund managers, to protect positions by hedging: What they gain (lose) in the cash market will be offset by the loss (profit) in the futures market.

The terms and rules of trading are set by the exchanges.

A financial futures contract is in essence a contract on an interest rate. The most popular are Treasury bills, bonds, and notes; Ginnie Maes; and CDs. They are sold through brokers or firms specializing in commodities. Contract sizes vary with the underlying security and the exchange, but they range from approximately $20,000 to $1 million. However, because margin requirements are low, sometimes only 5% to 10% of total value, your actual outlay is surprisingly little, relatively speaking.

The value of a financial futures contract is determined by interest rates:

- When rates rise, the price of fixed-income securities and the futures based on them fall.
- When rates decline, these investments rise in value.

☑ **HINT: Place stop orders with your broker. These provide instructions to close out your position when the price falls to a certain level, which will help limit any potential losses.**

U.S. TREASURY BOND FUTURES

Since their introduction in 1977, U.S. T-bond futures have become the most actively traded futures contract worldwide. Although there are various other financial futures traded, we will illustrate the principle with T-bonds and T-notes. (For Further Information at the end of this chapter lists more in-depth studies of trading financial futures.)

Like all futures contracts, T-bond futures contracts are standardized (see box on page 215). Their only variable is the price, which is established on the floor of the Chicago Board of Trade. Bond prices, of course, move in inverse relationship to interest rates: When rates rise, bond prices fall. Speculators and others use T-bonds to take advantage of anticipated interest rate changes; hedgers focus more on reducing and managing risk for their portfolios.

If You Expect Interest Rates to Fall

Such an expectation implies that bond futures will rise. This means you'll want to take a long position in order to take advantage of the potentially rising bond market (to be long on a contract is to buy it; to short a contract is to sell). For example, if bond futures are now trading at 72% of par, you go long one $100,000-face-value bond contract. If bond prices then rise to 74% of par, you offset your original long position by going short for a profit of 2 points, or $2,000.

> Long one contract @ 72 or $72,000
> Short one contract @ 74 or $74,000
> Profit: $2,000

If You Expect Interest Rates to Rise

You then take a short position. Then when bond prices fall to 69, you can offset your original position by going long for a $3,000 profit.

> Short one contract @ 72 or $72,000
> Long one contract @ 69 or $69,000
> Profit: $3,000

Spreads

Speculators usually trade financial futures by going long on one position and short on another with both contracts due in the same month. But you can also use spreads: buying one contract month and selling another. This technique is used when there's an abnormal relation between the yields and thus the prices of two contracts with different maturities. These situations don't come often, but when they do, they can be mighty rewarding, because the gains will come from a restoration of the normal spread.

Example: An investor notes that June T-bonds are selling at 80–11 (each 1/32% equals $3.125 of a standard $100,000 contract) and that September's are at 81–05. The basis for quotations is an 8% coupon and 15-year maturity.

Based on experience, he decides that this 26/32 difference ($81\frac{5}{32} - 80\frac{11}{32} = \frac{26}{32}$) is out of line with normal pricing. He sells the September contract and buys the June one. In a couple of weeks, prices begin to normalize: The September contract edges up to 81–08 and the June one surges to 80–24. Now he starts to cash in: He loses $\frac{3}{32}$ ($93.75) on the September contract but gains $\frac{13}{32}$ ($406.25) on the June one: $312.50 profit minus commission.

FOUR SMART RULES TO FOLLOW

If you have money you can afford to lose, time enough to keep abreast of developments in the financial world, strong nerves, and a trustworthy, knowledgeable broker, trading in financial futures may be rewarding and surely will be exciting. Of course, if you're involved with substantial holdings, you probably are already familiar with hedging, so you can stick to protective contracts. Otherwise, follow these rules:

U.S. Treasury Bond Futures

- Trading unit: $100,000 face value of U.S. T-bonds
- Deliverable: U.S. Treasury bonds with a nominal 8% coupon maturing at least 15 years from delivery date if not callable; if callable, not for at least 15 years from delivery date
- Delivery method: Federal Reserve book entry wire transfer system
- Par: $1,000
- Price quote: Percentage of par in minimum increments of $\frac{1}{32}$ point, or $3.125 per "tick," e.g., 74-01 means $74\frac{1}{32}$% of par
- Daily price limit: $^{64}/_{32}$ or $2,000 per contract above or below the previous day's settlement price
- Delivery months: March, June, September, or December
- Ticker symbol: US
- Traded on: The Chicago Board of Trade

1. Make dry runs on paper for several months. Interest rates change slowly. Pick different types of financial futures each week and keep practicing until you get a feel for the market and risks and, over at least a week, chalk up more winners than losers.
2. Buy long when you look for a drop in interest rates. With lower yields, the prices of all contracts will rise.
3. Sell short when you expect a higher cost of money. This will force down the value of the contracts, and you can cover your position at a profit.
4. Set a strategy and stick to it. Don't try to mix contracts until you are comfortable and making money.

☑ *HINT: Set stop and limit orders, not market orders. A market order is executed immediately at the best possible price. A stop order, to buy or to sell at a given price, becomes a market order when that price is touched. A limit order is the maximum price at which to buy and the minimum at which to sell.*

OPTIONS ON FUTURES

Another way to participate in the futures market is through options (see Chapter 16). A futures option is a contract that gives you the right to buy (call) or sell (put) a certain futures contract within a specified period of time for a specified price (called the premium).

Options on Commodities Futures

Options are traded on futures for agricultural commodities, oil, livestock, metals, etc. Quotes are listed in the newspaper under Futures Options. These involve far less money than contracts do: roughly $100 for an option compared to $1,800 for a futures contract. There are no margin calls, and the risk is limited to the premium, but these are for professionals and gamblers. If you ride a strong market trend, you can make a lot of money with a small outlay and rapid fluctuations, or you can make a modest profit by successful hedging.

💣 *CAUTION: Be careful and always limit your commitment. It's easy to con yourself into thinking you're a genius when you hit a couple of big winners fast, but unless you bank half of those profits, you will lose money over a period of time if only because of the commissions.*

Options on Financial Futures

Options are also traded on some interest-bearing securities, such as Treasury bills and notes. T-bond options, for example, are traded on the Chicago Board of Trade. The T-bond futures contract underlying the option is for $100,000 of Treasury bonds, bearing an 8% or equivalent coupon, which do not mature and are noncallable for at least 15 years. When long-term interest rates fall, the value of the futures contract and the call option increases while the value of a put option decreases. The opposite is true when long-term rates rise.

Contract Specifications of Futures

	U.S. TREASURY BONDS	10-YEAR U.S. TREASURY NOTES	GNMA-CDR	GNMA II
Basic trading unit	$100,000 face value	$100,000 face value	$100,000 principal balance	$100,000 principal balance
Price quotation	Full points (one point equals $1,000) and 32nds of a full point			
Minimum price fluctuation	$1/32$ of a full point ($3.125 per contract)			
Daily price limit	$^{64}/_{32}$ (2 points or $2,000) above or below the previous day's settlement price			
Date introduced	Aug. 22, 1977	May 3, 1982	Oct. 20, 1975	1984
Ticker symbol	US	TY	M	CT

SOURCE: Chicago Board of Trade.

Premiums for T-bond futures options are quoted in $1/64$ths of 1% (1 point). Thus $1/64$ point equals $15.63 ($100,000 × 0.01 × $1/64$). A premium quote of 2–16 means $2^{16}/_{64}$, or [(2 × 64) + 16] × $15.63, or $2,250.72 per option.

The profit is the premium you receive when the option is sold minus the premium paid when you purchased the option.

Setting Up Hedges

Options provide excellent opportunities to set up hedges if you plan your strategy and understand the risks and rewards. Here's an example cited in Forbes:

In March, the June T-bond contract is selling at 72–05 (72⁵⁄₃₂). Calls at 72, 74, and 76 are quoted at premiums of 2–06, 1–20, and 0–46, respectively; puts at 68, 70, and 72 are available at 0–30, 0–61, and 1–54. You think that the market will remain stable, so you make these paper projections of hedges with a margin of $3,000:

Sell June 72 call	$2,093.75
Sell June 72 put	1,843.75
Total income	$3,937.50

If the T-bond is still worth 72 on the June strike date, both options will expire worthless, so you have an extra $3,937.50 minus commissions.

Sell June 74 call	$1,312.50
Sell June 70 put	$1,953.13
Total income	$2,265.63

This is less risky, and profitable, because both options will expire worthless if the last-day price is between 70 and 74.

Sell June 76 call	$ 718.75
Sell June 68 put	$ 468.75
Total income	$ 1,187.50

If the final price is between 68 and 76, you will do OK. You swap a lower income for a broader price range.

STOCK INDEXES

You can also trade stock index options and stock index futures options.

These are the fastest-growing area of speculations and make it possible to play the market without owning a single share of stock. They combine the growth potential of equities with the speculative hopes of commodities.

With a stock index, you are betting on the future price of the composite of a group of stocks: buying if you anticipate a rise soon, selling if you look for a decline. You put up cash or collateral

Government Instrument Futures Contracts

COMMODITY	SYMBOL	ONE CONTRACT EQUALS
U.S. Treasury bonds	US	Face value at maturity: $100,000
10-year T-notes	TY	Face value at maturity: $100,000
GNMA	M	$100,000 principal balance
30-day Treasury repo	—	$2.5 million face value
90-day Treasury repo	—	$1 million face value
Zero coupon T-bonds	—	Discounted
Zero coupon T-notes	—	Discounted

SOURCE: Chicago Board of Trade.

equal to about 7% of the contract value versus 50% for stocks. All you need is a little capital and a lot of nerve. A minor jiggle can produce sizable losses or gains. There are also options that require even less money.

 CAUTION: *To emphasize the speculative nature of indexes, some brokerage firms advise their brokers to limit trading to individuals with a net worth of $100,000 (exclusive of home and life insurance).*

SIX GUIDELINES FOR SUCCESS

- *Follow the trend.* If the price of the index is higher than it was the day before, which in turn is higher than it was the previous day, go long. If the reverse, sell short.
- *Set stop-loss prices at 3 points below cost.* If they are too close, one erratic move can stop you out at a loss even though the market may resume its uptrend soon.

- *Recognize the role of the professionals.* To date, most contracts have been traded by brokerage houses active in arbitrage and spreads and in hedging large block positions. Only a handful of institutional managers have done more than experiment. So the amateur is competing with top professionals who have plenty of capital and no commissions to pay and who are in positions to get the latest information and make quick decisions.
- *Study the price spreads.* Contracts for distant months are more volatile. In a strong market, buy far-out contracts and short nearby months; in a weak market, buy the closer months and short the distant ones.
- *Be mindful that dividends can distort prices.* In heavy payout months, these discrepancies can be significant.
- *Use a hedge only when your portfolio approximates that of the index*: roughly a minimum of $250,000 (very rarely does a major investor buy only 100 shares of a stock). In most cases, any single portfolio has little resemblance to that of the index.

USING OPTIONS IN 1997

As we go to press the stock market is hitting record highs and the yield on the S&P 500 is at 2.22%. One way a sophisticated investor can address this scenario is to use index options.

FOR FURTHER INFORMATION

Books

Al Gietzen, *Real-Time Futures Trading* (Chicago: Probus, 1993).

Mark J. Powers, *Inside the Financial Futures Markets* (New York: John Wiley & Sons, 1991)

Edward W. Schwartz, *Financial Futures* (Homewood, IL: Dow Jones–Irwin, 1993).

Stock Indexes

These stock indexes currently have futures contracts and/or options on futures available:

- **Standard & Poor's 500 (SPX).** Stocks of 500 industrials, financial companies, utilities, and transportation issues, all listed on the NYSE. They are weighted by market value. This means each stock is weighted so that changes in the stock's price influence the index in proportion to the stock's representative market value. Contracts are valued at 500 times the index. They are traded on the Chicago Mercantile Exchange. Generally this is the index favored by big hitters, as contracts are extremely liquid, and it's widely used to measure institutional performance. Options on the SPX trade only on the Chicago Board of Options Exchange (CBOE).
- **Standard & Poor's 100 (OEX).** A condensed version of the S&P 500 index. It is weighted by capitalization of the 100 component corporations, all of which have options traded on the CBOE. The value is 100 times the worth of the stocks.
- **Standard & Poor's 100 LEAPS (OAX).** Capitalization-weighted index of 100 major stocks in the S&P 500. Options trade on the CBOE.
- **Standard & Poor's 500 LEAPS (LSW).** Capitalization-weighted index of 500 stocks. Options trade on the CBOE.
- **Value Line Composite (XVL).** An equally weighted geometric index of about 1,700 stocks actively traded on the NYSE, AMEX, and OTC. Contracts are quoted at 500 times the index. This tends to be difficult to trade because of a thin market on the small Kansas City Board of Trade. Options trade on the Philadelphia Exchange.
- **AMEX Market Value Index (XAM).** Measures the changes in the aggregate market of over 800 AMEX issues. The weighting is by industry groups: 32% natural resources, 19% high technology, 13% service, 11% consumer goods. No one company accounts for more than 7% of the total.
- **Major Market Index (XMI).** Based on 20 blue-chip NYSE stocks and price-weighted so that higher-priced shares have a greater effect on the average than lower-priced ones. Options trade on the American Exchange.
- **AMEX Oil & Gas Index (XOI).** Made up of the stocks of 30 oil and gas companies, with Exxon representing about 17%. Options trade on the AMEX.
- **Computer Technology Index (XCI).** Stocks of 30 major computer companies, with IBM accounting for about half and Hewlett-Packard, Digital Equipment, and Motorola another 16%. Options trade on the American Exchange.
- **NYSE Composite Index (NYA).** A capitalization-weighted average of about 1,500 Big Board stocks. Options trade on the New York Stock Exchange.
- **Standard & Poor's Computer & Business Equipment Index (OBR).** A capitalization-weighted average of a dozen major office and business equipment companies, with IBM about 75%, Digital Equipment, Wang, and NCR about 18%.
- **Technology Index (PTI).** A price-weighted index of 100 stocks of which 45 are traded OTC. Very volatile. Options trade on the Philadelphia Stock Exchange.
- **Gold & Silver Index (XAU).** Options trade on the Philadelphia Stock Exchange.
- **National OTC Index (NCMP).** Options trade on the Philadelphia Stock Exchange.
- **NYSE Beta Index (NHB).** Options trade on the New York Stock Exchange.
- **NYSE INDEX (NYA).** Capitalization-weighted index of all common stocks on the New York Stock Exchange; options trade on the NYSE.
- **Standard & Poor's Midcap (MID).** Capitalization-weighted index of 400 stocks with a median market value of about $1 billion. Options trade on the AMEX.

Stock Indexes *(cont.)*

- **NASDAQ-100 (MDX)**. Capitalization-weighted index of the 100 largest nonfinancial stocks traded on NAS-DAQ. Options trade on the CBOE.
- **Russell 2000 (RUT)**. Capitalization-weighted index of the 2,000 smallest companies in the Russell universe of 3,000 stocks. Options trade on the CBOE.
- **Russell 2000 LEAPS (ZRU)**. Capitalization-weighted index of the 2,000 smallest companies in the Russell universe of 3,000 stocks. Options trade on the CBOE.

Pamphlets

Contact the following exchanges for pamphlets on futures trading:

The Options Exchange
400 South LaSalle
Chicago, IL 60605
312–786–5600

Chicago Board of Trade
Literature Services Department
141 West Jackson Blvd.
Chicago, IL 60604
312–435–3500

Chicago Mercantile Exchange
30 South Wacker Drive
Chicago, IL 60606
312–930–1000

New York Mercantile Exchange
67 Wall Street
New York, NY 10005
212–363–7000

23

Splits, Spin-Offs, Small-Caps, Spiders, and Stock Buybacks

*T*his catchall chapter is simultaneously geared to experienced investors and those with money set aside to try their hand at some speculation in the market. Even if you decide against participating in any of these s-word opportunities, you'll find them interesting to read about.

Here's what you'll find in the next few pages:

- *Splits.* Companies that split their stocks can be excellent investments when these splits are justified by profitable growth. The techniques used in buying and selling, however, can be speculative: That is, when it appears that a company may split its stock, the price of its shares will usually rise rapidly and, after the split, fall sharply. The long-term investor who bought the shares when undervalued will probably benefit automatically. The speculative investor, however, buys as the prospects of a split catch Wall Street's fancy and sells at a quick profit right after the announcement.
- *Spin-offs.* When a company divests itself of a subsidiary, the investor in the parent company automatically owns stock in the new company as well. This provides possible price appreciation.
- *Small-caps.* Companies with a small number of shares can be profitable when you know, and have confidence in management and/or the owners. But many are extremely risky

because they have limited capital, no ability to expand, and declining sales.

- *Spiders.* A unit investment trust that tracks the performance of the Standard & Poor's 500 Stock Index. It trades on the American Stock Exchange.
- *Stocks of bankrupt companies.* Bankrupt stocks offer speculative investors an opportunity to make money if the company pulls itself together or restructures successfully.
- *Stock buybacks.* Companies often buy back their own shares to maintain control. This procedure often boosts the stock's price.

COMPANIES THAT SPLIT THEIR STOCKS FREQUENTLY

One of the most rewarding and exciting investments can be a corporation that increases the number of its shares of common stock: issuing 1 or more shares for each outstanding share.

Such splits usually occur when:

- The price of such a stock has moved to an historic high, so high, in fact, that many investors are simply unwilling or unable to buy shares. Psychologically, a stock trading at 50 will attract far more investors than one trading at 100.
- A small, growing company, whose shares are traded OTC, wants to list its stock on an

exchange where the rules for listing are far tougher. Such a listing broadens investment acceptance as many institutions prefer the liquidity of an established market, and more individuals can use the shares as collateral for margin loans.

- A corporation seeks to make an acquisition with minimal cash or debt.
- The price of the stock reaches $75 per share. The most attractive range for most investors is $20 to $45 a share, so few splits are declared when the stock price is that low.
- Management becomes fearful of an unfriendly takeover. When the top officials hold only a small percentage of the outstanding shares, a stock split will make more shares available at a lower price and thus, it is hoped, lessen the likelihood of a raid.
- Earnings are likely to continue to grow, which means that the price of the shares will keep rising. With more stock, the per-share profits will appear smaller—for a while.
- The company has a record of stock splits. This indicates that the directors recognize, and are familiar with, the advantages of adding shares to keep old stockholders and attract new ones.

SPIN-OFFS

What was perhaps the most famous of all spin-offs—AT&T's decision to split into three companies (telecom services, equipment and computers) made 1995 a record year for corporate divestitures. The trend has continued because U.S. corporations are under tremendous pressure to downsize, to increase shareholder values. And, for the most part, spin-offs wind up boosting the parent company's stocks.

Spinoffs take place when the parent company divests itself of a division, which may be unrelated to the rest of the business or may not fit into parent company's future plans. It's also a way for a company to get rid of a unit that's underperforming. The new division becomes an independent company, and often, once loosed from its parent, blossoms.

The parent company then issues shares in this new corporation to shareholders of the parent company in proportion to their original investment. Now they hold shares in two companies instead of one.

The theory behind a spin-off is that the division will be better off operating independently and that the parent company will be better off

---

Candidates for Stock Splits

Stocks that split tend to outperform those that don't. As we go to press, these 20 companies might announce splits in the coming months.

COMPANY	LAST SPLIT
Avery Dennison	1987
Hershey Foods	1986
Beckton Dickinson	1993
Hilton Hotels	1988
Boeing	1990
IBM	1979
Citicorp	1987
Kimberly-Clark	1992
Dover Corp.	1995
Knight-Ridder	1983
Dow Chemical	1989
Microsoft	1994
Emerson Electric	1987
Nike	1995
Exxon	1987
Reuters	1994
Genuine Parts	1992
SmithKline Beecham	1992
Harley-Davidson	1994
Williams Cos.	1993

SOURCE: Standard & Poor's, *The Outlook,* Spring 1996.

without this particular division. A prime example: General Mills' spin-off of its fashion and toy divisions. Similarly, after Allied Corp. and Signal Corp. merged, the parent company selected a number of businesses in which it was less interested and spun these off as an entity called Henley Group. Thus shareholder value was maintained and the parent company's objectives were met.

U.S. corporations are under tremendous pressure to increase shareholder value and this is one way to do it . . . so,

☑ *HINT: If you have a good sense of timing, you may be able to cash in on spin-offs. Most follow a fairly similar pattern:*

■ When a new stock is spun off, it tends to be sold by the shareholder recipients.

■ Afterwards, the spun-off stock tends to rise in price as its true value is realized.

If you own shares in a company that has announced a spin-off, you might want to wait until you sell them, or even consider buying some of the spun-off shares. Why?

The fact that corporate spin-offs create shareholder wealth has been verified by several studies. The Pennsylvania State University's Department of Finance found that performance of parent companies' shares outpaced the benchmark indexes, and in one out of seven cases, the spin-offs eventually attracted premium-priced takeover bids. A University of Texas Graduate School of Business study found that shares of spin-offs fell 4% to 10% during the first days of trading and then moved up. That time period is obviously optimum buying time.

A study done in 1995 by ZPR Investment Research in Florida found that, on average, spun-off stocks gained 30% more than the S&P 500 Index between the third and eighth month of their existence. The study consisted of 35 spin-offs launched since August 31, 1992. It also found that the parent company shares also outpaced the S&P 500, although by a smaller margin.

Stock Dividends: How to Benefit

Stock dividends are extra shares issued to current shareholders, usually on a percentage basis: That is, a 5% stock dividend means that 5 new shares are issued for every 100 old shares. Such a policy can be habit-forming, and most companies continue the extra distributions year after year because it conserves cash, keeps shareholders happy, and provides an easy, inexpensive way to expand the number of publicly owned shares and, usually, stockholders.

It's pleasant to receive such a bonus, but be sure that the payout is justified. The actual dollar profits of the corporation should keep rising. If they stay about the same or decline, stock dividends may be more for show than growth. To evaluate a stock dividend in terms of a company's earning power and the stock's current price:

1. Find the future earnings yield on the current stock price. Use anticipated earnings per share for the current year. If the projected profits are $3 per share and the current price of the stock is 50, the earnings yield is 6%: $3 ÷ 50 = 0.06.

2. Add the stock dividend percentage declared for the current year to the annual cash dividend yield. If the stock dividend is 5% and the cash dividend is 2%, the figure is 7%—the total dividend yield.

If the second figure (7%) exceeds the first (6%), a shareholder faces earnings dilution and probable price weakness unless the corporate prospects are strong.

But if the profits are $5 per share, the earnings yield is 10%. Since this is more than the total dividend yield (7%), the stock dividend is not excessive.

☑ *IF YOU DARE: Buy spin-off shares after they decline, if you have faith in the company, and hold for the long term or until they have rebounded close to their initial price.*

☑ *HINT: Two publications that periodically track potential spin-offs are:*

1. *Dow Theory Forecasts*
2. *S& P's The Outlook*

SMALL-CAP STOCKS

Small-cap companies typically have a capitalization of $150 million or less. With blue chips up in price, small-caps offer a defensive position against market corrections as well as a pleasant alternative to paying high premiums for quality stocks.

Small-caps have outperformed larger stocks in the early stages of the last eight bull markets. Statistics compiled by Ibbotson Associates show that since 1954, in every 12-month period following a recession, small-company stocks have outperformed large-company stocks.

Small-cap stocks are not without their problems, however. Many are not heavily followed (if at all) by analysts, which means little readily available research. The other side of that coin: They're often undiscovered and still low in price.

Because small-caps have performed well as a group and have gained a large following, Standard & Poor's introduced a new SmallCap 600 Index in late 1994. It consists of 600 U.S. issues that range in market value from roughly $46 million to $940 million. It complements the MidCap 400 and the larger-capitalization S&P 500. As a group, the 1,500 stocks in the three S&P indexes represent about 82% of the total market capitalization of stocks traded in the United States.

This index, like all the S&P indexes, is market-weighted (stock price times shares outstanding) which means the performance of one stock affects the index only in proportion to its market value. New York Stock Exchange-listed companies make up 43% of the issues in the index.

If you prefer to have a professional select small-cap stocks, then call for the prospectuses of the mutual funds listed in the box on the next page. If you want to do your own research, here are some ideas with which to begin. All trade on Nasdaq.

Six Fast-Growing Small-Cap Stocks for 1997

American President cos.
Cheyenne Software
Czech Republic Fund
First Mississippi
Global Marine
Ryan's Family Steak Houses

Out-of-Favor Spin-Offs, 1997

These companies, spun-off fairly recently, remain out of favor, but prices are likely to rise; only for risk-oriented investors.

COMPANY	BUSINESS	SPUN OFF BY
Crown Vantage	Paper products	James River
Gardner Denver	Indus equipment	Cooper Industries
Pitttston Brink's	Collection service	Pittston Services
US Industries	Housewares	Hanson plc

Small-Cap Mutual Funds

Although their returns continually gyrate, and usually more than with other types of equity funds, they're an excellent way to immediately have a diversified, albeit risky, portfolio of small cap companies.

☑ *HINT: To cushion the uncertainty related to small-cap companies: (1) Only put up to 25% of your equity money in these funds; (2) plan to stay invested a minimum of 3 years; (3) select small-cap funds that aim to preserve capital, such as those listed in the box below.*

SPIDERS

Leave it to Wall Street to come up with another animal product (see LYONS in Chapter 12). The Spiders crawled out of the financial web on January 29, 1993, when they became available on the American Stock Exchange.

SPDRs (Standard & Poor's Depository Receipts) are shares in a unit investment trust that tracks the performance of the Standard & Poor's 500 Index.

Their key advantage is that they enable you to buy the Standard and Poor's 500 just as if it were a single share of stock. They actually provide all the diversity and market-tracking ability of an index fund, and they have the plus of being liquid since they are a widely held and actively traded stock.

NOTE: Index funds are designed to give you an opportunity to earn market returns by buying all or a portion of the securities in a market index. See Chapter 6 for a discussion of index funds, including those that mimic the Standard & Poor's 500.

 CAUTION: Because Spiders trade like stocks, they are subject to price fluctuations. The Standard & Poor's 500 as of summer 1995 was around 559.05. Spiders at the same time were priced at approximately one-tenth of the index valuation, at $56. The symbol for Spiders, which trade on the American, is SPY.

How do you decide whether to buy a Standard & Poor's index fund or this Spider? It depends upon the amount of your investment and how long you plan to hold it. Keep these factors in mind:

- You buy shares in an index fund directly from the sponsor at the net asset value (the total of the fund's holdings divided by the number of shares outstanding).
- Spiders must be bought through stockbrokers, which entails a commission. They are also sold with a bid/asked spread.
- Index funds may have a load or sales fee or may be of the no-load variety.
- Spider management expenses are deducted from the quarterly cash distribution and are capped at ¹⁄₂₀th of 1%.
- Index funds often have an annual account maintenance fee—Vanguard's, for example, is $10.

Small-Cap Stock Funds That Take Low Risks

These funds purchase less-volatile, low P/E stocks and hold, on average, 35 to 40 stocks from a wide number of different industries.

FUND	TOTAL RETURN JAN–JUNE 1996	TELEPHONE
Fasciano	12.1%	800–848–6050
Fidelity OTC	27.4	800–544–8888
Nicholas II	16.1	414–272–6133
Pennsylvania Mutual	12.2	800–221–4268
Winthrop-Focus Aggressive Growth	11.7	800–225–8011

- Most people who invest in funds have their dividends reinvested.
- Spiders distribute all dividends on a quarterly basis, so you do not have the benefit of increasing your holdings through accrual.
- The Spider dividend rate, as of fall 1995, was only about 2.49%—about the same as bank savings rates.
- With an index fund, you pay taxes on capital gains distributions once a year.
- With Spiders, you pay tax on any capital gains only when you sell your position.

☑ *HINT: If you are a frequent trader: Spiders seem to be a better bet, even taking brokerage commissions into consideration. You can trade them all day long, while with index funds (or any funds, for that matter) purchases and redemptions are based only on end-of-the-day prices.*

The American Stock Exchange gives this example:

If you wanted to sell when the market opened on Monday, October 19, 1987, you could have sold Spiders (had they existed then) early in the morning when the Standard & Poor's 500 was at 270, down from the opening of 283, for only a 5% loss on the day. On the other hand, if you wanted to get out of a Standard & Poor's 500 index fund, you wouldn't have been able to do so until the end of the day at the closing price, which was 225. With a fund you would have had a 20% loss.

Index funds, however, are more cost-efficient over time. Of the nearly 30 funds that track the Standard & Poor's 500, the largest in which individuals can invest is the Vanguard Index Trust 500. Although it has no load, it takes 19 basis points off dividends for operating expenses and you must pay a $10 annual maintenance fee. With a Spider, you pay a brokerage commission, and a management fee of 20 basis points is taken out of dividends.

However, Vanguard limits its investors' trades to two purchases and sales a year. Buy and sell requests are mailed only, not relayed by telephone or fax. This creates a time lag between when transactions are ordered and executed. Most other index funds allow more frequent trades, but they have made these transactions very expensive in order to discourage them. This does not make them an appropriate choice for those who like to trade on a daily or even weekly basis.

By way of contrast, Spiders trade continually, so if you're the type who carefully tracks market movements, you can make profits during the day in a Spider.

STOCKS SELLING BELOW BOOK VALUE

Book value is the net worth per share of common stock: all assets minus all liabilities. When the stock price is below book value, it is at a bargain level in that: (1) the corporation may be worth more dead than alive: If it were liquidated, shareholders would get more from the sale of assets than the current value of the stock; and (2) the company may be a candidate for a takeover.

The usefulness of book value as a criterion depends on the type of corporation. Steel firms and manufacturers of heavy machinery have huge investments in plants and equipment, so they usually have a high book value. But they rarely make much money. By contrast, a drug manufacturer or retailer will have a low book value but will often have excellent earnings.

☑ *HINT: The trick in using book value effectively is to find a company whose stock is trading below that figure and is making a comeback that has not yet been recognized in the marketplace.*

In such a situation, you will get a double plus: buying assets at a discount, and a higher stock price due to better profits. Just make sure that the assets are real and that the earnings are the result of management's skill, not accounting legerdemain.

12 Stocks Selling Well Below Book Value

Book value can be seen as what shareholders would receive theoretically after all of a company's debts were paid. Stocks with low price-to-book value ratios are often overlooked bargains. On the other hand, stocks with high book values may be overpriced and due for a fall.

COMPANY	PERCENT PRICE-TO-BOOK VALUE RATIO
USF&G Corp.	1.07
ITT Hartford Group	1.16
Springs Industries	1.25
St Paul Companies	1.35
Allstate Corp.	1.38
Mead Corp.	1.40
Texas Utilities	1.58
Ryan's Family Steak Houses	1.74
Timken Co.	1.75
Boise Cascade	1.76
Dillard Dept Stores	1.78
General Re	1.78

SOURCE: Standard & Poor's *The Outlook,* Fall 1996.

STOCKS OF BANKRUPT COMPANIES

When corporations fall upon hard times, their misfortunes can signal investment opportunities for the strong-willed. Before these companies revive, their stocks and bonds are often available at bargain prices. What are your chances for success? Edward Altman, professor of finance at New York University's business school, released a report in early 1990 showing that investors who bought bonds of companies that declared bankruptcy or defaulted on meeting their payments averaged nearly 30% in compounded annual returns over the past 4 years.

If you'd like to select your own stocks, begin by looking at management. If a company has gone through restructuring and the new team is competent, the value of the stock will rise. It takes time for the improved performance to be recognized.

- *Look for corporations that have resources and a strong position in their field.* The broader the customer base, the greater the chance of success.
- *Diversify with at least three holdings.* If you're lucky, one will prove to be a winner, the second will stay about even, and the loss on the third will be small. Hopefully, that right choice will pay off well enough to make all the risks worthwhile.
- *Buy soon after emergence from Chapter 11.* At that point, there's the greatest uncertainty and maximum risk, but also a low base for future gains.

According to the National Institute of Business Management, investors can identify a company preparing for a strong comeback by looking for these traits:

- A large tax loss carryforward that can be written off against future earnings, thus sharply boosting after-tax profits
- Substantial saleable assets relative to debt, indicating that the securities will appreciate even if the company is partially or completely liquidated
- A new management team, especially one with turnaround experience
- Selling off of unprofitable divisions or buying of profitable new ones
- Restructuring of debt to improve cash flow
- Reduced leverage

☑ *IF YOU DARE: Because many institutions shy away from stocks of troubled companies, individual investors willing to assume the high degree of risk involved can sometimes make large profits in turnaround situations. To be on the safe side of an unsafe situation, wait until the company has announced a reorganization plan, or buy secured debt of the company.*

STOCK BUYBACKS

A corporate action that remains amazingly popular is the stock buyback. And as a shareholder you generally benefit when a company repurchases some of its shares. That's because buybacks are very often a sign that the company's cash flow is improving and that management views its company's stock as undervalued by the overall market. It also sees it as a way of creating shareholder value rather than increasing dividends or paying down debt.

During the first 6 months of 1996, according to Securities Data Corp., some 200 U.S. companies announced new or expanded stock repurchases, versus 268 for the prior year.

If the shares of repurchased stock are returned to the status of Treasury shares, then the number of the company's outstanding shares is reduced. This should eventually raise per-share profits and boost the price of the remaining outstanding shares.

Companies buy back their shares primarily for one of three reasons: to have stock available for employee stock-ownership programs, for executive stock options, or for making acquisitions.

By purchasing its shares in the open market, the company avoids diluting shareholder equity, which would be the case if it issued new stock.

Various studies show that the best price impact comes from what is called a Dutch auction. This is a type of self-tender in which the shareholder is asked to specify the lowest per-share price he will accept within a range set by the seller. A study at the University of Rochester's Graduate School of Business found that Dutch auctions generally provide returns of about 8% versus the Standard & Poor's 500, while open-market repurchases, which can take many months to complete, give excess returns of about 2%.

CAUTION: Not all corporate buybacks are a positive sign. If the company borrows money to reacquire its shares, it is taking on additional interest expenses, which may offset the benefit of increased per-share earnings.

HINT: Standard & Poor's weekly publication, The Outlook, *occasionally runs a list of stock repurchase programs, indicating which stocks they favor for investor's portfolios.*

FOR FURTHER INFORMATION

David Alger, *The Raging Bull: How to Invest in the Growth Stocks of the 90s* (Homewood, IL: Business One Irwin, 1992).

Dow Theory Forecasts (newsletter)
Dow Theory Forecasts, Inc.
7412 Calumet Avenue
Hammond, IN 46324
Weekly; $233/year

PART FIVE

You and Your Account

You might think you've done enough now that you've learned which investments are best and when to buy and sell them. Yet surprisingly, your education is not quite complete. After you've set your financial goals, selected various securities, and worked out a balanced portfolio, you need to correctly implement your plan, to put it into action in the most effective way possible.

The financial planner or broker you select, the firm you use, and the type of account you have make the difference between success and failure, between being in charge of your money or merely letting someone else, often a stranger, pull the strings. So, before you start trading securities, read this section carefully, or if, unfortunately, you are in the midst of a situation you're displeased with, study the suggestions for changing brokers and arbitrating disputes.

In this section you will learn:

- How to find, interview, and select the best professionals
- How to settle discord with your broker
- Whether to use a full-service broker or a discount broker
- The advantages of regional stockbrokers
- How to change brokers
- The type of brokerage account that's best for you
- What types of orders to use and when
- Easy ways to build a profitable portfolio
- Whether or not to have a margin account
- How to do your own research
- Dividend reinvestment plans
- Dollar cost averaging

24

Finding the
Best Professional Help

*E*ven if you are willing to spend time doing research and follow the sound investment principles outlined in this book, you're still going to need some professional help—to execute your trades if nothing else.

And, there are other times when professional help is useful, even essential: for direction when you are starting out; for confirmation when you become more experienced; and for management when you have sizable assets and no time to oversee them.

Nevertheless, you should be cautious about letting anyone else manage your money without first understanding your goals. It's your money, you worked hard to earn it, and in most cases, you know your risk tolerance and future needs better than anyone else.

There are three general categories of people whose job it is to help you with your investments: financial planners, stockbrokers, and investment advisers. Below are guidelines for selecting the best in each category, but a word of general advice first:

☑ **HINT: *Don't use a financial planner, broker, or investment adviser who:***

■ Has a criminal record or a history of securities-related complaints. Check with your state Securities Agency, or contact The National Association of Securities Dealers, 800–289–9999.

■ Has no staff or operates from a post office box or telephone answering service. Insist on visiting the office, and then check out the person's ties with other professionals. No one planner can master the U.S. Tax Code, pension laws, stocks, bonds, real estate, and insurance.

FINANCIAL PLANNERS—GETTING THE RIGHT ONE

If you feel you need help with your overall financial decision-making, you may want to turn to a generalist, known as a financial planner. Planners, unlike stockbrokers, become involved with all your assets—stocks, bonds, mutual funds, real estate, insurance, trusts, tax plans, even collectibles. Most planners work independently or in a group practice, although many are on the staffs of accounting firms, brokerage houses, banks, insurance companies, or mutual funds.

A good financial planner will begin by looking at your net worth, reviewing key documents relating to your assets and debts. He should have a checklist to be certain everything is covered: bank and brokerage firm statements, insurance records, mortgage papers, titles and deeds, tax returns, pension plans, a list of valuable objects, estimates of monthly living expenses, and so forth.

He next should review your goals. You need to be forthcoming about your investments, your job and possible promotions, what you might inherit, your retirement plans, as well as any major expenses you will be incurring. He should draw up, along with your help, a workable budget to help you meet your goals.

By putting all of this together, the planner can then advise you on appropriate investments, what insurance you do or do not need (health, disability, property, and damage), if you need to rewrite your will, set up trusts, or make other plans for passing your wealth to others.

He should also discuss whether or not you should invest in real estate, and if you are saving enough toward retirement. He should spot errors in how you've been handling your finances: if you have the wrong kinds of insurance, too risky a portfolio, a poorly executed will or estate plan, or sloppy tax returns.

This analysis is generally presented in writing, with suggestions on ways to improve your financial picture. Some planners then put into motion all aspects of the plan; others turn to professionals, such as an accountant for tax purposes, an attorney for trust plans, stockbrokers, insurance experts, and others.

These generalists, who help you develop an overall financial plan and then implement it with you, are not licensed or regulated by the government. Most work independently or in a small practice. Unless a planner is a stockbroker, he or she does not advise on stocks and bonds. Instead, the planner favors mutual funds or refers you to a broker.

At least 200,000 people call themselves financial planners, according to the Consumer Federation of America, but only 15% to 20% have ever completed a course in the field. With no federal regulations and no nationwide accreditation requirements, it's not easy to weed through the crop.

☑ HINT: *Before you turn your money over to a planner, read this section carefully. There are three basic categories of financial planners—determined by what they charge clients.*

- FEE-ONLY. A few years ago, advisers who charged only fees instead of commissions were difficult to find, but in the last couple of years their ranks have increased. Today there are an estimated 6,000 of them, up from 2,700 in 1992. Of this group, about 500 belong to the National Association of Personal Financial Advisors.

One reason for their increased popularity is that many people feel more comfortable turning to someone for advice who does not have a potential conflict of interest. Conflict can arise when an adviser earns a commission on the sale of investments, such as stocks, bonds, or insurance.

These planners charge either an annual fee, based on your assets and investment activity, or an hourly fee, ranging from $75 to $250. Annual reviews may be another 25% to 50% of the initial fee. Although fee-only planners do not sell you products, they will recommend them and, of course, eventually you will have to pay for any securities you purchase. You'll also be charged for the fee-only planner's plan, whether you choose to follow it or not.

- COMMISSION-ONLY. Some planners do not charge a fee but receive a commission on the investments they sell—for example, on a mutual fund or insurance product. With a commission-only planner, you benefit from one-stop shopping. Because any financial plan entails investments with a commission, you can do it all with the same person. However, the commission-only planner may have a vested interest in selling particular commission products. If you have a good relationship with your planner, this need not be a problem.

- FEE PLUS COMMISSION. Many planners charge a fee for their overall plan and a commission on investments you purchase.

In many cases the commission is lower than with a commission-only planner, simply because under this arrangement the adviser also receives a fee. In addition, the fee is almost always lower than with a fee-only planner.

Unless you have a complicated situation, don't pay more than 1% of the assets involved for a financial plan.

☑ *HINT: Always get a written estimate of what services you can expect for what price before making a commitment to a planner.*

Associations That Will Help You in Your Search

Unless you know an exceptional financial planner personally, confine your search to those who have demonstrated their seriousness by obtaining one of the several designations offered in the field. For example, those who have the designation CFP after their names have studied and been awarded this certification by the Certified Financial Planner Board of Standards. Other degree programs and designations are listed below. Although meeting the requirements is not a guarantee of brilliance, it does represent dedication to the field.

Most of these groups will provide a list of members in your area.

APFS (Accredited Personal Financial Specialists)

For: CPAs who concentrate on financial planning
Contact:
American Institute of CPAs
Personal Financial Planning Division
1211 Avenue of Americas
New York, NY 10036
800–862–4272

CFP (Certified Financial Planners)

For: The more than 232.000 planners listed with the Certified Financial Planner Board of Standards. To stay listed, CFPs must participate in continuing education. About 78 colleges offer courses to prepare students for the CFP exam—a comprehensive 10-hour, 2-day-long exam. The group does not provide referrals but you can call them to determine if a planner is licensed and to lodge a complaint about a planner.
Contact:
Certified Financial Planner Board of Standards
1660 Lincoln Street
Denver, CO 80264
303–830–7543 and 888–CFP–MARK

Institute of Certified Financial Planners

For: Over 10,000 CFPs make up membership in the Institute of Certified Financial Planners.
Contact:
3801 East Florida Avenue
Denver, CO 80210
800–282–PLAN

IAFP (The International Association for Financial Planning)

For: Some 14,150 members who must abide by a strict code of professional ethics.
Contact:
International Association for Financial Planning
5775 Glenridge Drive, NE
Atlanta, GA 30328
404–845–0011
NOTE: If you call 800–945–IAFP, you can get the names of planners in your area, drawn from a selected list of highly recommended professionals.

NAPFA (National Association of Personal Financial Advisors)

For: Fee-only planners.
    Contact:
    NAPFA
    355 West Dundee Road
    Buffalo Grove, IL 60089
    800–366–2732

Checking Up on a Planner's Reputation

If you have any reservations about a planner, you can contact these groups to see if any lawsuits or complaints have been filed:

1. The North American Securities Administrators Association, 202–737–0900
2. Your state attorney general's office
3. Your local Better Business Bureau

Although the financial planning field is not nationally regulated nor does it require a special license, more and more advisers are electing to register with the Securities and Exchange Commission which, in turn, keeps background information as well as a record of customer complaints.

Anyone who registers with the SEC must provide customers with a fee schedule and a list of services.

☑ *HINT: You can request a copy of the filing, which includes information on the planner's education and work history. You must supply the name of the adviser and his/her address and company name, if there is one. The cost is $0.24 per page.*

    Contact:
    SEC
    Public Reference Department
    450 Fifth Street, NW
    Washington, DC 20549
    or fax: 202–628–9001

For information on customer complaints against an adviser, write the SEC's Freedom of Information Act Officer at the above address, adding Room 2115.

STOCKBROKERS

These are representatives or agents who act as an intermediary between a buyer and a seller of securities. Brokers, who receive commissions for their services, are sometimes partners in a brokerage firm, but if not, they are called registered representatives (reps) and are regular employees. Brokers and registered reps must first be employed by a member firm of the National Association of Security Dealers (NASD) and then pass a comprehensive exam. Only upon successful completion of the exam is the broker registered and allowed to buy and sell securities for customers.

INVESTMENT ADVISERS

This professional may be a financial planner, but not all financial planners are investment advisers. An investment adviser recommends stocks, bonds, or mutual funds that are appropriate to your goals and risk level. If you give the adviser a discretionary account, he or she will buy and sell securities without first consulting you. Or you may require that he consult with you regarding trades. Many investment advisers require high minimums—at least $100,000. Annual fees start at 1½% to 2% of the assets up to $500,000, with a sliding scale of lower fees on heftier accounts. You also pay brokerage costs.

☑ *HINT: Ask your lawyer, accountant, or stockbroker for names of reliable investment advisers.*

    You can also get a list by writing to:
    Investment Counsel Association of America
    20 Exchange Place
    New York, NY 10005
    212–344–0999

INTERVIEWING A STOCKBROKER OR ADVISER

Select a stockbroker or financial adviser the same way you do your doctor: with great care and caution. Your financial well-being is second only to your physical health. Don't be tempted by tips you hear at cocktail parties or Little League baseball games. By following these steps, you will find the person best suited to guide your financial future.

Step 1. Ask for names from friends and colleagues whose business judgment you respect.

Step 2. Ask your lawyer and accountant for referrals.

Step 3. If you have a contact at a particular firm, ask the manager or president for the names of the best two or three brokers.

The number one consideration in choosing any type of investment adviser is comfort: Select someone you respect and whose advice you are willing to follow, who operates in a professional manner (with integrity, intelligence, and information), answers your questions, and eases your doubts and fears.

These criteria eliminate those brokers who are hustling for commissions, as well as salespeople who make quick recommendations without considering your assets, income obligations, and goals; and everyone who promises large, fast returns.

☑ *HINT: Look for the following:*

Performance Over the Long Term

Select someone with at least 5 years' experience in order to cover both bull and bear markets. Anyone can be lucky with a few stocks for a few years, but concentrate on an individual or firm whose recommendations have outpaced market averages by at least 2 percentage points: higher in up markets, lower in down periods. This applies to total returns—income plus appreciation or minus depreciation—and refers primarily to stocks, but it is a sound guideline for debt securities. A mini-mum expectation of return on investment from an investment adviser should range between 15% and 20%, including income and appreciation.

Superior performance should be a continuing criterion. Every 6 months, compare the returns on your investments with those of a standard indicator: for bonds, the Dow Jones Bond Average or, for tax-frees, the Dow Municipal Bond Average; for stocks, Standard & Poor's 500 (which is broader and more representative than the Dow Jones Industrial Average). Then subtract the commissions you paid to see whether you're getting your money's worth.

Reputation

Comments from old customers are most valuable for helping you learn how you are likely to be treated, including promptness and efficiency of service and reports. Is extra cash moved quickly into a money market fund? Are orders executed promptly and correctly? Are dividends posted immediately? Are monthly reports issued on time?

Compatibility

Choose advisers whose overall investment philosophy matches your objectives of income or growth. If you're conservative, stay away from a swinger who constantly comes up with new issues, wants you to trade frequently, suggests speculative situations, and scoffs at interest and dividends.

If you're aggressive, look for someone who keeps up on growth opportunities and is smart enough to recognize that no one should always be fully invested in equities and not recommend bonds or liquid assets under unfavorable stock market conditions.

Strategies and Techniques

Find out by asking questions such as these:

■ Where do you get investment ideas? From in-house research or from brokerage firms?

- What are your favorite stock-picking strategies? Out-of-favor stocks with low price-earnings ratios? Small company growth stocks? Larger corporations whose shares are now undervalued according to predictable earnings expectations?
- How diversified are the portfolios? Do you shoot for big gains from a few stocks or seek modest profits from a broader list?

Knowing When to Sell

Successful investing relies on two factors: how much you make and how little you lose. Check the composition of several portfolios for the past 5 years. If they are still holding glamour stocks bought at peaks and now near lows, move on! Don't stick with professionals who ignore their losses.

Just Say "No"

After you've made a choice, don't be afraid to say no if you don't understand or if you lack confidence in the recommendations. Nothing is more important than trust when you are dealing with money. You can forgive a few mistakes, but if they mount up, cancel the agreement. Remember, it is your money and you have every right to call the shots.

More about Interviewing Potential Planners, Advisers, and Brokers

Whatever you do, don't select someone to help you with your investments by walking into a firm cold off the street. And never sign on with the first person you talk with. Set up interviews with several candidates. Go to the interview prepared with a series of questions and compare how each of your potential advisers answers them.

Jay J. Pack, a broker and author of *How to Talk to a Broker,* suggests the following six basic questions:

1. What do you suggest that I do with my $25,000 (or whatever amount you have)? Beware of the person who suggests you put it all in one product.
2. How long have you been in business? With this firm?
3. Will you give me several references so that I may check on your record?
4. What will it cost me to use your help? Get specifics about fees and commissions, in writing.
5. What sort of return can I expect from my investment?
6. What research materials do you rely on?

And keep in mind that any good planner, adviser, or broker should:

- Be willing to meet with you in person for a free consultation
- Provide you with references or sample portfolios
- Ask you about your net worth, financial goals, and tolerance for risk
- Offer you several alternatives and explain them
- Be able to refer you to other professionals for specific help
- Set up a schedule for reviewing your securities, assets, and overall financial picture
- Answer your phone calls promptly

☑ *HINT: The NASD will tell you if a broker or his or her firm has been slapped with a disciplinary action or convicted of a crime. Unresolved complaints are not disclosed. Call: 800–289–9999.*

DISCOUNT STOCKBROKERS

If you like to make your own buy-and-sell decisions, do your own research, and can operate independently of a full-service brokerage firm, it is possible to save between 30% and 80% on your commissions by using a discount broker.

Commissions: Full-Rate vs. Discount Brokers

	200 SHARES @25	300 SHARES @20	500 SHARES @18	1,000 SHARES @14
Merrill Lynch	129.50	157.00	214.50	293.60
Shearson	128.00	154.25	222.25	347.75
Prudential	140.92	167.08	232.60	348.95
Dean Witter	122.13	145.52	205.86	322.82
Charles Schwab	81.00	87.00	96.00	111.00
Fidelity Brokerage	80.75	86.75	95.75	110.75
Quick & Reilly	60.50	65.00	81.50	94.00

These no-frills operations are able to offer lower rates because they do not provide research, they hire salaried order clerks and not commissioned brokers, and they maintain low overheads. Yet many have a surprisingly complete line of investment choices available: In addition to stocks and bonds, many handle Treasury issues, municipals, options, and mortgage-backed securities and will set up self-directed IRAs or Keoghs. The country's largest discounter, Charles Schwab & Co., also offers to trade mutual fund shares. Shearman Ralston and Securities Research have distinguished themselves in the field by publishing a monthly market report newsletter and offering modest amounts of research free to customers.

Several discounters have also moved into the computer field: Quick & Reilly, Charles Schwab, and Fidelity Brokerage Services market software programs enabling customers to place trades from their home computers, to receive stock quotes, and even to evaluate their portfolios.

As a general rule, you will be able to save $25 to $75 when doing a 300-share trade. But discounters set up varying schedules, so it definitely pays to shop around when selecting a firm. With some—called value brokers—the rates escalate with both the number of shares and their price. With others—called share brokers—rates are tied

solely to the number of shares traded. You will save more with lower-priced shares if you use a value broker and with higher-priced stocks if you use a share broker.

You should use a discount broker only if you:

- Like to select your own stocks
- Belong to an investment club
- Have inherited a few shares that you want to sell
- Have a portfolio of $100,000
- Trade at least twice a month in units of 300 shares or more
- Feel so confident of your stock market skill that you do not want someone else to monitor or question your decisions
- Are not involved with special securities such as convertibles, options, or warrants, here accurate information is difficult to obtain

---

Should You Use a Discount Broker?

YES, IF:

- You have investment savvy
- You enjoy following the stock market and have time to do so
- You have clear ideas about what to buy and sell, and when
- You subscribe to an investment service or to serious professional periodicals
- You follow technical indicators
- You read market news on a regular basis
- You trade often
- You are not afraid to make mistakes

NO, IF:

- You cannot decide what to buy and sell
- You require investment advice
- You are too busy to follow the market
- You are nervous about things financial
- You are inexperienced

SOURCE: Jay J. Pack, *How to Talk to a Broker* (New York: Harper & Row, 1985).

Don't assume that all discount firms are alike. Always ask what services are offered in addition to buying and selling stocks at a discount. For example, Charles Schwab & Co., headquartered in San Francisco, makes it possible for clients to:

- Purchase any of hundreds of no-load and low-load mutual funds through any of its branch offices
- Place buy and sell orders 24 hours a day
- Purchase fixed-income securities, including Treasuries, municipals, and corporate bonds
- Purchase some 200 no-load funds available without transaction fees
- Receive independent research reports by fax, phone, and mail
- Trade your account by modem and access stock market research through its software package, available to those with an IBM-compatible computer
- Get a no-fee CMA-type account, called the Schwab One Account, free checking, and a Visa debit card
- Trade stocks and mutual funds, get price quotes, and check on your account through TeleBroker, an automated service available to customers with touch-tone phones

REGIONAL STOCKBROKERS

Regional brokerage firms, those with home bases outside New York, are recognized for their personal touch, local knowledge, and independent nature. Many are excellent in picking stocks. That's because regional brokers are in positions to spot promising unnoticed stocks and bonds of local companies, ones Wall Street firms either ignore or do not follow closely. For you, this means a chance to buy a stock before the rest of the investment world becomes bullish.

The regionals also pride themselves on better service. Brokers tend to stay longer at these firms, which lessens the chances of a rookie or broker-

---

Leading Discount Stockbrokers

Baker & Co., Cleveland, Ohio
    800–321–1640; 800–362–2008 in Ohio
    $40 minimum
Fidelity, Boston, Massachusetts
    800–544–3939
    $38 minimum
Pacific Brokerage Services, Los Angeles, California
    800–421–8395
    $25 + $4 service fee minimum
Quick & Reilly, New York, New York
    800–672–7220
    $37.50 minimum
Charles Schwab & Co., San Francisco, California
    800–435–4000
    $39 minimum
Shearman Ralston, Inc., New York, New York
    800–221–4242; 212–248–1160 in New York City
    $40 minimum
Securities Research, Inc., Vero Beach, Florida
    800–327–3156
    $35 minimum
Muriel Siebert & Co., New York, New York
    800–872–0711
    $37.50 minimum
StockCross, Inc., Boston, Massachusetts
    800–225–6196; 800–392–6104 in Massachusetts
    $25 + 8.5¢ minimum per share
Jack White & Co., San Diego, California
    800–233–3411; 619–587–2000
    $33 + 3¢ minimum
Wilmington Brokerage Services, Wilmington, Delaware
    800–345–7550; 302–651–1011
    $39 minimum

---

of-the-day handling your account. They also have the freedom to sell products of other firms—mutual funds, unit investment trusts, limited partnerships, and so forth.

To check out a regional firm:

1. Read the annual report to see if it's been profitable during bull and bear cycles.

Regional Brokerage Firms

FIRM	TELEPHONE	FIRM	TELEPHONE
Advest Inc. 90 State House Square Hartford, CT 06103	860–509–1000 800–243–8115	Janney Montgomery Scott Inc. 1801 Market Street Philadelphia, PA 19103	215–665–6000 800–526–6397
J.C. Bradford & Co. 330 Commerce Street Nashville, TN 37201	615–748–9000 800–251–1060	Legg Mason Wood Walker 111 South Calvert Street Baltimore, MD 21202	410–539–0000 800–368–2558
Alex Brown & Sons Co. 135 East Baltimore Street Baltimore, MD 21202	410–727–1700 800–638–2596	McDonald & Co. 800 Superior Avenue Cleveland, OH 44114	216–443–2300 800–553–2240
Crowell, Weedon & Co. 624 South Grand Avenue Suite 2600 Los Angeles, CA 90017	213–620–1850	Piper, Jaffray Inc. 222 South 9th Street Minneapolis, MN 55402	612–342–6000 800–333–6000
Dain Bosworth Inc. Dain Bosworth Plaza 60 South 6th Street Minneapolis, MN 55402	612–371–2711	Raymond James Financial 880 Carillon Parkway St. Petersburg, FL 33716	813–573–3800 800–248–8863
D.A. Davidson & Co. P.O. Box 5015 Great Falls, MT 59403	406–727–4200 800–332–5915	Rauscher Pierce Refsnes, Inc. 2700 North Haskell Dallas, TX 75204	214–989–1000
Edward D. Jones & Co. 201 Progress Parkway Maryland Heights, MO 63043	314–851–2000	Sutro & Co. 201 California Street San Francisco, CA 94111	415–445–8500 800–652–1030
A.G. Edwards & Sons, Inc. One North Jefferson Avenue St. Louis, MO 63103	314–515–3000	Van Kasper & Co. 600 California Street San Francisco, CA 94108	415–391–5600 800–652–1747
Interstate/Johnson Lane 121 West Trade Street Charlotte, NC 28202	704–379–9000	Wheat First Butcher Singer 901 East Byrd Street Richmond, VA 23219	804–649–2311 800–627–8625

2. Call and ask for some sample research; read and compare with other firms.

3. Talk to smart investors in the area who are either customers of the firm or can tell you why they are not.

GETTING YOUR BROKER'S RESEARCH

The advantage of a full-service broker is access to investment research that separates companies on the rise from those that are heading down. Reports on individual companies as well as industry groups are prepared by analysts. Assigned to follow a particular industry, these security analysts interview corporate executives, study financial reports, and identify trends, potential problems, and new developments. Their reports are the basis of many of the investment decisions your broker makes.

Reports produced by analysts are a mixed bag—some are financial tables of little use to individuals, while others contain useful comments on a company's stock. Some are brilliant; some are ordinary. Many analysts tend to run with the pack. To overcome this tendency, take the advice to "hold" a stock and interpret it as "OK to sell."

If your broker recommends a stock, always ask for the most recent report on the company. Or, if you hear about a potentially interesting buy, find out if the firm has taken a position on it. If you are a regular customer, your broker should send you the firm's weekly or monthly roundup reports, which cover a number of stocks. If your broker resists sending these to you, maybe you should look for another broker. (However, don't expect the firm's best reports if you make only a handful of trades a year.)

The Top Research Sources

If you decide to do your own research or supplement what's offered by your stockbroker or adviser, three publication services will be enormously helpful. They are expensive, so you may want to use them at your library or broker's office before buying your own copies.

Beware of the Ponzi Scheme: 1997

Every year, as I revise this guide, I consider removing this warning; but then I meet someone who has been bamboozled by a fast-talking, usually good-looking, con artist. So, I leave in the following, hoping you'll read it and remember it when you next meet a Ponzi type at a dinner party, fund-raiser, auction, or your club. *And remember*, as you're thinking, "Hmm, this sounds good," that con artists come in male and female versions!

An amazing number of intelligent people are taken in by seemingly attractive, smart embezzlers through the Ponzi scheme—a swindle in which the first few investors are paid interest out of the proceeds of later investors. The latter end up with zero when the balloon breaks and the swindler pockets the remaining money. Ponzi schemes masquerade as tax shelters, deals in precious metals, gold and diamonds, real estate, and collectibles, as well as in putting together unique, tailor-made portfolios.

A sure sign: a guarantee of far higher interest rates or returns than the prevailing market is paying.

Moody's

Moody's Investors Service
99 Church Street
New York, NY 10007
212–553–0546
800–342–5647

A leading research and information service aimed primarily at the business community, Moody's (a Dun & Bradstreet Corporation company) is known throughout the world for its bond ratings and factual publications. It is not an investment advisory service.

Here's what it publishes:

Moody's Manuals

The company publishes eight manuals on an annual basis. Each is continually updated, some as often as twice a week. The manuals cover

20,000 U.S. and foreign corporations and 15,000 municipal and government entities. Each one gives financial and operating data, company histories, product descriptions, plant and property locations, and lists of officers. The eight are:

- *Bank and Finance.* Covers 20,000 financial institutions, including insurance companies, mutual funds, banks, and brokerage firms.
- *Industrial.* Covers industrial corporations on the NYSE and AMEX, plus others on regional exchanges.
- *OTC Industrial.* Covers 2,500 industrial companies.
- *OTC Unlisted.* Covers 2,200 hard-to-find companies not listed on Nasdaq's National Market System or on regional exchanges.
- *Public Utility.* Covers every publicly-held U.S. gas and electric utility, gas transmission, telephone, and water company and many privately held ones.
- *Transportation.* Covers airlines, railroads, oil pipelines, bridge and tunnel operators, bus and truck companies, and auto and truck rental and leasing firms.
- *International.* Covers 9,000 international corporations in 100 countries.
- *Municipal and Government.* Covers 15,000 bond-issuing municipalities and government agencies; includes bond ratings.

Moody's Handbooks

These softcover books, published quarterly, give concise overviews of 2,700 corporations. Useful for instant facts and financial summaries. They are called Handbook of Common Stocks and Handbook of NASDAQ stocks.

Other Publications

- *Moody's Dividend Record.* Detailed reports on current dividend data of 19,000 stocks; updated twice weekly.

- *Moody's Industry Review.* Ranks 3,500 leading companies in 137 industry groups.
- *Moody's Bond Record.* Monthly guide to 86,000 fixed-income issues including ratings, yield to maturity, and prices.
- *Moody's Bond Survey.* Weekly publication on new issues.

☑ *HINT: A Word About Moody's Bond Ratings. Their purpose is to grade the relative quality of investments by using nine symbols ranging from Aaa (the highest) to C (the lowest). In addition, each classification from Aa to B (for corporate bonds) sometimes has a numerical modifier: The number 1 indicates that the security ranks at the highest end of the category; the number 2, in the middle; and the number 3, at the lower end.*

Standard & Poor's

Standard & Poor's Corp.
25 Broadway
New York, NY 10004
212–208–8000
800–221–5277

For over 120 years Standard & Poor's has been providing financial information, stock and bond analysis, and bond rating and investment guidance. Its materials are used by investors as well as the professional and business community.

Major Publications

- *Corporation Records.* Seven volumes covering financial details, history, and products of 12,000 corporations. One volume, Daily News, provides continually updated information five days a week about these publicly-held corporations.
- *Stock Reports.* Analytical data on 4,400 corporations. Includes every company traded on the NYSE and AMEX plus 1,400 over-the-counters. There are two-page reports on each company.

- *Industry Surveys.* This four-volume looseleaf is continually updated and covers 21 leading U.S. industries. Surveys cover all aspects of an industry including market trends, earnings, and government regulations.
- *Stock Guide.* A small paperback containing 49 columns of statistical material on 5,900 stocks. A broker's bible.
- *The Outlook.* A weekly advisory newsletter covering the economic climate, stock forecasts, industry predictions, buy-and-sell recommendations, etc. Presents a "master list of recommended stocks" with various portfolios.
- *Trendline Publications.* Publishes marketing behavior charts providing investors with a visual look at a company's performance. Includes charts of indexes and indicators.

Other Publications

CreditWeek, Bond Guide, Commercial Paper Ratings Guide, Standard & Poor's *Register of Corporations, Directors and Executives,* and *Security Dealers of North America.*

Standard & Poor's Bond Ratings

S&P rates bonds from AAA (the highest) to D (bonds in default). Those with ratings between AAA and BBB are considered of investment quality. Those below BBB fall into the speculative category. Ratings between AA and CCC often have a + or – to indicate relative strength within the larger categories.

The company also rates stocks from A+ (highest) to A (high), A– (above average), B+ (average), B (below average), B– (lower), C (lowest), to D (reorganization). With the exception of banks and financial institutions, which are rated NR (no ranking), most publicly-owned corporations are listed. Never invest in any company rated below B+.

Value Line Inc.

220 East 42nd Street
New York, NY 10017
800–833–0046

An independent investment advisory, Value Line, Inc., publishes one of the country's leading investment advisory and research services, the *Value Line Investment Survey*, as well as several other publications and the Value Line index.

Value Line Investment Survey

Begun in 1935, it's a weekly advisory service published in a two-volume looseleaf binder. It analyzes 1,700 common stocks divided into 100 industry groups.

A report on each industry precedes the individual stock reports. Each stock is given two rankings: one for "timeliness" (the probable relative price performance of the stock within the next 12 months) and one for "safety" (the stock's future price stability and its company's current financial strength). Within these two categories each stock is assigned a rank from 1 (the highest) to 5 (the lowest). Here's what the rankings mean:

- VALUE LINE TIMELINESS
    Rank 1 (highest) Expect the stock to be one of the best price performers relative to the 1,700 other stocks during the next 12 months
    Rank 2 (above average) Expect better-than-average price performance
    Rank 3 (average) Expect price performance in line with the market
    Rank 4 (below average) Expect less-than-average price performance
    Rank 5 (lowest) Expect the poorest price performance relative to other stocks
- VALUE LINE SAFETY
    Rank 1 (highest) This stock is probably one of the safest, most stable, and least risky relative to the 1,700 other stocks

Rank 2 (above average) This stock is probably safer and less risky than most

Rank 3 (average) This stock is probably of average safety and risk

Rank 4 (below average) This stock is probably riskier and less safe than most

Rank 5 (lowest) This stock is probably one of the riskiest and least safe

Other Publications

- *The Value Line OTC Special Situations Service.* Covers fast-growing smaller companies. Published 24 times a year.
- *Value Line Options.* Evaluates and ranks nearly all options listed on the U.S. exchanges. Published 48 times a year.
- *Value Line Convertibles.* Evaluates and ranks for future market performance 585 companies and 80 warrants. Published 48 times a year.

SETTLING DISPUTES: ARBITRATION

As with all businesses, there are individuals who either deliberately or carelessly give poor advice. In the brokerage business, integrity is paramount—all the exchanges have strict rules, and most firms have compliance officers whose responsibility it is to monitor trading, make sure that full information is provided to all clients, and act promptly when there are deviations.

Generally, trouble develops when the customer does not understand an investment or when the broker is not clear about all the facts or has not made them clear to the client. When the price of the securities goes down, recriminations start. If you take a flier, you can't blame the broker for your mistake. But brokers may be at fault if they cross the line between optimism and misrepresentation, or, of course if they churn your account or are intentionally dishonest.

☑ *HINT: The areas most prone to problems are options, commodities, and margin accounts, or what are called "other, esoteric" investments. Every broker is required to know each customer and not put any customer in an inappropriate, high-risk investment. A client's net worth, income, investment objectives, and experience help determine what is suitable.*

If you have a problem with your broker, begin by trying to settle it informally with him or her. If the problem remains unresolved, take the following action:

Step 1. Talk to the broker's supervisor or branch manager. Brokerage firms do not want to earn bad reputations with the public or have a number of vociferous, complaining clients.

Step 2. Write a letter of complaint to the broker and the firm's compliance officer, with a copy to the branch manager. Request a written response from the compliance officer.

Step 3. Send a copy of the letter to the state securities administrator. The North American Securities Administrators Association is the national organization for all 50 state securities officials. Call NASAA for the person in your state: 202–737–0900.

Step 4. Contact the SEC, Office of Consumer Affairs, 450 5th Street NW, Washington, DC 20549. If your problem involves a commodities or futures contract, a copy of the complaint letter should go to the Commodity Futures Trading Commission, Office of Public Information, 1155 21st Street NW, Washington, DC 20581, or call: 202–418–5000.

Step 5. Send a copy to the exchange involved (see Appendix E for addresses).

Step 6. If you are unable to resolve your complaint through phone calls and letters—and if it involves a great deal of money, the next step is arbitration.

ARBITRATION

 CAUTION: When you opened your brokerage account, you signed a customer's agreement form of some sort. Many forms specify which arbitration body will hear a case if there is a dispute. Contact that body.

Arbitration panels sponsored by the industry's self-regulatory bodies consist of three people, and only one can be affiliated with the securities industry. Arbitrators have awarded punitive damages of as much as $1 million. They often also award attorneys' fees.

By contrast, the American Arbitration Association has absolutely no connection to the brokerage industry. Check your brokerage agreement. Although it may be more impartial, filing with the AAA is also more costly—from $500 for a dispute involving $10,000 or less to $5,000 for disputes of $1 million or more. At the National Association of Security Dealers, it is $30 for $1,000 or less and $1,250 for amounts over $500,000.

☑ *HINT: The U.S. Supreme Court has upheld a ruling that allows securities dealers to refuse to open accounts for clients who do not agree in advance to settle disputes through arbitration rather than by suing. Arbitration is generally quicker and less costly than a long court battle. See "For Further Information" on page 243.*

AN OUNCE OF PREVENTION

It's nice to know arbitration is available for resolving disputes, but it's nicer still to avoid them in the first place. Here's how to reduce the possibility of the need for arbitrating:

Put in writing to your broker:

- Your financial objectives
- Your income, assets, liabilities
- Your financial obligations to others

How to Protect Yourself

- Keep track of all your trades, including monthly statements.
- Note all important conversations with your broker in a diary.
- Contact your firm's manager if there's a problem—the company wants to keep, not lose customers.
- If you're not satisfied, contact an experienced lawyer; ask about fee structure.
- Figure out your brokerage losses plus the lawyer's fee. Is it worth taking the next step?

Before You Undertake Arbitration. . .

Arbitration is a long and often unpleasant procedure and should never be entered into casually. According to Jay J. Pack, author of How to Talk to a Broker:

- The odds for an arbitration settlement in your favor are typically 50–50.
- You will improve your chances if you are prepared ahead of time. Gather proper documentation and other evidence to support your case.
- In 1987 the SEC ruled that arbitration results are binding. Therefore, if you decide to go to arbitration and the case is not decided in your favor, you cannot turn around and sue your broker.
- Act immediately if you are planning to go to arbitration. Arbitrators won't look favorably upon your complaint if you wait to see whether the investment in question goes up in price.

  For further information, see sources listed at the end of this chapter.

- Directions for trading your account
- Where you can be reached during trading hours to confirm buy or sell positions

And, always:

- Read your monthly statement, trade slips
- Call quickly if there's a problem

- Know whether your account is up or down in value over the previous month, over a year ago at the same time

Once a year, review with him or her:

- Changes in your financial situation
- The performance record of your account
- Your net worth and income tax bracket
- Ask your broker and accountant to communicate about your tax situation

THE ABUSIVE BROKER RULING

On March 6, 1995, the U.S. Supreme Court ruled 8–1 that brokerage firms cannot deny investors punitive damages in securities arbitration cases. Until that point, the industry found a way to impede arbitrators from awarding punitive damages through the agreement that customers sign when they open an account.

Most agreements say that in arbitration, the laws of New York State will prevail. And that state law prohibits arbitrators from awarding punitive damages. The Supreme Court has ruled that these agreements did not clearly state that customers were giving up this right.

Of course, brokerage firms could revise the agreements to make it clear that arbitration awards will be limited to compensatory, not punitive damages. That, however, would be tough since the New York Stock Exchange and the National Association of Securities Dealers both have rules that say brokerage firms can not limit relief in contracts.

FOR FURTHER INFORMATION

Arbitration

Director of Arbitration
New York Stock Exchange
20 Broad Street
New York, NY 10005
212–656–3000

Director of Arbitration
National Association of Security Dealers
33 Whitehall Street
New York, NY 10004
212–480–4881

Office of Consumer Affairs
Securities & Exchange Commission
450 Fifth Street NW
Washington, DC 20549
202–942–7040

American Arbitration Association
140 West 51st Street
New York, NY 10020
212–484–4000

The Administrative Directory
North American Securities Administrators Association
One Massachusetts Avenue NW
Washington, DC 20001
202–737–0900; $5
Lists telephone numbers and addresses of state administrators and federal agencies.

Brokers

Jay J. Pack, *How to Talk to a Broker* (New York: Harper & Row, 1985).

Financial Planners

Mastering Money: Secure Your Financial Future
International Association for Financial Planning
5775 Glenridge Drive NE
Atlanta, GA 30328
404–845–0011; free

Selecting a Qualified Financial Planning Professional
Institute of Certified Financial Planners
3801 East Florida Avenue
Denver, CO 80210
800–282–PLAN; free

Tips on Financial Planners
Council of Better Business Bureaus, Inc.
Publications Dept.
4200 Wilson Boulevard, 8th floor
Arlington, VA 22203
$2

How to Choose a Financial Planner
National Association of Personal Financial
Advisors
355 West Dundee Road

Buffalo Grove, IL 60089
800–366–2732; free

Investment Swindles: How They Work and How to Avoid Them
National Futures Association
Public Affairs Dept.
200 West Madison Street
Chicago, IL 60606
312–781–1300; free

25

Managing Your Brokerage Account

*I*n the previous chapter you learned how to select a top-notch pro to help you buy and sell securities and manage your overall portfolio. Once you've lined up this adviser, you're not off the hook. You still have some decisions to make—such as what type of account to use, what types of orders to place, and the degree to which you want to be involved in running your account, all topics covered in this chapter.

Please read this chapter carefully—whether you are opening your first account or already have an established relationship with a broker.

YOUR ACCOUNT—WHAT TYPE?

First, you must decide between a *margin account* and a *cash account*. Most investors should and do use a cash account. In a cash account you pay for your securities within 3 business days after the transaction.

A margin account is not only more risky, because it involves borrowing, but it can lead to actual dollar losses if you do not monitor your position on a regular basis. Margin accounts are discussed in detail later in this chapter.

Discretionary or Nondiscretionary Accounts

If you are just beginning to work with your broker, do not, repeat, not sign a discretionary account agreement. This type of account gives the broker the power to buy and sell securities without consulting you first. Discretionary accounts should be used only with brokers you have worked with for a number of years and you trust more than your own mother. Not surprisingly, discretionary accounts often cause problems—customers think the broker is churning their accounts (executing too many trades merely to rack up commissions) or not buying the right types of securities. The customer may or may not be right. Mismanagement of an account is hard to pinpoint, but it does indeed happen. So don't let it become a possibility—stick with a cash account instead.

In Street Name

Your broker will also ask you if you want your securities held in "street name"—that is, held with the firm—or if you want them registered in your own name with the certificates sent directly to you. If you decide to take physical possession of your securities, you will have to wait several weeks for them to arrive. If they are in street name, they become simply a computerized book entry at your firm, and your dividends and any stock splits are automatically collected and recorded for you.

☑ *HINT: If securities are in the broker's custody, transfer of shares when you sell them is easier than if the stock is registered in your name. Then you have to get the stocks out of your safe deposit box and deliver them to the broker's office.*

⊙ CAUTION: *If your travel or trade often, you certainly should not hold your own certificates—it makes selling shares quickly to take advantage of the market almost an impossibility.*

JOINT ACCOUNTS

Before you open your account, check with your lawyer, especially if you are married, have children and/or are involved in estate planning. You may want to establish a joint account.

- *In a joint tenancy with the rights of survivorship,* if one person dies, the other receives all the securities and cash in the account. The assets bypass probate and go directly to the survivor, although estate taxes may have to be paid.
- *In a tenancy-in-common account,* the deceased's share of the account goes to the deceased's heirs, not to the joint account holder. The survivor must then open a new account.
- If you have children, you may want to open a *Uniform Gifts to Minors* account. Whoever establishes the account names a "custodian" for the minor—very often they name themselves. All trading activity is then done by the custodian for the child's benefit. When the child reaches majority (age 18 or 21) he or she can legally take control of the account.

Wrap Accounts

A product of the nineties, the Wrap Account is designed to put your money decisions in the hands of a professional. Wrap accounts are offered by many brokerage firms, financial planners, and some banks. They manage your money for a fixed annual fee—instead of charging you commissions whenever you buy or sell something.

In other words, you pay a fixed percentage of your assets every year to a brokerage firm, instead of commissions. All your expenses, including the expense of hiring an outside, professional manager to pick your investments, are "wrapped" into that one, single fee.

Sounds good—but before you leap in consider the fact that doing so will cost you about 3% of your assets per year.

In a way, wrap accounts wrap you up in several layers of money management. First of all, your money is invested by private money managers in individual stocks and bonds and/or in a mixture of mutual funds.

Secondly, you're also paying part of your fee to the stockbroker or financial planner who referred you to the professional manager. Some brokerage firms try to talk customers into hiring an in-house manager; but a good wrap program should offer several outside managers who are not part of the firm.

⊙ CAUTION: *You may wind up paying the fee, year after year, for services that you need only now and then.*

Wrap programs make sense sometimes:

1. If there's a private money manager you like and this is the only way you can get access to him/her
2. Managers often require a minimum of $1 million but in a wrap program that minimum might be dropped to $100,000, or in the case of a wrap program that uses mutual fund managers, to $25,000.
3. To avoid transaction charges if you do lots of trading
4. To have someone else pick and monitor your mutual funds

☑ HINT: *Before signing on, if you want a one-step, one-decision plan run by a professional, compare a wrap account with an asset-allocation fund offered by the mutual fund companies. Fidelity and T. Rowe Price, for example, both have such funds in which your money is allo-cated among the company's various mutual funds. Fees are less than in a wrap account.*

HOW TO SWITCH BROKERS

One of the most time-consuming and sometimes awkward tasks investors face is switching brokers. Transferring assets from one firm to another ought to be easy, but it often occurs at a tortoise-like pace. Delays sometimes last weeks or months, and occasionally investors lose money because securities dropped in value during the transit process.

Here's how to head off delays and trouble:

- Your new broker will ask for a list of what's held in your old account. Have that ready. Give him a copy of your last monthly state-ment, or fax it to him to accelerate the process. Under the rules of the National Association of Securities Dealers and the New York Stock Exchange, the old broker must deliver the holdings in 5 to 10 days.

- If that deadline cannot be met, the old bro-kerage firm must send the new one cash equaling the market value of the securities under what is called a "fail-to-deliver con-tract." This money enables the customer to trade. When the securities arrive, the money is returned. (Fail-to-deliver contracts are required by the NASD under a 1986 ruling adopted because of the number of customer complaints about transfers.)

Handling Snags

Problems, of course, do arise. The key reasons are that (1) assets cannot be moved quickly, such as an IRA that requires a change of custodians or proprietary investments, such as a mutual fund run by the transferring brokerage firm; (2) the account has assets with virtually no value—bank-rupt companies or companies with other technical problems; or (3) the old broker stalls—he or she may be annoyed that you're leaving, on vacation, or no longer with the firm. Talk first with the old broker, then with the supervisor. Ask why there is a hang-up. Prod gently, then firmly. You'll find most firms are accustomed to making this type of transaction within two weeks.

Solutions

- If a serious delay occurs, you can complain to your old broker's supervisor, the NASD, and the SEC.

    Complaints to the NASD should be filed with the district office nearest the receiving broker. Contact the NASD in Gaithersburg, Maryland (800–289–9999), for the address of its nearest office.

    The SEC will contact the brokers and ask for an update.

    To complain, contact the Office of Consumer Affairs, SEC, 450 Fifth Street NW, Washington, DC 20549 (202–942–7040).

- If you lose money because of a delay and your former broker won't help out, your only recourse is to use the NASD's arbitration ser-vice. For the proper forms, write to the NASD's Arbitration Office, 33 Whitehall Street, New York, NY 10004 (212–858–4488). Expect to spend between $30 and $1,800, depending on the amount involved. Cases take about 6 to 10 months to complete, and the decision is binding.

TYPES OF STOCK MARKET ORDERS

Once you have opened your account you're ready to trade. Although both dividend reinvestment plans and dollar cost averaging, discussed later on, are sensible ways to buy shares of stocks or mutual funds without using a broker, they only work for securities you already own. When adding to your holdings or selling stocks, you need to know what type of order to place.

Most investors simply call their broker and place an order, called a market order. However, there are several other ways to go about it. Armed with a little more information, you can place a specific type of order and thereby protect your portfolio.

Market Order

This is the most common type of order. It tells your broker to buy or sell at the best price obtainable at the moment, or at the market. If the order is to buy, the broker must keep bidding at advancing prices until a willing seller is found. If the order is to sell, the broker offers it at increasingly lower prices. With a market order, you can be certain that your order will be executed.

Limit Order

Usually a market order is sufficient, but when prices are fluctuating, it is wise to enter a limit order, which tells the broker the maximum price you're willing to pay, or if you're selling, the minimum you'll accept. For example, if you put in a limit order to buy a stock at 20 when the stock is trading at 22, your order will not be filled unless the stock falls to 20 or lower.

Day Order

This is an order to buy or sell that expires unless executed or canceled the same day it is placed. All orders are day orders unless you indicate otherwise. The key exception is a "good-until-canceled order."

Good-Until-Canceled Order

Also known as an open order, this is an order that remains in effect until executed or canceled. If it remains unfilled for long, the broker generally checks to see if the customer is still interested in the stock should it reach the designated or target price.

Sale Order

An order to buy or sell specified amounts of a security at specified price increments. For example, you might want to buy 5,000 shares but in lots of 500, each in stages of ¼ points as the market falls. Not all brokers will accept scale orders because they involve so much work.

Stop Order

An order to buy (or sell) if the stock trades at a certain price. If the stock reaches this price your order is automatically triggered and becomes an order to buy (or sell) "at the market." A stop order may also be placed with a price limit to avoid its being executed at a substantially different price than the price of the stop.

Stop Loss Order

An order that sets the sell price below the current market price. Stop-loss orders protect profits already made or prevent further losses if the stock falls in price.

 CAUTION: Both the New York and American stock exchanges have the power to halt stop orders in individual stocks to prohibit further sell-off in a declining stock. However, they very rarely use this power and in fact did not do so during the 1987 market crash.

HOW TO USE STOP ORDERS

Stop orders basically provide protection against the unexpected by forcing you to admit your mistakes and thus cut your losses. In effect, they say that you will not participate above or below a certain price. For example, if you bought a stock 6 months ago at $50 per share and it's now at $75, you can set a stop-loss order to sell at $60. Then, should it fall in price, you know that your broker will sell you out at $60. Stop orders are useful for the following purposes.

To Limit Losses on Stocks You Own

You buy 100 shares of Allied Wingding at 50 in hopes of a quick gain. You are a bit queasy about the market, so at the same time you enter an order to sell the stock at 47⅜ stop. If AW drops to 47⅜, your stop order becomes a market order and you've limited your loss to 2⅜ points per share.

Traders generally set their loss targets at 10% below cost or recent high. Those who are concerned with long-term investments are more cautious and prefer a loss figure of about 15%: say, 42⅜ for a stock bought at 50.

☑ *HINT: For best results, set stop prices on the down side and have courage enough to back up your decisions. Once any stock starts to fall, there's no telling how far down it will go. Cut losses short and let your profits run.*

To Ensure a Profit

A year ago you bought 100 shares of a stock at 42 and it is now at 55. You are planning a vacation trip and do not want to lose too much of your paper profit, so you give your broker an order to sell at 51 stop, good until canceled. If the market declines and the sale is made, you will protect most of your 9-point-per-share gain.

Similarly, the stop order can protect a profit on a short sale. This time, you sell short at 55. The price falls to 40, so you have a $15-per-share profit. You look for a further price decline but want protection while you're away. You enter a buy order at 45 stop. If the stock price does jump to 45, you will buy 100 shares, cover your short position, and have a $1,000 profit (assuming that the specialist is able to make the purchase on the nose).

To Touch Off Predetermined Buy, Sell, and Sell-Short Orders

If you rely on technical analysis and buy only when a stock breaks through a trend line on the up side and sell, or sell short when it breaks out on the down side, you can place advance orders to "buy stop," "sell stop," or "sell short stop." These become market orders when the price of the securities hits the designated figure.

Example: Your stock is at 48¾ and appears likely to shoot up. But you want to be sure that the rise is genuine, because over the years there's been resistance at just about 50. You set a buy stop order at 51⅛. This becomes a market order if the stock hits the price 51⅛.

HOW TO SET STOP PRICES

Broadly speaking, there are two techniques to use:

- SET THE ORDER AT A PRICE THAT IS A FRACTION OF A POINT ABOVE THE ROUND FIGURE. At 50⅛, for example. Your order will be executed before the stock drops to the round figure (50), which most investors will designate.

💣 *CAUTION: There is no guarantee that your stock will be sold at the exact stop price. In a fast-moving market, the stock may drop rapidly and skip the stop price, and thus the sale will be at a lower figure than anticipated.*

- RELATE THE STOP PRICE TO THE VOLATILITY OF THE STOCK. This is the beta. In making calculations, the trader uses a base of 1, indicating that the stock has historically moved with the market. A stock with a beta of 1.1 would be 10% more volatile than the overall market; one with a beta of 0.8 would be 20% less volatile than the market. If your stop price is too close to the current price of a very volatile stock, your order may be executed prematurely.

Use these guidelines for relating your stop order to the volatility or beta of your stock:

- Under 0.8, the sell price is 8% below the purchase price

- Between 0.8 and 1, the stop loss is set at 10% below the cost or recent high
- 1.1 to 1.3: 12% below
- 1.4 to 1.6: 14% below
- Over 1.6: 16% below

Example: XYZ stock is acquired at 50. Its beta is 1.2, so the stop loss is set at 44: 12% below 50. If the market goes up, the stop is raised for every 20% gain in the stock price. At 60, the sell order would be 53: 12% below 60.

The lower the price of the stock, the greater the probable fluctuations; the higher the price of the stock, the smaller the swings are likely to be.

Thus Teledyne, at 150 with a 1.1 beta, would normally have a stop-loss price of 132, but because of its high price, it would probably be about 139.

SELLING SHORT

Selling short is a technique that seeks to sell high and buy low—or reverse the order of what most investors seek to do. It's speculative but can be used as a protective device. You sell stock you do not own at the market price in anticipation of a drop in price. You borrow the stock from your broker, who either has it in inventory, has shares in the margin account of another client, or borrows the shares from another broker. If the stock drops to a lower price than the price at which you sold it short, you buy it, pocket the profit, and return the stock you borrowed to your broker.

Example: The stock of Nifty-Fifty, a high-technology company, has soared from 20 to 48 in a few months. A report from your broker questions whether NF can continue its ever-higher earnings. From your own research—of the company and the industry—you agree and decide that after the next quarter's report, the price of the stock will probably fall sharply. You arrange with your broker to borrow 500 shares and sell these shares at 48.

Two months later, the company announces lower profits, and the stock falls to 40. Now you buy 500 shares and pocket a $4,000 profit (less commissions). Or if you're convinced that the price will continue to go down, you hold out for a lower purchase price.

This technique seems easy, but short selling is one of the most misunderstood of all types of securities transactions and is often considered un-American and dangerous, as indicated by the Wall Street aphorism "He who sells what isn't his'n buys it back or goes to pris'n." Yet when properly executed, selling short can preserve capital, turn losses into gains, defer or minimize taxes, and be profitable.

With few exceptions, the only people who make money with stocks in a bear market are those who sell short.

Here's another *example.* Say that in anticipation of a bear market, you sell short 100 shares of AW at 50. To reduce your risk if you are wrong and the market rises, you enter an order to buy 100 shares of AW at 52⅞ stop. If the stock price advances that high, you'll limit your loss to $287.50 (plus commissions).

With a stop-limit price, you specify a price below which the order must not be executed. This is useful with a volatile stock in an erratic market. Then if the price of the stock slips past the stop price, you won't be sold out.

Say you enter an order to sell 100 AW at 50 stop, 50 limit. The price declines from 50½ to 50. At that point, your order becomes a limit order at 50, not a market order. Your stock will not be sold at 49⅞, as can happen with a stop order at 50.

Short selling is not for the faint of heart or for those who rely on tips instead of research. You may have some nervous moments if your timing is poor and the price of the stock jumps right after you sell short. But if your projections are correct, the price of that stock will fall—eventually. You must have the courage of your convictions and be willing to hang on.

Rules and Conditions for Selling Short

Because it's a special technique, short selling of all securities is subject to strict operational rules:

■ MARGIN. All short sales must be made in a margin account, usually with stock borrowed from another customer of the brokerage firm under an agreement signed when the margin account was established. If you own stock, you can sell "against the box," as explained in the box on page 252. The minimum collateral must be the greater of $2,000 or 50% of the market value of the shorted stock.

☑ *HINT: For those who want to feel more comfortable with a short sale, it's best to maintain a margin balance equal to 90% of the short sale commitment. This will eliminate the necessity for coming up with more cash.*

■ INTEREST. There are no interest charges on margin accounts.

■ PREMIUMS. Once in a while, if the shorted stock is in great demand, your broker may have to pay a premium for borrowing, usually $1 per 100 shares per business day.

■ DIVIDENDS. All dividends on shorted stock must be paid to the owner. That's why it's best to concentrate on warrants and stocks that pay low or no dividends.

■ RIGHTS AND STOCK DIVIDENDS. Because you are borrowing stock, you are not entitled to rights or stock dividends. You must return all stock rights and dividends to the owner.

　　If you know or suspect that a company is going to pass or decrease its payout, you can get an extra bonus by selling short. The price of the stock is almost sure to drop. But be careful: The decline may be too small to offset the commissions.

■ SALES PRICE. Short sales must be made on the uptick or zero tick: That is, the last price of the stock must be higher than that of the previous sale. If the stock is at 70, you cannot sell short when it drops to 69⅞, but must wait for a higher price: 70⅛ or more.

☑ *EXCEPTION: The broker may sell at the same price, 70, provided that the previous change in the price was upward. There might have been three or four transactions at 70. A short sale can be made when the last different price was 69⅞ or lower. This is called selling on an even tick.*

Picking Stocks for Short Sales

Ask your broker for recommendations and then take a look at these fairly simple indicators:

■ INSIDER TRANSACTIONS. If officers and directors of the corporation have sold stock in the previous few months—the assumption is that when the number of insiders selling exceeds the number buying, the stock is at a high level and these knowledgeable people believe a decline is ahead.

■ VOLATILITY. As measured by the beta of the stock. This is the historical relation between the price movement of the stock and the overall market. A stock that moves with the market has a beta of 1.0; a more volatile issue is rated 1.5 because it swings 50% more than the market.

　　The more volatile the stock, the better it may be for short selling. You can hope to make your profit more quickly.

■ RELATIVE STRENGTH. Or, how the stock stacks up with other companies in the same or similar industries. This calculation takes into account the consistency and growth of earnings and whether the last quarter's profits were lower or higher than anticipated by Wall Street. These data are available from statistical services such as *Value Line* and Standard & Poor's *Earnings Forecast*.

When corporate earnings are lower than the professional forecasts, the stock will almost always

Selling Against the Box

This is a favorite year-end tactic that can freeze your paper profits and postpone taxes. You sell short against shares you own. The short sale brings in immediate cash and the profit (loss) is deferred until the short position is covered—next year. Here's how it works:

On March 1, Mary buys 100 shares of XYZ Corp. at 40. By July the stock is at 60, but the market is weakening and Mary gets nervous. She sells short 100 shares of XYZ with her own shares as collateral.

Her long position (the 100 shares bought at 40) remains in a margin account, where it represents collateral.

Her short position is made in a different "short account."

What are Mary's choices?

1. If the stock stays around 60, she may elect to deliver her stock against her short sale, which was made at 60, after January 1. This will postpone taxes until the new year and will also give her a 20-point profit ($60 - 40 = 20$). Note: that determination of long-term or short-term depends on date of short sale, not on date of actual delivery.

2. If the stock drops from 60 to 50, she can deliver her stock and take a 20-point profit ($60 - 40 = 20$) as in choice 1, or she can take a 10-point profit by buying back her short sale. In this case she remains an investor in the company with the original stock at a cost of 40.

Commissions should be considered in selling against the box; they become a factor.

Under the wash sale rule (see Chapter 32), there will be no tax loss if the short sale is covered by buying the same or identical securities within 30 days before or after the date of the original short sale. In other words, if Mary sells short at 60 and then her stock moves up in price within a short period of time and she covers the short sale by purchase within 30 days, the loss is not a tax loss; it is simply added to her original cost (40 per share). If she covers the short sale by purchase after 31 days, the loss is valid for tax purposes.

SOURCE: Joel Fein, ISI Group, Inc.

fall sharply. Catching such a situation so that you can sell short early will depend on your own projections, which can be based on news stories or information that you have gleaned from your personal contacts.

What to Sell

As a rule of thumb, the best candidates for short selling are (1) stocks that have zoomed up in a relatively short period; (2) one-time glamour stocks that are losing popularity—after reaching a peak, these stocks will be sold rapidly by the institutions, and because these "professionals" follow the leader, the prices can drop far and fast; (3) stocks that have begun to decline more than the market averages—this may be an indication of fundamental weakness; (4) warrants of volatile stocks, which are selling at high prices.

What Not to Sell

The least attractive stocks for short selling are (1) thin issues of only a few hundred thousand outstanding shares—a little buying can boost their prices, and you can get caught in a squeeze and have to pay to borrow, or buy back, shares; and (2) stocks with a large short interest: more than the volume of 3 days' normal trading; they have already been pressured downward, and when the shorts are covered, this extra demand will force prices up.

Guidelines for Succesful Short Selling

- *Don't buck the trend.* Do not sell short unless both the major and intermediate trends of the market—or, on occasion, those of an industry—are down. Make the market work for you. You may be convinced that an individual stock is overpriced, but do not take risks until there is clear, confirmed evidence of a fall in the market and for the stock you're considering.
- *Don't sell short at the market when the stock price is heading down.* Place a limit order at the lowest price at which you are willing to sell short.
- *Do set protective prices, on the up side,* 10% to 15% above the sale price, depending on the volatility of the stock. In most cases, a quick small loss will be wise.
- *Don't short several stocks at once* until you are experienced. Start with one failing stock; if you make money, you will be ready for another.
- *Do rely on the odd-lot selling indicator.* This is available from several technical advisory services or can be set up on your own. It is calculated by dividing the total odd-lot sales into the odd-lot short sales and charting a 10-day moving average. When the indicator stays below 1.0 for several months, it's time to consider selling short. When it's down to 0.5, start selling.

  On the other hand, when the indicator rises above 1.0, do not sell short and cover your positions. And if you hesitate, cover all shorts when a 1-day reading bounces above 3.0.
- *Do set target prices* but be ready to cover when there's a probability of an upswing. There will usually be a resistance level. If this is maintained with stronger volume, take your profit. You can't afford to try to out-guess the professionals.

BREAKING EVEN

Before you hang on to a stock in hopes that its price will rise so that you can break even, check the following table. A stock must rise 100% to correct a 50% decline! If your stock declines from 100 to 50, it has dropped 50%. But it will take a doubling in price (a 100% increase) to rise from 50 back to 100. Moral: Take losses early; set stop orders to protect profits; stop dreaming.

PROGRAM TRADING

An ongoing situation individual stock investors should be aware of is "program trading," a complicated strategy used by institutions whereby computers trigger buy and sell orders.

It is less of a problem than in the past although it does add to market volatility and was blamed for much of the market's drop in October 1987.

Program trading is the result of the introduction of index options, index futures, and computers to Wall Street. It takes advantage of the price gap between index futures and option prices and the market value of the stocks making up the indexes.

The trader uses computers to follow the price differentials and then to sell automatically at a specified point. When a number of big institu-

IF A STOCK DROPS THE FOLLOWING PERCENTAGE	IT NEEDS TO RISE THIS PERCENTAGE FOR YOU TO BREAK EVEN
5% (100 to 95)	5% (95 to 100)
10% (100 to 90)	11% (90 to 100)
15% (100 to 85)	17% (85 to 100)
20% (100 to 80)	25% (80 to 100)
25% (100 to 75)	33% (75 to 100)
30% (100 to 70)	42% (70 to 100)
40% (100 to 60)	66% (60 to 100)
50% (100 to 50)	100% (50 to 100)
60% (100 to 40)	150% (40 to 100)
75% (100 to 25)	300% (25 to 100)

tions follow the same strategy, the market swings can be large.

Here are two typical trading situations:

- If the value of the S&P 500 futures contract drops below the market price of the stocks that make up the index and the spread (or price gap) becomes wide enough, computers send out automatic signals to sell stocks. This huge sell order can lead to a drop in the price of the stocks.
- If the prices of the S&P 500 stocks fall behind the futures on the index, the computers will signal to buy these stocks and sell the futures when the spread reaches a certain amount. This can lead to a rise in stock prices.

SPACE YOUR TRADES

If you are making a large investment (500 shares or more) in any one stock, consider spacing out your purchases over a period of several days or even weeks. The commissions will be higher, but you'll gain a time span in which to review your investment decisions without committing all your funds. And if you decide that your choice was wrong, you can cancel the rest of the order.

CHECK THE EX-DIVIDEND DATE

Always check the ex-dividend dates before you sell. This will ensure extra income benefits.

The Triple Witching Hour

Four times a year, three "items" expire on the same day: stock index futures, index options, and stock options. Program traders take offsetting positions, and a burst of buying and selling takes place, sometimes just before the market closes. There's no way to determine if the result will push the market up or down. This occurs on the third Friday of March, June, September, and December.

Ex-dividend means without dividend. On the stock tables, this is shown by the symbol "x" after the name of the company in the "sales" column.

The buyer of a stock selling ex-dividend does not receive the most recently declared dividend. That dividend goes to the seller. With Consolidated Edison, the date is shown in Standard & Poor's *Stock Guide* as in the table on page 255.

Once a dividend is ex-dividend, shareholders then look to the next dividend to be declared.

Going ex-dividend is actually a two-step process. The new dividend is payable to those who are "holders of record" as of a certain date. To be a holder of record, one must buy the stock at least 5 business days before the record date. On the fourth business day prior to the record date, the stock trades ex-dividend; that is, without dividend. Step two involves payment of the dividend by the corporation to the holders of record. This payment occurs 2 or 3 weeks after the official record date.

Once you have decided to sell a stable stock, you may want to delay the sale until a few days after the ex-dividend date, so you can earn the dividend. On the ex-dividend date, the stock will usually drop by the amount of the dividend but will tend to make it up in the following few days.

Ex-rights means without rights. As outlined in Chapter 17, rights offer stockholders the opportunity to buy new or additional stock at a discount. The buyer of a stock selling ex-rights is not entitled to this right after the ex-right date.

AUTOMATIC WAYS TO BUILD YOUR PORTFOLIO

The simplest, easiest way to buy shares of a stock—once you own it, that is—is through a dividend reinvestment plan, so we'll discuss that approach first. Dollar cost averaging is another automatic way to add to your portfolio holdings.

NAME OF ISSUE	DECLARED	EX-DIV.	RECORD	PAYMENT
Consolidated Edison	1/25	2/10	2/16	3/15/97

Neither dividend reinvestment nor dollar cost averaging requires a great deal of work or thought on your part once you've actually purchased the stock or mutual fund for your portfolio.

Dividend Reinvestment Plans

In this plan, offered by most blue-chip companies, dividends are automatically reinvested in shares of a company's stock without a brokerage fee. A number also offer a 5% price discount on new stock purchases. This service is offered by corporations to strengthen stockholder relations and raise additional capital at low cost; for investors, it is a handy, inexpensive means for regular saving. It avoids the nuisance of small dividend checks and forces regular investments. It's good for growth but not for current income, because you never see the dividend check. Many corporations permit extra cash deposits, ranging from $10 to $3,000 each dividend reinvestment time. There is usually an annual cap ranging anywhere from $10,000 to $100,000 per year.

Under such a plan, all dividends are automatically reinvested in the company's stock. The company then credits the full or fractional shares and pays dividends on the new total holdings.

Because these cash dividends are reinvested automatically at regular quarterly intervals, they resemble dollar cost averaging and turn out to be a way to buy more shares of a stock when its price is low. Full as well as fractional shares are credited to your account.

 CAUTION: *You must pay income taxes on the dividends reinvested just as though you had received cash. If you buy the stock at a discount from its current market price, the difference is regarded as taxable income.*

Dollar Cost Averaging (DCA)

This, the most widely used direct-investment formula plan, eliminates the difficult problem of timing when to buy and sell. You purchase a fixed dollar amount of stocks at specific time intervals: 1 month, 3 months, or whatever time span meets your savings schedule. Consequently, your average cost will always be lower than the average market price. This is because lower prices always result in the purchase of more shares.

For example, if you invest $100 per month regardless of the price of the shares, the lower the market value, the more shares you buy. The stocks you buy fluctuate in price between 10 and 5 over 4 months. The first month you buy 10 shares at $10 each for a total of $100. The second month you buy 20 shares at $5 each, and so on. At the end of 4 months you have acquired 60

Companies with Dividend Reinvestment Plans

AT&T	Kroger Co.
Bell South	McDonald's
Bristol-Myers Squibb	MMM
Citicorp	Morgan (J.P.)
Clorox	NYNEX
Commonwealth Edison	PepsiCo
Duke Power	Piedmont Nat. Gas
Du Pont	Raytheon
Exxon	Sears, Roebuck
General Electric	Southwestern Bell
Green Mountain Power	Texas Utilities
Hawaiian Electric	United Water Resources
Heinz	Wells Fargo
IBM	WPL Holdings
Illinois Power	Xerox Corp.
Indiana Energy	

shares for your $400 at an average cost of $6.67 per share (400 ÷ 60).

NOTE: During this same period, the average price was $7.50.

☑ **HINT: With DCA, the type of stock acquired is important. You want quality stocks that have these general characteristics:**

■ *Volatility.* But not too much. Preferably, the 10-year-high price should be 2½ times the low. These swings are more common with cyclical stocks such as motors, machinery, and natural resources, but they can also be found with industries whose popularity shifts: drugs, electronics, and food processors.

> Total invested: $400
>
> 40 shares @ $5   =$200
> 20 shares @ $10 = 200
> $400

In bear markets, your dollars buy more shares, but your paper losses on stock already held will be high, so you will have to have a stout heart and confidence enough to maintain your commitment. That's where quality counts.

■ *Long-term growth.* These are stocks of companies that can be expected to continue to boost revenues and earnings and outperform the overall stock market. If your stock fails to keep pace with the market comeback, you will lose the main advantage of DCA. Look for stocks that are more volatile on the up side than on the down side.

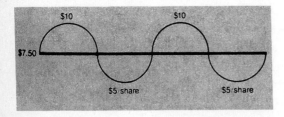

■ *Steady, ample dividends.* It is true that dividends, as such, have little to do with formula plans, but they can help to provide regular sums needed for periodic investments, especially when you find it difficult to scrape up spare cash.

With the right stocks and modest commitments, you may find that in a few years, the dividends will be enough to meet those periodic payments.

When you use margin, you can buy more shares with the same savings, but you will have to pay interest on your margin account. However, the interest charged will be partially offset by the dividends you receive.

☑ **HINT: Start your program a week or two before the date you expect to receive a dividend check from the company whose stock you plan to buy.**

■ *Better-than-average profitability.* The average profit rate of the company over a decade should be at least 10%. It's fine to be able to buy more stock when the price is low, but there's little benefit if its value does not move up steadily over the years. Corporations able to show consistent profitable growth will always be worth more in the future. With DCA, you are striving to accumulate greater wealth. This can always be done best by buying stocks of companies that make better-than-average profits.

■ *Good quality.* This means stocks of companies rated A− or higher by Standard & Poor's. With such criteria, you will avoid companies with high debt ratios and, usually, those whose prices swing sharply.

☑ **HINT: Shares of mutual funds are excellent vehicles for DCA. They provide diversification, generally stay in step with the stock market as a whole, and usually continue to pay dividends.**

Reverse Dollar Cost Averaging

This is a technique that is best used after retirement when you begin to liquidate shares of a mutual fund. Instead of drawing a fixed dollar amount (as most retirees do), you sell a fixed number of shares. The average selling price will come out higher that way.

For illustration only, the box below shows the values of fund shares that fluctuate widely over a 6-month period. To get $100 income, you must sell 10 shares in the first month, 20 in the second, etc. Over the half-year, you liquidate 75 shares at an average price of $8.

But if you sell a fixed number (10) of shares each month, your income will vary: $100 in month 1, $50 in month 2, $200 in month 4. Overall, you will cash in only 60 shares at an average redemption price of $10.

This can be dangerous for two reasons: (1) You won't get the same dollars every month, but over the same period of time you will receive as much and have more shares still invested. Yet when the price of the shares drops, you will have to unload more shares and will have fewer assets invested in the fund. (2) You cannot know in advance the correct number of shares to sell; if you have to change the formula, you may be in trouble.

☑ *HINT: This system is arithmetically correct but may be difficult for people who do not have additional income to live on in months when fund per-share price is low.*

Advantages

Over the years, the average cost of all shares will be less than the average price at which you bought them. But you lose the fun and pride of judgment-based investing.

 CAUTION: When stock prices are falling, consistent purchases are a form of averaging down—generally a poor policy unless you are convinced that there will be a turnaround soon.

Disadvantages

Formula plans sound simple, but they can be difficult to maintain. Most investors cannot convince themselves to sell when things are going well and buy when the market action is unfavorable. These

---

Stocks for Dollar Cost Averaging: 1997

American Home Products	Long's Drug Stores
American Int'l Group	McDonald's
Anheuser-Busch	Merck & Co.
Becton Dickinson	PepsiCo, Inc.
Boeing	Pfizer, Inc.
British Telecom (ADR)	Procter & Gamble
	Reader's Digest
Caterpillar	Rockwell Int'l
Clorox Co.	Rollins, Inc.
Coca-Cola	Rubbermaid, Inc.
Disney (Walt)	Seagram, Co.
Exxon	Smucker, J.M.
General Electric	Texaco
Goodyear Tire	Tootsie Roll Indus.
Heinz	Upjohn Co.
Iowa Gas & Electric	Winn Dixie Stores
Johnson & Johnson	Wrigley (Wm.)
	Xerox Corp.

Reverse Dollar Cost Averaging

SHARE PRICE	$100 PER MONTH: NO. SHARES SOLD	10 SHARES PER MONTH: INCOME
10	10	$100
5	20	50
10	10	100
20	5	200
10	10	100
5	20	50
	75	$600
Average redemption price per share	$8	$10

plans will seldom let you achieve a big killing, but they can stop you from being killed.

ALL-IN-ONE ACCOUNTS

If you have a brokerage account, a money market fund, and a major credit card, as well as some type of checking account, you may find it useful and economical to wrap it all together and put it into a combo, or asset management account. In this way, all your financial transactions will be handled under one roof—at a bank or brokerage firm— which saves you time, red tape, and sometimes money, too.

A typical central assets account consists of one versatile package that can include stocks, bonds, your IRA, a money market fund, and credit or debit card transactions. But you must be able to meet the minimum amount set by the brokerage firm or bank, which ranges from $5,000 to $20,000.

For a yearly fee (zero to $200) the sponsoring bank or brokerage firm will provide unlimited check-writing privileges on a money market account; an American Express, Visa, or MasterCard account; a line of credit; a securities brokerage account; and an all-inclusive monthly statement. An important additional benefit, known as the "sweep" feature, automatically transfers or sweeps any idle cash (from the sale of a security, a CD that matured, or dividends) into a high-paying money market fund. This system not only relieves you of keeping track of the money, but, more importantly, prevents any loss of interest between transactions.

A central asset account comprises seven basic ingredients:

- A brokerage account in which securities can be bought and sold at regular commissions
- Automatic investment of idle cash into money market funds
- A checking account, usually with free checks; minimum amounts vary
- A debit or credit card that can be used for purchases, loans, or cash
- A line of credit, that is, the privilege of borrowing against your credit or debit card
- Quick loans secured by the margin value of the securities held in the account, with interest charged at slightly above the broker call rate
- Composite monthly statements showing all transactions and balances

How a Central Assets Account Works

Let's say you have 300 shares of Eastman Kodak that you want to sell. You call your broker with directions to make the transaction. Money from the sale is immediately invested in a money market fund, where it earns around 4%. The transfer of money from your securities account to the money market fund is done automatically by computer.

Then a few weeks later you write a check for $800. You do so against your money market fund, leaving a balance of several thousand dollars. You felt this was an adequate balance—and it was, until you had a sudden emergency and needed to use that amount plus $1,500. So your broker arranged for a loan using your remaining securities as collateral. This was done in your margin account. By having an umbrella account, you avoided hours of time and miles of red tape that are customarily involved in obtaining a bank loan.

Many of the larger brokerage firms offer customers one of several funds in which to park their idle cash: a regular money market fund; a U.S. government fund, which is slightly safer but also has lower yields; and a tax-free money fund for those in high-tax brackets.

The traditional monthly statement includes:

- A list of securities held in the account
- Securities bought or sold with an indication of profit or loss
- Amount of commission paid to the broker
- Dividends received

- Interest received from the money market fund
- Number of money market fund shares
- Amount of margin loans either advanced or paid off
- Credit and debit card transactions
- Data required in preparing your income tax returns

CAUTION: You should also keep in mind some of the disadvantages of this type of account. First of all, most components of a combo account are available elsewhere. Credit card holders already have credit lines and cash advances. Debit cards can be a disadvantage, because they provide a shorter "float period"—that is, less free credit time than for a standard credit card. With the latter, you can stretch your credit or payment time up to at least 30 days, sometimes 60 or 90.

Easy access to credit means those without a lot of self-control can zoom through their credit line without even thinking about it. If you fall into

Directory of Central Assets Accounts

Citicorp: Citigold Account
    (800–285–1701)
Dean Witter: Active Assets Account
    (800–869–3326)
A.G. Edwards: Total Asset Account
    (800–677–8380)
Fidelity: Ultra Service Account
    (800–343–8721)
Merrill Lynch: Cash Management Account
    (800–262–4636)
PaineWebber: Resource Management Account
    (800–762–1000)
Prudential-Bache: Prudential Command Account
    (800–222–4321)
Charles Schwab: One Account
    (800–421–4488)
Smith Barney: Financial Management Account
    (800–221–3434)

this category, steer clear of the central assets account.

The Better Business Bureau in many areas has free material on central asset accounts, banks, and brokerage services. Contact your local office.

MARGIN ACCOUNTS

Leverage—using borrowed funds to supplement your own commitments—is a key factor in making money make money. With real estate, it's making a small down payment and having a large mortgage; with securities, it's buying on margin: using cash, stocks, convertibles, bonds, etc., as collateral for a loan from your broker. When the borrowing is kept at a reasonable level and the interest costs are modest, buying on margin can enhance profits, because your money is working twice as hard because you put up only part of the cost. Margin, then, is trading on credit and a way of using borrowing power to take a larger position in the stock market.

Leverage in the stock market is not as simple as it sounds. Successful use of margin requires sophistication, sufficient resources to absorb substantial losses when the prices of the securities decline, and the temperament to handle debt.

The Rules

When you open a margin account and sign a margin agreement and loan consent, you are giving your broker permission to lend the securities in your account.

Your stocks in a margin account are held "in street name," which means in the broker's firm. Therefore, you cannot put your stock certificates in your vault. You may also be subject to "margin call" if you use the assets in your account to the point where you have no more credit, or if the value of your portfolio falls below a minimum amount. Then your broker will ask you to reduce some of the loan. If you cannot come up with the

Calculating Your Yield When Buying on Margin

To determine exactly what yield you get by buying on margin, you must ascertain the return on your actual investment: the *margin equivalent yield*. You can calculate this from the accompanying formula. The *cash yield percent* (CY%) is the return on securities bought outright. The same formulas can be used for both pre-tax and after-tax yields.

$$MEY = \left(\frac{100}{\%M} \times CY\%\right) - \left[\left(\frac{100}{\%M} - 1\right) \times DI\%\right]$$

where MEY = margin equivalent yield
%M = % margin
CY% = cash yield %
DI% = debit interest %

Example: You are on a 50% margin base, receive 12% cash yield from dividends, and pay 20% in your debit balance.

$$MEY = \left(\frac{100}{50} \times 12\right) - \left[\left(\frac{100}{50} - 1\right) \times 20\right]$$

$$MEY = (2 \times 12 = 24)$$
$$- [(2 - 1 = 1) \times 20 = 20]$$
$$MEY = 24 - 20 = 4\%$$

Thus the 12% return, with margin, dwindles to 4%.

Exchange and Federal Margin Requirements

Assuming you put up cash in the amount of $10,000 in each case, you could buy on margin:

- $20,000 worth of marginable stocks
- $20,000 worth of listed corporate convertible bonds

You can invest on margin in nearly every issue on the New York and American stock exchanges and in nearly 2,000 over-the-counter securities. To open an account, you must sign a margin agreement that includes a consent to loan securities. The margin account agreement states that all securities will be held "in street name"; that is, by the broker. The consent to loan means that the broker can lend your securities to others who may want them for the purpose of selling short.

cash or additional securities, your broker may have to sell some of your remaining stock.

Margin accounts are governed by the Federal Reserve Board's Regulation T, the New York Stock Exchange, the National Association of Securities Dealers, and individual brokerage house rules.

1. Under the rules set forth by the Federal Reserve Board, the initial requirement for margin on stocks is 50%. So to buy $10,000 worth of securities you must put up at least $5,000. Greater leverage is allowed on government bonds, where you can borrow up to 95%.

2. The New York Stock Exchange, however, has stricter requirements. It asks members to

demand that investors deposit a minimum of $2,000 in cash or its equivalent in securities in order to open a margin account. That means that if you want to buy $3,000 in stock, your initial margin requirement is actually 66⅔%, or $2,000, rather than the $1,500, or 50%, that the Federal Reserve Board requires.

3. Some brokers set even higher requirements.

NOTE: All brokers hold securities purchased on margin in "street name."

The New York Stock Exchange also requires that the equity in the account be maintained at 25% to 30% at all times. This is called a "minimum maintenance margin." When the value of your portfolio drops below this level, your broker will issue a margin call, and you will have to come up with more cash or the broker will sell enough securities in your account to bring it up to the required level.

Example: Let's say you want to buy 200 shares of a $50 stock. In a regular cash account, you would put up $10,000 ($50 × 200 = $10,000). But in a margin account, you only have to put up 50%

of the purchase price, or $5,000 plus commission. Your broker lends you the other $5,000 and charges you interest on it.

The Loan Rate

Mounting interest charges can take a big chunk out of profits in a margin account, especially if you hold your stocks a long time. You are charged interest daily based on the broker call rate, the rate the banks charge brokers for money. The interest the broker then charges you may run from 0.5% to 2.5% above the broker loan rate, which currently ranges from 6¼ to 7¼%. The more active and the larger your account, the lower the rate is likely to be. Dividends, of course, can help offset some of the interest.

☑ *HINT: The interest you pay on your margin account is tax-deductible to the extent that it is offset by investment income—dividends, interest, and capital gains. So to deduct $2,000 in interest, you must report at least $2,000 in investment income. NOTE: Since 1993, capital gains are no longer classified as investment income for purposes of investment interest deduction unless the taxpayer elects to have all or part of the gains subject to the 28% maximum tax classified as investment income to offset additional investment interest. But, in that case, the gains are subject to ordinary income tax rates which can be as high as 39.6%.*

☛ *CAUTION: The New York Stock Exchange may set special margin requirements calling for more cash or securities or require full cash payments in very volatile stocks.*

Special Miscellaneous Account

If you have excess cash or equity in your margin account, this is known as a special miscellaneous account (SMA). It is created by the deposit of more than 50% of the purchase price of stocks or securi-

---

Margin Call

If your firm requires a 30% minimum maintenance rather than 25%, to find out if you're approaching a call, multiply the price of the stock at the time you purchased it by 0.71. If it's reached that price, your phone will ring.

---

ties bought on margin, by the accumulation of dividends, or by a rise in the value of the margined portfolio. As long as the value of your margined portfolio is at or above the minimum maintenance margin, you may use your SMA to buy additional securities, but if your account is below the minimum margin maintenance requirement your broker will use your SMA to meet the margin call.

☑ *HINT: If you use margin, don't let your equity fall below 50%. In a volatile market, you can get in trouble very fast.*

Additional Regulations

■ Margin rules have been extended to some mutual funds.
■ Individuals are allowed to have more than one margin account at the same brokerage house

---

Do Not Have a Margin Account If:

■ You lack the temperament
■ You are dealing in small amounts of money
■ You cannot absorb a loss
■ Your portfolio consists primarily of income equities
■ You tend to buy and hold stocks

To Minimize Risks:

■ Set stop orders above the 30% loss point
■ Borrow less than the maximum
■ Buy on margin only in a bull market
■ Watch for increases in the broker loan rate
■ Check the prices of margined stock once a week to avoid a surprise margin call

under certain circumstances, which vary from firm to firm. Check with your broker.

- Not all securities traded over-the-counter are marginable. Stocks under $5 usually cannot be margined.
- The NYSE sets special loan limits for individual issues that show unusual volume, price fluctuations, or rapid turnover, to discourage undue speculation.
- Customers whose accounts show a pattern of "day trading" (purchasing and selling the same marginable issues on the same day) are required to maintain appropriate margin before the transactions are made.
- Each brokerage firm sets its own margin requirements for nonconvertible bonds, municipal bonds, and U.S. government bonds.

☑ *HINT: You may use your margin account to borrow from your broker for purposes other than to buy stocks and bonds. The rates are almost always lower than a consumer bank loan, and ther is no monthly repayment of the loan payments.*

FOR FURTHER INFORMATION:

Buying Stocks Without a Broker, Charles B. Carlson (New York: McGraw-Hill, 1995); $16.95 + $3

shipping, from: Dow Theory Publications, Inc., 7412 Calumet Avenue, Hammond, IN 46324.

DRIP Investor Clearinghouse
800–774–4117

This 24-hour hotline service provides a single source for enrollment information for a number of direct stock purchase plans. It is a free service to subscribes of the DRIP Newsletter. Among the companies you can receive information on:

- Amoco
- Bob Evans Farms
- Central & Southwest
- Duke Realty
- Eastern Company
- Energen
- Houston Industries
- IES Industries
- McDonald's
- Morton International
- Nevada Power
- Northern States Power
- Piedmont Natural Gas
- SCANA
- Union Electric
- York International

PART SIX

Financing Your Lifestyle

Whether you're a baby boomer, new parent, empty nester, or member of the senior-something crowd; or whether you're single or living together, you need to arrange your finances to suit your lifestyle. In this section we look at the most important areas of financial planning as they relate to your particular needs:

- Housing: residential, rental, second homes
- Mortgages: how to get the best rate
- Paying for college: for your kids and yourself
- Adjusting to adult children returning home
- Helping aging parents
- Retirement plans, IRAs, Keoghs, 401(k)s
- Getting the most out of Social Security
- Understanding GICs
- Insurance and annuities
- Retirement living: adult communities, nursing homes, reverse mortgages
- Investment gifts

26

Housing and Real Estate Investments

The ongoing downsizing of corporate America, the fallout effect of the recession and the general feeling of economic uncertainty in various geographical areas of our country have combined to make real estate predictions extremely difficult. Property values in many parts of the United States are still well below what they were in the heydays of the 1980s when many approached their highs.

However, these situations can also make for excellent buys—especially if mortgage interest rates don't go sky high.

The purpose of this book, and more specifically this chapter, however, is to advise you on investing and managing your money—not on what house to buy. However, the various bits of information and advice given below will help you make a wise real-estate investment and, as a result, have more money with which to invest and fund the other aspects of your life.

WHAT TO DO IN THIS REAL ESTATE MARKET

If you want to buy:

1. *Distress sales and auctions.* The slump in residential and commercial property contnues to create what's known as the "distress sale." You won't find as many troubled properties for sale as in the previous years, but this is still fertile territory for savvy buyers.

- Public notices of default sales are generally announced in local newspapers and, in some places, posted at the city hall. You can also find out about such sale properties from local real estate dealers—take time to let several know of your interest. Realize, however, that you can seldom find a house in a hurry using this approach.

☑ *HINT: For a list of foreclosed properties offered by Fannie Mae (Federal National Mortgage Association), call 800–732–6643.*

2. *Rental property.* If you're investing for rental income, pick a location within a day's drive; it's easiest to be a landlord if your property is nearby.

3. *Refinancing.* With lower interest rates, the question of refinancing your mortgage pops up. The rule of thumb is do not refinance unless the new rate is at least 2 percentage points lower than the old one. This guideline, however, overlooks a critical factor: how long you plan to stay in your home. The sooner you intend to move, the greater the rate differential between the two loans must be in order for refinancing to pay off. Why? You will probably pay 3% to 4% of the total loan in points and closing fees on a new loan, and it will take 2 to 4 years to recoup the up-front charges (see the example in the box below).

4. *Consider a lease option.* If you own a house you would like to sell but haven't been able to, or if you want to buy but can't quite afford the down payment, a "lease-option" plan may solve the problem. Under this arrangement, the potential buyer moves into the house as a tenant, paying monthly rent. The rent, however, is considerably higher than normal, sometimes even double. The extra is credited toward the down payment. Some landlords also require an up-front cash payment. At the end of a specified time, typically 1 to 4 years, the tenant finds a mortgage and buys the house. If he cannot, the owner keeps the extra payments. Most of these arrangements are made through ads in local newspapers.

CAUTION: Make certain the lease includes an exclusive contract that the property will be sold to the tenant for a set price when the lease expires and states whether or not the deposit is refundable. An option to buy could prove worthless unless a sales contract is attached to the lease and the contract has been signed in advance by the seller.

5. *Buying in an unknown area.* Whether it's rental property or a home for yourself, get a "destination appraisal" before buying in unfamiliar territory. Otherwise you might move in and find out six months later that an office building is going to be built nearby. Prepurchase appraisals range in price from $200 to $400. They let buyers know about hidden problems as well as give them an idea of the going prices.

HINT: To find a qualified appraiser, contact the Appraisal Institute, 875 North Michigan, Suite 2400, Chicago, IL 60611. Call 312–335–4100 and request the Directory of Designated Members.

6. *Investing in vacant lots.* With the price of land relatively low, this is a good time to consider land as a long-term investment. You can avoid a lot of problems if you know what your legal rights are—so take time to read the Department of Housing and Urban Development's brochure, *Buying Lots from Developers*, available from:

HUD
Program Information
451 7th Street SW, 8th floor
Washington, DC 20410
202–708–1420
Free.

SORTING OUT THE MORTGAGE MAZE

One thing that has not changed over the years is the fact that getting a mortgage is one of the largest financial commitments most people make. To help get through the mortgage maze, review these most popular types. It helps to understand the lingo when applying for a loan and negotiating terms.

Fixed-Rate Mortgage

The old standby, the 30-year fixed-rate mortgage, remains the most popular type of real-estate loan.

Where to Find Bargains in Rental Real Estate

- Someone desperate to sell, who has already moved, is being transferred, or has purchased another piece of property
- An REO (real-estate owned), also known as a foreclosure. Local bankers maintain listings. Prices are often well below market.
- Estate liquidations and family breakups
- Distressed properties sold through sheriff's sales, IRS seizures for back taxes, and other forced sales
- Discounted mortgages. These are existing loans sold by the lender for less than the balance owed. Check with real-estate brokers, or place an ad in the newspaper. Review state foreclosure laws carefully.

Interest rate and monthly payments are fixed for the life of the loan, which protects buyers from increased monthly payments when interest rates rise. On the other hand, when rates drop, it often pays to refinance this type of mortgage in order to get lower monthly payments.

☑ *HINT: Shop carefully for a fixed-rate mortgage, because even a small rate difference affects your monthly payments.*

This mortgage is generally considered a good choice for those planning to remain in their houses a number of years. The borrower knows what the payments will be, and equity builds up steadily over time.

A variation on this theme is the 15-year fixed-rate mortgage. The good news here is that the debt is paid off in half the time it would be with a 30-year mortgage, and the total interest cost of the loan is lower. The bad news: Monthly payments are higher. On a $100,000 loan, for instance, the monthly payment would be $1,106 on a 15-year mortgage at 10.5% versus $953 on an 11%, 30-year loan. The major advantage of a 15-year mortgage is that you build equity faster and save on interest costs. This makes it a logical choice for those near retirement who want to be free of mortgage payments and/or those with sufficient disposable income to handle higher monthly payments.

Biweekly Mortgage

This is another way to build equity more quickly and reduce interest costs. Instead of paying down your mortgage on a monthly basis, you do so every 2 weeks. The biweekly payments are half of what a monthly payment would be, but there's the equivalent of one more monthly payment per year. In other words, 26 biweekly payments equal 13 monthly payments. Most lenders require that biweekly payments be automatically deducted from your bank account.

Adjustable-Rate Mortgages

Called ARMs for short, this mortgage generally offers lower initial rates than fixed-rate home loans, but the interest rate and the monthly payment are adjusted periodically according to terms specified by the lender. Most peg the rate to an index based on short-term Treasury bill rates. Many ARMs are adjusted annually, semiannually, or once every 3 years over a 5-year period, and thereafter remain fixed. With others, the rate remains fixed for one or more years and then is adjusted annually. In most cases, the increase in interest is capped and cannot be adjusted by more than 2 points over the life of the loan. Some ARMs have a conversion feature allowing borrowers to convert (for a fee) to a fixed-rate mortgage, usually between the second and fifth year.

☑ *HINT: ARMs are particularly well suited to young people who anticipate growth in income and those who do not plan to stay in the same home for more than a few years.*

Seven-Year Two-Step

It may sound like a dance, but it's a mortgage with fixed monthly payments for the first 7 years at a rate ¼ to ½ a percentage point less than those on a 30-year fixed. After 7 years, the rate is adjusted to market level.

MORTGAGE POINTS

Regardless of what type of mortgage you wind up with, make certain that any "points" you pay in connection with your mortgage are for interest (1 point equals 1% of the loan amount). As long as you pay points up front with a separate check or if the seller pays the points, they are tax-deductible in the year you buy the property. Points that are really origination fees are not deductible until you sell your property for a profit. And then, they would be deductible if based on a percentage of the loan in exchange for a lower interest rate. On the "Uniform Settlement Statement," they may be called "points," "loan origination fees," "loan discount," or "discount points." Points paid for refinancing a mortgage are not deductible in full in the year they were paid. They must be deducted over the term of the mortgage. This is particularly important because lenders send reports to the IRS.

ESCROW PAYMENTS

In late May of 1995, a new Department of Housing and Urban Development ruling went into effect, specifying how escrow payments must be calculated and how much surplus a lender may collect.

Under the guidelines, monthly escrow payments may not be more than one-twelfth of the total due annually for taxes and insurance premiums, plus enough for a 2-month surplus. (Previously, some lenders kept a surplus of up to 8 months.)

☑ *HINT: If your lender overcharged you (HUD says this may be the case with 5 million homeowners), you should get a refund or an adjustment made on future payments. Check with your lender and if you have problems, contact your area HUD office.*

MORTGAGES—BEYOND YOUR FRIENDLY BANK

Government agencies and mortgage lenders also often list with local brokers; many accept smaller-than-usual down payments.

- *FHA-Insured Loans.* Require down payments of only 5%; check with your lender to see if you qualify.
- *VA (Veterans Administration) Loans.* Now available not only to vets, but also members of the National Guard and military reservists with 6 or more years of service. Low or no down payments required. Check your regional VA office.
- *Fannie Mae Loans.* The Federal National Mortgage Association, the nation's largest

source of mortgage money, has some loans that require interest-only payments in the first year, plus a variety of other loans.

For info and list of lenders, call 800–732–6643.

- *Farmers Home Administration.* Helps low- and moderate-income people who live in rural areas with loans.

☑ *HINT: For information, contact your area's Farmers Home Administration Office, listed under "Department of Agriculture" in your phone book, or write: Farmers Home Administration, U.S. Department of Agriculture, Washington, DC 20250, for a list.*

- *Mortgage brokers.* These intermediaries match you with a mortgage banker or commercial bank; they will save you time and are helpful for those having difficulty getting a mortgage. You usually pay a flat fee or an additional point or two for the service.

☑ *HINT: For information, call the National Association of Mortgage Brokers at 703–524–0664.*

- *Public agencies.* Local real-estate brokers and lenders can tell you about state-run programs, such as the Community Homebuyers Program, that make below market-rate financing available to low- and moderate-income buyers.

Also, contact: The National Council of State Housing Agencies for more info at 202–624–7710.

TIPS ON FINDING THE RIGHT MORTGAGE

Although the purpose of this chapter is to discuss real estate as an investment, a key part of successful investing is leverage—that is, your mortgage. For current rates and information, keep up-to-date by reading the popular press and talking to bank loan officers. To help you make informed decisions, consult these sources.

How to Avoid Drowning in a Mortgage

1. **Shop around.** Call several banks and mortgage companies and find out what they are offering. Compare details carefully. Don't rely only on your real-estate broker's recommendation.
2. **Do your math.** You must figure out the exact amount you will pay each month for each type of mortgage. When doing the numbers for ARMs, assume interest rates will rise to the maximum.
3. **Look for hidden traps.** Read the mortgage document before signing on. Among the traps to look for in the fine print: a bank that requires permission for borrowers to obtain a second mortgage or a home equity line of credit; a clause requiring you to sell your old house before the bank will let you close on a new one; any add-on charges and fees.
4. **Make extra payments.** Assume a mortgage only if it lets you make payments above the stated required amount. This reduces the length of your mortgage and will save you thousands of dollars in interest, since the prepaid amount is applied to the principal.

Comparing Mortgage Rates

HSH Associates
1200 Route 23
Butler, NJ 07405
800–UPDATES

This group operates a mortgage hotline (201–838–8197), which lists the national average rates on a variety of mortgages. For $20 HSH will send you a listing of mortgage rates in your area plus a 44-page planning kit. HSH covers 50 metropolitan areas.

Refinancing

Tables to determine whether you should refinance or pay off your mortgage early appear in *Consumer's Guide to Refinancing Your Mortgage,* available from:

Mortgage Bankers Association of America
1125 15th Street NW, 5th fl.
Washington, DC 20005
202–861–6500

Prepayment

Design your own mortgage prepayment plan with *The Banker's Secret.* The book ($17.95) or book-and-software package ($42.95) is available from:
Good Advice Press
P.O. Box 78
Elizaville, NY 12523
914–758–1400; 800–255–0899

Adjustable-Rate Mortgages

For a copy of *Introducing a New ARM for Today's Homeowner,* contact:
Public Information
Federal National Mortgage Association
3900 Wisconsin Avenue NW
Washington, DC 20016
800–732–6643; 202–752–7124

YOUR HOME AS A TAX SHELTER

Once you own a home, you can easily use it to shelter taxes . . . here's how:

1. You can postpone gains made on the sale of your principal residence as long as you buy another that costs at least as much as the net proceeds of the one you sold within 2 years of the sale date. If the new home costs less, you must pay taxes on the lesser of either the house sale profits or the difference between the sale proceeds of the old home and the cost of the new home.
2. You can continue to defer these taxes, provided you do not move more frequently than once every 2 years, unless the move is job-related.
3. When you reach age 55, you can take advantage of a special one-time tax break: a $125,000 capital gains exemption from your

The Benefits of Refinancing Your Mortgage

Follow these basic points to determine how refinancing pays off. You can also order a software package called "The Banker's Secret Loan" that will run the calculations for your particular situation; it's $42.93 and available from Good Advice Press, 800–255–0899.

Point #1. If you have a $150,000 mortgage, payable over 30 years at 9.5%, your monthly payments are $1,261. If after four years you refinance the balance, about $145,712, at 7.5% (for a new 30-year term), your monthly payment will drop to $1,019, for a savings of $242 each month.

Point #2. However, you must take into account administrative fees and other expenses: refinancing your $142,712 balance will cost $2,686 ($500 in fees and $2,186 for your 1.5% points, a percentage of the loan amount).

Point #3. Then, balance that against what you save in monthly payments: your refinancing costs will be recovered in just 11.1 months ($2,686 divided by $242 = 11.1 months).

Point #4. After that, your gross monthly cash flow is boosted by $242.

> ☑ *HINT: Put that $242 into prepaying your mortgage each month and you'll actually wind up saving over $107,000 in interest expenses—and reducing your loan term by 12 years and 10 months. And, that's in addition to nearly $27,000 in interest expenses saved by refinancing.*

SOURCE: The Banker's Secret.

taxes. You must have lived in the home for 3 out of the past 5 years, unless you've been living in a nursing home. In that case, you must have lived at home for just one of the previous 5 years to escape tax on a sale. You can claim the $125,000 exclusion only once, and a married couple cannot claim the break when one spouse has already used his or her exclusion before the marriage. However, only one spouse must be over 55 to claim the exclusion on a jointly-held home. When the home is not jointly owned, the spouse whose name is on the deed must be over 55 at the time of sale.

4. To make certain you whittle down the size of any eventual tax bill, keep good records. When your home is sold at a profit, the difference between the net sale price and the seller's "basis" in the property is the amount that is subject to tax. The basis is calculated as the price paid for the property plus closing costs, such as title insurance, incurred in making the purchase. Add to this expenses for capital improvements made over the years, but subtract any depreciation or casualty losses claimed. A capital improvement is anything that adds to the value of the property, for example, a roof that has been replaced, fences, gates, central air-conditioning, or a burglar alarm. Painting and repairs are maintenance expenses, however, and do not increase the owner's basis in the property. So keep canceled checks, copies of invoices relating to capital improvements, and notices of co-op apartment assessments.

> ☑ *HINT: Call the IRS at 800–TAX–FORM (829–3676) to get a copy of Publication #523,* **Selling Your Home.**

HOME EQUITY LOANS

Interest on up to $100,000 of a home equity loan or a home equity line of credit is fully deductible as long as the loan is secured by your principal home or a second home that you own.

The elimination several years ago of the deductibility of personal interest (on credit card loans, for example) has added to the appeal of home equity loans. And because this type of loan is secured by your home, interest rates are often lower than those charged on other borrowing.

> ☑ *HINT: Call the IRS at 800–TAX–FORM (829–3676) to get a copy of Publication #936,* **Home Mortgage Interest Deduction.**

Banks often promote these "credit line" types of loans to pay for big-ticket items such as cars, college education, and vacations.

☉ *CAUTION: Use a home equity line of credit only if necessary. Your home could be repossessed if you fail to make payments.*

With a home equity line of credit, the bank allows borrowers to apply for a loan, pay closing costs just once, and then borrow money as needed. You can usually borrow up to 80% of the home's appraised value minus any existing mortgages. Interest is higher than on first loans, but it is assessed only on money you actually draw. Fees and closing costs tend to be low because of lender competition.

☑ *HINT: Because interest rates are usually tied to prime, look for a loan with an interest rate cap.*

THE JOYS OF RENTAL INCOME

Rental property—whether it's a condo in Florida, a ski house in Montana, or a center-hall colonial in the suburbs—if bought after January 1, 1987, does not fare as well as earlier purchases.

First of all, it must be depreciated over a longer period of time—the write-off period, formerly 19 years on residential property, has been stretched out to 27½ years (31½ years for commercial property), or 39 years if acquired after May 13, 1993.

Second, you must take deductions in equal amounts each year over 27½ years, whereas previously, as a landlord, you could deduct the total value of your investment over 19 years, writing off greater amounts in the first years.

NOTE: Depreciation can only be taken on the cost of the buildings, not on the underlying land.

If your property produces rent, the income or losses generated are considered "passive," which means you cannot offset salary or investment income with your rental losses, with one excep-

tion: If your adjusted gross income is under $100,000 ($50,000 for married couples filing separately), the tax law allows you to write off up to $25,000 a year in rental property tax losses against other income, including your salary—provided you actively manage the property. This special $25,000 allowance is phased out as you become wealthier; if your adjusted gross income exceeds $150,000 ($75,000 for married couples filing separately, there is no such break.

☉ *CAUTION: If at least one-half of your personal services are performed in rental real-estate business and you materially participate for at least 750 hours, the $25,000 limit does not apply.*

☑ *HINT: Recalculate the return you receive on any property. If your property generates a loss and your income is less than $150,000, make certain you satisfy the IRS requirement of being an "active" participant in order to get the loss allowance.*

To be considered an active manager, you must own 10% of the property involved as well as make decisions on repairs, rents, and tenants. If you hire a manager but provide guidance, you will still be considered active provided you can document your involvement to the IRS.

In considering rental property, keep in mind that the restrictions for deducting losses mean you must invest in property that produces a positive cash flow; that is, rents must be greater than costs.

If you make more than $150,000 annually, you can still reap some benefits, because the changes pertain to tax reporting, not to your cash flow. This means that if your rental income covers mortgage payments, the only plus you've lost is the tax shelter aspect. In the meantime, keep a running account of your losses and apply them when you eventually sell the property or to offset passive income from limited partnerships or other rental income.

> ### Deductions You May Take on Rental Property
>
> - Maintenance
> - Depreciation
> - Repairs
> - Utility bills
> - Insurance
> - Advertising

VACATION HOMES—FOR PROFIT AND FUN

If you have a ski condo, beach cottage, or fishing shack, or something much grander, read on so you'll be certain to take all the tax breaks possible on your property. Find the category that applies to your particular situation regarding renting or not renting.

- *If you do not rent out* your vacation home, you can deduct interest on your mortgage, in the principal amount, up to the original purchase price plus the cost of improvements.
- *If you use your vacation property personally* for more than 14 days a year or more than 10% of the time you rent it out (at a fair market rate), whichever is greater, then the IRS considers it a "residence." In that case, any time that you spend on repairs and upkeep does not count toward personal or rental use. Deductions for rental expenses on a "residence" are for the most part limited to the income received. The IRS formula is precise; check with your accountant.
- *If you rent out for no more than 14 days a year,* the income is tax-free and you are not even required to report it, but the expenses, other than property taxes and interest, are not deductible.
- *If you rent out more than 14 days or 10% of the time,* the house is classified as rental (not residential) property. If the property was placed in service prior to January 1, 1987, you can still use the 19-year accelerated depreciation

schedule, which allows larger deductions in early years. Otherwise, you must use the 27½-year depreciation schedule.

Rental expenses, under these circumstances, cannot be used to offset regular income because they are considered passive losses. Under the 1986 law, these expenses can be deducted only from passive income from other rental properties or from limited partnerships and not from your wages, salary, or portfolio income. *NOTE:* There is an exception for those whose adjusted gross income is $150,000 or less, as explained earlier.

☑ *HINT: If your income is too high to benefit from the $25,000 active rental allowance, you may be better off converting a "rental" vacation home into a "residential" property and writing off the full amount of the mortgage interest.*

TIME-SHARES

Time-sharing, which combines vacationing with a very small degree of investing, should be viewed cautiously if not with complete skepticism. When you buy a time-share, you purchase the right to use a studio, apartment, or house in a vacation complex year after year. Time-shares are usually 1- to 4-week periods. For example, you may purchase a 2-week time slot in Aspen for a fixed period, say the first 2 weeks in January, or for a floating period that changes from year to year.

> ### The Seafaring Loophole
>
> Although tax reform eliminated interest deductions on most consumer credit loans, yacht owners and houseboat dwellers got a break. If your boat qualifies as a personal residence by having a head, galley, and sleeping facilities, you can probably deduct interest on any loan you take out to buy the floating home. Have your accountant check Code section 163(h) 5(A) (i) II, which governs interest deductions for qualified residences.

The primary advantage is cost. It's an affordable way to vacation—1 week can range from $2,000 to $25,000+ depending on the location, season, and facilities. There is often an annual maintenance fee as well. You pay only for the days you use your space, and in most situations you can sublet if you are unable to occupy your time-share. The interest on your mortgage is tax-deductible.

Many time-share investors have been disappointed that their property did not escalate in value as much as traditional real estate. The resale potential of time-shares depends on their location, how well they're managed, and the market.

CAUTION: Buy a time-share for vacationing, not primarily as an investment.

The concept of time-sharing is less popular today than when it first came to the public's attention more than 20 years ago. Since then it has suffered as a result of industry mismanagement and a period when dishonest operators were more common than they are now. Federal and state regulations now protect the investor, so it is possible that time-sharing will regain some popularity. However, with the widespread trend toward co-ops and condos, this remains a less-than-timely investment.

HINT: Call or write:
The American Resort Development Association
1220 L Street NW, 5th floor
Washington, DC 20005
202–371–6700
They have a number of consumer publications on time-shares.

SWAPPING PROPERTY

The 1986 tax law gave a boost to a rather obscure yet legal technique that allows real-estate investors to sell one piece of investment property and buy another while deferring capital gains taxes. In fact, you can swap any number of times and not pay taxes until you actually sell for cash. The exchange must be completed within 180 days.

HINT: Discipline yourself to invest the money that would have gone to pay the capital gains tax.

To qualify for this tax deferral you must:

- Exchange like pieces of property
- Use the property for business or hold it as an investment; your home does not qualify, nor does an interest in a real-estate limited partnership

If the two pieces of property involved in a swap are not of equal monetary value, cash or an additional piece of property is used to make up the difference.

NOTE: The cash or extra property is a taxable transaction.

HOW TO REDUCE YOUR PROPERTY TAXES

Experts estimate that 60% of all homeowners pay too much property tax. Take time to study your taxes and if you suspect you're being overcharged, file a challenge.

The Most Common Mistakes

Errors in paperwork and/or math are amazingly widespread. So go in person to the tax assessor's office and ask to see the worksheet used when your property was evaluated. You have a legal right to examine this document. Check for:

1. *Typographical errors.* The assessment amount on the worksheet should match the assessment on the tax bill.
2. *Measurements.* Dimensions and square footage should be accurate.
3. *Evaluation.* After checking out the figures, look at how your property was evaluated. The assessed value of property, adjusted by the local tax assessment office, is almost always lower than the market value.

To find out if you are being overassessed, ask what the *adjusted* assessment value is plus what *multiplier* was used to make the adjustment.

For instance, if your tax bill shows an assessed value of $100,000 and the multiplier is 2, then your home is really assessed at $200,000.

Using this example, if you believe your home is worth less than $200,000, you would want to challenge the assessment by following these steps:

1. *Find out the assessed values* of comparable property in your neighborhood. This is public information.
2. *Get the actual selling prices* of similar homes in the "Recorder of Public Deeds" office at your town hall.
3. *Locate copies* of any existing professional appraisals of your property. (Your bank is likely to have this document.)
4. *Arrange a new appraisal* to document the fact that the value of your home is lower than its appraised value.

Then present these facts to the assessor. If your appeal is denied, you can present your case to a board of review for an impartial opinion. Ask the assessor for an appeal form and the filing deadline.

☑ *HINT: About half the homeowners who question their assessments through official appeals win reductions of 10% or more. Prepare for your appeal by reading* How to Fight Property Taxes, *from:*

National Taxpayers Union
108 North Alfred Street
Alexandria, VA 22314
703–683–5700
$2

INVESTING IN REAL ESTATE STOCKS

Investing in real estate stocks and mutual funds, like any other market industry, has a degree of risk—and in this particular case, the degree of risk is substantial. However, there are some interesting opportunities provided you can keep a close watch on the eye on the condition of real estate—both residential and commercial. One of the easier ways to own a diversified, hence less risky, real estate portfolio is through REITS—Real Estate Investment Trusts.

REITs are like mutual funds—they own a variety of properties or mortgages on properties. Their shares trade on the stock exchanges. While some are high in risk, many are considered relatively sound investments, offering an easier way to participate in commercial real estate than direct ownership, say of an office building.

REITs frequently focus on specific geographical areas and on particular property types. As we go to press, health care REITs are among the best investments. Three of the top performers with impressive dividend yields are:

- Nationwide Health Properties (NHP); $23/share; 6.5% yield
- Meditrust (MT); $35/share; 8.0% yield
- Health & Retirement Properties (HRP); $17/share; 8.0% yield
- Another consideration: American Strategic Income Portfolio (NYSE: ASP), which has a yield of 9.0%, and is selling at $11 per share. This closed-end fund invests 70% to 75% of its portfolio in discount mortgages, such as those of the Resolution Trust Corp., and the rest in government-backed mortgages, such as those issued by Ginnie Mae and other government agencies.
- New Plan Realty Trust (NPR), with a yield of 6.5%, is selling at $22 per share. It owns shopping centers and apartments and over the past decade has nearly tripled its book value. Another point in its favor: the company has raised its dividend for 64 consecutive quarters.
- In May 1996, Vanguard introduced a mutual fund specializing in REITs. Called the

Vanguard REIT Index Portfolio, it uses a passive approach and invests in stocks that comprise the Morgan Stanley REIT Index, a benchmark of more than 90 U.S. property trusts (REITs) that invest in some 7,000 properties. The fund is designed for long-term investing. Let's see how it's doing within a year.

■ ARMs. Adjustable rate mortgage mutual funds are a relatively new and fast-growing type of investment vehicle that invests primarily in adjustable rate mortgage securities issued by Ginnie Mae, Fannie Mae, and Freddie Mac (see Chapter 12). Because the rates on ARM securities are adjusted period-

ically, prices are less volatile than fixed-income securities. However, some investment uncertainty is created by the varying patterns of mortgage prepayment by property owners.

The yield on ARM securities generally tracks the ebb and flow of short-term interest rates, but is typically 1.5% to 2% higher.

☑ *HINT: Two ARM mutual funds that impose no sales charges are Benham's Adjustable Rate Government Securities (800–345–2021) with a 5.54% yield, and T. Rowe Price's Short Term U.S. Government Bond Fund (800–541–8832) with a 6.01% yield as of September 1996.*

27
Family Finances

THE HIGH COST OF CHILDREN

For many people, nothing is ever as exciting as having a baby—or as expensive. It's certainly one of life's most costly endeavors. Depending on where you live and how extravagant you want to be, raising a child from birth to age 18 can set you back anywhere from $40,000 to $150,000 . . . and that's before college bills. So there's no question that having a baby will drastically change your financial life.

The best way to enjoy parenthood is to have enough money to care for your child, maintain the lifestyle you and your spouse had before baby made three, and minimize as many financial sacrifices as possible. The biggest sacrifice for most couples is the loss of the mother's income, because the majority of women take 3 to 6 months off for the first child. Yet, armed with a sensible financial plan, you can minimize the dollar drain and fully enjoy the newest member of your family.

Prenatal to Age 2

As soon as you know you'll be having a baby, both you and your spouse should find out what your respective firms offer in terms of maternity leave, including possible benefits for the father. Then check your health coverage. Whether you have a private policy or one sponsored by your firm, determine precisely what medical costs for the first 2 years are covered.

☑ *HINT: Borrow maternity and baby clothes as well as equipment from friends, or buy from secondhand shops, discount stores, and outlets. And don't be shy: Encourage baby showers. Your family and friends may pitch in and purchase some of the big-ticket items for you. Use family members to baby-sit, or join a baby-sitting cooperative and share the task with other parents.*

Build up your savings as soon as you know you'll be having a baby. Stash all or part of one salary in a money market fund and practice living on one salary, which will be the case when the baby arrives.

If you already have a nest egg, divide it into two categories: Put half into a money market fund so you can draw on it to pay immediate bills when the baby is born, and put the remainder into a revolving certificate of deposit program, purchasing CDs with staggered maturity dates. Save all cash gifts the baby receives. You'll need to get the baby a Social Security number to put them in his or her name.

Ages 2 To 5

Now that the start-up costs of having a baby have been absorbed, use these years to replace or add to your savings, especially if you plan to move to a larger home. If you have not done so, you and your spouse should try to put at least 3% to 5% of your take-home pay in safe investments, such as Treasuries. You'll also need this money if you have a second child. Make certain you have adequate life and disability insurance to provide for your child, up to and through college. Finally, make out your wills and name guardians for the baby.

Elementary School Years

When your child reaches age 6, you have approximately 12 years left in which to save money for college. Begin immediately adding to the college fund established when he or she was born. An early start will pay off. For example, a zero coupon Treasury that matures in 18 years can be purchased for approximately $150. When it comes due you will receive $1,000.

Junior and Senior High School

Encourage your child to earn his or her own money. Do not pay for everything. Instead, teach

Savings Bonds Pay for College

The earlier you start saving, the more you will have when your child is ready for college.

	VALUE AT AGE 18, BASED ON MONTHLY ALLOTMENTS OF:	
CHILD'S AGE	$50	$100
1	$14,579.32	$29,158.64
6	9,233.20	18,466.40
10	5,656.16	11,312.32
12	4,069.28	8,138.56

The values in this table are based on the guaranteed interest rate of 4% per annum, compounded semiannually.

SOURCE: The Treasury, U.S. Savings Bond Division, 1996.

your child how to save and pay for certain items. And remember, children learn by what they see regularly—make sure you are not living off credit and neglecting to save while encouraging your child to do so.

☑ HINT: *Start to investigate financial aid for college by ordering a copy (25¢) of* Planning for College, *from the Investment Company Institute, 1401 H Street NW, Washington, DC 20005.*

PAYING FOR YOUR KID'S COLLEGE

Most children have plenty of toys, clothes, bikes, and even cars, but very few have a nest egg to pay for one of life's biggest expenses: a college degree. It takes more than good grades to get through school: It takes a lot of cash.

Early planning certainly eases the pain, as the time value of money works to everyone's advantage. For instance, if you want to accumulate $35,000 by the time your child reaches age 18, based on a fixed interest rate of 9%, compounded monthly, you must save $73.08 per month, if your child is now 1 year old. If you wait until the child is 14, that figure jumps to $608.48 a month.

Yet the picture's not all that hopeless. There are a number of ways to stockpile money and find financial aid. Here's what parents and grandparents can do to meet college costs.

Step 1. Know who should own the nest egg. Money earmarked for college can be held in an adult's name, in the child's name, or in trust with the child named as beneficiary. Putting the money in the adult's name is, of course, the easiest, and it gives the adult complete control over the money and how it is used. It's also advantageous when it comes to seeking financial help: Most financial aid formulas require the student to contribute 35% of his or her assets to college costs annually, while parents are expected to contribute far less, usually only 5%.

Money can be put in the child's name through the Uniform Gifts to Minors Act (UGMA), adopted in almost all states, and the Uniform Transfers to Minors Act (UTMA), available in over 30 states. The key difference between them is the type of property an adult can transfer to a child. UTMA allows any kind of property—real estate, personal property, securities, cash—to be given as a custodial gift, whereas UGMA restricts custodial gifts to bank deposits, securities (including mutual funds), and insurance policies.

Both are simple to set up and administer. Almost any bank, mutual fund company, stockbroker, or attorney can do so. The custodian, who can be a parent or someone else named by the person funding the trust, controls the money until the child becomes of legal age (18 or 21, depending on the state). The custodian can invest, manage, or even dispose of the gifted property on the minor's behalf.

CAUTION: At age 18 or 21, the money must be turned over to the child, who can then use it any way at all—to buy a car, join the circus, or, ideally, pay for college.

There are other types of tax-advantaged trusts for sizable amounts of money that an accountant or attorney can explain.

Step 2. Understand the tax law. The so-called kiddie tax seriously affects college nest eggs. Study the box on page 279 and talk to an accountant or tax lawyer before deciding who should hold the assets for college. The current ruling is: If your child is under age 14 and receives more than $650 a year in unearned income (from investments and savings), the next $650 will be taxed at the child's rate, usually 15%. But, be aware: all unearned income above $1,300 per year will be taxed at the parent's top marginal rate, which could be as high as 39.6%.

Then when your child turns 14, all income he or she receives will be taxed at his or her rate, again typically 15%.

HINT: As the rules stand now, if your child is under age 14, it's advantageous to put the money in the child's name, only as long as the income it earns does not exceed the annual income cap.

Step 3. Consider gifts. A parent, grandparent, or anyone else can give a child up to $10,000 a year without paying gift taxes. If parents or grandparents have sizable estates that they plan to leave to the family, such a gift reduces future estate taxes. Grandparents can also make cash gifts in any amount and pay no gift tax as long as the gift goes for tuition and is paid directly to the college. And a grandparent can give an additional $10,000 free of gift tax to pay for room and board directly to the college or university.

Step 4. Set up a savings plan. Save a certain amount every month. Parents who find this difficult or who lack the discipline to do so on their own can establish an automatic payroll-deduction plan at work so that a set amount is taken out of paychecks on a regular basis and is used to purchase EE savings bonds or is transferred to a high-yielding money market fund. Both are low in risk.

The current yield on money market funds is between 4% and 5½%.

For the current yield on EE Savings Bonds, call your bank or 800–US–BONDS. Although the interest on these bonds has always been exempt from state and local taxes, it's now exempt from federal taxes if the bonds are purchased after January 1, 1990, and are used to pay college tuition. However, the parents' total income must fall below a certain dollar amount when the bonds are cashed in. This income cap is adjusted annually for inflation.

CAUTION: EE Savings Bonds purchased in this tax-free college education plan cannot be held in the child's name.

HINT: What if you've already purchased Series EE Bonds in your child's name—is there any way you can get this tax break? Perhaps. Try filing a

How a Child's Money Is Taxed

IF THE CHILD IS:	THEN
Under age 14	The first $650 of income is tax-free; $651 to $1300 of income is taxed at the child's rate, usually 15%
Age 14 or older	All income is taxed at the child's rate

Reissue Form PD F4000 with the Bureau of the Public Debt. This is a request to reissue the bond in the name of a different owner. Send the form, along with a letter stating that you initially purchased the bonds for education and you didn't know they had to be in your name.

However, skip the whole process if your adjusted gross income is over $95,250 (couples) or $58,500 (single parent), as the tax breaks are phased out at those levels. And, of course, don't bother if you purchased bonds before 1990 when this education tax break was launched.

Your request will be considered on a case-by-case basis.

Step 5. Pick other investments. Certain investments are particularly suited for a college nest egg because they grow in value over time. One of the most popular is zero coupon bonds, described in Chapter 12. Growth stocks and mutual funds are suitable for long-term investments. Conservative choices include certificates of deposit and Treasury bonds and notes. Deferred annuities can be purchased so that they start paying out income when tuition bills come due. An added advantage: Earnings inside an annuity grow tax-deferred until the money is paid out.

Step 6. Look into Baccalaureate Bonds. A growing number of states offer special municipal zero coupon bonds to help parents. They are sold at a discount from face value and do not pay interest until they mature. At that time, the bond-

holders receive the principal plus earned interest in one lump sum. Their great advantage: Parents know exactly how much money is coming due on a certain date. Some states even pay a cash bonus when the bonds mature if the child attends a state college. These bonds are exempt from federal taxes and, for state residents, from state and local taxes. Call your stockbroker or your state's treasury department for current details.

Step 7. Investigate special college deals. Tuition prepayment plans allow parents to pay a flat one-time dollar amount that is guaranteed to cover the cost of schooling later on. These plans eliminate the risk that inflation will boost tuition bills out of sight.

☑ HINT: *Before signing up, ask the following questions: Can the money be transferred to another member of the family? What does the plan cover—tuition only, or other costs? Is the plan insured or guaranteed? Is there an on-campus residency requirement? Is the money available in an emergency? What if the child elects to go to another school?*

Many schools will also arrange for bills to be paid on an installment basis, typically with monthly payments over a 10-month period, for a nominal fee.

Step 8. Apply for financial aid. Although it's tough to get, some financial aid is available, even to middle-income families. When visiting college campuses or writing for catalogs, ask each school about its financial aid packages. A statement of the family's financial resources must be submitted along with the application.

⊘ CAUTION: *Keep in mind that shifting money into a child's name may jeopardize aid, as explained above.*

Many people assume incorrectly that they won't qualify for financial aid. The three most common misconceptions about aid are:

Crunching the Numbers for Tuition

According to the College Board, the average private college in the United States costs almost $19,000 a year, while for public schools, it's nearly $9,000.

Assuming an 8% after-tax return, here's approximately how much you'll need to invest per month to pay for your son or daughter's college. (Assumes a 6% increase in college costs.)

AGE	PUBLIC	PRIVATE
Newborn	$188	$392
5 years old	$248	$517
10 years old	$381	$794
15 years old	$974	$2,030

1. The money I've saved in my retirement account will count against my child's chances of getting aid. Wrong: Money from 401(k)s, IRAs, and Keoghs is not counted in the formula for determining aid.
2. If one child was rejected, the other will be too. Wrong: Families with more than one child in school often have a better chance than those with just one in college.
3. Older people returning to college or those who are going for the first time aren't financial aid candidates. Wrong: Older students are just as eligible as traditionally-aged students.

Step 9. Borrow if you need to. Meeting the staggering costs may mean borrowing. Check these relatively low-cost sources first:

1. Many companies allow employees to borrow from their 401(k) retirement plans to pay college bills. The major advantage: Interest payments are made into the account, not to a bank.
2. Borrow against a universal life insurance policy. Policyholders pay premiums to the company, which are then invested in an account where they grow tax-deferred. When it's time to pay tuition, policyholders can withdraw the cash balance or borrow against it. Loan rates are almost always lower than bank rates.
3. Home equity loans offer a tax break in that the interest is tax-deductible.
4. PLUS (Parent Loan for Undergraduate Students) loans do not require parents to show financial need, although they must have a good credit history. These loans are made by private financial institutions, not the government. Generally the parents can borrow up to the full cost of education minus any other estimated financial aid received by the student. Other similar loans are available. The college financial aid office will give you information on them.

☑ **HINT:** *Using life insurance for college lets you take advantage of current formula used by colleges to calculate financial aid. The equity in your home, your retirement plans, annuities and life insurance policies are currently excluded from being counted as assets or toward the amount you are expected to contribute to tuition. To put it another way, life insurance and annuities help you avoid being penalized for saving for your kid's college.*

Step 10. Insist your child help out. Encourage children to shoulder some of the expenses by saving money from jobs or working part-time. Another cost-cutting choice: Attend a school that offers a work-study program in which students alternate working and attending classes, so they earn money as they go along. Among the leading such schools are Drexel in Philadelphia, the University of Detroit, and Northeastern University in Boston. Students can also commute and eliminate the cost of room and board, or attend a community college for the first two years, where the tuition is much lower than at a four-year school. Military schools supported by the government, such as West Point, Annapolis, or the Air Force Academy, provide free education if, in return, the student pledges a certain number of years of military service. These schools are difficult to get into, but most other colleges and universities offer ROTC, which is open to all and covers most school expenses.

Step 11. Use software. The program, *Scholarships 101* by Pinnacle Peak Solutions of Scottsdale, Arizona, lists thousands of scholarships and grants. You punch in your child's interests, family income, hobbies, academic record, etc., and out comes a list of potential scholarships with addresses for getting more material. The program is $69.95 for the DOS and Windows version and $99.95 for Macintosh. Phone: 800–762–7101.

Step 12. High school moves. By the time your kids are freshmen or sophomores you need to make some smart moves.

Get financial aid forms—the two most popular are the FAF (Financial Aid Form) from the College Board in Princeton, New Jersey, and the FAFSA (Free Application for Federal Student Aid) available from the Education Department's Federal Student Aid Information Center, 800–433–3243. And, obtain copies when your child is a junior so you'll know how to answer the questions when he or she is a senior.

Also, by junior year you want to reduce the income held in your child's name as financial aid formulas count 35% of a student's assets as being available for tuition, but only 5.6% of yours.

FOR FURTHER INFORMATION

- *Paying for College: A Guide for Parents*, $14, along with other publications on financial planning, from: The College Board, Box 886, New York, NY 10101; 212–713–8150.
- *Don't Miss Out; The Ambitious Student's Guide to Financial Aid*, Octameron Press, Box 2748, Alexandria, Virginia 22301; 703–836–5480; $7.50 + $2 shipping.
- *Paying for College: A Step by Step College Planning Guide*, free from T. Rowe Price, 800–638–5660.

A Mortarboard Mutual Fund

This no-load fund is designed to help finance your child or grandchild's undergraduate degree.

Twentieth Century Giftrust Investors buys stocks of small companies with very high growth rates. Consequently, it is a very volatile fund and does not perform well in down markets. However, its 10-year compounded annual return was 23.3%.

- This fund is an irrevocable living trust, which means you can buy shares only in someone else's name and that someone cannot be your spouse. Your initial investment cannot be withdrawn for at least 10 years or until the beneficiary reaches the age of majority (18 or 21), whichever is longer.
- Because each Giftrust account terminates on a fixed date, the portfolio manager knows when every dollar invested will be redeemed. This eliminates panic selling in jumpy, down markets.
- The first $100 in annual income or short-term capital gains is free of state and federal tax. Beyond that amount, it is taxed at federal trust rates, which move up faster than individual rates—reaching 39.6% at $7,501 in income versus $79,640 for a single filer.
- Long-term capital gains are taxed at 28%. Taxes are paid by selling shares of the fund. You must also file IRS Form 709, although you will not owe any gift tax until all your gifts exceed the lifetime estate gift exemption of $600,000.
- Twentieth Century charges a flat 1% of assets to run the fund; there's no trustee fee and the minimum investment is $250.
  Call: 800–345–2021.

- *Federal Student Guide*, free from Federal Student Financial Aid Information Center, 800–433–3243. Explains eligibility requirements on government loans and grants.

BOOMERANG KIDS, OR ADULT CHILDREN WHO COME BACK HOME

Your child may wend his or her way back home after college, bringing the stereo, posters, and a pile

Financial Aid Primer

Take this list of key programs with you when visiting colleges; discuss with the school's financial aid officer.

- Pell Grant. A federal award of up to $3,900 to help needy undergraduates. More than 4 million recipients annually; does not have to be repaid.
- Federal Supplemental Educational Opportunity grants. A college-administered program that awards up to $4,000 to needy students.
- Federal College Work Study. Colleges provide 10 to 15 hours of work per week, on/off campus to some students.
- Federal Stafford loans. These low-interest loans are backed by the federal government and available regardless of need. Needy students may also qualify for a subsidized loan—on which the government pays the interest while the student is in school plus 6 months after graduation. On the unsubsidized version, repayment begins 6 months after the student graduates or leaves school. And you must pay interest while in school. First-year dependent students can borrow up to $2,625.
- Federal Perkins loan. Low-interest loans of up to $3,000 for needy students.

of dirty clothes. He or she may plan to stay just for the summer or longer—until landing an apartment, a job, a spouse, or all three. Or your child may have no plan at all. You face a philosophical decision about money at this point: Should you be an indulgent parent and provide free housing, a car, spending money, a lavish wardrobe? Even though you say it's because you're a loving parent, such moves actually encourage dependence and continue to keep your son or daughter in the role of child. Alternatively, you can treat the stay as you would that of any other adult boarder: charging room and board, drawing up a simple contract, and encouraging adult behavior and self-reliance.

Check insurance coverage for adult children living at home:

- *Medical.* If the plan where you work does not include grown dependents, then your child will need individual coverage, unless he or she is working and is covered there.
- *Automobile.* Drivers under age 25 typically add to the premium costs of family vehicles.
- *Personal liability.* You may want to take out an umbrella policy that will supplement your coverage for accidents around the house as well as in the family car.

From time to time, even when the nest is empty, you may receive requests for additional financial help—for graduate school, a down payment on a car or house, or a wedding. If your child has a trust fund or a secure job, encourage the child to use his or her own money, perhaps with some help from you. If you're in a quandary about how much to help, set dollar and time limits and divide the responsibility. You may want to make a no- or low-interest loan. At this point, you must also think about your own financial needs, about saving for retirement or to help your elderly parents if they need it. Although you want to be supportive, emotionally, and financially, you also want to encourage self-reliance—what you set out to do when you taught your toddler how to cross the street and tie shoelaces.

These judgment calls are not easy to make: They are filled with emotion. It's particularly hard to say no to your own children. But keep in mind that setting limits is sensible and reasonable, for both of you. Regardless of the choice you make, when you make a loan you should get a written IOU spelling out the amount of the loan, interest, and terms of repayment.

FOR FURTHER INFORMATION

- *Boomerang Kids: How to Live with Children Who Return Home,* by Jean Okimoto and Phyllis Steggal (Boston: Little, Brown and Co., 1987).
- *Your First Financial Steps: How to Manage Your Money When You're Just Starting Out,* by Nancy Dunnan (New York: HarperCollins, 1995).

TRADING PLACES: HELPING YOUR PARENTS

When age or a serious illness hits one's parents, adult children must step in and come to their rescue. Yet, as in anything financial, the results will be far superior if some planning takes place before a crisis hits. Your parents have three sources of support: their own assets, help from their children or other relatives, and the government. Here's what you can do to make certain all three are fully used.

First, talk. While your parents are still fit, discuss their plans for the future.

☑ *HINT: If you need help breaking the ice, refer to these pamphlets:* **Miles Away and Still Caring: A Guide for Long Distance Care Givers** *and* A **Checklist of Concerns/Resources for Care Givers,** *free from The American Association of Retired Persons, AARP Fulfillment, 601 E Street NW, Washington, DC 20049.*

Take time to discuss these important and sometimes emotional topics with your parents, but in a helpful not intruding fashion. Let them know you care and want to make certain that if and when they need your help you'll be armed with the information you need to step in and protect them, both financially and medically.

Among the topics to cover:

- *Assets and liabilities.* Ask parents to make a complete list of bank accounts, stocks, bonds, mutual funds, CDs, life insurance policies, safe deposit boxes, real estate, and other holdings. Debts should be listed as well.

☑ *HINT: If they are reluctant to share this information with you, honor that wish, but ask them to make the list anyway and simply let you know where it's kept in case of an emergency.*

- *Income.* Review sources of income: Social Security, investments, pensions.
- *Wills.* Each parent should have a separate will and all wills should have been updated since

the 1986 Tax Reform Act, following relocation to a new state; a death, divorce, or birth in the family; retirement, disability, a change in income.

- *Important papers.* Where are documents stored? Who has the key to the safe deposit box? Get names and telephone numbers of attorney, accountant, stockbroker, insurance agent, financial planner, and clergy. Is there a burial plot? Where is the deed?
- *Insurance.* Determine whether parents are adequately insured or overinsured. Parents 65 or older are eligible to enroll in Medicare, a federal health insurance program. Still, supplemental insurance may be required to fill in the gaps.

☑ *HINT: For an explanation of benefits and exclusions under the Medicare program, ask your doctor for a copy of* **Medicare: What It Will and Will Not Pay For,** *published by the American Society of Internal Medicine.*

- *Housing.* Be prepared to help your parents move to a new, smaller home, a retirement community, or perhaps even a nursing home.

☑ *HINT: Read* **Choosing a Nursing Home: A Guide to Quality Care,** *free from the American Association of Homes and Services for the Aging, 901 E Street NW, Washington, DC 20004 (see also Chapter 28).*

- *Incapacity.* If no provisions are made for physical or mental incapacity, the court can declare parents incompetent and appoint a guardian or conservator. So get a lawyer to draw up one or more durable powers of attorney to ensure that a person the parents trust will manage their financial and medical welfare if they cannot. Parents can confer the power on each other and also name, as successor, one of their children. The powers can be broad or narrow: The appointed individual can manage all finances, for instance, or merely have check-writing privileges. A medical durable power of attorney enables an appointed trustee to make health care decisions on the parents' behalf.

Three additional, important tips:

- Short of getting power of attorney, a joint checking account, usually with a spouse or child, can provide funds for an incapacitated individual.
- Discuss drawing up a living will that specifies medical measures to be taken or not taken in case of terminal illness.
- Consult a knowledgeable attorney regarding joint ownership of property and various types of trusts. A revocable living trust, for example, in which a parent is the trustee but makes provisions for a successor trustee, provides money management in case the parent becomes mentally or physically disabled.

Providing Financial Help to Parents

Review these suggestions with a lawyer familiar with estate planning.

- *Hire parents.* Children who own a business can hire parents to work on a part- or full-time basis. This is a good way to provide fit parents with income while receiving tax benefits.
- *Make tax-free gifts.* Anyone can give as much as $10,000 ($20,000 if given jointly with a spouse) without incurring a gift tax. If parents don't want to accept a gift, try making a loan instead. The money can eventually be repaid from the estate or sale of their home.

CAUTION: Beware there may be income tax consequences of below-market interest loans of over $10,000.

- *Increase investment income.* Money in low-yielding bank accounts or CDs should be transferred to higher-yielding money market funds.

- *Tap equity in their home* (see Chapter 28).

HINT: One final note—you are not alone. Thousands of children face similar situations. Children of Aging Parents, Woodbourne Office Campus, 1609 Woodbourne Rd., Suite 302A, Levittown, PA 19057, will put you in touch with a support group in your area. Membership is $20 a year, or send a SASE. Call: 215–945–6900.

Sources of Help:

- ElderCare Locator, 800–677–1116
  This helpline, sponsored by the National Association of Area Agencies on Aging, will refer you to appropriate AAA offices near your parents' home. The AAA has information ranging from adult day care centers to legal assistance.
- National Association of Professional Geriatric Care Managers, 602–881–8008
  This group will provide you with the names of people who evaluate a parent's situation and then advise on the appropriate type of care. They also locate professionals who help the elderly.
- National Academy of Elder Law Attorneys, 520–881–4005
  Free information on how to choose an estate planner or elder law attorney.
- National Organization of Claims Assistance Professionals, 708–963–3500
  Locates professionals who will help you or your parents with health and medical care paperwork and red tape.

GOING BACK TO SCHOOL AS AN ADULT

Some say that youth is wasted on the young. The same might be said about a college education, which is one reason why so many adults return to school with enthusiasm, absorbing new information and skills. If you're planning to return to college or professional school, be prepared for the fact that tuition is probably higher than when you last sat in a classroom. And, keep in mind that raising money takes time; start as early as possible. Here are some tips for funding your schooling:

- *Ask the school* you're applying to about special tuition deals. Many state institutions reduce tuition for nontraditional and/or adult students.
- *Contact the school's financial aid officer* as soon as you're accepted. This person typically knows the most about sources of money.
- *Look into state loan programs* for students pursuing careers as teachers, with "forgiveness" features for those who wind up in the classroom, as well as incentives for professionals the state needs—usually medicine, nursing, and special and bilingual education.

☑ HINT: *Write to the appropriate state department of higher education. For addresses see: Need a Lift? Educational Opportunities, Careers, Loans, Scholarships, Employment, $4.95, from the American Legion, Box 1050, Indianapolis, IN 46206; 317–630–1200.*

- *Perkins Loans* are available for both undergraduates and graduate students. They are istributed by the school's financial aid office.
- *Stafford Student Loans* are federally-guaranteed student loans made by banks, S&Ls, and credit unions. Interest rate is 3.1% above the 91-day T-bill rate, with an 8.25% cap. Get a loan application from a lender and send it to the college.

☑ HINT: *For quick information about loans and procedures, call 800–4–FEDAID; for information about other public student loans, call College Credit, at 800–831–5626.*

- *Private loans*, unlike public funds, do not carry income limits or have needs tests provisions. Approval is based on the creditworthiness of the applicant or, if necessary,

on the participation of a reliable cosigner. The three leading sources are:

- *Nellie Mae loans:*   800–634–9308
- *CONCERN/PLATO loans:*   800–767–5626
- *TERI loans:*   800–255–8374

AT-HOME STUDENTS

If you're working or home with children, check out various "Weekend Colleges" designed to meet your specific needs. Classes are held on Friday evenings, Saturdays, and Sundays, depending upon the school. Some, like Trinity College in Washington, DC, provide on-campus baby-sitting and rent dorm rooms for only $15/night. Others, like The College of St. Catherine in St. Paul, Minnesota, allow adult students to pay tuition using their Visa or MasterCard and spread out the bills over three payment periods—for which there is a small interest charge.

☑ HINT: *Read* IRS Publication 508, Educational Expenses, *in order to learn what expenses qualify as income tax deductions.*

INVESTMENTS GIFTS TO GIVE TO OTHERS

Financial gifts are a wonderful, easy way to defray the cost of raising a family, buying a house, paying for college, even funding retirement. The next time you're asked, "What do you want for your birthday?," or when you're wondering what to give a recent graduate, a newlywed couple or a retiree, the answer may be a financial gift. Throughout this book we have suggested specific stocks, bonds, and mutual funds—any that fall within the conservative category make sound presents. To simplify matters, here are nine suggestions.

- *Stock in a company the recipient knows.* Suggestions: one's local public utility company, the chewing gum maker, William Wrigley & Co.; the cereal giant, Kellogg Co.; Nike, Disney, Microsoft, PepsiCo, Toys R Us, Harley Davidson and CocaCola.

☑ *HINT: Check with several discount brokers to compare the commissions for buying a small number of shares (see list on page 236 or use A.G. Edwards (314–289–3000), where one-share commission on trades of $100 or less is only 16% of the stock's price.*

■ *EE Savings Bonds.* Available at your local bank with no commission or fee. These ultra-safe bonds earn a floating interest rate and are available for as little as $25. (See Chapter 9 for more on using savings bonds as a tax-deferred investment.)

■ *Mutual fund shares.* Pick a no-load fund with a good track record. The Franklin Money Market Fund and the Berger Funds both have $500 minimums; if you can spring for a $1,000, you'll get a slightly better yield with the Strong Money Market Fund. (See Chapter 6 for more fund suggestions.) Many well known no-load funds will reduce their minimum investment requirement (usually $1,000 to $2,500) for uniform Gift To Minor Accounts. Check with Vanguard and T. Rowe Price.

■ *SteinRoe Young Investor.* This mutual fund buys companies children know about, often those who have well-known brand names, such as McDonald's and Wrigley. The fund has some excellent literature for kids, aimed at teaching them about saving and investing. Details: 800–338–2550.

■ *Utility stock or bond.* Your local utility company is a known entity. And most utilities are generally recession-proof, and have above-average yields. Some utilities sell shares of stock (but not bonds) directly to investors, so you avoid a brokerage commission.

■ *Zero coupon bonds.* These sell at a substantial discount from the $1,000 face value, yet the owner will receive the full $1,000 when the bond matures. Treasury zeros are especially safe. (See Chapter 12 for details.)

■ *Tuition.* A course in investing or financial planning is always a wise choice. Check local colleges, YMCAs, and other schools in your area. Beware of courses taught by financial products salespeople; some may be prospecting for customers.

■ *Session with a financial planner.* Call the International Association for Financial Planning (800–945–IAFP or 404–395–1605) or the National Association of Personal Financial Advisors (800–366–2732) for referrals to planners in your area.

■ *Subscription to a financial publication.* (See page 2 for suggestions.)

■ *Financial software.* These programs, such as Quicken, will balance a checkbook, prepare budgets, and track investments. For the Record stores your personal history, financial and estate plans, and lists where to find key documents and possessions. (See Appendix A for additional software information.)

28

Retirement Living

As retirement draws near, most people begin to reevaluate their housing needs. So should you, if you haven't already done so. The house you bought 20, 30, or 40 years ago may indeed be your most valuable asset, one that you can put to active use to provide income and security as well as shelter.

TO MOVE OR NOT TO MOVE

That is indeed the question everyone faces as they get older.

Your wonderfully rambling three-story Victorian was perfect for raising the family, but now it seems to be empty most of the time. You're thinking about selling it and moving to smaller quarters, all on one floor, with no driveway to plow and re-pave. Then some days it seems as though you'd like to stay put but make better use of the space.

Either way, you can certainly profit from the fact that you own a major asset.

Among the investment-related alternatives to consider are:

- Selling and moving to a less expensive, smaller house or apartment
- Renting out part of your house
- Sharing your house with a friend or relative, especially if you live alone
- Remodeling to create a separate, self-contained apartment, either to live in or to rent

- Selling and moving to a retirement or planned community

☑ *HINT: If you're thinking of this last possibility, be certain that you want to live with people all the same age. If so, select a place where you have friends or can easily make new ones, where you are near work if you would like to work part-time or as a consultant, and where you have the kinds of activities you enjoy close at hand—golf, swimming, schools, etc. Adequate transportation and health facilities are also important when relocating.*

If you buy into a community, select one that is accredited by the American Association of Homes for the Aging, preferably one that has a waiting list. Both are indications of a well-run establishment. Among the other points to check out before making a financial commitment are:

- Management's experience and reputation
- The corporation's balance sheet
- Potential price increases
- Restrictions on use of the property (pets, children, car space, visitors)
- Any deed restrictions

☑ *HINT: If you are age 55 or older, $125,000 of the proceeds of the sale of a house that is your primary residence is tax-free. This is a once-in-a-lifetime tax break.*

FREEING UP THE ASSETS IN YOUR HOUSE

Here is a thumbnail sketch of techniques that can turn your house into a source of income. For more on each one, check the source list at the end of this chapter. And regardless of which path you take, consult your accountant or tax lawyer well in advance. Laws change, and state regulations vary widely.

Selling to the Children

You can sell your house to your children and then lease it back, paying them a fair market value. This gives them the tax advantages associated with real estate as well as your rental money with which to meet their costs. You can invest the money from the sale, perhaps in an annuity or other vehicle that provides you with a steady stream of income.

Move to a Rental that May Go Co-op or Condo

Check the local and state laws first. In many areas, when a rental building converts to co-op or condo, tenants over a certain age can stay on forever as renters. This is known as a non-eviction plan. If the rent is modest, this could be to your financial advantage.

Take Out a Mortgage on Your Home

. . . then invest the proceeds. You can deduct the interest portion of your mortgage payments.

Be cautious about selling your home, especially to someone outside your family, and certainly if it is your only residence. Your house is immune from claims by the government, even if you or your spouse apply for Medicaid, particularly if one of you lives in it. Cash is not.

Get a Reverse Mortgage

This is a home loan in reverse that allows you to take the equity in your home and turn it into regular monthly income without giving up your property. A reverse mortgage is designed to help elderly homeowners who are house-rich but cash-poor. The monthly amount is deducted with interest from the accumulated equity in the home. Each month the equity declines. The loan is paid off when the house is sold or the owner dies.

Nationally about 150,000 home equity conversion loans have been made since they began in the early 1980s. Of these, about 10,000 have been made through private banks. Federally-insured reverse mortgages are available in 41 states.

On the face of it, they sound ideal—instead of writing a monthly mortgage check, the bank sends you a check. And, this money does not jeopardize your Social Security benefits, Medicare, or your pension.

To qualify, you must own your home (or nearly so) so you can borrow against it without selling. You can use your monthly, nontaxable payments for living expenses or take a lump sum. In some cases, you can use a reverse mortgage simply to get a line of credit to pay for medical bills, home repairs, or taxes, or even to adapt your house for living there—putting in a wheelchair ramp or special safety devices.

"Short-term" reverse mortgages tend to run 3 to 10 years, which can be a problem if you outlive the loan—you must repay the loan in full, refinance, or sell.

"Long-term" reverse mortgages establish payments until the owner dies or sells the house. The amount received monthly is based on the value of your home, your age, prevailing interest rates, and the percentage of future increases in the value of the house that you agree to share with the lender or bank. If, for example, you own a $100,000 house and are 65 years of age, depending upon the type of reverse mortgage you take out, your monthly check could range from $207 to $496.

CAUTION: Keep in mind that a reverse mortgage means leaving less for heirs. Any remaining equity in your home belongs to you or your heirs. But, before signing any papers, have a lawyer and an accountant review all terms.

The Negatives

The downside to these reverse mortgages is that you may run into extra fees and costs, such as closing costs, insurance, an up-front fee and, of course, interest on the money you're borrowing. How much all this will come to will depend on your age, the value of your home, who your lender is, and how long the mortgage runs for. It could be a financial disaster if you have to move shortly after taking out a reverse mortgage.

Which Reverse Mortgage Is Best?

The least risk at this date is a Federal Housing Authority (FHA)-Insured Loan. These loans apply to houses valued at under $150,000. They come with credit lines and/or monthly advances at adjustable rates, and advances are guaranteed even if the lender goes bankrupt. The FHA writes the reverse mortgage and gives free loan counseling in all states except Alaska, South Dakota, and Texas.

The New Fannie Mae Reverse Mortgage

Fannie Mae recently rolled out a "Home Keeper" reverse mortgage for owners of properties appraised up to $203,150; they have adjustable interest rates and are available in every state except Texas. Loan processing time is one month or less.

☑ *HINT: If you live a long time and use up all the equity in your house, neither you nor your heirs will incur any debt larger than the market value of the property. Counselors at Fannie Mae, 800–732–6643, will answer telephone inquires and refer you to approved lenders.*

CONTINUING CARE RETIREMENT COMMUNITIES

If you are concerned that your parents, or you, may need nursing services but not a nursing home, consider CCRCs, a flexible, although fairly expensive, form of long-term care. As of early 1995, over 300,000 Americans, with an average age of 82, were living in these communities. CCRCs offer a range of leisure activities as well as residential and nursing services.

In a typical CCRC, you do not purchase your home, but you pay a hefty entry charge plus a monthly fee. The fee covers some or all nursing care for residents who need it. If you don't need the care, or if you move out, it is very unlikely that you will get your money back because you are not making a real-estate purchase as much as you are buying a service.

For example:

- *Type A facility* provides unlimited nursing care. Median entry charge for a one-bedroom apartment is $72,000 with a monthly fee of $1,150. At the high end of the range: $195,000 to $250,000 for two bedrooms with a monthly fee of $4,200.
- *Type B facility* provides specified level of long-term care, often 60 days a year; after that you pay $50 to $150 per day for care. Median entry charge is $51,000; monthly fee is $1,000.
- *Type C facility* provides a "fee-for-service" plan with access to nursing facilities—but you pay full rate. Medicare will cover short-term care only. In some facilities, residents pay for meals. Median entry price: $42,000 plus a $800 monthly fee.

Predicting your illness or that of your parents is not easy to do. But your decision can be guided by other more "known" factors. For instance: Can you or your parents afford to pay the monthly fees for as long as the CCRC resident lives? Select a CCRC that's in sound financial shape; ask to see its audited financial statement and review it with a knowledgeable accountant. Know under what circumstances the monthly fees can rise, or if there are any refunds in the event you or your parents move or do not need long-term care. Determine what happens to the fee and the unit if one parent moves to the health center.

CAUTION: *Choose a CCRC that has a seal of approval from the American Association of Homes and Services for the Aging (AAHA). Of the 1,000 CCRCs in the United States, about 190 have been so accredited. For a list, send a SASE to: CCRC, 901 E Street NW, Washington, DC 20004.*

SHARED AND CO-HOUSING

If you don't want to live alone or can't afford to, and yet you're not ready for a nursing home/retirement type institution, you may want to join with others in a shared nest. A growing number of such communities and housing arrangements exist nationwide. Two helpful sources of information are:

- The American Association of Retired Persons, 800–424–3410 (202–434–2277 in the Washington, DC, area)
- National Shared Housing Resource Center, 410–235–4454

RETIRING ABROAD

If you decide to retire outside the United States, keep in mind that:

- *Medicare* does not cover health services in foreign countries, with the exceptions of Canada and Mexico. Medicare, for example, will pay for emergency care in a qualified Canadian or Mexican hospital for U.S. residents if that facility is closer than an American hospital.
- *U.S. citizens* can receive Social Security benefits outside the country as long as they are eli-

gible. The same is true for eligible dependents and survivors who live abroad—they, too, can collect benefits based on your Social Security record.

- *If you are not a U.S. citizen,* in some countries checks may not be sent to your dependents or survivors unless they have already met specific residency requirements in the United States. And, in certain countries, your checks will stop after you've been out of the country 6 months.

HINT: *Check out the facts in the Social Security pamphlet,* **Your Social Security Checks While You Are Outside the United States;** *for updated info, call 800–772–1213.*

CLOSING UP YOUR HOUSE FOR THE LAST TIME

If you do decide to move, you'll find cleaning out years of scrapbooks, photo albums, clothes, and furniture will be time-consuming and, of course, emotional. However, it will ease the burden if you also view it as an opportunity to lighten up on possessions and to make some money.

Some downsizing tips:

- *Have an auctioneer* look at your furniture, collections, and jewelry and give you estimates.
- *Get estimates* also from used-furniture dealers.
- *Then hold a garage sale* for items that the auctioneer and furniture dealer do not want.
- *Finally, have a reliable charity* pick up what doesn't sell and you don't want to move. Be certain you get a receipt for tax purposes.

HINT: *Be smart and request the IRS Publication 526,* **Charitable Contributions,** *well in advance; call 800–829–3676.*

And, before you move to another state:

- *Look into state laws.* If you maintain residences in two states, say one in the south and one up north, you could wind up paying taxes in both. Know how many days spent in each makes you a resident for tax purposes.

- *Change* your driver's license and voter registration.
- *Review your municipal bonds.* If you own municipal bonds in your home state you'll have to pay income tax on the interest when you move to a new state, provided the new state has an income tax. That's because bonds are tax-free only in the state in which they were issued, with the exception of bonds issued by Puerto Rico.
- *Read: The State Tax Laws Guide,* free from AARP Scudder Mutual Fund Company; call 800–322–2282. It includes information that relates to senior citizens as well as each state's tax rulings.

NEW LAW RELATING TO STATE TAXES

In January of 1996, President Clinton signed a bill that's taken the sharp bite out of what was known as the "source tax," making it easier for older people to relocate to states with little or no income tax and be free of their tax obligations where they originally lived.

Prior to the law change, residents who moved from one state to another and who had tax-deferred pensions were frequently made to pay taxes to their former state and if they did not were penalized—even though they no longer resided in the old state.

The new law affects retirement income received after December 31, 1995, and covers IRAs, 401(k)s and other tax-deferred employer-sponsored retirement savings plans.

This means residents of California, New York, Massachusetts and other high income tax states can retire to Florida, Texas, Nevada, Alaska, Washington, Wyoming, and South Dakota where there's no income tax. New Hampshire and Tennessee tax only dividend and interest income—

and no longer worry about filing in their former state every year they receive pension income.

☑ *HINT: You should also be aware of the fact that 25 states and the District of Columbia, exclude Social Security benefits from taxation, including:*

- California
- Arizona
- Georgia
- Michigan
- New York
- New Jersey
- South Carolina

Some states give 100% pension-income exclusions, among them:

- Alabama
- Hawaii
- Illinois
- Massachusetts
- Mississippi
- Pennsylvania

☑ *HINT: If you're thinking of moving, find out what the income tax rulings are for various states and ask your accountant to find out where you can keep the most of your pension dollars.*

IF YOU RETIRE EARLY OR ARE FIRED OR LAID OFF

In recent years a great many American corporations have eliminated thousands of blue- and white-collar jobs. No one, not even top executives, are immune to cutbacks. Those who planned to glide into retirement are cast adrift. Those on the fast track are suddenly being derailed. If you're one of the many Americans who has been "let go," you face a number of important financial decisions. Although it is beyond the scope of this book to guide you through this period in your life, the following financial tips may help make life a bit easier.

1. *Make a realistic budget and stick to it.* Prepare for leaner times. Cut back on luxury items, eating out, taxis, and the like.
2. *Keep any severance pay in a liquid account,* such as a money market fund. If you received a sizable amount, put half in a fund and half in T-bills.
3. *If you are given the choice* of taking severance in a lump sum or payments, it's generally best to opt for the lump sum and invest it so it starts earning interest. This way you won't need to worry about your ex-employer's financial condition. If it's near year-end, it may be better to schedule payments so you can defer income into the next year.
4. *Do not make the common mistake* of using the severance check to pay off the mortgage. You may need this money, and a mortgage is usually one of the lowest-rate loans around with interest being tax-deductible.
5. *If you receive a large sum* from your 401(k) or other retirement plan, try not to touch it. That money has never been taxed. If you take it out now, you will pay income tax on it plus a 10% penalty if you're under age 59½. In many cases, profit-sharing and stock option plans can be left with the company. However, if you suspect that your pension might be underfunded, provide for a direct transfer to your IRA to avoid the 20% withholding. It will continue to grow on a tax-deferred basis with no penalty. Keep this IRA money separate from any other IRAs; if you take a new job, you can roll it over into the new employer's plan.
6. *Don't be too proud* to take unemployment insurance if you were fired. (You cannot collect if you leave voluntarily.) You and your employer have helped fund this benefit over the years; now you're certainly entitled to use it.
7. *In a true emergency* you may have to use some of your retirement savings.

8. *Keep track of job-hunting expenses;* some of these may be deducted from your taxable income as "miscellaneous itemized deductions." Check with your accountant for details.

☑ HINT: *Among the expenses to track are recruitment and agency fees, transportation, telephone calls, and résumé preparation.*

9. *Keep your health insurance.* In 1986 a federal law was enacted requiring employers sponsoring group health plans to offer employees and their dependents the opportunity to extend their health coverage at group rates. This is called "continuation coverage" and it lasts for 18 months, longer if you are disabled. You will have to pay the costs, but they will be far less than taking out your own policy. If you are forced to take out your own policy, look into group rates offered by professional associations, unions, or an alumni association.

☑ HINT: *If you are self-employed, look into membership in the National Association for the Self-Employed; call 800–232-NASE.*

10. *Don't panic.* Most problems have solutions and people willing to help you find them. Join a local group composed of others who are out of work. There's much to be gained by sharing your situation with others. The worst thing you can do is to bury your head in the sand and hide from the reality of what has happened.

   NOTE: Suggestions for working after retirement are given in the next chapter.

FOR FURTHER INFORMATION

Reverse Mortgages

For a list of reverse mortgage programs and a fact sheet, send a self-addressed, stamped envelope to the National Center for Home Equity Conversion —address below.

The Center also has a useful book, *Your Retirement Nestegg: A New Consumer Guide to Reverse Mortgages*, available at libraries or for $4.50 from the Center.

National Center for Home Equity Conversion
7373 147 Street West
Apple Valley, MN 55124
612–953–4474

HomeMade Money: Consumers' Guide to Home Equity Conversion
AARP Home Equity Information Center
601 E Street NW
Washington, DC 20049

General Information on Housing Issues

Free literature and a directory of members from:

American Association of Homes and Services for the Aging
901 E Street NW
Washington, DC 20004
202–783–2242

Selecting Retirement Housing
American Association of Retired Persons
601 E Street NW

Washington, DC 20049
202–434–2277
Free.
Lee Rosenberg, *50 Fabulous Places to Retire in America* and *Retirement: Ready or Not*

Retiring Abroad

Discusses contracts, payment plans, and financial matters, plus how to evaluate communities.

Tax Information for Older Americans
IRS Publication 554
800–TAX–FORM
Free.

Retire in Mexico
40 Fourth Street
Suite 203
Petaluma, CA 94952
$1.95 for four issues/year.

Mexico Retirement & Travel Assistance
Box 2190–23
Parhump, NV 89041
$25 for four issues/year.

International Living
105 West Monument Street
Baltimore, MD 21201
410–223–2605

29

Social Security, Retirement, and Pension Plans

The time to start planning for a financially secure retirement is the day you receive your first paycheck, although few of us ever do. But don't agonize over the fact; just avoid further delays and start now. This chapter is not intended to be a complete retirement guide, but the information here will help you lay the financial groundwork that makes the difference between merely getting along and continuing life at full tilt.

HOW MUCH MONEY WILL YOU NEED?

Retirees are living much longer now—a person retiring in 1997 at age 60 is expected to live about another 25 years or more. This means that accumulating enough money to carry you through those years is critical. The combination of a pension and Social Security may equal only 40% to 60% of preretirement income, so the balance must come from personal savings and/or part-time work. In addition, the higher your annual earnings, the less percentage-wise may be replaced by Social Security in the future. Inflation, too, will erode retirement funds: At 4% a year, $1,000 will be worth only $380 in 25 years.

Rule of thumb: To maintain your current standard of living, your pension, investment income, and Social Security must add up to 70% to 80% of your last year's salary.

☑ *HINT: To retire at your current standard of living, begin saving 10% of your income while you're in your twenties and thirties. As soon as possible— and certainly by age 40—begin increasing that by at least 1% each year. When your children are out of college, boost savings to 15% per year until retirement.*

And aim to have your mortgage paid off by the time you retire.

WHAT DIFFERENCE DOES $1,000 MAKE?

You might not think that just $1,000 a year could make a difference in your retirement nest egg— it's a little less than $20 a week. Yet if starting on your 45th birthday you save $1,000 each year and earn 6% annually, by the time you're 65 you'll have almost $39,000, not taking into consideration income taxes. Obviously your best bet is to save the money in a tax-exempt investment or

Annual Interest Rate	20 years	10 years	5 years
5%	$33,775	$13,124	$5,794
6%	38,993	13,972	5,975
7%	44,211	14,810	6,156
8%	49,423	15,645	6,335

SOURCE: Case Western Reserve University.

294

tax-deferred account such as an IRA, SEP, or Keogh.

SOCIAL SECURITY

How Social Security Works

Although we all spend a lot of time talking and thinking about Social Security, few of us know how the system works. It is a social insurance program that provides old-age benefits for retirees and their survivors, disability insurance for workers, and survivor benefits for dependents. It is called an "entitlement" because Congress has set eligibility requirements—age and the number of years worked. The system is financed by matching contributions from employers and employees.

In order to plan your retirement intelligently, start by taking a close look at your Social Security situation. Then build around this basic data. It may seem like a nuisance, but ignoring Social Security records could lead to lower benefits than you're legitimately entitled to, because benefits are based on the Social Security Administration's records of what you have earned. It's up to you, and not the folks in Washington, to find out if your records are accurate. Serious errors could cost you thousands of dollars in benefits.

For Help with Social Security

To reach one of the several thousand Social Security representatives who help the public, call 800–772–1213. The lines are least busy early in the morning, later in the week, and later in the month. Social Security representatives can answer most questions and will also send you helpful publications.

Hundreds of lawyers specialize in resolving Social Security problems related to disability benefits. They are members of the National Organization of Social Security Claimants' Representatives, which operates a nationwide referral service. For a member in your area, call 800–431–2804.

Four Simple Steps You Absolutely Must Take

Step 1. Request a written statement of earnings. Call the Social Security Administration, 800–772–1213, or visit your local office to get a copy of Form SSA–7004, "Request for Social Security Earnings and Benefit Estimate Statement." Fill it out, sign it, and mail it back. In a few weeks, you will receive a computerized statement showing all earnings credited to your account. It will give a year-by-year listing of earnings, with an estimate of your monthly benefits.

Step 2. Check the information for errors. If you suspect a mistake, contact your Social Security office. Provide them with copies of as much data as possible, including dates of employment, wages received, employer's name and address, copies of W–2 forms, and paycheck stubs. The most common error results from incorrect reporting by your employer, unreported name changes because of marriage, or clerical errors at the Social Security Administration.

☑ *HINT: If for some reason you cannot find your old W–2 forms, try to get copies from the employer you had at the time of the error. If you fail, you can get a certified copy of any tax return from the last 6 years for $14 by sending Form 4506 to the Internal Revenue Service Center where you filed your return.*

In 1989, Congress virtually eliminated the 3-year statute of limitations on errors, so you can now correct mistakes, even those the Administration previously refused to address.

Step 3. Request this statement periodically, especially if you have changed employers, or if you have more than one employer.

Step 4. File an application 3 months before you want retirement benefits to begin. You should file for disability or survivor benefits as soon as possible after disability or death occurs. Start any application by calling 800–772–1213. Social Security will not start sending your benefits until you file an application. Most applications can be taken by telephone. If you are late in filing an application, it's possible you may be paid only some of your benefits. Social Security seldom goes back more than 12 months, no matter how long ago you could have started receiving benefits had you filed on time.

Now that you know what you're likely to receive from Social Security, you're undoubtedly impressed with the fact that you will need a great deal more to continue a comfortable lifestyle after age 65! Other ways to build a retirement nest egg are covered later in this chapter.

YOUR INCOME TAXES AND SOCIAL SECURITY

If you have relatively high income, believe it or not, you might have to pay taxes on your Social Security benefits. Up to half of your annual Social Security benefit is subject to federal income tax if your "provisional income" exceeds $25,000 if you're single, or $32,000 for married couples filing jointly.

Provisional income consists of: your adjusted gross income plus nontaxable interest income (such as municipal bond income) and half of your Social Security benefits.

CAUTION: The 1993 Tax Act made it even worse: Single taxpayers with provisional income above $34,000 and married couples filing joint returns with provisional income above $44,000 can have as much as 85% of their benefits taxed. If you're in the situation, consult with your accountant and/or estate lawyer.

WHEN TO RETIRE—EARLY OR LATE?

The Pros and Cons of Early Retirement

Should you take early retirement? It's not an easy yes or no. It depends . . . and so, before making a decision, consider these facts:

- You can begin receiving Social Security at age 62, but if you do, your benefits will be permanently reduced by 20% of the amount you would have been paid had you waited to collect until age 65.

- Taking early retirement could also affect the amount your spouse receives, if you are taking combined benefits. The maximum your spouse can receive at age 65 if you file as a couple is 50% of your benefits. So, if you were due to collect $10,000, the most your spouse would get is $5,000.

- If you begin receiving benefits early, at age 62, your spouse's portion will be reduced (if your spouse is under 65) from 50% to 37.5%.

Taxes on Social Security Benefits

IF YOUR PROVISIONAL INCOME IS:	THIS % OF YOUR SOCIAL SECURITY BENEFITS COULD BE SUBJECT TO FEDERAL TAX
• Single taxpayers	
$25,001–$34,000	50%
Above $34,000	85%
• Married couples filing jointly	
$32,001–$44,000	50%
Above $44,000	85%

(As of June 1996)

Should You Retire Late?

Well, again, it depends. Here are the facts:

- If you retire after age 65, you can receive additional Social Security "credits" for each year you work up to when you're 70. If you turn 65 in 1996, you will have 5.7% more for each year until age 70.
- If you decide to put off collecting Social Security, be certain to apply for Medicare when you turn 65. Medicare coverage does not begin automatically.
- Signing up for Medicare Part A is a no-brainer. That insurance covers hospital and skilled nursing care and is free to anyone over age 65 who is eligible for Social Security. *NOTE*: Medicare B, which covers doctors' and outpatient hospital services, currently costs $42.50 a month.

Should You Work After Retirement?

Well, it depends. One out of five beneficiaries age 65 and older today has some earned income. Some points to consider:

- If you continue to work and you don't need the extra income, you can contribute up to 2,000 a year in an IRA until the year before you reach age 70½.
- If you are self-employed, you can contribute to a Keogh plan—as much as 25% of your earned income, up to $30,000. Contributions to a Keogh can be made even when you are over age 70½.
- If you do keep working after retirement, it could affect your Social Security benefits and your tax situation, but not your Medicare benefits. That means:
- If you are between the ages of 65 and 69 and have more than $12,500 in earned income, your Social Security benefits will be reduced by $1 for every $3 of earned income above this amount.

- If you are under age 65, you will lose $1 in benefits for every $2 of earnings above $8,280.
- The money held back by Social Security is not a total loss. You get a "delayed retirement credit," which pads your benefits slightly after your earnings drop or you turn 70.
- If you are 70 or older, you can earn any amount you like.
- If you're working and you don't need your Social Security, delay your application past age 65. Whether or not you are working, Social Security will adjust your benefit. If you were born in 1929 or 1930, the benefit will be increased by 4.5% per year of delay beyond normal retirement age. This increases by 0.5% every 2 years until it reaches 8% per year for workers hitting retirement age in 2009, when it will be age 66 and age 67 for people born in 1960 and later.
- The current tax law is in favor of waiting for full benefits if your income, including half of your Social Security benefits, is high enough to trigger a tax on your benefits. If your income is over $32,000 on a joint return or $25,000 on a single return, as much as 85% of your benefits will be taxed.

☑ HINT: *An easy-to-follow guide,* Understanding Social Security, SSA Publication #05–10024; *is free, by calling 800–772–1213.*

INDIVIDUAL RETIREMENT ACCOUNTS (IRAs)

If you work for yourself or someone else, you should take advantage of an IRS—through it you can build a retirement nest egg on a tax-deferred basis. In fact, if you've been stashing away $2,000 a year since 1981, when IRAs were made available to all workers even if they had a pension plan, you have a sizable amount of money on hand. However, an IRA should not be regarded passively, as some sort of savings account that can be ignored or placed in a CD. It is an important investment—one requiring diversification and thoughtful management.

What to Invest Your IRA In

How best to invest your IRA depends on several factors: the current economic environment, your age, other sources of income, and your appetite for risk. The closer you are to retirement, of course, the less risk you should take. You must also decide if you are temperamentally suited to manage your account or if you need a professional. In general, high-yield conservative investments should form the basic core of most IRAs, but there are exceptions and variations. A part of your IRA should go into other vehicles such as growth stocks, which protect your nest egg from reduced returns when interest rates are low and yet take advantage of a rising stock market.

Only a few investments are excluded by law from IRAs: collectibles (such as gems, stamps, art, antiques, and Oriental rugs), commodities, and leveraged investments (those made with borrowed cash). Interestingly, you can include U.S. legal tender gold and silver coins acquired after December 31, 1986, but they must be held by a custodian, not the IRA owner.

☑ *HINT: You may borrow money to put in your IRA, but margined stocks, commodity futures, and mortgaged real-estate are out. Among the tax-advantaged investments that make no sense in an IRA are municipal bonds, tax shelters, and deferred annuities.*

Years ago, the $2,000 annual deduction was available to all who earned at least that much in salary form. That's not been true for some time. Now:

■ If your adjusted gross income (before IRA contribution) is over $50,000 ($35,000 for singles) and you or your spouse is an active participant

in an employer's pension plan, you are no longer entitled to any IRA tax deduction, but you can make nondeductible contributions.

■ If your gross adjusted income (before IRA contribution) is between $40,000 and $50,000 ($25,000 to $35,000 for singles) and you or your spouse is an active participant in an employer's pension plan, your IRA deduction is reduced.

■ If you or your spouse is not an active participant in such a plan, you can still deduct the full $2,000 IRA contribution.

■ The full $2,000 deduction is available to workers who are active participants in employer-maintained retirement plans only if their adjusted gross income is below $25,000 for singles and $40,000 for those filing jointly.

■ The following retirement programs disqualify you from making a fully deductible IRA contribution: Keogh, SEP, money-purchase pension plan, profit-sharing plan, defined-benefit plan, 401(k), employee stock option plan, government employee retirement plan, 403(b) (teachers' annuity), 457(s) (municipal employee retirement plan), and Taft-Hartley plan (union employee retirement plan).

Should You Have an IRA?

If you no longer qualify for the $2,000 tax deduction, you may decide it's not worth contributing to your IRA anymore. *THIS IS A BIG MISTAKE FOR MOST PEOPLE.* Over the long run, your money will accumulate on a tax-deferred basis, more than offsetting the fact that it's not an

---

A Nice Freebie for Readers of this Book

Oppenheimer Fund Management has free a calculator that lets you determine the growth of an IRA depending on the size of annual contributions, the number of years contributions are made, and various assumed rates of return. Call 800–525–7048.

immediate tax deduction. And, of course, it is a forced way of saving. In general, the higher the rate you earn on your IRA and the higher your tax bracket, the more valuable this shelter is. And there's no guarantee that Congress won't raise the tax brackets before you retire.

☑ **HINT:** *Contributions that do not qualify as a tax deduction should be paid into a separate IRA to avoid confusion.*

IRA Basics

- Annual contribution: $2,000 of earned income if under age 70½
- You can wait until April 15 to make your contribution for the previous year.
- If you and your spouse both work, you may each have an IRA.
- Beginning in 1997, a married couple can contribute up to $4,000/year, even if one spouse has little or no income.
- IRA money must be invested with an IRS-approved custodian, such as a bank, savings and loan, stockbroker, mutual fund, or insurance company.
- You can open as many IRA accounts as you like using a different custodian or investment each year and thus spreading out your risk.
- There is a 10% penalty for withdrawing money before you are 59½. There is an exception to penalty for withdrawals in the form of equal periodic payments over life expectancy. Two other exceptions: to pay for certain medical expenses and to purchase medical insurance if you've been receiving unemployment for at least 12 weeks.
- Money withdrawn from IRAs funded by deductible contributions is taxed as ordinary income. (Only the earnings from IRAs funded by nondeductible contributions are taxed as ordinary income upon withdrawal.) If you withdraw before age 59½, you pay both the tax and the 10% penalty.
- You must withdraw money starting at age 70½ or be penalized.

Some Painless Ways to Fund Your IRA

- You don't have to pay all $2,000 in one lump sum; divide $2,000 by twelve months and you get $166.66—so aim to put that amount in each month.
- Make your IRA contribution as early as possible in the new year—this will boost the value of your account in the long run. Most people delay until April 14 to fund their IRA because they either feel that they can't spare the $2,000 or they can't decide where to invest the money.
- Use an automatic plan with a mutual fund or your stockbroker. Plan to deposit $167 each month, even if it's into a money market fund. You will have accumulated $2,000 within a year, painlessly.
- If you can only make nondeductible IRA contributions, consider a deferred annuity contract in which you accumulate interest and dividend earnings tax-free. Two added pluses: There is no limitation on the amount you can invest.

NOTE: The 10% early withdrawal penalty applies to annuities—but only to the amount includable in income, which is less than the total amount of withdrawal.

Self-Directed IRAs

When your IRA contains $5,000 to $10,000, you're ready to benefit from diversification. Consider doing so through a self-directed account, which can be set up at a brokerage firm for $25 to $35 plus a yearly fee. It allows you to invest in stocks, bonds, limited partnerships, options, Treasuries, zeros, or mortgage-backed securities. If you want advice on managing the portfolio, use a full-service broker; otherwise, save on commissions with a discount broker. A self-directed account takes time and vigilance on your part, yet it offers the greatest degree of flexibility along with the greatest potential for appreciation. It also involves the most risk.

Six No-Load Growth Funds for Your 1996 IRA

Unless you're very close to retirement, you can afford to devote 20% to 40% of the total amount of your IRA to low-to-moderate-risk stock or balanced funds; the latter hold both stocks and bonds. The following five funds charge low IRA custodial fees and have had high average annual returns.

Baron Growth & Income
Lexington Corporate Lenders
Stein Roe Cap Opportunities
Strong Growth
Vanguard Index Growth
Warbug Pincus Cap Appreciation

CAUTION: Avoid investments that are attractive largely for tax advantages, such as tax-exempt municipal bonds. Because IRAs are already sheltered from taxes, the exemption is wasted. In addition, all income, including tax-free yields, will be taxed when withdrawn.

 HINT: The Cleveland Electric Illuminating Co. was the first company to establish an IRA for those who buy the stock through its dividend reinvestment plan. There are no brokerage commissions, and dividends can be automatically reinvested. Check with the electric utility company in your area.

Your IRA and Your Heirs

If you're blessed with sufficient income from other sources, you may want to leave IRA funds to your heirs. Although the IRS views IRAs primarily as a retirement benefit, not a death benefit, the mortality tables help those who want to leave money behind by making it possible for them to withdraw less money from their IRAs — you must, of course, start withdrawing money by April 1 of the year after you turn 70½; otherwise, you face a stiff 50% excise tax on excess accumulations.

It's a good idea to check with your accountant or financial planner to determine your required withdrawal amounts.

CAUTION: An IRA left to a beneficiary is fully taxable to the heir. If it is left to an heir under age 14, it is taxed at the parents' rate. And, this money cannot be rolled over (see below) and thus the tax benefit is eliminated.

IRA Rollovers

If you receive a partial or lump-sum distribution from a qualified retirement plan or tax-sheltered annuity, you may roll it over into an IRA. The amount you roll over may not include your after-tax contributions to the plan, but you may roll

How an IRA Can Pay Off

If you invest $2,000 a year and you are in the 28% tax bracket, here's what you'll earn in an IRA versus in a taxable investment. The figures assume that you'll earn 7% annually on the money invested.

	IN AN IRA	IN A TAXABLE INVESTMENT
5 years	$12,306	$11,617
10 years	29,567	26,473
15 years	53,776	45,469
20 years	87,730	69,759
30 years	202,146	140,537

SOURCE: Chase Manhattan Bank.

over all or only part of the distribution that would otherwise be taxable.

Once in the IRA rollover, the savings continue to accumulate tax-free until payouts start—permissible after age 59½, mandatory at 70½. The transfers must be made within 60 days after the distribution.

☑ *HINT: Be extremely careful when rolling over or transferring these funds, especially if the transfer is to yourself. The safest method, in order to not incur a tax penalty, is from trustee to trustee.*

NOTE: Rollover from a single IRA can be made only once in a 1-year period (1-year waiting period between distributions applies separately to each IRA), but for direct trustee-to-trustee transfers, the 1-year waiting period does not apply.

To Avoid Any Tax Penalties

If for some reason you have inadvertently put too much money into your IRA, take it out immediately. For each year the excess remains in the account a 6% excise tax is levied on both it and

15 Stocks for Your IRA: 1997

An IRA holds plenty of appeal for building retirement funds. These stocks combine good capital gains potential with attractive yields, dividend growth prospects, and above-average safety.

STOCK	REASON
Abbott Laboratories	Growing overseas profits
American Home Products	Top dividend record
Bristol-Myers Squibb	Attractive drug issue
Citizens Utilities B	Impressive dividend and growth
Coca-Cola	Solid overseas sales
A.G. Edwards & Sons	Well run securities firm
Gibson Greetings	Strong cash flow
Heinz, H.J.	Continued earnings growth
Kellogg	Major multinational
McDonald's Corp.	In emerging markets
Royal Dutch Petroleum	Energy play; high yield
J.M. Smucker	Leader in jams and jellies
Southwestern Bell	Appeal of cellular business
Tootsie Roll	Well managed; low debt
WPL Holdings	Expanding via acquisition

Four Income Funds for Your IRA

FUND	YIELD	TELEPHONE
T. Rowe Price GNMA	7.27%	800-638-5660
Vanguard Preferred Stock	7.23	800-662-7447
T. Rowe Price Short-Term Global	6.00	800-638-5660
Wellesley Income (Vanguard)	6.03	800-662-7447

(As of October 1996)

earnings. Earnings on the excess must be reported as income in the year earned. The excess and earnings on the excess may also be subject to a 10% penalty when withdrawn.

YOUR COMPANY PENSION PLAN

The next scheduled stop on your road map for an enjoyable retirement should be your company pension plan. The crash of 1987 and the severe correction of 1996 proved to all of us that the value of even the best-run pension plan can decrease, just as a personal portfolio can. So even if you have little or no control over where your plan is invested, you need the facts. Ask. Find out what you can expect to receive. The answer will help you determine what additional savings you will need to live comfortably in your later years.

Here are 13 questions you should gather the answers to during the course of 1997:

1. Am I eligible to receive retirement benefits? If not now, when will I be?
2. What type of retirement plan do I have, defined benefit or defined contribution? (A defined-contribution plan gives you some flexibility regarding where the money is invested, but it doesn't guarantee you any set amount when you retire. A defined-benefit plan is less flexible, but it guarantees you a certain amount when you retire.)
3. What choices do I have about where my pension is invested? How many times a year can I move my money from one place (usually a mutual fund) to another?
4. What are the penalties for early withdrawal?
5. Can I borrow money from my plan? How much? At what rate? For what purposes? For how long?
6. Can I make contributions to my plan to build up the dollar amount? How much? How often?

7. Does the company contribute to my plan? If so, how much?
8. How much is my plan worth today?
9. How much do you estimate it will be worth when I retire?
10. How will the benefits be paid out? What are the advantages and disadvantages of taking it in a lump sum?
11. What happens if I become disabled? If I die?
12. What happens to my pension if the firm is bought by another company or if the firm closes down?
13. What is the estimated amount I will receive on a monthly basis when I retire?

☑ *HINT: If you have no pension plan, you're not alone. According to AARP, thousands of Americans are in this situation. The organization has two booklets that will help you:* **Working Options** *and* **Planning Your Retirement.** *Order from: AARP Fulfillment Office, 601 E Street NW, Washington, DC 20049.*

ALCOA—A Leading 401(k) Plan

Compare your company's plan with Alcoa's, one of the best in the nation.

■ Matching. Each division determines how much it will match; it ranges from 50% to 100% of up to 6% of the employee's salary.

■ Investments choices:
  1. Guaranteed investment contracts (GICs)
  2. American Balanced (a growth and income fund)
  3. Investment Company of America (a growth and income fund)
  4. Amcap (a growth fund)
  5. New Perspective (a global fund)
  6. Alcoa stock

■ Features. Automated phone system for account balance and for executing transactions. Sales fees on all mutual funds are waived.

Types of Retirement Plans

There are several basic types of retirement programs available to employees, described below. Programs for the self-employed—Keoghs and SEPs—are discussed later on in this chapter.

- *Defined-benefit plan.* The most traditional type of pension plan. Pays a fixed retirement benefit, such as 50% of your final salary, determined by a formula. The advantage: You know what your final pension will be.
- *Defined-contribution plan.* Popularly called a profit-sharing plan. The company decides how much it wants to contribute each year and then specific amounts are contributed to individual employee accounts. The employee's final benefit is not determined in advance, but depends upon the amount of money accumulated in his or her account prior to leaving the company. In a self-directed plan, you, the employee, assume responsibility for whether the money is invested in stocks, bonds, or money market accounts.
- *Money-purchase plan.* The company contributes a fixed percentage of your salary into an individual benefit account. You decide how it should be invested.
- *401(k) plan.* You voluntarily contribute part of your own salary into individual accounts. The tax advantages are explained below. The

company often supplements your contribution by matching a percentage of employee contributions.

- *Combination plan.* Your company may set up more than one plan, say, for example, a pension plan and a profit-sharing plan. The most common combination is a money-purchase plan to which the company makes an annual contribution equal to, say, 10% of salary, combined with a profit-sharing plan to which the company has the option of contributing up to another 15%.
- *Medical benefit plan.* Some companies pay medical benefits to retirees.
- *Employee stock ownership plans (ESOPs).* An ESOP is a retirement program that invests contributions in the company's own stock. The ESOP buys company stock with money obtained from a third-party lender, thus giving the company, in effect, the proceeds of a bank loan. The bank loan is repaid through annual contributions to the SOP.

401(K) PLANS

This plan, also known as a "salary-reduction" plan, is offered by nearly four out of five major firms. Employers like it because it reduces the firm's pension costs by encouraging employees to save more themselves. Employees like it because they can set aside untaxed dollars in a special account and their employer will add to their contribution.

How They Work

1. Your employer sets up the plan with a regulated investment company, a bank trust department, or an insurance company.
2. You set aside part of your salary into a special savings and investment account. You have several options, typically a guaranteed fixed-rate income fund, a stock fund, a bond fund, or short-term money market securities. The

Allocating Pension Money

As more companies offer more investment choices, it becomes more difficult to decide how to allocate your pension money. For 1997, use these guidelines:

- Treasuries or Treasury bond fund   10%
- Corporate bonds or bond fund   20%
- Small-cap stocks or stock fund   15%
- Blue-chip/growth stocks or stock fund   30%
- Foreign stocks/multinationals/fund   10%
- Money market fund or GIC   15%

amount set aside is not counted as income when figuring your federal income tax. For example, if you earn $50,000 and put $5,000 into a 401(k), you report only $45,000 compensation. In addition, earnings that accumulate in the 401(k) plan do so free of tax until withdrawn.

3. Many companies match employee savings, up to 5% or 6%. Most often a firm chips in 25¢ to 50¢ for each $1 the employee saves. Employer contributions can be up to 25% or $30,000, whichever is less.

4. The maximum you can currently contribute is $9,500 for 1996. There is a 10% penalty for withdrawing funds before age 59½. The maximum contribution is adjusted annually for inflation, so check it for the existing tax year.

5. If you change jobs or take out the balance in a lump sum after age 59½, you can take advantage of 5-year averaging, another tax break. (You treat the total payout as though you received it in five annual installments.) Entire tax calculated under 5-year averaging is payable in 1 year.

You can withdraw money without paying a penalty under certain circumstances:

■ When you reach 59½
■ If you separate from service and you are age 55 when the distribution occurs
■ If you are disabled
■ If you need money for medical expenses that are greater than 7.5% of your adjusted gross income

WHAT TO INVEST YOUR PENSION IN

As with any investment portfolio, make it a point to diversify. If your plan does not offer many choices, you can diversify in your IRA or regular brokerage account.

If you are 10 years or more from retirement, a large portion of your 401(k) should be in stocks or stock mutual funds. Over almost any 15-year period, they have outperformed interest-paying investments. So don't shy away from stocks because of the risk involved. (See box of suggested stock funds on page 301.)

As retirement approaches, gradually swing more toward conservative investments, but do not completely abandon stocks. Stocks continue to protect you from inflation. The percentage of your stock portfolio should equal 100 minus your age. (See suggested income funds in Chapter 6.)

CAUTION: Don't overinvest in your company's stock. You've seen what has happened to even the bluest of the blue chips: stocks of IBM, General Motors, and other major companies at various times have taken nosedives. It's a serious mistake to have more than 40% of your assets in your company's stock, because your job is also dependent upon the company.

Many 401(k) plans offer the same mutual funds that are sold to the public, in which case getting information on their performance is not difficult. But some plans put money into funds run by banks, insurers, or private money managers. In this case you must turn to your benefits director for information. Ask for each vehicle's investment objective, largest holdings, fund manager's name, and long-term and year-to-year performance records. If you can't get adequate answers, don't invest in that particular fund.

HINT: There are about 600 private-label mutual funds sold only through insurance companies and pension plans. Some of them have names that sound like those of banks or other funds, yet you will not find their performance figures listed in most financial publications. To track their performance records, read Morningstar's Variable Annuity/Life Performance Report, $195/year, 800–876–5005; or read Barron's.

Taking Money out of Your 401(k)

Regulations that went into effect January 1, 1989, make it tough to take money out of your 401(k). Even if you meet the so-called hardship qualifications, you must have no other sources of income reasonably available, and you will still have to pay the 10% early withdrawal penalty unless the money is going for medical expenses that exceed 7.5% of your adjusted gross income.

Hardship reasons that will satisfy the IRS are:

- Medical expenses for you, your spouse, or dependents
- Down payment on your principal home
- Post-secondary tuition for you, your spouse, or dependents
- Prevention of foreclosure on or eviction from principal residence
- Funeral costs for a member of the family

You will have to pay a 10% early withdrawal penalty unless: the money is going for medical expenses that exceed 7.5% of your adjusted gross income, you have reached 59½, you separate from service and are age 55 when the distribution occurs, you are disabled.

Borrowing from Your 401(k)

Balances up to half the funding but no more than $50,000 can be borrowed under many plans. You pay interest on the loan to your own account, typically a percentage point less than what banks charge on secured personal loans, which, as we go to press, averages just below 11.90% nationally. By law, 50% of your balance must stay in the account as security against the loan. The loan must be repaid at least quarterly and fully within 5 years, unless the money goes for buying a principal residence.

CAUTION: You lose tax-deferred compounding until you repay the loan, so if you own a home, get up to $100,000 from a tax-deductible home equity loan instead.

Whatever amount you borrow usually must be paid back within 5 years, although extensions are usually granted if the loan is helping you purchase your principal residence.

Leaving Your 401(k)

Before you leave your company, find out the exit rules. In general, here's what you'll be faced with:

- If you take the money from your 401(k), you'll owe taxes on everything except any after-tax contributions made.
- If you are under age 55, there is also a 10% penalty on the taxable amount.
- You may be able to leave your money in the company's plan after you leave.
- You may be able to have it transferred to the 401(k) of your new employer.
- You can shift the money into an IRA through an IRA rollover.

CAUTION: If you decide to do this, make certain the money is transferred directly from the 401(k) to the IRA and NOT TO YOU. If you personally take the payout and roll it over into an IRA, 20% of your money will be withheld for taxes by the IRS.

And, take care not to add any other money to the special IRA created for your 401(k) rollover funds. If you do, you lose the right to transfer the funds into a new employer's 401(k) later on should you get a new job.

IF YOU HAVE A 403(b) OR 457 PLAN

Some 17 million Americans are eligible for these two plans that differ slightly from 401(k)s.

- *403(b) Plans.* Designed specifically for employees of colleges, universities, hospitals, research institutes, schools, and other nonprofit organizations. In fact, the country's largest retirement plan—the $114-billion Teachers Insurance and Annuity Association and College Retirement

Equities Fund (TIAA-CREF), is a 403(b). Rules for contributions, rollovers, withdrawals before age 59½, and hardship withdrawals are almost identical to those for a 401(k). The maximum annual contribution is $9,240.

■ *457 Plans.* These are sponsored by state and local governments and nonprofit organizations. They are considerably different from 401(k)s in that matching contributions from the employer are rare and the maximum you can contribute annually is the lesser of $7,500 or 33⅓% of includable compensation. The money you contribute remains the property of the employer until you leave your job and thus is subject to the claims of the employer's creditors.

Rules for taking money out under hardship conditions are tougher than with a 401(k)—buying a house or paying for college do not qualify. Nor can you borrow from a 457. When you leave your job, you cannot make a tax-free rollover of your funds to an IRA. The one advantage: There's no penalty for withdrawing funds if you leave your job before you turn 59½.

Guaranteed Investment Contracts (GICs)

Few people realize that the most popular investment in most 401(k) and company pension funds is a guaranteed investment contract, or GIC. A GIC is a contract between an insurance company and the pension plan that guarantees a specific rate of return on the invested capital over the life of the contract. The life or time period is typically 1 to 5 years. They are the life insurance industry's equivalent of bank CDs, although they are not federally insured. They tend to yield ⅔ of a percentage point more than Treasuries.

How GICs Work

The insurance company invests the cash it raises in a number of conservative investments, such as long-term bonds, public utility bonds, real estate,

and mortgages, and, to some extent, stocks. The rate of return is guaranteed by the issuer, i.e., the insurance company, but no specific pool of funds backs a GIC, and despite the use of the word "guarantee" they are not backed by federal insurance or government guarantees. Instead, the assets of the insurance carrier back the principal contract, so any default of an underlying issue or drop in interest rates is absorbed by the insurance company.

Most employees who select where to invest their retirement funds select GICs but know little about them, because the contracts are sold to the pension plan and not individuals. You should be aware that they also go by other names, such as "guaranteed fund," "stable return fund," or "benefit accumulation contract."

☑ HINT: *If rates rise, as with any fixed-income vehicle, you are locked into a lower yield. If rates fall, you benefit.*

Check the Quality

As a member of a 401(k) plan you are legally entitled to at least annual reports from your plan manager on how your plan is performing. When you receive yours, check for the name of the insurance company that sold your plan its GICs.

Then contact one of the independent rating companies given in the HINT below for a financial evaluation of the soundness of the insurance company. Do not invest in GICs of a parent company ranked below A.

You should also call the state insurance commissioner for the state where the insurer is domiciled to find out if the state requires the bailout of a failed insurer. Many states, such as New York, do require this type of protection.

☑ HINT: *For information on the financial health of an insurance company, call A.M. Best, 800–424-BEST (you will be charged for the call); Weiss Research, 800–289–9222; Moody's, 212–553–0377; or Standard & Poor's, 212–208–8000.*

CAUTION: GICs guarantee only the interest rate; the ability to pay is not guaranteed and depends upon the creditworthiness of the insurance company.

And insurance companies can face problems—during 1990, for example, First Executive Corp. of California ran into financial trouble because it had more than 5% of its assets in junk bonds.

PLANS FOR THE SELF-EMPLOYED: KEOGHS & SEPs

If you run an unincorporated business, either full-time or part-time, you can reduce your income tax by funding a qualified retirement plan with your earnings. The two most popular choices are a Keogh or a simplified employee pension (SEP). The money you contribute grows on a tax-deferred basis and, in fact, is not taxed until you withdraw it.

To qualify for a Keogh plan or a SEP, your earnings must come from your business or from fees for services you provided. The IRS will recognize you as self-employed if the companies that paid you send you Form 1099-MISC, which is used to report non-employee compensation, instead of the Form W–2.

How Much Income You Can Put Away

KEOGH DEFINED-CONTRIBUTION PLANS

Money-purchase: The lesser of 20% or $30,000
Profit-sharing: The lesser of 13.0435% or $30,000

KEOGH DEFINED-BENEFIT PLAN

Amount necessary to provide benefit of no more than $120,000.

SEP

Regular plan: The lesser of 13.0435% or $30,000
Salary-reduction plan: The lesser of 15% or about $9,240.

Keogh Plans

Keoghs work much like IRAs but have several added advantages. You can put away as much as $30,000 a year and, as with an IRA, your Keogh contribution is deductible from income when calculating your taxes. Earnings are not taxed until withdrawn. If you have a Keogh, you may also have an IRA. *NOTE:* Because the maximum compensation limit is $150,000, the maximum contribution has been effectively limited to $22,500, although the IRS still uses the $30,000 figure.

To get your annual deduction, however, you must have the Keogh officially set up by the end of that year, although dollar contributions don't have to be completed until you file your income tax return.

 CAUTION: One disadvantage to keep in mind: If you, as a self-employed person, establish a Keogh for yourself, you must extend its benefits to your employees. In fact, employees must get comparable benefits on a percentage basis: For example, if you put in 15% of earned income for yourself, you must match that 15% for each employee.

There are five types of Keoghs:

- *Defined-contribution plan.* In this type, you decide how much to put in. In other words, the annual contribution is predetermined and what you receive upon retirement is variable, depending on how well you've invested the deposits. You can contribute up to a maximum of 25% of compensation, not to exceed $30,000 a year. This plan may be either a profit-sharing plan or a:
- *Money-purchase plan.* The amount you can contribute is sometimes given as 20% of earned income or as 25% of compensation minus your Keogh contribution, which works out to 20% of net earnings. The limit is the lesser of $30,000 or 20% of an individual's self-employed net earnings. For example, if

you make $100,000, you can contribute $20,000 ($100,000 minus $20,000 contribution = $80,000 compensation; 25% of $80,000 = $20,000). In a money-purchase plan you must heed to this percentage no matter how hard-pressed you may be. In other words, the percentage contribution initially established must continue in the future. Although this plan gives you the most mileage by letting you determine the annual contribution at a fixed rate that is as high as 20% (25% of "net" income), you must stick to this percentage in lean years as well as prosperous ones.

- *Profit-sharing plan.* The most you can contribute and deduct here amounts to the lesser of $30,000 or 13.0435% of your net self-employed earnings. This plan gives you the flexibility to contribute less than the maximum or even nothing at all, from year to year.

- *Combination plan.* To keep your right to make maximum contributions without committing yourself to them every year, you can open two accounts: a profit-sharing and a money-purchase plan. Set your obligatory money-purchase plan at 7% of income. Then, in good years, you can put up to 13% in the profit-sharing plan.

- *Defined-benefit plan.* If you've only recently started to make a high income, you can shelter much of it. The current limit on benefits is the lesser of $120,000, or 100% of the average compensation for the highest 3 consecutive years of self-employment income, in a defined-benefit plan. This plan is best for those with surplus income. For example, if you're earning $55,000 from a sideline business, you may be able to shelter it all from taxes. A defined-benefit plan is designed to pay a predetermined benefit each year after you retire. A pension actuary determines how much you need to deposit each year to provide for your benefits. This amount is adjusted for inflation. This type of Keogh is smart for those over 50, since there are fewer years left in which to put aside retirement funds.

Withdrawals

You must start taking money out of your Keogh or SEP by April 1 of the year after you turn 70½. (You can keep contributing after that date, however.) Lump-sum withdrawals from Keoghs after age 59½ (but not from SEPs) are eligible for 5-year forward averaging, which can reduce your tax bite. If you were born before 1936, you can use the even more advantageous 10-year averaging.

Simplified Employee Pension Plans (SEPs)

There is another type of tax-saving retirement plan for the self-employed that has received far less publicity than either the IRA or Keogh, yet it permits employer contributions greater than $2,000 a year. Called a Simplified Employee Pension plan, it is suitable for small businesses and sole proprietors. Designed to cut red tape, it's considerably easier to set up and administer than a Keogh. Although its initial purpose was to encourage small and new firms to establish retirement programs, self-employeds without Keoghs can use it too. The deadline for setting up a SEP is April 15, just as it is with a regular IRA or the extension date if you file for one. (With a Keogh, the date is December 31.)

When an employer—which can be you as a sole proprietor—establishes a SEP, the employee then opens an IRA at a bank, brokerage firm, mutual fund, or other approved institution. The employer can put up to 15% of an employee's annual earnings in the SEP, to a maximum of $30,000, effectively limited to $22,500 because of the reduction of compensation limit to $150,000. Presumably this limits the owner–employee's contribution to a maximum of $19,565. The contributions made on your behalf are not included in

> ## Moving Your IRA, SEP, or Keogh
>
> As your account grows or as market conditions change, you may want to invest your dollars elsewhere. The IRS has strict rules to follow.
>
> ### A TRANSFER
> - If you arrange for a direct transfer of funds from one custodian to another, there is no limit on the number of switches you can make.
> - Plan on transfers taking at least a month. Banks, brokerage firms, and even some mutual funds are often backlogged with paperwork.
> - Get instructions early on, ideally in writing, from both the resigning and accepting sponsor. Pay fees and notarize necessary papers immediately. Keep track of details as well as deadlines; don't depend on the institution to do this for you.
>
> ### A ROLLOVER
> - You may take personal possession of your money once a year for no more than 60 days.
> - If you hold the money longer than 60 days, you'll be subject to the 10% penalty.

total wages on your W–2, and no deduction for the amount contributed in your behalf is allowed.

NOTE: Contributions for an owner–employee are limited to 13.0435% of contribution to a maximum of $30,000.

Annuities and Your Pension

If you're close to retirement or changing jobs, you're faced with the issue of how to handle the balance in your pension account. There are three basic choices: (1) cashing it in for a lump-sum distribution, (2) taking it in monthly payments, and (3) rolling it over into an IRA. Your accountant should be consulted prior to making a final decision.

To help you have an intelligent conversation with him/her, you should know that:

- *With a lump-sum payment,* you will have control over your investment choices and you may also be able to take advantage of the 5- or 10-year averaging tax formula.

- If you decide on *monthly payments,* your employer uses your pension dollars to buy an annuity. As discussed in the next chapter, annuity returns vary widely. Find out. Of course, you can also buy your own individual annuity.

- With an *IRA rollover,* your money will grow tax-free until withdrawn, starting no later than age 70½.

- If you elect *an annuity,* you can specify how your pension savings will be invested: for fixed income, where the holdings will be bonds and mortgages to provide a set sum each month, or variable income, where the investments are split between bonds and stocks and the returns will vary, depending on how well the portfolio performs.

- If you have *a defined-benefit plan* (see page 308), in which the amount of distribution is guaranteed, you will probably have these four choices:

1. *Straight-life (single-life) annuity.* This is the classic annuity in which you get a fixed monthly payment for the rest of your life, whether you live 5 days, 50 years, or more. Best for: singles with no dependents and people with dependents who are unlikely to outlive them. It offers the highest monthly payment. Some plans also offer a guaranteed minimum of 5 years of payment, which are made to your beneficiary if you die within 5 years of retiring.

2. *Joint and survivor annuity.* You get a fixed monthly payment during your lifetime, and if you predecease your spouse, he or she receives a set percentage of that monthly amount for the rest of his or her life. However, the younger your spouse and the higher his or her percentage, the smaller the current payment you'll receive. Since 1984,

this plan is required by law to make a minimum 50% payment to the surviving spouse of married retirees. A married person can select a different option only if the spouse provides written consent within 90 days of the person's retirement date.

3. *Period-certain annuity.* This annuity makes payments for your entire life, but if you die within a certain number of years, your surviving dependent receives your full monthly pension for the remaining years.

☑ *HINT: Best for: those who need to provide for a current dependent who will eventually become independent. Also ideal for people with spouses who are expected to live only a few years.*

4. *Lump-sum certain.* Although this is not usually offered in defined-benefit plans, you should know its ramifications. Here you relieve your company of its legal obligation to pay you a lifetime monthly retirement benefit. In exchange, it gives you one large lump sum. This single payment is based on the average life expectancy for someone your age and a given interest rate. Of course, the older you are and the higher the rate, the lower the lump sum.

☑ *HINT: Best for: retirees with other resources who are not terribly dependent on their pension, and for those in poor health who will not be receiving annuity payments for very long.*

FINDING WORK AFTER YOU OFFICIALLY RETIRE

By now you may be thinking, "I'll never have enough money to really retire; or perhaps you're the type that doesn't like to spend the day fishing, golfing, watching the sitcoms on TV.

According to a study by the Commonwealth Fund, a New York philanthropic group, about 2 million retired Americans over age 50 want to work, but they're not looking for jobs—they think

employers will say they're too old. Wrong! The study points out that certain employers are clamoring for mature workers. The best jobs are found by word of mouth—so talk to everyone about your interest in working.

- *Banks.* Older workers are excellent as tellers and customer service representatives. The Bank of America, Citibank, and others actively seek older workers.
- *Hotels.* Over one-third of Days Inn's employees are 55 and older. Their absentee rate is only 3%. Other chains, including Marriott and Holiday Inns, are following Days Inn's example.
- *Home health care.* Demand for home health aides is soaring—physical therapists, companions, preparation and delivery of meals.
- *Travel agencies.* Because one in four pleasure trips is taken by someone age 55 or older, the gray-haired employee is a plus in this industry. Take a 6- to 8-week course at a travel agent school. And you get extra perks: reduced hotel rates and airfares.
- *Hardware stores.* Builders Emporium, Hechinger, and Home Depot all rely heavily on older employees who have fix-up experience.
- *Tax return preparers.* The IRS hires people during tax time; so do accounting firms.
- *Temp agencies.* Kelly, Adia, and Volt actively recruit employees over 55. Demand for accountants is strong during the first quarter of the year; engineers can land short-term projects; office assignments are unending.

☑ *HINT: If you work as a temp you can get around the fact that Social Security benefits are cut when annual wages are over $8,250 for someone under age 65 or $11,520 for someone age 65 to 69—when your income reaches that amount, you simply delay going to work until next year.*

You should know that it is unlawful to be turned down for a job because of age, if you're 40 and older. If you feel you've been discriminated against because of age, write:

Equal Employment Opportunity Commission (EEOC)
1801 L Street, NW
Washington, DC 20507

SETTING UP YOUR OWN RETIREMENT BUSINESS

You may also wish to start your own business. Ideally it should be based upon expertise you already have. One of the least expensive routes to take is to become a consultant, working from a home office.

If you like or can do any of the following, you're apt to find plenty of work:

- Appliance, car, computer/printer/fax repair
- House-sitting and housecleaning
- House/apartment repairs
- Lawn and garden care
- Pet care/kennel
- Child and elderly care
- Research and clipping service
- Catering

FOR FURTHER INFORMATION

General Retirement Material

Retirement Planning Kit from:
T. Rowe Price
800–638–5660
Free

Retirement Planning Guide and Retirement Investment Strategies Workbook from:
Fidelity Investment
800–544–8888
Free

Retirement Plans for the Self-Employed
IRS Publication 560
800–TAX–FORM (829–3676)
Free

Pension Checkups

Your Guaranteed Pension
What You Should Know About the Pension Law
Consumer Information Center
Box 100
Pueblo, CO 81002
Free

A Guide to Understanding Your Pension Plan
American Association of Retired Persons
Fulfillment Dept.
601 E Street, NW
Washington, DC 20049
Free

Taxes and Retirement

Tax Information for Older Americans
IRS Publication 554
800–TAX–FORM (829–3676)
Free

Tax Information on Social Security Benefits
IRS Publication 915
800–TAX–FORM (829–3676)
Free

Working after Retirement

How Work Affects Your Social Security Benefits;
Free from your local Social Security office

Working Options—How to Plan Your Job Search, Your Work Life, #D12403, from:
American Association of Retired Persons
AARP Fulfillment Center
601 E Street NW
Washington, DC 20049

Lisa Rogak and David Bangs, Jr., *100 Best Retirement Businesses* (Dover, NH: Upstart Publishing Co., Inc.), $15.95 + $5 shipping; 800–235–8866.

Social Security Benefits

Social Security, Medicare & Pensions by Joseph
Matthews
Nolo Press, 800–992–6656
A guide to rights and benefits for those 55
and older

*The Social Security Book: What Every Woman
Absolutely Needs to Know*
AARP
Fulfillment Center
601 E Street, NW
Washington, DC 20049
Free
This 32-page booklet is full of advice on how
to get all your benefits.

30

Insurance and Annuities

In this chapter we will cover life insurance, annuities, and touch briefly on medical and nursing home insurance.

LIFE INSURANCE

What It Is

A life insurance policy is a contract between the insurance company and you, the policyholder, in which the company agrees to pay a specified amount to the beneficiary you name upon your death, provided you die while the policy is in force. The amount paid to your beneficiary when you die, known as the "proceeds" is not taxed.

To fund this cash payout to your beneficiary, you must pay the company premiums.

LIFE INSURANCE AS A TAX SHELTER

Life insurance is one way you can turn your life into a tax shelter. Certain types of life insurance not only cover your life, providing money for your heirs, but they can also double as an investment and as a tax-deferred way to save.

That's because back in 1986 when Congress passed the Tax Reform Act it preserved the tax-free buildup of savings (called "cash value") inside both insurance policies and annuities, making them one of the few ways left to defer taxes.

(Other ways to defer taxes: IRAs, Keoghs, SEPs, 401(k)s and other types of qualified pension plans.)

Other advantages to this type of tax shelter:

- In a crisis you can cash in your policy and get most of your money back.
- With some policies, you can withdraw part of your cash value.
- With many you can borrow the cash portion at fairly low rates.

☑ *HINT: If you decide to purchase either life insurance or an annuity, deal only with a financially stable company, one rated A or A+ by A.M. Best Co. or Weiss Research, two independent nationwide rating services. (For telephone numbers, see "For Further Information" at the end of this chapter.)*

💣 *CAUTION: This is not idle advice: In 1991, First Executive Corp., a Los Angeles-based holding company that owns four life insurers with $18 billion in assets, failed and was taken over by the state of California.*

But before you even think of speaking to an insurance agent, you need to protect yourself by knowing what products are out there; otherwise you could be a sitting duck—buying and paying for something you don't need.

THE TWO TYPES OF LIFE INSURANCE

There are two basic types of life insurance plans—term and cash (which is also called permanent), as well as a hybrid known as universal life.

Term

Term provides only life insurance—only coverage for your beneficiary. It is also the least expensive type of insurance, giving coverage only for a specified time or "term" as its name indicates, usually 1, 5, 10, or 20 years, or up to age 65. It has absolutely no savings feature. If you die during the term of the policy, then your beneficiary receives the full face value of the policy.

On the other hand, if you die and you have not kept your policy alive, there's no payout at all to your family or other named beneficiary.

There are some variations on term insurance:

- Although your policy must be renewed at the end of every "term," with premiums increasing each time, you can instead purchase what is known as a "level premium" term policy in which your payments are fixed for the entire term, say 5 or 10 years. Your initial premiums will be higher with a "level premium" policy, but they don't rise during the term and could save you money over a longer period of time.
- Although there is no cash buildup—that is, no savings—inside a term policy, you can buy a "convertible" term policy that can be converted, for a higher premium, into permanent insurance, without a medical exam. *NOTE*: Permanent insurance, discussed below, has a savings element.
- You can also purchase "decreasing term" in which the cost of your premiums will remain the same—a tradeoff for the fact that the death payout will decline.

Because it has no savings features and no extras, term is less expensive than permanent or cash insurance, at least when you are young. However, because the premiums rise significantly with age, a rule of thumb has evolved:

☑ *HINT: Buy term if you need insurance for 10 years or less, because the premiums will be lower than those for cash or permanent insurance.*

Like all rules of thumb, it's not perfect, but generally the older you are the less insurance coverage you will need, and so when that point in your life arrives, you can then end your term policy.

The bottom line: Term is best for those who need coverage for a certain term or time period—parents of young children or home buyers, for instance, who do not want to spend as much as permanent insurance costs—who need coverage but are not cash-rich.

☑ *HINT: If you select term, make certain you buy a policy that has a "renewable provision" so you do not have to prove you are insurable at the end of each term. Also get a "convertible" term policy that gives you the option to convert to permanent insurance, if you wish, also without a physical exam. Both will boost your premium slightly, but it's worth it, especially if you should develop health problems.*

Permanent Life (Cash) Insurance

This type of policy is part insurance and part investment. Unlike term, it has a tax-deferred savings feature. It is called permanent because, as long as you pay your premiums, it provides coverage — that is, it does not end at a certain point as does term insurance.

Your premium is based on your age when you purchase the policy; you pay it monhly, annually, or quarterly. During the early years, the premium exceeds the insurance company's estimated cost of insuring your life.

Then after several years the surplus and interest are channeled into a cash or savings-like fund.

You do not select where your cash value is invested—the insurance company does it for you, usually in conservative, fixed-rate, long-term bonds and mortgages, and blue-chip stocks. The insurance company uses part of this cash fund to pay administrative costs and any agent's commission. If you cancel your policy, you receive the cash value back in a lump sum.

Because of the cash reserve feature and the fact you are getting permanent, lifelong coverage, premiums for whole life insurance are higher than those for term.

One advantage permanent has over term is that you can borrow from your cash reserve, typically at low rates, currently in the neighborhood of 5% to 8%, and still be insured. You don't have to pay back the loan, but if you don't the amount due will be subtracted from the death benefit.

Types of Permanent Life Insurance

- Modified life: Premium is relatively low in the first several years but escalates in later years. Designed for those who want whole life but need to pay lower premiums when they are young.
- Limited-payment whole life: Provides protection for the life of the insured, but the premiums are payable over a shorter period of time. This makes the premiums higher than for traditional whole life.
- Single-premium whole life: Provides protection for the insured's life, but the premium is paid in one lump sum when you take out the policy.
- Combination plans: Policies are available that combine term and whole life within one contract. Generally premiums for combination plans do not increase as you get older.
- Universal life: Can pay premiums at any time in virtually any amount subject to certain minimums.
- Variable life: The cash value fluctuates according to the yields earned by the fund in which the premiums are invested.

☑ *HINT: You should consider permanent insurance only if you need to protect your spouse; if you have small children; if your spouse does not work; if you had children late in life; if you need to cover estate taxes; or if you are wealthy.*

Within this broad category of insurance there are three basic types of coverage: whole life, universal, and variable life.

Whole Life

This is the most traditional type of cash value coverage. The premiums remain the same for the entire life of the policy, which has given rise to the name "straight life." The policy remains in place until you die, at which time the company pays a set or predetermined death benefit. You accumulate a cash reserve within the policy, but the insurance company, not you, decides where it is invested—typically in safe, often low-yielding securities.

Universal Life

Universal life, launched in the late 1970s, is popular because of its unique and flexible features:

- The death benefit, i.e., the face value, can be increased or decreased while the policy is in force.
- The premium payments can vary, subject to a basic minimum. You can lect to pay annually, quarterly, or monthly.
- You can use money from your cash buildup value to meet premium payments.
- You can borrow against the cash value at low interest rates.
- You can cash in the policy at any time and receive most of your savings.

With universal life, part of each premium is used to cover sales commission and administrative fees; this is called a load charge. The rest of your premium is invested in various low-risk vehicles. With some universal life policies you can designate how much you want to go for insurance and how much into savings. The company, however, determines the rate of return, which is often tied to an index, such as the Treasury bill rate. Rates generally are guaranteed for 1 year, but when changed will not fall below the minimum stated in the policy—about 3%.

Some companies now offer a variable universal life plan that lets you switch your investments among several mutual funds sponsored by the insurance company.

At the present time, standard universal life policies are paying between 5 and 7%, although the yield is actually less after fees and commissions are deducted.

CAUTION: Sales fees and other costs can eat up as much as 50% of your first year's premium and between 2% and 5% annually thereafter. So plan to hold your policy at least 10 years.

No-load universal life is sold by a handful of companies. The premiums are less because, of course, there are no commissions. No-load, however, does not mean no-cost. There are still administrative costs and other fees.

Low- and No-Load Universal Life Policies

The following companies have low- or no-load universal policies. This list is not an endorsement, but serves merely to start you on your search for information.

- American Life of New York (no-load) (212–224–1600)
- Ameritas Life Insurance (low-load) Houston, Texas (800–552–3553)
- USAA Life (no-load) San Antonio, Texas (800–531–8000)

Variable Life

This hybrid type of cash value insurance is designed basically for investment growth. To accomplish that aim, the cash portion is invested in mutual funds that you, not the company, select from a menu of funds. Most companies offer several stock, bond, and money market funds as well as the opportunity to switch from one to another. Consequently, the death benefit and the cash value vary based on how successfully your cash reserve is invested.

With this type of insurance, you have the potential of a far greater return than with other types of cash value policies, but there is also substantially more risk in that your cash value is uncertain.

CAUTION: If your investment choices turn out to be poor, you could conceivably wind up with less cash value in a variable policy than with other types of insurance.

There are two types of variable: scheduled premium and flexible premium. Premiums in the scheduled premium plans are fixed, both in timing and dollar amount. With a flexible premium plan, you can change both the timing and the amount.

TERM OR PERMANENT?

That is the question. And not such an easy one to answer. An even bigger question is whether to buy life insurance at all. Only you can be the final determinant . . . take care not to let an insurance agent talk you into either, and before you meet with him or her, consider the following points:

- Commissions are higher for permanent life. Agents, aware of this fact, may try to steer you away from term, saying it is really only a temporary solution. However, term almost always provides the most insurance coverage for the price and is initially cheaper.

- However, term premiums become extremely expensive as you get older. If your family is adequately covered by your pension and other sources of income, you could conceivably drop term in your later years.
- Term tends to be best for those who need large amounts of coverage for a given time span: parents of young children, for example, or homeowners with a mortgage.
- If you purchase a term policy, make certain it is convertible and renewable. Then switch to whole life as your age and family circumstances change.

ARE YOU TOO OLD FOR TERM?

It's easy to hang on to term insurance long after it's smart. It provides a lump sum upon death, but has no investment value. Unlike investment-type insurance policies, whose premiums tend to remain about the same, term insurance premiums start low and begin to rise rapidly when you hit midlife. For example, State Farm Insurance charges a nonsmoking male in good health about $350/year for a $100,000 policy at age 50. When he hits 60, the cost is $920 and at age 70, $2,504.

At some point you may be too old for term. Consider giving up term insurance if:

- You have educated your children
- Your spouse is not dependent solely on your income
- Your mortgage is paid off
- You are independently wealthy
- You have a sizable pension

FIVE INSIDER PROTECTIVE TIPS

A recent study by the Federal Trade Commission concluded that (1) life insurance is so complicated that the public is practically unable to evaluate the true costs of various policies; (2) the savings portions of cash value policies that do not pay divi-

dends offer an extremely low rate of return; (3) prices for similar policies vary widely; and (4) the public loses large amounts of money when they surrender cash value policies within the first 10 years.

As a result of these FTC conclusions, the CFA, an independent consumer advocacy group, devised these guidelines for selecting an insurance policy:

1. Don't buy if you don't need it. If you are without dependents you probably don't need life insurance, and don't buy a policy to cover your children's lives.
2. Buy only annual renewable term insurance. If you buy term, purchase only this type.
3. Don't buy credit life insurance. This is useless insurance, marketed to pay off a particular loan, often a mortgage. It is way, way overpriced in most states, although New York is an exception. Instead, purchase a term policy to cover your loan.
4. Don't buy mail-order life insurance unless you compare its price to annual renewable term and find it less expensive.
5. Don't let an agent talk you into dropping an old policy. If it still pays dividends, you may be better off borrowing out any cash value and reinvesting it elsewhere at higher rates.

SHOPPING FOR THE RIGHT COVERAGE

If you decide you need coverage, shop for it as if you were buying a car or household appliance. Compare features and prices. Your employer may already offer you life insurance as part of your benefits package. This is usually the best deal you can get, even if you have to pay some of the premiums. You may also be able to increase your coverage through your company—ASK.

☑ *HINT: If you live in Connecticut, New York, or Massachusetts, look into low-cost term and cash value insurance offered through savings banks.*

Low-load policies, sold directly to the public, have lower fees because there is no sales commission (see box on page 316).

Finally, a good insurance agent should be able to show you several policies; of course, make certain you're working with a reliable person.

You can also turn to:

Insurance Quote Firms

They provide four or five of the lowest-cost policies in their computer files. Most deal only with highly rated companies. Some operate in all states; others are licensed only in certain areas. For further information, contact:

- Insurance Information
      Cobblestone Court #2, Rte. 134
      South Dennis, MA 02660
      800–472–5800
- Insurance Quote
      3200 North Dobson Road, Building C
      Chandler, AZ 85224
      800–972–1104
- SelectQuote
      595 Market Street
      San Francisco, CA 94105
      800–343–1985

SWITCHING YOUR LIFE INSURANCE POLICY

Before changing your policy, take time to compare the death benefit, annual premium, initial rate of cash buildup, and, most importantly, the net yield—what your money earns after all charges and fees.

For help analyzing the rate of return, write:
Consumer Federation of America's Insurance Group
      414 A Street SE
      Washington, DC 20003
      202–547–6426
For $40 for the first proposal and $30 for each

additional one, CFA will analyze the rate of return on your current cash value policy.

Or, contact Insurance Information, Inc., 800–472–5800. They will do a search of term rates for a $50 fee, with a guarantee that they will save you at least $50 over your current policy, or the $50 will be refunded.

HOW MUCH INSURANCE DO YOU REALLY NEED?

When you decide to buy any kind of insurance, don't automatically rely on an agent's advice. They have an inherent desire to sell you as much coverage as possible. Instead, begin with these general guidelines and then adapt them to your particular situation.

Life

The amount of life insurance you should have is related to other sources of coverage (pension, social security, investments, etc.) and of course to how old you are and how many people need your financial help. If you have several small children, you want enough coverage to support them until they are 18 or through college, but if you are single, put your money elsewhere.

☑ *HINT: The rule of thumb is 65% to 75% of the breadwinner's income—but this does not all have to come from life insurance. Factor in other savings, Social Security benefits, pension, property, and investments. Because insurance needs are so individual, even the old formula—which said your coverage should equal five times your total annual take-home pay—no longer holds.*

☑ *HINT: Before you purchase life, assess your assets, liabilities, and income requirements using the easy-to-follow worksheet in* A Consumer's Guide to Life Insurance, *available free from the* American Council of Life Insurance, *202–624–2000.*

Health

You need a major medical policy that covers at least 80% of doctor and hospital bills above your deductible. Avoid a policy that has exclusions for expensive diseases such as cancer.

Disability

Get a policy that replaces 60% to 80% of your net income. Select one that will pay out when you cannot work at your own occupation, not when you cannot do any type of work.

Medigap Insurance

This supplemental policy is designed to fill the gaps between your medical bills and what Medicare covers. Before you buy such a policy, be clear about what Medicare now covers:

- Hospital stays after a deductible and co-payments; check for limitations
- Up to 100 days in a skilled nursing facility; with some co-payments
- Hospice-care benefits for the terminally ill; check for certain limitations
- Home health care
- 80% of approved doctor's charges after a $100 deductible

NOTE: The rulings are continually being revised.

☑ *HINT:* **The Medicare Handbook** *has complete explanations of coverage. Call 800–772–1213 for a free copy, or stop in at your local Social Security Office.*

Whether or not you need a Medigap policy depends on what other coverage you already have. Review your existing policies carefully, and take full advantage of the "free look" provision recommended by the National Association of Insurance Commissioners (NAIC), which gives you 30 days to change your mind after purchasing a policy.

Most states have adopted this provision. Follow these guidelines:

- Buy one comprehensive policy, not several with possible overlapping coverage.
- Buy a policy that is guaranteed renewable for life.
- Find out about exclusions for preexisting conditions and waiting periods.
- Turn down any policy that says it is government-sponsored or guaranteed; it's not.
- Write a check only to the insurance company, not the agent. If your policy does not arrive in 30 days, call your state insurance office.

Auto

Meet these minimums: $100,000 for one injury; $300,000 total per accident, and $50,000 for property damage. If your car has lost at least one-third of its initial value, consider canceling collision. Your state may require you to be covered against uninsured motorists. Ask if discounts are available for safe drivers, nonsmokers, honor-roll students, graduates of driver education courses, and owners of cars with airbags.

Homeowners

Be covered for at least 80% of the replacement cost of your home, not including land value, plus a minimum of $100,000 for liability. Ask if discounts are available for those with smoke alarms, deadbolt locks, and fire extinguishers.

Umbrella Policy

If your assets are above $100,000; you have a swimming pool, throw lots of parties, or race cars; or you are vulnerable to lawsuits, take out an umbrella policy for $1 million.

NURSING HOME INSURANCE

As you (or members of your family) approach your late 60s or 70s, part of retirement planning should deal with long-term care. Depending on your financial situation, you may want to consider this new type of insurance. According to the Health Insurance Association of America, the national average for nursing home costs are $110 a day, or about $40,000 a year. Many senior citizens incorrectly believe that Medicare will pick up the total bill. It does not.

Although an insurance policy may initially seem the logical solution, this particular field is complex and riddled with problems. Read the brochures listed at the end of this chapter before purchasing a policy.

Some 120 companies now sell long-term care coverage, according to the Health Insurance Association of America. And although the National Association of Insurance Commissioners has issued guidelines for policies, insurers are not legally forced to abide by them. This means you must do some serious research before purchasing a long-term care policy. The companies listed in the box below may be a good place to begin gathering information, as are the sources listed at the end of this chapter. Before taking out a policy, discuss the matter with your insurance agent or financial planner and study at least two, preferably three, different plans before making a final decision.

The downside of long-term health care policies is that if you never need this care, the premiums paid are not recoverable. However, a new type of policy, which uses the structure and guarantees of whole life insurance, recently came onto the market. With a single premium of $10,000 or more, you can purchase a death benefit that also doubles as an account for paying for the cost of long-term care. It is available on a single life or joint basis, and if an insured needs nursing home care, the policy will pay up to 2% (4% for both insureds) of the death benefit for these costs.

☑ *HINT: For information, call The Golden Rule Insurance Company in Lawrenceville, Illinois: 800–950–4474.*

Key Nursing Home Insurance Rulings

Many long-term insurance care policies have flaws. To address them, the National Association of Insurance Commissioners adopted new guidelines in 1993 and some states are adopting some of the rules on a voluntary basis. Meanwhile, you should look for policies that already meet the NAIC standards.

One rule requires insurers to let buyers designate up to three people to be notified if a policy is about to lapse because of nonpayment. (The designees would not be liable for payment.) The new rules also require an insurer to reinstate a policy for a period of at least 5 months after termination if the lapse was due to mental or physical impairment of the insured.

NOTE: AMEX Life Assurance, for example, offers a 9-month reinstatement period, but not all insurers do.

Another new rule would bar insurers from describing premiums as "level" unless they are set for life. Many insurers use the term even though they have the right to raise rates.

Three Nursing Home Insurance Providers

CNA
Box 305090
Nashville, TN 37230
800–775–1541

AMEX Life Assurance Co.
Box 2060
San Rafael, CA 94912
800–456–7766

John Hancock
Box 111
Boston, MA 02117
800–543–6415

General Insurance Tips

DO:

- Take the maximum deductible you can afford
- Ask if you qualify for a discount
- Get coverage through a group when possible; it's cheaper

DON'T:

- Buy narrow policies; they frequently duplicate coverage you may have in other policies
- Switch from one policy to another without studying the costs; fees and commissions are high
- Use life insurance only for an investment; your first goal is coverage, then investment

☑ *HINT: For more information, get a copy of the free booklet,* A Shopper's Guide to Long-Term Care Insurance, *by writing to: NAIC, 120 West 12th Street, Suite 1100, Kansas City, MO 64105.*

Tips for Evaluating Nursing Home Insurance Policies

Be certain you select a policy that:

- Covers these three areas: skilled, intermediate, and custodial care
- Does not require being hospitalized before receiving long-term care. Those with Alzheimer's, for instance, are not usually hospitalized before entering a home.
- Covers long-term care in the home
- Guarantees renewability for life
- Covers "organically based mental conditions" (e.g., Alzheimer's)
- Has an inflation clause—you want to have your benefits ride up with the cost of living
- Covers any type of health-care facility, not just a Medicare-certified nursing home

ANNUITIES: AN IMPORTANT ALTERNATIVE FOR TAX-DEFERRED SAVINGS

If you'd like to stockpile tax-deferred savings for your retirement years, then take a close look at an annuity—it's one of the few investment vehicles that survived the 1986 Tax Reform Act relatively unscathed.

Annuities have all the benefits of an IRA, but no $2,000 cap on annual contributions, and with most you can continue to invest on an after-tax basis beyond age 70. The minimums are low, often only $1,000, and with most you can invest as much as you like. However, annuities are complicated, riddled with fees, charges, rules, and restrictions, so do your homework first.

The Basics

An annuity is simply a contract between you and an insurance company in which you pay a sum of money and in return receive regular payments, for life or for a stated period of time. The money grows on a tax-deferred basis until you begin receiving it, typically after age 59½. At that point you can postpone the tax bite by annuitizing, that is, converting your assets into a monthly stream of income. Then, only that portion of the payout representing growth or interest income is taxed.

Annuities are often confused with life insurance. They are not the same. An annuity provides a steady stream of income while you are alive, while a life insurance policy pays off upon your death and benefits your heirs.

There are two key types of annuities: fixed and variable.

Fixed Annuities

With a fixed annuity the premiums are invested in fixed-rate instruments, usually bonds or mortgages. Your money earns a fixed rate of return that is guaranteed for a certain time period, anywhere from 1 to 5 years, occasionally longer. After the guarantee period is over, your assets are automatically rolled over for a new time period at a new rate. The new rate will have moved up or down, depending upon the general direction of interest rates.

☑ HINT: *Fixed annuities are best in times of high interest rates, when you can lock in good yields.*

Most fixed annuities have a "floor" or guaranteed rate below which your return will not drop. This floor, often tied to the T-bill rate or other index, lasts the life of the annuity.

💣 CAUTION: *Watch out for any plan that entices investors with an initially high teaser rate and then reduces it drastically when the guarantee period is up. And make certain when you roll over that the new rate is equal to that being paid to new customers.*

Variable Annuities

A variable annuity, which works rather like a tax-deferred mutual fund, has more pizzazz as well as more risk. Your premiums are invested in stocks, bonds, real estate, money market instruments, and

Questions to Ask an Insurance Company about Annuities

Before purchasing an annuity, read the contract, have your accountant or financial adviser review it as well, and make certain you know the answers to these questions:
- What is the current interest rate?
- What were the rates for the last 3 to 5 years?
- How long is the rate guaranteed for?
- How is the rate determined?
- What are the bond ratings in the portfolio? (Select a policy with bonds rated A or above.)
- How long has the insurance company been selling this particular annuity?
- What is the company's A.M. Best rating? (Again, it should be A or above.)

Variable Annuities with Their Ratings

COMPANY/INSURER (CONTRACT NAME) TELEPHONE	S&P RATING
MFS/Sun Life (Compass 2-NY-VA) 800–343–2829	AAA
ITT/Hartford Life Ins. (The Director-VA) 800–862–6668	AA+
Guardian Ins. & Annuity (Guardian Investor-VA) 800–221–3253	AAA
Keyport Life Ins. Preferred Advisor 800–437–4466	AA-
ITT/Hartford Life Ins. (Putnam Capital Mgr-VA) 800–862–6668	AA+
Nationwide Life Ins. (Best of Amer 4) 800–321–6064	AA+

(As of June 1996)

managed portfolios, thus offering the potential of a higher return than with a fixed annuity. You can direct your assets among portfolios (or have the insurance company do so for you). Your return varies, depending upon the portfolio's performance, hence the name variable annuity.

Ways to Pay for an Annuity

You can select either a single-premium annuity, in which case you make a one-time payment, or an installment or flexible premium, which you pay for in stages over time. You can also purchase an annuity long before you retire, which is known as a deferred annuity, or close to retirement, known as an immediate annuity. An immediate annuity, in which payments begin almost at once, is often used by those who receive a lump-sum payment from a company pension plan. In a deferred payment annuity, no payments are made until at least a year or more after you've paid your premium.

Getting Your Money Back

When you reach 59½ your money is returned to you in one of several ways: in a lump sum, in regular monthly payments, or as lifetime income for you and your spouse. Payments vary depending on the amount you have contributed, your age, the length of time your money has been compounding, and the rate of return on the portfolios. Taxes must be paid on all payouts.

☉ *CAUTION: If you withdraw money before age 59½, there is a 10% IRS tax penalty.*

Here are the basic types of payouts:

- *Lump sum.* Withdrawal of all the annuity's assets upon retirement. You'll have to pay taxes and reinvest your money somewhere else. And, you're tossing aside one of the major advantages of an annuity—a guarantee of lifetime income.
- *Systematic withdrawal.* This keeps most of your money invested; you take a fixed amount at regular intervals—let's say $300 a month, until all assets have been withdrawn. How long this takes depends upon how well your investments performed. This method spreads out your tax payments.
- *Annuitization.* With this option you get payments for life, either fixed or variable amounts, depending upon your annuity. Even if your investments perform poorly, insurance companies generally guarantee to pay you at least 3% to 5% annually.
- *Lifetime Income, Life Income, or Life Only.* You receive payments for life but payments end when you die.
- *Life with Period Certain.* If you die before the preset period of payments has ended, the remaining payments continue on to your named beneficiary.

- *Joint and Survivor or Lifetime Income for Two.* Designed primarily for married couples, upon death of either, payments continue to the survivor. Payments to the survivor can remain the same, or be greater while both of you are alive.

Cashing in Early

Cashing in your annuity early is expensive. As mentioned above, there's a 10% IRS penalty for money taken out before you reach 59½. In addition, most insurance companies let you take out only up to 10% of your assets before they impose a surrender charge. Go beyond that 10% and you'll be slapped with a fee, typically 6% of the withdrawal during the first year, going down to 0% by the seventh year.

☑ *HINT: One plan, The Golden Select from Golden America in Wilmington, Delaware, lets you cash out up to 15% with no fee. Call 800–243–3706.*

The combination of surrender charges and a 10% penalty means an annuity must be viewed as a long-term investment.

☉ *CAUTION: Look for a plan that has a "bailout" clause so you can cash out with no surrender charge if the insurer lowers the renewal rate by more than 1% below the initial rate.*

PICKING OUT THE BEST ANNUITY

Annuities are not federally protected or guaranteed. If you need that type of security, you should purchase a bank CD, which is covered by FDIC insurance, or Treasury securities, which are backed by the full faith and credit of the U.S. government. With an annuity, you must depend on the financial strength of the insurance company. It should have an A or A+ A.M. Best rating. (Most large libraries carry this rating book, or you can ask the insurance company what its rating is.)

It's a good idea to check the ratings periodically, because insurance companies can be downgraded. Remember, Baldwin United, which filed for bankruptcy just over 6 years ago, once had an A+ rating! (The company had approximately $3.4 billion in annuities. The investors did not lose their principal, but a great many did not have access to it for several years.)

☑ **HINT:** *If your company's rating drops, you can make a tax-free exchange into another annuity. Called a 1035 exchange, it is similar to a tax-free IRA rollover.*

Additional protection is provided in all 50 states—but not in Washington, DC. If one insurer goes bankrupt, the state fund assesses charges against other insurance companies in the state to cover investor losses. Call your state insurance commission to determine whether you live in one of these states. Coverage is generally limited to $300,000 per life insurance policy or $100,000 per annuity—Find out!

Checking Up on an Annuity's Performance

Before selecting an annuity, gather information on the parent insurance company, consulting one of the sources listed below in "For Further Information" at the end of this chapter. After selecting an A-rated company, you should then get its performance figures, using one or more of these services:

■ The current rates and performance records for over 180 fixed annuities are tracked by *Comparative Annuity Reports* (P.O. Box 1268, Fair Oaks, CA 95628). A copy of the monthly newsletter, which provides an overview of the top 100 programs, is $10; a full report, $50. Call: 916–487–7863.

■ Returns on variable annuities are tracked by Lipper Analytical Services (New York; 212–393–1300) and then reported weekly in *Barron's*.

■ *Morningstar's Variable Annuity/Life Performance Report,* available at libraries; for subscription information, call: 800–876–5005.

 CAUTION: The tax-deferred advantages of an annuity do not come cheap. Sales charges, surrender fees, management costs, and other expenses can eat away at your return. You can reduce some of these costs by purchasing a no- or low-load annuity.

FOR FURTHER INFORMATION

Life Insurance

Glenn Daily, *The Individual Investor's Guide to Low-Load Insurance Products* (New York: International Publishing Corp., 1991), $22.95.

What You Should Know About Buying Life Insurance
National Insurance Consumer Helpline
800–942–4242
Free

Term Life Insurance—The Simplified Buyers Guide
800–778–2001
For a list of publications, as well as "Rate of Return" data, contact:
Consumer Federation of America's Insurance Group
414 A Street SE
Washington, DC 20003
202–547–6426

Long Term Health Care Insurance

Long Term Care: A Dollars and Sense Guide
United Seniors Health Cooperative
1331 H Street NW
Washington, DC 20005
202–393–6222
$11.50

Consumer's Guide to Long Term Care Insurance
Health Insurance Association of America
555 13th Street NW
Washington, DC 20008
202–824–1600
The Association will also send you a list of private insurers offering long-term health care policies in your state.

Medigap Insurance

Medigap (#D14042)
AARP Fulfillment
601 E Street NW
Washington, DC 20049

Guide to Health Insurance for People with Medicare
Healthcare Financing Administration
Publications Dept.
7500 Security Blvd.
Baltimore, MD 21244

Insurance Company Ratings

The insolvencies of several companies have highlighted the importance of dealing with an A-rated company. To determine a company's financial soundness you can get reports, for a fee, from:

Best's Insurance Reports
A.M. Best Co.
Oldwick, NJ 08858
800–424-BEST
$2.95 per call plus surcharges.

Standard & Poor's Insurance Rating Service
25 Broadway
New York, NY 10004
212–208–8000

Weiss Research, Inc.
4176 Burns Road
Palm Beach Garden, FL 33410
800–289–9222

PART SEVEN

Taxes and Your Investments

The U.S. Congress is continually overhauling the tax code. Unless you know the basic current rulings, you could unwittingly lose hundreds of dollars to the IRS. It is particularly crucial that every financial decision you make be made only after reading the following two chapters and consulting with your tax adviser.

These chapters explain the pertinent parts of the law and how it relates to investments, and also show you how to take advantage of the current rules. Among the topics covered are:

- The tax rates
- Margin loans
- AMT
- Taxes on investments
- Sources of tax-free income
- Last-minute tax savers
- Shifting income to children
- Deductions for investors
- Choosing the right tax preparer
  and perhaps most importantly,
- Year-End Tax Moves for 1997

31

Dealing with Your Taxes

*I*n this chapter we cover four aspects of taxes and investments:

- Key points in the tax act
- Smart end-of-the-year tax moves you can make
- Tax deductions available to investors
- 10 sound sources of tax-free income

KEY POINTS IN THE TAX ACT

By a slim margin—two votes in the House and the vice president's tie-breaking vote in the Senate—the Omnibus Budget Reconciliation Act was passed back in 1993. It remains in effect today. Here are the points you need to know about the Act that relate to your investments and financial planning for 1997–1998. You will also want to read the sections of personal relevance in the next chapter.

At the end of this chapter you will find a checklist of end-of-the-year moves you can make to keep your taxes to a minimum.

INDIVIDUAL TAX RATES

There are now five individual income-tax rates: 15%, 28%, 31%, 36%, and 39.6%. The 36% rate applies to taxable income over:

- $147,700 for married couples filing jointly
- $121,300 for single taxpayers

- $134,500 for heads of household
- $73,800 for married individuals filing separate returns

The 39.6% rate results from a 10% surtax for 1996 imposed on taxable income over $263,750 ($131,875 for married persons filing separate returns.) This surtax effectively raises the top individual tax rate to 39.6%.

ALTERNATIVE MINIMUM TAX

This tax was designed to make certain that Americans with high incomes and high deductions would still have to pay an appropriate amount of income tax. That means, no matter how rich you are, no matter how many loopholes or tax shelters you participate in, if you have sufficiently high income, you still must pay a minimum amount of federal income tax.

The AMT is actually a separate, parallel tax system under which many of the deductions and credits allowed under the regular tax are modified or eliminated.

The AMT calculation begins with your regular taxable income as reported on Form 1040, to which certain AMT "adjustments" and "tax preference items" are added. You must pay the AMT only if it exceeds your regular income tax. The 1993 Act increased the AMT and now a two-tier structure exists: A 26% rate applies to the first

$175,000 of AMT income above an exemption amount; and, on amounts above $175,000, the rate is 28%. The level of income exempt from AMT is:

- $45,000 for married filing a joint return
- $33,750 for unmarried individuals
- $22,500 for married individuals filing separate returns

How do you know if you're subject to AMT? The most common way to incur the AMT is to make investments that take advantage of (or even exploit) tax shelter provisions of the tax code, such as accelerated depreciation methods for real estate or passive losses from passive activities. However, other more common situations may make you subject; for instance, if you:

- Own private activity municipal bonds (direct ownership or in a mutual fund)
- Exercise incentive stock options granted by your employer
- Own real-estate investment trusts (REITs) that use accelerated depreciation on their holdings
- Report substantial itemized deductions for state and local income and property taxes paid or miscellaneous deductions

ALL ABOUT CAPITAL GAINS

You can take some comfort in the fact that the maximum tax rate on net capital gain (i.e., net long-term capital gain less net short-term capital loss) is still at 28%. This is good news because the 28% rate widens the spread between the tax due on ordinary income and the tax on capital gains to as much as 11.6% for individuals in the 39.6% income-tax rate.

Therefore you should consider making investments that will generate income from capital gains, such as individual growth stocks, mutual funds that invest in growth stocks, real estate, and other assets that are likely to appreciate in price. You will not owe tax on the appreciation of these

assets until they are sold, so in effect your taxes are being deferred while your personal wealth is growing.

There's another related tax break you should be aware of: the maximum capital gains tax rate on profits earned by individual investors in certain small businesses, when stocks in these companies are held for 5 years or longer, is just 14%.

HINT: Ask your stockbroker for a list of small business stocks to consider.

To qualify, the stock must have been issued after the date of the enactment of the 1993 Tax Act. The gain eligible for this break is limited to the greater of 10 times the stock's basis, or $10 million of gain. The issuing corporation must meet a $50 million or less "aggregate gross assets" test to qualify.

CAUTION: Don't let the appeal of this low, 14% capital gains rate, sometimes expressed as a 50% capital gains exclusion ($28\% \div 2 = 14\%$), make you oblivious to the high risks involved in investing in start-up businesses. Experts estimate that nearly half of the nation's new businesses fail within the first few years of operation.

TAXATION OF SOCIAL SECURITY BENEFITS

As dreadful as it may seem, very often Social Security recipients must pay income tax. The maximum percentage of Social Security benefits subject to tax is 85% for "provisional income" in excess of:

- $34,000 for unmarried persons
- $44,000 for married persons filing jointly
- $0 for married persons filing separately

A 50% exclusion rule applies when their income is between:

- $25,000 and $34,000 for singles
- $32,000 and $44,000 for married couples filing jointly

"Provisional income" is essentially adjusted gross income plus all tax-exempt interest income and one-half of Social Security or Railroad Retirement Tier 1 benefits.

- *Salary deferral.* Under the new rulings, up to $9,240 can be contributed on a pretax basis to 401(k) plans and SEPs that offer a salary-deferral feature.
- *Retirement limits.* The maximum compensation level to be considered in making qualified retirement plan contributions is $150,000.
- *Estimated taxes.* These rules have been somewhat simplified. You can avoid penalties by basing your estimated tax payments on:
- 90% of the current year's tax
- 100% of the prior year's tax if adjusted gross income is $150,000 or less ($75,000 for married filing separately), or
- 110% of the prior year's tax if adjusted gross income is over $150,000 ($75,000 for married filing separately)

YEAR END TAX MOVES TO MAKE FOR 1997

Despite New Year's resolutions and other good intentions, most of us still wind up putting off organizing our tax return materials until the first week

How to Cut Taxes on Stock Gains

- Hold onto a stock for a year so it will be subject to capital gains treatment. Stocks held less than a year and sold at a profit are taxed as regular income, often at a higher rate than the capital gains rate.
- Sell at a gain and then find other stocks to sell at a loss. Up to $3,000 of excess losses is deductible against ordinary income annually and the remainder can be carried forward for use in the future.
- Sell appreciated shares in this order: the shares you paid the most for first so your capital gain will be smaller.

in April. But if you're really serious about reducing your tax bite, you should start at the end of the year. In fact, there are a number of fairly easy steps you can take to improve your tax picture. So, come November and December, review this list carefully and also check the clip and save calendar pages at the end of this book for other tax savings ideas.

Take a Stock Loss

If you own stock in a corporation whose long-term outlook is favorable but your shares have

1996 Tax Rates and Brackets

	SINGLE TAXPAYERS	MARRIED TAXPAYERS FILING JOINTLY
15 %	$0–24,000	$0–40,100
28%	$24,001–58,150	$40,101–96,900
31%	$58,151–121,300	$96,901–147,700
36%	$121,301–263,750	$147,701–263,750
39.6%	over $263,750	over $263,750
	HEADS OF HOUSEHOLD	**MARRIED FILING SEPARATELY**
15%	$0–32,150	$0–20,050
28%	$32,151–83,050	$20,051–48,450
31%	$83,051–134,500	$48,451–73,850
36%	$134,501–263,750	$73,851–131,875
39.6%	over $263,750	over $131,875

dropped in price, consider selling at a loss for tax purposes, but without giving up your position entirely. Here's how: Buy more stock now at the lower price and sell your original holdings 31 days later.

NOTE: You must wait the 31 days in order to avoid the "wash sale rule," which prevents loss deductions on the sale and repurchase transactions made within 31 days. (You can buy back the stock after 31 days.)

CAUTION: *The risk involved, of course, is that the stock could continue to fall in price.*

The wash-sale rule applies only to losses. A wash sale occurs when an investor sells a security at a loss and purchases securities that are substantially identical to those sold within a 61-day period, beginning 30 days before the sale and ending 30 days after the sale. You cannot get a loss deduction under those circumstances.

HINT: *You can avoid a wash sale by purchasing an equivalent amount of the same security, holding both lots for 31 days and then selling the original security at a loss. Or, you can invest in securities that are not substantially identical, such as those of another company in the same industry.*

Lock in Profits

If you own a stock that has gone way up in price and you think it's near its peak, you can lock in your profit but not pay taxes this year by "selling short against the box" (see page 252 for details on how to do this).

Use Bond Swaps

Another year-end strategy that can help save on taxes is a bond swap. Under certain circumstances it pays to sell a bond worth less than its initial cost in order to set up a tax loss, and then reinvest that same money in a similar bond. By converting a

paper loss into an actual loss, you can offset any taxable gains you earn in other, more profitable investments. In the process of swapping, you may also be able to boost your bond yield.

CAUTION: *Don't wait until the last days of the year. It may take your broker several days or even a week to locate an appropriate bond for swapping.*

Bond swaps involve two steps:

1. Selling bonds that have declined in price
2. Replacing these bonds with similar (but not substantially identical) bonds

By immediately purchasing similar bonds for approximately the same price as the ones you sold, you restore your market position and your income.

Tax Breaks

Even if you didn't make a killing in the market this year, if you took some investment profits, a bond swap can help reduce your tax bite. Here's how it works:

If you own bonds purchased when interest rates were lower, they are probably worth less in the secondary market today. If you sell them, you can take a loss that can be used, dollar for dollar, to offset any capital gains. If you have no long- or short-term capital gains, the loss can be used to offset up to $3,000 of taxable income, on a dollar-for-dollar basis. If your loss is greater than that, it can be carried over into the next year.

In order for the IRS to recognize a loss for tax purposes, you must buy bonds of a different issuer or with a substantially different maturity date or coupon.

State Income Tax

A bond swap is also useful if you move from a state with no income tax to one that has an income tax. Buy municipal bonds issued by the new state that are not subject to state taxes.

Swapping Costs

Unlike stocks and most other securities, where commissions are noted separately from the purchase or sale price, municipal bonds have their commission included in the price of the bond. Commissions range from $5 to $20 per $1,000-face-value bond, which means that a swap involving $50,000 worth of bonds could entail a commission somewhere between $500 and $2,000.

Shift Income to Children

Any unearned (or investment) income of a child aged 14 or less is taxed to the child, but at the parent's rate when this income exceeds $1,300 per year. The first $650, however, is not taxed at all and the next $650 is taxed at the child's rate. Then when the child is over 14, all income is taxed at his or her rate, which is presumably a lower rate than the parent's.

If you wish to give money to a child under 14 but you don't want it to be taxed at your rate, you are limited to a handful of choices: tax-free municipal bonds and bond funds, low-dividend-paying stocks, and EE Savings Bonds. In the latter case, interest is not taxed until the bonds mature or are cashed in. Then, when your child turns 14, you can change the portfolio mix to higher-yielding taxable investments and periodically cash in the bonds, because the income will be taxed at the child's rate.

☑ *HINT: You can still make a tax-free loan of up to $10,000 ($20,000 per couple) to each member of your family per year. It is also possible to loan up to $100,000 if tax avoidance is not one of the principal purposes. Imputed interest is then limited to the borrower's investment income. This is a popular way for parents to help children buy property.*

If you are involved in income shifting, keep careful records indicating that you have separate accounts for your children.

Shift Other Income

You have until December 31 to shift money to reduce your taxable income for the following year and, at the same time, avoid the gift tax. The law allows you to give anyone up to $10,000 a year ($20,000 for a married couple) tax-free. Although there is no gift tax on the transfer, there will be income tax on any earnings the gift generates. (Gifts are not a deduction from income.) *NOTE:* The recipient of the income must have immediate access to the funds transferred. Check with your accountant for exceptions.

It may be advantageous for you, if you are in a high tax bracket, to transfer appreciated property or income-producing property to your children ages 14 and older to take advantage of their lower tax bracket. A child claimed as a dependent can earn up to $650 of investment income without incurring a tax liability.

Set Up a Keogh Plan

If you have income from your business or freelance work, set up a Keogh retirement account at a bank, brokerage firm, or mutual fund. The dollar amount you contribute is tax-deductible directly from your taxable income, and the principal grows on a tax-deferred basis. Unlike an IRA, which can be established up until April 15th, a Keogh must be opened before the end of the year to qualify for a tax deduction. However, you do not need to make a dollar contribution until you actually file your tax return—on April 15th or extension dates. *NOTE:* You can have a Keogh even if you have a 401(k) or other retirement plan if you have self-employment income.

Contribute Early to Your IRA

Fund your IRA, SEP, or Keogh plan as soon as possible. Tax is deferred on the income earned from the day you contribute it up until you withdraw it. If you delay making your contribution until the last minute, you are giving up months of compounded tax-deferred income.

Fund Your 401(k) Plan to the Max

The contribution is not counted in your income.

Add Up Your Deductions

Take time to determine if you have spent enough on tax-deductible items to qualify for write-offs: (1) Miscellaneous deductible expenses must be greater than 2% of your adjusted gross income in order to be itemized. (2) Unreimbursed medical expenses must add up to more than 7.5% of your AGI to be deductible. If you are still far away from these minimums (known as "floors"), try to postpone these expenses until next year when you may have enough to deduct them. On the other hand, if you are near these thresholds, consider making additional expenditures that will lift you above the floor.

Establish a Charitable Remainder Trust

Feeling philanthropic? Consider a remainder trust in which you give appreciated securities, such as stocks, bonds, or property, to a charity in exchange for a qualified annuity. You can retain the income from the property for life or for a set number of years as well as get a tax deduction. The deduction amount is determined by IRS tables. Another advantage: This type of annuity is not subject to premature withdrawal penalties or to the new pension excise tax. Because rulings are complex, work out this particular tax move with a knowledgeable accountant.

Defer Capital Gains Tax on Property

Until Congress decides otherwise, you can still swap one piece of investment property for another, deferring capital gains tax until the property is actually sold for cash. The pieces exchanged must be comparable and used for business or investment purposes. (That means your home does not qualify.) If the two properties are not of equal value, and cash or an additional piece of property has been included in the swap to make up the difference, both are taxable.

File Correct Estimates

Figure out if you withheld enough during 1996, because if you underestimated you will be subject to hefty penalties. Or, if you overestimate, you then lose the earning power of that money. So to be safe, estimate 100% or 110% of last year's tax liability, or 90% of what you owe this year. Check with your accountant. It's not too late to get your employer to withhold more.

Pre-Pay Property and State and Local Income Taxes By December 31st

If you pay 100% of your state tax liability by December 31st, you can deduct it on this year's federal income tax return.

Make Charitable Contributions with Appreciated Investments

If you are thinking about making a charitable contribution, do so by December 31st and use appreciated investments, such as stocks, bonds, antiques, paintings, etc., that you've held at least 1 year. The advantage of doing so: You can deduct the full market value of the gift and your capital gains tax will be forgiven.

Defer Income

If it is to your advantage to reduce this year's income, delay receipt of self-employment income or year-end bonuses; or delay billing customers so payments are made to you after December 31st. This is a smart move if you expect to be in the same tax bracket from one year to the next because you'll have use of money you otherwise would have paid in taxes. And, if you drop to a lower bracket in 1998, you'll actually reduce the amount you must pay in taxes. Lastly, this move may also keep you from inching up into a higher bracket, something to be avoided at all costs. You can also defer income by transferring money out of investments paying current interest—money market funds, savings accounts, etc.—into Treasury bills or bank CDs that mature within a year or less and that won't pay interest until 1998.

Don't miss these four tax deductions:

1. *State and local taxes.* Except for sales tax, these taxes continue to be fully deductible.

Tax Deductions for Investors

You can deduct the amount over 2% of adjusted gross income for certain expenses incurred to produce and collect income and to manage or maintain property held to make income. Among these deductible-as-itemized deductions are:

- Subscriptions to investment publications
- Cost of books on investing and taxes
- Clerical expenses
- Insurance on investment property
- Safe deposit box rent or home safe, if used to hold securities
- Fees for accounting or investment advice and for legal advice if related to tax or investment matters; includes: cost of tax preparation, cost of tax preparation software, and fees paid to file electronically
- Expenses directly related to tax (but not investment) seminars, including transportation
- Travel expenses to visit your broker, your safe deposit box, and your tax accountant or lawyer for investment or income-tax purposes
- Computers. The cost of a computer used in managing your investments is sometimes deductible. (If you use your computer for business over 50% of the time, you can depreciate it over 5 years.)
- IRA, SEP, or Keogh account custodial fees if paid by a separate check
- Appraisal fees for charitable deductions

2. *Investment expenses.* These expenses, including tax planning, the cost of this book, tax-return preparation, investment publications, and other miscellaneous items are deductible, but only for amounts in excess of 2% of your adjusted gross income.

3. *Charitable deductions.* Get a receipt and remember, you must itemize on your tax return in order to deduct your charitable contributions.

4. *Medical expenses.* You can deduct unreimbursed medical expenses, but only if they exceed 7.5% of your adjusted gross income.

TEN SOURCES OF TAX-FREE INCOME

By carefully planning your investment strategies, you can easily increase the amount of tax-free or tax-deferred money you receive every year. Here are 10 sure-fire ways to do just that:

1. *IRAs.* You don't pay any tax on the earnings inside an individual retirement account until you withdraw the money. Interest earned is reinvested and thus continues to compound on a tax-deferred basis.

2. *Life insurance.* As with an IRA, the interest income earned inside a life insurance investment is tax-deferred until you cash in the policy. Proceeds paid to your beneficiary upon your death are free of income taxes.

3. *Disability insurance.* If you paid your own disability insurance premium, the benefits from accident or health insurance policies are tax-free. (However, if your employer paid the premiums, any income you receive from the policy is taxable.)

4. *Municipal bonds.* Interest earned on muni bonds is free from federal income tax. You may have to pay a state income tax if you purchased bonds issued by a state other than your state of residence—for example, if you live in Minnesota and purchase a bond for New York State, you may have to pay Minnesota tax on the income.

◉ CAUTION: *Some municipal bonds are subject to the AMT; check with your accountant.*

5. *Real estate.* Some real-estate investments yield depreciation deductions over the life of the property.

6. *Savings plans, annuities, and pension plans.* Any investment made with after-tax income is tax-free when you withdraw it or when you receive a payment that represents the return of your investment. Or, to state it another way, the principal is tax-free, although the income earned on the principal is generally taxed.

7. *Social Security.* Disability, retirement, or surviving spouse income may be tax-free, depending on your other income. Taxpayers with income greater than $32,000 ($25,000 for singles) have to pay tax on up to half of their Social Security income

   A maximum of half of this income is tax-free. *NOTE:* Under the 1993 law, up to 85% is taxable if couples have income over $44,000 and for individuals, over $34,000.

8. *Tax-deferred annuities.* (Sometimes called single-premium deferred annuities.) The money invested with an insurance company in this type of annuity and the interest earned is deferred until you cash in and receive that income.

9. *Tax-free money market funds.* Mutual funds whose portfolios consist of municipal notes offer tax-free income.

10. *U.S. Treasury issues.* Treasury bonds, notes, bills, and savings bonds are exempt from tax at the state and local levels no matter what state you live in. However, you must pay federal income tax on these investments.

FOR FUTHER INFORMATION

These publications are available free of charge at your local IRS office or by calling 800–TAX–FORM (829–3676).

523, *Selling Your Home*

527, *Residential Rental Property*

530, *Tax Information for First-Time Home Owners*

550, *Investment Income and Expenses*

554, *Tax Information for Older Americans*

560, *Retirement Plans for the Self-Employed*

564, *Mutual Fund Distributions*

575, *Pension and Annuity Income*

590, *Individual Retirement Arrangements (IRAs)*

915, *Social Security Benefits*

   For a complete list of all IRS brochures, ask for Publication 910, *Guide to Free Tax Services.*

32

Alphabetical Directory of Your Investments and Their Tax Status

*T*he information that follows is general in scope and intended as an introductory explanation of how taxes affect your investments. To begin with, keep in mind that the IRS recognizes three types of income:

- *Portfolio or investment income:* dividends and interest
- *Active income:* salaries, wages, fees, commissions, and personal services
- *Passive income:* from businesses you don't actively manage and from rental property.

NOTE: Passive losses cannot offset active or portfolio income; they can only offset passive income.

ANNUITIES

- Interest earned can accumulate tax-free until withdrawn. When it is withdrawn, only the interest earned is taxed, not your initial investment.
- If you withdraw money prior to age 59½, there is a 10% tax penalty. With qualified employer-sponsored annuities, there is no 10% penalty if you immediately transfer the money to a qualified annuity with another company.
- For other rulings, check your policy.

ANTIQUES, ART, COINS, GEMS, STAMPS AND OTHER COLLECTIBLES

Profits made upon sale are subject to federal income tax at the regular rate of 15%, 28%, 31%, 36%, or 39.6%. If the asset is held long-term, the maximum capital gains tax is only 28%. The purchase price, of course, is subject to state and local sales tax.

BONDS (AGENCY ISSUES)

- Interest income is subject to federal tax.
- Interest income on some agency issues is exempt from state and local taxes. Ask your broker or accountant.

BONDS (CORPORATE)

- Interest income is subject to federal, state, and local taxes.
- Gains made when bonds are sold are taxed at regular rates with a maximum rate of 28% if held long-term.
- Losses can be used to offset other net gains you may have, plus up to $3,000 of wages, salary, and other "ordinary" income.

BONDS (DISCOUNT)

Gains on disposition of bonds purchased at a discount from face value (also called "market discount") is ordinary interest income to the extent of accrued market discount. You can elect to include market discount in your gross income for years to which it is attributable. This included discount is then added to the original cost.

BONDS (MUNICIPAL)

- Interest earned on most munis is exempt from federal income tax and from state and local taxes for residents of the state where the bonds are issued.
- Most states tax out-of-state bonds.
- Bonds issued by the Commonwealth of Puerto Rico and the District of Columbia are exempt from taxes in all states.
- Interest earned on certain "private activity" bonds that were issued after August 7, 1986, is regarded as a tax preference item and is included in the calculation of the alternative minimum tax. If you are not subject to the AMT, you will not pay taxes on these particular bonds.
- Some municipal bonds are subject to federal tax but remain exempt at the state and local levels. These include bonds to help finance convention centers.
- Illinois, Iowa, Kansas, Oklahoma, and Wisconsin tax any municipal bonds issued in their state.
- Interest earned on fully tax-exempt bonds can be taxed when held by a retiree receiving Social Security. If you are retired and if your adjusted gross income plus half your Social Security plus all your tax-exempt interest income is over $25,000 for a single return or $32,000 for a joint return, interest earned on the tax-exempt bond is effectively taxable.

BONDS (PREMIUM)

If you purchase a bond at a premium, you can only use any amortizable premium to offset your investment income. In other words, you cannot use the premium as a deduction against other types of income. The amortized premium is subtracted directly from the interest you earn on the bond, rather than deducted as a separate expense subject to the investment interest expense limitations.

NOTE: Amortization of premium is not required for taxable bonds, but is required for tax-exempt bonds to prevent deduction of the premium as a loss upon sale or maturity.

BONDS (ZERO)

- Taxes must be paid on the so-called imputed interest that accrues annually, even though, of course, no interest is actually paid to the bondholder.
- Because you must pay tax as though you had received interest, zeros are well suited for IRAs, SEPs, and Keoghs where interest income is deferred from taxes until withdrawn, and for children over age 14 who are no longer subject to the kiddie tax.
- Zero coupon municipals are usually exempt from federal taxes and from state and local taxes when bonds are issued in the investor's state.
- Zero coupon Treasuries are exempt from state and local taxes.

CERTIFICATES OF DEPOSIT (CDS)

- Any interest earned is subject to federal, state, and local taxes.
- Interest is taxed in the year it is available for withdrawal without substantial penalty, whether or not you withdraw it.

NOTE: Interest can be deferred on a CD with a term of 1 year or less. For example, if you invest in a CD before July 1, the entire amount of interest is paid 6 months later and taxable in the year paid out. However, if you invest in a CD after June

30th, only the interest actually paid out or made available for withdrawal without penalty is taxable in the year issued. The balance is taxable in the year of maturity—the next year. The interest, however, must specifically be deferred to the year of maturity by the terms of the CD.

CHILDREN'S INVESTMENT INCOME

Unearned income of children under the age of 14 is taxed at the marginal rate of their parents, as if the parents had received the income, rather than at the child's lower rate. This income falls under special rules: The child can use $650 of his/her standard deduction to offset unearned income. The next $650 of unearned income is taxed at the child's tax bracket. Unearned income over $1,300 is taxed as if it were included in the parent's return. *NOTE:* Form 8615 is required for this purpose.

See also Savings Bonds.

COMMERCIAL PAPER

- Any interest earned is subject to federal, state, and local taxes.
- *Exception:* Commercial paper issued by state and local governments is usually, but not always, exempt from federal as well as state and local taxes.

COMMODITIES AND FUTURES CONTRACTS

- Profits and losses are taxed at 60/40 rates, 60% long-term and 40% short-term, and reported at the end of the year. Losses may be carried back to the 3 prior years to offset any regulated futures contract gains (but not other income) from those years.
- Profits become taxable at the end of the year, even if you have not closed out your position. The IRS, in effect, will tax you on your paper profits.
- In some cases, you can deduct paper losses, even of positions that are still open. These

rules may apply to contract subject to the mark-to-the-market rule. Check with your accountant.

CONVERTIBLE STOCKS AND BONDS

There is no gain or loss when you convert a bond into a stock or preferred stock into common stock of the same corporation, if the conversion privilege was granted by the bond or preferred stock certificate.

CREDIT UNION ACCOUNTS

Even though depositors are actually shareholders of the credit union and the money earned is known as a dividend, your earnings are regarded as interest and subject to federal, state, and local taxes.

DIVIDEND INCOME

Dividends and interest you receive are reported to the IRS by the company on various versions of Form 1099: dividends on Form 1099-DIV; investment interest on Form 1099-INT; and original issue discount on Form 1099-OID. You will receive copies from the company and must report the amounts shown on your tax return. The IRS will use its forms to check the income you report.

- *Cash dividends.* If you receive dividends from Exxon, Dial Corp., General Electric, or any other corporation, the amount is reported by the company directly to the IRS. You, in turn, receive Form 1099-DIV from each corporation stating precisely how much you received for the year.
- *Stock dividends.* If you own common stock in a company and receive additional shares as a dividend, it is usually not taxable. Exceptions: If you can take either stock or cash or if it is a taxable class of stock. The company will notify you if it is taxable.

- *Dividend reinvestment plans.* If you sign up to have your dividends automatically reinvested in the company's stock and if you pay fair market value for these shares, the full cash dividend is taxable. The IRS maintains that because you could have had cash but elected not to, you will be taxed the same year you receive the dividend.
- *Return of capital.* Corporations sometimes give a return of capital distribution. If this is the case, it will be so designated on your 1099 slip. Most return of capital is not taxed; however, your basis of stock must be reduced by whatever the amount is. If a return of capital exceeds basis, the excess is taxable and the basis is reduced to zero.
- *Insurance dividends.* Any dividends you receive on veterans' insurance are not taxed, and dividends received from regular life insurance are generally not taxed. However, if you are in doubt, check with your accountant or insurance company.
- *Other types of dividends.* Money market mutual funds pay what is called a dividend and you should include it as such on your tax return.

EQUIPMENT LEASING PARTNERSHIPS

- Income is subject to federal, state, and local taxes.
- Because it is a partnership, items of income and deductions are passed through and are thus subject to the at-risk rules. Interest expense may be used to the extent of interest, dividend, and other net investment income.
- Deductions generated by the partnership will help shelter some of the income derived from lease payments. The key deduction is depreciation for the cost of equipment. If the partnership borrows to pay for the equipment, interest may also be deductible.
- When deductions are greater than income, resulting losses cannot be used to shelter your

salary, wages, interest, and dividend income or profits made in the stock market. The partnership losses can only be used to shelter income from other passive activities.
- If the partnership is publicly traded, income and loss require special treatment; check with your accountant.

FOREIGN INCOME

- If you have a foreign bank account or a foreign securities account, you must indicate this on Form TDF 90–22–1, if the value of the account at any time during the year was over $10,000.
- Foreign dividends may be subject to a withholding tax by the payer. You must also include the gross amount of the dividend on your U.S. income tax return, but you can deduct or receive a tax credit for the taxes paid to the foreign country.

GINNIE MAE, FREDDIE MAC, AND FANNIE MAE CERTIFICATES

- The interest portion of the monthly payments you receive is subject to federal, state, and local taxes.
- Profits from the sale of any mortgage-backed security are taxed as well.

GOLD AND SILVER

- If you buy gold or silver coins or bullion, most states impose state and local sales tax. In many cases you can sidestep this tax if you do not take delivery but leave the metal with the dealer and hold certificates instead.
- Profits from the sale of gold and silver are taxed at regular rates.
- Dividends from precious metals stocks and mutual funds are taxed at regular rates.
- Profits from futures and options: *See* Commodities.

■ An exchange of gold for gold coins or silver for silver coins usually qualifies as a tax-free exchange of like-kind property, for example, if you exchange Mexican pesos for Austrian coronas. However, exchanging silver for gold is not tax-free nor is exchanging collectible coins for bullion coins (i.e., exchanging coins whose value is based on rarity for coins whose value is based on the weight of metal).

HISTORIC REHABILITATION OF PROPERTY

■ The credit is 20% or 10% of qualified rehabilitation expenditures, depending on the building—10% for nonresidential buildings put into service prior to 1936 and 20% for all certified historic structures.

■ This tax credit is not a deduction: It provides a dollar-for-dollar reduction in the actual amount of income you owe.

■ This tax credit is applicable only to depreciable buildings—those used in a trade or business or held for the production of income, such as a commercial or residential rental property. A nondepreciable building may qualify as a certified historic structure if it is the subject of charitable contributions for conservation purposes.

   NOTE: The amount of the credit reduces the cost basis of the building for depreciation, thus reducing the amount of the deduction for depreciation.

■ A certified historic structure is any structure that is listed individually in the National Register of Historic Places, maintained by the Department of the Interior, or located in a registered historic district and certified by the Secretary of the Interior.

INVESTMENT CLUBS

■ If the club is considered a corporation, it reports and pays a tax on the club's earnings.

As an individual member, you report dividend distributions made to you by the club.

■ If the club is a partnership, the club files a partnership return that includes the tax consequences of its transactions and the shares of each member. The club does not pay a tax. You and the other members pay tax on your shares of dividends, interest, capital gains, and any other income earned by the club. You report your share as if you earned it personally.

NOTE: You may deduct as itemized deductions your share of the club's investment expenses, subject, of course, to the 2% AGI floor.

IRAS, SEPS, AND KEOGHS

See Chapter 29.

LAND

■ Any profits made when land is sold are taxable.

■ Rental income is subject to regular tax, although it may be partially offset by deductible expenses, property costs, and mortgage interest payments.

■ Land does not qualify for depreciation deductions.

■ Check with your accountant regarding the status of income-producing land vis-à-vis the current passive loss rules, as these rules are complex.

LIFE INSURANCE

■ When you purchase whole life insurance, part of your premium goes toward the purchase of insurance; the rest is an investment. The earned income on the investment portion builds up tax-deferred until you cash in the policy. If you die before you cash in, and the benefits are paid to your children or spouse, this buildup becomes completely tax-free, not just tax-deferred.

💣 *CAUTION: Single-premium annuities or life insurance policies, where you pay only one premium, no longer qualify for this tax-deferred treatment.*

- If you purchased a single-premium contract after June 30, 1988, and you borrow from the contract, the loan is treated as a distribution of income on which you must pay regular income tax, and in most cases, a 10% penalty on the taxable portion. (There's no 10% penalty if distributions are made after you reach 59½, or if you are disabled, or if the distribution is part of a life annuity.)
- The same rules apply to a partial surrender of the contract, a cash withdrawal, or the distribution of dividends that are not retained by the insurance company as a premium if received on or after the annuity starting date. If received before the annuity starting date, special rules apply. Check with your accountant.
- These rules generally apply also to any life insurance plans ("modified endowment contract") that you fund with fewer than seven annual payments of equal size.
- You must also pay income tax on distributions from single-premium contracts purchased on or after June 21, 1988, to the extent that the distributions exceed your contract investment. Distributions of less than $25,000 made after your death to cover your burial are not taxed.

LOW INCOME HOUSING

- Tax credits are available to those who buy, build, or rehabilitate low-income housing.
- The credits can offset regular income tax, subject to certain limits, but are phased out if your adjusted gross income is over $200,000. If your income exceeds $250,000, there are no credits. This income limitation does not apply to property placed in service after 1989.

- The annual credit is adjusted monthly for projects placed in service after 1987.

💣 *CAUTION: This can be a high-risk investment and should be examined by a professional. Avoid projects of inexperienced developers.*

MARGIN LOANS

- Interest you pay on money borrowed from your broker for investment purposes is deductible only to the extent that it is offset by investment income (from dividends, interest income, and royalties). For example, if you want to deduct $1,500 worth of interest on your margin loan, you must report at least $1,500 of investment income to the IRS.
- You must use the money borrowed to make an investment in order to deduct the interest. Keep careful records to document this fact.

💣 *CAUTION: If you borrow to buy municipal bonds or any other tax-exempt investment, interest (or margin) expense is not deductible.*

MONEY MARKET DEPOSIT ACCOUNTS

Interest earned is subject to federal, state, and local income taxes.

MONEY MARKET MUTUAL FUNDS

- Interest is subject to federal, state, and local income taxes.
- With tax-exempt money market funds, interest is exempt from federal tax and possibly from state and local tax if the fund buys tax-exempt securities in the investor's state.

MUTUAL FUNDS

- Dividend income and capital gains distributions are usually taxed at federal, state, and local levels, except for tax-free or municipal bond funds.

- Income from municipal bond funds is exempt from federal tax and is also exempt from state and local taxes if the securities in the portfolio are issued in the taxpayer's state.
- Mutual fund companies must send investors a year-end statement documenting all distributions and their tax states: Form 1099-DIV and/or Form 1099-B.
- A dividend declared in December by a mutual fund is taxable in the year declared (i.e., that year) if it is paid before February 1st of the following year.
- All capital gains distributions are considered long-term.
- When you sell your fund shares at a profit, the gain is taxed at your rate: 15%, 28%, 31%, 36%, or 39.6%, with the maximum rate of 28% for shares held long-term.
- Losses can be used to offset gains and up to $3,000 in salary, wages, and ordinary income.
- Most funds make their largest distribution at the end of the year; call the toll-free number to verify. Avoid buying fund shares just before major distributions. The fund's NAV or share price immediately drops by the amount of the distribution. By waiting for a fund to go ex-dividend, you can buy in at a lower price and avoid paying some taxes.

☑ HINT: *Consult IRS Publication 564,* Mutual Fund Distributions.

OPTIONS

Rulings are extremely complicated. Consult your accountant.

POINTS

See Real Estate.

PUBLIC LIMITED PARTNERSHIPS

- If a limited partnership trades publicly, income earned is not passive but is consid-

ered portfolio income, and current losses cannot be used to offset income from other public partnerships.
- Because a partnership is a pass-through entity, reportable income may be greater than actual cash distributions.

REAL ESTATE

- *Acquisition debt.* This is money used to purchase or substantially improve a residence. You may deduct all mortgage interest costs on up to a total of $1 million in acquisition debt for primary and secondary residences purchased or refinanced after October 13, 1987.
- *Home equity debt.* This is money you borrow using your home as collateral. You may deduct interest on home equity loans up to $100,000. The proceeds of this loan can be used for any purpose.
- *Points.* Lenders charge "points" above the regular interest rate to increase their fees and get around state limits. The rules on points seem to be continually changing; check with your accountant and/or lender and in all cases, always pay points with a separate check. Currently, you may deduct points if the payment is solely for your use of the money and not for services performed by the lender, which are separately charged. Points associated with refinancing a loan are not fully deductible in the year paid, but must be deducted ratably over the life of the loan.
- *Gain on the sale of your principal residence* may be deferred if the proceeds are invested in another principal residence that you buy or build within a time period beginning 2 years before the date of the sale and ending 2 years after the sale date. To defer the full amount of the gain, the cost of the new residence must be at least equal to the adjusted sales price of the old residence.

■ *The $125,000 capital gains exclusion.* If you are age 55 or older you are allowed a one-time exclusion of capital gain up to $125,000 ($62,500 in the case of a married individual filing a separate return). To qualify, you must be 55 before the date of the sale and must have owned and occupied the residence for 3 out of the previous 5 years. Married individuals are entitled to only one lifetime exclusion per couple.

NOTE: If you are physically or mentally incapable of self-care during the 5-year period and you lived in a residential care facility, the 3-out-of–5-year rule is altered: In this case, if you lived in your principal residence for 1 out of the 5 years before it was sold, you may still claim the exclusion.

REAL ESTATE INVESTMENT TRUSTS

■ Most dividends you receive are taxable, even those that represent capital gains distributions from the sale of property held by the REIT.

■ There is an exception: Dividends paid out of the shareholder's equity and treated as a return of your original investment are not taxed.

■ When you sell your REIT stock, any gains made are taxed at the regular rates; at 28% for long-term holdings.

■ Losses from a REIT stock can be used to offset gains, plus up to $3,000 of salary, wages, and ordinary income.

REAL-ESTATE LIMITED PARTNERSHIPS

Check with your accountant.

RENTAL REAL ESTATE

■ Rental income and profits when property is sold are taxed at regular rates.

■ Much rental income can be sheltered by deductions and expenses, such as mortgage interest, property taxes, depreciation, maintenance, repairs, and travel to and from the property. You can write off the cost of residential rental properties over a period of 27½ years, or 39 years for commercial property placed in service after May 13, 1993.

■ Up to $25,000 per year in tax losses can be used to offset your wages, salary, and other income, provided that your adjusted gross income is under $100,000. This $25,000 cap is reduced 50 cents for each dollar by which your adjusted gross income exceeds $100,000. By the time your income hits $150,000, the cap is at zero. You must, however, pass the active participation test to receive this break.

■ If your adjusted gross income is over $150,000, you can use tax deductions only up to the amount of rental income received that year. If there are any excess losses, they can be carried over until such time as you have excess income. These losses, however, can be used to offset income from other passive losses.

■ To claim losses, you cannot have less than 10% ownership in rental property.

SAVINGS ACCOUNTS

Interest earned is taxable even though you do not present your passbook to have the interest entered.

NOTE: Dividends on deposits or accounts in some institutions are reported as interest income: mutual savings banks, cooperative banks, domestic building and loan associations, and savings and loan associations.

SAVINGS BONDS

■ Interest is exempt from state and local taxes.

■ Federal income tax can be deferred on Series EE bonds until the bonds are redeemed or mature, or you can report the income annually as it accrues.

- If you roll over your Series EEs into Series HHs, federal tax on the accrued EE series interest can again be deferred until the HH bonds either mature or are redeemed.

- Interest on Series HH bonds is taxed each year. HH bonds pay interest semi-annually and must be reported in the year in which it is paid.

- If you elect to pay the federal tax due each year on EE bonds, you pay on the annual increase in redemption value of the bond. However, once you begin paying, you must continue doing so for the bonds you presently own plus any new ones you buy.

- Children's accounts. If a child is under age 14, the first $650 of investment income is not taxed. The next $650 is taxed at the child's rate. Any investment income over $1,300 per year is taxed at the parent's rate, which is presumably higher. Starting at age 14, the income is taxed at the child's lower rate. By timing bonds to come due after the child turns 14, you can save on taxes.

- EE Savings Bonds purchased after January 1, 1990, by a bondholder at least 24 years old, and used to pay college tuition for the bondholder, his or her spouse, or dependent children, are free from federal income tax provided the bondholder falls within certain income guidelines at the time the bonds are used to meet college costs. Since these income guidelines are inflation-indexed, check with your accountant or bank to see if you qualify for this tax break. *NOTE:* This break is not available if you are married and filing separately.

STOCK INDEX OPTIONS AND FUTURES

- Profits are generally taxed the same as commodities: 60/40 rule for gains and losses and a 3-year carryback for losses.

- Profits on futures and options become taxable at the end of the year, even if you have not closed out your position. In effect, the IRS will tax you on your paper profits.

- In some cases, you can deduct paper losses, even of positions still open. Check with our accountant.

STOCK RIGHTS

- If you sell your rights, the profit is taxed.
- If you exercise the rights, you will eventually pay tax, but not until you sell the new stock.
- If you receive stock rights (as opposed to purchasing them in the market) and then let them expire, you cannot claim a deduction for the loss.
- If you purchase rights in the market and let them expire as worthless, you can deduct the loss.

STOCK SPLITS

Stock splits are not dividends; they do not represent a distribution of surplus funds as do stock dividends. Therefore, stock splits are not taxable.

STOCKS

- Profits from the sale of stocks and dividends earned are taxed at regular rates, and at a maximum of 28% on long-term gains.
- Losses from sale may be used to offset any gains you have plus up to $3,000 of salary, wages, and other income.
- Interest on margin loans may be claimed as an itemized deduction. See Margin Loans.
- Gain on the exchange of common stock for other common stock (or preferred for other preferred) of the same company is not taxable. An exchange of preferred stock for common, or common for preferred, in the same company, is generally not tax-free, unless the exchange is part of a tax-free recapitalization.
- Worthless stock. You may deduct as a capital loss the cost basis of securities that became worthless during the year.

NOTE: It is deductible only in the year it became completely worthless. To support this deduction, you must show that it had some value the previous year and that it became worthless in the current year—showing that the company went bankrupt, stopped doing business, or is insolvent. Check with both your stockbroker and accountant.

STOCKS (FOREIGN)

- If you have foreign tax withheld from dividends of a foreign stock, you are entitled to a tax credit. To determine how much, divide your taxable foreign income by your total income, then multiply by the amount of U.S. tax. Example: You receive taxable foreign income of $5,000 and your total taxable income is $100,000. Divide $5,000 by $100,000 and multiply that by $28,000 (the estimated U.S. tax on $100,000). The maximum tax credit you could claim in this situation would be $1,400.

  Your credit would be the lesser of the amount withheld and the maximum credit calculated. Any amount disallowed in the current year may be carried forward.
- You can also list foreign taxes as an itemized deduction on line 7 of Schedule A, but you must choose one method or the other.

TREASURY BILLS

- Interest income is subject to federal tax, but not state and local taxes.
- The income earned is subject to taxation the year in which the T-bill matures or in which you sell it.
- With T-bills, the dollar difference between the original price and the amount you receive when you redeem the bill is regarded as the interest income.
- You can defer income from one year to the next by purchasing a T-bill that matures in the next calendar year.

TREASURY BONDS AND NOTES

- Interest is subject to federal tax, but free from state and local tax.
- Any profit made when T-bonds or notes are sold is taxed, with 28% being the maximum or long-term gains.
- Losses from sales can be used to offset any capital gains you have plus up to $3,000 of salary, wages, and other ordinary income.

VACATION HOMES

- If a home is solely for personal use, you can deduct mortgage interest and real-estate taxes, as you can with your principal residence. Mortgage interest is not deductible on third or fourth homes unless they are rental properties.
- You can deduct mortgage interest on loans up to the amount of your original purchase price plus improvements. Special rules apply to refinancing.
- If a home is used for pleasure and for rental purposes, your tax liability varies. If you rent it out for no more than 14 days per year, the rental income is not taxed. You do not even have to report it.
- If you use your home more than 14 days a year or 10% of the number of days rented, whichever is greater, your property qualifies as a second home. Mortgage interest and property taxes become deductible. Rental expenses can be deducted, but only up to the amount of rental income. However, if you have excess expenses, they can be carried forward.
- If you use your house 14 days or less a year or 10% of the number of days the house is rented out, whichever is greater, the house then becomes rental property, not property used as a home, in which case see Rental Real Estate. Although expenses, including mortgage interest and real-estate taxes, must be apportioned according to actual days of per-

sonal use and rental use, rental expenses in excess of gross rents might be used to offset other income.

   NOTE: This is a fairly complicated situation; check with your accountant.

- When you sell a vacation home, profits are taxed at regular rates. They do not qualify for the preferential treatment that your primary residence does. With a primary residence, taxes on the profits of a sale can be deferred as long as the profits are reinvested in a principal residence that costs at least as much as the sale price of the previous home. And, the special one-time $125,000 tax exemption of gains from the sale of a primary residence available to those age 55 or older is not granted in the case of the sale of a vacation home. Any loss from the sale of a vacation home is not deductible.

WARRANTS

- Profits made when warrants are sold are taxed at regular rates.
- If your warrant expires worthless, the cost of the warrant can be used to offset capital gains plus up to $3,000 of salary, wages, and other ordinary income.
- If the warrant is converted to stock shares, no taxes are due on the transaction. Cost of the warrant, if any, is added to the cost of the stock purchased.

PART EIGHT

Your Customized Portfolio

You've now read over 300 pages about investing, provided you started at the beginning and plowed straight through to this point. Yet all reading and no action won't make you rich.

It's now time to actually pick specific investments that will work for you. In this special section you will find suggestions for what to buy—and why. Although I've divided the sample portfolios according to age and lifestyle, you should really read all of them and then mix and match according to your goals and income level.

If you're worried or nervous about making a move, I urge you to resist the temptation to merely sit on the sidelines. It may appear that doing so is safe, that earning 3% in a bank savings account means you're fully protected; but it's not smart because bank savings accounts barely equal the rate of inflation.

So, calm your investment jitters by heeding the advice of our great cowboy-humorist, Will Rogers:

"Even if you're on the right track, you'll get run over if you just sit there."

Individual sample portfolios follow for those of you who are:

- Just out of school
- Newly married or living with a significant other
- Raising a family
- Empty nesters
- Retired or just about to be
- Have, or are starting, a business

Plus, you'll find solid information on how to protect your portfolio during tough economic times.

33

What to Invest in . . .

*O*ften we spend more time thinking about what car or personal computer to purchase than we do about what to buy for our portfolio. We pore over consumer magazines, talk to friends, test drive endless models, read the ads. Well, you need to spend the same time and enthusiasm researching and finding the right stocks, bonds, and mutual funds.

The investments you should own, like a car, depend upon lots of personal factors—your age, your income, your family situation, your feeling about risk, and what other securities you already own.

Bear in mind that as you grow older your investment needs will change, along with your income and your fiscal responsibility to others. That means, of course, that you must review your portfolio on a regular basis. Your financial goals, too, will change over time. So stocks, bonds, or mutual funds that do not meet your changing goals should be sold and replaced with ones that do.

The following sample portfolios contain ideas that are geared toward the various stages of your life. Many of them, particularly the stocks, should be held at least a year or more; the bonds should be held until maturity or their call date.

I've divided the portfolios into six lifestyle categories:

- Just out of college
- Newly married or coupled

- Having/raising a family
- Empty nester
- Approaching or in retirement
- Owning your own business

☑ *HINT: Read all the portfolios even though you may fall into only one category; the investment recommendations are indeed transferable.*

SECTION 1

IF YOU'RE JUST OUT OF SCHOOL

This is a time for new beginnings—you're on your own, perhaps for the first time in your life, and although your income is probably modest, it's likely to increase quite quickly. Your responsibilities are limited, too—perhaps only to you and your cat—so you can focus your financial attention on building up a solid cash base.

Follow these 10 steps to achieve financial independence:

Step 1. Set financial goals (see suggestions on the next page).

Step 2. Open a bank account. If you're new in the area, use the same institution your company uses.

Step 3. Get a credit card and pay all bills on time to establish a good credit rating.

Step 4. Open a money market mutual fund. A list of high-yielding funds appears on page 22.

Portfolio for the Recent Grad

INVESTMENT	AMOUNT	DETAILS
Money market account	3-months' living expenses	Add cash gifts, bonuses, freelance income
Certificates of deposit	Due in 3 and 6 months	Roll over only if rates go up
Company you work for	100 shares	Use employee stock purchase plan
or. . .		
Boston Chicken, Staples, The Gap Anheuser-Busch	100 shares	Monitor carefully and reinvest the dividends
Electric utility stock	100 shares	Reinvest all dividends
IRA	$1,000	Stock, CDs, Treasuries

Step 5. Sign up for the automatic payroll savings plan where you work and have 3 to 5% of your paycheck transferred into your money market fund.

Step 6. After you've accumulated cash enough to cover three months' worth of living expenses, you're ready to invest. (Aim to keep housing costs to 30% or less of your take-home pay.) Begin by purchasing several short-term bank CDs with different maturities, either at a local bank for convenience or with an out-of-the-area bank that has higher rates. Check the financial section of the newspaper for a list of the nation's top-yielding bank CDs.

Step 7. Purchase 100 shares of stock in the company you work for, if you have faith in its future, using the company's stock purchase plan, if one exists. You'll avoid a broker's commission and you may be able to buy shares at a discount.

Alternative: Buy 100 shares of a company whose product you use or like, or one that is within the industry where you work. *Suggestions:* Coca-Cola, IBM, Kellogg, Border's, Oxford Health Plans, Boston Chicken, Staples, Carnival (Cruise) Corp., Procter & Gamble, The Gap. Use this as a learning experience, as your introduction to the stock market.

Step 8. Study the financial condition of your local electric or gas utility company. Read the annual report and check the rating in *Value Line.* If Value Line rates the utility a #1 or #2 in safety,

add 100 shares to your portfolio. If your particular utility is not a smart investment, select one of those listed in Chapter 15.

Step 9. After a year or two you can afford to take greater risks with your money. Consider the sample portfolios that follow and incorporate those choices that you find appealing, keeping in mind that it is essential to diversify—between types of investments as well as types of industries.

Step 10. Open an IRA so that 50 years from now you'll have a sizable retirement fund. Put in $2,000 all at once or in small monthly or quarterly payments.

☑ *HINT: Look into a "Smart Loan" Account, which enables college grads to consolidate their student loans into a single loan. Monthly payments in the first four years (when interest is typically higher) are cut by nearly 40%. Students can stretch repayment terms from 10 to 15 years, although you should realize that doing so may boost the total cost of the loan. For more info: Sallie Mae, 800–524–9100.*

SECTION 2

IF YOU'RE NEWLY MARRIED OR LIVING WITH A SIGNIFICANT OTHER

Now that you've added someone else to your life, review and revise your financial goals. Decide

Portfolio for the Newly Coupled

INVESTMENT	AMOUNT	DETAILS
Company you work for	100 shares	Use employee stock purchase plan
Electric utility stock	100 shares	Reinvest all dividends
U.S. Treasury notes or zeros	$5,000 minimum	Hold until maturity
Municipal bond fund or UIT	$1,000 minimum	Hold until maturity
Neuberger & Berman Partners Fund	$1,000 minimum	Call 800-367-0700
IRA	$2,000/year	Stocks, CDs, Treasuries
Coca-Cola	100 shares	Price: $50
		Yield: 1.0%
Sysco Corp.	100 shares	Price: $32
		Yield: 0.5%
Montgomery Street Income Securities	200 shares	Price: $17
		Yield: 7.9%
Intel	100 shares	Price: $80
		Yield: 0.3%

(Prices as of October 1996)

whether to invest jointly or separately, or do a little of both, keeping in mind that your dual incomes give you doubled investing and saving power.

Step 1. Review the portfolio for the recent grad. All suggestions there should be part of your financial life, too.

Step 2. Focus on the housing issue. You've probably been renting, but now together, by putting aside 3 to 5% of both your salaries, you can save a sizable amount for a down payment on a house or co-op. Begin by purchasing Treasury notes with two- to four-year maturities. Put the semiannual monthly interest payments in your money market fund. Don't spend them! This cash plus your CDs can be combined with your Treasuries when the latter come due, making a nice downpayment.

Step 3. Because you have many years left for building assets, the securities you own should be primarily for growth, not income. Check the list of suggested stocks in the box on this page. Regard them as long-term holdings, but monitor earnings trends twice a year and be prepared to sell.

Step 4. If you are in the 28% tax bracket, put 10 to 15% of your investments in municipal bonds, or in a tax-free unit investment trust.

Step 5. If you and your spouse spend weekends going to flea markets, auctions, or garage sales, consider becoming a knowledgeable collector. Every year, the "Investor's Almanac" section of this book contains ideas for building a savvy collection. Check your library for previous editions.

- COCA-COLA (KO). This leading soft-drink company has huge international earnings.
- SYSCO CORP. (SYY). This company distributes food to restaurants, hospitals, hotel chains, and educational institutions and is recession-resistant.
- MONTGOMERY STREET INCOME SECURITIES, INC. (MTS). These shares, with their impressive 7.9% yield, are suitable for conservative investors regardless of age.
- INTEL CORP. (INTC). A leading manufacturer of integrated circuits; benefits from the ongoing explosion in sales of PCs and notebooks.

SECTION 3

IF YOU HAVE A FAMILY

Nothing is ever quite as exciting or as expensive as raising a family. Once you know you're going to have kids:

Step 1. Check your firm's maternity leave policy as well as your health coverage. Make certain you're adequately insured.

Step 2. Put all or part of the mother-to-be's salary in a money market fund and practice living on one salary, which is likely to be the case when the baby arrives, at least at the beginning.

Step 3. Then put half of your money market fund into a series of bank CDs, staggered to come due at various dates—for example, one every two months after the baby is born. This will provide an influx of much-needed cash.

Step 4. Start a college education fund before the baby leaves the hospital nursery. You'll need to get your child a Social Security number for savings bonds and other financial presents. (See Chapter 27 for the tax implications of holding securities in a child's name versus your name.)

Step 5. At this stage, your portfolio should be both income- and growth-oriented—income to cover the extra costs of the family, and growth to make it possible to move into a larger home, add on to your present one, save for college tuition, and finance any expansion of your family. See the suggested stocks and bonds listed below.

- DREYFUS STRATEGIC INCOME (DSI). This closed-end bond fund states its investment objective to be income and conservation of capital. It invests largely in government bonds—U.S. and foreign. Hold for its 8.7% yield.

- HERSHEY FOODS CORP. (HSY). This premier candy and chocolate maker has moved into the popular field of low-fat foods; it also owns and operates a highly successful resort and convention center in Hershey, PA.

Portfolio for Those with a Family

INVESTMENT	AMOUNT	DETAILS
Company you work for	100 shares	Use employee stock purchase plan
Electric utility company	100 shares	Reinvest all dividends
Municipal bond fund or UIT	$1,000 minimum	Hold until maturity
Neuberger & Berman Partners Fund	$1,000 minimum	Sell when you've reached your profit point (800-367-0770)
U.S. Treasury notes or Treasuries	$5,000 minimum	Time to mature when you buy a house or pay tuition bills
IRA	$2,000/year	Stocks, CDs, Treasuries
Dreyfus Strategic Income	200 shares	Price: $9 Yield: 8.0%
Hershey Foods	100 shares	Price: $87 Yield: 8.0%
Abbott Labs	100 shares	Price: $45 Yield: 2.1%
Wrigley (Wm)	100 shares	Price: $54 Yield: 1.3%

(Prices as of October 1996)

- ABBOTT LABS (ABT). Leading maker of health-care products, drugs, and diagnostic tests, including Similac, Sucaryl, and Murine. Recent development of a drug to help AIDs patients boosting visibility and per share price.
- WRIGLEY (WWY). The world's largest manufacturer of chewing gum has no debt and no pension liability, but does have a steady growth rate. The family owns about 27% of the stock. Conservatively managed, it offers a continually popular, cheap, disposable product. Moves into foreign markets have been very successful.

SECTION 4

IF YOU'RE AN EMPTY NESTER

These are the peak payout years of your life, whether you are married or single, with or without children. You can now afford to focus on maintaining a comfortable lifestyle, caring for your own aging parents, or fueling an expanding business or career.

During this period, your income is probably the highest it will ever be, which enables you to make more aggressive investments than when you were footing the bill for college education or just getting started. Look at purchasing a second home or rental property, additional growth-oriented stocks and even some high yielding bonds. Be sure to fund your 401(k), Keogh, and/or IRA to the fullest and take time to set up a tax-deferred annuity.

- TOOTSIE ROLL INDUSTRIES (TR). This low-debt, well-run company, like Wrigley (see left) offers a continually popular, relatively low-priced disposable product.
- MEDITRUST (MT). One of the nation's largest health-care REITs, it owns well over 100 properties, including nursing homes. Management continually raises the dividend.

SECTION 5

IF YOU'RE RETIRED OR ABOUT TO BE

Now the emphasis should be primarily on income plus some growth. Safety is critical—so add top rated bonds, blue chip stocks, and high yielding securities to your portfolio. But keep in mind that the average American lives twenty years after retirement, so you will want some growth stocks as well.

In addition to the specific suggestions given in the box below, take a look at the list of high yield bonds on pages 129 and 130 and add to your portfolio if you can assume the extra risk.

Portfolio for the Empty Nester

INVESTMENT	AMOUNT	DETAILS
Tootsie Roll Ind.	100 shares	Price: $35 Yield: 0.8%
Meditrust	200 shares	Price: $34 Yield: 8.1%
AT&T 7s, 2005, 101	5 to 10 bonds	Reinvest income for retirement or to buy real estate
Duke Power 7s, 2005, 99	5 to 10 bonds	Reinvest income
Government zeros	5 to 10 bonds	Pick maturity date to match your retirement

(Prices as of October 1996)

Also, load up on zero coupon Treasuries, timed to come due at various stages of your retirement years. You can read about zero coupon bonds in Chapter 12.

- TREASURY BONDS. As we go to press U.S. Treasury bonds due in 30 years are yielding close to 6.85%.
- HIGH-YIELD BONDS. If you are willing to assume some risk, put a portion of your portfolio in these bonds. See Chapter 1 for a recommended list.
- ZERO COUPON BONDS. Use to mature at or soon after your retirement. Remember, zeros do not pay annual interest, but you must pay annual taxes on the imputed income.
- GINNIE MAES OR FANNIE MAES. These pay high yields through monthly checks. Most pass-throughs are fully paid out in less than 15 years, so time your certificates to coincide with your retirement.

- SCHERING-PLOUGH (SGP). Worldwide manufacturer of prescription and over-the-counter drugs; plus biotech products.
- GENESIS HEALTH VENTURES. These bonds are issued by a company specializing in long-term health care and rehab facilities.
- ROYAL DUTCH PETROLEUM (RD). Major player in the international energy field with solid management.

SECTION 6

IF YOU HAVE OR ARE STARTING A SMALL BUSINESS

More and more Americans in 1997 are working at home, freelancing, or running their own incorporated businesses. This has become increasingly common with the advancement of computers, E-mail, and the art of communications. And it has been exacerbated by the general downsizing of corporate America.

Portfolio for Those Retired or About to Be

INVESTMENT	AMOUNT	DETAILS
American Electric Power	100 shares	Price: $42 Yield: 5.8%
AT&T 7 1/8s, due 2002, 99	5 to 10 bonds	Use interest income or reinvest; non-callable
1838 Bond Debenture Fund	150 shares	Price: $20 Yield: 7.9%
Schering-Plough	100 shares	Price: $56 Yield: 2.4%
Genesis Health Venture, 9 3/4s, 2005	5 to 10 bonds	Use interest income or reinvest
Long Island Lighting pfd C	100 shares	Price: $92 Yield: 8.3%
Royal Dutch Petroleum	50 shares	Price: $149 Yield: 3.7%
U.S. Treasury notes	$1,000 minimum	Hold until maturity
Ginnie Mae certificate	$25,000	Hold until maturity

(Prices as of August 1996)

Before either starting a business or expanding an existing one, I suggest you follow these steps:

Step 1. Address personal financial needs. No one should be in business for themselves if there's any question about where money for the kids' education or the next mortgage payment is coming from. I have increased my rule of thumb for business owners: You should have enough money set aside in a money market fund or in CDs to cover at least one year's worth of personal living expenses. (Under ordinary circumstances, that time frame is three to six months, depending upon the economy and one's age.)

Step 2. Take care of medical and disability insurance. Under federal law you have the right to continue medical coverage for 18 months after leaving a job, at your expense. Because premiums for a group policy are lower than for individual coverage, it is wise to arrange to continue coverage by paying the premiums yourself.

Bear in mind that various benefits—health, life, and disability insurance plus paid vacations—make up almost one-third of most employee's annual salaries. So for you to just stay even, your business must generate more than only your salary.

Portfolio for Business Owners

INVESTMENT	DETAILS
Money market account	9-months' living expenses
and/or	
Certificates of deposit	9-months' living expenses
IRA	$2,000/year
IRA SEP or Keogh Plan	See Chapter 29
Dreyfus Strategic Govt. Inc. (DSI)	Price: $9
	Yield: 8.0%
American Electric Power (NYSE:AEP)	Price: $42
	Yield: 5.8%
AT&T 7 1/8s due 2002, selling at 100	Solid utility bond
Long Island Lighting pfd C	Price: $92
	Yield: 8.3%
1838 Bond Debenture Fund	Price: $20
	Yield: 7.9%
Webb (Del) 9 3/4s due 2003 selling at 99	Hold for income
Safeway Stores 10s due 2001 selling at 110	Hold for income
Meditrust (NYSE: MT)	Price: $34
	Yield: 8.1%
Montgomery Street Income Securities (NYSE: MTS)	Price: $17
	Yield: 8.0%
Weingarten Realty (NYSE: WRI)	Price: $44
	Yield: 6.3%
Putnam Premier Income Trust* (NYSE: PPT)	Price: $7
	Yield: 8.7%

*Some of this yield is actually a return of capital. Portfolio has some high risk holdings.

(Prices as of October 1996)

Step 3. Order these free IRS publications by calling 800–829–3676:

334 *Tax Guide for Small Business*
584 *Starting a Business & Keeping Records*
587 *Business Use of Your Home*
917 *Business Use of a Car*

Step 4. Gear your portfolio to provide income to weather any downturns in your business and to provide collateral should you wish to use part of it to obtain a loan.

There are two ways to finance a business: debt financing consists of loans that the business must repay; equity financing consists of money given to a business in exchange for an ownership in the business, commonly done through selling shares of stock. In most cases, a balance between the two is ideal. Too much debt necessitates a huge cash flow to pay the interest on the loans and too much equity means you've given away control and perhaps too much ownership.

The suggestions in the box on page 357 are aimed primarily at providing income as well as securities that can be used as collateral for a loan, or sold if you should need an infusion of capital. Please note: The first three securities suggestions should be taken care of before attempting the rest.

PROTECTING YOUR PORTFOLIO DURING HARD TIMES

The ongoing downsizing of corporate America, with layoffs in virtually every industry, has affected all of us. Some of us have lost jobs, others have had to face frozen salaries or a cutback in hours. It's not surprising that many Americans are worried about their finances. Whether or not you're dealing with a personal cash flow struggle, it's smart to know what steps to take to protect your family's money during tough times, now or in the future. Here are some tips for doing just that.

BUILD UP YOUR NEST EGG

If you're worried about your job security, start now to built up enough cash to see you through the hard times. Without fail you should set aside a monthly sum immediately after paying the rent or mortgage. Don't wait to save until later. Useful steps:

1. *Use automatic savings plans.* Sign up for payroll deduction programs. Arrange for automatic transfers from checking to savings or to a money market fund. Purchase EE Savings Bonds this way as well.
2. *Pay cash for purchases.* Avoid using credit cards, which often lead to overspending, debt buildup, and high interest rate charges.
3. *Reduce and/or pay off the loan with the highest interest rate.* Make this a priority. Then tackle the next highest rate loan.
4. *Fund your 401(k) or other retirement plan.* If you're ever really pressed, you can borrow from these plans and pay back yourself rather than a bank. You'll also be reducing your tax bite.
5. *Increase tax withholding.* Get a bigger tax refund by boosting salary withholding. Then save the refund.

 CAUTION: *Do this only if you will save the money; otherwise you're just giving Uncle Sam an interest-free loan because no interest is paid on your refund check.*

OTHER STRATEGIES

If you are experiencing financial difficulties:

1. *Go on a crash budget.*
2. *Review avenues of income and fixed and variable expenses.*
3. *Trim variables, such as entertaining, travel, eating out, dry cleaning.*
4. *Stop outrageous spending.*
5. *Talk to the children.* If you or your spouse has lost a job or has a sudden cutback in

For Any Portfolio: The Top-Yielding Stocks in the Dow

At any time when you have accumulated enough cash, use this simple strategy that almost always beats the market: on a given day, say January 2 or your birthday, buy equal amounts of the 10 highest-yielding stocks in the Dow Jones Industrial Average. Then, replace any that have fallen out of the top 10.

Stock	Yield (%)
Philip Morris	5.3
Exxon Corp.	3.8
Texaco, Inc.	3.7
J.P. Morgan & Co.	3.7
Chevron Corp.	3.6
General Motors	3.2
MMM	2.8
Du Pont, E.I.	2.7
AT&T Corp.	2.5
Int'l Paper	2.5

(As of September 1996)

Alternative Portfolio Suggestions for All Ages

- BUY: Beverly Enterprises, bonds, 9¼s, due 2004, selling at $980. The bonds will cost $9,600. Annual income from these high yield bonds will be $900.
- BUY: Puerto Rico Electric Power Authority bonds, 6s due 2015, selling at $1,000. Total cost for 10 bonds will be $10,000. Annual income will be approximately $600. Puerto Rican municipals are exempt from local, state, and federal taxes in all 50 states.
- BUY: U.S. Government (Treasury) zeros, due August 2005, with a yield of 7.0%. Cost per bond is $550; total cost for $10,000 worth of bonds will be $5,500. In August 2005 your zeros will mature and you will receive the full $10,000.
- BUY: Dreyfus Strategic Gov't. Fund (DSI). This closed-end bond fund trades on the NYSE and invests in U.S. and foreign government debt. Its shares in September 1996 were $9, for a yield of 8.0%.
- BUY: Fidelity's Capital Income Fund. Invests in corporate and convertible bonds; minimum investment $2,500; yield as of late September 1996 was 9.7% (800–544–8888).

income, it's important to let the children know the truth, but without frightening them. After all, they will be affected too. Reassure them that hard times won't last forever.

6. *Claim benefits.* If you are laid off and entitled to unemployment compensation, do not be embarrassed to collect. After all, you've been paying to fund the system for many years.

7. *Reduce debt.* Paying off high-rate loans, such as credit card debt, is critical. Pay all credit card balances within 30 days to avoid interest charges. Consolidate high-rate debt if you can get a lower interest rate by doing so.

8. *Pinch pennies.* You'll know where to do so. Start by leaving your credit cards at home.

9. *Eat home more.* Or, if dining out, have drinks and dessert at home.

Finding Extra Cash

Don't be surprised if you need extra cash to tide yourself over until you get a job, a raise, or your spouse is employed. Here are four tips:

1. *Review your portfolio and first sell securities that are not performing well.* If need be, slowly sell other securities, holding until last the best performers.

2. *Consider a home equity line of credit.*

CAUTION: It is virtually impossible to get this type of loan when you are out of work. If you fear losing your job, process the loan now. There's no obligation to use it, although you will incur some expenses in setting it up.

3. *Borrow against the cash value in any life insurance policies.*

4. *As a last resort, borrow from your 401(k) plan.* Hold off tapping this source as long as possible because it's hard to replace these funds, which you will need when you retire. Most companies let employees borrow up to 50% of the amount vested, or $50,000, whichever is less. Typically you repay the money in installments through payroll deductions.

Finance charges are based on current market rates—expect to pay prime plus one or two percentage points. Terms and conditions vary, so check with your benefits officer.

CAUTION: *Don't withdraw money from your IRA or Keogh plan if you are under age 59½. Not only will you pay regular income tax on such withdrawals, but there's also a 10% penalty on top of that.*

Investment Analysis and Information Sources

Now that you are well acquainted with the various types of investments available, the next step, of course, is deciding which ones to select for your personal portfolio. Do you want common stocks? If so, which ones? Perhaps you would benefit from bonds or convertibles. Yet selecting the best and avoiding the worst require skill and knowledge. That's where investment analysis enters the picture.

In this section you will learn the various techniques used by the experts in selecting all types of securities. You will come to know how to recognize the potential profit in stocks, bonds, and mutual funds and how to spot the winners and avoid the losers. Among the topics covered are:

- Reading a company's balance sheet and annual report
- Getting the most out of statistics
- Following technical analysis
- Studying the charts
- Using software programs and investment newsletters

In Parts Three and Four we explained the various types of stocks and the analytical tools for evaluating securities. You may want to review these points as you now learn precisely how to select top-quality securities on your own, including:

Knowing the stock exchanges, indexes, and averages

A

Managing and Investing Your Money with a Computer

A personal computer can be a helpful tool for financial planning, investing, and even preparing tax returns. It not only does the obvious—make number crunching faster and easier—but with the right software you can gain access to a large amount of research that until recently was the private domain of the professionals on Wall Street.

NOT A SUBSTITUTE FOR THINKING

There's all sorts of help available—programs for writing checks, filing taxes, getting current stock and mutual fund data, doing a budget, even talking to other investors and experts. No one program, however, does it all and no combination of programs can replace intelligent, sensible decision-making. So look upon your computer as an additional way to improve your financial bottom line, and not as a substitute for thinking. Use it in conjunction with the basic investment guidelines you've learned by reading this book and other resources.

Following is an overview of some of the best software and on-line programs, starting with the simplest programs first—those that do check-writing. Read what we have to say, talk with knowledgeable friends who use financial software programs, check your public library (many have programs you can practice with), and then call the sources for the promotional literature. *NOTE:* Prices for software range widely depending upon where you purchase the program.

Before purchasing any software you need to consider two things: (1) how complex are your financial affairs; and (2) what format does your computer accept—DOS, Windows, or Macintosh?

CHECKBOOK MANAGEMENT

- *Microsoft Money.* Has a great deal of built-in assistance for keeping track of your checkbook and budget. Its on-screen graphic resembles a checkbook. You fill in the necessary information and the calculations are done automatically.
- *Quicken.* This best-seller is just about the easiest to learn and use. It sorts financial information into budgeting and tax categories for record-keeping purposes. The data can then be transferred to most major tax-preparation software packages. Small businesses can add on a payroll program, QuickPay, for an extra $60.
- *Quicken for Windows.* This version has an extra feature for the same price called "Intelli-Charge": Users can apply for a Visa Gold Card; all charges placed on the card are then electronically sent via modem to your computer and automatically sorted into the two categories.
- *QuickBooks.* Similar to Quicken, but with a simple accounting program that is useful if you have a home office or small business. It uses the same checkbook entry plan as Quicken, but

adds on business features such as invoicing, accounts payable, and accounts receivable.

FINANCIAL PLANNING

Andrew Tobias's Managing Your Money. One of the most comprehensive and popular financial planning packages available. In addition to doing checkbook, budget, and portfolio management, it tracks stocks, has an address keeper, a calendar, a to-do list, a simple word processor, and a tax planner. The program also calculates mortgage payments and can help you determine whether it's better to buy or lease a car or home. A well-written and enjoyable-to-read manual.

TAXES

You'll have to spend about two hours learning a tax program, but it does make filling out returns easier. And, the math is almost always correct. Other advantages: You have to enter the data in only one place, information is transfered quite easily to state forms, the good ones do some analysis of your return and help locate errors.

However none of the programs answers every question—you may still have to consult IRS publications or even a professional. Don't get too smart for your own good and assume that now that you can use a software program you also know all the ins and outs of the tax code.

Among the best:

- *Andrew Tobias's TaxCut.* A question-and-answer format that gets you to the right IRS forms and then leads you through the forms with help screens. Keeps track of important receipts and tax information throughout the year. Prints out IRS-approved forms on any printer.
- *Kiplinger Taxcut.* This takes the Andrew Tobias' TaxCut program and adds material from the tax editor of *Kiplinger's Personal Finance* magazine. This extra help, written in

easy-to-follow language, makes calculations much easier. The package also includes the "Kiplinger TaxEstimator" program for tax planning and a copy of Kiplinger's 476-page tax guide, *Sure Ways to Cut Your Taxes.*
- *MacInTax.* Has a question-and-answer format and a useful, easy-to-follow help program. For another $19.95, you can file tax returns electronically for faster refunds.
- *Personal Tax Edge* from Parsons, *TaxCut* from Meca, and *TurboTax* from Intuit are also effective.

RETIREMENT PLANNING

If you're retiring soon, you can expect to live 25 to 30 years—what a difference from the 1960s, when many Americans worked up until they turned 65, automatically retired, and died in their early 70s. In order to finance this much longer life you need to undertake some serious financial planning—and there's some easy-to-use software now available. The best to date is:

Retirement Planning System put out by Price Waterhouse. Available in both DOS and Windows versions. The full version can be ordered directly from the accounting firm for about $45 (call 800–752–6234); or, a simplified version for about $19. The program has a lot of "what-if" scenarios with results; it also gives advice on investment choices, spousal benefits, and estate planning.

ON-LINE TRADING AND FINANCIAL SERVICES

With a home computer and a modem, you can tap into the telephone lines and into an amazing amount of up-to-the-minute financial information—stock prices, mutual fund values, earnings estimates, analysts' opinions, historical information, and research reports. You can even place stock orders through on-line discount brokerage firms, or you can join a discussion group and ask your financial questions of on-line experts.

Once you have the necessary hardware, you pay an initial setup fee and an as-you-go fee or a flat monthly fee. Here's data on several of the leading on-line services for investors.

CompuServe

No start-up costs. First month free. Monthly fee, $9.95 for five hours; additional hours @ $2.95. Additional surcharges for other features. Details: 800–848–8199.

This service is vast, and offers current and historical market quotes, fundamental and technical data on U.S. and foreign stocks, and mutual funds, as well as material from newsletters and journal articles.

The monthly fee covers basic quotes and company earnings data, information on mutual funds, news, sports, and weather. The FUNDWATCH area, co-sponsored by *Money Magazine,* enables you to search for mutual funds that meet your goals from a database of 4,800 funds; at present there's no extra cost for this service.

For other information and browsing, including research on stocks, there's an hourly connect-time fee. The "Company Analyzer," which searches all the financial databases for data on a single company, is also additional.

Its "Executive News Service" scans seven new wire, including Dow Jones, the Associated Press and Reuters and will get your stories about your stocks, funds, etc. You'll pay 25 cents/minute to download the ones you want to read, but even at that, it's cheaper than others that offer the same or similar scanning.

Rosebud, an add-on service ($39.95) from Magee Enterprises (800–662–4330) retrieves news on any company, industry or market that you specifically request. It also updates your portfolio's value.

If you travel a lot, Rosebud has a $25 program that will let you know, via a pager, about important developments in your portfolio—such as a sharp movement up or down in a stock's price.

Another CompuServe add-on, called "Stock Tracker" from Virgil (415–433–9025) will get quotes and news on up to 25 stocks and mutual funds.

Dow Jones News/Retrieval

No start-up costs. Monthly fee for eight hours of non-prime-time access to quotes and news or to selected stock and mutual fund info is $29.95. Access to historical data on thousands of other issues during non-prime time is $1.50 per 1,000 characters. Details: 609–452–1511.

Although designed for professionals and serious investors, a flat-fee, after-hours arrangement enables you to access what otherwise is an expensive, top-notch service, getting Dow Jones news as well as current and historical stock quotes, Standard & Poor's reports. Additional surcharges for other data bases.

Prodigy

Is free for the first month and you get 20 free hours; then, $9.95 for 5 hours of basic service; beyond that it's $2.95 per hour and another $14.95 for "Strategic Investor." Details: 800–776–3449.

A general on-line, graphic-intensive service with numerous charts. The monthly fee gives you most of the service, news, weather, shopping, current stock market news, quotes, libraries of investing articles, and discussion forums with experts providing answers to financial questions.

☑ *HINT: There's no need to sign up for an on-line service if you only want electronic banking; a growing number of banks are offering electronic services through Quicken and Money for Windows—for less than you pay to get on line.*

This is the best choice for checking your bank balance because it has some 18 banks on its system, including Chemical Bank and Wells Fargo. America Online has Bank of America and First National Bank of Chicago. And, with BILLPAY, for $9.95/month you get 30 checks per month—one of the better deals around.

America Online

No start-up fee; the first month you get free service for 10 hours and then for $9.95/month, 5 hours of usage; each additional hour costs $2.95. Details: 800–827–6364.

The simplest to use, with access to stock quotes, company profiles, mutual fund information, and commodity prices. Two pluses: an investment bulletin board and the ability to create and track your own personal portfolios.

On-line stock trading, mutual fund purchases, and other brokerage services are available through Quick & Reilly, E. Trade, Fidelity, and Charles Schwab.

Use the keyword PERSONAL FINANCE and you'll get a continually updated chart showing the DJIA. To add an investment to your list you just type in the name or click the "Add to Portfolio" button. Once you do, you'll get an updated quote every time you open your America Online portfolio screen.

If you're tracking a large number of investments, go for the Quote Track service; it costs an extra $2.95/hour from 9 AM to 4:20 PM weekdays; you get a lot more options.

ON-LINE STOCK TRADING

Thanks to the computerization of our world, you can now tap into a number of on-line brokerage services that plug you into the floors of the major stock exchanges. Fees start as low as $15 per trade.

This type of trading is best for people who don't need hand holding. They are not perfect; there are reports of hidden fees (requesting a stock certificate, for instance) and higher prices than elsewhere. But the firms that offer on-line trading say it keeps their labor costs down and eliminates a lot of mistakes.

Some facts:

1. You need a Net account which will run $5 to $30/month.

2. Settlements are still done by check
3. Access is by Netscape Navigator 2.0, a Web browser that is pretty good at protecting security breaches.

The leading brokers offering reasonably priced on-line trading:

- Accutrade 800–228–3001
- Aufhauser 800–368–3668
- Charles Schwab 800–435–4000
- E Trade 800–786–2575
- National Discount 800–888–3999
- PC Financial 800–825–5723

ON-LINE MUTUAL FUND TRADING

With almost 6,000 mutual funds out there, picking the right one is not easy. However, specialized software andonline services will help you narrow the choices. Some alert your to the best buys and sells, others will match your risk level and goals with the right funds.

Call and get literature first or a trial subscription.

The best to date:

- MUTUAL FUND EXPERT 800–237–8400. Screens 6,000+ funds including money market funds; $30 trial; $95/year for quarterly updates. Windows/DOS.
- MORNINGSTAR PRINCIPIA 800–876–5005. Screens 6,250 funds with information taken from its weekly publication. $45 for trial; Windows.
- MORNINGSTAR MUTUAL FUNDS ON FLOPPY 800–876–5005. For each fund, shows its entire portfolio holdings and monthly returns; $95/year for quarterly disk updates or $495/year for the DC-ROM; DOS
- AAII's QUARTERLY MUTUAL FUND UPDATE 312–280–0170. Ideal if you want only no-low and low-load funds; screens 900 of them; $50/year for quarterly updates; DOS

B

Behind the Scenes:
How to Read Annual Reports

Annual reports can be one of the most important tools in analyzing a corporation to determine whether to buy, hold, sell, or skip its securities. In a few minutes you can check the corporation's quality and profitability and learn about the character and ability of management, its methods of operation, its products and services and, most importantly, its future prospects.

If you own securities of a corporation, you will receive a copy of its annual report about 3 months after the close of the fiscal year. If you don't own securities, you can get a copy from your broker or by writing to the company—get the address from Standard & Poor's, Value Line, or Moody's, copies of which are in most libraries.

First, skim the text; check the statement of income and earnings to see how much money was made and whether this was more or less than in previous years. Review the list of officers and directors for familiar names.

An annual reports statements will always be factually correct, but the interpretations, especially those in the president's message, will naturally be the most favorable possible, within legal and accounting limits.

If you are considering a stock to buy, look at 3 years' worth of annual reports. Here are the key points to be aware of:

Trends

In sales, earnings, dividends, accounts receivable. If they continue to rise, chances are that you've found a winner. Buy when they are moving up; review when they plateau; consider selling when they are down.

Information

From the tables: corporate financial strength and operating success or failure. From the text: explanations of what happened during the year and what management projects for the future. If you don't believe management, do not hold the stock.

Positives

New plants, products, personnel, and programs. Are the total assets greater and liabilities lower than in previous years? If so, why—tighter controls or decreases in allocations for R&D, marketing, etc.?

If the profits were up, was the gain due to fewer outstanding shares (because of repurchase of stock), nonrecurring income from the sale of property, or higher sales and lower costs?

Negatives

Plant closings, sales of subsidiaries, discontinuance of products, and future needs for financing. Not all of these will always be adverse, but they can make a significant difference with respect to what happens in the next few years.

If the profits were down, was this because of the elimination of some products or services? Price wars? Poor managerial decisions?

Footnotes

Read these carefully because they can point out problems. Be cautious if there were heavy markdowns of inventory, adverse governmental regulations, rollovers of debt, and other unusual events.

Balance Sheet

To see whether cash or liquid assets are diminishing and whether accounts receivable, inventories, or total debts are rising. Any such trend can serve as a yellow flag, if not a red one.

Financial Summary

Not only for the past year but for the previous 5 years. This will provide an overall view of corporate performance and set the stage for an analysis of the most recent data.

In the stock market, past is prologue. Few companies achieve dramatic progress or fall on hard times suddenly. In most cases, the changes have been forecast. The corporation with a long, fairly consistent record of profitable growth can be expected to do as well, or better, in the years ahead and thus prove to be a worthwhile holding. The erratic performer is likely to move from high to low profits (or losses), and the faltering company will have signs of deterioration over a 2- or 3-year period.

READING THE REPORT

When you review the text, you will get an idea of the kind of people who are managing your money, learn what they did or did not do and why, and be able to draw some conclusions about future prospects.

Begin with the Shareholders' Letter

This message from the chairman outlines the company's past performance and its prospects. Compare last year's letter with this year's facts. Did the company meet its previously stated goals? Beware of the chairman who never mentions any problems or areas of concern. If there were failures, there should be logical explanations.

To Translate the President's Message

Here are some of the techniques used in writing annual reports to phrase comments in terms that tend to divert the reader's attention away from problems.

WHAT THE PRESIDENT SAYS	WHAT THE PRESIDENT MEANS
"The year was difficult and challenging."	"Sales and profits were off, but expenses (including executive salaries) were up."
"Management has taken steps to strengthen market share."	"We're underselling our competitors to drive them out of the market."
"Integrating the year's highs and lows proved challenging."	"Sales were up; profits went nowhere."
"Management worked diligently to preserve a strong financial position."	"We barely broke even but were able to avoid new debts."
"Your company is indebted to the dedicated service of its employees."	"We don't pay 'em much, but there's not much else to cheer about."

Consolidated Statement: Fred Meyer, Inc.

	FISCAL YEAR ENDED ($ IN THOUSANDS EXCEPT PER-SHARE AMOUNTS)		
	JANUARY 31, 1996	FEBRUARY 1, 1996	FEBRUARY 2, 1996 (53 WEEKS)
Net sales	$1,688,208	$1,583,796	$1,449,108
Cost of merchandise sold	1,200,379	1,135,836	1,053,689
Gross margin	487,829	447,960	395,419
Operating and administrative expenses	430,469	397,841	354,914
Income from operations	57,360	50,119	40,505
Interest expense, net of interest income of $1,679, $2,983, and $3,090	11,945	17,652	19,565
Income before income taxes and extraordinary items	45,415	32,467	20,940
Provision for income taxes	21,350	13,000	8,000
Income before extraordinary items	24,065	19,467	12,940
Extraordinary items	(1,530)		2,649
Net income	$ 22,535	$ 19,467	$ 15,589
Earnings per Common Share			
Income before extraordinary items	$ 1.15	$ 1.06	$ .73
Extraordinary items	(.07)		.15
Net income	$ 1.08	$ 1.06	$ .88
Weighted average number of common shares outstanding	20,870	18,355	17,790

Management is not always right in its decisions, but in financial matters, frankness is the base for confidence. If previous promises were unfulfilled (and that's why you should keep a file of past annual reports), find out why. If the tone is overly optimistic, be wary. If you are skeptical, do not hold the stock or buy.

Watch for Double-Talk

Clichés are an integral part of business writing, but they should not be substitutes for proper explanations. If you find such meaningless phrases as "a year of transition" or some of the locutions listed in the box on page 368, start getting ready to unload. There are better opportunities elsewhere.

Study the Balance Sheet

This presents an instant picture of the company's assets and liabilities on the very last day of the fiscal year. Divide the current assets by the current liabilities to get the current ratio. A ratio of 2:1 or better signals that there are enough assets on hand to cover immediate debts. (we return to balance sheets in Appendix C.)

Look at Long-Term Debt

Divide long-term debt by long-term capital (i.e., Long-term debt plus shareholders' equity). If it is below 50%, the company is probably solid, but of course, the more debt, the less cash to help weather rough times.

Review Accounts Receivable

Listed under current assets, this figure reflects the payments for products or services that the company expects to receive in the near future. If receivables are growing at a faster pace than sales, it may indicate that the company is not collecting its bills fast enough.

Look at Current Inventories

If inventories are rising faster than sales, the company is creating or producing more than it can sell.

Look at Net Income per Share

Note if this figure, which reflects earnings, is trending up or down.

Compare Revenues and Expenses

If expenses are greater than revenues over time, management may be having trouble holding down overhead. Discount earnings increases t hat are due to a nonrecurring event, such as sale of a property or division. Nonrecurring items should be explained in the footnotes. The footnotes also reveal changes in accounting methods, lawsuits, and liabilities.

Study the Quality and Source of Earnings

When profits are entirely from operations, they indicate management's skill; when they are partially from bookkeeping, look again. But do not be hasty in drawing conclusions. Even the best of corporations may use "special" accounting.

Examples: In valuing inventories, LIFO (last in, first out) current sales are matched against the latest costs so that earnings can rise sharply when inventories are reduced and those latest costs get older and thus lower. When oil prices were at a peak, Texaco cut inventories by 16%. The LIFO cushion, built up over several years, was a whop-

ping $454 million and transformed what would have been a drop in net income into a modest gain.

Such "tricks" are one reason why stocks fall or stay flat after annual profits are reported. Analysts are smart enough to discover that earnings are more paper than real.

Read the Auditor's Report

If there are hedging phrases such as "except for" or "subject to," be wary. These phrases can signal the inability to get accurate information and may forecast future write-offs.

Look at Foreign Currency Transactions

These can be tricky and often difficult to understand. Under recent revisions of accounting rules, it's possible to recast them retroactively when, of course, they can be favorable. One major firm whose domestic profits had been lagging went back 4 years with its overseas reports and boosted its per-share profits to $7.08 from the previously reported $6.67 per share.

Most international corporations have elaborate systems for hedging against fluctuations in foreign currencies. These are relatively expensive, but they tend to even out sharp swings in the value of the dollar.

Check for Future Obligations

You may have to burrow in the footnotes, but with major companies, find out about the pension obligations: the money that the firm must pay to its retirees. One way to boost profits (because this means lower annual contributions) is to raise the assumed rate of return on pension fund investments.

Calculate the Cash Flow

Add after-tax earnings and annual depreciation on fixed assets and subtract preferred dividends, if any. Then compare the result with previous years. Cash flow is indicative of corporate earning power because it shows the dollars available for profits, new investments, etc.

Beware of Overenthusiasm about New Products, Processes, or Services

Usually it takes 3 years to translate new operations into sizable sales and profits—and the majority of new projects are losers.

Pay Special Attention to the Return on Equity (Profit Rate)

This is the best measure of management's ability to make money with your money. Any roe above 15% is good; when below, compare the figure with that of previous years and other firms in the same industry. Some industries seldom show a high rate of return: for example, heavy machinery because of the huge investment in plants and equipment, and utilities because of the ceiling set by public commissions.

Watch Out for Equity Accounting

Where earnings from other companies, which are more than 20% owned, are included in total profits. There are no cash dividends, so the money cannot be used for expansion or payouts to shareholders. This maneuver can massage the reported earnings, but that's about all. Teledyne, a major conglomerate, reported $19.96 per share profits, but a close examination revealed that $3.49 of this was from equity accounting—phantom, not real, earnings.

FOR FURTHER INFORMATION

How to Read a Financial Report (pamphlet), free from any Merrill Lynch office, or call: 800–MERRILL.

George T. Friedlob and Ralph E. Welton, *Keys to Reading an Annual Report* (Hauppauge, NY: Barron's Educational Series, 1989).

C

Balance Sheets Made Simple

DETERMINING VALUE

The idea is to buy low and sell high. This sounds easy, but it isn't. You must determine what is low and, to a lesser degree, what is high. That's where value comes in. The surest way to make money in the stock market is to buy securities when they are undervalued and sell them when they become fully priced. Value shows the range in which a stock should be bought or sold and thus provides the base for investment profits.

Value itself is based on financial "facts," as stated in the corporate reports. Projections, by contrast, are based on analyses of past performance, present strength, and future progress. When you select quality stocks on the basis of value (or undervaluation), you will almost always make money—perhaps quickly with speculative situations, more slowly with major corporations. You can identify value if you understand the basics of financial analysis, our next step.

HOW TO ANALYZE FINANCIAL REPORTS

Financial analysis is not as difficult as you may think, and once you get into the swing of things, you can pick the few quality stocks from the thousands of publicly-owned securities. If you are speculation-minded, you can find bargains in securities of mediocre or even poor corporations.

Several basic figures and ratios show the company's current and prospective financial condition, its past and prospective earning power and growth, and therefore its investment desirability or lack of desirability.

Publicly-owned corporations issue their financial reports on an annual, semiannual, or quarterly basis. Most of the information important to the investor can be found in (1) the balance sheet; (2) the profit and loss, or income, statement; and (3) the change in financial position or "flow of funds" data. In each of these three sections you should look for:

- The key quantities: net tangible assets, changes in working capital, sales costs, profits, taxes, dividends, etc.
- The significant rates and ratios: price-earnings multiples, profit rates, growth in net worth, earnings, dividends, etc.
- The comparison of a corporation with a standard: that of its industry, the stock market, the economy, or some other broader base.

The following data and explanations are digested from Understanding Financial Statements, prepared by the New York Stock Exchange. They do not cover every detail, but will get you started. For a copy, write to the address given on page 400, or ask your broker for one.

Income and Retained Earnings

Here's where you find out how the corporation fared for the past year in comparison with the two previous annual reporting periods: in other words, how much money the company took in, how much was spent for expenses and taxes, and the size of the resulting profits (if any), which were available either for distribution to shareholders or for reinvestment in the business. Income and retained earnings are the basis for comparisons, both between years for this company and between firms in the same or similar business.

Sales

How much business does the company do in a year? With public utilities, insurance firms, and service organizations, the term "revenues" is often used instead of sales. In the past year, corporate sales in the sample corporation shown were up $5.8 million, a gain of 5.3%, not quite as good as the 5.5% rise the year before. Net income per

Statement of Income and Retained Earnings ($ millions)

"YOUR COMPANY"

	DECEMBER 31 YEAR-END		
	CURRENT YEAR	**PREVIOUS YEAR**	**2 YEARS AGO**
SALES	$ 115.8	$ 110.0	$ 104.5
Less:			
COSTS AND EXPENSES			
Cost of goods sold	$ 76.4	$ 73.2	$ 70.2
Selling, general, and administrative expenses	14.2	13.0	12.1
Depreciation	2.6	3.5	2.3
	$ 93.2	$ 89.7	$ 84.6
OPERATING PROFIT	$ 22.6	$ 20.3	$ 19.9
Interest charges	1.3	1.0	1.3
Earnings before income taxes	$ 21.3	$ 19.3	$ 18.6
Provision for taxes on income	11.4	9.8	9.5
Net income (per common share for year: current, $5.24; last, $5.03; 2 years ago, $4.97)[*]	$ 9.9	$ 9.5	$ 9.1
RETAINED EARNINGS, BEGINNING OF YEAR	42.2	37.6	33.1
Less dividends paid on:	$ 52.1	$ 47.1	$ 42.2
Preferred stock ($5 per share)	(.3)	(.3)	—
Common stock (per share: this year, $3.00; last year, $2.50; 2 years ago, $2.50)	(5.4)	(4.6)	(4.6)
RETAINED EARNINGS, END OF YEAR	$ 46.4	$ 42.2	$ 37.6

*After preferred share dividend requirements.

share (middle) was also just slightly better: $0.4 million (to $9.9 from $9.5), +4.2%. Check these figures against those of the industry and major competitors. They may be better than they appear.

Costs and Expenses

- COST OF GOODS SOLD. The dollars spent to keep the business operating. The $3.2 million more was less than the $5.8 million increase in sales.
- SELLING, GENERAL, AND ADMINISTRATIVE EXPENSES. The costs of getting products or services to customers and getting paid. These will vary with the kind of business: high for consumer goods manufacturers and distributors because of advertising; lower for companies selling primarily to industry or government.
- DEPRECIATION. A bookkeeping item to provide for wear and tear and obsolescence of machinery and equipment, presumably to set aside reserves for replacement. The maximum calculations are set by tax laws. Typically, a straight-line accounting method might charge the same amount each year for a specified number of years.

With companies in the natural resource business, the reduction in value is called depletion, and it too is calculated over a period of years.

By changing the type of depreciation, a company can increase or decrease earnings, so always be wary when this happens.

Operating Profit

Operating profit consists of the dollars generated from the company's usual operations without regard to income from other sources or financing. As a percentage of sales, it tells the profit margin: a rising 19.5% in the last year compared with 18.5% the year before.

- INTEREST CHARGES. The interest paid to bondholders. It is deductible before taxes. The available earnings should be many times the mandated interest charges: in this case, a welcome 17 times before provision for income taxes (i.e., $22.6 \div $1.3 = 17.3$).
- EARNINGS BEFORE INCOME TAXES. The operating profit minus interest charges. When companies have complicated reports, this can be a confusing area.
- PROVISION FOR TAXES ON INCOME. The allocation of money for uncle sam—a widely variable figure because of exemptions, special credits, etc., From about 5% for some companies to 34% for industrial corporations.
- NET INCOME FOR THE YEAR. The bottom line. This was 4.2% better than the year before—about the same as recorded in the previous period. This was no record-breaker and works out better on a per-share basis: $5.24 versus $5.03.

One year's change is interesting, but the true test of management's ability comes over 5 years.

Use this figure to make other comparisons (against sales: 8.5% versus 8.6% the year before) and then relate this to returns of other companies in the same industry. The average manufacturing corporation earns about 5¢ per dollar of sales, but supermarkets are lucky to end up with 1¢ against share-owners' equity: the profit rate (PR). Here, the PR was a modest 13%.

To find the earnings per share, divide the net income (less preferred dividend requirements) by the average number of shares outstanding during the year. This is the key figure for most analysts. It is also used to determine the price-earnings (P/E) ratio: divide the market price of the stock by the per-share profits. If the stock was selling at 30, the P/E would be 10—slightly above the average of most publicly-owned shares.

■ RETAINED EARNINGS. The dollars reinvested for future growth, always an important indication of future prospects. If the company continues to boost this figure, its basic value will increase. At the same pr, earnings will increase, and eventually so will the value of the common stock.

Here the company keeps plowing back more: $4.6 million in the current year versus $4.5 million the year before. (Subtract the retained earnings at the beginning of the year from retained earnings of the previous year: $37.6 – $33.1 = $4.5.)

■ DIVIDENDS. The amount paid out to shareholders for the use of their money. The $5 per share paid on the preferred stock is fixed. The payments for the common move with profits: last year up 50¢ per share to $3 from the flat $2.50 of the 2 prior years.

Note that this statement shows earnings retained as of the beginning and end of each year. Thus the company reinvested $46.4 million for the future.

BALANCE SHEET ITEMS

Now that you know what happened in the last year, it's time to take a look at the financial strength (or weakness) of the corporation. On this page is a typical balance sheet. Use it as the basis for reviewing annual reports of the companies in which you own, or plan to own, securities. The headings may vary according to the type of industry, but the basic data will be similar—and just as important.

Current Assets

Items that can be converted into cash within 1 year. The total is $48.4 million this year, $4.2 million more than last year.

■ CASH. Mostly bank deposits, including compensating balances held under terms of a loan—like keeping a savings account to get free checking.

■ MARKETABLE SECURITIES. Corporate and government securities that can be sold quickly. In the current year, these were eliminated.

■ RECEIVABLES. Amounts due from customers for goods and services. This is a net amount after a set-aside for items that may not be collected.

■ INVENTORIES. Cost of raw materials, work in process, and finished goods. Statements and footnotes describe the basis, generally cost or current market price, whichever is lower. To handle the additional business, these were up over those of the previous year.

Property, Plant, and Equipment

The land, structures, machinery and equipment, tools, motor vehicles, etc. Except for land, these assets have a limited useful life, and a deduction is taken from cost as depreciation. With a new plant, the total outlays were $11.6 million more, with depreciation up $2.6 million.

Other Assets

Identifiable property is valued at cost. Intangibles such as patents, copyrights, franchises, trademarks, or goodwill cannot be assessed accurately, so they are omitted from the computation of tangible net worth or book value.

If an increase in sales does not follow an increased investment, management may have misjudged the ability to produce and/or sell more goods, or the industry may have reached overcapacity. If a company's plant and equipment show little change for several years during a period of expanding business, the shareholder should be cautious about the company's progressiveness. In this example, both fixed and total assets grew steadily.

Balance Sheet ($ millions)
"Your Company"

	DEC. 31 CURRENT YEAR	DEC. 31 PRIOR YEAR		DEC. 31 CURRENT YEAR	DEC. 31 PRIOR YEAR
ASSETS			**LIABILITIES AND STOCKHOLDERS' EQUITY**		
Current Assets			**CURRENT LIABILITIES**		
Cash	$ 9.0	$ 6.2	Accounts payable	$ 6.1	$ 5.0
Marketable securities	—	2.0	Accrued liabilities	3.6	3.3
Accounts and notes receivable	12.4	11.4	Current maturity of		
Inventories	27.0	24.6	long-term debt	1.0	.8
Total current assets	$ 48.4	$ 44.2	Federal income and other taxes	9.6	8.4
			Dividends payable	1.3	1.1
PROPERTY, PLANT, AND EQUIPMENT			Total current liabilities	$ 21.6	$ 18.6
Buildings, machinery, and					
equipment, at cost	104.3	92.7	**OTHER LIABILITIES**		
Less accumulated depreciation	27.6	25.0	Long-term debt	3.6	2.5
	$ 76.7	$ 67.7	5% sinking-fund debentures,		
Land, at cost	.9	.7	due July 31, 1990	26.0	20.0
Total property, plant, and			**STOCKHOLDERS' EQUITY**		
equipment	$ 77.6	$ 68.4	5% cumulative preferred stock		
			($100 par: authorized and		
OTHER ASSETS			outstanding, 60,000)	6.0	6.0
Receivables due after 1 year	4.7	3.9	Common stock ($10 par:		
Surrender value of insurance	.2	.2	authorized, 2,000,000;		
Other	.6	.5	outstanding, 1,830,000)	18.3	18.3
Total other assets	$ 5.5	$ 4.6	Capital surplus	9.6	9.6
			Retained earnings	46.4	42.2
TOTAL ASSETS	$ 131.5	$ 117.2	Total stockholders' equity	$80.3	$76.1
			TOTAL LIABILITIES AND STOCKHOLDERS' EQUITY	$ 131.5	$ 117.2

Liabilities

Divided into two classes: current (payable within a year) and long-term (debt or other obligations that come due after 1 year from the balance sheet date).

■ ACCOUNTS PAYABLE. Money owed for raw materials, other supplies, and services.

■ ACCRUED LIABILITIES. Unpaid wages, salaries and commissions, interest, etc.

■ CURRENT LONG TERM DEBT. Amount due in the next year. This usually requires annual repayments over a period of years.

■ INCOME TAXES. Accrued federal, state, and local taxes.

■ DIVIDENDS PAYABLE. Preferred or common dividends (or both) declared but not yet paid. Once declared, dividends become a corporate obligation.

■ TOTAL CURRENT LIABILITIES. An increase of $3 million needed to finance expansion of business.

- LONG-TERM DEBT. What's due for payment in the future less the amount due in the next year. Although the total was reduced to $20 million, an additional $6 million of debentures was issued.

Stockholders' Equity (or Capital)

All money invested in the business by stockholders, as well as reinvested earnings.

- PREFERRED STOCK. Holders are usually entitled to dividends before common stockholders and to priority in the event of dissolution or liquidation. Dividends are fixed. If cumulative, no dividends can be paid on common stock until the preferred dividends are up to date.

    Here each share of preferred was issued at $100, but its market value will move with the cost of money: up when interest rates decline, down when they rise.

- COMMON STOCK. Shown on the books at par value, an arbitrary amount having no relation to the market value or to what would be received in liquidation.

- CAPITAL SURPLUS. The amount of money received from the sale of stock in excess of the par value.

- RETAINED EARNINGS. Money reinvested in the business.

- TOTAL STOCKHOLDERS' EQUITY. The sum of the common par value, additional paid-in capital, and retained earnings less any premium attributable to the preferred stock: what the stockholders own. The increase of $4.2 million is a rise of about 5%—not bad, but not as much as should be the mark of a true growth company.

CHANGES IN FINANCIAL POSITION

This presents a different view of the financing and investing activities of the company and clarifies the disposition of the funds produced by operations. It includes both cash and other elements of working capital—the excess of current assets over current liabilities.

The balance sheet shows that the working capital has increased by $1.2 million (current assets of $48.4 million exceeded current liabilities of $21.6 million by $26.8 million at the end of the year versus $25.6 million the year before).

Sales and net income were up; the contribution to working capital from operations decreased to $13.6 million versus $15 million the year before. This was narrowed to $0.4 million by the proceeds of the $7 million in long-term debt, $1 million more than the proceeds from the sale of preferred stock the year before.

The difference between the funds used last year and the year before was $1.1 million, reflecting a heavier investment in productive capacity against a larger repayment of long-term debt the year before.

With increased capacity, the company should be able to handle higher sales. The additional cash may be a good sign, but when too much cash accumulates, it may indicate that management is not making the best use of its assets. In financially tense times, cash is still always welcome.

SEVEN KEYS TO VALUE

1. *Operating profit margin (PM).* The ratio of profit (before interest and taxes) to sales. As shown on the statement of income and retained earnings, the operating profit ($22.6) divided by sales ($115.8) equals 19.5%. This compares with 18.5% for the previous year. (Some analysts prefer to compute this margin without including depreciation and depletion as part of the cost, because these have nothing to do with the efficiency of the operation.)

    When a company increases sales substantially, the PM should widen, because certain costs (rent, interest, property taxes, etc.) are pretty much fixed and do not rise in proportion to volume.

Statement of Changes in Financial Position ($ millions)
"Your Company"

	DEC. 31 CURRENT YEAR	DEC. 31 LAST YEAR	DEC. 31 2 YEARS AGO
FUNDS PROVIDED			
Net income	$ 9.9	$ 9.5	$ 9.1
Changes not requiring working capital:			
Depreciation	2.6	3.5	2.3
Increase in other liabilities	1.1	2.0	1.4
Funds provided by operations	$ 13.6	$ 15.0	$ 12.8
Proceeds from long-term debt	7.0	—	—
Proceeds from sale of 5% cumulative			
preferred stock	$ —	6.0	$ —
Total funds provided	$ 20.6	$ 21.0	$ 12.8
FUNDS USED			
Additions to fixed assets	$ 11.8	$ .5	$ 6.2
Dividends paid on preferred stock	.3	.3	—
Dividends paid on common stock	5.4	4.6	4.6
Payments on long-term debt	1.0	15.0	—
Increase in noncurrent receivables	$ .8	$ .1	$ .3
Increase in other assets	$ .1	$ —	$ .2
Total funds used	$ 19.4	$ 20.5	$ 11.3
Increase in working capital	$ 1.2	$ .5	$ 1.5
CHANGES IN COMPONENTS OF WORKING CAPITAL			
Increase (decrease) in current assets:			
Cash	$ 2.8	$ 1.0	$ 1.1
Marketable securities	(2.0)	.5	.4
Accounts receivable	1.0	.5	.8
Inventories	2.4	1.0	1.3
Increase in current assets	$ 4.2	$ 3.0	$ 3.6
Increase in current liabilities:			
Accounts payable	$ 1.1	$ .9	$ .6
Accrued liabilities	.3	.5	.2
Current maturity of long-term debt	.2	.1	.5
Federal income and other taxes	1.2	1.0	.8
Dividends payable	.2	$ —	$ —
Increase in current liabilities	$ 3.0	$ 2.5	$ 2.1
Increase in working capital	$ 1.2	$ .5	$ 1.5

2. *Current ratio.* The ratio of current assets to current liabilities is calculated from the balance sheet: $48.4 ÷ $21.6 = 2.24:1. For most industrial corporations, this ratio should be about 2:1; it varies with the type of business. Utilities and retail stores have rapid cash inflows and high turnovers of dollars, so they can operate effectively with low ratios

Seven Stocks with Strong Balance Sheets

COMPANY	5-YEAR GROWTH RATE	LONG-TERM DEBT
Abbott Labs	13%	9%
Dollar General	39	1
Home Depot	27	2
Int'l Flavors	11	1
Kelly Services	3	0
Old Kent Financial	10	0
Wilmington Trust	6	0

Keys to Value

	CURRENT YEAR	PRIOR YEAR
1 Operating profit margin	19.5%	18.5%
2 Current ratio	2.24	2.38
3 Liquidity ratio	41.7	44.1
4 Capitalization ratios:		
Long-term debt	19.7	20.8
Preferred stock	6.0	6.3
Common stock and surplus	80.3	72.9
5 Sales to fixed assets	1.1	1.2
6 Sales to inventories	4.3	4.5
7 Net income to net worth	12.3	12.5

When the ratio is high, say 5:1, it may mean that the company has too much cash and is not making the best use of these funds. They should be used to expand the business. Such corporations are often targets for take-overs.

3. *Liquidity ratio.* Again referring to the balance sheet, the ratio of cash and equivalents to total current liabilities ($9 ÷ $21.6 = 41.7%). It should be used to supplement the current ratio, because the immediate ability of a company to meet current obligations or pay larger dividends may be impaired despite a high current ratio. This 41.7% liquidity ratio (down from 44.1% the year before) probably indicates a period of expansion, rising prices, heavier

capital expenditures, and larger accounts payable. If the decline persists, the company might have to raise additional capital.

4. *Capitalization ratios.* The percentage of each type of investment as part of the total investment in the corporation. Though often used to describe only the outstanding securities, capitalization is the sum of the face value of bonds ($26) and other debts plus the par value of all preferred and common stock issues ($18.3 + 6.0 = $24.3) plus the balance sheet totals for capital surplus ($9.6) and retained earnings ($46.4).

Bond, preferred stock, and common stock ratios are useful indicators of the relative risk and leverage involved for the owners of the three types of securities. For most industrial corporations, the debt ratio should be no more than 66⅔% of equity, or 40% of total capital. Higher ratios are appropriate for utilities and transportation corporations.

In this instance, looking at the balance sheet, the long-term debt plus preferred stock ($26 + $6 = $32) is 87.2% of the $27.9 equity represented by the common stock ($18.3) and surplus ($9.6), and 30.1% of total capital.

5. *Sales-to-fixed-assets ratio.* Using both the statement of income and retained earnings and the balance sheet, this ratio is computed by dividing the annual sales ($115.8) by the year-end value of plant, equipment, and land before depreciation and amortization ($104.3 + $0.9 = $105.2). The ratio is therefore 1.1:1. This is down from 1.2:1 the year before.

This ratio helps to show whether funds used to enlarge productive facilities are being spent wisely. A sizable expansion in facilities should lead to larger sales volume. If it does not, there's something wrong. In this case, there were delays in getting production on stream at the new plant.

6. *Sales-to-inventories ratio.* Again referring to both statements, you can compute this ratio

by dividing the annual sales by year-end inventories: $115.8 ÷ $27 = 4.3:1. The year before, the ratio was 4.5:1.

This shows inventory turnover: the number of times the equivalent of the year-end inventory has been bought and sold during the year.

It is more important in analyzing retail corporations than in analyzing manufacturers. A high ratio denotes a good quality of merchandise and correct pricing policies. A declining ratio may be a warning signal.

7. *Net-income-to-net-worth (return on equity) ratio.* One of the most significant of all financial ratios. Derived by dividing the net income from the statement of income and retained earnings ($9.9) by the total stockholders' equity from the balance sheet ($80.3). The result is 12.3%: the percentage of return that corporate management earned on the dollars entrusted by shareholders at the beginning of each year. Basically, it's that all-important PR (profit rate).

This 12.3% is a slight decrease from the 12.5% of the prior year. It's a fair return: not as good as that achieved by a top-quality corporation but better than that of the average publicly-held company. The higher the ratio, the more profitable the operation. Any company that can consistently improve such a ratio is a true growth company. But be sure that this gain is a result of operating skill, not of accounting legerdemain or extraordinary items.

RATIOS AND TRENDS

Detailed financial analysis involves careful evaluation of income, costs, and earnings. But it is also important to study various ratios and trends, both those within the specific corporation and those of other companies in the same industry. Analysts usually prefer to use 5- or 10-year averages. These can reveal significant changes and, on occasion, point out special values in either concealed or inconspicuous assets.

■ OPERATING RATIO. The ratio of operating costs to sales. It is the complement of profit margin (100% minus the pm percentage). Thus if a company's PM is 10%, its operating ratio is 90%. It's handy for comparing similar companies but not significant otherwise.

PMs vary with the type of business. They are low for companies with heavy plant investments (Ingersoll-Rand) and for retailers with fast turnovers (The Limited) and high for marketing firms (Gillette).

■ INTEREST COVERAGE. The number of times interest charges or requirements have been earned. Divide the operating profit (or balance available for such payments before income taxes and interest charges) by the annual interest charges.

According to the statement of income and retained earnings, the interest (fixed charges) was covered 17.4 times in the past year and 20.3 times in the previous year. This is a high, safe coverage. If earnings declined to only 6% of the past year's results, interest would still be covered. As a rule, a manufacturing company should cover interest 5 times; utilities, 3 times.

Keep in mind that when a company (except utilities or transportation firms) has a high debt, it means that investors shy away from buying its common stock. To provide the plants, equipment, etc., that the company needs, management must issue bonds or preferred shares (straight or convertible to attract investors). There are some tax advantages in following such a course, but when the debt becomes too high, there can be trouble during times of recession. All or most of the gross profits will have to be used to pay interest, and there will be nothing or little left over for the common stockholders.

By contrast, speculators like high-debt situations when business is good. With hefty profits, interest can be paid easily, and the balance comes down to the common stock. Typically, airlines with heavy debt obligations for new planes do well in boom times. An extra 10% gain in traffic can boost profits by as much as 30%.

■ PAYOUT RATIO. The ratio of the cash dividends to per-share profits after taxes. Fast-growing corporations pay no or small dividends because they need money for expansion. Profitable companies pay out from about 25% to 50% of their profits. Utilities, which have almost assured earnings, pay out more. But be wary when those dividends represent much more than 70% of income.

It's pleasant to receive an ample dividend check, but for growth, look for companies that pay small dividends. The retained earnings will be used to improve financial strength and the operating future of the company … and they are tax-free.

■ PRICE-TO-BOOK-VALUE RATIO. The market price of the stock divided by its book value per share. Since book value trends are usually more stable than earnings trends, conservative analysts use this ratio as a price comparison. They check the historical over- or undervaluation of the stock, which in turn depends primarily on the company's profitable growth (or lack of it).

Because of inflation, understatement of assets on balance sheets—and, in boom times, the enthusiasm of investors—often pushes this ratio rather high. On the average, only stocks of the most profitable companies sell at much more than twice book value. Investors believe that these corporations will continue to achieve ever-higher earnings. But if the stock prices rise too high, their decline, in a bear market, can be fast and far.

■ PRICE-EARNINGS (P/E) RATIO. Calculated by dividing the price of the stock by the reported earnings per share for the past 12 months.

■ CASH FLOW. A yardstick that is increasingly popular in investment analysis. Reported net earnings after taxes do not reflect the actual cash income available to the company. Cash flow shows the earnings after taxes plus charges against income that do not directly involve cash outlays (sums allocated to depreciation, depletion, amortization, and other special items).

A company might show a net profit of $250,000 plus depreciation of $1 million, so cash flow is $1,250,000. Deduct provisions for preferred dividends (if any), and then divide the balance by the number of shares of common stock to get the cash flow per share.

Two types of cash flow are important:

■ *Distributable cash flow:* the amount of money that the company has on hand to pay dividends and/or invest in real growth. If this is negative, there are problems. If it's positive, fine, unless the company pays out more than this figure in dividends and is thus liquidating the firm.

■ *Discretionary cash flow:* distributable cash flow minus dividends, that is, how much

---

Companies with Strong Cash Flows

COMPANY NAME	LINE OF BUSINESS
• Abbott Laboratories	Health care products
• Bristol-Myers Squibb	Drugs
• Chase	Banking
• General Motors	Automobiles
• A.G. Edwards & Sons	Securities broker
• Gibson Greetings	Greeting cards
• J.M. Smucker	Jams and jellies
• Tootsie Roll Industries	Candy

(As of October 1996)

money is left to grow with, after allocations for maintenance and dividends. Companies do not actually set aside such funds, but they must ultimately have the money in some form—cash savings or borrowing.

HOW TO DETERMINE A PRUDENT P/E RATIO

Analysts usually justify their recommendations by adjusting the multiple of the price of the stock by estimated rate of future growth or by cash flow per share rather than by reported earnings. In both cases, these are attempts to justify a predetermined decision to buy. The projections appear plausible, especially when accompanied by tables and charts and computer printouts. But in most cases, they are useful only as background and not for the purpose of making decisions on the proper level to buy or later to sell. The calculations depend a good deal on market conditions and your own style, but here's one approach for those "supergrowth" stocks that will be suggested by your friends or broker.

Example: According to your financial adviser, the stock of a "future" company now selling at 40 times its recent earnings will be trading at "only 16 times its projected earnings 5 years hence if the company's average earnings growth is 20% a year."

If you are speculating with this type of "hot" stock, you should compare it with other opportunities and on some basis decide how reasonable this projection really is.

A handy formula is

Prudent P/E ratio = GRTQM

G = growth
R = reliability and risk
T = time
Q = quality
M = multiple of price to earnings

■ GROWTH. The company's projected growth in earnings per share over the next 5 years.

The basic compound interest formula is (1 + G), where G is the projected growth rate, as shown in the price evaluator and prudent p/e multiples table below. This omits dividend yields because they are usually small in relation to the potential capital appreciation.

■ RELIABILITY AND RISK. Not all projected growth rates are equally reliable or probable. A lower projected growth rate is likely to be more reliable than a very high projected one (30% to 50% a year).

Logically, you can assign a higher reliability rating to a noncyclical company (utility, food processor, retailer) than to a corporation in a cyclical industry (aluminum, machinery, tools).

■ TIME. Another factor is the assumed length of the projected growth period. If you can realistically anticipate that the company will continue its rate of growth for the next 10 years, a 10% rate for its stock is more reliable than a 15% rate for a company whose growth visibility is only 3 to 5 years.

If you are uncertain about the corporation's consistency, you should assign it the greater risk.

■ QUALITY. As you know, this is the single most important investment consideration.

■ MULTIPLE OF PRICE TO EARNINGS. This is a comparative measurement. The first step is to determine the p/e for an average quality nongrowth stock. This is done by relating the current yield on guaranteed, fixed-income investments (savings accounts, corporate bonds) to the p/e multiple that will produce the same yield on the nongrowth stock.

$$P/E = \frac{D}{IR}$$

P/E = price/earnings ratio
D = dividend as percentage payout of earnings
IR = interest rate

Thus a stock yielding 8% on a 70% payout of profits must, over a 5-year period, be bought and sold at 7 times earnings to break even on capital and to make as much income as could be obtained over the same period via the ownership of a fixed-income investment continually yielding 10%:

$$P/E = \frac{7}{10} = .7$$

NOTE: This is not a valid comparison in terms of investment alone. Because the non-growth stock carries a certain amount of risk in comparison to the certainty of a bond or money market fund, the stock should sell at a lower multiple, probably 5 to 6 times earnings.

Other key items used in analysis are:

■ EARNINGS GROWTH RATE. A formula that gives the rate at which a company's profits

Prudent Price-Earnings Multiples for Growth Stocks

IF YOU PROJECT EARNINGS PER SHARE (AFTER TAXES) TO GROW IN NEXT 5 YEARS AT AN AVERAGE COMPOUNDED RATE OF:	WITH THESE QUALITY RATINGS* THESE ARE APPROXIMATE PRUDENT MULTIPLES THAT REPRESENT THE MAXIMUM CURRENT PRICE TO PAY:				
	B	B+	A-	A	A+
5%	12.0	12.9	13.7	15.0	16.7
6	12.5	13.4	14.3	15.8	17.4
7	13.0	14.0	14.9	16.5	18.2
8	13.6	14.5	15.6	17.1	18.9
9	14.1	15.1	16.2	17.8	19.7
10	14.6	15.7	16.8	18.5	20.4
15	17.4	18.7	20.1	22.0	24.5
20	20.2	21.8	23.4	25.7	28.6
25	23.0	24.7	26.6	29.3	32.7
30	25.2	27.3	29.4	32.5	36.2
35	28.5	31.0	33.5	37.1	41.5
40	31.9	34.8	37.7	41.7	46.7

*Standard & Poor's designations. If not rated, use B; if a new, untested firm, use a conservative rating based on comparison with similar companies, preferably in the same industry.

have increased over the past several years. You can find the earnings growth rate in annual reports or from your broker. Then divide it by the P/E and compare this number with the Standard & Poor's 500 to decide whether to buy or sell. Keep in mind that in good years the average growth rate for the Standard & Poor's 500 stock index has been 16% and the average P/E 8, so the index for the purposes of this formula should be divided by 2.

For example, let us assume that Company XYZ has an earnings growth rate of 40% per year. Its P/E is 20; its index is therefore 2, only equal to the Standard & Poor's average—nothing to get excited about.

Another company, the LMN Corporation, has an earnings growth rate of 40% also; however, its P/E is 15, so its index comes out to be 2.6. Because this ratio is above the Standard & Poor's index of 2, it is an apparent bargain.

■ PERCENTAGE BUYING VALUE. This is a variation of the formula developed by John B. Neff of the windsor fund. It uses the current yield plus the rate of earnings growth divided by the current P/E ratio. If the result is 2 or more, the stock is worth buying:

CY = current yield
EG = earnings growth
P/E = price/earnings ratio
PBV = percentage buying value

$$\frac{CY + EG}{P/E} = PV$$

$$\frac{1.4 + 20}{22} = 9.7\% = buy$$

$$\frac{8.6 + 2}{7.7} = 1.32\% = sell\ or\ do\ not\ buy$$

■ RETURN ON EQUITY AND P/E: TOTAL RETURN. Most investors tend to think about their gains and losses in terms of price changes and not dividends, whereas those who own bonds pay attention to interest yields and seldom focus on price changes. Both approaches are mistakes. Although dividend yields are obviously more important if you are seeking income, and changes in price play a greater role in growth stocks, knowing the total return on a stock makes it possible for you to compare your investment in a stock with a similar investment in a corporate bond, municipal, treasury, mutual fund, etc.

To calculate the total return, add (or subtract) the stock's price change and the dividends received for 12 months and then divide that number by the price at the beginning of the 12-month period.

Example: An investor bought a stock at $42 per share and received dividends for the 12-month period of $2.50. At the end of 12 months, the stock was sold at $45. The total return was 13%.

> Dividend $2.50
> Stock price change + *$3.00*
> $5.50 ÷ $42 = 13%

■ CORPORATE CASH POSITION. Developed by Benjamin Graham, granddaddy of fundamentalists.

Subtract current liabilities, long-term debt, and preferred stock (at market value) from current assets of the corporation.

Divide the result by the number of shares of common stock outstanding to get the current asset value per share.

If it is higher than the price per share, Graham would place the stock on his review list.

CHECKPOINTS FOR FINDING UNDERVALUED STOCKS

■ A price that is well below book value, asset value, and working capital per share
■ Ample cash or liquid assets for both normal business and expansion
■ Current dividend of 4.5% or more

■ Cash dividends paid for at least 5, and preferably 10, years without decrease in dollar payout
■ Total debt less than 30% of total capitalization
■ Minimum current dividend protection ratio of at least 1:4 ($1.40 earnings for each $1.00 in dividends), preferably higher
■ A P/E ratio lower than that of prior years and preferably below 10 times projected 12-month earnings
■ A company that sells at 4 or 5 times cash flow and that generates excess cash, which can be used to expand or repurchase its stock
■ Inventories that are valued lower than their initial cost or their immediate market value (check *Value Line* or Standard & Poor's *Outlook* for figures)

Low P/Es Pay Off

Investors often get excited about stocks with high P/Es. They figure the stocks are so popular that their prices will keep on rising. But the facts prove otherwise: Stocks with low P/Es (seemingly those with the worst prospects) outperform those with high multiples.

Low P/Es are often found in mature industries, in low-growth and blue-chip companies. In

Ten Stocks with P/E Ratios below Ten

COMPANY	PRICE	P/E
Stone Container	$16	6.4
Cyprus Amax Minerals	27	6.6
Timken Co.	40	8.4
Union Carbide	46	9.3
Bank of New York	47	9.4
IBM	107	9.4
ITT Hartford Group	46	9.8
Bank of Boston	48	9.8
St Paul Compapnies	54	9.8
First Union Corp.	61	9.9

(As of October 1996)

general, low-P/E companies pay higher dividends, although there are many exceptions.

High P/Es, by contrast, tend to be found in newer, aggressive growth companies, which are far riskier than those with lower P/Es.

☑ *HINT: Look for companies with high sales per share in cyclical industries (auto, aluminum, rubber) that are temporarily depressed. When industry conditions change and profit margins increase, the turnaround in earnings can be dramatic.*

Companies Repurchasing Their Stock

When corporations set up a program to buy back their shares, it's a bullish sign. Over a 12-month period, one survey showed, 64% of such stock outpaced the market.

Repurchase of a substantial number of shares automatically benefits all shareholders: Profits are spread over a smaller total, there's more money for dividends and reinvestments, and there's a temporary price increase for the stock in many cases.

FOR FURTHER INFORMATION

Charles H. Brandes, *Value Investing Today* (Homewood, IL: Dow Jones–Irwin, 1989).

Rose Marie Bukics, *Financial Statement Analysis* (Chicago: Probus Publishing Co., 1992).

D

Using Technical Indicators

*T*echnical analysis (TA) is a way of doing securities research using indicators, charts, and computer programs to track price trends of stocks, bonds, commodities, and the market in general. Technical analysts use these indicators to predict price movements.

If you understand the basics of both technical and fundamental analysis, you'll have a great advantage as an investor.

TA is neither as complex nor as esoteric as many people think. It's a tell-it-as-it-is interpretation of stock market activity. The technician glances at the fundamental values of securities but basically concentrates on the behavior of the market, industry groups, and stocks themselves—their price movements, volume, trends, patterns; in sum, their supply and demand.

Basically, TA is concerned with what is and not with what should be. Dyed-in-the-wool technicians pay minimal attention to what the company does and concentrate on what its stock does. They recognize that over the short term, the values of stocks reflect what people think they are worth, not what they are really worth.

Technical analysts operate on the assumption that (1) the past action of the stock market is the best indicator of its future course, (2) 80% of a stock's price movement is due to factors outside the company's control and 20% to factors unique to that stock, and (3) the stock market over a few weeks or months is rooted 85% in psychology and only 15% in economics.

THE DOW THEORY

There are a number of technical theories, but the granddaddy is the Dow theory. It is the oldest and most widely used. As with all technical approaches, it is based on the belief that stock prices cannot be forecast accurately by fundamental analysis but that trends, indicated by price movements and volume, can be used successfully. These can be recorded, tracked, and interpreted because the market itself prolongs movements: Investors buy more when the market is rising and sell more when it's dropping.

This follow-the-crowd approach enables the pros to buy when the market is going up and to sell or sell short when the market turns down. For amateurs, such quick trading is costly because of the commissions involved and the need for accurate information. But when properly used, TA can be valuable in correctly timing your buy and sell positions.

The Dow theory is named after Charles H. Dow, one of the founders of Dow Jones & Company, Inc., the financial reporting and publishing organization. The original hypotheses have been changed somewhat by his followers, but broadly interpreted, the Dow theory signals both the beginning and end of bull and bear markets.

Dow believed the stock market to be a barometer of business. The purpose of his theory was not to predict movements of security prices but rather to call the turns of the market and to forecast the business cycle or longer movements of depression or prosperity. It was not concerned with ripples or day-to-day fluctuations.

The Dow theory basically states that once a trend of the Dow Jones Industrial Average (DJIA) has been established, it tends to follow the same direction until definitely canceled by both the Industrial and Railroad (now Transportation) Averages. The market cannot be expected to produce new indications of the trend every day, and unless there is positive evidence to the contrary, the existing trend will continue.

Dow and his disciples saw the stock market as made up of two types of "waves": the primary wave, which is a bull or bear market cycle of several years' duration, and the secondary (or intermediary) wave, which lasts from a few weeks to a few months. Any single primary wave may contain within it 20 or more secondary waves, both up and down.

The theory relies on similar action by the two averages (Industry and Transportation), which may vary in strength but not in direction. Robert Rhea, who expanded the original concept, explained it this way: "Successive rallies, penetrating preceding high points with ensuing declines terminating above preceding low points, offer a bullish indication ... and vice versa for bearish indication .... A rally or decline is defined as one or more daily movements resulting in a net reversal of direction exceeding 3% of either average. Such movements have little authority unless confirmed by both Industrial and Transportation Averages ... but confirmation need not occur in the same day."

Dow did not consider that his theory applied to individual stock selections or analysis. He expected that specific issues would rise or fall with the averages most of the time, but he also recognized that any particular security would be affected by special conditions or situations.

These are the key indicators of the Dow theory:

- *A bull market is signaled as a possibility* when an intermediate decline in the DJIA stops above the bottom of the previous intermediate decline. This action must be confirmed by the action of the Transportation Average (DJTA). A bull market is confirmed after this has happened and when on the next intermediate rise both averages rise above the peaks of the last previous intermediate rise.
- *A bull market is in progress* as long as each new intermediate rise goes higher than the peak of the previous intermediate advance and each new intermediate decline stops above the bottom of the previous one.
- *A bear market is signaled as a possibility* when an intermediate rally in the DJIA fails to break through the top of the previous intermediate rise. A bear market is confirmed (1) after this has happened, (2) when the next intermediate decline breaks through the low of the previous one, and (3) when it is confirmed by the DJTA.
- *A bear market is in progress* as long as each new intermediate decline goes lower than the bottom of the previous decline and each new intermediate rally fails to rise as high as the previous rally.

A pure Dow theorist considers the averages to be quite sufficient to use in forecasting and sees no need to supplement them with statistics of commodity prices, volume of production, car loadings, bank debts, exports, imports, etc.

Interpreting the Dow Theory

Interpreting Dow theory leaves no room for sentiment.

- *A primary bear market* does not terminate until stock prices have thoroughly discounted the worst that is apt to occur. This decline requires three steps: (1) "the abandonment of hopes upon which stocks were purchased at inflated prices," (2) selling due to decreases in business and earnings, and (3) distress selling of sound securities despite value.

- *Primary bull markets* follow the opposite pattern: (1) a broad movement, interrupted by secondary reactions averaging longer than 2 years, where successive rallies penetrate high points with ensuing declines terminating above preceding low points; (2) stock prices advancing because of demand created by both investors and speculators who start buying when business conditions improve; and (3) rampant speculation as stocks advance on hopes, expectations, and dreams.

☑ *HINT: A new primary trend is not actually confirmed by the Dow theory until both the DJTA and the DJIA penetrate their previous positions.*

Criticism

There are analysts who scoff at the dow theory. They point out that the stock market today is vastly different from that in the early 1900s when dow formulated his theory. The number and value of shares of publicly-owned corporations have increased enormously: in 1900, the average number of shares traded annually on the NYSE was 59.5 million. Now that's the volume on a very slow day.

The sharpest criticism is leveled against the breadth, scope, and significance of the averages. The original Industrial index had only 12 stocks, and today's 30 large companies do not provide a true picture of the broad, technologically oriented economy. Critics point out that the Transportation

Average is also unrepresentative, because some of the railroads derive a major share of their revenues from natural resources, and the airlines and trucking companies are limited in their impact. Add the geographic dispersal of industry, and Transportation is no longer a reliable guide to the economy.

Finally, the purists argue that government regulations and institutional dominance of trading have so altered the original concept of individual investors that the Dow theory can no longer be considered all-powerful and always correct.

To most investors, the value of the Dow theory is that it represents a sort of think-for-yourself method that will pay worthwhile dividends for those who devote time and effort to gaining a sound understanding of the principles involved.

PSYCHOLOGICAL INDICATORS

Keeping in mind that the stock market is rooted 15% in economics and 85% in psychology, some analysts predict the future by using such technical indicators as these:

Barron's Confidence Index (BCI)

This is published weekly in the financial newsmagazine Barron's. It shows the ratio of the yield on 10 highest-grade bonds to the yield on the broader-based dow jones 40-bond average. The ratio varies from the middle 80s (bearish) to the middle 90s (bullish).

The theory is that the trend of "smart money" is usually revealed in the bond market before it shows up in the stock market. Thus, Barron's Confidence Index will be high when shrewd investors are confident and buy more lower-grade bonds, thus reducing low-grade bond yields, and low when they are worried and stick to high-grade bonds, thus cutting high-grade yields.

If you see that the BCI simply keeps going back and forth aimlessly for many weeks, you can probably expect the same type of action from the overall stock market.

Overbought–Oversold Index (OOI)

This is a handy measure, designed by indicator digest, of a short-term trend and its anticipated duration. Minor upswings or downturns have limited lives. As they peter out, experienced traders say that the market is "overbought" or "oversold" and is presumably ready for a near-term reversal.

Glamour Average

Another indicator digest special, this shows what is happening with the institutional favorites, usually trading at high multiples because of their presumed growth potential and current popularity (in a bull market). By and large, this is a better indicator for speculators than investors.

Speculation Index

This is the ratio of AMEX-to-NYSE volume. When trading in AMEX stocks (generally more speculative) moves up faster than that in NYSE (quality) issues, speculation is growing. It's time for traders to move in and for investors to be cautious.

BROAD-BASED INDICATORS

Odd-Lot Index

This shows how small investors view the market, because it concentrates on trades of fewer than 100 shares. The small investor is presumably "uninformed" (a somewhat debatable assumption) and so tends to follow established patterns: selling as the market rises; jumping in to pick up bargains when it declines. The signal comes when the odd-lotter deviates from this "normal" behavior.

When the small investor distrusts a rally after a long bear market, that investor gives a bullish signal: Initial selling is normal, but when this continues, it's abnormal and a signal to the pros to start buying.

Moving Average Lines

You can also watch the direction of a stock by comparing its price to a moving average (MA). A moving average is an average that's periodically updated by dropping the first number and adding in the last one. A 30-week moving average, for example, is determined by adding the stock's closing price for the current week to the closing prices of the previous 29 weeks and then dividing by 30. Over time, this moving average indicates the trend of prices.

A long-term moving average tends to smooth out short-term fluctuations and provides a basis against which short-term price movement can be measured.

Moving averages can be calculated for both individual stocks and all stocks in a group—say, all those listed on the NYSE or all in a particular industry. Technical analysts use a variety of time frames: 10 days, 200 days, 30 weeks, etc. In most cases they compare the moving average with a regular market average, usually the Dow Jones Industrial Average. For example:

- As long as the DJIA is *above* the MA, the outlook is bullish.
- As long as the DJIA is *below* the MA, the outlook is bearish.
- A confirmed downward penetration of the MA by the base index is a *sell* signal.
- A confirmed penetration of the MA is a *buy* signal.

Beware of false penetrations, and delay action until there is a substantial penetration (2% to 3%), upward or downward, within a few weeks. In other words, don't be in a hurry to interpret the chart action.

MAs are vulnerable to swift market declines, especially from market tops. By the time you get the signal, you may have lost a bundle, because prices tend to fall twice as fast as they rise.

If you enjoy charting, develop a ratio of the stocks selling above their 30-week MA. When the ratio is over 50% and trending upward, the out-look is bullish. When it drops below 50% and/or is trending down, there's trouble ahead.

☑ *HINT: The longer the time span of the MA, the greater the significance of a crossover signal. An 18-month chart is more reliable than a 30-day one.*

Buying Power

Buying power basically refers to the amount of money available to buy securities. It is determined by the cash in brokerage accounts plus the dollar amount that would be available if securities were fully margined. The bottom line: the market cannot rise above the available buying power.

The principle here is that at any point investors have only so much money available for investments. If it's in money market funds and cash, their buying power is stored up and readily available, not only to move into stocks but to push up prices. By contrast, if most investor buying power is already in stocks, there's little left for purchasing more stocks. In fact, in this situation investors could actually push the price of stocks down should they begin to sell.

Buying power is shown by these indicators:

■ Rising volume in rallies. Investors are eager to buy, so the demand is greater than the supply, and prices go up.

■ Shrinking volume on market declines. Investors are reluctant to sell.

With this technical approach, volume is the key indicator: It rises on rallies when the trend is up and rises on reactions when the trend is down.

☑ *HINT: Volume trends are apt to reverse before price trends. Shrinking volume almost always shows up before the top of a bull market and before the bottom of a bear market.*

One other measure of buying power is the percentage of cash held in mutual funds. The Investment Company Institute in Washington,

DC, publishes this figure every month. In general, the ratio of cash to total assets in mutual funds tends to be low during market peaks, because this is the time when everyone is eager to buy stocks. The ratio is high during bull markets.

☑ *HINT: When cash holdings, as compiled by the Investment Company Institute, are above 7%, it's considered favorable; 9% to 10% is out-and-out bullish.*

Most Active Stocks

This list is published at the top of daily or weekly reports of the NYSE, AMEX, and NASDAQ, and it gives the high, low, and last prices and change of 10 to 15 volume leaders. Here's where you can spot popular and unpopular industry groups and stocks.

Forget about the big-name companies such as Exxon, GE, and IBM. They have so many shares outstanding that trading is always heavy. Watch for repetition: of one industry or of one company. When the same names appear several times in a week or two, something is happening. Major investors are involved: buying if the price continues to rise, selling if it falls.

Watch most-actives for:

■ Newcomers, especially small- or medium-sized corporations. When the same company pops up again and again, major shareholders

---

London's Financial Times Index

The Financial Times Index is a British version of the Dow Jones Industrial Average. It records data on the London Stock Exchange: prices, volume, etc. Because it reflects worldwide business attitudes, it's a fairly reliable indicator of what's ahead, in 2 weeks to 2 months, for the NYSE.

There are, of course, temporary aberrations due to local situations, but over many years it has been a valuable technical tool. Since London is 5 hours ahead of New York, early risers benefit the most.

are worried (price drop) or optimistic (price rise). Because volume requires substantial resources, the buyers must be big-money organizations. Once they have bought, you can move in, if the other fundamentals are sound.

- Companies in the same industry. Stocks tend to move as a group. Activity in computer retailers such as IBM and Apple could signal interest in this field.

NYSE Biggest % Movers

WINNERS

NAME	VOLUME	CLOSE	CHANGE	% CHG.
AppliedMagn	52689	$17\frac{1}{2}$	$+5\frac{1}{2}$	+45.8
USAirGp	177734	$10\frac{3}{4}$	$+2\frac{3}{4}$	+34.4
Chyron	13236	$2\frac{3}{4}$	$+\frac{5}{8}$	+29.4
SafegrdSci wi	157	$42\frac{1}{4}$	$+8\frac{5}{8}$	+25.7
Chaus	3027	$6\frac{1}{8}$	$+1\frac{1}{4}$	+25.6

LOSERS

NAME	VOLUME	CLOSE	CHANGE	% CHG.
CoramHlthcr	56239	$3\frac{5}{8}$	$-1\frac{1}{2}$	−29.3
TelexChile	11521	$9\frac{3}{4}$	$-2\frac{1}{2}$	−20.4
KimminsEnvr	5435	$4\frac{1}{8}$	$-\frac{7}{8}$	−17.5
NordRes	3161	$2\frac{1}{4}$	$-\frac{3}{8}$	−14.3
Handleman	8796	$8\frac{3}{8}$	$-1\frac{1}{4}$	−13.0

SOURCE: Barron's.

AMEX Biggest % Movers

WINNERS

NAME	VOLUME	CLOSE	CHANGE	% CHG.
HastingMfg	160	26	$+7\frac{1}{2}$	+40.5
GloblOcean	681	$4\frac{1}{2}$	+1	+28.6
Transcisco	1151	$3\frac{9}{16}$	$+\frac{3}{4}$	+26.7
HovnanEnt	6879	$7\frac{7}{8}$	$+1\frac{9}{16}$	+24.7
HiShearTch	2414	14	$+2\frac{3}{4}$	+24.4

LOSERS

NAME	VOLUME	CLOSE	CHANGE	% CHG.
PlainsRes	11920	$8\frac{5}{16}$	$-2\frac{7}{16}$	−22.7
Belmac	1797	5	$-1\frac{1}{8}$	−18.4
IntrCityPdt	3435	$1\frac{7}{8}$	$-\frac{3}{8}$	−16.7
IntellgSys	384	$1\frac{3}{4}$	$-\frac{1}{4}$	−12.5
AmTechCeram	1799	$13\frac{1}{64}$	$-1\frac{47}{64}$	−11.8

SOURCE: Barron's.

Nasdaq Biggest % Movers

WINNERS

NAME	VOLUME	CLOSE	CHANGE	% CHG.
Biospheric	4786	14	$+7\frac{1}{2}$	+115.4
TransdSvcs	23490	$6\frac{5}{8}$	$+2\frac{3}{8}$	+55.9
DevcnInt	2400	$8\frac{5}{16}$	$+2\frac{3}{16}$	+51.1
Xylogics	43803	$50\frac{3}{8}$	$+15\frac{3}{4}$	+45.5
CyrixCp	135853	$48\frac{3}{16}$	$+14\frac{3}{16}$	+43.3

LOSERS

NAME	VOLUME	CLOSE	CHANGE	% CHG.
vjNuclrSpt	1748	1	−2	−66.7
HappinesExp	27614	$6\frac{1}{2}$	$-4\frac{1}{2}$	−40.9
RockBottm	33957	$17\frac{3}{4}$	$-7\frac{1}{2}$	−29.7
Forstmann	66	$1\frac{1}{2}$	$-\frac{1}{2}$	−25.0
CasinoAm	17966	$11\frac{1}{8}$	$-3\frac{3}{8}$	−23.3

SOURCE: Barron's.

Percentage Leaders

This list is published weekly in several financial journals. It's primarily for those seeking to catch a few points on a continuing trend.

Although the value of the percentage leaders list has diminished recently because of the high gains scored by takeover or buyout candidates, it is still a way to spot some potential winners and to avoid losers. If you're thinking about making a move, check this list first. You may find several yet undiscovered stocks moving up in price.

Advances vs. Declines (A/D)

This is a measure of the number of stocks that have advanced in price and the number that have declined within a given time span. Expressed as a ratio, the A/D illustrates the general direction of the market: When more stocks advance than decline on a single trading day, the market is thought to be bullish. The A/D can be an excellent guide to the trend of the overall market and, occasionally, of specific industry or stock groups. The best way to utilize A/D data is with a chart where the lines are plotted to show the cumulative difference between the advances and the declines on the NYSE or, for speculative holdings, on the AMEX. The total can cover 1 week, 21 days, or whatever period you choose, but because you're looking for developing trends, it should not be too long.

NYSE Advances and Declines: Highs and Lows

NYSE	WED	TUE	WK AGO
Issues traded	2,267	2,282	2,268
Advances	821	1,010	883
Declines	881	698	829
Unchanged	565	574	556
New highs	72	62	91
New lows	13	19	10

SOURCE: Wall Street Journal.

The table on page 391 shows a week when the advance/decline ratio was approximately 10 to 7, generally a positive trading day. On Wednesday, declines outnumbered advances by a small percentage, but new highs outnumbered new lows by a greater amount than on the prior day.

Many analysts prefer a moving average (MA) based on the net change for the week: 3,484 advances and 4,403 declines, for a net difference of 919. To make plotting easier, you can start with an arbitrary base, say 10,000, so the week's figure would be 9,081 (10,000 – 919).

The following week there's a net advance of 1,003, so the new total would be 10,084, etc. When you chart a 20-week MA, divide the cumulative figure by 20. When you add week 21, drop week 1. Result: a quick view of market optimism or pessimism.

To spot trouble ahead, compare the A/D chart with that of the DJIA. If the Dow is moving up for a month or so but the A/D line is flat or dropping, that's a negative signal. Watch out for new highs and lows on the A/D chart. Near market peaks, the A/D line will almost invariably top out and start declining before the overall market. At market lows, the A/D line seldom gives a far-in-advance warning.

Be cautious about using the A/D line alone. Make sure that it is confirmed by other indicators or, better yet, confirms other signals.

Volume

Trading volume, or the number of shares traded, is an important indicator in interpreting market direction and stock price changes. Changes in stock prices are the result of supply and demand, that is, the number of people who want to buy a stock and the number who want to sell. The key point here is that a rise or fall in price on a small volume of shares traded is far less important than a move supported by heavy volume. When there's heavy trading on the up side, buyers control the

By Dollar Volume: NYSE

NAME	VOLUME	CLOSE	CHANGE
MicronTch	22834268	$89\frac{7}{8}$	$+13\frac{1}{2}$
IBM	20353360	$98\frac{7}{8}$	$-3\frac{7}{8}$
TexInstr	8178621	$78\frac{3}{4}$	$+6\frac{1}{4}$
Chrysler	7634676	$57\frac{3}{4}$	$+3\frac{1}{8}$
Motorola	7270874	$79\frac{5}{8}$	$+5\frac{1}{8}$

SOURCE: Barron's.

market, and their enthusiasm for the stock often pushes its price even higher.

☑ *HINT: Volume always precedes the direction of a stock's price.*

Momentum

This indicator measures the speed with which an index (or stock) is moving rather than its direction. Index changes are seldom if ever abrupt, so when an already rising index starts to rise even faster, it is thought likely to have a longer continuing upward run.

To measure momentum effectively you need to compare current figures to an index or previous average such as a 30-week moving average or the S&P 500.

New Highs or Lows

Every day the newspaper prints a list of stocks that hit a new price high or low for the year during the previous day's trading activity. Technical analysts use the ratio between the new highs and the new lows as an indication of the market's direction. They believe that when more stocks are making new highs than new lows, it's a bullish indication. If there are more lows than highs, pessimism abounds.

☑ *HINT: You should not use these figures as an absolute prediction of the future course of the*

market, because for a while a number of the same stocks will appear again and again. Also, the further into the year it is, the more difficult it is for a stock to continually post new highs.

These figures are most effective when converted to a chart and compared with a standard average. As long as the high and low indicators stay more or less in step with the Dow Jones Industrial Average or the S&P 500, they are simply a handy confirmation. But when the high–low line starts to dip while the average moves up, watch out: Internal market conditions are deteriorating.

This index of highs and lows exposes the underlying strength or weakness of the stock market, which is too often masked by the action of the DJIA. In an aging bull market, the DJIA may continue to rise, deceptively showing strength by the upward moves of a handful of major stocks; but closer examination will usually reveal that most stocks are too far below their yearly highs to make new peaks. At such periods, the small number of new highs is one of the most significant manifestations of internal market deterioration. The reverse is the telltale manner in which the total number of new lows appears in bear markets.

USING THE INDICATORS

Never rely on just one technical indicator. Only rarely can a single chart, ratio, average, MA, or index be 100% accurate. When an indicator breaks its pattern, look for confirmation from at least two other guidelines. Then wait a bit: at least 2 days in an ebullient market, a week or more in a normal one. This won't be easy, but what you are seeking is confirmation. These days a false move can be costly.

This emphasis on consensus applies also to newsletters, advisory services, and recommendations. If you select only one, look for a publication that uses—and explains—several indicators. Better yet, study two or three.

CHARTS: A VALUABLE TOOL FOR EVERYONE

Charts are a graphic ticker tape. They measure the flow of money into and out of the stock market, industry, or specific stock. They spotlight the highs and lows and point up how volume rises and falls on an advance or decline, illustrating the long-term patterns of the market and individual stocks.

Charting is simple, but interpretation can be complex. Even the strongest advocates of technical analysis (TA) disagree about the meaning of various formations, but they all start with three premises: (1) what happened before will be repeated, (2) a trend should be assumed to continue until a reversal is definite, and (3) a chart pattern that varies from a norm indicates that something unusual is happening. More than almost any other area of TA, chart reading is an art and a skill rather than a solid body of objective scientific information. It is an aid to stock analysis, but not an end.

Charts are not surefire systems for beating the market, but they are one of the quickest and clearest ways to determine and follow trends. However, all charts provide after-the-fact information.

The best combination for maximum profits and minimum losses is fundamental analysis supplemented by graphic technical analysis. Charts report that volume and price changes occur. Proper interpretation can predict the direction and intensity of change, because every purchase of every listed stock shows up on the chart.

Watch the bottom of the chart as well as the progress lines. This shows volume, and volume precedes price. A strong inflow of capital eventually pushes up the price of the stock; an outflow of dollars must result in a decline. To the charted results, it makes no difference who is doing the buying or selling.

Keeping in mind that charts are not infallible. Use them to:

- *Help determine when to buy and when to sell* by indicating probable levels of support and supply and by signaling trend reversals
- *Call attention, by unusual volume or price behavior,* to something happening in an individual company that can be profitable to investors
- *Help determine the current trend:* up, down, or sideways, and whether the trend is accelerating or slowing
- *Provide a quick history of a stock* and show whether buying should be considered on a rally or a decline
- *Offer a sound means for confirming or rejecting* a buy or sell decision that is based on other information

☑ *HINT: Charts are history. By studying past action, it is often possible to make a reasonably valid prediction of the immediate future.*

WIDELY USED CHARTS

The most commonly used types of charts are point-and-figure (P&F) and bar charts. For best results, they should be constructed on a daily or weekly basis.

POINT AND FIGURE CHART

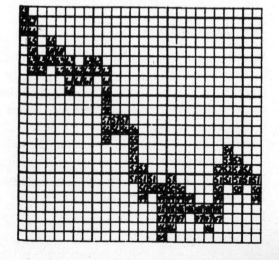

If you have time, charting can be fun and highly educational. All you need is a pad of graph paper: plain squares for P&F charts, logarithmic or standard paper for bar charts.

P&F Charts

P&F charts are one-dimensional graphics. They show only price changes in relation to previous price changes. There are no indications of time or volume. The key factor is the change in price direction.

Some professionals think that P&F charts are oversimplified and consider them useful only as short-term guides and as a quick way to choose between two or three selections.

In making a P&F chart, the stock price is posted in a square: one above or below another, depending on the upward or downward movement of the price. As long as the price continues in the same direction, the same column is used. When the price shifts direction, the chartist moves to the next column.

In the chart shown on page 394, the stock first fell in a downward sequence from 68 to 67 to 66. Then it rose to 67, so the chartist moved to column 2. The next moves were down to 62, up to 63 (new column), and so on. Most chartists start the new column only when there is a distinct change, typically 1 point, but for longer projections, 2 or 3 points.

Note how a pattern is formed with various resistance levels where the price of the stock stayed within a narrow range (57–56 and later 48–47). The chart signals each shift from such a base: down from 56 to 51; up from 47 to 52.

The best way for an amateur to learn about P&F charts is to copy them. Take a stock that has been plotted for many years and slowly recopy its action on a piece of graph paper. Then draw in the trend lines: the uptrend line on the high points, the downtrend line along the low points. Then draw your channels, which are broad paths created by the highs and lows of a definite trend. (Without a trend your channel will be horizontal.)

P&F charts have disadvantages: They do not portray intraday action or consider volume. The financial pages report only the high (62), low (59¼), and close (61½). This does not show that the stock might have moved up and down from 60 to 62 several times during the day.

Despite the omission of volume on P&F charts, many technical analysts feel that volume should always be checked once there is a confirmed trend on the chart. Rising volume on upward movements and dwindling sales on the downside usually indicate that the stock has ample investor support. It's always wise to be on the same side as volume.

Bar Charts

These graphics record changes in relation to time. The horizontal axis represents time—a day, week, or month; the vertical coordinates refer to price. To follow volume on the same chart, add a series of vertical lines along the bottom. The higher the line, the greater the volume. On printed charts, adjustments are made so that everything fits into a convenient space.

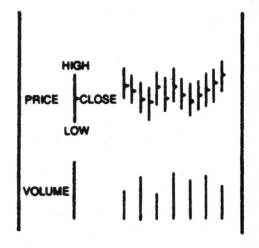

BAR CHART

In plotting a bar chart, enter a dot to mark the highest price at which the stock was traded that day; add another dot to record the low. Draw the vertical line between the dots to depict the price range, and draw a short horizontal nub to mark the closing price. After a few entries, a pattern will begin to emerge.

Head-and-Shoulder Charts

Almost every chartist has favorite configurations. They include such descriptive titles as the rounding bottom, the flag, the pennant, the tombstone top, the Prussian helmet formation, the megaphone top, and the lattice formation. One of the most popular formations is head and shoulders (H&S).

Oversimplified, the head-and-shoulders chart portrays three successive rallies and reactions, with the second reaching a higher point than either of the others. The failure of the third rally to equal the second peak is a warning that a major uptrend may have come to an end. Conversely, a bottom H&S, formed upside down after a declining trend, suggests that an upturn lies ahead.

Left Shoulder

This forms when an upturn of some duration, after hitting a climax, starts to fall. The volume of trading should increase with the rally and contract with the reaction. Reason: people who bought the stock on the up-trend start to take profits. When the technical reaction takes place, people who were slow to buy on the first rally start buying on the technical reaction.

Head

This is a second rally that carries the stock to new highs and is followed by a reaction that erases just about all the gain. Volume is high on the rally, yet lower than when forming the left shoulder. Reason: Investors who missed both the earlier actions start buying and force new highs.

This is followed by another drop as those who hesitated earlier see the second reaction and start acquiring the stock as it is sold by early buyers.

Right Shoulder

The third rally fails to reach the height of the head before the reaction. This is a sign of weakness. Watch the volume. If it contracts on a rally, it's likely that the price structure has weakened. If it increases, beware of a false signal.

Breakout

This occurs when the stock price falls below the previous lows. At this point, most of the recent buyers have sold out—many of them at a loss.

No H&S should be regarded as complete until the price breaks out below a line drawn tangent with the lows on the left and right shoulders. This is called the neckline.

INTERPRETING CHARTS

The charts from Securities Research Company (SRC) shown in this chapter are typical of those available from technical services. They can be valuable tools to improve the selection of securities and especially the timing of purchases and sales. Similar graphics are available for industry groups and stock market averages.

HEAD-AND-SHOULDERS CHART

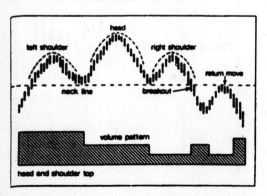

Do not buy any stock when the chart shows a confirmed downtrend. Buy up stocks in up groups in an up market. And unless you are holding for the long term, consider selling when there's a downtrend in the stock, the industry, and the market.

SRC offers two books of charts on stocks: blue for long-term trends over 12 years and red for short-term trends over 21 months. By using both, you get a better idea of the character, history, and probable performance of the stock.

Long-Term Charts

Capitalization

Information on the corporation: dollars of bonds and preferred stocks (in millions); number of common shares outstanding (in thousands); and book value per common share.

Earnings and Dividends

Per-share data scaled from $1.40 to $5.50.

Dividends

The annual rate of interim dividend payments. The circles mark the month in which the pay-

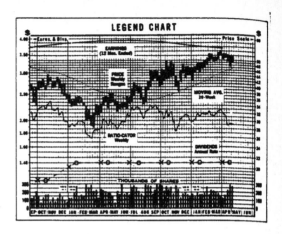

ments were made. Extra or irregular payouts (not shown) are typed in.

Earnings

On a per-share 12-month-ended basis as shown by the solid black line. Dots indicate whether the company issues quarterly, semiannual, or annual earnings reports.

Monthly Ranges

Shows the highest and lowest prices for the stock each month. Crossbars indicate the closing price.

Price Scale

This shows the dollar price of the stock, against which the monthly ranges are plotted.

Ratio-Cator

A guideline used by SRC. The plottings are obtained by dividing the closing price of the stock by the closing value of the djia on the same day. The resulting percentage is multiplied by a factor of 4.5 to bring the line close to the price bars and is read from the right-hand scale. The plotting indicates whether the stock has kept pace, out-performed, or lagged behind the general market.

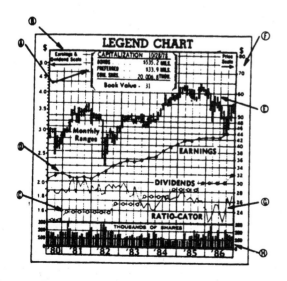

Volume

The number of shares traded, in thousands, each month on an arithmetic scale. Volume comes before price.

Short-Term Charts

Here the data are similar to those of the longer-term charts, but cover the action for only 21 months.

Earnings

For the last 12 months. Read from the left border to find the changes in dollar-per-share profits.

Dividends

On an annual basis; X indicates the ex-dividend date, 0 the dividend payment date.

Moving Average for 39 Weeks

Each dot represents the average of the closing prices of the 39 most recent weeks. When used with the price bars, it helps you determine trends as well as buying and selling points.

Ratio-Cator

Shows the relative performance of the stock. It is calculated by dividing the closing price of the stock by the closing value of the DJIA on the same day and then multiplying by 7.0.

NOTE: In plotting the short-term chart, the price range, earnings, and dividends are shown on a uniform ratio scale: that is, the vertical linear distance for a 100% move is the same any place on the chart regardless of whether the rise was from $5 to $10 or from $20 to $40. Thus all charts of all stocks are comparable.

USING TREND LINE CHARTS

The key to the successful use of charts, and most technical analysis, is the premise that a trend in

force will persist until a significant change in investor expectations causes it to reverse itself—or as Martin Pring puts it, "on the assumption that people will continue to make the same mistakes they have made in the past." To discern that trend, the chartist draws lines connecting the lowest points of an upward-moving stock and the highest points of a downward-moving stock. This trend line is a reliable indicator about 80% of the time, because it predicts the immediate action of the stock or market.

The shrewd investor rises with the trend: buying when there's a confirmed upward move, considering selling when there's a definite down-swing. Generally, the stock will move along that line—regardless of the direction. There will be interim bounces or dips, but most stocks hold to that pattern until there is a clear change.

Trend lines establish bases. The uptrend line becomes a support level below which an upward-moving stock is not likely to fall. The downtrend line marks a resistance level above which the stock is not likely to rise.

HINT: Before you invest—or speculate—in any stocks, check the chart and draw trend lines. Buy when the trend is up; hold or do not buy when it is moving down. The best profits always come when you buy an up stock in an up industry in an up market—clearly evident from trend lines on charts. And, of course, when you sell short, it's the opposite.

Technical analysis, especially charts, can be a valuable aid to timing if you remember these three points:

- Unless you are extremely optimistic and can afford to tie up your money for a while, never buy any stock until its chart is pointing up.
- Always check the chart action before you sell. You may think that the high has been reached, but the chart may disagree and make possible greater gains.

- If the chart shows a downtrend, consider selling. If it's a good investment, you can buy the stock back later at a lower price. If it's not, you'll save a lot of money.

Properly employed, technical analysis can be an important adjunct to fundamental investing and, more often than not, it will keep you humble!

FOR FURTHER INFORMATION

Robert D. Edwards and John Magee, *Technical Analysis of Stock Trends* (Boston: John Magee, Inc., 1992).

Martin Pring, *Technical Analysis Explained*, 3rd ed. (New York: McGraw-Hill, 1991).

T.H. Stewart, *How Charts Can Make You Money: Technical Analysis for Investors*, 2nd ed. (Chicago: Probus Publishing, 1990).

Robert W. Colby and Thomas A. Meyers, *The Encyclopedia of Technical Indicators* (Homewood, IL: Business One Irwin, 1992).

Where, What, When:
Exchanges, Indexes, and Indicators

*I*n keeping with Wall Street jargon and financial reporting, initials are used frequently. Here are some of the most widely used:

EXCHANGES

NYSE: New York Stock Exchange 11 Wall Street, New York, NY 10005; 212–656–3000. This is the oldest and largest exchange in the United States. To be listed, a corporation must:

- Demonstrate earning power of $2.5 million before federal income taxes for the most recent year and $2 million pre-tax for each of the preceding 2 years
- Have net tangible assets of $40 million
- Have market value of publicly held shares of $40 million
- Report a total of 1.1 million common shares publicly held
- Have 2,000 holders of 100 shares or more

AMEX: American Stock Exchange 86 Trinity Place, New York, NY 10006; 212–306–1000. These corporations are generally smaller and less financially strong than those on the NYSE. The firm must have:

- Pre-tax income of at least $750,000 in its last fiscal year or in 2 of the last 3
- Stockholders' equity of $4 million
- 500,000 shares of common, exclusive of holdings of officers or directors

- 800 public stockholders or a minimum public distribution of 1 million shares together with a minimum of 400 holders of 100 or more shares
- Market price of $3 minimum with $3 million public market capitalization

NASDAQ: This is the market for securities that are not listed on major exchanges. The trading is conducted by dealers who are members of NASD (National Association of Securities Dealers, 1735 K Street NW, Washington, DC 20006; 202–728–8000) and who may or may not be members of other exchanges. Trading is by bid and asked prices. The primary market is Nasdaq (National Association of Securities Dealers Automated Quotations), which consists of about 6,090 of the most actively traded issues. Some 13,000 other stocks are quoted in daily financial summaries.

CBOE: Chicago Board Options Exchange 400 South La Salle at Van Buren, Chicago, IL 60605; 312–786–5600. The major auction market for calls and puts, primarily on NYSE stocks, and recently for special types of options such as those on Treasury bonds and on the S&P 100 and 500.

ACC: AMEX Options Exchange 86 Trinity Place, New York, NY 10006; 212–306–1000. The division of AMEX that trades puts and calls, almost entirely on NYSE-listed and OTC stocks.

CBT: Chicago Board of Trade 141 West Jackson Boulevard, Chicago, IL 60604; 312–435–3500. A major market for futures contracts: commodities, interest rate securities, commercial paper, etc.

CME: Chicago Mercantile Exchange 30 South Wacker Drive, Chicago, IL 60606; 312–930–1000. Futures contracts for commodities.

NYCE: New York Cotton Exchange 4 World Trade Center, New York, NY 10048; 212–742–5800. Trading in futures in cotton and orange juice.

KCBT: Kansas City Board of Trade 4800 Main Street, Suite 303, Kansas City, MO 64112; 816–753–7500. Trades in futures of commodities and Value Line futures index.

NYFE: New York Futures Exchange 4 World Trade Center, New York, NY 10048; 212–938–4940. A wholly owned subsidiary of the NYSE that trades in the NYSE Composite Index futures contract.

NYME: New York Mercantile Exchange 4 World Trade Center, New York, NY 10048; 212–748–3000. Trading in futures of petroleum, platinum, and palladium.

FEDERAL AGENCIES

SEC: Securities and Exchange Commission 450 Fifth Street NW, Washington, DC 20549; 202–942–7040. A federal agency established to help protect investors. It is responsible for administering congressional acts regarding securities, stock exchanges, corporate reporting, investment companies, investment advisers, and public utility holding companies.

FRB: Federal Reserve Board 20th and C Streets NW, Washington, DC 20551; 202–452–3000. The federal agency responsible for control of such important investment items as the discount rate, money supply, and margin requirements.

FDIC: Federal Deposit Insurance Corporation 550 17th Street NW, Washington, DC 20429; 800–934–3342. An agency that insures bank deposits.

Savings Association Insurance Fund 550 17th

Other Stock Exchanges

U.S.

Boston Stock Exchange 1 Boston Place, 38th floor Boston, MA 02108	617–723–9500
Chicago Stock Exchange 440 S. LaSalle Street Chicago, IL 60605	312–663–2222
Pacific Stock Exchange 301 Pine Street San Francisco, CA 94104 or	415–393–4000
233 South Beaudry Avenue Los Angeles, CA 90012	213–977–4500
Philadelphia Stock Exchange 1900 Market Street Philadelphia, PA 19103	215–496–5000

CANADA

Alberta Stock Exchange 300 Fifth Avenue SW Calgary, Alberta T2P 3C4	403–974–7400
Montreal Stock Exchange 800 Victoria Square (4th floor) Montreal, Quebec H4Z 1A9	514–871–2424
Toronto Stock Exchange Exchange Tower 2 First Canadian Place Toronto, Ontario M5X 1J2	416–947–4700
Vancouver Stock Exchange 609 Granville Street Vancouver, British Columbia V7Y 1H1	604–643–6590
Winnipeg Stock Exchange 620 One Lombard Place Winnipeg, Manitoba R3B 0X3	204–987–7070

Street NW, Washington, DC 20429; 800–934–3342. An agency that insures deposits with savings and loan associations.

CFTC: Commodity Futures Trading Commission 2033 K Street NW, Washington, DC 20581; 202–254–6387. This is a watchdog for the commodities futures trading industry.

STOCK MARKET AVERAGES

These indicators are used to measure and report value changes in representative stock groupings. An average is simply the arithmetic mean of a group of prices. An index is an average expressed in relation to an earlier established base market value. Indexes and averages may be broad-based—that is, made up of many stocks—or narrow-based: made up of stocks in a particular sector or industry.

DOW JONES INDUSTRIAL AVERAGE (DJIA). The oldest and most widely used stock market average. It shows the action of 30 actively traded blue-chip stocks, representing about 15% of NYSE values.

This popular indicator of the direction of the stock market was devised in 1884 by Charles H. Dow, a founder and first editor of the *Wall Street*

Stocks in Dow Jones Averages as of October 1996

INDUSTRIALS (DJIA)

Alcoa*	Du Pont, E.I.	Minnesota Mining & Manufacturing
Allied Signal	Eastman Kodak	J.P. Morgan
American Express	Exxon Corporation	Philip Morris Co.
AT&T	General Electric	Procter & Gamble
Bethlehem Steel	General Motors	Sears, Roebuck, & Co.
Boeing	Goodyear Tire	Texaco, Inc.
Caterpillar	International Business Machines	Union Carbide
Chevron	International Paper	United Technologies
Coca-Cola	McDonald's Corp.	Westinghouse Electric
Disney (Walt)	Merck & Co.	Woolworth (F.W.)

TRANSPORTATION (DJTA)

Airborne Freight	ConRail	Santa Fe Pacific
Alaska Air Group	CSX Corp.	Southwest Airlines
American President Lines	Delta Airlines	UAL Corp.
AMR Corp.	Federal Express	Union Pacific Corp.
Burlington Northern	Norfolk & Southern	U.S. Air
Carolina Freight	Roadway Service	XTRA Corp.
Consolidated Freightways	Ryder Systems	

UTILITY (DJUA)

American Electric Power	Houston Industries	Peoples Energy
Centerior Energy	Niagara Mohawk Power	PECO Energy
Commonwealth Edison	Noram Energy	Public Service Enterprises
Consolidated Natural Gas	Pacific Gas & Electric	SCE Corp.
Detroit Edison	Panhandle Eastern Corp.	Unicom Corp.

*Aluminum Co. of America

Journal. At that time it was simply a list of the average closing prices of 11 railroad and manufacturing stocks, published in *The Customer's Afternoon Letter*, a forerunner of the *Journal.*

The Dow average is determined by adding up the closing prices of the component stocks and using a divisor that is adjusted for splits and stock dividends. The average is quoted in points, not dollars. Initially the divisor was 11; in the 1920s it became 30, when the number of stocks was increased from 11 to 30; today it is .38610730. Each Dow Jones Average—transportation, utility, and industrials (see box)—measures the stocks' performance during one day. The Dow Jones Composite Index, also called the 65 Stock Average, combines the other three indexes and consists of 30 industrials, 20 transportation, and 15 utility stocks. It is not widely followed.

For many years the Dow Jones Industrial Average hovered around 100, peaking at 386 in 1929 just before the crash. Afterwards it climbed back up slowly, never moving much past 200 until World War II, when it hit 700. In 1966 it reached 1,000. It fell again to 570 in 1974 only to return to 1,000 two years later. In August 1987 the Dow posted an all-time high of 2,722.42, but two months later, on October 19, it plunged a record 508 points to 1,738.74. Since then there have been numerous ups and downs. In early July 1988 the Dow reached 2,158.61, the highest point since the October crash. A year later, in July 1989, it was 2,456.56. As we went to press in October 1996, it was over 6,000!

The Dow is often criticized for the fact that a high-priced stock has a greater impact on the average than lower-priced issues. In other words, the stocks are not equally weighted, so on any given day, a fluctuation of significance in one or two high-priced stocks can distort the average. The Dow, then, captures absolute price movement without regard to current share price or market capitalization. A $1 change in the price of a lower-priced stock has the same effect as a $1 change in a higher-priced stock.

As a result, the Dow is useful for tracking the direction of the market over the long term, but is often less reliable on a daily or even weekly basis. With only 30 stocks, it is also regarded by many as too small.

STANDARD & POOR'S COMPOSITE INDEX OF 500 STOCKS. This index addresses some of the criticism of the Dow. Unlike the Dow, the S&P 500 is market-weighted—that is, its component stocks are weighted according to the total market value of their outstanding shares. The result: The impact of any single component's price change is proportional to its overall market value. Devised in 1957, the S&P 500 covers 500 stocks and is computed by multiplying the price of each stock by the number of shares outstanding. This gives larger and more influential corporations more weight and, many think, makes it a better general measure than the Dow.

The 500 stocks consist mainly of NYSE-listed companies, with some AMEX and OTC stocks. There are 400 industrials, 60 transportation and utility companies, and 40 financial issues. Options on this index trade on the Chicago Board Options Exchange and futures on the Chicago Mercantile Exchange.

STANDARD & POOR'S 400 MIDCAP INDEX. Introduced in June 1991, this index is comprised of 400 domestic companies. The median market capitalization of stocks in the index is $610 million versus about $2.2 billion for stocks in the S&P 500. It is a market-weighted index (stock price times shares outstanding).

STANDARD & POOR'S 100 STOCK INDEX. This consists of stocks for which options are listed on the Chicago Board Options Exchange. Options on the 100 Index are listed on the Chicago Board Options Exchange and futures on the Chicago Mercantile Exchange.

WILSHIRE 5000 EQUITY INDEX. This is a value-weighted index derived from the dollar value of 5,000 common stocks, including all those listed on the NYSE and AMEX and the most active OTC issues. It is the broadest index and thus is more representative of the overall market. Unfortunately, it has not received adequate publicity. The Wilshire is prepared by Wilshire Associates in Santa Monica, California. No futures or options are traded on the Wilshire.

NYSE COMPOSITE INDEX. A market-value-weighted index covering the price movements of all common stocks listed on the Big Board. It is based on the prices at the close of trading on December 31, 1965, and is weighted according to the number of shares listed for each issue. The base value is $50. Point changes are converted to dollars and cents to provide a meaningful measure of price action. Futures are traded on the NYFE and options on the NYSE itself.

NASDAQ-COMPOSITE INDEX. This represents all domestic OTC stocks except those having only one market maker. It covers a total of 3,500 stocks and is market-value weighted. No futures or options are traded.

VALUE LINE COMPOSITE INDEX. This is an equally weighted index of 1,700 NYSE, AMEX, and OTC stocks tracked by the Value Line Investment Survey. Designed to reflect price changes of typical industrial stocks, it is neither price- nor market-value weighted. Options trade on the Philadelphia Exchange and futures on the Kansas City Board of Trade.

AMEX MAJOR MARKET INDEX. Price-weighted, which means that high-priced stocks have a greater influence than low-priced ones, this is an average of 20 blue-chip industrials. It was designed to mirror the Dow Jones Industrial Average and measure representative performance of these kinds of issues. Although produced by the AMEX, it includes stocks listed on the NYSE. Futures are traded on the Chicago Board of Trade.

AMEX MARKET VALUE INDEX. This is a capitalization-weighted index that measures the collective performance of more than 90% of AMEX-listed companies, including ADRs, warrants, and common stocks. Cash dividends are assumed to be reinvested. Options are traded on the AMEX.

DOW JONES BOND AVERAGE. This consists of bonds of 10 public utilities and 10 industrial corporations.

BARRON'S CONFIDENCE INDEX. Weekly index of corporate bond yields published by Barron's, the financial newspaper owned by Dow Jones. It shows the ratio of the average yield of 10 high-grade bonds to the Dow Jones average yield on 40 bonds. The premise is that when investors feel confident about the economy they buy lower-rated bonds.

BOND BUYER'S INDEX. Published daily, it measures municipal bonds.

Market Indicators, Indexes, and Averages

Whether you're bullish, bearish, or uncertain, you can get a reading on the direction of the market, interest rates, and the overall economy by following some of the key statistics (or indicators) regularly churned out by Wall Street and Washington. These should be regarded not as gospel but rather as tools to help you make informed and intelligent decisions about your investments and for timing moves between stocks, bonds, and cash equivalents. Make a point of jotting down these numbers on your own chart and track the trends. You will see definite patterns between the market, interest rates, and the money supply. (The indicators are presented in alphabetical order.)

ECONOMIC INDICATOR	COMPOSITION	WHAT IT PREDICTS
Consumer price index (CPI)	The average price of consumer goods and services	The direction of inflation and changes in the purchasing power of money

ECONOMIC INDICATOR	COMPOSITION	WHAT IT PREDICTS
Dollar index	The value of the dollar as measured against major foreign currencies	Domestic corporate profits and multinational earning power
Dow Jones Industrial Average (DJIA)	30 major companies whose stock is held by many institutions and individuals; index is price-weighted so that moves in high-priced stocks exert more influence than those of lower-priced stock	Action of the stock market, which in turn anticipates future business activity
Employment figures and payroll employment	Number of people working or on company payrolls	Potential consumer spending, which in turn affects corporate profits
Gross domestic product (GDP)	Total goods and services produced in United States on an annual basis; inflation can distort the accuracy of this figure, so subtract inflation from GDP to get "real" GDP	General business trends and economic activity
Index of industrial production (IIP)	Shown as a percentage of the average, which has been tracked since 1967; base is 100	Amount of business volume
Money supply: M1	Currency held by the public plus balances in checking accounts, NOW accounts, traveler's checks, and money market funds	Extent of consumer purchasing power and liquidity of public's assets, used by Federal Reserve as a gauge for predicting as well as
M2	M1 plus time deposits over $100,000 and repurchase agreements	controlling the pace of the economy; when M1 shows a big
M3	M2 plus T-bills, U.S. savings bonds, bankers' acceptances, term Eurodollars, commercial paper	increase, the Fed usually reduces the money supply, which sends interest rates up; Fed reduces M1 by selling Treasuries; tightening of M1 serves to curb inflation; an increase in M1 fuels inflation
Standard & Poor's 500 stock index	Indexed value of 500 stocks from NYSE, AMEX, and OTC; more useful than the Dow Jones Industrial Average because it's broader; includes 400 industrials, 40 public utilities, 20 transportations, and 40 financials; stocks are market-value weighted; that is, price of each stock is multiplied by the number of shares outstanding	Direction of the economy and the market; good leading indicator because the market tends to anticipate future economic conditions
3-month Treasury bill rate	Interest rate paid to purchasers of T-bills	General direction of interest rates; gives indication of the Federal Reserve system's fiscal policy; for example, during a recession, the Fed

ECONOMIC INDICATOR	COMPOSITION	WHAT IT PREDICTS
		increases the amount of to lower the T-bill rate; during inflation, currency is reduced and the T-bill rate rises; rising interest rates tend to reducecorporate profits because of the increased costs of borrowing; therefore, a continual rise in T-bill rates presages a decline in the stock market; falling rates help stock and bond prices
Wage settlements	Percentage changes in wages that come about because of new labor contracts	Price changes for goods and services; sharply higher wage settlements result in higher inflation rates

Glossary:
Wall Street Jargon Made Simple

adjustable rate mortgage (ARM): A mortgage whose interest rate shifts, typically twice a year, to reflect general changes in interest rates.

after-tax contributions: Money that you've paid income tax on that is contributed to your savings plan; also called voluntary contributions. Because you have paid taxes on this money when you earned it, it cannot be mingled with the pretax money you or your employer contributed to your savings plan.

all or none order (AON): An order in which the customer wants to execute an entire buy or sell at once price. The order does not have to be executed immediately, but it must be executed in its entirety on the same transaction.

alternative minimum tax: A special income tax for high earners with certain tax-exempt investments.

American Depository Receipts (ADR): A security, created by a U.S. bank, showing ownership of a certain number of shares of a foreign stock; certificates are held in a depositary in the country of the issuing company.

amortization: Gradual reduction of a debt by a series of periodic payments. Each payment includes interest on the outstanding debt and part of the principal.

annuity: A contract, usually sold by an insurance company, that makes periodic payments to the person who holds it (the annuitant) at a future date, usually beginning at retirement. A fixed annuity pays a guaranteed rate; a variable annuity produces investment returns that are tied to the perfor-

mance of the market. An immediate income annuity begins income payments right away. A deferred annuity can be fixed or variable and keeps your investment growing, shielded from taxes until you begin withdrawals.

arbitrage: Profiting from price differences when a security, currency, or commodity is traded on different markets. Also, to buy shares in a company that is about to be taken over and sell short the shares of the acquiring company.

asked price: The lowest price at which a security is offered for sale.

asset: A possession that has present and future financial value to its owner.

asset allocation fund: A mutual fund that allocates its assets among stocks, bonds, and money market securities. As the market and economic conditions change, the fund manager shifts assets among the particular industry categories to maximize returns and protect the principal.

ATMs: Automated teller machines, located primarily at banks. Upon insertion of a magnetically coded bank identification card, the computer-controlled machine dispenses cash that you request or deposits money to your account and indicates the status of your account on a viewing screen. No teller is necessary. The majority of ATMs are open 24 hours.

automatic dividend reinvestment (ADR): A plan in which shareholders can elect to have their dividends automatically used to purchase additional shares of stock instead of receiving a cash dividend payment.

back-end load: A commission paid when you sell mutual fund shares; also known as redemption fees. They may be eliminated after you've owned your shares a certain number of years.

balance sheet: A statement showing the financial condition of a company at a given point in time. It includes assets, liabilities and net worth. The term comes from the fact that assets always equal, or balance, the liabilities plus net worth.

basis point: One hundredth of 1%; used in discussing bond yields. For example, 1% equals 100 basis points, and a yield rise from 5.40% to 5.50% is a 10 basis-point increase.

bear market: A sharp, prolonged decline in the price of stocks, usually brought on by a slowing economy. A bear fights by slapping downward with his paws, thus the phrase for a downward market.

bearer bond: A bond certificate held by the owner with coupons that are detached and presented in order to collect the interest due. It is not registered to an owner on the books of the issuer; it is owned by the person holding or bearing the certificate.

beneficiary: The person(s) named to receive your benefits in the event of your death.

beta: A number that compares the price volatility of a stock with that of the overall market. A beta of less than one indicates less volatility and risk than the market; a beta of over one indicates higher risk than the market.

bid price: The highest price which a buyer is willing to pay for a security.

block trade: A purchase or sale of a large quantity of stock, usually 10,000 shares or more.

blue chip: The common stock of a well-known national company with a history of earnings growth and dividend increases, such as Exxon or General Electric.

blue-sky laws: State laws that require issuers of securities to register their offerings with the state before they can be sold to its residents.

bond: A security that represents debt of the issuing corporation. Usually the issuer is required to pay the bondholder a specified rate of interest for a specified time and then repay the entire debt (also known as face value) upon maturity.

book value: The current net worth of a company—i.e., its assets minus its liabilities divided by the number of shares on the market. If a stock's price is lower than its book value and the company is financially solid, it is considered a bargain.

bull market: A sharp, prolonged rise in the price of stocks that usually last at least several months, often much longer, and consists of high trading volume. A bull attacks by thrusting upward, thus the term for an upward market.

bullion: Gold or silver sold in bars called ingots.

bullion coins: A coin whose value resides only in the precious metal it contains. See also Numismatic Coins.

call: An option for the right to buy a stock.

call date: A feature of many bonds giving the issuer the right to call in or redeem the bonds before their maturity date.

capital: Also called capital assets; property or money from which a person or business receives some monetary gain.

capital gains: Profits from the rising price of an investment.

capitalization: A firm's capital structure, composed of total securities issued by a corporation, including bonds, debentures, preferred and common stock, and all surpluses.

cash equivalents: The generic term for assorted short-term instruments such as U.S. Treasury securities, CDs, and money market fund shares, which can be readily converted into cash.

cash flow: Net income plus other non-cash charges, such as depreciation and amortization. Cash flow determines a company's avility to pay its dividends to shareholders.

cash flow multiple: Price of a stock divided by its cash flow per share.

central asset or combo account: Brokerage, money

market fund, and checking account combined with a credit card. Offered by both banks and brokerage houses, some central asset accounts include forms of life insurance, mortgages, traveler's checks, and other special features.

certificates of deposit: Also called CDs or "time certificates"; official receipts issued by a bank stating that a given amount of money has been deposited for a certain length of time at a specified rate of interest. CDs are insured by the U.S. government for up to $100,000.

charts: Records of price and volume trends as well as the general movement of stock and bond markets, economic cycles, industries and individual companies, updated continually. Chartists believe that past history as expressed on a chart gives a strong clue to the next price movement. They "read" the lines to determine what a stock has done and may do.

closed-end fund: Mutual funds that issue limited numbers of shares and then are traded on stock exchanges as common stocks.

commodities: Anything in which contracts for future delivery may be traded, such as precious metals, food, grain, oil, U.S. Treasury securities, foreign currencies, and stock indexes.

common stock: See Stock, Common.

compound interest: The amount earned on the original principal plus the accumulated interest. With interest on interest plus interest on principal, an investment grows more rapidly.

confirmation: A printed acknowledgment of the purchase or sale of a security, sent to the customer by the brokerage firm or mutual fund company.

convertibles: Bonds, debentures, or preferred stock that may be exchanged or converted into common stock.

correction: A reverse downward in the prices of stocks, bonds, or commodities.

cost of living adjustment: A boost in wages, Social Security, or a pension designed to offset the impact of inflation.

credit card: A plastic card issued by a bank or financial institution that gives the holder access to a line of credit to purchase goods or receive cash. Repayment may be required in full in 30 days or in installments. Compare with Debit Card.

current assets: Cash, inventory, accounts receivable and other assets that can be converted to cash in a relatively short time, usually within a year.

CUSIP number: A nine-character code on the face of each stock certificate that is assigned to a security by Standard & Poor's Corp. It helps expedite the settlement process. It stands for Committee on Uniform Security Identification Procedures.

custodian: The financial institution responsible for the safekeeping of your investment assets.

day order: A buy or sell order that is valid only until the close of trading on the day it is placed.

debenture: An unsecured bond backed only by the general credit of the company.

debit card: A deposit access card that debits the holder's bank account or money market account immediately upon use in purchasing. There is no grace period in which to pay; payment is transferred immediately and electronically at the moment of purchase.

defensive stock: A stock not subject to changes in the business cycle, such as food stores and manufacturers, utility companies.

defined-benefit plan: A pension that promises to pay a specified amount to all employees who complete a set number of years of work. In many plans, employers make all the contributions and invest them.

defined-contribution plan: Usually called a 401(k) or salary-reduction plan. It allows employees to contribute up to 10% of their pretax salaries to various investment funds. The account grows tax-free, but employees who select funds that perform poorly have no recourse.

depreciation: An accounting method for recovering the cost of fixed assets, such as plant and equipment. The cost is amortized over the depreciable life of the assets and is considered a noncash expense.

derivative: A financial instrument whose value derives

from the performance of an underlying asset, such as a stock, bond, currency rate, or market index.

discount rate: The interest rate the Federal Reserve charges member banks; it provides a floor for interest rates that banks then charge their customers.

discretionary account: A brokerage firm account in which the customer gives the broker permission to buy and sell securities on the customer's behalf.

distribution: The income and capital gains paid by a mutual fund to its shareholders.

disinflation: A reduction in the rate of ongoing inflation.

dividends: A portion of the company's net profits distributed to its shareholders; usually a fixed amount for each share of stock held and paid quarterly in cash; dividends also may be in the form of property, script, or stock. Dividends must be voted on by the company's directors before each payment.

DJIA (Dow Jones Industrial Average): Price-weighted average of 30 blue-chip stocks, representing overall price movements of all stocks on the New York Stock Exchange.

downtick: A transaction executed at a price lower than the preceding transaction in the same security; opposite of an uptick.

earnings per share: A company's net income divided by the total number of outstanding shares.

effective annual yield: Rate of return earned on your savings if you do not incur service charges or penalties.

employee stock ownership: Called an ESOP plan, it encourages workers to buy their employer's stock, usually at a reduced price.

equity: Stocks or ownership interest held by shareholders in a corporation as opposed to bonds. In a brokerage account, the market value of securities minus the amount borrowed.

ex-dividend date: The date on or after which a security begins trading without the dividend included in the contract price.

face value: Value of a bond or note when issued. Corporate bonds are usually issued with $1,000

face value; municipals with $5,000; T-bills with $10,000. Also called par value.

FDIC (Federal Deposit Insurance Corporation): An independent agency of the U.S. government whose basic purpose is to insure bank deposits.

financial futures: Contracts to deliver a specified number of financial instruments at a given price by a certain date, such as U.S. Treasury bonds and bills, GNMA certificates, CDs, and foreign currency.

401(k) plan: One that allows an employee to contribute pretax dollars to a company pool, which is invested in stocks, bonds, or money market instruments; also known as a salary reduction plan.

front running: A trader knowing in advance of a block trade that will affect the price of a security and buying to profit from the trade.

fundamental analysis: The study of a company's past record of sales, earnings, assets, management and other factors to predict its future.

futures: See Commodities.

going public: When a private company first offers shares to the public.

good until canceled: An order to buy or sell a stock at a specific price that is left in force until executed or canceled by the customer.

guaranteed investment contract: Known as a GIC, it is a contract between an insurance company and a corporate savings or pension plan that offers a fixed rate of return on the capital invested over the life of the contract. It is not federally insured.

index: A statistical yardstick that measures a whole market by using a representative selection of stocks or bonds. Changes are compared to a base year. Futures are sold on stock indexes, such as the S&P 500.

index arbitrage: Profiting from the difference in prices of the same security. In program trading, traders buy and sell to profit from small price discrepancies, using computers that monitor both the S&P 500 stock index and futures contracts on the index. When there is a larger than normal gap, the computers notify the traders to sell.

index future: A contract to buy or sell an index (S&P

500, for example) at a future date. An index is not an average. See also Index.

individual retirement account: Called an IRA, this personal fund defers taxes on the money put in and any income it generates until the owners begin withdrawing their money, which they cannot do without penalty before the age of 591Ú2.

inflation: An increase in the average price level of goods and services over time.

institutions: Organizations that trade huge blocks of securities, such as banks, pension funds, mutual funds, and insurance companies.

interest: Money paid for the use of money. See also Discount Rate; Prime Rate.

investment banker: The middleman between the public and a corporation issuing new securities. He/she usually buys a new issue of stocks or bonds directly from the issuing corporation and sells them to individuals and institutions. Investment bankers also act as agents to distribute very large blocks of stocks and bonds.

IPO: Initial public offering; a company's offering of stock, not previously issued, for sale to the public.

IRA rollover: A technique allowing employees to avoid taxes by transferring lump-sum payments from a 401(k) or a profit-sharing plan into an IRA within 60 days.

junk bonds: High-risk, high-yielding bonds, rated BB or lower.

LBO (leveraged buyout): The purchase of a corporation by using a large amount of debt, much of it short-term bank loans secured by the assets of the company being acquired. After the buying is completed, the acquired company issues bonds to pay off a portion of the debt taken on in the takeover.

liability: A debt; something owed by one person or business to another.

limit order: An order to buy or sell a security at a specific price or better. A buy limit order is placed below the market price while a sell limit is placed above the market price.

limited partnership: Investment organization in which your liability is limited to the dollar amount you invest; a general partner manages the project, which may be in real estate, farming, oil, and gas.

liquid: Cash or investments easily convertible into cash, such as money market funds or bank deposits.

lump-sum distribution: Payment of a retirement account's complete holdings at once, usually when one leaves a job.

"Mae" family: Various mortgage-backed securities either sponsored or partially guaranteed by a handful of government agencies or private corporations, such as the Government National Mortgage Association (GNMA, or "Ginnie Mae") and the Federal Home Loan Mortgage Corporation ("Freddie Mac").

margin: The amount a client deposits with a broker in order to borrow from the broker to buy stocks.

market order: An order to buy or sell a certain number of shares of a stock at the best possible price at the time the order is given.

mark to the market: The value of any portfolio based on the most recent closing price of the securities held.

material news: Information given out by a company that might affect the value of its stocks or bonds or influence investors' decisions; example: tender offers, very poor or good earnings, a stock split, a corporate event.

mature: To come due; to reach the time when the face value of a bond or note must be paid.

money market fund: A mutual fund that invests only in high-yielding, short-term money market instruments such as U.S. Treasury bills, bank CDs, and commercial paper. Shareholders receive higher interest on their shares than in a bank money market deposit account.

Moody's: A trademark for issuance of ratings on the relative investment quality of corporate and municipal bonds and for the company's financial publications.

multiple: Price-to-earnings ratio.

municipal bonds: Debt obligations of state and local entities. For the most part, the interest earned is free from federal income tax and often from state and local taxes for residents.

mutual fund: An investment company in which investors' dollars are pooled with those of thousands of others. The combined total is invested by a professional manager in a variety of securities; shares are sold to the public.

net asset value (NAV): The price at which you buy or sell shares of a mutual fund on a given day. To determine NAV, mutual funds compute their assets daily by adding up the market value of all securities owned by the fund, deducting all liabilities, and dividing the balance by the number of shares outstanding. The NAV per share is the figure quoted in the newspaper.

net worth: Total value (of cash, property, investments) after deducting outstanding expenses and amounts owed.

no-load fund: An open-end investment company that sells shares directly to customers without applying a sales charge.

odd lots: A stock transaction that involves less than 100 shares.

open order: An order to buy or sell a stock that remains in effect until it is either canceled by the customer or executed.

option: The right to buy (call) or sell (put) a certain amount of stock at a given price (strike price) for a specified length of time.

over-the-counter (OTC) stock: A security not listed or traded on a major exchange. Transactions take place by telephone and computer network rather than on the floor of an exchange.

point: A measure of a price change. With a stock, a point change means a change of $1; with a bond that has a $1,000 face value, it refers to a $10 change.

points: Up-front fee charge by the lender in a real-estate deal; separate from interest but designed to increase the overall yield to the lender. A point is 1% of the total principal amount of the loan; on a $100,000 mortgage, 2 points would equal $2,000.

preferred stock: See Stock, Preferred.

premium: Amount by which a bond sells above its par or face value.

price/earnings (P/E) ratio: Price of a stock divided by its earnings per share. Also known as the multiple, it gives investors an idea of how much they are paying for a company's earnings power.

prime rate: Interest rate banks charge their largest and most financially solid business clients; lower than rate charged to consumers.

principal: Face amount of a debt or mortgage on which interest is either owed or earned; balance due on an obligation as separate from interest.

profit-sharing plan: An agreement by which a company makes annual contributions out of its profits to an account for each employee. This money is invested in stocks, bonds, or money-market securities. The funds are tax-deferred until the employee leaves the company.

prospectus: A printed summary of data that is also a registration statement filed with the SEC in conjunction with a public offering of securities, including mutual funds. It contains information about the company and its business that enables investors to evaluate the security and decide whether or not to buy. Among the data included is information about the company's products, services, facilities, management, and the risks involved. SEC regulations determine what must be set forth in every prospectus.

proxy statement: Information required by the SEC to be given to a corporation's stockholders in order to be able to solicit votes.

public float: The portion of a corporation's outstanding shares that are owned by public investors; in other words, shares not held by the company's officers, directors, or investors who hold a controlling interest in the company.

put: An options contract giving the investor the right to sell a specified number of shares by a certain date at a certain price.

real return: The inflation-adjusted rate of return on an investment. If an investor earns a 12% return during a year when inflation is 3%, the real return is 9%.

red herring: A preliminary prospectus issued by underwriters to determine interest in a prospective offering. It must contain a warning, printed in red, that the document does not contain all the information and that some of it may be changed before the final prospectus is made public.

registered representative: A stockbroker. All stockbrokers must be registered before they can do business with the public and must pass qualifying exams given by the NASD.

Regulation T: A Federal Reserve Board rule that governs how much credit stockbrokers can give to customers to purchase securities in margin accounts.

round lot order: An order to buy or sell stock in multiples of 100 shares; the generally accepted unit of trading.

seat: Term for membership on an exchange, such as the New York Stock Exchange or the American Stock Exchange; gives the holder the right to trade securities on the exchange floor.

SEC (Securities and Exchange Commission): A federal agency with power to enforce federal laws pertaining to the sale of securities and mutual fund shares and the governing of the exchanges, stockbrokers, and financial advisers.

SEC Rule 13d: Requires that anyone acquiring 5% or more stock in any one company file certain disclosure papers with the SEC.

sharedraft: Interest-bearing checking account at a credit union.

shares outstanding: Shares of a corporation that have been issued to common shareholders.

secondary: The market in which existing securities are traded after their initial public offering. Also called the aftermarket.

selling short: Sale of a security that must be borrowed to make delivery. Usually involves the sale of securities that are not owned by the seller in anticipation of making a profit from a decline in the price of the security.

SIPC (Securities Investor Protection Corporation): An independent agency established by Congress to provide customers of most brokerage firms with protection similar to that provided by the FDIC

for bank depositors, in the event that a firm is unable to meet its financial obligations.

split: Division of outstanding shares of a corporation into a larger number of shares. Splits can be 2 for 1, 3 for 1, etc.

spread: The difference between the bid and asked prices of a security; the difference in yields between two fixed-income securities.

stockbroker: An agent who handles the public's orders to buy and sell stocks, bonds, commodities, and mutual funds. A broker may be a partner of a brokerage firm or a registered representative, who is an employee of a brokerage firm. Brokers charge a commission for their services.

stock, common: A security that represents ownership in a corporation.

stock, preferred: A stock that pays a fixed dividend and has first claim on profits over common stocks for payment of that dividend. The dividend does not rise or fall with profits.

stock right: A short-term privilege issued by a corporation to its existing stockholders granting them the right to buy new stock at a stated price.

stock symbol: A letter symbol assigned to a security that is used to identify issues on stock tickers and in automated information-retrieval systems.

street: Jargon for Wall Street and the financial services industry.

strike price: The dollar amount per share at which an option buyer can purchase the underlying stock or a put option buyer can sell the stock. Also called the exercise price.

takeover: When the controlling interest of a corporation is taken over by a new company. Takeovers can be friendly or hostile.

tax bracket: The point on the income tax rate schedules where one's taxable income (income subject to tax after exemptions and deductions) falls. It is expressed as a percentage to be applied to each additional dollar earned over the base amount for that bracket. The current tax brackets for individuals are 15%, 28%, 31%, 36%, and 39.6%.

tax-deferred: Taxes postponed until a later date. Pretax money invested in retirement plans is tax-deferred but not tax-exempt or tax-free, which means that no taxes will ever have to be paid.

tax shelter: An investment that allows one to realize tax benefits by reducing or deferring taxable income.

total return: Dividend or interest income plus any capital gain; a better measure of an investment's return that just dividends or interest. For a mutual fund it is an historical measure of the fund's overall performance, reflecting dividends and capital gains distributions, if any, and the increase (or decrease) in net asset value over a specific time period.

trading halt: Suspension of trading in a security while certain "material" news about the company is being disseminated, giving all investors an equal chance to evaluate the news and make buy or sell decisions. See Material News.

Treasuries: Bills, notes, and bonds backed by the U.S. government and sold through the Department of the Treasury. The interest they pay investors is exempt from state and local taxes.

triple tax-exempt bonds: Municipal bonds exempt from federal, state, and local taxes for residents of the states and localities that issue the bonds.

underwriter: An investment banker who agrees to purchase shares of a new issue of securities and sell them to investors. The underwriter makes a profit on the spread—the difference between the price paid to the issuer and the public offering price.

vested benefits: The nonforfeitable dollar amount in a pension plan that belongs to the employee even if he/she leaves the job. An employee typically becomes vested after 5 years with the same firm.

warrant: A security, usually issued with a bond or preferred stock, giving the owner the privilege of buying a specified number of shares of a stock at a fixed price, usually for a period of years.

yield: The income paid or earned by a security divided by its current price. For example, a $20 stock with an annual dividend of $1.50 has a 7.5% yield.

zero coupon bond: A bond that pays no current interest but is sold at a deep discount from face value. At maturity, all compounded interest is paid and the bondholder collects the full face value of the bond (usually $1,000). EE savings bonds are zeros.

PULL-OUT FINANCIAL GUIDE AND PERSONAL CALENDAR

YOUR OWN NITTY-GRITTY

Name _____   Social Security # _____

Address _____   Telephone # _____

_____   Fax # _____

Employer _____   Telephone # _____

Address _____   _____

_____   _____

In an emergency, contact:

_____   _____

_____   _____

_____   _____

Blood type _____   Allergic to _____

Doctor _____   Hospital _____

Address _____   Address _____

Telephone # _____   Telephone # _____

LOCATION OF PERSONAL PAPERS

- Social Security card

- Will

- Executor

- Attorney

- Burial instructions

- Deed to burial plot

- Birth certificate

- Citizenship papers

- Power of attorney

- Real estate deeds and rental lease

- Marriage license

- Divorce papers

- Military records

- Passport

- Previous tax returns

- Other

BANKING INFORMATION

• CHECKING ACCOUNT

Bank _____   Telephone # _____
Address _____   Officer _____
_____   Account # _____
Who may sign _____   Location of canceled checks _____
_____

• SAVINGS ACCOUNT

Bank _____   Telephone # _____
Address _____   Officer _____
_____   Account # _____
Book kept _____   Statements kept _____
Value as of Jan. 1st: _____   Value as of June 1st: _____
_____   _____

• SAFE DEPOSIT BOX

Bank _____   Box # _____
Address _____   Telephone # _____
Key kept _____   Access _____
Contents _____   _____
_____   _____
_____

MONEY MARKET FUND OR ACCOUNT

Firm/Bank _____   Account # _____

Address _____   Telephone number 800 _____

_____   Current yield _____ %

Value as of Jan. 1st $_____   Value as of June 1st $_____

CERTIFICATES OF DEPOSIT

Bank _____   CD # _____

Address _____   Amount: $ _____

_____   Maturity date _____

Telephone # _____   Automatic rollover yes/no _____

Interest rate _____ %   Certificate kept _____

Early withdrawal penalty _____   Features _____

_____   _____

MUTUAL FUNDS

Company _____   Name of fund _____

Address _____   Account # _____

_____   Telephone # _____

Value as of Jan. 1st $_____   Value as of June 30th $_____

Total return

• Year-to-date: _____ %   • 3 years: _____ %

• Last year: _____ %   • 5 years: _____ %

BROKERAGE ACCOUNT

Firm _____   Broker _____

Address _____   Telephone # _____

_____   Fax # _____

Account # _____   Type of account _____

Value as of Jan. 1st $_____   Value as of June 30th $_____

ANNUITY

Company _____   Policy #   _____

Address _____   Face Value $ _____

_____   Type/term   _____

Agent _____   Policy kept   _____

Telephone #_____   Current yield _____ %

Beneficiary _____   Withdrawal/loans $_____

Payout begins _____   Value as of Jan. 1st $_____

LIFE INSURANCE

Company _____   Type/term   _____

Address _____   Face Value $ _____

_____   Policy #   _____

Agent _____   Telephone #   _____

Premium $_____   Premiums due _____

Beneficiary _____   Policy kept   _____

Loan rate _____ % Value as of Jan. 1st $_____

HEALTH INSURANCE

Company _____   Type/coverage _____

Address _____   Policy #   _____

_____   Telephone #   _____

Agent/contact_____   Family members covered _____

Covers _____   Excludes _____

Co-payment _____   Other   _____

Premium $_____   Premiums due _____

Policy kept _____   Features   _____

401(k) OR RETIREMENT PLAN

Held with _____

Address _____

_____

Contact _____

My contribution $ _____

Employer's contribution $ _____

Total return last year _____ %

Type _____

Account # _____

Telephone # _____

Date started _____

Years until vested _____

_____

Value as of Jan. 1st $ _____

IRA

Custodian _____

Address _____

_____

Total return last year _____ %

Account # _____

Date opened _____

Telephone # _____

Value as of Jan. 1st $ _____

MORTGAGE

Lender _____

Address _____

_____

Telephone # _____

Monthly payment $ _____

Rate _____ %

Type _____

Date taken out _____

Original amount $ _____

Length (years) _____

Payment book _____

Date due _____

Interest rate cap _____ %

Rate tied to _____

YOUR 1997 FINANCIAL CALENDAR

Clip and save this calendar and consult it all year round to avoid incurring tax penalties, wasting your hard-earned money, and generally being financially foolish. *Note*: Those marked with an asterisk are tax-related actions that must be taken by that date.

SECTION 1

JANUARY

- Do your annual Net Worth Statement.
- Determine your financial goals for the year; write them down.
- Set up file folders for 1099s, W-2 form, tax-related documents; give up the old shoe box or shopping bag you've been using.
- Put business-related receipts for 1996 in a separate folder used to document tax deductible business expenses when you file next year's returns. Include: receipts for taxis, tolls, gas, telephone and fax charges, rent, stationery, equipment, books, professional dues, etc.
- Read IRS publications: #917, "Business Use of a Car"; #535, "Business Expenses"; and #463, "Travel, Entertainment and Gift Expenses"; All are free by calling 800–829–3676.
- Buy holiday cards and wrapping paper on sale.
- Pay off holiday credit card debt.
- ** January 15: Your final estimated tax payment for 1996 is due if you did not pay your income tax (or enough of your tax) for that year through withholding.

    Use Form 1040ES.
- **** January 31: If you did not pay your last installment of your estimated tax by January 15, file your income tax return for 1996 by the 31st to avoid late payment penalty for the last installment.

    Use Form 1040 or 1040A.

NOTES _____
_____
_____
_____
_____
_____

SECTION 2
FEBRUARY

- Call any banks, brokerage firms, mutual funds, or employers that have not sent you their IRS records by the end of the month.

- Make an appointment with your accountant to discuss taxes. The earlier, the less stressed out he/she will be, and the more attention your return will receive.

- File income tax early and use any refund to reduce credit card debt and/or your car or any other loan that doesn't have a prepayment penalty.

- Visit or call your local IRS office for copies of free booklets on preparing your tax return; avoid the March and April rush.

    To order by phone, call 800–829–3676.

- Shop Presidents' Day sales for winter clothes.

- For a list of outlets in your area where prices are 25% to 70% less, call Outlet Bound, 800–336–8853.

- Get organized to swap your house or apartment for this summer's vacation and thus eliminate hotel bills. Contact: Vacation Exchange Club, 800–638–3841; Intervac, 800–756–HOME; or if you're a teacher, Teacher Swap, 516–244–2845.

**** February 15. If your child/student is working but will not earn enough to owe any tax, this is the last date to file a Form W-4 with his/her employer so taxes will not be withheld.
   Note: You can file a new Form W-4 to adjust your withholding allowance any time of the year. Check with your accountant or benefits officer.

NOTES

_____

_____

_____

_____

_____

_____

_____

_____

SECTION 3

MARCH

- Challenge your property tax bill. Most states allow appeals in early spring. About half the homeowners who question their assessments through official appeals win reductions of 10%.
- Read "How to Fight Property Taxes," from National Taxpayers Union; $2; 703–683–5700.
- Finish preparing your tax return. If you're doing your own return but need last-minute help, call the National Association for Enrolled Agents, 800–424–4339, for the names of those in your area; certified by the IRS, they are less expensive than CPAs.
- See Chapters 31 and 32 on taxes and investments.
- Buy air conditioner and fan before prices go up; you'll save anywhere from $50 to $250 per appliance.
- **** March 1. If you're a farmer or fisherman, file your last year's tax return to avoid an under-payment penalty for the last quarter of 1996 if you were required to pay estimated taxes on January 15.

  Use Form 1040.

NOTES

_____

_____

_____

_____

_____

_____

_____

_____

_____

_____

_____

_____

_____

SECTION 4
APRIL

- Move this month if it's part of your plan. Costs are 40% to 50% cheaper between October 1 and May 1 and highest during the summer months when kids are out of school.

- Insist your mover give you the booklet, "Your Rights and Responsibilities When You Move," by the Interstate Commerce Commission. Read it before signing a contract.

- Save all receipts if your move is job-related; some expenses may be tax-deductible.

- Read IRS publication 521, "Moving Expenses"; free by calling 800–829–3676.

- Support Earth Day, April 22nd. Reduce cost of garbage pick-up and recycling by contacting: Mail Preference Service Direct Marketing Association, Box 9008, Farmingdale, NY 11735; 212–768–7277. They will remove your name from most mailing lists. To get off all lists, consult "Stop Junk Mail Forever," a $3 pamphlet from: Good Advice Press, Box 78, Elizaville, NY 12523, 914–758–1400.

**** April 15. File your income tax return for 1996.

>   Use Form 1040, 1040A, or 1040 EZ, and pay any tax that is due.

**** April 15. This is the last day you can fund your IRA.

>   See Chapter 29 for investment suggestions.

**** April 15. Fund your Keogh or SEP if you have self-employment income and are not filing for an extension.

**** April 15. If you are not filing your taxes, get an automatic 4-month extension by filing Form 3868. And pay any tax you estimate will be due.

Note: If you get an extension, you can't file Form 1040 EZ.

An extension applies to the filing time but not to the time for paying any taxes due. You'll be penalized if the total tax you've paid including withholding, estimated payments, and the check you send on April 15 does not equal at least 90% of the tax you owe for 1996.

**** April 15. If you made any taxable gifts during 1996 (those that were more than $10,000 per donee), file a gift tax return for that year.

>   Use Form 709 or 709(A) and pay any tax due. Or, for an automatic 4-month extension, file Form 4868.

**** April 15. Pay the first quarterly installment of your 1997 estimated tax if you're not paying your 1997 income tax (or enough of it through withholding tax).

- Use Form 1040-ES.
- Pay your IRS trustee or custodial fee with a separate check so it is tax-deductible.
- Call 800-829-1040 for last-minute help in filing your return. To hear tax recorded info on 140+ topics, call TeleTax at 800–829–4477.

NOTES

SECTION 5

MAY

- Get your air conditioner overhauled, clean and/or replace the filter to increase efficiency.
- Make spring cleaning pay off. If your power company has two-tier pricing, run the dishwasher and wash and dry curtains, bedspreads, and cotton rugs in the evening when rates are lower.
- Do some spring financial cleaning. Take an inventory of your household possessions and check insurance coverage. Items should be covered at their replacement value, not what they cost initially. Make a written or videotaped inventory of your possessions; for jewelry, antiques, collections and other valuables, get an appraisal.
- For the name of a local appraiser, call the American Society of Appraisers, 703–478–2228.
  ☑ *HINT: Keep a copy of your inventory at work or in your safe deposit box.*
- Book summer vacation hotel/resort and airline tickets now to avoid last-minute, outrageously high rates.
- Cut vacation costs by reserving space early in a national park.
- Call Destinet reservation system, 800–365–2267; or contact The National Park Service, Box 37127, Washington, DC 20013; 202–208–4747.
- Check your frequent flier miles now and use to get limited space on planes for the summer months.

NOTES

_____

_____

_____

_____

_____

_____

_____

_____

_____

SECTION 6

JUNE

- Do a semi-annual review of your investments. Note the total return figures and yields and compare them with those of January 1st and of one year ago. Then:
- Meet with your stockbroker and/or financial adviser to review your account; decide what securities to hold or to sell.
- See Part 8 in this book for specific portfolio suggestions.
- Give a garage or yard sale. Invest the cash you take in.
- See Chapters 3 and 5 on where to invest small amounts of money and get high, safe yields.
- Donate what you don't sell to charity for a tax deduction. Get a receipt.
- Read IRS Publication #526, "Charitable Contributions"; free; 800–829–3676.
- Discuss finances and house rules with any adult children returning home to live with you after graduation (or for any other reasons).
- Read *Never Call Your Broker on Monday,* Nancy Dunnan, New York: HarperCollins, 1997.
- See Chapter 27 for suggestions on handling family finances.
- Rent, don't buy wedding dress, bridesmaid clothes, or tuxedos; you'll save at least 50%.
- Get a tune-up for your car; check air conditioning, water, coolant, and tires, especially if you're driving on a trip.
- **** June 17. Pay the second installment of your 1997 estimated tax.
       Use Form 1040-ES.
- **** If you have a bank, securities, or other financial account in a foreign country that's worth more than $10,000, you must file Form TDF 90-22-1 with the Department of Treasury by June 30.

NOTES

_____

_____

_____

_____

_____

_____

_____

_____

SECTION 7

JULY

- Read a good investment book on the beach or in the mountains.

    ☑ *HINT: Keep the receipt, it may be tax-deductible.*

- Save patriotically. EE Savings Bonds, tops in safety, cost as little as $25, and there's no sales fee.

- For info and current yields, call 800–US–BONDS.

    See Chapter 9 for more details on bonds.

- Call your nearest Federal Reserve Bank or Branch to find out how to purchase U.S. Treasuries without a fee.

    See Chapter 9 for telephone numbers.

- Talk to colleagues or friends about starting an investment club in the fall. During the summer read the information published by the National Association of Investment Clubs.

    Call 810–583–6242 for material.
    See Chapter 5.

- Study your cash flow situation during this lazy month.

    Use the worksheet on page 15 to see just where your money is going and then resolve to cut back by September if you need to do so.

NOTES

_____

_____

_____

_____

_____

_____

_____

SECTION 8
AUGUST

- Go for good deals on lawn and patio furniture, bathing suits, lawnmowers, barbecues, and camping and ski equipment.
- Prepare your child or grandchild going off to college. Discuss checking accounts, credit cards, and budgeting for the school year.
- Visit a stock exchange or federal reserve bank/branch while traveling in the United States or abroad. See Appendix E for a list with addresses and phone numbers. Most have excellent books and pamphlets in their gift shops.

  ☑ *HINT: Good place to take kids and grandchildren and introduce them to "live investing."*

- Take steps to get last-minute money for your child's college tuition payments.

  See Chapter 27 for a list of loan sources and ideas of meeting educational expenses.

**** August 15. If you filed for an automatic 4-month extension, your 1996 income tax return is now due.

  Use Form 1040 or 1040A, and pay any tax, interest, and penalties due.

**** August 15. Last date to file for a further 2-month extension.

  Use Form 2688.

**** August 15. If you filed for an automatic 4-month extension on your gift tax return for 1996, file the return by this date and pay any tax, interest, and penalties due.

  Use Form 709 or 709A.

  Or, if you need an additional extension, check the "Gift Tax" box on Form 2688.

NOTES

_____

_____

_____

_____

_____

_____

_____

_____

_____

SECTION 9
SEPTEMBER

- ■ Go back to school. Take a class in financial planning, investing, or money management.
- ■ Figure out what your child earned from a summer job. Ask your accountant if he/she needs to file a return.
- ■ Read IRS Publication #4, "Student's Guide to Federal Income Tax"; free by calling 800–829–3676.
- ■ Weatherize your home. Call your local power company for a free (or inexpensive) winter energy audit.
- ■ Read "How to Weatherize Your Home or Apartment," $4.25, from: Massachusetts Audubon Society, Educational Resources, 208 South Great Road, Lincoln, MA 01773.
- ■ Begin your investment club, as discussed in the month of August.

    See Chapters 13 and 14 on picking stocks.

**** September 16. Pay the third installment of your quarterly 1997 estimated tax.

    Use Form 1040-ES.

NOTES

_____

_____

_____

_____

_____

_____

_____

_____

_____

_____

_____

_____

_____

SECTION 10
OCTOBER

- Review your will. Since this is a slow month regarding taxes, take time to re-read (or make) your will.
- Update if: you've gotten married, separated, or divorced; if you've had a child or grandchild; if your income has changed significantly; if you've moved to a new state; if a close relative or someone named in your will has died; if the tax laws have changed.
- Service your furnace. Replace disposable filters or clean permanent ones.
- Caulk around windows and doors to reduce heating costs.
- Get your flu shot or checkup before cold season; good health is one way to cut medical costs. If your doctor prescribes medication, buy your drugs at a discount through a mail-order pharmacy, such as the one operated by the American Association of Retired Persons.

  ☑ *HINT: You don't have to be retired or a member to participate. Call 800–456–2277 for prices.*

**** October 15. If you received both a 4-month and additional 2-month extension for your 1996 income tax return, file now and pay any tax, interest, and penalty due.

   Use Form 1040 or 1040A.

**** October 15. This is the last day to make a Keogh or SEP contribution for calendar year 1996 if you were granted an additional extension of time to file your return.

NOTES

_____

_____

_____

_____

_____

_____

_____

_____

_____

_____

_____

_____

SECTION 11

NOVEMBER

- Talk with your broker about year-end tax swaps and what securities you may want to sell before the year end.

    See Chapters 31 and 32 on taxes.
- Make charitable contributions for tax deduction.
- To find out if a charity is approved by the National Charities Information Bureau, write to them at: 19 Union Square West, New York, NY 10003, or call 212–929–6300.

> ☑ *HINT: If your gift is more than $250, a canceled check is no longer adequate proof. You must possess a written acknowledgment of your donation from the charity in order to be able to deduct it. If your gift is property, not cash, it must include a description of the property.*

- Buy a car this month. Dealers, forced to clear their showrooms for next year's models, start offering reduced prices, rebates, and good financing deals. Or buy a used car.

    To find the current value of a used car, call: The Consumer Reports Used Car Price Service, 900–446–1120; $1.75 per minute.
- Quit smoking during the American Cancer Society's "Great American Smokeout Week" this month. At $2/pack, one pack a day is $740 a year. And you'll cut the cost of your life insurance premiums.
- Begin making Christmas and Hanukkah cards and gifts.
- Get free firewood. If you live in one of the 155 national forests, you may be able to pick up several cords of firewood free, or for a small fee. (A cord of wood regularly runs $85 to $125, depending upon where you live.) Check with your regional office of the U.S. Forest Service or call the Federal Information Number, 800–688–9889, for your area number.

NOTES

_____

_____

_____

_____

_____

_____

_____

SECTION 12

DECEMBER

- Empty closets and cupboards and give away items to charity for an end-of-the-year tax deduction.
- Review last year's tax return; it will remind you of the tax-deductible expenses you took and can probably take again.

     See Chapter 31 for a list of deductions.
- Review financial documents. This is the best way to avoid automatically renewing policies, especially life insurance.

     See Chapter 30 on insurance.
- Play Santa Claus. You can give up to $10,000 to any number of people and not pay a gift tax.

     ☑ *HINT: Checks should be cashed before the end of the year.*
- Push investment income, bonuses, and freelance earnings into next year to delay paying income taxes; you'll also have use of the money for a year.
- Implement stock or bond swapping for tax purposes.

     See Chapters 8 and 31 for instructions on how to do swaps.

     ☑ *HINT: For other last-minute tax-savers, see Chapter 31.*
- **** December 31. This is the last day to set up a Keogh Plan for 1998, if you're self-employed. You don't need to put money in the plan, merely do the official paperwork.

     See Chapter 29 for everything you need to know about Keoghs.
- **** December 31. This is also the last day to pay deductible items, such as state estimated taxes, and still get a deduction.

NOTES

_____

_____

_____

_____

_____

_____

_____

_____

_____

_____

Securities Index

This listing includes closed-end funds since they trade as stocks on the exchanges.

Only securities mentioned more than once within the book are listed.

Mutual Fund Index

Index